LET'S LOOK AT OUR DEMOCRACY

Boy!, Have We Been Fooled!

(A book with videos)

Dr. Robert O'Connor

TOTAL HEALTH PUBLICATIONS

Oslo, Norway

ACKNOWLEDGEMENTS

A special thanks to Paul Ritterbush for his comprehensive editing of content as well as his outstanding copy-editing. In my forty years of writing for publishers big and small, I have never worked with an editor as competent.

Doctors Chuck and Jean Hon helped immensely with Part Four, on education. Their lifelong experience as secondary and college teachers and administrators has deepened and widened my own impressions of our problems with our educational systems—or, perhaps we should say the lack of systems!

VIDEOS The Videos illustrate the spoken words of some of the subjects of the book. If you are reading the e-book version, merely click the link. If you are reading a print version, write the link address into the address bar of your digital device.

What a gullible lot we are!! Throughout history we have been sold on multiple ideas of how we were created and where we are going after we die. One God, many gods, no god. Elect Herbert Hoover in 1928 and the Republican Party promised that "there will be a chicken in every pot and the car in every garage." Seven months later we were hit by the Great Depression. In January of 1941 FDR told us that we are entitled to four freedoms: freedom of speech, freedom of religion, freedom from want, and freedom from fear. Included in this was the expressed need for adequate healthcare. Three quarters of a century later and we still do not have it.

Each of these messages, like the thousands before and the thousands after, are delivered with authoritative hope-- but without verifiable evidence or concrete policies. But like the wild ostriches with their heads on the sand--we hope, and we believe. Package the message effectively and we will believe anything!

On Halloween night, in 1938, Orson Welles delivered a radio broadcast that convinced thousands of us that the Martians had invaded New Jersey. For those listening at the beginning of the program, it was clear that this was a drama. For those who listened to the ending remarks, it was clear that it was a drama. But for those who tuned in late or didn't listen to the ending remarks, many were convinced that our Earthly humanity was imminently doomed.

Throughout our human history we have been the gullible audiences for snake oil salesmen who will sell us an elixir that will cure whatever physical or mental problems we have. Leaders or "wannabe" leaders tell us that we are the master race, we can be great again, we can be safe again, we can be rich again, we take care of our own lives, and that moving back to we thought life used to be is better than life is now.

Mitch McConnell, the Senate Majority Leader has told us that the health insurance we have now is "good for the American people." He doesn't say how. Since we pay 40 to 50% more than any other country for our health delivery systems and our reward is the 38th best health delivery system in the world, the worst of any developed country—how is this good for the American people?

Nigel Farage and Boris Johnson told us how easy would be to negotiate with the EU after the UK left it. Oh my! The reality is more than slightly different! Did they ever think that negotiating with someone who doesn't like you anymore, and who has everything you want, will be a sympathetic and generous negotiator? Has Brexit made a Robinson Crusoe of the British Isles?

Politicians promise. That is their stock-in-trade. But should their promises be even remotely possible to secure? Evidence clearly shows that cutting taxes increases the national debt. Trump promised that his tax cuts would reduce it. He just didn't say how. Now it looks like they will add $10 trillion to our ever-expanding national debt. He promised to make America great again by stopping or even reversing immigration. How many generations back shall we reach to draw the line? Should we go back to 1905 when Donald Trump's grandfather was deported from Bavaria but welcomed in the U.S.? Should we draw the line somewhere between 1850 and 1880 when my forebears fled the Emerald Isle? Lucky for Donald and me that the American presidents in those days didn't brand all Germans and Irishmen as drug dealers and rapists. Maybe we should we toss out all the immigrants and their offspring who have crowded out the Native Americans in the last 500 years? Was that the time when America was great?

Somebody called us "homo sapiens," Latin for "thinking man." Certainly there have been a few thinkers emerge as we stumbled down the path of human history. One of them discovered how to tame fire. Another invented the wheel. Along the way we have had our Aristotles, Confusiuses, Newtons, and Einsteins. But we have also had our inquisitors who tortured or killed us if we would not join them in believing the unbelievable.

A messiah promises us a new view of life everlasting. So we give his priests tithes. A politician promises us a utopia. So we donate to his campaign. A tub-thumping orator promises us riches if we will only buy his book, buy his products, or join his pyramid club.

We are so full of hope that we will follow the pie-in-the-sky piper like so many non-thinking Hamlin rats. So let's look at how we have been "dumbed down" by politicians bypassing our intellects with the promises of hope that will conquer our fears and anger.

In this book we aim to look at: how we have been manipulated in recent elections; some things we should clarify and change is we really want a government "of the people", then a glimpse of how our educations can be re-ordered to increase our chances of developing a democratic government that is shaped by a thinking electorate.

WHERE ARE WE?—ANOTHER PREFACE

Events change so fast in this time: of populist politics challenging the globalized world, of free speech advocates protecting fake news and other lies, of party politics hampering the good of the nation and the world, and of opinions or "alternate facts" of the propaganda of fossil fuel moguls holding more credence than scientifically verified facts.

Now we have another major problem in global politics. Whenever people with deeply entrenched psychic problems seize power, either by election or by other means, their politics can be directed by their unconscious mental states rather than by intelligent analysis and the logical projection of possible outcomes. Hitler, Napoleon, and Pope Urban II and his Crusades, come to mind.

Donald Trump's political directions often are manifestations of his lifelong inferiority complex which have long been exhibited as narcissistic and bullying traits. Political pundits attempt to analyze his tweets, programs, appointments and pronouncements as if they were well thought out ideas. This is often a major mistake. They may be American executive policy because of his position, but they derive from his unconscious mind, not from national or global realities and well-thought-out solutions to real problems.

Some of his ideas do come from his experience, like the concepts that business is more important than people, or that the rich should keep more of their money and should be able to pass it all along to their children. He is not alone in these beliefs. In fact, his major financial backers have the same primary concerns.

So it is a mistake to think that all of his policies emanate from the personality problems in his unconscious mind. But it is equally erroneous to believe that all of his agenda items have a well thought out and consistent orientation toward making America great again. Many of his ideas spring directly from his superiority complex and the ensuing bullying behavior. These, often contradictory, ideas however are masked by his rationalizations and lies. This combination of unconscious motivations, personal selfish ideas, his business oriented views of the world, lack of experience in government, aversion to reading, aversion to advice by experienced people, and his impulse to win at any cost—make his "leadership" harmful to the U.S. and its allies. It makes it very difficult to find consistency in his policies and his nominations of the people whom he expects to carry out his ideas. The journalist or pundit must consistently change lenses from being a philosopher, to being a psychologist, to being a political scientist.

His erroneous views: of science, as seen in his rejection of the fact of climate change; his inconsistent ideas that outlawing abortion can be done while lowering taxes; or that tax cuts can decrease the national debt--can readily be seen by most informed people.

On the other hand, he seemed quite presidential in his press conference in Singapore with Kim Jong Un. If what happened in the past is prologue, like Jong Un killing his half-brother, or his father's reneging on his agreement to stop his production of nuclear arms during the Clinton administration in 1994—he might be a little skeptical of his newfound friend. Has the North Korean tiger really changed his stripes permanently? If so, was it that he had encountered a bigger bully with a bigger red nuclear button? Was is it the United Nations heavy sanctions that had done it? Was it the pressure from China—it's biggest trading partner? Was it just because he liked our Donald? Or was the real reason that he wanted a McDonald's in his capitol city? The facts are that we have two bullies who can change their minds faster than Superman can stop a speeding bullet. So we'll just have to wait and see! The essential requirement is that there be no regime change in North Korea. Too bad for the North Korean citizens, but it does keep Kim out of prison and off the welfare rolls.

In his summit with Putin in 2018, he was as confrontive in pursuing America's interests as Mary's little lamb. His professed admiration for his country's major enemy throughout his campaign and into the post-meeting press conference revealed a pussycat cowering to the wolfhound. His body language clearly revealed that he was a sheep in lamb's clothing. It brought back the familiar belief that Putin has something on him. With every Russian hotel surveilling it's guests with audio and video technology, and with his well-known penchant for paying for sex, we can fix the likelihood of Russian blackmail at something north of 99%!

His normal method of dealing with friends and adversaries is to degrade them before meeting them, then as any bully with his inferiority complex challenged, play nice when he meets them. As in his meeting with Theresa May the week before, he showed his bullying and his distain for her in an interview with the Sun, then couldn't compliment her enough in the press conference.

His often irrational behavior, stemming from his deep-seated inferiority complex, becomes American governmental policy—which it is. Some of his policies, such as his taxation interests, stem from the selfish interests of him and his financial backers. This makes a perfect taxation policy from their points of view. The policy to make NATO members pay the agreed 2% of their GDP has been a consistent American goal—perhaps his bellicose behavior will speed it up. But his continual negative remarks about Merkel and Trudeau do not seem to endear him to them or to their countrymen. His apparent trade motto seems to be that, "You catch more flies with vinegar than with honey," And, the aforementioned Putin policy seems diametrically opposed to American interests.

Most of Trump's predecessors, whether liberal or conservative, had relatively consistent sets of policies. They were generally easily understood—and might be relatively easily criticized using internal or external criteria. The problem with Trump's policies and programs, tweets and threats, actions and inactions are that we must seek different causes for what we see. Unconscious motivations, conscious selfishness, varied business or personal experiences, and campaign promises that were made off-the-cuff-- have the pundits pondering their consistency. There is no consistency!

OUR CONVOLUTED PATH TO A MODERN DEMOCRACY

Because of the very complicated natures of our minds and of our government, it is impossible to go straight from A to Z as most books do. Their focus is usually to make one point—and make it well. In this book we have to zig and zag on our way from A to Z— just bear with us, the zigs and zags are absolutely necessary to arrive at Z --knowing how we got there. We will periodically address certain issues that we should think about more deeply.

➢ Why have our voting preferences changed from economic issues to identity issues?

➢ Why has our empathy for the less fortunate immigrants and war refugees diminished or disappeared?

➢ Why are we retreating from the national confederations and globalization which have reduced the urge to war as national interests were somewhat sublimated to regional economic and peaceful goals?

➢ Why does the U.S. Supreme Court address so narrowly the wording of the amendments to the Constitution when the reason for the Constitution, to "promote the general welfare," is neglected. What about "establishing justice" or insuring "domestic tranquility?"

➢ In what way is the Electoral College "just" in today's democratic world? In what way do AK47s promote domestic tranquility?

➢ In what way does bringing unwanted children into the world promote the general welfare?

➢ In what way does increasing the national debt through unbalanced national budgets "establish justice" or "promote the general welfare?"

➢ In what way does the lack of a comprehensive public health program, such as all other advanced countries have, "promote the general welfare?"

➢ Since America's happiness rating has been falling, as has its international evaluation of a fully functioning democracy, are the branches of government failing to consider the primary reasons for our Constitution?

➢ Since American schoolchildren are far down the list in the international knowledge tests of mathematics, science, and reading; and, American adults lag well behind other countries in their knowledge of reading and mathematics-- are our 14,000 public school districts and our 35,000 private schools maximally "promoting the general welfare?"

There are many other such questions that we will discuss throughout the book.

Just a glance at the Preamble to our Constitution, in case you have forgotten some of the reasons for our great document.

"We the People of the United States, in Order to form a more perfect Union, establish Justice, insure domestic Tranquility, provide for the common defence, promote the general Welfare, and secure the Blessings of Liberty to ourselves and our Posterity, do ordain and establish this Constitution for the United States of America."

But there are so many other factors that have "dumbed us down." Our knowledge of how we are manipulated through our subconscious minds and our lack of a basic knowledge of psychology. Our lack of a basic knowledge of logic, logical fallacies, and the scientific method hamper us from being able to differentiate between real news and fake news and hamper us from finding the truth in politicians' statements and the probabilities of their promises.

Luckily, we still have some honest politicians. The late John McCain clearly illustrated this in a primary Republican gathering when he was running for president against Barak Obama. Typical unknowledgeable Americans looking for McCain's approval by spouting their faulty beliefs about the Democratic opponent were sternly corrected by McCain, who insisted on honest debates about real issues. His response was classic for a thinking statesman, as opposed to the hack politician who wants to win at all costs. To see and hear his comments, click:

https://vimeo.com/286871294/4ae8cce87e

As you noticed, some booed him and some cheered him. We never like to be shown that our erroneous beliefs are wrong. How could we ever possibly be wrong! The world is flat. There is no global warming. Zeus leads his gods from his throne on Mount Olympus. World War I was the war to end all wars.

We must be able to grasp the whole truth of our political and global realities and hold them tightly in our grasp or the sand and stones that cement our nation will fall from our fists with the speed and abandon of an avalanche and the dreams of a government by and for the people will become the nightmare of the rule of Big Brother!

WHY THIS BOOK?

This book was originally published as "Dumbing Down Democracy." This edition of the book adds some videos and has been updated in a number of sections.

The objective of writing this book was to get us thinking about saving our governmental system and make it more effective. As French President Macron told the U.S. Congress in April of 2018—for democracy to survive we must be able to make rational decisions in our pursuit of a better world society and for world peace. But several recent elections have by-passed the rational and have manipulated us through our unconscious motivations. At this point in time, these elections have had negative earth-shattering consequences because we have abandoned verifiable evidence and reason.

In addition to being able to see how we are manipulated into governmental programs that are actually detrimental to our countries, we need to look further ahead to anticipate problems and minimize them before they overwhelm us with tragedies. We were late in recognizing the problems of global warming resulting in climate change and of our disposing refuse in the oceans which threaten both the fish and us--when we need to fish.

Our unbounded hope that nothing will go wrong continues to be hammered senseless. Wars and terrorism still abound. The world is getting warmer. The world is overpopulated. Millions of people are unhappy in their nations and seek to leave for economic or safety reasons. Empathetic peoples have often welcomed them in, but the inns are now filled. Should we have seen the problem? Could it have been prevented? Would any preventative methods have been welcomed by the burgeoning populations?

Climate change is a verifiable fact but in the summer of 2018, four senators worked to prevent more research in the area, calling it propaganda. All four senators come from states that are far below the average in scientific achievement in their schools. How much education do we need for the majority of the population to recognize present and future problems and arrive at solutions? Where will be the end of empathy when sub-Saharan African countries cannot produce the food they need because of global warming and the lack of rain? The rise of right-wing parties in Europe and the United States is already closing the doors to economic migrants and war refugees.

Empathy is not inexhaustible. When people cannot afford to feed, educate, or psychologically nourish one child—should they have five children, There are not enough people or funds to take of the deserving young ones. Good intentions do not always come with overflowing purses.

Let us explore the problems of today and their projected ramifications for tomorrow. What unseen traditions, assumptions, or ignorance cloud our thinking? These are the questions that this book will now investigate.

But there is more!

The book was not written to make money. For this reason the e-book version is free, where the sales channels allow free books. In print books the price is the lowest allowed by the seller.

ON MOUNT OLYMPUS—AND YET ANOTHER PREFACE

Zeus, Brahma, Odin, and Jupiter relax with their fellow chief gods on their clouds and laugh in amazement at what humans have done-- for themselves-- and to themselves. Since the dawn of homo sapiens we have had the battles for power between the various kings of the jungle. The Olympians chuckled when we earthlings discovered fire and the wheel. They were flattered by the temples and cathedrals to themselves-- the Parthenon, the Pantheon, Chartres, St. Peter's, The Temple of Kukulkan at Chichen Itza, Angkor Wat, and the many golden temples in the East.

They were amazed by the monuments to the human hope of immortality-- the pyramids, the golden grave of Philip of Macedon, the sepulcher of Suleiman, and the heavenly ecstasy of the Taj Mahal.

But the human frailties were a continual source of amusement. Jealousy and pleasure continue to thwart men's conquests. John Kennedy lost some luster when he flaunted Marilyn Monroe. Bill Clinton suffered impeachment after a highly successful presidency because of Monica. Profumo and Schwarzenegger were decidedly embarrassed, but nothing compared to Attila who died in rapture upon his honeymoon bed.

But nothing brings smiles and laughter to Olympus more than the continuous comedic manipulation of today's supposedly advanced societies. The puppet masters of the media make our populations move to their whims. Fear, anger, and hope move us. "Loki misnamed them as homo sapiens, 'thinking humans'" mumbles Thor. "I gave that job to Dionysus," roared Zeus. "He was undoubtedly drunk as usual," roared Zeus. "And I always blamed Kokopelli," mused Tawa, the creating god of the Hopi.

Jupiter interjected, "Whoever it was he should have named them homo smartphonus because that is their essential appendage!

Through electronics the "Big Brother" masters control the thinking of their Nietzschean herd. They make them jump through invisible hoops. They force them to stupidly gaze at unreachable stars while falling lemming-like into the political and financial abyss of their masters' creation. The ease of manipulating those humans is about as difficult as getting Miss Piggy excited about a date with Brad Pitt.

"And these mortals thought they could rule themselves!"

CHAPTER 10.   HOW DID GEORGE W. BUSH MANIPULATE US –

AND WHERE DO WE GO FROM HERE?

PART III. WHAT KIND OF GOVERNMENT DO WE WANT?

CHAPTER 11 NO OTHER COUNTRY HAS SUCH LEGALIZED CORRUPTION AS THE U.S.

SOME QUESTIONS TO CHEW ON
HOW HAVE WE BEEN "DUMBED" AND WHAT CAN WE DO ABOUT IT?

When we subtitled the book "Boy, Have We Been Fooled" we meant to imply that most of us are not going deep enough into the critical areas of thinking that affect us and our society. We tend to believe what is on the surface.

➢ What mother told us,
➢ What our traditions tell us,
➢ What our minister or mufti told us,
➢ What our friends told us,
➢ What our elected representative told us..

None of them have all the answers, but they often think they do!

Not only have we been hampered by a lack of information and by the motivation of our subconscious minds by politicians using techniques that whiz right by our intellects, now we are manipulated through our psychological profiling by several social media companies and by the misinformation they furnish through their advertising, fake news, and the forwarding and the re-tweeting of the propaganda.

➢ Will we continue to have democratic elections? YES
➢ Will these elections be decided by voters who are informed about the pros and cons of the issues and have projected the possible effects of those proposals into the future? HIGHLY UNLIKELY!

We, as a society, must understand the issues, and understand them thoroughly. And where should we start? In our underfunded, poorly equipped, and under-staffed classrooms.

But we're getting ahead of ourselves. We can't come out of the tunnel before we go in. So let's prepare a bit before we start into the tunnel. Are you ready? Then as the Seven Dwarfs sang, "Hi ho, hi ho, it's off to work we go." (Let's hope it isn't all work!)

WHAT HAPPENS WHEN OUR PSYCHOLOGICAL DRIVES MEET THE ETHICAL IMPERATIVE!

Certainly, we are all content that what we know is absolutely true. Being shown verifiable facts will seldom replace our "alternative facts." And, why consider, or even think about values other than those learned at mother's knee? Why waste time reading and thinking, when there are sports on my TV, games on my smartphone, and music in my earphones?

Current research verifies and amplifies the work of Freud and his cohorts. Our unconscious minds don't merely deal with seeking pleasure—they are critically important in influencing how many of us vote in democratic elections. Sadly, for many, the facts don't matter—rather, it is their feelings— anger at immigrants, fear of losing one's job or status, and a hope for the good old days.

With Alfred Adler, we can see the essential nature of our drives for power—power which can be used for ethical or unethical ends. Why do people bully, why do men and women harass and abuse? Power! Why do men and

women create or lead great companies? Power! Why do people want to amass fortunes? Power! Why do they want to hold elective office? You guessed it. Some men drink for power. The drunker man is obviously more *macho*!

We are conversant with the methods of using power as: "power over" or "power to." "Power over" is seen the most often. It is seen in spousal arguments, childhood bullying, sexual harassment, and Trump's tweets. "Power to" is commonly found in the success stories in our world that pull us upward—Gandhi, King, Gates, Edison, and Curie are among the stars of our galaxy that focus our dreams, and allow us to dream beyond our dreams and often excel beyond our expectations.

But most of us are cursed by the more primitive and sub-conscious need to feel power by sublimating another person. Recently we have seen the long awaited, "Me too" movement? The harassment and abuse of women by men has been endemic. But why? Men have traditionally had most of the power, so why not? The "why not" is because the psychological drive for power must be measured against the higher human ethical standard. Immanuel Kant probably expressed it the most clearly, "Always treat people as ends in themselves, not as means only." Of course, every religion enunciates the Golden Rule in varying versions of "Do unto others as you would have them do unto you."

So how do we handle this problem? How do we eliminate bullying, harassment and abuse in our personal lives, in our elections, in the workings of our government and in our society? The ideal would be to have every child loved effectively so that he or she will recognize every other person as being important "selfs" as Erich Fromm has clearly shown us in his book, "The Art of Loving." Sadly, the development of humanitarian love it quite rare, since parenting is the world's most demanding profession and requires many rare qualifications and abilities.

Consequently, we must rely on punishments for abusers. Embarrassment, job loss, fines, prison terms, and isolation are available and finally being used in this singular unethical area of sexual harassment and abuse. Education has finally caught up with the reality and may make some headway in the battle. But the drive for power is not limited to the sexual areas.

OUR UNCONSCIOUS NEEDS HAVE OVERPOWERED THE ESSENTIAL ETHICAL CONSIDERATIONS IN OUR RECENT ELECTIONS

In recent elections in the US and the UK, it was often the needs felt in the unconscious minds of the voters, rather than the thoughtful evaluation of facts and predictions, that guided their hands in marking their ballots. It was not enough to blindly prod our unconscious minds with the whips of fear and anger at targets real and imagined. The shrewd politician must offer an all-encompassing hope—usually without any foundation of realism. Put blinders on the voter's eyes and he will follow you anywhere.

But these recent elections in the US and UK have even gone beyond the "pie in the sky" promises. Data mining and profiling the possible voters allowed social media to go well beyond the traditional political arguments and to influence voters to go to the polls or stay home—depending on their probable voting choices.

Fake news joined in the battle. Our unconscious minds were probed and stimulated far more than any time in history. It seems that these advanced psychological weapons won the recent battles. But the war isn't over. Are you ready to grab your weapons and fight for a better tomorrow?

However, it is not only the voter's mind that is directed by unconscious motivations—our representatives are often similarly moved by unconscious forces rather than well thought-out programs for the good of the nation. The anger at opponents, the fear of losing the next election—with the accompanying loss of status, and the hope for advancing up the political and social ladders. Each prod the politician.

Is it possible for us to hone our intellects so that they will silence the screams of our unconscious minds?

➤ Perhaps we CAN think deeper.

➤ Perhaps we CAN question our representative's facts and motives.

➢ Perhaps we CAN reroute our democracy and put it back on the road that our Founding Fathers fashioned.

➢ Perhaps we CAN again have a government of thinking and thoughtful citizens who elect representatives concerned with "promoting the general welfare" of our country.

WHERE ARE WE GOING WITH THIS BOOK?

Our democracy is being dumbed down because we are not thinking deeply enough.

➢ We see things and discuss them based on what is obvious, rather than what is their cause and their deeper and projected meanings.

➢ Our psychological needs and drives influence us much more than we realize.

➢ Our unconscious minds are much larger than our conscious minds but because they are below the surface, we are not aware of their influence.

➢ British political analyst Ian Dunt reached into his Freudian sack to describe Donald Trump as "a rolling ball of 'id'."

➢ Genetics, neuroscience, epigenetics give us hints as to what is in our unconscious minds

➢ We all develop our inferiority complexes when we are very young.

➢ Most of us seek power through different avenues to overcome our inferiorities.

➢ Some of us, because of superior parenting, are capable of being truly loving.

➢ Being able to love, in the deepest sense, overcomes the drive for power.

➢ Our values dictate much of what we do.

➢ The values we live by generally have deeper basic assumptions that we may not understand.

➢ Because the sources of our needs, drives, and values are generally hidden in our minds, we are often targets of manipulation by politicians and advertisers.

➢ We are increasingly being manipulated through our

manipulation is enhanced as the knowledge of psychology is increased and the potential for data mining and uses of social media are exploited.

➢ By combining the drive for power with other conscious and unconscious realities such as: anger, fear, and hope-- recent elections have hijacked the issues away from the good of the nation and deposited them in the wallets of the self-centered billionaire elites. (Not all billionaires fall into this category.)

We must therefore understand:

➢ How we have been manipulated

➢ What kind of society we really want, and

➢ What are the best ways to achieve this.

And there you have it—the outline of the book.

WHAT HAVE WE GOT OURSELVES INTO?

From the ideas of the thinkers of the Enlightenment in the 18th century, to the fruition of many of their ideas in our fundamental law, The Constitution of the United States, it was reason, not emotion, that laid the foundations for the American Constitution that has been a beacon for the world. It is true that the emotions of fear and anger ignited the Revolution, but it was the intellectual planning for a government for all of the American people, that captured the hopes of large bodies of citizens of other nations during the last 200 years.

Our knowledge of history shows us that neither biological nor intellectual evolution will be smooth. Two steps forward and one step back may be expected, but the dialectic of ideas must not retreat 500 years, erasing the achievements of the enlightened intellect.

But recently, we have seen:

➢ A decaying ideology conquering the intellectual, emotional appeals conquering the evolution of our intelligent progress,

➢ Appeals to the unconscious mind bypassing the intellect, and

➢ Falsehoods trampling truth.

WE NEED RESPONSIBLE CTIZENS*!*

We must retake the reins and steer our democracies back on track. The world is becoming more globalized. Ignoring this is to be trampled by the time we have invested. The world is becoming safer. Ignoring this can bring this back to the tribal wars that have defined our human history.

In April of 2018, Martin Wolf of the Financial Times, echoed his concern. "The threat is the decadence of the West, very much including the US — the prevalence of rent extraction as a way of economic life, the indifference to the fate of much of its citizenry, the corrupting role of money in politics, the indifference to the truth, and the sacrifice of long-term investment to private and public consumption."

Are we willing to commit our time and resources to solving the problems that face us? Overpopulation causes climate change—which threatens us all. Fossil fuels cause climate change—which threatens us all. Unloved, uneducated, and unemployed youth provide the seeds for terrorism.

Our oceans are threatened with warming, acid, and plastic. Shall we continue to destroy the mother of our evolution?

There are issues that threaten our survival that may be even more important than the interests of business and industry. The economy is only one small piece of the planetary puzzle. It is true that a job puts food on the kitchen table. But there is another room—one called the "living" room. Have we forgotten to live up to our potential? Is this why the Scandinavians are so much happier than the Americans and the Brits?

WHERE ARE OUR LEADERS?

Where are the statesmen and stateswomen who will lead us by our intellects, not by our emotions and our subconscious fears? And if they attempt to rouse us, will we turn our backs on them and follow the simpletons who have all the answers, but do not understand the questions?

Could it be that my country, my world, and my government should also have a slice of my mind-- and more than a bit of my time? Has my fire been sparked by the incendiary zeal of the survivors of the Parkland High School massacre? Has my long-darkened lamp been lighted by the need to reignite the hope of democracy? Has my myopic view of today miraculously morphed into a realistic vision of the future? If so, where do I start?

HOW ABOUT STARTING WITH CLEAR THINKING?

In the pre-Brexit debates people were told that they were sending 350 million British pounds to the EU every week and that this could be sent to the national health programs instead and help the people of Britain. When the people who wanted to remain in the European Union said this was not true, the Brexiteers said they did not know what they were talking about. It turns out that the "remainers" were right.

When Donald Trump said he would build a wall and Mexico would pay for it, many people believed it. Mexico will not pay for the wall. The only way that it could be done would be with tariffs on Mexican goods. The tariffs, of course, would be paid in the increased price of the goods. So, if a wall is built, the Americans will really pay for it—either in tariffs or in taxes.

Maybe there are some questions we should ask ourselves!

➢ Is Donald Trump psychologically fit to be the President of the United States? James Comey wrote that he is morally unfit.

➢ Why do many in the American government tell us that climate change is not real, and if it is, that it is not caused by people.

➢ In both the referendum to leave the European Union and in Donald Trump's campaigns, data mining was used to sway potential voters to or away from the ballot box. This was aided by Russian hackers and their government, who paid for ads in the social media-- like Facebook. Is this what we want in our democracy?

➢ If we are to be intelligent we need to look beyond what is said and what are our traditions to find how much truth is in the messages we hear.

➢ Is there economic inequality? Should it be changed? How?

➢ Is the Bible true? Is the Koran true? Are these books factually true or is it only their message on morality that we should consider?

➢ Is democracy the best form of government? Or should it be changed?

➢ If the American president has approval ratings in the 30% range and the Congress has approval ratings below 20%--does America have a representative democracy?

➢ Can we believe in equality and liberty, and if so what we mean by them?

➢ Is equality of opportunity an essential goal for a dynamic society?

If we are not content with the directions our "democratic" governments are going, should we do something about it? What?

Of course, there are many more questions that we will discuss at greater lengths. But, will we only be discussing our own opinions or shall we look beyond our opinions to come closer to verifiable truths?

To approach truth with more verifiable evidence, we need a greater knowledge of: world history, our national history, logic, semantics, psychology, sociology, political science, environmental science, religions, and other disciplines depending on the opinions we are investigating.

To determine Trump's fitness for the presidency, we need to look at psychology and possibly political history to see whether or not his policies are negative to the country and the world.

To look at the pronouncements of most politicians, we need a knowledge of semantics, inductive and deductive logic, and knowledge of whatever political, religious, moral, or scientific area that are pontificating about.

To understand how British and American voters were swayed by data mining, we must understand the process by which it is done and the messages that they are trying to convey.

So, looking beyond the obvious is a way to slow down the dumbing of our democracies.

What do we want?

➢ The survival of the fittest.

➢ The survival of the richest.

➢ The survival of the wisest.

➢ The survival of the liars.

PART I OUR GOVERNMENT, OUR REPRESENTATIVES, OUR PROBLEMS--AND US

While playing the jigsaw puzzle of life we expect a favorable picture of our future appear through our rose-colored glasses. But there are seldom enough pieces of the puzzle to get the whole picture. Some are hidden, some are stolen, some have been lost. Why?

So it is with our idealized idea of democracy. No Pericles on the Pnyx urging his compatriots to forge a stronger city-state through laws. Intelligent persuasion was the method of democracy in the golden age of Athens. The citizens knew the issues and the realities. How different from today where data mining selects and influences the mob that the avaricious billionaires used to have their way.

tear down the citizen-protecting regulations enacted by the legislators. Who needs tax reduction? The super-rich! Who cares about the national debt? The lenders.

In this section we will explore a bit about what we might want in our society-- and how we can intelligently direct those changes. In this section we must:

➢ Learn a bit about our minds, because unscrupulous politicians and billionaires are using modern technologies to control us;

➢ Arm ourselves with our knowledge of our minds and the tools of logic to be able to resist the mental manipulations we have seen in the Bush, Brexit, and Trump elections;

In subsequent sections, we will look at exactly how we have been manipulated. We already see the results:

➢ The Iraq war, a cost of a trillion dollars, 4500 American and a half million Iraqi lives lost, and the rise of ISIS—because we were told that Saddam Hussein had weapons of mass destruction;

➢ The significant financial problems developing in the UK; and,

➢ The total incompetence of Donald Trump as a leader in the world.

Without a thorough understanding of the contents of this section, both the knowledge of psychology and of logic-- it will be impossible to analyze the subsequent sections. Too bad artificial intelligence isn't smart enough to help us yet!

We are going to look at "being fooled in our concept of democracy," in order to do this, you must look at how we are manipulated by politicians and the billionaires that often control them. Our task is to look beyond the obvious to find the real reason for certain behavior. For example, when a jihadist says it is for Allah, in most cases the real reason is a deeper psychological need, such as the need for the psychological power required to overcome our nearly universal inferiority feelings. This inferiority is the result of the inadequacy we felt as infants when we couldn't walk, talk, or change our own diapers. (We all think we are in total control of our lives, but I doubt it! We will discuss this later.). This need to overcome our inferiorities is in the unconscious mind so cannot be understood by the perpetrator—the bully, the terrorist, or the harasser. News reporters and politicians usually accept the reasons that are mouthed by terrorists, politicians, and other bullies—and assume that it is the true reason for the behavior.

When a black hooded man, who calls himself an Antifa, lashes out at an observer, or even a participant, in a peaceful Nazi rally, and along the way throws rocks through shop windows and burns cars-- we have a person with a mental problem. It is certainly good to be antifascist, but the label may not disguise one's real motivations that are based on their need for power because of their deep-seated feelings of inferiority. When Kim Jong Un threatens to bomb America for its imagined threats to his country and is faced with severe economic sanctions, can it be said that he is a thoughtful leader for his people? No! He is a bully motivated by a deep-seated feeling of insecurity and inferiority. As bad as he is, he pales in comparison with the great bully of the West, Donald Trump.

It is not unusual to see leaders of nations demonstrating their psychological impairment. Maduro in Venezuela and Putin in Russia may be criticized from within and without, but their drives for power are at least understood rationally, if not ethically.

We need to understand the workings of the mind to be able to see through the rationalizations and understand the motivations for the behavior of those seeking to manipulate us. But we had better understand ourselves, too. We can prepare our minds to see through these political puppeteers. We can prepare our minds so that we can pull our own strings. We can prepare our minds to think positively and creatively in terms of what is needed for an effective and fair society, Then, we can prepare our minds to make it happen!

KNOW YOURSELF, KNOW THE WORLD

Since one major task of this book is to indicate how we have been manipulated in recent elections, in order to do this, we must first look at how our brains and minds function so that we can understand how the big money interests often work to direct our own voting choices towards outcomes that are not good for us.

To combat this, we should understand a bit about how our brains work and how a major function of our brains, our minds, may be constructed. Psychologists and neuroscientists have been working on these questions for many years-- and do not yet have definitive answers. However, they do indicate some directions and possibilities. Many years ago, advertisers were quick to understand the motivating forces of needs, drives, and values in directing our behavior into buying their products.

The late Roger Ailes, founder and longtime head of Fox News, realized the impact of moving us through our conscious and unconscious minds when he said that the message must be emotional, not intellectual. Keep on themes, he said, but avoid details. He taught this to Ronald Reagan in 1984 and had been advising Republicans since. The people he brought to Fox News had to make an immediate impression on the viewers, because he thought that viewers would determine within seven seconds whether or not they would watch a program. Forty percent of Trump voters relied on Fox and its news. Yes, it was propaganda-- and yes it was effective. His message was aimed at older white men in the blue-collar belts of America. He was famous for developing conspiracy theories to make his audience suspicious of the bad guys. Who needs evidence when we are dealing with emotions?

Politicians soon understood the value of the findings of psychology. They generally try to influence us through our intellects as well as our conscious hopes and unconscious fears. Until recently, it was primarily haphazard guesswork as to which promises should be made and which fears should be emphasized. Now, through data mining the social media, they have found far more reliable ways of pinpointing which voters should be attacked with which messages, so that we will vote FOR what they want.

Concurrently, they now have ways of discouraging voters from going to the polls if they were likely to cast their votes AGAINST them.

LOOKING DEEPER

In the opening chapters we will look at the brain and some of the influences on it such as: genetics, epigenetics, and the environment.

Then we will look at the mind as a function of the brain, looking briefly at: the intellect, the conscious mind, the subconscious and unconscious mind and the needs, drives and values that may motivate us.

In looking at our values, we must also look deeper--looking at the basic assumptions that we might use in making our life decisions. Here we will look at: self-centered basic assumptions, God-based assumptions and society-based assumptions. Any of these can influence our behavior partially or totally.

A major thesis of this book is that we are often motivated to actions and manipulated by unconscious needs and drives. But our defenses for our actions often rely on rationalizations, that is false reasoning, that can mask our real motivations by claiming that our actions were motivated by higher values. Jihadists, motivated by power or anger, say it is what Allah wants. Trump, motivated by power, says he wants to "make America great again."

Commentators in the media seem to take at face value what the newsmakers say-- as the reasons for their actions. Psychologists often look beyond the obvious for deeper reasons. A large number of mental health professionals have criticized Donald Trump's actions as indicative of pathology, particularly narcissism and a superiority complex.

He blames the media, Muslims and Mexicans for the problems he sees and for his own inadequacies. While Kim Jong-un is too far removed geographically for us to see many of his actions and pronouncements, what we do see indicates the same type of neurotic and selfish power drive that we see in Trump. Of course, he blames the US for his irrational and nation-threatening actions.

The pundits try to make sense of the illogical tweets and speeches that Trump gives- where he continually contradicts himself and does a great deal of potential harm to the internal and external interests and workings of the American government. Similarly, commentators take jihadist terrorists at their word that their actions are for the advancement of Islam and the elimination of blasphemers and nonbelievers are acting counter to what the Qur'an espouses. It is nearly always the experience of having some kind of power that their inferiority complexes crave.

Naturally these people don't know why they do it. Can you imagine a bully saying, "I have an inferiority complex because I was never really loved, that's why I'm going to make fun of your big nose." Can you picture Harvey Weinstein saying, "Although I am extremely successful in the film business, I have a huge inferiority complex that can be temporarily satisfied if you take off your clothes and watch me take a shower."

It is our contention that many, if not most, of these actions are based on inferiority complexes that require the person to exhibit power in some area of their lives. Many jihadists are angry at their societies because they have not achieved or have been prejudiced against. Anger is a major motivator. Hope is another. Jihadist preachers promise paradise if they die advancing the cause of Allah. Paradise would be nice, if it existed and if the Qur'an could backup the preachers' promises-- which it doesn't. So a nonreligious psychological drive results in the murder of innocents, but it is rationalized by a perversion of a religion.

Trump has tweeted and spoken of the terror that North Korea will experience if they attack the US or its allies. "They will be met with fire, fury and frankly power the likes of which this world has never seen before." Was this a well-conceived attempt to scare North Korea? Some commentators thought so. Was it merely an explosion of self-importance and bullying? If so, it was likely generated from the unconscious mind.

Nearly everyone has inferiority feelings based, to a large degree, on our total helplessness when we were infants. This inferiority was then enlarged as we went through school and were subject to teachers, parents, and other students who reminded us that we didn't know everything. It is highly likely that, as much as we don't want to believe it, the great majority of us still carry some feelings of inadequacy. When I think of people who may have completely escaped their prisons of immaturity, only a few names come to mind-- Bill Gates, Sergey Brin, and Mark Zuckerberg are possibilities. But then, as far as I know, none of them finished the academic degrees they originally sought before becoming genius entrepreneurs. There are probably some extremely creative researchers in the world who may also qualify. Barack and Michelle Obama certainly qualify.

There are a number of ways that people compensate for their feelings of inferiority. They may attack the society as bullies or braggarts, as gang members or terrorists, or as criminals. Rapists, Mafia members, and murderers-- especially mass murderers-- are the ultimate extensions of bullying behavior. One of the ways that some people try to overcome their inferiorities is by developing a superiority complex. This is often exhibited in either bullying behavior or narcissism. Donald Trump exhibits both to a large degree.

Some people attempt to combat their inferiority feelings through withdrawing from life, such as: excessive daydreamers, many drug abusers, many neurotics and psychotics, and the ultimate withdrawal-- suicide. Instead of a quest to develop "power to" they take the easy way, "escape from."

Luckily, for the good of the individual and the society, most people attempt to achieve personhood by achieving in socially acceptable ways, such as: studying, playing sports, finding a good job and doing well at it, or developing a happy and successful relationship or family.

So, these first few chapters will look at our minds, both the rational and the irrational aspects of them, and look at how we might be more rational if we would hold to the findings of philosophers in terms of understanding logic--from semantics to inductive and deductive reasoning.

Then we will look a bit deeper into the values that people commonly hold. Here we are in another area of philosophy. Every value we hold is based on assumptions—most of which are not provable. We believe that if a value is held, the holder should know what assumptions are basic to that value. So whether you are a Catholic, a Democrat, a socialist or a capitalist—you should know exactly what and why you hold that belief. It reminds me of a TV interview I saw with a Tea Party member. When asked about his definition of socialism, he said, "I don't know what it is, but I'm against it!"

If you are conversant with the basic understandings of psychology and with the areas of philosophy that deal with ethics and logic, you might well skip these first few chapters. If not, they are critical to understanding how we have recently been enticed to vote in contradiction to our best interests. We voted for Bush and got a trillion dollar war, the rise of ISIS, and many thousands of deaths and injuries to Americans and to foreigners. We voted for Brexit and shot ourselves in our financial feet. We voted for The Donald and have seen no end of trouble.

CHAPTER 1   WHY THIS BOOK?

My political-mental indigestion began in 2000 when matador Bush gored his more experienced, more far-thinking, more ethically-minded opponent for the presidency. And 49.3% of Americans didn't care enough to vote.

The 2004 campaign had me belching fire when another supremely intelligent and courageous candidate bit the dust in the corrida of modern politics. And 44.3% of Americans could not have cared less.

Then sanity returned for a short while before it was frustrated by an avalanche of adversity from extreme partisan politics. And little was accomplished because of party politics and the need to frustrate those on the other side of the aisle was more important than solving the problems of the country.

Then came the June 23, 2016 referendum results in Britain, and Brexit became a reality. 28% of the British voters didn't care enough to go to the polls.

Later that year the improbable, in fact the unbelievable, happened. Again with 45% of Americans not caring who led their country--as they watched football or reruns of "Fraser," the talk-show psychiatrist. Unreality TV soon began beaming from our TV screens.

For too many of our elected officials, political power is now more important than patriotic performance for the good of the nation. Frustrate your foes so that you look better. All is fair in love and politics-- so lie, cheat, and steal to get yourself, or your lackey, to the ruling rung of the state power ladder. Then reward your financial backers by rolling back regulations that interfered with their businesses and cut their taxes by borrowing from the national pension funds. It makes absolute sense to be corrupted absolutely when you have the power to turn on the financial faucet.

LOOKING BEHIND AND BEYOND

Among the major reasons for the book were to look beyond the conscious and obvious messages of a number of politicians and see how they motivated voters to back their causes. The verbal message, and the nonverbal communication, often stimulates deeper unconscious needs that may be more important in rallying the voter than the actual message. Psychologically, according to Alfred Adler, our nearly universal interiority complexes develop in us a need to feel power. While we would like to think that everything we do is well thought out, a deeper psychological understanding shows that it is not quite that simple.

For example, Donald Trump as a candidate, promised many outcomes. He promised to:

> - Drain the swamp,
> - Build a wall between the USA and Mexico and have Mexico pay for it,
> - Eliminate "Obamacare" and replace it with something cheaper and better,
> - Massive tax breaks for the middle class,
> - More coal mining and steel factory jobs,
> - Great expansion of the national infrastructure,
> - Tariffs on Chinese and Mexican imports,

Some of these may have been lies aimed at getting votes. But many people believed him. However, his bombastic style and sarcasm against his opponents excited many people and appealed to both the conscious and the unconscious message levels. On the conscious level, he reminded many voters that they were out of a job, poorly educated, and angry at the government for not taking care of them.

At the unconscious level, we often feel powerless. So, when Donald Trump belittled people in government in the primaries, it made us feel good because they were being taken down—which obviously raised us psychologically. It didn't really matter that Mexico wouldn't pay for the wall, that the tax breaks were for the rich, that coal mining jobs did not come back, that there was no movement on building infrastructure, or that parts of Obamacare, that gave federal subsidies to us were eliminated.

His behavior in office which isolated the US, his not wanting to take immigrants from 'shithole" countries, his defense of Neo-Nazis and the KKK, didn't matter to his base. What was important was that he kept blaming others for his failures. His base recognized many of his unfulfilled promises and his unpresidential demeanor. What was important was that he continued to blame others so that his base could feel superior to those he was debasing.

Also, when you have been so strongly for a person or an idea, you may want to protect your position until your dying day! This is true of dearly held habits or traditions, whether they are new or generations old. Your religion, your political party, your family traditions, are very difficult to change. Even if you want to change, your family and friends provide a huge bulwark against it. Our deeply held, often contradictory, beliefs and values are not easily swayed.

John Stuart Mill, one of philosophy's most perceptive paragons, wrote that humanity's greatest problem is deluding itself by continually believing unverifiable beliefs. People must think deeply about the most pressing beliefs of how we do, and should, live— our ethical beliefs—and their ramifications. This would also include the pillars of most religions—where we came from and where we may go after we live out our earthly years. Science clearly has verifiable evidence of the Big Bang and the evolution of life since. So far science hasn't proven an afterlife of any sort. But as long as we hope, we often accept what religious teachers tell us about our options for the future. And we tithe dearly for the guarantee of a rosy future.

Through the book we will often digress to illustrate some possible chinks in our intellectual armor. Sometimes this will be in looking deeper into religious beliefs, sometimes into our beliefs of democracy, sometimes into our beliefs in liberty or equality, sometimes into our society structures-- like education.

WHERE ARE WE GOING WITH PARTS I AND II OF THE BOOK

Looking at the trifecta from Bush to Brexit to The Donald, it was obvious that the method of moving voters was becoming less and less intellectual and more and more emotional. The gateway to the immense expanse of our unconscious minds was being opened by the keys to the psyche. Fear and anger played on the keyboard of hope.

Two days before going to press, a study reported in the National Academy of Sciences was published validating the ideas I had been writing about during the previous seventeen months. It was not so much about not having a job—rather it was the fear of non-Anglos becoming more powerful, of Islam threatening Christianity, and of women threatening the patriarchy. (Read the article at:
http://www.pnas.org/content/early/2018/04/18/1718155115)

Monstrous lies and continual logical fallacies were used to manipulate the mob of those who saw themselves as disenfranchised. Promises of small tax breaks and the possibility of an industrial age job in a digital society found eager ears. Meanwhile, the self-centered financial moguls extracted promises of real riches through massive tax cuts for the rich and deregulation of their corporations. In return they bankrolled their cohorts, the candidates who were supposed to represent us.

The original idea for the book was to show how these political puppeteers manipulated our subconscious strings and made us move to their music. Logical arguments became less important as it became clearer that tugging at our unconscious minds was more effective in swaying the potential voters.

Evidence indicates that reliable facts are becoming less and less important in American political campaigns. We are hammered with –

➢ Perceptions rather than facts,
➢ Propaganda rather than truth,
➢ Mudslinging rather than concrete proposals,
➢ Impossible promises rather than reasonable plans,
➢ Short term objectives rather than long term goals,
➢ Inconsistent proposals.

Candidates run on: balancing the budget, reducing the national debt, keeping entitlements, and cutting taxes. It is, of course, impossible to balance the budget while cutting taxes. It is impossible to cut taxes and not increase the national debt.

Candidates run on eliminating abortion, reducing crime, reducing taxes, and increasing freedoms. This, too, is impossible. Every unwanted baby will cost taxpayers $120,000 to get that child to high school graduation. Evidence is clear that unwanted children are more likely to cost taxpayers more in law enforcement costs and foster care costs.

Donald Trump campaigned with the charge to 'make America great again." He has not yet told us his criteria for his evaluation that it is not great— and his concrete proposals for fixing the country, unless getting more money to our impoverished millionaires and billionaires is our major stumbling block to greatness!

Understanding our minds, and being able to see through the untruths being beamed at the public, required some explanations of how the mind works and how our intellects can be confused by logical fallacies-- ideas that are untrue but are continually being used to convince us that they are true. So an explanation of some basic psychology and philosophy seemed needed for those without backgrounds in these two fields. Consequently, a brief explanation of these academic areas was added as Part I and the original idea for the book became Part II.

In Part I we first look at the brain and the mind. While many politicians will appeal to our conscious minds in their policies, today we are finding more electioneering geared at moving us through our unconscious minds. The data mining of firms such as Cambridge Analytica developed psychological profiles so that political teams would know how best to attack each individual voter. It then gave addresses so that the appropriate voters could be contacted with advertising, real or fake news, bot messages, or as targets for trolls.

So social media, particularly Facebook and Twitter, were both the source of the psychological profiles and the delivery system that brought the appropriate messages to the selected voters.

Often times politicians are thought to be somewhere south of normal in their politicking or leadership styles. People like Hitler, Napoleon, Pol Pot, Maduro, and Trump come to mind. If they do stray into psychosis, neurosis, or personality problems—that difference may be found in their genetic inheritance, in epigenetic transferring, or in the malfunctioning of the nervous system. To understand the possible causes of such abnormal behavior, we should understand, at least minimally, how these abnormal behaviors might occur. Donald Trump is a featured guest in this psychological segment.

Then we look at logic in our philosophical segment. We illustrate many of the logical fallacies and how they were used in the various campaigns--particularly those of Donald Trump. Then we jump to another area of philosophy, how we choose our values, and to ethics, which deals with how we should treat others.

Only by understanding some basic psychology, logic and ethics and how we choose our values--does Part II become clearer.

A GLANCE AT PART III

But then, it did not seem to be enough to show how we had been hoodwinked by illogical rantings and spurious arguments. So, it was decided to look at some of the obstacles to democracy that have become fixtures in our American method of modern politics. If we are to sincerely believe that our Constitution is designed to enhance "the general welfare" of our population, we have been led down a primrose path to a haunted house!

The intelligence of our Founding Fathers, which laid the foundations for an intelligent and enduring mode of government, has been converted to a Pandora's box of power politics where the elites of business and government have built walls and dams designed to protect their interests and forcibly frustrate the general welfare of the people. Special interests, rather than a functioning democratic republic which would improve and endure, became the soul of the governing elites. This then became Part III of our work.

In Part III, we look at some of the obvious impediments to a just and efficient democracy. Among the areas we discuss are such things as: lobbying, gerrymandering, and the obstacles to an effective checks and balances theory of government-- which has become too partisan to be maximally effective.

There are several suggestions we make to remedy the unseen problems that our 18th-century founders could not have anticipated.

One major emphasis of this book is to look beyond the obvious. Most of us see the surface problems but do not understand what lies behind them. Why does Donald Trump continually lie? We need to look beyond what he says to understand why he is saying it. Political pundits often criticize his policies as if they were well thought out rather than being actions done to satisfy his deep unconscious inferiority feelings.

But there is more than just the policies of The Donald. People continually shout for their "rights." But often these "desires" are only that, not rights. We talk about justice. But one's concept of justice is based to a larger degree on the ideals of liberty or equality. But these are often antithetical ideals. For example, when one has the liberty to make as much money as possible, why should an equalitarian ideal such as a graduated income tax, a minimum wage, or a guaranteed annual income be allowed? Liberty and equality are often conflicting ideals, as most political philosophers have long understood.

We argue opinions without understanding the fundamental assumptions that our opinions rest upon. We will therefore examine briefly the underpinnings of our assumptions that lead to our opinions and our actions.

Another area to consider is whether we want happiness or low taxes. Denmark is generally found to be the happiest country in the world—although this year it is Finland, with Norway, last year's winner at second place, and Denmark 3rd. Denmark's total tax burden is over 50%. America's is about half that. Norway's is generally about 42%, much higher that America's 26% However, America is number 18 in the UN's happiness survey, having dropped from 14th in 2017, and 11th a few years ago. Apparently making America great again is also making it sadder!

Perhaps the United States should determine its basic objectives before working on its legislative endeavors. Americans pay nearly twice as much for their medical coverage as most countries, yet their medical delivery system is rated at about the 37th best in the world, the worst of any developed country. This is because private enterprise and stockholders must take their cut from the insurance premiums. Is it the duty of the American government to put private profits ahead of public interest?

Still another major concern is whether we should put present day concerns ahead of future concerns. Since the United States legislators and public think primarily of "now," the future is impacted. Year after year the federal deficit limit is increased to cover wars, tax reductions, or entitlement spending. Our national debt is one of the highest in the world as a percentage of our gross domestic product (GDP). Are we willing to reduce our future pensions to pay for this? Are we willing to have our children pay for our selfishness? Are we willing to have our dollars worth less in the future? Are we willing to endure the future pains because of our living beyond our means today?

PART IV

So now we have criticized the way we have been manipulated and have looked at some ways that our democracy can be improved. And what is the best way to do this? Obviously, it is through an effective education if we want to be intelligent and economically productive citizens. Vocational education seems to be the primary concern of governments across the globe. It is certainly important. But today, more than ever, we need education for citizens. Here, it seems, that with few exceptions, our governments are not concerned. The American system of education is so far behind most of the world that it would be laughable if it were not so tragic. It is the Mr. Bean of international academia. So, Part IV of this work deals with modernizing the system and energizing its content. The question is whether we want to continue to be "dumbed down" or if we want to energize our democratic souls and lift our democracies to the heights envisioned by Jefferson and Washington.

The historian Arnold Toynbee reminded us that great civilizations arise when elite individuals lead their tribes to confront and successfully meet the challenges that face them. King George was an absent irritant to the development of the colonies-- and intelligent courageous men worked successfully to excise the mutilations of George's monarchy.

What would Athens have been without Pericles, Assyria without Sargon, Israel without Moses, modern China without Mao? History is the record of great leaders. But they pass on, and their baton will not be passed on indefinitely as the race between those working for a thriving civilization, those with a passion for self-aggrandizing power, and those bathing in the joys of parentally-produced riches—strive for control.

Then, as Toynbee has observed, when societies die they usually commit suicide-- each falling on its rusty sword, rusted by the apathy in the face of challenges and decayed by the lack of dynamism. Dull the senses with psychoactive drugs. Dull the intellect with electronic Ecstasy. Dull the pursuit of achievement with a blanket of calming platitudes.

The historian concluded that, "Man achieves civilization, not as a result of superior biological endowment or geographical environment, but as a response to a challenge in a situation of special difficulty which rouses him to make a hitherto unprecedented effort."

AND FINALLY, PART V—DO WE WANT TO DO ANYTHING ABOUT IT?

We can sit on our hands, vote intelligently, run for office, or work to amend our Constitution. Many of America's problems can only be permanently remedied by changes to the Constitution. You may think that flying to Jupiter is difficult! Try amending the Constitution by referenda! Successful amendments always start in Congress. But a balanced budget is essential to our country. Why didn't Congress vote to start it on its way to adoption? Easy! It will require us to pay for what we use now. No more kicking the financial can down the road so our children will pay for what we have spent. No more of politicians making election promises of tax cuts without considering who will pay for them. Infants around the country are wetting their diapers with delight. They pee with glee 'cuz now they're almost debt-free.

SO WHAT DO WE NEED TO DISCUSS?

Let's quickly glance at a few of the issues that our country faces. We will address these, and others, in more detail as we move forward.

THINKING DEEPER—TO UNDERSTAND "WHY?

One of the major problems in "REALLY" thinking is about how do we base our opinions on any issue. If we take a step into the deeper reasons for an opinion we come to an unprovable idea. We call this a basic assumption. The deepest reason for us to hold an opinion, or a value, comes down to a self-centered reason, a God-based reason, or a society-based reason. Quite often our opinions conflict within ourselves. Also, quite often, a reason that we hold as primary does not really back up what we think it does. Let's look briefly at some issues where thinking more deeply might shed more light on a possible solution.

SHOULD WE BEND OR BREAK TRADITIONS?

➤Is your political party on the same page as you are in terms of: taxation, entitlements, education issues, abortion, climate change, death penalty, or freedom of speech?

➤Are the values of your religion aligned with how you live your life? If not, you should do some hard thinking—and either live your religion, or find one more in line with how you live.

➤Are you expected to work in the family business? Will this fulfill your life? Or is there an occupation or a hobby that is in line with your real interests?

➤If your family and friends seem to be interested in things that don't interest you, find your real calling: in college, in eclectic reading, in traveling.

HAPPINESS OR LOW TAXES

For those of you who are interested in some of the factors used in determining the "happiness" rankings in the 2018 summary, here are a few: the median GDP per capita (as opposed to the mean or average, which is inflated when all the billionaires' money is averaged in), social support, freedom to make life choices, healthy life expectancy, perceptions of corruption, and one's propensity to be generous.

Finland ranks number one, followed by: Norway, Denmark, Iceland, Switzerland, the Netherlands, Canada, New Zealand, Australia, and Sweden. Israel was 11th, Costa

Rica 12th, United States 18th (having fallen from 12th a few years ago) and Ireland 15th (rising four places from last year's survey). Germany was 16th, United Kingdom 19th, Mexico 25th, Singapore 26th, France 31st, Russia 49th, Japan 51st, Turkey 69th, Hong Kong 71st, China 79th, Pakistan 80th, Venezuela 82nd, Greece 87th, Somalia 93rd, South Africa 101st, India 127th, and Central African Republic last at number 155.

A quick glance at these figures may bring to mind that democratic socialism, as found in the top 10 countries, may be a significant factor in their happiness. These countries are also rated very low in government and business corruption, which is a major factor in determining the happiness of citizens.

The total taxes paid (income, social security, value added taxes), as a percent of GDP, are: Denmark 49%, France 48%, Finland 44%, Sweden 43%, Norway 42%, Iceland 38%, Greece 36%, New Zealand 37%, Japan 32%, Canada 32%, Turkey 30%, Switzerland and Australia 28%, the United States 26%, Ireland 24%, and Mexico 18%.

The Mideast and Africa are areas in which there are large families, very high unemployment, and a large amount of both emigration and terrorism.

Addressing these negative forces is one focus of this book.

ABORTION—PRO-LIFE OR PRO-CHOICE?

Many people believe that the abortion of a fertilized ovum is against the wishes of the Judeo-Christian God. They often cite Job 1:21 which says that the Lord has given and the Lord has taken away. But of course, Job was not pregnant, he was just besieged with troubles. In fact, the Old Testament is quite clear that life starts at birth.

The New Testament says nothing about abortion. It does, however, give the power to Peter to change the tradition that God has revealed-- if he wishes. In Matthew 16:19 Jesus tells Peter that he will build his church upon him and whatever he shall bind on earth shall be bound in heaven and whatever he shall loose on earth shall be loosed in heaven. The Roman Catholics believe that their pope is the spiritual progeny of Peter so when speaking of faith and morals the Pope can add, delete, or clarify what God should have enunciated. So, in 1869 Pope Pius IX determined that the soul entered the ovum at the instant of fertilization. This undid centuries-old teachings that the soul entered the body one or two months after fertilization. So we can understand why Catholics might be against any abortion. But why have the evangelical Protestants so tightly grasped this Catholic idea?

The idea of when life starts is merely a human definition. Religions usually assume some sort of spiritual entity, such as a soul, in the body that survives one's death. Some religions believe that life starts when that soul enters the body. Ensoulment has been assumed to take place at various times: at the instant of conception, when the fertilized ovum attaches to the placenta, one or two months after conception, at birth, or even sometime after birth. In fact, there was a serious debate in early Christianity about whether or not girls even had souls!

Various medical definitions may surmise that life starts with the first heartbeat or with the first brain waves. The point is, that one's opinion as to when life starts is only a definition and not a verifiable eternal truth.

WE OFTEN HOLD VIEWS THAT CONFLICT

Candidates, and their constituencies, often desire, or even require, incompatible ideas or ideals. Forbidding abortion, while lowering taxes, is an example, so is private versus public health insurance. Here are some examples of conflicting desires.

OUTLAW ABORTION WHILE LOWERING TAXES

This undefined unknowable concept has been a disruptive gadfly in American politics. Recently the Governor of Ohio, John Kasich, who has a reputation for being pro-life and anti-taxation, became the third governor to sign into law that it was illegal to abort a fetus that was diagnosed with Down Syndrome. Down Syndrome, as you know, is a chromosomal problem where there are three chromosomes in the 21st group. There should be only two. This factor results in a number of physical and mental problems. For example, the average IQ is 50. This means that out of a thousand people, 999 would have a higher IQ than 50. The average IQ for the entire population is 100. This would mean that a person with an IQ of 100 would have 500 people out of a thousand with higher IQs.

There are a number of physical differences from the average person also. According to the government's Center for Disease Control, the average Down Syndrome person requires 12 to 13 times more money spent for healthcare than the average person. While some Down Syndrome children can attend regular classes, many require special education which is more expensive than the average spent per year per child for education from kindergarten through high school of $12,000 per year.

There are other questions relative to one's value to society, especially as the types of jobs needed in the future will generally require a university education. This is an example of the possible conflicts in values previously noted. If the parent wants a Down Syndrome child, that parent's self-centered desires will be fulfilled. The Down Syndrome child is usually quite pleasant and docile. If the pregnant parent does not want such a child, her self-centered values would be thwarted by the religious governor's decision.

Using a God-based value, we can say that it was God's plan to have the child as it is. Using a society-based assumption, the aforementioned problems of increased costs for healthcare and education, and reduced economic value of the person to the society would be major factors. So, the Catholic Governor's advocacy would be against the self-centered desires of those who did not want a Down Syndrome child and against the good of society in terms of reducing its costs and increasing its economic efficiency.

It is quite common for conservatives to be against aborting unwanted children while being for lowering taxes. They do not tell us why more unwanted children are needed for the society. They do not mention the fact that unwanted children are more likely to run afoul of the law -- with its extra expenses of police, foster homes, courts, and prisons.

So we have conflicting ideals and ideas among many in the society regarding requiring unwanted children to be born while advocating lower taxes. We have similar problems with wanting better infrastructure for roads and bridges while keeping gas taxes low. We have the call for "equality of opportunity," while increasing the cost of university education. Legislators continually call for a balanced budget, but are unwilling to cut the ever-increasing entitlement spending, military spending, or to increase the taxes. So spending limits and our national debt must be increased annually.

There is the stated desire by many politicians to reduce the national debt, but spending cuts or tax increases are out of the question. So the debt must be increased annually from a few hundred billion dollars, then increased by trillions if there is a war to finance, a reduction of taxes for the rich, or a recession to spend our way out of!

The important factor is that legislators must be re-elected so they need the lobbyists' bribes and the approval of their voters for their needs today. Larry Legislator told me, "Why worry, I'll be retired in style when the chit hits the fan."

The Bishop of Liverpool has criticized American Christians' support of Trump because he is marginalizing the poor. He says that they should review the tenets of their faith. The Archbishop of Canterbury echoed the criticism. Eighty percent of white evangelicals voted for Trump and 75% still support him. Supporting right wing populism is certainly an option, but doing it and calling it Christian is illogical.

The preachings of Christ exalt the poor, but President Trump works to degrade them—taking away their health coverage and marginalizing them. The non-citizen poor he deports if they are in the country, and bars them from entering if they reside outside—even if they are refugees from wars. At the same time, he enriches the wealthy.

The gospels are very clear that it is an impossible task for the wealthy to be saved. Matthew 19:24, Mark 10:25, and Luke 18:22-25 are clear. Here is the version in Luke; "When Jesus heard this, He said to him, 'One thing you still lack; sell all that you possess and distribute it to the poor, and you shall have treasure in heaven; and come, follow Me.' But when he had heard these things, he became very sad, for he was extremely rich. And Jesus looked at him and said, 'How hard it is for those who are wealthy to enter the kingdom of God! For it is easier for a camel to go through the eye of a needle than for a rich man to enter the kingdom of God.'"

There is some question about whether the Greek word used by the Evangelists should have been translated as "camel" or "rope," but either way, it would not pass through the eye of the needle. Most scholars believe that he meant "camel," probably paraphrasing a Babylonian phrase about how impossible it was to move an elephant through the eye of a needle. There are Christians who preach the gospel of wealth as being what God wants. They try to find other explanations for the camel story, but religious scholars are agreed that Jesus talked about a camel.

Is Trump's avowed love of money a truly Christian pursuit? Luke (12:15) clearly disagrees. "And He said to them, 'Take heed and beware of covetousness, for one's life does not consist in the abundance of the things he possesses.'"

The Golden Rule (Luke 6:31, Matthew 7:12) "Do unto others as you would have them do unto you," is a fundamental rule in most religions and ethical theories. How has Donald followed this rule?

The federal government filed a complaint against Trump, because he had violated the Fair Housing Act, part of the Civil Rights Act of 1968, by discriminating against tenants and potential tenants based on their race. Trump has also had several bankruptcies where his creditors had to eat their loans to him. Do unto others <u>before</u> they do unto you! Christians might wonder, with Mark (8:36), "For what will it profit a man if he gains the whole world, and loses his own soul?"

We might wonder about his admitted "pussy grabbing." Using the Golden Rule, was he hoping that the women would also "do this unto him." The same might be asked about his alleged sexual harassment. Was he hoping that they would harass him?

How does he measure up against the Seven Deadly Sins?

Lust—the longing for sexual pleasures, is shown in his multiple sexual harassment charges and his admitted pussy grabbing. Then there was his violation of the 7th Commandment when he had an adulterous relationship with Marla Maples when still married to his first wife, and his affairs with the porn star, Stormy Daniels, and Karen McDougal, former Playboy Playmate, in the early years of his marriage to Melania. Evangelical women interviewed on TV about Trump's adultery and his paying for sex (prostitution) said that his extramarital sexual activities were between him and God. They apparently believe that his billions create an exception to the "Thou shalt not" message that Moses brought down from Sinai carved in stone. I wonder how much money God requires in order to be released from his Commandments.

Pride—has been exhibited since he began his primary wars, and even before that. His speech where he said "only he could fix America" are prime examples of pride. His diagnosed narcissism indicates his extreme amount of pride.

Wrath-- is another of his deadly sins that are continually being exhibited. His uncontrolled feelings of anger and hate toward anyone who opposes him, especially Hillary Clinton and the major news networks.

Envy-- has been shown relative to his losing the popular vote to Hillary Clinton and to having a smaller than normal turnout for his inauguration.

Greed--has been obvious throughout his life as he pursued material possessions. It has probably been his hallmark goal in life.

Well that is only 5 out of 7. But it certainly seems that he has done an impeccable job paving his way to Hell! Dare his base follow him chanting "Downward Christian Soldiers" as they see him descend into Dante's Inferno?

Prominent supporters when asked about his adulterous behaviors say, "it's between him and his God." But God was quite clear in writing "Thou shalt not." He didn't say, "these are only recommendations, check with me if do some.' There's that adultery proscription that he violated with Marla Maples during his first marriage, and a slew of instances during his third marriage. Then there is that command not to bear false witness, that violated when he charged Barack Obama with tapping his phone. And how about playing golf on the Sabbath and not inviting God to play along?

Or will they follow the British bishops' beacons and look upward where their Testament points? Populism or evangelism is the choice—they can't be piggy-backed! Or, perhaps it is because his followers have the same sins, or wish for them? If so they are not really Christians, but calling themselves Christian gives them a feeling of superiority--- which salves their inferiority complexes.

WE HAVE AN OVERPOPULATION PROBLEM-- BUT TO PAY THE PENSIONS
AND HEALTH COSTS OF THE GREYING POPULATION SHOULD WE ENCOURAGE MORE BIRTHS OR RAISE THE RETIREMENT AGE

We continually hear of the necessity of having more children to pay the retirements of the older workers. This it is heard from the legislators who have not effectively funded public retirements as our life expectancies have increased at a rate of one year more of life for every six calendar years. But our retirement age has increased only one year in the last 80.

As I remember, one of those messages carved in stone on Mount Sinai was that we should be able to retire at age 65. Most blasphemous countries allow it to be between 55 and 60. I hope there's enough oil under their workplaces to support 30 years of retirement!

China recently increased the number of children allowed per family to two. There were several reasons for this. One of which was to provide a workforce to support the aging population. Lifespan in China has increased from 35 years in 1948 to 66 years in 1976 to 76 years today. Retirement age is between 50 and 55 for women and 6o for men. How much will these young workers need to contribute for their extra 15 to 20 years of retirement?

Tradition continually blocks our thinking about issues. For China, rather than having more children, they might raise the age of retirement to 68 or 70 for both men and women. In the US when Social Security was enacted, the retirement age was 65 and the average lifespan was 64. We have recently raised the retirement age to 67, for those born since 1960, but our lifespans are in the early 80s—and increasing.

Our retirement contributions are generally used up by our early 70s. The government must then make up our lack of contributions for 5 to 10 more years of our retirement.

If we continue to increase the population, with 5 to 7 new workers to pay for the older workers, we will need geometrically more workers every generation. So if we need five more workers now to support each retiree, in 20 to 40 years we will need 25, Then 40 more years 125 workers to support the 25 of the last generation. All this while the number of employees needed is reducing because of robotics, computerization, 3D printing, and artificial intelligence.

Pragmatic politicians, know that older people vote more than younger people. Realistic politicians know that we must either raise the retirement age to about 72 or raise the retirement contributions to nearly double what they are now. These options would be sure fire losers—and politicians want to keep their jobs. Consequently they opt for more children to support the greying voters. Doubling the population of our severely overcrowded planet thereby quadrupling the droughts, forest fires and storms of climate change is the better option—How can you blame politicians for "acts of God?"

WE SAY WE WANT EQUALITY OF OPPORTUNITY, BUT MANY PEOPLE START A THOUSAND MILES AHEAD OF OTHERS.

True equality of opportunity would require equally loving and supportive parents, equal education to the degree possible, and equal financial means. It would seem that to approach such equality we would need: parent licensing to attempt to insure loving knowledgeable parents; a national education system to increase and equalize the offerings; and, 100% taxes on inheritances.

The problems are that: tradition allows anyone to be a parent, no matter what their competence is in parenting; the Constitution, which is silent on education, appears to give the states the responsibility for education, then the states give a good bit of freedom to the local communities—thereby insuring unequal education; and the most unlikely of these requirements is to be eliminated, inheritance taxes because the rich have a huge amount of control over the legislation-- largely through their lobbyists.

I WANT CHEAPER, BETTER HEALTH INSURANCE—BUT NOT SOCIALIZED MEDICINE!

We have the national goal of healthcare for all, or nearly all, while requiring private insurance which must pay its investors and administrators high returns. This results in far higher costs than a government program which has no investors and no multi-million dollar CEOs.

Americans have an aversion to socialism and communism. But what are they? One definition is that in communism the government owns all of the means of production, and in socialism, the government owns the major means of production. But in practice there are few illustrations of these definitions. For example, in Norway, the government owns: the postal system, the airports, the major airline (along with Sweden and Denmark), the hospitals, a number of other businesses, and the liquor stores. It has part ownership in: oil and mining companies, theaters, some banks, research facilities and a number of other enterprises. These provide much of Norway's employment and the profits go into reducing debt, rather than into the pockets of capitalists as in the so-called capitalist countries. There are, of course, many multimillionaire business people in Norway. These often owned shipping companies, hotel chains and many other businesses.

The definition of communism that I like is Karl Marx's definition that, "communism is from each according to his abilities, to each according to his needs." The definition of socialism that I like is Vladimir Lenin's, that socialism is, "from each according to his ability, to each according to his work."

Using these definitions, Medicare and Medicaid and parts of Social Security, like survivor benefits and disability insurance, are actually communistic according to Marx. The pension system of Social Security is socialistic. You get at pension based on how much you made while working.

The American government also occasionally becomes socialistic, such as when the government bailed out General Motors in the recent recession. It took back stock in the company, which it then sold back when the company was solvent again. Banks have also been similarly saved by temporary government loans and ownership.

So we have socialistic and communistic elements of our government that people are excited about and will not let them be privatized. But few people seem to understand that they fall into the hated categories of socialism and communism. So let's continue to think a bit deeper into what we believe.

Since America spends 30 to 50% more of its gross domestic product than any other advanced country on healthcare, but has the poorest medical system of any advanced country, rating 38th in the world according to the World Health Organization, there must be a reason. The obvious reason is that the lobbying of health insurance companies, malpractice insurance companies, lawyers' lobbies, and other medical and pharmaceutical groups continue to strongly influence legislators. The rich also lobby against a national healthcare system because increased taxes in some cases, such as income and inheritance, would hit them harder.

All other advanced countries have a socialized system to cover all or a large part of medical expenses, with no problem regarding pre-existing conditions. Taxes must be raised for this to happen, but the total amount paid by the middle-class and poorer citizens from their paychecks would be minimized. The total amount that they would pay out would be about half of what they pay now. Taxes would be higher but payroll deductions would be much lower.

OVERPOPULATION IS RESPONSIBLE FOR CLIMATE CHANGE

Well-informed people are aware that our climate has changed rapidly. Geologically we should be moving into a colder period, but nearly every year we set temperature records. Environmental scientists are nearly unanimous (98%) that humans are causing it. Carbon dioxide and other greenhouse gases warm the atmosphere which increases the air's ability to absorb water vapor— an even more potent greenhouse gas. Whether we burn wood, oil, or natural gas--we add carbon dioxide to the air.

As you know, this melts the polar icecaps which are raising the sea level, wiping out low lying islands and soon submerging coastal cities. Malibu, Balboa Island, New York City, and Amsterdam are just a few of the threatened areas.

So, all countries with intelligent leadership are working to reduce their CO_2 emissions. Great idea! But who is putting that CO_2 in the air? My assumption is that it is the 7,500,000,000 people who have overpopulated the planet!

So by going one level deeper, from excessive CO_2 emissions, to the excessive number of people who are using fossil fuels to generate electricity or power their machines, we can see the real cause of our dilemma.

But there are other population related problems. Irreplaceable natural resources are rapidly diminishing. Garbage disposal is uncontrolled. Landfills emit methane, another greenhouse gas. Plastic clouds the seas and is consumed by the fish. The oceans have absorbed a large amount of CO_2 reducing the ultimate amount they can handle—and they become more acidic as they do.

WE WANT KILLERS BROUGHT TO JUSTICE—BUT THE USE OF DNA MAY ALTER CITIZENS' PRIVACY

The Golden State Killer was brought to justice in April of 2018 because of the police using genetic records of relatives who had sent their genetic records to ancestry web sites to check for links to their ancestors. DNA samples from items left at crime scenes as long as 42 years earlier, long before DNA testing was even dreamed of, were matched with distant relatives, then closer relatives, then with Joseph DeAngelo. He has been charged with at least eight killings, and is a suspect in 12 murders, 45 rapes and 120 burglaries throughout California in the 1970s and '80s. Which value should be primary? Should the right to privacy of the relatives be primary, if any of them object to their genetic records being used to catch a criminal? Should the suspected criminal have a right to the privacy of his own genetic material? Should society's interest in justice be primary? Should the survivors of the murdered victims, the rape victims, or the victims of the burglaries be primary? What if these genetic data bases were used to identify certain people for a planned genocide?

This may seem like a "no brainer," but immediately after his arrest, privacy rights lawyers began to cry "foul." As we will discuss later, ethical values are based on either an individual's desires, society's concerns, or God-based assumptions. The Ten Commandments forbid murder and stealing, and the Golden Rule would certainly proscribe rape. Is the right to privacy a superior value? Some people seem to think so!

WE WANT LOWER TAXES BUT WE CANNOT ALLOW EUTHANASIA

The government spends $50 billion dollars a year on treating the terminally ill during their last two months of life. Do we let the dying go a month or two earlier, if they want to, or do we increase taxes to pay for the treatment of the terminally ill?

AND OUR LEADERS INFER "SOLVE TODAY'S PROBLEMS—DON'T THINK ABOUT THE FUTURE! OUR TRADITIONS WILL SAVE US!"

Don't improve education. It will cost money and smart people would vote many legislators out. But a much higher quality of education is needed if we are to compete in today's and tomorrow's world. International tests show that our students are well down the list in reading, mathematics, science, and problem solving. Similarly, our adults are way down the list in literacy.

Cut people's taxes so they will continue to vote for the "ins." It doesn't matter that the national debt is increased. The legislators will be retired or dead by the time adversity hits. Just increase the national debt a few hundred billion dollars a year—and keep your head in the sand!

REDUCING THE POPULATION

The obvious ideal solution to reducing greenhouse gases is to reduce the population significantly. However, the tradition of having children, as being a right, makes it next to impossible to require population reduction. In China in 1980, with a strong autocratic government—using a society based values assumption--, the one child policy reduced the expected population by 400 million births. This was a factor in spurring Chinese economic growth and in allowing for more state funds to be allotted to education at every level. Nearly 40 years later we see a highly technological society with large numbers of university educated citizens. Was this a miracle or intelligent planning?

Generally speaking, the more advanced economic societies have significantly reduced their fertility rates already.

OVERPOPULATION PROBLEMS

The tradition of having large families to help on the farms and to support their aging parents is difficult to change. This is particularly true when the religion of the people encourages more children as is particularly true with the Catholics, the Mormons, and some Muslims.

The results of having more children than the family or the nation can support result in economic migrations to the more economically advanced countries. Both Europe and the United States have encountered problems because of the migration of the poorly educated and of refugees. The rise of populist anti-immigrant populist parties throughout Europe and the US is making significant changes in the politics in these countries. The well of empathy is rapidly running dry.

One solution might be to require the organizations desiring more children to pay for them through college age. The Catholic and Mormon churches are very rich and could do this, and the Mideast oil would go a long way in educating newly born Muslims. When individuals or groups dictate how we will behave, should they put their money where their mouths are?

Of course, we could use the traditional methods of population control: war, famine, disease-- and to a lesser extent, natural disasters like earthquakes and storms.

REDUCING BIRTHS

Rather than war, we could attempt a world-wide one child per family limitation. Good luck with that! Demagogues want more soldiers for their armies. Capitalists want more customers for their products.

Still another suggestion has been to license parents to have children. There are probably no jobs as difficult as parenting. It requires not only financial means, since it costs about $235,000 to raise a child to college-age in the US, but also knowledge about such things as nutrition, health, exercise, and how to handle the psychological stages that children must conquer through their childhood and teenage years. Then there are the college expenses. But what is essential is the ability to love unselfishly. This is probably the most important, and the most often lacking, essential of parenting.

It has been relatively simple to require licensing for such essential jobs as barbering and cosmetology, and for other desires such as driving or owning a dog. But tradition has probably erected an impenetrable wall here. Can you imagine a democratically elected official suggesting such an intelligent requirement that would give many children the chance at a better life? After all, the only consideration for having children should be a parent's desire-- or an accident of sexual intercourse. The life of a child should never be a consideration! The UN Declaration of Human Rights grants everyone the right to start a family. (Article 16) The unborn, or the young children, are obviously not important to the United Nations. They have no rights!

WE MUST KEEP LOCAL CONTROL OF OUR SCHOOLS BUT WE WANT THE BEST EDUCATION FOR OUR CHILDREN

Education for citizenship? If we don't have educated citizens, our vocations may not mean much in a crumbling economy. The splintered thousands of school boards can't possibly deliver equal educations, so the future citizens suffer.

Do most politicians want voters who are broadly educated and can think for themselves? It's easier to get elected when the gullible swallow any bait! Let's stay with traditions: The Electoral College, partisan politics, religions influencing the state, lobbyists, and the golden promises of politicians that pave the yellow brick road to Never-Never Land -- and Oz.

CHAPTER 2   BEYOND THE OBVIOUS

To understand the second part of this book, we must understand the underpinnings of what our devious leaders have done to undermine our democracy while seducing our votes by appealing to our unconscious minds and bypassing our intellects with fear, anger, and hope—based on lies, half-truths, and advertising tricks that violate the rules of logic.

We are going to look at democracy, primarily at politics and politicians. One of the larger problems today is violence --- violence within democracies. So, we will look at that too. It is easy to see what today's politicians do. It is easy to see the damage done by jihadist terrorists. We hear them say why they do what they do-- but that is seldom the real reason.

We need to go back to the basics, to the causes. It is easy to deal with the obvious, but much more difficult to find the hidden causes and deal with them. That's where we want to go-- to explore the "whys" of the "whats." We know what has happened. But to really understand why, we must go beyond what they, the politicians and terrorists, say are the reasons.

Let's take as an illustration an American football quarterback who completes only 30% of his passes and has 10% intercepted. That's terrible! But why? Perhaps his receivers did not run the right patterns, but he threw the pass correctly. This happened a few times in a recent Super Bowl game. Maybe the cause was that the coaches had not prepared him for the opponent's type of secondary coverage. But perhaps the coaches did not know about that particular type of coverage. If so it may not have been the quarterback who was so much to blame as his coaches or the opposing coaches who developed the defense he had just seen, so the quarterback could not make the adjustments necessary. So the cause may not have been the obvious, the quarterback or the receivers. It may have been something quite different that was not obvious to the thousands who saw the game.

But in this book we are not talking about football. We are often talking about elements of behavior that cause the obvious problems-- but which are unseen. So we see a terrorist bomber and blame his religion. We see ineffective politicians and blame their lack of experience or intelligence. We see voters manipulated through their unconscious minds and by their lack of knowledge of the future. Some people will see the drive for power behind all of these actions. But there is a deeper reality still. It is the unconscious mind and the feelings of inferiority. And what caused that inferiority? Can we dig deeper into the "why"? To do this we must understand the physical brain—and its function, the mind. Then, we can better understand how we have been manipulated.

As with so many of the words we often throw around, like--democracy, God, justice, socialism, and prejudice--we often haven't looked deeply enough at the meaning of the word and its relationships to other concepts used in our society.

Let us now look at behavior and peek behind the obvious.

THE BRAIN AND THE MIND

What we call the mind is really the product of the brain. You might say that the brain is the noun and the mind is the verb. Memories and values are things that we say are part of our minds. However, they are located in our brains in different areas. Electrically stimulating different parts of the brain can bring up a memory, intense pleasure, hunger, an hallucination, or can make your arm move.

The brain contains just about all of our thinking power. But not all of it "thinks." We think we are in control of everything that we think and of all of our actions, but sadly, the truth is that we are not. While some of our mind is conscious to us, much of it is below the conscious level. It is in the brain, but we cannot access it alone. Sometimes through effective psychotherapy some of our mind can be brought to the surface.

Some of our behavior is inherited through our DNA. Some of our behavior is influenced by recent ancestors' behavior. This is a relatively new field of study. It is called epigenetics. Whether it is inherited in our DNA, or inherited RNA, it can significantly affect our behavior.

As science advances, we can evaluate more behavior and often we are able to categorize it as within the normal bounds-- or outside of them. If we are wondering about our politicians we are more likely to have creditable evidence after the representative is in office. Sometimes we can see behavioral characteristics in candidates before the election. Let us take a few minutes here to look more deeply into factors that may be crucial in our voting.

We need to look at the brain and how it functions as our mind. That functioning is partially inherited, some estimate as high as 50% of our behavior is inherited. But a very good part of our mind is determined by how our brain has been programmed by what has happened in our lives-- our environment.

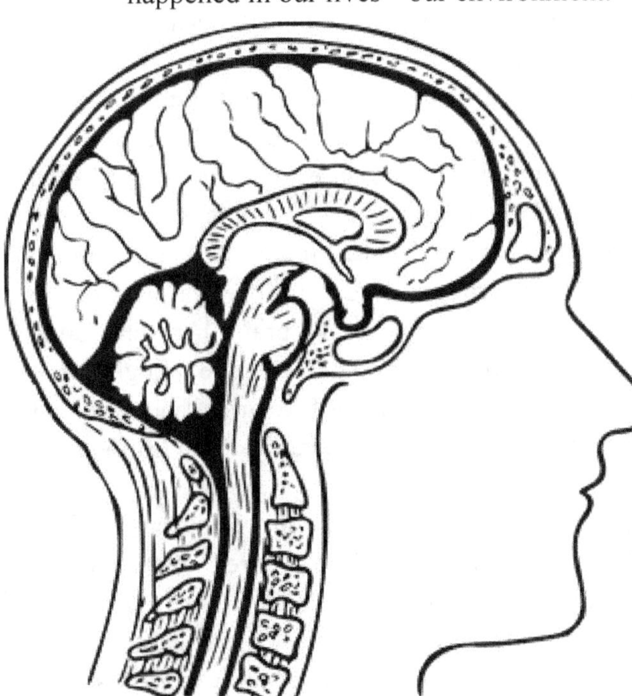

Our experiences, our evaluations of them, and our independent thinking are registered in different areas of the brain through electrical impulses in the nerves and

The following paragraphs are necessary to understand what will come later. If you have a background in neurophysiology, skip these paragraphs.

THE BRAIN AND NERVOUS SYSTEM

In the picture above, the frontal lobe is on the right and is part of the external cerebral cortex. The hippocampus, limbic system and amygdala are in the lower middle area and on the inside of the brain.

We must start with the nervous system, particularly the brain. Throughout the body we have nerves (neurons) that transmit electrical impulses both to and away from the spinal cord and the brain. There are about 85 billion neurons in the brain. We have nerves that carry impulses to the brain and are registered there and we have nerves that go from the brain to the body to make us move and talk. There are about 100,000 miles of nerves that carry these impulses. There are also about 100 trillion connections or "synapses" that are the gaps between the neurons.

Our memories, according to recent research, are stored primarily in the prefrontal area in the front of the brain and also in the hippocampus. However, they can be stored throughout much of the brain. The memory seems to strengthen in the frontal cortex while often weakening in the hippocampus. (Science, April, 2018) Memories may also be stored in the amygdala, which tends to give an emotional meaning to them.

So, your memories are merely bunches of chemicals in different areas of the brain. Doesn't that make you feel warm inside?

Many psychoactive drugs commonly act in the limbic system and amygdala by changing the normal chemical and electrical activity in the area.

HOW THE NERVE IMPUSES WORK

The electrical impulse travels down the nerve at about 268 miles per hour. At the end of the nerve (neuron) there are a number of terminals. Each of these terminals releases a chemical, a neurotransmitter, which moves across the microscopic gap of the synapse and stimulates the dendrites on the next neuron. This gap between the terminals of one segment of the neuron to dendrites of the next segment is called the synapse. You can imagine the delicacy and speed of the electric impulse to chemical release to a new electrical impulse. There are often thousands of nerves and synapses involved in a thought or an action. So:

ELECTRIC IMPULSE > NEUROTRANSMITTERS > NEW IMPULSE

NEUROTRANSMITTERS

Different nerve terminals release different neurotransmitters. There are well over 100 neurotransmitters so far discovered. Among the major ones are: acetylcholine, serotonin, dopamine, GABA, and norepinephrine. A slight increase or decrease in the release of a neurotransmitter can have effects, sometimes serious, on the behavior of a person. It is not just the type or the amount of neurotransmitter that is released, but the area of the brain in which the impulse is occurring.

For example, hunger is usually found in the area of the hypothalamus. Vision occurs in the rear of the brain. Much of balance is controlled in the cerebellum. Much of thinking occurs in the forward part of the cerebrum. The pleasure center is deeper in the brain in what is called the medial forebrain bundle and the nucleus accumbens.

All of our sensations, such as pain or joy, are registered on our brains through the action of electrical impulses and the release of neurotransmitters in different parts of the brain. All of our conscious movements are similarly started in the brain then sent to the muscles that we want to contract. So, if you want to take a bite of steak, the thought starts in your brain, probably in the front section, then through a series of electrical and chemical actions in your nervous system the impulses move your arm and hand and you lift the food to your mouth.

Every thought we have similarly moves through different brain pathways with the same series of electrical and chemical actions and is settled into an area where we can remember it. But quite often we "forget" thoughts or experiences. They still may influence our behavior after we have "forgotten" them. Often, very negative experiences, such as being gang raped or witnessing the murder of a loved one, are forgotten in our conscious mind. These, however, are still stored in the brain. While they exist, they can influence our behavior, we are not aware of them. They are in what we call the unconscious area of the mind.

It may be interesting for those not knowledgeable about neurotransmitters to relate the various effects from the use of mind altering drugs-- both legal and illegal. Psychoactive drugs, such as: marijuana, cocaine, heroin and the many prescription drugs, stimulate or depress our nervous systems. They work by increasing, decreasing, or preventing the neurotransmitter from being reabsorbed into the terminal so that it can be

released with the next neural impulse. When it is not reabsorbed, it has the effect of strengthening the amount of electrical current in the next nerve.

Alcohol can also alter behavior by the increase or decrease of several different neurotransmitters, but also by the deadening effect on the nerves which will inhibit the transmission of the electrical current.

Marijuana seems to affect the release a number of neurotransmitters including: GABA, noradrenaline, dopamine, and acetylcholine. The most likely areas to be affected are: the cerebellum, hippocampus and neocortex. The brain also has receptors for elements in the marijuana that are separate from the neurotransmitter effects. So its actions are more difficult to study.

Every psychoactive drug releases different amounts of different neurotransmitters and in different parts of the brain. Personality traits, such as narcissism and compulsive lying, similarly can caused by the action, or inaction, of the various neurotransmitters in different parts of the brain.

Having said this, the brain needs to be in good working order for our mind to work properly at its full potential. If there are areas of the brain that are damaged, that particular part of the mind will be affected. As in the case of brain-damaged people who hallucinate because a certain part of their brain is not functioning properly. Psychoactive drugs, both legal and illegal, will affect the brain's functioning. Poor nutrition from the womb to the present may affect functioning—proteins are essential in brain and neurotransmitter development.

GENETIC INFLUENCES ON OUR MINDS—AND BEHAVIOR

The normal human has 46 chromosomes, some of us have one or two, more or less. These chromosomes carry the 20,000 genes that determine who we are, and may even influence our behavior. About half of our genes come from each parent. They determine how tall and how smart we might become, our potential— but our environment usually determines how much of our potential we might reach. Our genes might make us more susceptible to a mental or physical disease, but out environment or epigenetic transfers might increase or decrease the genetic potential in each gene.

EPIGENETICS

Epigenetics is a relatively new area of study. "epi" means above, that is it somehow controls the DNA which was inherited. Epigenetic changes may be passed down from parents or even earlier generations or they may be developed after a child is born. These epigenetic changes can do this by changes in the DNA, changes in certain proteins affecting the workings of the DNA, or by the actions of RNA—which can turn on or off the functioning of a gene's DNA, so the inherited gene may or may not work.

It is theorized that some cancers may be affected by epigenetics. If a tumor producing gene is turned on by the RNA it might induce a cancer. Similarly, if a tumor suppressing gene is turned off by RNA it might allow tumors to develop. A link to prostatic cancer has been found. Some forms of lupus and rheumatoid arthritis in women have epigenetic links.

Stresses of varying types may cause such epigenetic changes. Child abuse has been shown to develop epigenetic changes in certain genes. In one study of people with post-traumatic stress, the people with certain epigenetic changes had 12 times the number of negative cases.

With mice, a loud noise has elicited epigenetic changes in the offspring. You can imagine that starvation is a stress. In the Netherlands after World War II, there were a large number of underweight babies born to women who had been severely undernourished because of the lack of food during the war. Their babies were severely underweight. This might be expected because of the condition of the mother. But the second-generation were also born underweight even though their mothers had been very well nourished.

Epigenetic changes have been found with many types of psychoactive drugs, such as: alcohol, nicotine, cocaine, heroin, and marijuana. Teenage binge drinking has been found to change the DNA methylation patterns in the hypothalamus of offspring who have never been exposed to alcohol. It is this DNA methylation that is one of the three major factors in epigenetic transferring from parent to child.

On the other hand, positive changes have been found in children who have been breast-fed. The physical closeness is at least as important as the human milk.

At this point in time, there have not been enough studies of the human genome to document which genes might be affected by which types of stresses--stresses such as violence or drug usage. Both alcohol and cannabis show changes in the genes of habitual users. Studies are being done that may indicate epigenetic links to the children and grandchildren of psycho-active drug users. When we see the incredibly rapid rise of childhood autism, ADHD and auto-immune diseases we might wonder if there might be a link with some drugs, both illegal and prescribed.

Epigenetic behavior changes have been hypothesized for over 50 years, but it is only recently that the human genome has been available for study. Violence, personality disorders and even psychoses may be epigenetically caused—schizophrenia is currently being studied and some links are promising.

LEARNED BEHAVIOR

Most of us think, along with Freud, that either we thought our way to our behavior or it is a result of our learning throughout our lives. There is no question that what we have experienced will have an influence in how we react.

As Freud also emphasized, most of our behavior is in the unconscious mind. It is filled with memories that we have forgotten but that still influence our behavior.

HOW MIGHT OUR BRAINS AFFECT VIOLENCE

As an illustration of how these influences might affect the violent behavior we see so often, let's look at these above influences, or possible influences, on violence.

THE ROOTS OF VIOLENCE

To illustrate the possible causes of behavior let us look at a common concern of today. You are undoubtedly familiar with the studies of rats and mice done by Dr. John Calhoun with the National Institute of Mental Health in the 50s and 60s. Starting with four pair of mice in a perfect environment, the population doubled every 55 days for several generations. Then the growth slowed. Eventually the entire population died out. In the stages where the population was approaching its maximum, there were no places for the young to become important. This, Calhoun called "the behavioral sink." in this period there was less interest in reproducing and the females became less motherly. They abandoned their young, they did not complete weaning, they chased the newborn from the nest, and they became more aggressive. The males, not finding important places in the society, were more likely to become homosexual, withdrawn and self-absorbed, or violent. This would be a possible environmental cause of behavior changes, such as violence.

Some would make comparisons with our human condition today. In Europe, the fertility rate of women (1.58 per woman) is below the population replacement level of 2.1. There is often more of interest for mothers to do, such as working productively in the commercial workplace, than raising little "rug rats" effectively. We certainly see that there are not enough places for the males to exert their power in today's society. Unemployment among youth is a major societal problem. This leaves them free to make mischief-- even violent mischief!

In some overpopulated areas, like the favelas of Rio or the ghettos and barrios of L.A., gang membership can give meaning to the lives of many young men and women. Violence is increased in the first or second generations of immigrants in many Western countries. Jihadism is another illustration of an avenue that is taken by some disenfranchised young people.

But there might be genetic influences increasing violence. In the 1960s, Robert Ardrey, a commentator on anthropology and psychology, wrote that we humans have an instinct to violence. We also have an instinct to gain territory and to protect it. If we have such instincts we must look to genetics to clarify the puzzle.

(See his books: "African Genesis" and "The Territorial Imperative" For well documented accounts of his theories.)

Here is some evidence of genetic influences on producing violent behavior. The MAO-a gene seems to increase violent behavior, especially if the boys had been mistreated as children or are stressed. Other people, without this gene, with similar stresses might withdraw from the situation rather than attack. A study in Finland, found that in about 10% of the murderers this gene was present.

The DAR1 gene is also associated with violence. It seems to change the activation of the neurotransmitter dopamine in the synapse between the nerve cells.

The DRD2 gene can increase the tendency to violence if there is a stress such as: family problems, lack of success at school, or being unpopular.

These genes may increase the likelihood of violence by as much as 50%.

Other personality traits or behaviors are caused by, or influenced by, our heredity, our epigenetic transfers, or our environment.

THE BRAIN AND MENTAL ILLNESS

Serious problems such as schizophrenia or depression can be caused by a lack or an excess of neurotransmitters in certain areas of the brain. Forty-four genes related to depression have been found so far. Anyone, from world leaders, to your neighbor, your child—or you—can be seriously affected. Mental illness may be genetically caused. It may also be caused by emotional stress. The type of mental illness may also be determined by how your genetic makeup reacts to your environmental stresses.

OUR MINDS—THINKING OR REACTING

We wonder how the world started. Then we come up with creation myths-- and that is enough. We don't ask who created Yahweh, or God, or Allah. They are the first cause.

But when people express a political position or act in a positive or negative way, we accept it as indicative of why and what they believe. Sometimes psychologists or sociologists will go a step beyond. For example, we used to think that rape was caused by sexual desire. A number of years ago we went beyond the act and looked at "power" as the cause—the use of power in a sexual context. But why does that person need power? There must be another reason or two beyond that.

It is always simplest to look at the obvious and say that it is the explanation. For example, when Donald Trump chastised both sides in the Charlottesville white supremacy confrontations, people said he was siding with the alt-right. And most people were anti-Nazi so they chastised their president.

But why did he seem to support these reactionary groups? They were chanting anti-Semitic slogans, and his daughter and son-in-law are Jewish. Some of his best friends are Jewish. Was he really supporting the far right? Was he trying to calm the situation? But when the members of the business advisory and art advisory committees that he had set up, resigned; when his ratings dropped even more, did he change his position? No. Because he is always right. And why is he always right? We need to go another step deeper. Many in the mental health field have called him narcissistic. If so, why?

We must go back another step. Psychiatrist Alfred Adler gave us the reason-- inferiority complex. His narcissism is an attempt to overcome his feelings of inferiority.

One more step back and we come to his parenting. We have no idea of how he was raised, but we know that he displayed bullying tendencies early in his life.

Maybe there's even one more step back. Could it be that his narcissistic and bullying behaviors are the result of genetic or epigenetic influences where his genes are somehow involved?

As we look at some issues in this book we will be attempting to go beyond the obvious and look for the real causes, some real results and even suggest some intelligent solutions. Unhappily, the most effective solutions will not be possible for the same reasons that the problems have arisen—changing he unconscious mind is far more difficult than changing the intellect.

> our inferiority complexes,
> our self-centered values, and
> our rose-colored glasses that obscure the realities!

HOW DO OUR MINDS WORK-- AND HOW CAN WE BE CONTROLLED?

First, we have to realize that our physical brain is the major source of what we call our mind. Stimulating the brain electrically can bring out thoughts and emotions that can give us an idea of where in the brain some of the functions of the mind are stored.

As an example, in the 1960s James Olds did some studies with rats. He put food on one side of a hot electrified grid. The hungry rats would not cross the grid for the food. He then inserted an electrode into a pleasure center of the brain of the rat, the medial forebrain bundle. Once the rat learned that it would receive a stimulus to its reward area, it would cross the hot grid. (This area of pleasure centers is the same as those stimulated by some upper drugs, like cocaine.)

We think that we are in total control of our thoughts and behavior. We are often wrong. Over 100 years ago, Freud popularized an older idea that we have a large part of our mind that is not conscious to us. If Freud was right, this subconscious or unconscious part of our mind is much larger than our conscious mind-- the things we can think of now. He compared it with an iceberg, where 90% of it is underwater.

If it is indeed larger, it may have great control over us. Shrewd politicians, as well as advertisers, have often used our unconscious minds to direct us to do what they want.

So, we have a conscious mind and an unconscious mind. But these can be further subdivided. Using a combination of psychological and philosophical labels we can categorize the functions of the brain-mind form and function. The levels of the mind might be:

The conscious mind-- contains memories, consciously held values, and the intellect—where we believe we are thinking independently.

The unconscious mind-- contains both the pre-conscious minds (subconscious) which may sometimes become known, such as through dreams, and the deeper unconscious mind. This deeper part of the unconscious mind may exert some control over our behavior. These unconscious areas of the mind also contain memories and values—they influence our behavior but we don't know they are there.

Genetic, epigenetic, and hypothetical substrates—such as instincts— influences on our minds that we did not experience, as opposed to the conscious and unconscious that contain memories that we have experienced. These would be the deepest level of the mind.

CONSCIOUS MESSAGES AND THEIR SUBLIMINAL MEANINGS

When politicians deliver their messages, they appeal through our conscious minds, even occasionally to our intellects. The message may remain in our conscious mind, but may seep into our unconscious. Sometimes a message can go directly into the subconscious through subliminal perception.

Other times the message is delivered to the conscious mind, but an implied message goes directly into the unconscious. For example, the National Rifle Association (NRA) continually harps on the idea that we must keep our freedoms, such as the Second Amendment guarantees. They play on the fear that you must be free to defend yourself from intruders in your home. (This freedom was not a concern in the original Bill of Rights, and was not made a "right" until 2007 by the Supreme Court.) The subliminal message was that you are more powerful with a firearm. And you certainly want to equal the power of Wyatt Earp or Billy the Kid! What a great way to reduce your inferiority complex. (More on this in a few pages.)

THE CONSCIOUS MIND

The conscious mind is a combination of experiences and thoughts, some of which we can control and some of which we cannot. Memories, such as familial or societal traditions are extremely important. It is the part of our mind that we experience when we remember events, when we choose values, and when we make conscious choices. A problem often develops when we forget that we, and others, are directed only by our conscious mind. The unconscious mind is apparently much larger than our conscious mind, but we cannot admit this. Our unconscious mind is more likely to react and to behave in a non-thinking manner. It is this part of the mind that politicians and advertisers often target with their messages. Will discuss this soon. But first we will deal with the part of our conscious mind should be able to think.

CONTENTS OF THE CONSCIOUS LEVEL OF THE MIND
➢ Memories
➢ Conscious values
➢ Stored knowledge
➢ Intellect--ability to use verified facts and logic
•Ability to analyze accurately
•Ability to rationalize or lie

TRADITIONS AND HABITS

Let's start with some stumbling blocks to clear thinking. Tradition is the major stumbling block—probably even more of a problem than a lack of learning. It reminds me of the opening song of the classic musical "Fiddler on the Roof." The hero Tevye leads the cast in the rousing reminder that we are all caught in the quicksand of our cultures. While Tevye was reminiscing about his state as a Jew in the later years of czarist Russia in the early 20th century, we are each dragged by our own anchors as we attempt to sail the sea of life. And here is what Tevye recognized:

"Because of our traditions, we've kept our balance for many, many years.

Here in Anatevka, we have traditions for everything.

How to sleep. How to eat. How to work. How to wear clothes. For instance, we always keep our heads covered,

and always wear a little prayer shawl. This shows our constant devotion to God.

You may ask, how did this tradition get started? I'll tell you. I don't know. But it's a tradition.

And because of our traditions every one of us knows who he is and what God expects him to do."

Political traditions are often strong. He's a Kennedy. I'll vote for him. He's a Bush. I'll vote for him. My family has always been Republican, so you know where my vote goes. My family has always been Democrat, so you know where my vote goes.

How many voters across the world step into the voting booths with the knowledge necessary to vote intelligently for their own enlightened self-interest? Did those who voted for the UK to leave the EU realize that the British pound would drop significantly? Did they know that their vacations to Greece and the Canaries will cost 10-20% more? Did they know that their imported groceries would go up in price because of the falling pound? Did they know that their retirees living in Spain and France and other EU countries will probably be forced back to the UK because their health bills will not be paid from the EU coffers? This could add another half billion pounds to the cost of Brexit. How much did they really know?

Did those who voted for Donald Trump realize that millions would lose their health insurance? Did they realize that they were seriously damaging the relationship between America and the EU? Did they realize that he would reveal classified information to the Russians? Did they realize that some of his close associates had had secret communications with the Russians?

What about the candidates who want to run our government? How many candidates understand the pressing issues of the world or the nation? How many are in it for the glory, the power, or the opportunity to make life better for themselves-- with tax breaks, opportunities for corruption, and the pursuit of riches?

Americans are upset when people criticize their way of life. This is not unusual because we all become upset when our ways of life are criticized-- our religion, our politics, our children, our parents, our grammar, our favorite team, our favorite restaurant, our chosen job-- in fact about everything we do. When Michael Moore in his movie, "Where Shall We Invade Next," pointed out that:

➢ Finnish schools are in session fewer hours than American schools and that they don't have homework, but still score significantly better than Americans on international tests,

➢ Norwegian prisons are much more open and caring that American prisons but they have half the recidivism rate of American prisons,

➢ French students have school lunches that are gourmet four course menus that are very healthy,

➤ Italians get more than one month paid vacation and get an extra paycheck to pay for it,

➤ Italian women get five months paid maternity leave,

➤ Women legislators and bankers in Iceland had done a far better job than the men.

What Moore didn't say was that,

➤ Estonia gives about 80 weeks of maternity leave; Norway, is only the 10th most generous country but it still gives you 11 months to the mother and one to the father; there are 38 countries that give paid maternity leave to mothers, only the United States does not.

➤ Most countries give four weeks of paid vacation, plus holidays, America has no law requiring paid vacations.

➤ The glass ceiling is still evident in most countries, where it is minimized or eliminated the countries do better.

When Donald Trump said "we have to make America great again," he did not say how. But we have our traditions. Prisons are for punishment not for rehabilitation. Schools need inexpensive teachers, no supplies, and lots of homework. Men must be in the positions of authority, because that is the way it has always been. Saying that we are Christian is the main thing, acting lovingly is not really important. Keep it the way it "was," if it was good enough for my grandparents, it is good enough for me.

THE INTELLECT

One part of the conscious mind we usually call the intellect. This is the part of the mind that can reason and find the truth, or the probable truth, of a theory or idea. Most people believe that their opinions are arrived at intellectually. The next four chapters will examine how savvy politicians use techniques, such as data mining and propaganda, to influence us to act and vote in a certain way. We think we are acting intelligently and on the evidence, but we are often acting on unconscious drives that are stimulated in our unconscious minds by falsified evidence, or propaganda.

The intellect is that part of the mind that poses questions and searches for solutions. We might imagine that many thousands of years ago our Neanderthal and Homo Sapiens ancestors thought about how they could best hunt for food or gather munchies. They sometimes put their thoughts on their cave walls with ochres and charcoals. Undoubtedly they asked, "where did I come from," and, "where do I go after I die."

If we can develop our intellects, we can probably determine ways to make our lives more fulfilling, and our societies more responsive to the well-thought-out needs of the citizens-- which is the purpose of this book.

If we have the evidence necessary, we might choose to listen to the opera Carmen rather than to Justin Bieber. We might choose to avoid the psychoactive drugs that interfere with our abilities to run our lives maximally. We might be concerned with the choosing of intelligent, socially concerned representatives to run our society. It may take some intellectual coaxing to choose to read Plato's "Republic" or Machiavelli's "Prince," rather than Patterson's "The Store" or Grisham's "The Whistler"-- as enjoyable as these popular books are, they may not make it into the classics of Western civilization.

The intellect, if properly used, can help us sort the good from the bad, the true from the false, and the beautiful from an ugly. In this book, a major concern is using the intellect to help us choose the best government possible. With the proper tools of logic, it should be able to help us sort out real news from fake news and realistic promises from pie-in-the-sky fanciful dreams.

With the tools for understanding ourselves, from psychology, and the tools to think more clearly, from philosophy, we should be able to become much more effective thinkers. Of course, we need a great deal of knowledge to be able to make intelligent decisions today. The tools of logic, from philosophy, can tell us how to define ideas more clearly and to determine their truth or falsity more effectively. But we need to have the knowledge of the area being discussed, such as: economics, globalization, climate change, world history, psychology, sociology, etc. If we don't have such knowledge, we must be willing to find it in books, the internet, or in discussions with learned people.

As most of us know, not everything we see, hear, or read is true. We are bombarded from the right and the left with truths, half-truths, and lies. The candidates are not always the best source of truth.

The job of the intellect is complicated. One is to use the tools of logic to understand the meanings of the words being used, Second, look at the truth or falsity of statements, and determine the probability of proposed ideas. Thirdly, if there are arguments, follow the rules of deductive logic. Another job, which is particularly important in questions of value such as ethics and morality, is to understand the basic assumptions, the non-provable starting points, of oneself and one's intellectual opponents.

Because of this, the intellect has its own chapter.

THE UNCONSCIOUS MIND—THE SOURCE OF MOST OF OUR BEHAVIOR

Sigmund Freud, who popularized the idea of us having part of our mind outside of our conscious control saw our minds as icebergs, with about 90% of our minds below the conscious level. Freud did not invent the terms unconscious or subconscious. Paracelsus in this book "About Illnesses," published in 1567, was probably the first to recognize it in the West. Many physicians and philosophers recognized it throughout the 18th Century, and we can find the idea in Hindu scriptures from 4,000 years ago.

The field of psychology separated from philosophy in 1880. Freud's development of his theories began about ten years later. Research into this invisible, yet highly evident entity, continues today with brain scanning and other techniques

CONTENTS OF THE UNCONSCIOUS LEVEL OF THE MIND

➢ Memories that are not conscious but can influence our behavior.

➢ Values below the conscious level—from traditions or forgotten memories from our earlier life.

➢ Unconscious motivations (based on unconscious memories and values).

➢ Genetic and epigenetic propensities for normal or abnormal behavior, such as: lying or other personality proclivities or mental illnesses.

➢ Instincts, if we have them—such as for violence or supremacy

THE FEELINGS OF INFERIORITY ARE UNIVERSAL

Now we leave Freud's idea of an unconscious mind and look to one of his contemporaries, Alfred Adler, who disagreed with Freud in the makeup of the unconscious. Freud thought that our major unconscious drive was for pleasure. Adler saw it as being the need to show power because of our deep feelings of inferiority—the inferiority complex.

This feeling of inferiority developed early in our childhoods because we really were inferior. We couldn't eat or drink without help. We couldn't walk or talk. We couldn't control our excretions. We were totally dependent on other people to survive. Added to that, perhaps we did not get the affection that was needed to make us feel desirable and loved. Perhaps we were punished for actions that we had no control over. Perhaps we did not have people around us to minister to our needs when we needed them. Perhaps we saw our parents fighting. Maybe we were sexually abused.

One in five girls and one in twenty boys have been sexually abused, and 90% of them knew their abuser, according to the US Health and Human Services' Children's Bureau. And there is much more abuse that is non-sexual, but often violent.

We were all really inferior to the adults around us. As we grew up we often accomplished things that made us feel good about ourselves. We may have been successful in school in academics or athletics. We may have written a published book or become an Eagle Scout. We may have been president of a club. We may have been hired for a job we really wanted. These are among the more psychologically uplifting accomplishments that a person may achieve. There are many things that we have done that may make us feel less inferior or even a bit superior.

OUR DRIVE FOR POWER IS OUR ATTEMPT TO OVERCOME OUR INFERIORITIES

The drive for power, emphasized by Alfred Adler, is probably the major motivational force for most people.

The very simplest way that many people have of showing power is in owning a gun. You can understand why people do not want to part with their pistols and rifles. But it is more than just owning the gun, if you use it for target practice, your power is increased every time you hit the bull's-eye or shoot a beer can off the fence. Whether or not you ever expect to use it, you have it. In your home, you may feel safer because of it. On hunting trips, you feel safe because the animals you are hunting don't have guns. And if you shoot one, what a macho feeling you will have. For some people, having a pistol is enough. For others, having the most powerful firearm available increases their feeling of power.

You can see why they fight for their newly enunciated Second Amendment rights. And we can all be proud of them when they march with their militias, ready to fight King George if he tries to invade us again. Oops! That was the original Second Amendment, not the one the Supreme Court wrote eleven years ago.

For high schoolers, having a car is a major conquering of one's inferiority. And for many, the faster the car-- the more powerful you are. Getting a job is a big deal. And getting one with Boeing as a vice president is even better than flipping burgers at McDonald's.

Moving away from home is a big deal—a real showing of independence and power. As you get older, owning a house probably fulfills a lifelong dream of independence and power.

Just to illustrate a few more common behaviors of people around us using their impulses for power: driving fast, driving aggressively, spousal and child abuse, yelling in frustration, harassing employees, sexual harassment, being a good cook, striving for success in business, identifying with a sport team, putting down your children, putting down others (even if it appears to be as a joke), sky diving, etc. You get the picture! Just observe the interactions of people around you. You will see actions of "power over" or "power to" continually. Some of the more anti-social illustrations of power include: joining a violent gang, raping someone, hacking a computer, or becoming a serial killer

But the drive for power is also used for positive goals. On the positive side, your drive for power may push you to study harder, to practice your sport with more intensity, to start a business, to run for an office. As I see it, the drive for power is our major motivator.

Working for an environmental organization, a political party, or a service club are socially acceptable groups that can give us some status. So, can our religion—especially if we are "saved" like evangelical Christians or fundamentalist Muslims.

Our need for power can be seen in many areas where you wouldn't expect it. Take gambling, for example. If you win, you can certainly brag about it because you have overcome the odds. But even if you lose big, you can brag about how much you lost.

Comedy is an even better example, look at how often you laugh because you feel superior to the butt of the joke. The late Don Rickles "schtick" was to make fun of those in his audience. Of course, you could laugh because you felt superior to his target. How about Polish, Irish, Catholic, or Jewish jokes. You may laugh at any or all of them. But you probably laugh harder if you are not in the group showing stupidity.

Jokes about Trump are a natural because most people don't lie as much or have the power to do so many ridiculous things. Some comedians make fun of themselves, their noses, their ears, their ethnicity, their gender—as long as you make the audience feel superior, they will laugh.

Knowledgeable advertising executives, mental health therapists, as well as politicians, understand that we are commonly motivated by our fears, anger and hopes that are reactions to our real or imagined feelings of inferiority. By tapping into the prevailing fears and anger of the various portions of the electorate the successful politician can develop loyalty from enough voters to win an election.

Donald Trump corralled many business owners by promising to cut regulations and reduce business taxes. He generated enthusiasm among the jobless by promising to bring back mining and factory jobs. And as a businessman he knew how to do it—he promised! One way was to deport illegal Mexicans who were taking the jobs. Not only would he deport them, but he would build a wall to keep others out! For the evangelical Christians, he would stop abortions any way possible. (He had once approved of abortions, but that was before he ran for office!) Then for the Christians, who had the true religion, he would keep out those infidel Muslims. That idea also appealed to those who were afraid of terrorism, which was a real threat.

THE NEED FOR POWER

Mental health professionals often see the need for power as the reason for much of our behavior. It is obvious when we look a little deeper at both socially valuable and socially destructive actions. I have no doubt that Warren Buffet feels a bit of a power surge when a company he buys does exceptionally well. Similarly, we can imagine Bill Gates' feeling of power and accomplishment when he finally finished his work in developing the Windows operating system. But the same feeling of power, though probably far less intense, can be found when a gang member shoots somebody in a drive-by or when a terrorist kills one or more people in an attack on innocents.

Whether socially positive or negative, the feeling of power exists. This is what social psychologist Arie Kruglanski called "the search for significance." If one can then associate the search for significance with a "higher" cause, it makes it more noble. Whether it be public acclaim, personal satisfaction, riches, a place in paradise, or the accolades of one's gang—there is often a reward--the feeling of power.

If the mind is 90% under the surface of consciousness, is it any wonder that psychological submarines have such a huge target to influence our behavior? Advertising agencies target our conscious and unconscious needs primarily with appeals to our need for power:

> Nike's "Just do it" stimulates one to find the power to escape one's feelings of inferiority and gives hope that one can conquer one's fears.'

> Dos Equis: The Most Interesting Man in the World. He is in control. He smokes Cuban cigars and drinks Dos Equis beer. Again, we have the appeal to power.

> Clairol: Does She, or Doesn't She? When this ad was released only 1 in 15 women colored their hair. Within a few years, it was 1 in 2. Power again, but this time aimed at women. Looking younger gave them more power in many areas of life.

> L'Oreal's power appeal to women was similar with their, "Because you're worth it."

The drive for power is not only more universally felt, it is more easily portrayed by advertisers and more easily elicited by politicians. As we will later see, some people will overcome the self-centered need for power and become altruistic "lovers." For some that selflessness extends only to members of one's family, for others it includes all of humanity. We talk about "love" so much that we think we know what it means. Generally, we mean "I want you" rather that the humanitarian idea of "what can I do for you to make you a better person." (We will discuss this more fully in a few pages.)

Because the experience of unselfish love is fairly rare, it is not often used in advertising or politics. In December, the holiday season may make us more susceptible to a message of love. Hallmark cards often do a good job in their Christmas ads. Procter & Gamble tried a "Thank You, Mom" ad that was successful.

If you pay attention to ads you will notice that the appeal to "power" is the dominant theme for men and women. It may be reflected in riches, sexual attractiveness, or athletic success. If you will only drink the right beer, smoke the right cigarette, drive the right car, or wear the right clothes—you too can be powerful.

Political ploys attempt to influence us the same ways. "Drain the swamp," "Make America great again," blame those who are different, blame other countries that are more successful, blame those who don't agree with us—we should have more power because we are right!

The Republican Party, much more than the Democrats, has been able to utilize the basic psychological tools that motivate most people.

Many think that the Democrats have actually been able to come up with better plans for a modern nation. Modernizing the infrastructure, providing adequate healthcare and retirement benefits, and relating to the globalized world are of primary importance to the better educated of the electorate.

However, the promises of Trump of creating jobs gives us all hope. But if the jobs are in steelmaking, when the Chinese make it much cheaper; in coal mining, when climate change threatens us and when alternative energy sources are multiplying like photovoltaic bunnies--these promises can have no fruition. Trump's promises to businesses to deny climate change, to cut regulations, and to reduce taxes were powerful in the lead up to the election and are even more powerful now that he has done these. Many businessmen are solidly behind him because making America great means stimulating business and increasing bank accounts.

It seems that to be politically successful today a party needs to be able to attract the less educated people with psychological spears of promises and hopes. Then they must be able to appeal to the business owners and the more educated among us with policies and practices that can make those promises come true. This of course requires controlling both the legislative and the executive branches of government. Donald Trump has trumped all candidates in our American and English histories in his approach to rouse the voting rabble.

THE LESSONS OF HISTORY

History is replete with the power people running our world. Kings and bishops, the Rothchilds and Rockefellers, Napoleons and Charlemagnes, have sought to control us today and into posterity. Whether they inherited their thrones or had them bestowed by God, they have not always been on the right side of the ethical roadway. In the olden days, we peasants and serfs were illiterate and thankful for whatever crumbs or promises we were given. But today many of us can think as well, or even better than our "betters."

Today, many of us can see a light at the end of the tunnel. And it is not a train intent on running us over! It is a beacon beckoning us to enter the full light of day. It is the spark that stimulated Gandhi. It is the spirit that guided Martin Luther King. It is the hope and the courage that spurred Barack Obama, Emmanuel Macron, Colin Powell, Thomas Edison, Frederick Chopin and many others. It tells us that, "We can." But are there enough of us to do what is necessary to save our nation?

Modern-day parliaments and congresses are elected. But it is the political parties that usually control the finances necessary for their elections. A girl I went to high school with, Roz Weiner, set her sights on being elected to the Los Angeles City Council after she graduated from college. She knocked on nearly every door in her district and introduced herself. No money, but lots of work, got her elected. While on the Council, she was instrumental in bringing the Dodgers from Brooklyn to LA. For Brooklyn, it was tantamount to a capital crime.

The election of Donald Trump, and the referendum for Brexit, stimulated many people to arise from their sofas and get involved in the political process. The hundreds of "marches of women," enticed many women to run for office. The publishing of the sexual assaults of Harvey Weinstein set off the "Me, too" movement around the world.

There have been many thousands of women who were just "not going to take it anymore." Women in Iran cast off their hijabs. Women in Saudi Arabia began to drive their cars, illegally. Citizens in Venezuela, Zimbabwe, and South Africa erupted in violence against their elected leaders.

There is a threshold for each of us that will stimulate us to act-- to act with our whole selves. Many cry and complain after each school shooting where innocent children and teenagers are killed with automatic weapons. How many will run for office or work to elect those who will to call for a constitutional convention to undo the 5 to 4 decisions of the 2007 Supreme Court that totally reversed the thinking of the Founding Fathers and many previous Supreme Court decisions on the right to own firearms. The single shot muskets and pistols of the 18th Century, that were needed to repel a future invasion from the Continent, are now replaced with automatic weapons. And we all feel so much safer, as do our children in school!

HOW ASTUTE POLITICIANS USE OUR REACTIONS TO OUR INFERIORITIES

The inferiorities we feel may be different depending on whether: we were raised in a truly loving home, we have a good job, we had an effective education, we had approving friends, we did socially rewarding work, we have been foster children, we are deeply religious, or any of a number of positive or negative influences on our past or present lives.

Our inferiorities are basic in our minds. They then elicit conscious and unconscious fears and angers. These then give rise to hopes. The skillful advertiser or politician--just as many parents, teachers, and bosses-- understand what motivates us and how we can motivate others. Advertisers and teachers often rely on motivating us through hope, religious seers through fears and hopes, while wily politicians use anger, fear, and hope to prod us to the voting booth.

This chart may clarify this concept. We will revisit this chart as we analyze the Trump, Bush and Brexit manipulations of the electorates.

HOPE—that things will improve (better job or marriage, go to heaven)

FEAR—that things will not improve

ANGER—that things are not better

INFERIORITIES IN THE CONSCIOUS OR SUB-CONCIOUS MIND

Adulthood—Job situation or no job, no satisfactory social relationship, poor economy

↑

High School—Poor grades, poor physical skills, few or no friends

↑

Elementary school-Can't master subjects, few or no friends, poor athletic ability

↑

Infants—Can't walk, talk, feed themselves

HEROS AND IDOLS

The media can give us heroes. Sport and film stars are ever-present. They probably also have a lot of money. But then there are heroes that are not marked by their wealth: Gandhi, Martin Luther King, the Dalai Lama, or Desmond Tutu.

Because of their fame, such people may be more easily elected to governmental offices. Ronald Reagan is a prime example of moving from film to government. George Murphy, a song and dance movie favorite, moved to the US Senate. Hall of Fame basketball player Bill Bradley became a US Senator. Pro-football players Steve Largent and Jack Kemp became members of the House of Representatives. But there were many others in the Congress. And of course, we have real estate mogul and reality TV star, Donald J. Trump.

DIMMING THE GLOW OF THE GOLDEN GODS AND GODDESSES

Donald Trump's ghostwriter, Tony Schwartz, for the book "The Art of the Deal," said that "it's impossible to keep him focused on any topic, other than his own self-aggrandizement." He also said that Trump had a deep black hole in his psyche that needed to be filled with praise. That is another way of saying that he had a huge inferiority complex.

In our financially fixated world, how could any billionaire have an inferiority complex? The answer is simple. It is the emotional warmth of loving parents that is likely to develop a solid unconscious mind with which we can feel secure. The warmth of a bankbook in our breast pocket doesn't fill the bill psychologically.

For those who find fault with the beliefs and actions of Scientology, the celebrity of Tom Cruise and John Travolta may have lost some glow. Similarly, professional sports stars accused of spousal or child abuse may lose their jobs and their endorsements.

JOINING ANTI-SOCIAL GROUPS

What about school dropouts who have joined gangs? What about children whose parents are not capable of loving them?

Of course, we see other efforts that people make to become more superior or less inferior that may be less desirable socially. These are the simpler accommodations that people may do to attempt to reduce their inferiorities. Body piercing, tattooing, cursing, wearing gang clothes, joining fan clubs, wearing hairstyles which are not common are among the many simple ways that people try to become acceptable to some fringe groups that may accept them. Joining a fringe group that may give one status such as: Black gangs like the Crips or Bloods; white gangs like the Aryan Brotherhood, Skinheads or neo-Nazis: Latino groups like the Mexican Mafia or Salvadorian Mafia; and many other groups that are commonly antisocial. If joining a group is not possible or not considered, individual or small group efforts at being superior will most likely be attempted. This is where individual bullying and abuse come into play. Check the anonymous comment to issues on the Internet where inane and vulgar comments and put-downs allow bullying without fear of reprisals. It is a perfect medium for cowards with well-deserved inferiority complexes!

But nobody has been able to do everything he or she has wanted. Barack Obama, while president of the most powerful country in the world, could not get many of his ideas passed by a confrontational Congress. Vladimir Putin was thwarted when he wanted to re-annex the Ukraine. The leader of China, Xi Jinping, could not stop financial troubles in his country and has been castigated by others for abusing human rights—rights often guaranteed in other countries. Of course, Western "guarantees" often don't evolve from paper promises to practical practices—but criticizing China still feels good.

The most powerful people in politics, business, or society do not have total control over getting their desires satisfied. And so it is with us mere mortals!

In a survey in the UK in 2016 it was found that 43% of 30 year olds still lived with their parents. Large numbers describe themselves as worn down (42%), lacking self-confidence (47%) and feeling worried about the future (51%). 54% of 30-year-old women said they lacked self-respect. For men, it was 39%. Lack of work and low pay were major factors in their inferiority feelings.

Think of how much worse it is for school children who have not yet accomplished very much on their road to successful adulthood. Bullying has its birth in these childhood and teenage inferiorities that have long sought a safe place to explode. Good luck on trying to put down your father or mother as a way to feel power when you are four years old! Wait until you are in the first grade then find a small kindergartner with a fat belly or big ears.

So, we all feel inadequate to some degree at some times. Having a strong belief in the truest sect of the truest supreme being is a common method of removing one's inadequacy. Going to the best college or joining the best fraternity or sorority is another one. Having the most expensive or fastest car is another one. So our mental adjustments may be positive, negative or neutral in terms of contributing to our society.

LOVE AS A HUMAN NEED

The ability to love, if we are to believe Erich Fromm, is developed when we are loved as children. True lovers get a deep satisfaction from helping others. One of

America's must beloved social thinkers, Ashley Montagu, writing for the Encyclopedia of Mental Health has attempted to solve this enigma with his definition that:

"Love is the communication to another person of one's deep involvement in that person's welfare, of one's profound interest in him as a person, demonstrated by acts that support, stimulate, and contribute to the realization of that person's personality and its fulfillment."

With this definition in mind, he then echoes Freud's idea that, "Mental health is the ability to love and the ability to work." This is exactly what modern politicians are asking of their countries' citizens today. Most of our recent presidents have been very clear in their desire that people should take responsibility for their own lives and that they should work to improve the lives of others in their communities.

We can better understand what Montagu meant by breaking down the definition into its component parts:

"Love is the communication to another person." How do we communicate? If I say "I love you, baby." to a newly-born infant, the idea would vary according to the tone of my voice. If I coo it softly, the baby will receive a positive message; if I snarl it sharply, the baby will receive a negative message. So it is not only the actual words spoken that reveal the message, but also the tone of the voice used and one's body language.

Adults often cannot actually love because their inferiority complexes and power drives get in the way. Real love between adults is shown where each person helps the other to be the best that he or she can be. It means helping them to fulfill worthwhile goals, helping them to eliminate harmful habits, saying things that make them feel good, and making them feel worthwhile. But love is not so much what you say, but rather what you do. How often have we said, "I love you, " when we really meant, "I want you." Our basic selfishness must be overcome before we can be a real "lover."

I see it on a continuum, with the need for power on one end and the ability to love unselfishly on the other.

Ability to love Unselfishly (ie. Humanitarian love, ideal spousal or parental caring)	<	Ability to feel empathy to feel with or for others	<	Power TO do important things	<	Power OVER others (spouse, children, employees others)	<	Selfishness inferiority

Because this loving ability is not nearly as common as the drive for power, it is not used often as a political motivator. Kennedy used it when he said, "Ask not what your country can do for you, but ask what can you do for your country." Obama used it when he said, "I'm asking you to believe. Not just in my ability to bring about real change in Washington. I'm asking you to believe in yours."

Another relatively rare source of motivation is what Victor Frankel termed "the need to find meaning in life." When John Kennedy was attempting to fight the grassroots programs of Russia which were dedicated to developing communists and an allegiance to the USSR, he decided to develop the Peace Corps which mobilized American youth who had that ability to love and the need to find more meaning in their lives. It was highly successful for Kennedy, for America, and for the host countries— and was also an extremely valuable experience for the members of the Corps.

Appealing to the idealism of youth was a major factor in the success of Bernie Sanders in 2016. Socialism, along with free college tuition, sounds very good to the youth.

But the American ideal of making money tends to make older adults more cynical and selfish. They want cheaper health care and lower taxes.

So, if you want to appeal to youth, you might consider any political messages that included either power, love, or meaning. But to appeal to older Americans political messages are better centered on power--on jobs, tax cuts, higher wages, and better pensions.

Internationally we can see the selfishness and "power over" behaviors in third world countries like in corrupt African countries and the drug cartels and gang violence in some Latin American countries. In the U.S. there has been an emphasis on the selfish right side of the spectrum=="'gimme" more and tax me less. Of course we have a number of people in each category. Gangs, many bosses, and some law enforcement people are in the "power over" group. The social media tech giants, many teachers, and some parents illustrate the "power to" category. Many Peace Corps volunteers, as well as Bill and Melinda Gates represent the "humanitarian love" category. The welfare state nations, particularly in Scandinavia, illustrate the more loving national attitudes.

LEARNED BEHAVIOR AND VALUES

Through most of the history of psychology and psychoanalysis, it was the learned behavior that was the only factor considered. It is obviously very important, probably the most important. If memories and values are crucial in our mental makeup, certainly our experiences are critical. But as we learn more about epigenetics, we wonder how many learned experiences have changed the ability of our genes to work to their fullest capacity.

At this time, it would certainly seem that our values are learned, often early in life, and our memories are important in our decisions and our behavior.

If some of our memories and values sink into the unconscious mind, we can understand how they may be influential in our behavior.

Long before the importance of genetics entered the field of psychology, it was only the learned behavior that was studied. Freud thought that we were primarily pleasure seeking animals, while Alfred Adler thought we were power driven as a way to overcome our inferiorities that started in our infancies because we really were inferior. We could not eat by ourselves, walk, talk, or change our diapers. As we grew up our parents and teachers and ministers continued to show their superiority over us.

The drive for power has been noticed by many thinkers throughout the ages. We can certainly see such drives in those who would like to lead us. Since each one knows best what is ideal for our society, or ideal for themselves, you can understand why they will do whatever they can to be elected. As we will indicate in succeeding chapters, their methods of attaining power have been moved from appealing to our intellects to manipulating our unconscious minds. This is done primarily by developing anger at the status quo, fermenting a fear of the future, then finally giving us hope in their leadership, because only they can deliver what we and our society need.

WHAT MOTIVATES US?

In attempting to understand politicians or political movements we tend to look only at what they say, rather than why they say it, and how we digest it. Throughout history politicians have lied to us and we have believed them. When Machiavelli wrote "The Prince" he was observing what he had seen relative to the principles used in gaining and holding power. Many have read the book and criticized it as being unethical. But people commonly gain power and keep it unethically. The principles of power generation are psychological, not ethical. Ethics is concerned with treating others equally, as ends in themselves. Politics is nearly always concerned with the politician being the only "end" of concern, and the populace is the means to that end.

Occasionally a politician becomes a statesman. When this happens, the "self" with which he is concerned is the state—the good of the state. So the "end" with which he is concerned is the common good, not with self-promotion. Still the population may serve as means to that end, but the end is the common good. So, sending soldiers to die for the common good is ethical— when defending the country. A war of aggression is obviously quite a different thing, and is usually unethical.

Our human desire to gain power is probably as old as the most primitive human community. We can guess that the best hunter in the tribe became its chief.

We can see the power of the people assuaging their intellectual inferiorities in the judgment of the mob that found that Socrates was corrupting the youth of ancient Athens. We see it in the Caesars, in Brutus and his gang. We see it in the power of religion to convert people and to appoint kings. We see it in the kings holding power because of their "divine right."

As the unwashed mobs became more educated and armed, democratic republics were born. There was the hope of ethical government. But the urge to power is only sometimes achieved by following an ethical path. It is a sad fate that the ideal of democracy is not often accompanied by the virtue of honesty as it evolves. But politicians seldom want us to think rationally. It is easier to plan their power ascent if they can count on us reacting positively to their baseless promises of hope. They certainly don't want us to be educated or truthfully informed.

It is often said that we need an educated electorate to run a functioning democracy. With the rapid increase in the knowledge of psychology and how people can be easily manipulated, the knowledge of advertising and the awareness of how to rig an election have increased exponentially. Advertisers have told us that "real men smoke Marlboro cigarettes" and "real men drink Budweiser." these nudge our male drive for power which is fundamental in humans. Not to be left out, women are influenced by being told that "they are worth it," so they should buy L'Oréal products. "We've come a long way, baby" was a powerful advertising slogan for a woman's cigarette. Ya!, women want power, too.

If we are going to vote intelligently we need to develop the higher level of our minds, our intellects, so that we can analyze ideas, discard false promises, and accurately predict our future based on the arguments that are made by politicians.

With this in mind we need to understand a bit about semantics, what is meant by a word or a sentence.

We then need to determine how probable an argument is. We need to look at the argument and not the arguer. A basic fallacy of logic is to run down the person making the argument, then assume that the argument is therefore false. Trump did this continually making fun of his primary rivals like: Ted Cruz, Jeb Bush, Marco Rubio, Ben Carson-- in fact all of them! Then he did the same with Hillary. His opponents acted civilly. They answered with rational arguments. And, you see where it got them.

Huge numbers of people are motivated psychologically, not logically. The poorly educated, blue collar Rust Belt voters fall into this group. Others are motivated by self-centered values. Trump's business base falls into this category. Bernie Sanders' college students fell into this self-centered group because they wanted free tuition. Many college educated women wanted to make their own choices of whether or not to have a child. So they were in Hillary's camp for self-centered reasons. Many evangelical Christians believed that God was against abortions, so they followed Trump and Pence because of their God-based values.

What can be done to make voters more informed? How can they be enticed to vote with enlightened self-interest? We will make some recommendations after looking at how these problems have affected our present-day lives.

OUR UNCONSCIOUS MIND OFTEN RULES

In May of 2017, Greg Gianforte, a Republican candidate for Congress, attacked a journalist from the well-respected UK newspaper, The Guardian. Since Greg did not like the questions being asked, he body slammed the reporter--causing some injuries and breaking his glasses. The reporter was taken to the hospital in an ambulance. Gianforte was cited by the sheriff for misdemeanor assault. Two local newspapers withdrew their endorsements of him but about half of the votes had already been returned as absentee ballots. A few days later he won with 50.1% of the vote. He later apologized.

His actions illustrate the unconscious level of our behavior. Had his intellect been in control, he would have answered the questions, or possibly just left the room. This is an obvious illustration of one's unthinking unconscious mind attempting to satisfy his power drive-- that is necessary to reduce his inferiority complex. His inferiority was challenged when he did not want to answer a question. Ethical behavior, that is acknowledged by our intellects, commonly loses out in our battle for overcoming our feelings of inferiority.

As we move through the book we will attempt to show, what psychologist Alfred Adler popularized—that we all start with feelings of inferiority that are rooted in the first years of our lives. This feeling of inferiority may be a catalyst to our becoming "whole" people, or it may linger throughout our lives and create a number of problems. There may be a few among us who have: observed bosses who are domineering, observed spouses trying to make the other into an image of themselves, or parents attempting to control their children into paths that they had never been able to traverse.

CHAPTER 3   GAUGING CANDIDATES' MENTAL HEALTH

Just a quick look at the way people might unhealthily adjust to stresses or to feelings of inferiority. They may attack or withdraw from the real world. This is often called "fight or flight." People typically use one method of adjustment primarily, so they will usually attack when their ego is threatened by something stressful, or they will withdraw when a stress occurs.

Behavior is often variable, moving from normal to abnormal, depending on the situation. You have heard the legal term "temporary insanity." It refers to a person who is fairly normal but on this occasion, was aggravated sufficiently in a situation to do something he might not otherwise consider—like killing someone.

You may not have noticed that politicians are also human! As such, they may react to negative situations irrationally. They may succumb to sexual invitations. And they may even sexually harass or abuse people around them. But the fact that they are in the public eye, their behavior is more publicized than yours or mine.

ATTACKING ADJUSTMENTS

When attacking as a reaction to stress, they may use what we call: Displacement—One type of displacement is called "scapegoating" which is attacking someone or something that was not the cause of the problem. For example, mass shootings are experienced far too often in America. Many people maybe killed who were not the cause of the stress. Using vehicles to run down innocent people have been used in the US, France, and Germany. The abduction of schoolgirls in Nigeria by Boko Haram is another illustration. The 9/11 destructions in New York was a major one. Hate groups are often joined, such as: ISIS for Muslims, Jewish Defense League (Jews), Ku Klux Klan (whites) are just a few of the organizations. The unconscious attacking adjustment may be blind violence with no selected target, or there might be people who influence you to target a special group, like: Muslims, non-Muslims, Jews, whites, blacks, or the gang that controls another street.

The "package bomber" in Austin, Texas in early 2018 is a good example of senseless non-targeted attacking. He espoused no cause, like ISIS terrorists do. He did have a conservative religious view, probably from his parents and his home schooling. He was against abortion and homosexuality, and for the death penalty. He called himself a psychopath, saying he had many problems growing up. His bombs killed two black men and injured two white men. His actions are a crystal-clear example of attacking violently, with no special target in mind, as an adjustment to mental stresses.

But not all violence is displacement. The use of poison gas in Syria was against the Articles of War but was probably geared to winning the war. However, we can never be sure. It is possible that the Syrian president's drive for power was threatened, so he acted in a psychologically unhealthy displacement reaction.

So, we cannot always see whether an attacking reaction is psychologically or intellectually generated. We can certainly see how Hitler's inferiority feelings, after being rejected three times by the University of Vienna, may have played out in his displacement of his inferiorities in his death camps for the Jews and other "undesirables."

We see this continually in Donald Trump's antics. Blaming the lack of steelmaking jobs on illegal Mexican immigrants. His attacking of the free press is another.

His continual blaming of Barack and Hillary, and even George Bush for things he can't do is probably a psychological defense mechanism.

But he commonly uses a legal attack when he is challenged. Attorney Roy Cohn had been a lead attorney with Senator McCarthy's anti-communist hearings of the 1950s. He became Trump's attorney later, before he was disbarred. His legal advice to Trump was to always attack when challenged. Donald has continually followed this advice. When the Federal government found him in violation of the Fair Housing laws, he sued, then settled. Women who have accused him of sexual abuse are threatened with legal action. When people sued Trump University for fraud and other felonies, he countersued then settled for many millions. When a Los Angeles Times journalist took the classes then wrote an expose' Trump threatened to sue. These legal threats were not psychological adjustments, they were well-thought-out business practices designed to eliminate the threat. So, some of his attacking has been psychological adjustments that are signs that his mental problems were not being handled effectively. But some of his attacking uses often practiced legal maneuvers. They may unethical, but they are legal and were intelligently utilized.

President Erdogan of Turkey has recently attempted to purge Western language from the language of the Turks. This is an attack on an outside influence that may threaten his Muslim directed power-push that appeals largely to his non-city, non-educated power base. Was this action prompted by an intelligent political technique to maintain power, or by a feeling of inferiority because the European Union continually thwarted his attempts to join. We cannot know—only guess.

Verbal abuse may also be used when one is frustrated or is attempting to increase his or her status. One of the few times that President Trump was calling together members of the two parties in order to enact meaningful legislation that would reduce the number of school shootings and other mass shootings. He was making good headway, but he could not resist blaming Presidents Bush and Obama for not being able to produce meaningful legislation in these areas. Yep! Another psychological attempt to bolster his fragile ego.

THERE ARE ALSO WITHDRAWING TYPES OF BEHAVIOR

Withdrawing behavior is behavior that separates the person from the problem. It can be: denying the problem, trying to make up for problem, using chemicals such as alcohol and psychoactive drugs to forget the problem, or ultimately, committing suicide. Just as the attacking behaviors can be unconscious adjustments or rational reactions, withdrawing behaviors can also be unconscious or rational.

When President Putin denies Russia's involvement in meddling in the elections in the West, it is a rational reaction. He knows he is lying. When Hitler and his top aides committed suicide, I can see that as being rational. If you can imagine what they would have gone through in court cases, imprisonment, and possibly capital punishment-- the suicide pill was certainly an easier way out.

So, when we see someone lying in denying that they were at fault, it may be rational or irrational. If it is rational, it is certainly dishonest. It is therefore unethical, but not necessarily an unconscious reaction. When Putin lies, he knows exactly what he is doing. When Trump lies, we are never sure if he is aware of the lie or if it is an unconscious defense mechanism.

The most common ways of withdrawing from reality are: distorting reality, such as in rationalization; atoning for reality, compensating in some mental or physical way to make up for the real world; forgetting reality, such as in daydreaming; and retreating from reality, such as in drugs, alcohol, and suicide. For the purposes of this book we will only look at the first two of these.

Distorting reality can include such behaviors as: rationalization (giving false reasons for one's behavior, but believing them true), projection (blaming someone else for our own problems), and denigration (seeing someone much worse than they actually are.)

Nations or national leaders seldom take the blame for their evil actions or mistakes. When Otto Warmbier, an American college student, was released after over a year in a North Korean prison he was in a coma and died within a week after his return. The North Korean government expressed surprise that he was in a coma and didn't take any responsibility for it.

Trump's continual demeaning of Obama, even accusing him of tapping his phones or his continually saying, "I inherited a mess" are prime examples of distorting reality. His taking full credit for firing FBI Director Comey, then after Comey's damning testimony indicating that Trump was obstructing justice, he blamed the Attorney General's office for recommending the firing. These completely opposite ideas of reality were about a month apart. Does he lie, or is it just the beginning stages of Alzheimer's?

Trump is a master at denigration. The way he insulted his primary opponents, then Hillary Clinton in the presidential race, are examples far in excess of anything we have ever seen in Western politics. ISIS and other jihadists do the same thing, claiming that all of their opponents are guilty of blasphemy.

Atoning for reality is often done by: egocentrism (thinking of oneself primarily, bragging, showing off), a superiority complex (thinking oneself better than all or most others), and negativism (seeing good ideas as bad). Oh my goodness! More examples from The Donald!

Donald Trump exhibits what Adler would call a superiority complex. This is not because he is actually superior, but it masks his deep feelings of inferiority. The fact that he has made a lot of money makes it easy to carry off this superiority complex. It is rather difficult for a homeless man to do the same, but in mental institutions this complex is not uncommon.

Some would say he has delusions of grandeur. He has achieved the billionaire status, which may allow for some such feelings—but neither are preferable to the alternative lifestyles of Bill Gates nor Warren Buffet, who are many times richer, but don't exhibit such behavior, and both were self-made. Of course, being the President of the US is a bit of a grand accomplishment. But Trump seems to flaunt his achievements to an abnormal degree. Some believe his behavior borders on the psychotic. It seems to me that it is commonly outside of the normal range of behavior, often pushing into the area of neurosis—but generally he exhibits what we call personality disorders.

Having logic tight delusions can be a psychotic trait. But it is difficult for me to place him on the normal to abnormal scale. Are his refutations of proven facts, like human caused climate influences or finding invisible jobs for coal miners, really neurotic rants or merely political techniques used to influence the voters.

You may have heard the story of the psychiatrist visiting a patient. He asked the patient what was his name. "Napoleon," he replied. "And who told you that you are Napoleon?," the psychiatrist asked. "God told me," was his answer. "I did not!," shouted the voice from the next bed. We all like to think that we are important, but some people overdo the urge to escape their infantile prison of inferiority.

So what is left? People adjust to problems by attacking reality—or withdrawing from it. You can attack by words or deeds. Soccer hooligans from England and Russia seek out physical violence. Politicians, and others, are more likely to rationalize their failures or blame others. Only mature ethical people will take the blame for their mistakes.

The unconscious mind was enough for Freud to explain much of our behavior, appealing to unconscious motivations, such as increasing our power, because we don't have enough control of our lives. The appeals to the unconscious minds of the electorates in recent elections may also explain much of the success of recent campaigns.

THE UNCONSCIOUS MIND'S CHOICES OF A REACTION PATTERN

Why would one person attack reality and another person withdraw from reality? There may be genetic or epigenetic reasons, but it would appear that the society in which one lives is usually a determining factor. If your family was abusive and often yelling or fighting, it is highly likely that you will react the same way to stresses. If the people in your family drank to drunkenness or relied on heroin to release them from the realities of life, it is likely that you will follow that path.

Today, we are continually bombarded with violence in films and television. Seeing this violence gives us permission to follow this path as a way to react to our inferiority feelings, our angers, and our frustrations. We have come a long way from the Lone Ranger of the 1940s and 1950s. He would never draw his gun first, then when somebody did draw, he would shoot the gun out of their hand. He never killed anyone! Now we see several people jumping out of a truck armed with automatic weapons and shooting everyone in sight.

There was a time, more than 50 years ago, when there was a film rule that people who were shot had to move a little to show that they were not dead. I rather doubt that that did any good!

The availability of guns, combined with the amount of violence that we see, including spousal abuse, fighting, and verbal abuse, gives us more permission to use these attacking behaviors to react against our own feelings of inferiority and anger.

Writing a script for a movie or TV program is much simpler if there is a great deal of violence, many shootings and explosions, and cars flipping over each other. It is far more difficult to write a comedy program that has a real depth of meaning-- such as, Mash, The Cosby Show, or Frasier. Even pure comedies, like Cheers or Seinfeld are difficult to write.

Naturally the availability of guns makes today's attacks more deadly. Then the publicity that mass shooters gain can give them the feeling of power that their inferiority complexes were seeking. For this reason, some commentators will not release the names of the mass shooters because the fame attached to the shooter may stimulate others to follow that adjustment pattern.

By the same token, the availability of psychoactive drugs (including alcohol and marijuana) make withdrawing from reality also relatively easy.

Not all attacking or withdrawing adjustments are abnormal. A person might "attack" by studying harder after performing poorly on a test. One might play a sport more intensely as a way of gaining power. One might work on being a good cook or on performing well in a job. One might even do normal things to an abnormal degree. I had a patient who cleaned her house several times a day and would not let her family into the living room because they might get it dirty.

Withdrawing behavior might also be done within the normal range of behavior. A glass of wine before dinner after a trying day at work; a "white lie" to shield someone from a hurtful experience; or, an occasional few minutes of daydreaming—are all within the area of normal withdrawing.

A DEEPER LOOK AT TRUMP'S PERSONALITY

Donald Trump obviously has a huge inferiority complex. It is strange that this has developed because he was born with a silver apartment key in his mouth. He was given several millions of dollars to start his business. He was lucky that the housing boom happened as he was growing up so he had a particularly fertile ground to use his money. He also had a father who was in the business and a mother who apparently loved him. In addition to this he was reasonably good-looking and a fair athlete.

The history of psychology makes us want to assign environmental causes to psychological effects. But in the last few of years, genetics has been becoming more and more important as we can link genes with mental and physical diseases either because they cause them or they make us more susceptible to them.

While it is not possible to make a comprehensive diagnosis from afar, it seems that The Donald has an inferiority complex, as nearly all of us do to some degree. While some people will wall themselves off in a corner and feel sorry for themselves, others will use alcohol or other drugs to forget it. Some will withdraw to reading, video games or even studying—yes, you can do normal things to an abnormal degree! And, as we see— some use attacking behavior continually as a way to deal with their inferiorities.

TRUMP'S SUPERIORITY COMPLEX

Trump's basic inferiority has been manifest in a superiority complex to mask the inferiorities that are locked in his unconscious. This is not uncommon. His superiority feelings have been enabled to a large degree from his business successes and his television productions. But there seem to be at least two more personality problems in his makeup. Narcissism is a frequent companion of a superiority complex. A number of people in the psychology and psychiatry fields have written about his obvious narcissism.

It is now reported that President Trump has news releases showing positive news treatments of his behavior brought to him every morning and afternoon. This behavior even goes beyond classic narcissism.

The narcissism of Trump becomes even more evident when we see that he is not willing to negotiate disagreements but is more concerned with "saving face." His biggest problem is that in the campaigns he promised to build a wall and have Mexico pay for it. But communications recorded between him and the Mexican president show that he was more concerned with having Mexico "say" that they would pay for the wall even though he admitted that they did not have to do it. Trump said, "The fact is we are both in a little bit of a political bind, because I have to have Mexico pay for the wall – I have to." And later, referring to the Mexican president's insistence that he would not pay, Trump said: "You cannot say that to the press. The press is going to go with that and I cannot live with that. You cannot say that to the press because I cannot negotiate under those circumstances."

At about the same time he was talking to the Prime Minister of Australia. They were discussing a swap of refugees that Obama and Turnbull had agreed to, Muslims to US and Hispanics to Australia. Trump refused to carry it out. "This is going to kill me," he said to Turnbull. "I am the world's greatest person that does not want to let people into the country. . . This deal will make me look terrible."

Contrast Donald Trump's immature behavior trying to protect his superiority complex, with 100-meter world record holder Usain Bolt's loss in the finals of the world championships in London in 2017. His 9.95 time was only good enough for third place, 0,03 of the second behind the winner and 0.37 seconds behind his world record. Did he sulk or make excuses? No! He could have blamed his bad back which he had had treated in Germany. He could have blamed his slow start, which was even slower than his normal starts. He could have blamed the water on track, but all the runners ran on the same track. He had no excuses. He smiled immediately. The first thing he did was to embrace the winner, his longtime rival, Justin Gatlin. It was not the typical quick hug that is so common among track athletes. It was a caring and loving embrace. He whispered to the winner his congratulations and his displeasure with the way the crowd treated the winner. He then jogged around the track smiling, bowing, and waving to the crowd of 60,000 people, most of whom had come to see him win his last race.

What a difference between the legitimately elected of the president of the world's most powerful country and the icon of athletics! If you make an educated guess about the parenting of each person you may surmise some of the reasons for the vastly different behaviors of the two to their setbacks, or imagined setbacks.

A person with a superiority complex commonly is narcissistic. He or she may also become a bully if their temperament, physical strength, or station in life allows it. Compulsive lying, or even psychopathic lying, are often found with narcissism. Trump's pronouncements definitely include lying. (The New York Times counted over 3,000 Trump lies in the first five months of 2018.) Other untruths that he has spoken or written may or may not be lies. Some may be rationalizations, that he really believes are true, some untruths may be put out there because he thinks they serve a political end.

Trump's lies are legion!

➢ Trump said that the NFL had sent him a letter complaining about debate dates and the conflicts they posed with football games. The NFL said that it hadn't sent him a letter.

➢ He said that his mind was made up to fire Comey before the letter from the Deputy Attorney General. A few weeks later he said that the letter was why he fired him.

➢ Trump said China stopped manipulating its currency on several different dates: when he announced his candidacy, during the campaign, after the election, and after the inauguration.

➢ In June of 2017 he said that the US was one of the highest taxed countries. In truth, its 26% rate is about half of the 52% rate of Denmark, traditionally ranked as the happiest country in the world. The US is third from the bottom in the percent of GDP tax ratio of the 34 advanced OPEC countries. Only Mexico and Korea are taxed less.

His statements during the campaign were found to be blatant lies or totally untrue about 50% of the time. Less than 10% of his statements were totally true.

If you would like to hear some from his own lips—click
https://vimeo.com/285107263/916e249336
Still not convinced? Click
https://vimeo.com/285107192/8ae2ae7415
Mental health therapists, like psychiatrists, seem to be nearly unanimous in their judging him to be seriously narcissistic. Narcissistic people are very self-centered and tend to lack the ability to be sympathetic.

It may be difficult to separate those who are very self-centered as being narcissistic and those who are acting superior to hide their inferiority feelings. This is particularly true with men, who tradition tells us should always be superior to women. Of course, we should also be superior to people of other races and religions and even to people who root for different sport teams, or support different political candidates!

The narcissistic personality disorder may have genetic roots. Studies of identical and fraternal twins indicate that narcissism can be inherited. However environmental influences may be essential in its eventual development. Relatively few psychological disorders appear to be inherited, but narcissism shows the most heritability. According to a study in a 2007 issue of the International Journal of Neuropsychopharmacology, a specific gene called tryptophan hydroxylase-2 may be implicated in the development of certain personality disorders, including the narcissistic personality disorder. Tryptophan hydroxylase-2 helps regulate the production of serotonin, an important brain neurotransmitter involved in mood regulation.

COMPULSIVE LYING

At the University of Southern California neuroscientists have found the first genetic link to partially explain pathological liars--and possibly people with related personality problems who cheat and manipulate others. (Reported in the October 2017 issue of the British Journal of Psychiatry) Previous studies have shown increased activity in the prefrontal cortex-- an area of the brain that allows people to feel remorse and to learn moral behavior.

Pathological liars can't always tell truth from falsehood and contradict themselves often. They are manipulative and they often admit that they prey on people. They are brazen in terms of their actions, but very cool when talking about this. The study included: 12 pathological liars, 16 people with other mental problems, and 21 psychologically normal people.

The researchers used Magnetic Resonance Imaging to explore structural brain differences between the three groups. The liars had almost 26% more prefrontal white matter and slightly less gray matter than those with other mental problems and 14% less gray matter than the normal people. The increase in white matter might explain how liars are able to conjure up their deceitful behavior, since "lying takes a lot of effort," said Dr. Raine, one of the major researchers in the project. The variations in the percentages of white and gray matter may explain how the liar can appear cool and controlled while overcoming the normally expected moral behavior of truthfulness. In normal people the gray matter may keep any desire to lie in check. Liars are not so inhibited, possibly because the prefrontal cortex, where concerns about morality are usually made, does not have as much thinking power because of the significantly fewer brain cells. The researchers were clear that this is not the whole cause of being able to lie, but it may be a significant genetic factor.

TRUMP'S ATTACKING BEHAVIOR

Whether his attacking behavior is genetic, epigenetic, or learned-- it is impossible to say. But it did seem to start reasonably early in this life. This was the reason that his parents sent him to military school when he was young. Later, his attorney, Roy Cohn advised him to always attack harder when he was attacked. Threaten, sue, or do whatever is necessary to attempt to weaken the resolve of the adversary. This seems to have worked well for him.

DO MENTAL HEALTH PROFESSIONALS HAVE A DUTY TO WARN THE PUBLIC OF PSYCHOLOGICAL ILLNESSES OF POLITICIANS?

The best people to evaluate mental health are usually the mental health professionals. Back in the days of the Cold War, Senator Barry Goldwater was a strong advocate of being tough on communism. The magazine Fact published a story titled, "The Unconscious of a Conservative: A Special Issue on the Mind of Barry Goldwater." (Fact magazine, 1964 (Vol. 1, Issue 5), was the source of the APA's Goldwater rule. Scribd has the full text at https://www.scribd.com/document/322479204/Fact-Magazine-Goldwater-1964)

In a survey of psychiatrists, 1,189 believed he was unfit to be president, while 657 believed that he was fit. 571 said that they didn't know enough about him to make an evaluation. Some of the evaluations were that his personality was paranoid, and akin to people like Hitler and Stalin. Other evaluations were more of a philosophical, rather than psychological, point of view. The liberal psychiatrists just didn't like him. Of those who supported him, he was called a realist. Others called the whole concept of the article as being asinine.

Goldwater sued the publisher of the magazine and was awarded $75,000, equivalent to about a half million dollars today. The Supreme Court refused to review the case. Because of the decision, the American Psychiatric Association decided that it was unethical to give a professional opinion about public figures that have not been examined in person. The so-called "Goldwater Rule," was adopted by that association, it states:

"On occasion psychiatrists are asked for an opinion about an individual who is in the light of public attention or who has disclosed information about himself/herself through public media. In such circumstances, a psychiatrist may share with the public his or her expertise about psychiatric issues in general. However, it is unethical for a psychiatrist to offer a professional opinion unless he or she has conducted an examination and has been granted proper authorization for such a statement."

There are several organizations of mental health therapists. The American Psychiatric Association (APA) is only one. The American Psychological Association (APA) is another. It also is concerned with protecting the individual being commented on. However, it does not seem to be quite as strict as the psychiatric association's. Another is the American Psychoanalytic Association (APsaA). It recently told its membership "that the responsible use of professional expertise in public affairs is permissible."

Varying mental health professionals have observed the behavior of Donald Trump and publicly stated that he has an assortment of personality problems, particularly: narcissism, a lack of empathy, and a superiority complex, or grandiosity. Some have said that he has a dangerous mental illness.

All known mental problems and illnesses are listed and explained in the "bible" of mental health therapists, the Diagnostic and Statistical Manual of Mental Disorders of the American Psychiatric Association. It is now in its fifth edition. (DSM 5 is the abbreviated title.) Under, "Narcissistic Personality Disorder" (Section 301.81) it is written that the narcissistic personality disorder (NPD) is becoming better known. There is not as much written about it as there is other personality disorders, but it is quite prevalent in the offices of therapists. . . These patients could not be classified as psychotic, and they were not typically neurotic, and were generally not responsive to conventional therapeutic treatment. It seems to be more common with males than females.

The symptoms are: grandiosity, seeking excessive admiration, and the lack of empathy. From the outside these patients act as if they are in control and are always right, and show condescending attitudes towards others. They cannot accept criticism. Even though some may achieve very high in some societal areas, they battle with strong feelings of low self-esteem and inadequacy.

Any five of these nine symptoms below is a strong indication of clinical narcissism. (American Psychiatric Association, 2013)

1.   Grandiose logic of self-importance
2.   A fixation with fantasies of infinite success, control, brilliance, beauty, or idyllic love

3.	A credence that he or she is extraordinary and exceptional and can only be understood by, or should connect with, other extraordinary or important people or institutions

4.	A desire for unwarranted admiration

5.	A sense of entitlement

6.	Interpersonally oppressive behavior

7.	No form of empathy

8.	Resentment of others or a conviction that others are resentful of him or her

9.	A display of egotistical and conceited behaviors or attitudes

Donald Trump seems to exhibit all of these symptoms. In the general population, we expect to see this personality problem in less than 1% of the cases. However, in the clinical settings of therapists, we find this in 2 to 16% of patients.

In a public statement he said "Actually, throughout my life, my two greatest assets have been mental stability and being, like, really smart." He also said he "would qualify as not smart, but genius ... and a very stable genius at that!"

The psychiatrists who abide by the Goldwater rule, and lawyers, who are not mental health specialists ask how can therapists express a diagnostic opinion without ever having met him face-to-face in a therapy session? A well-known television personality, who is also a trial lawyer, has said that such diagnoses would never be allowed in a court of law.

Well, that trial attorney has not practiced diagnosing mental abnormalities. A face-to-face meeting or interpreting ink blots are not the only possible methods for making a diagnosis. A number of other options can give conclusive diagnoses. For example: Rorschach inkblots, word association and free association are often used as adjuncts to diagnosis. Paper and pencil answers to questions or drawing varying situations may also be used. But the best method of diagnosis is quite often merely observing.

In family counseling, it is rather common to have the therapist watching from behind a one-way mirror to see how the family members interact with each other. It is well-known that when a person with sub-psychotic problems knows he is being evaluated for mental health, he is often sufficiently aware enough to give desirable answers to the questions of the therapist. This is quite different from psychotic with a logic tight delusion. A patient who thinks he is Napoleon all the time will probably not hide this from the diagnosing therapist.

The Army's Field Manual on Leadership, lists the five crucial qualities of a leader: "trust, discipline and self-control, judgment and critical thinking, self-awareness, and empathy. Leaders must shape the objectives and ethical behavior of their followers. The core values of a leader include: loyalty, duty, respect, selfless service, honor, personal courage, and integrity."

Any objective evaluation of Donald Trump shows lying, a lack of self-control, huge gaps in critical thinking, selfish motivation, and a number of similar absences of leadership qualities.

CHAPTER 4   HONING THE INTELLECT

With the phalanxes of fake news and false or impossible promises, along with the fake history and highly unlikely predictions for our futures that many politicians have promulgated—it might protect our futures if we could sort through them and separate the wheat from the gaffe.

Intelligent people know that there are few answers to important questions that are certain—they therefore have doubts. They have questions. Certainty is most often the result of not knowing the issues completely or being unable or unwilling to understand the complexities of an important issue. What is meant by: "let's make America great again" or "all men are created equal?" As gadflies to stimulating action they may be powerful—but as principles of governing, they are meaningless.

Look at the naïve certainty of Farage, Johnson, and Trump. "Leaving the EU will be simple, we hold all the cards." Or, "We will replace Obamacare with something better and cheaper." True? Easy to do?

The discipline of philosophy, through its sub-discipline of logic, has taught us how to think more effectively by having a clearer understanding of the words and phrases we use (semantics), by evaluating the probability of a statement (induction), and by evaluating structure of an argument to determine whether or not a conclusion follows from the premises used in the argument (deduction).

SEMANTICS

Like every organized body of knowledge, semantics has many sub-parts and is itself a sub-part of the general area of thinking effectively.

We often use "Google" to mean any web searching, even if we are using another search engine. In England, they use "Hoover" to mean any vacuum cleaner. But Hoover is an American company that was a pioneer in producing vacuum cleaners. So, a Londoner might be using an Electrolux, but would still be "hoovering."

We hear arguments using different meanings continually. Look at the abortion arguments. The pro-life people often call a one day old embryo a child.

Many people are against abortion because it can kill a child, but they are for war and do not mind when young adults are sent off to die. We often hear of a bombing killing innocent women and children and do not worry about soldiers who were killed. It might be one thing if the soldier had volunteered for the Army and understood that he might be killed in a war. But others were drafted into the Army or were forced into military service for a year or two when they were about 18. Are not the lives of these unwilling warriors equal to the lives of women and children? And what about the 1400 American children killed annually with guns? Are not their lives worth as much as a month-old embryo? Yet we must allow nearly all citizens to own guns!

Many "pro-lifers" cite the biblical commandment that they think says "thou shalt not kill." Modern biblical scholars know that earlier translations of the Jewish word were wrong and that the commandment should read "thou shall not murder." Certainly, not all killing is murder. A killing in self-defense is not murder. Most killings in traffic accidents are not murder. Killing in war is not murder. Is it murder to abort a six-week-old embryo? If so, God is the biggest murderer of all because spontaneous abortions or miscarriages, are far more prevalent than medical abortions.

There are probably very few people who have exactly the same meanings for the word "democracy." Does it include one person one vote? Should voting be at age 14, 16,

18, 20? Is capitalism a fundamental of democracy? What about socialized medicine? If you were to talk to a Scandinavian about their definitions of democracy they would probably lean more toward socialized medicine and a strong welfare state along with some ownership of major industries by the government. But if you talk to someone from the Republican Party in Texas she would be more likely to be for private ownership of all property and no socialized medicine. There would be a number of other differences also.

When we have different meanings for words such as: killing, democracy, equality, diversity, capitalism, socialism or many other words which do not have a completely and universally understood meaning-- we have problems. If I say that 2+2 = 4, that is pretty well understood. But when I say "democracy is the best political system," it has thousands of possible meanings.

Even a word like "blue" can have a number of meanings. It can be the wavelength of color, a depressed feeling (I'm feeling blue), it can be a number of hues close to the agreed-on wavelength so can be: light blue, navy blue, turquoise blue, etc. And what if your listener thought you were talking about the homonym "blew?"

In semantics, meaning is called "signification." Exactly what does the word being used signify? If we are going to discuss nearly any important question, we need to be clear on what we mean by the terms we are using. In the political arena, this is very difficult because there are so many meetings and each person believes that the others in the discussion have the same meaning as the person speaking.

Something as simple as the word "snow," which for most of us has one meaning, is much more complicated for the Sami people (the Laplanders) of northern Norway. They have 100 different words for "snow." It might be very light, very wet, very early in the year, from the north, from the south, etc.

We hear people calling others "fascist," do they know what they mean? The word was defined and expanded in essay titled, "The Doctrine of Fascism" by Giovanni Gentile in 1935. Benito Mussolini added a bit to the end of the essay. Gentile rejected democracy, liberalism, and Marxism. People are not equal, so they should not have an equal say in governing. In fact, the state is primary. When a liberal is called a fascist, the name caller doesn't understand what he or she is saying.

The author of "Animal Farm," George Orwell, warned that the English language "becomes ugly and inaccurate because our thoughts are foolish, but the slovenliness of our language makes it easier for us to have foolish thoughts." But he said that "the process is reversible." I sure hope so!

Today, as we often do, my wife and I were discussing the meaning of a word. She is the leading researcher and political specialist in the area of sexual harassment and sexual abuse in sport. She has been doing this for 30 years, so her concern predated the "Me too" movement by a number of years. (Of course, since males showing superiority over females in just about every walk of life has gone on for thousands of years, we are all quite tardy in our response!) She was getting ready for a conference for Safe Sport International, an organization which she helped to found. She was wrestling with the idea of the meaning of sexual violence.

The World Health Organization defines sexual violence as: "the intentional use of physical force or power, threatened or actual, against oneself, another person, or against a group or community, that either results in or has a high likelihood of resulting in injury, death, psychological harm, mal-development, or deprivation." It then goes on to categorize different types of violence as: self-directed violence (in which the person injures himself); interpersonal violence (violence between one or a few people) and; collective violence in which larger groups can be violent for social, political, or economic violence. They further divide this into family or community violence and further break it down into: physical, psychological, sexual, and neglecting categories.

When researchers in the area write about sexual abuse or harassment, they may use terms like: bullying, mobbing, hazing, harassment, gender harassment, sexual harassment, verbal abuse, rape, child abuse, spousal abuse, and many others. Some differences are obvious, some are not. For example, spousal abuse can be harassment, physical abuse, or even rape. What about bullying? Is somewhat similar behavior labeled bullying if it is in elementary school, hazing in high school or college, then harassment in the workplace? The point is, that when we are discussing important concepts, we must be on the same page. We must know the exact meaning of the words or terms we are using.

My reaction was that the one word was far too comprehensive to have any real meaning. When we consider neglect as a form of violence we are probably way out of bounds. The Latin root for the word is "vi" which means "force."

I looked up "violence" in the Merriam-Webster dictionary and it said:

➢ Behavior involving physical force intended to hurt, damage, or kill someone or something.

➢ The legal definition was similar: The unlawful exercise of physical force or intimidation by the exhibition of such force.

➢ A third definition dealt with the force of emotion.

So I wondered whether neglect could be considered violent, or even psychological stress, if it was not engendered by the threat of force.

Some people call American football violent. It had been long considered a "contact" sport. One coach I knew called it a collision sport. Certainly, contact can run the gamut from tango-ing to tackling.

Individuals, groups, or organizations may take a commonly used word or phrase and give it a new meaning. Usually the meaning is expanded. This gives listeners to people speaking about the newly changed concept a more limited meaning. Consequently, it is not understood.

I mentioned to my wife that I had taken a graduate-level course in semantics from one of the world's experts in the area, Dr. Abraham Kaplan, the chairman of the Philosophy Department at UCLA. In our 30 years, I had never mentioned it. It gave me new status because I was criticizing meaning from the position of someone who has studied the area, and not just an ignorant husband!

It has often bothered me when people take a perfectly well understood word and give it an entirely new meaning. This is particularly true with the word "gay." Gay has meant "merry and carefree" for many, many years. A favorite saying from over 100 years ago was "Have yourself a gay old time.

Many Christmas songs have the same word with the same meaning. "Have yourself a Merry Little Christmas, make the Yuletide gay."

And my favorite songs, from my favorite composer Sigmund Romberg use the word quite often. From New Moon, the love song "Softly as in a Morning Sunrise" Begins "Love came to me gay and tender, love came to me, sweet surrender." From his "Desert Song," the female lead sings "Ah, this is a humdrum world, But when I dream I set it dancing. When life is gray, I have a way to keep it gay, Passing the time of day romancing." And from the "Student Prince," the marching song of the students, "Come boys let's all be gay boys, for education should be scientific play boys."

In Leonard Bernstein's "West Side Story," when Maria falls in love she sings, " I feel pretty, and witty, and gay."

But what do the dictionaries say? Merriam-Webster says:

As an adjective:

1. a) happily excited: <u>merry</u> in a gay mood

   b) keenly alive and exuberant: having or inducing high spirits

2. a) <u>bright</u>, <u>lively</u>

   b) brilliant in color

3. given to social pleasures; also: <u>licentious</u>

Recent usage as a noun or an adjective:

4. a) <u>homosexual</u>, gay men

So, I'm mostly right in my understanding of the word!

Oh no! The Oxford Dictionary reverses Merriam-Webster, putting the more recent usages first.

1. Noun--(of people, especially men) sexually attracted to people of the same sex synonym <u>homosexual</u> gay men I didn't know he was gay. Is she gay? He is openly gay. opposite <u>straight</u>. Oxford Collocations Dictionary

2. Adjective before a noun--connected with people who are gay a gay club/bar the lesbian and gay community the gay and lesbian section in the bookstore Oxford Collocations Dictionary

3. Stand-alone adjective (slang, disapproving, offensive) (used especially by young people) boring and not fashionable or attractive. She didn't like the ringtone—said it was gay. That is so gay! He likes skiing but thinks snowboarding is gay.

4. Adjective—(traditional usage) happy and full of fun gay laughter She felt lighthearted and gay.

5. Adjective—(traditional) brightly coloured The garden was gay with red geraniums.

6. Without thinking about the results or effects of a particular action, "with gay abandon"

So a word with a commonly accepted meaning may be appropriated by some and take on a totally different meaning. Then, that new meaning may eventually become the commonly accepted meaning.

Donald Trump kept repeating his battle-cry, "We will make America great again." The semantics here are difficult to pin down. What is meant by "we?" Is it just those following Trump? Is it all Republicans? Is it only rhetorical and really only means Donald Trump?

The statement appears to indicate that America is not great. What criteria are used to determine greatness? The US has the leading economy in the world. Its unemployment rate was the lowest since 1973. It had come out of the recession of 2008 better than any country in the West. On the other hand, if we compare it with the growth in China it is far behind. Or is the meaning of "greatness" the number of victories in wars or against terrorists. Or does it mean winning more Olympic medals? In most Summer Olympics, the US leads in medal count. But in the Winter Olympics it is far below Norway's medal count—and Norway has less than 2% of the population of the US. If America is to be great in the Winter Olympics, we need more college scholarships for skiers and ski jumpers! Let's just reduce the engineering classes to make room.

Remember when James Comey testified to the Senate Intelligence Committee, in June of 2017, that he was in a room with several top level presidential advisors. Donald

Trump herded all the other people out of the room, among them Jeff Sessions who was Comey's boss. He then said to Comey, "I hope you can let the Flynn investigation go." Comey assumed that this was a strong desire of the President. But under Congressional investigation, a Republican Senator argued that "hope" only means a kind of a wish. Comey heard "hope" meaning a strong desire--a Presidential order. The Republican Senator indicated that it would only be a weak wish.

NON-VERBAL COMMUNICATION

What we mean by what we say is not only based on our words, but also on our body language, our tone of voice and the setting in which it is said. For Comey, clearing all of the advisors of the President and the Attorney General out of the room before making his statement indicated to Comey that it was a command and not a wish. After the conversation Comey immediately wrote down what had transpired in the conversation.

When we look at various definitions of "hope," Comey's assessment is probably closer to the definitions than the senator's—especially when you consider Trump's clearing the room before making his "hope" known. Of course, we have no picture of the body language or tone of voice of the President when he did his "hoping."

DEFINING "HOPE"

Here are some dictionary definitions of the word "hope."
> to look forward to with desire and reasonable confidence
> to feel that something desired may happen
> to cherish a desire with anticipation
> to desire with expectation of obtainment or fulfillment
> to expect with confidence

Here is the exchange between Senator Risch and Comey:

RISCH: You wrote down the words so we can all have the words in front of us now. There's 28 words there that are in quotes, and it says, quote, "I hope" — this is the President speaking — "I hope you can see your way clear to letting this go, to letting Flynn go. He is a good guy. I hope you can let this go." Now those are his exact words, is that correct?

COMEY: Correct.

RISCH: And you wrote them here, and you put them in quotes?

COMEY: Correct.

RISCH: Thank you for that. He did not direct you to let it go.

COMEY: Not in his words, no.

RISCH: He did not order you to let it go.

COMEY: Again, those words are not an order.

RISCH: He said, "I hope." Now, like me, you probably did hundreds of cases, maybe thousands of cases charging people with criminal offenses. And, of course, you have knowledge of the thousands of cases out there that — where people have been charged. Do you know of any case where a person has been charged for obstruction of justice or, for that matter, any other criminal offense, where this — they said, or thought, they hoped for an outcome?

COMEY: I don't know well enough to answer. And the reason I keep saying his words is that I took it as a direction.

RISCH: Right.

COMEY: I mean, this is the President of the United States, with me alone, saying, "I hope" this. I took it as, this is what he wants me to do.

Now I — I didn't obey that, but that's the way I took it.

RISCH: You — you may have taken it as a direction, but that's not what he said.

COMEY: Correct. I — that's why...

RISCH: He said — he said, "I hope."

COMEY: Those are exact words, correct.

RISCH: OK, do you— you don't know of anyone that's ever been charged for hoping something. Is that a fair statement?

COMEY: I don't, as I sit here.

Looking at the previous discussion. clearly, we can't have meaningful discussions if we don't agree on the meanings of the words or phrases we are using.

Another semantic problem that Comey faced occurred when he was promoting his book and making the rounds of the talk shows. Twice I heard the host asking him about leaking his conversation with the President. He was emphatic that he had not leaked anything. He had shared recollections s about a private conversation he had with Donald Trump. The TV hosts felt that was a leak. But he responded with the legalized FBI definition that, "a leak is the unauthorized release of a classified document." Both hosts that I saw wanted to argue with him using their own idea that a leak is the release of a private conversation. We can't argue about a word if we have very different ideas of what a word means.

INDUCTIVE LOGIC

A second area of logic is called inductive logic. Here we look at how probable is the truth of your statement. An opinion does not make it true, but of course your opinion may be true. If you say "all Mexicans are illegal immigrants." This is of course false because there are millions of people from Mexico who are American citizens. Some may be only American citizens, others may hold dual citizenship. Remember that the southwestern states of the USA, from Texas to California, were owned by Mexico prior to the 1840s. The US went to war to aggressively gain a great deal of Mexican territory. I'll bet the Mexicans wish they had built a wall from northern California across to Colorado and down to Texas before the war. Even if they had paid for it themselves, they would be way ahead financially!

So, we are looking at the argument, and not who said it. Very often we assume something is true because of who said it: the Pope, the king, the candidate. What is the probability that United Kingdom will be better off if it leaves the EU? What was the probability that invading Iraq and getting rid of Saddam Hussein would give birth to ISIS? What is the probability that Donald Trump can make America safer?

There are always people who are not happy with all that the government is doing. They may want: better primary education, better roads, free college tuition, a war with Iran, higher taxes on the rich, lower taxes, higher wages, better and cheaper healthcare, and a number of other wishes. No government can make everyone happy, so in every election cycle the is the opportunity for the "out" politicians to promise the moon. When the "ins" haven't delivered it, we vote back in the rascals we voted out in the last election.

It is standard political procedure to play on the anger and disappointment of the population and promise them hope, if they will vote for you. In the West, in recent times, we have had some semblance of rationality in the political discourse. In the last several years we have had George W. Bush, Brexit, and Donald J. Trump strike down rational thinking and promise us things that sound good but are highly detrimental to our nations.

TALK ABOUT UNINFORMED VOTERS

➤ 40 percent of Trump voters insist that he won the national popular vote.

➢ 60 percent of Trump voters think that Hillary Clinton received millions of illegal votes.

➢ 73 percent of Trump voters believe that George Soros is paying anti-Trump protesters.

➢ 29 percent of Trump voters don't think California votes should be allowed to count in the national popular vote.

➢ 67 percent of Trump voters think the unemployment rate went up under President Barack Obama. Only 20 percent accurately believe it went down.

➢ 39 percent of Trump voters think the stock market went down under Obama. And 19 percent are unsure.

➢ 14 percent of Trump voters think Hillary Clinton is connected to a child sex ring run out of a Washington pizzeria. Another 32 percent aren't sure one way or another. Only 54 percent are certain that Pizzagate was a myth.

Millions of people vote straight party lines or they vote on information that is not correct. Those who believed Trump were believing statements that were found to be 50% totally false, 20% mostly false, and less than 20% of what he said was true or partially true. There was plenty of publicity on the truth and falsity of the statements by both presidential candidates, but the Rust Belt voters either didn't know or didn't care. What does this say about intelligently voting in our democracy?

People who want to lead a nation or to vote intelligently for representatives need much more information today than ever before. We need an extensive knowledge of world history, macroeconomics, natural science, biological science, the theory of science, philosophy of religion, comparative religions, political science along with some knowledge of psychology and sociology and an understanding of ethics. Armed with a strong background in basic knowledge we can then effectively criticize or agree with propositions that are held by candidates who want to run our governments.

Donald Trump is an anti-intellectual politician. He changes his position on major issues from week to week, possibly depending on the audience he is addressing. Changing a position is not wrong if you have additional evidence to make you change your mind. Ethically it is wrong if you're only changing it for political motives and do not plan to follow through with policies that implement your position.

About a month after taking office Trump cited a Muslim terror incident in Sweden two days prior. The fact was that there never was such an incident, it was a fabrication. When asked about it he said that someone had told him. He did not name the someone. Conversely, less than a week later an article appeared in the New York Times from an unknown source that criticized him. He insisted on the source being named. This waffling back and forth based on his actions and words and how they are reported and negatively impact on him has created not only concerns but also a number of questions about his psychological health.

There are a large number of fallacies that relate to inductive logic. Often, they are not used to deceive, but the arguer has opinions that do not stand up to scrutiny. When Tea Party advocates were "definitely" against socialism, but could not define what it was that they were against? It was just ignorance-- not malice.

INDUCTIVE FALLACIES IN RECENT ELECTIONS

Because a number of inductive fallacies have been used extensively lately, we will give you an abbreviated list to give you an idea of how so many magicians of the mouth have attempted to pull the wool over our brains in their quests for political power.

When listening to candidates who are attempting to become elected today, we often hear statements that are not true, fake news, and promises that are impossible to fulfill. Many of these can be analyzed in terms of their truth or falsity. Many of these are what we call "logical fallacies." Here are just a few illustrations.

One common type of fallacy is called an **argumentum ad hominem**. (The argument is false because of the person who said it.)

Donald Trump criticized former Florida governor Jeb Bush in this way several times. He said that Bush: "had no honor," "was a hypocrite," "has no clue," and a number of other epithets that had nothing to do with the arguments that Bush was making. At various times, he called him: sad, desperate, a total disaster, a low energy guy, a sad sack, a low energy stiff and in many other negatives without criticizing his arguments. Bush was a major candidate with good credentials but was embarrassed out of the primary race.

Among the positions that Jeb Bush had taken were:

➢ No litmus test for judicial appointees,
➢ Abortion OK if the life of the mother was at risk,
➢ Defund Planned Parenthood,
➢ Aim for 4% national economic growth,
➢ Bank bailouts were necessary,
➢ For a balanced-budget,
➢ Let businesses express religious freedom against homosexuals,
➢ Lower tax rates on businesses,
➢ For school vouchers,
➢ A skeptic on global warming.

These conservative-reactionary positions actually agreed with Trump on many of the conservative-reactionary Republican positions. If an intelligent debate were going to be accomplished they needed to argue about those areas in which they disagreed. Instead Bush was personally attacked, but his issues were not discussed.

Trump called US Senator Marco Rubio "a lightweight" 19 times that I counted.

On John Kasich, the Governor of Ohio Trump called him: a typical politician, poor, doesn't have what it takes, can't debate, dummy, one of the worst presidential candidates in history, a total failure, so easy to beat, total dud, pathetic.

Trump's major approach to winning the primaries and the general election was in criticizing his opponents, usually without any proof. While this is not sound, as an inductive argument, it works because so many people are primarily moved by their unconscious minds and their inferiority complexes. It makes us feel good when somebody else is put down. And research often shows that when you hear something about 20 times—you generally accept it as true.

Another type of logical fallacy is the **"argument from ignorance."** In this line of thinking of the person claims that something is true because it cannot be disproven. This is an argument often used in religion to prove God. Trump said he could increase the Gross Domestic Product by 3% and maybe as high as 6%. The first quarter growth in 2017 was only 1.2%, the lowest in three years. For the year, it was 2.3%. The first quarter of 2018 is predicted to be 1.8 to 2.0%.

Brexit voters were told that their economy would improve. Their 2017 GDP rise was 1.5%, lowest of all EU countries—which averaged a 2.7% gain for the year. Of course, they're not out of the EU yet. Oh well, ignorance!

Another type of fallacy is called **"the appeal to the stone."** Here someone else's argument is dismissed because I say so, without any proof. I counted 27 times that Trump called Ted Cruz a liar. He also called him a number of other negatives like: hypocrite, not nice, cheater, nasty, desperate, and a big problem.

Ted Cruz had many of the same views as Trump. He was a free-trade advocate, against abortion, for gun rights, against the Affordable Care Act, hard line on immigration, denied climate change, and saw Iran as an enemy.

He did vary from Trump in advocating a flat tax and abolishing the IRS, and being against a higher minimum wage, Cruz also proposed eliminating the departments of: Energy, Education, Commerce and Housing and Urban Development. Should these issues have been discussed, or was it enough to forget them? Here we have a combination of dismissing the arguments because of who said them (ad hominem fallacy) and because Trump said so.

Sometimes fallacies are implied. For example, what is called the **anecdotal fallacy** deals with a personal experience that is supposed to counter the available evidence. Since Donald Trump was worth over $3 billion he must've been successful. That success in business would obviously carryover to success in government. Of course, there is no evidence of this would happen--only conjecture. (Actually, businessmen who have become presidents have been among our least effective presidents. We'll come to that in a few moments.)

Apparently, no one in history disregarded provable facts anywhere near as much as Donald Trump, his statements will be used extensively to indicate some of the fallacies that run counter to verifiable scientific or historical facts.

There is also the "**appeal the probability**" fallacy. Here the arguer postulates that this would probably be the case. In the Brexit campaign, it was held that a return to sovereignty by leaving the EU would bring all sorts of positive effects. Trump's slogan "to make America great again," somehow assumed that the United States was not great even though it was the world's greatest economic power and it had the world's greatest military force. Trump gave no reasons why the country was not great, although we can assume that it meant that we needed more coal mining jobs and more steelmaking jobs.

The" **conjunction fallacy**" assumes that if one outcome is probable, so are many others. Trump made his case for "making America great again," this one slogan was supposed to carry over into creating jobs for coal miners and steelworkers, cutting down the murder rates in Chicago, moving illegal immigrants back to their home countries, cutting taxes for the rich, and marginalizing Muslims.

Then there is the type of fallacy that tries to link a possible positive outcome to a previous but unrelated positive outcome. It can also be used to link a negative outcome to a possible negative outcome. For example, claiming that Hillary Clinton was responsible for the killing of an ambassador in Benghazi would therefore make her unreliable as a president. Clinton could have brought up the more than a thousand cases in which Trump was a defendant. Some of these were cases involving federal laws which he had violated. Some were cases in which he did not pay his contractors.

When Hillary was asked why she didn't attack him the way he attacked her she said that, Michelle Obama had told her that "when they go low we go high." She assumed that a higher level of ethical behavior would win when contrasted with his baseless fallacies. She was wrong. Most people say they want ethics in government, but the truth is that for many, their most basic needs and their need to fulfill their power drives is primary when it comes to voting. In the future politicians should say, "when they go low, we will go lower."

There is another type of "ad hominem" argument which is called "**poisoning the well**." If Hillary had done anything wrong in the past, she would do everything wrong in the future. This is without proving that anything was wrong with her emails or the Benghazi situation. Trump continued to bring these up as if they were major concerns for a future president. Another type of this argument is to abuse the arguer rather than answer the argument. This has been a major approach of Donald Trump.

Another common fallacy is called **incredulity** that is a lack of belief. If I don't believe something, it can't be true.

Trump did not believe that the Obama care health program was any good. Of course, he did not understand that what Obama wanted and what he got from Congress were two very different programs. When Trump worked to get a healthcare program through the House of Representatives, he said, "who knew that healthcare could be so complicated!"

Still another fallacy is called the **argument from silence**. Here my argument must be true because there is no evidence against it. I am a good businessman therefore I will be a good president. There is no evidence against this since I am not aware of any. Actually, the evidence is that in the US in the last hundred years, businessmen have been among our worst presidents.

Another fallacy is called **equivocation**. Here a word with more than one meaning is used to confuse the issue. For example, when creationists say that "evolution is only a theory" they are confusing a common use of the word with the scientific use of the word "theory"-- which means an established highly probable idea based on extensive research. Einstein's theories of relativity are examples. The creationists are using a different definition of theory which really means just guessing. "I have a theory that if I bet on black on the roulette wheel five times I will win at least twice."

"Let's make America great again." What does "great" actually mean in Trump's pronouncements? Does it mean to go to war with Mexico again, like we did in the 1840s, and take more of their land so that we can be a larger country? Does it mean going back to the past when religions were stronger and abortion was not possible? Does that mean going back to the 1950s and 1970s when laborers' earnings were a relatively large percentage of the CEO's earnings?

"**False attribution**" is the use by an arguer of unqualified or fabricated statements to back up his position. Trump did this when he cited a Muslim flare-up in Sweden to prove his anti-Muslim ideas. The problem was that there had been no Muslim flare-up in Sweden. George W. Bush did this with his false accounts of John Kerry's lack of heroism in Vietnam. The Brexiteers did it when they asserted that the EU workers were using the healthcare system more than the British, so were tapping unjustly into the coffers of the UK. The truth was that European workers did not use the health service as much as the British did. They were also told that they could have the same deal with the EU that Norway had. But Norway's deal cost almost as much as the UK paid and Norway was required to take in EU workers and migrants—the same conditions the Brexiteers wanted to eliminate.

"A **false dilemma**" is presented when only two possibilities are given for a solution when there may be many possibilities. For example, saying that there are only two ways to deal with Islamic terrorism. Let them all in or keep them all out. In reality, there was already a very strong vetting process in place by the US government.

The fallacy of "**a single cause**" is another oversimplification of the facts in a very complicated world. Illegal Mexican immigration has brought in both hard-working contributing people and a criminal element. They did come illegally so can be returned, but what if they are contributing to the society? Is it the best option for America? A few years ago in Norway an Indian family was sent back to India because they were no longer in danger. The parents had responsible jobs, the daughter was in medical school and the son had the highest grades in his high school. Did Norway hurt itself in this action?

An **"incomplete comparison"** is a fallacy in which not enough information is given to make an accurate comparison. Trump continually said that he had "inherited a mess" but the truth was that: the unemployment level was under 5%, the lowest since the 70s, the stock market had gone up for seven years, most of the soldiers had been brought back from the Mideast, and President Obama was respected around the world as a peacemaker. Trump brought up no evidence for his claim.

As of this month (August 2018) American wages are up 3%. Hooray! But inflation is us 2%. Boo! So buying power is up 1%. Big deal! In the EU wages are up 2%. But inflation is 1.5%, so the net in purchasing power is only 0.5%. So do the politicians use the high number or the honest number in their speeches? As of now the Trump tariffs and the retaliatory tariffs are just beginning to be felt. In addition, central banks are tightening interest rates so inflation will increase. Will our leaders tell us the whole truth or just cite the wage increases as evidence that we are getting richer?

The **"red herring"** fallacy occurs when the arguer does not answer the question but brings up another, often unrelated, situation and emphasizes that. Trump and his advisers do this continually. The press brings up the possible collusion with Russia in the election, and Trump answers that there were millions of illegal voters, or he answers that he supports Article 5 in the NATO agreement.

Still another type of fallacy is based on the idea that because it has been repeated so many times it must be true--**argument by repetition**. "Hillary is crooked." Trump said this 192 times that I counted. This was in addition to calling her a liar, corrupt, a fraud and incompetent. His basis for this seemed to be primarily her emails on a private server and the fact that she had made a great deal of money speaking-- often to Wall Street firms. The fact that he had made more money borrowing from Wall Street firms did not seem to be an issue, at least to him. But, of course, in politics as he saw it, there are no rules except to win.

This is a major problem in the process of electing representatives in many democratic republics. Repeat the lies about the faults or your opposition or your own accomplishments, usually with a controlled press, and your chances of winning are increased. Zimbabwe with Robert Mugabe, South Africa with Jacob Zuma, and Putin in Russia are just a few of the elected dictators around recently. It is almost unbelievable that two are now gone because of the people's strong opposition to them. Venezuela's poor voted for a spreading of the wealth in 1998, but much of the educated part of the country left and the mismanagement of President Maduro left the citizens starving and ill.

The solutions to major problems are not as simple as politicians, or our limited knowledge, lead us to believe. In the 2500 years of democracies, some people have gained power by honestly proposing ideas that should improve the society. But there have certainly been large numbers of presidents and representatives who had lied to gain power and often maintain their power through the strong arms of the police and army. The ideal of "government of the people, by the people and for the people" is too often "government of the powerful, by the powerful and for the powerful." And gaining that power is not always done ethically!

There can be overlaps in these fallacies in that something that is said violates more than one fallacy type.

"I believe in God, everybody does and nobody can disprove it." While God may well exist, the fact that the idea cannot be disproven or that everyone believes it, does not prove it.

DEDUCTIVE LOGIC

The third area of logic is the deductive. Here the argument is analyzed as to whether or not the conclusion follows from the two premises of the argument. It is possible to have a conclusion that is true even if the premises are false-- as long as the rules of deduction are followed.

While inductive logic looks at the possible or probable truth of a statement. deductive logic looks at the structure of the argument to see if the conclusion follows from the premises.

When statements are put together to arrive at a more advanced level of knowing, this is called deductive logic. There are rules for arguments to be "valid." Deductive logic does not deal with truth as much as with whether or not the statements used in the argument follow the rules of sound thinking. The classic syllogism of deductive logic is:

All men are mortal.

Socrates was a man.

Therefore, Socrates was mortal.

The first two sentences are called the premises. The last sentence is called the conclusion. If it is true that all men are mortal, then the first premise is true. But not all people have died who have been born, so we don't know for sure that the first premise is true. But since all people who were born at least 200 years ago are now dead, it would appear to be true.

The second premise "Socrates was a man" is true if he actually existed. There is some historical basis for this fact.

There are several rules that must be followed for an argument to be valid. One such rule is that the term that appears in both premises (in this case it is man or men) must include all of the group in at least one premise. In this case, it is "all men."

When we look at the premises and the conclusion we have three terms: Man, Socrates and Mortal. When we are looking for relationships between these we must know just how much of each we are talking about. So we use modifiers which may not be in the premises or the conclusion. the modifiers are: all, some (one or more), or none. So the above syllogism would be:

- ➢ All men are (some of) mortals
- ➢ (All) Socrates was (some of) men
- ➢ Therefore (all of) Socrates was (some of) mortals.

But here is an example of an argument that is valid and the conclusion is true but the premises are not true.

- ➢ The moon is made of green cheese.
- ➢ All things made of green cheese are round.
- ➢ Therefore, the moon is round.

The conclusion is true but the premises are false. They don't pass the test of inductive logic. The rules of deductive logic have been followed.

The premises did not pass the standards of truth needed for an argument that might be used in seeking election. We might also look at the semantics of the premises. Which moon are we talking about? The moon of Earth, one of the moons of Saturn or some other moon? What do we mean by green cheese? And what do we mean by round? Do we mean a globe, a circle, something that is nearly a globe—like the Earth, which is really an oblate spheroid.

A similar syllogism from the Trump campaign might be:
- ➢ All businessmen can be effective American presidents.
- ➢ Donald Trump is a businessman.
- ➢ Therefore, Donald Trump can be an effective American president.

The argument is valid. The problems are with the premises. So it is an inductive problem. While this argument was not made in this form to the voting public, it was strongly inferred. And many Americans, not being aware of history, bought into it.

The problem with the first premise is that from the 1900s businessmen who became presidents have ranked the lowest of all presidents in terms of effectiveness: Hoover, Coolidge, George W. Bush and Harding are all at the bottom of the list of effective presidents. All were successful businessmen.

The second premise also has some problems. Donald Trump has not been a particularly effective businessman. His hotels and casinos have had four bankruptcies. His ownership of: a USFL football team, Trump Steaks, Trump Magazine, Trump Vodka, Trump Airlines, Trump Mortgage, Trump University, Trump's Travel Website-- all ended in failure. Add to that his many court cases in which he broke federal laws or contracts and we have some real doubts as to his business acumen and his ethics.

Just as in inductive logic, there can be fallacies when developing a deductive argument. You can have only three terms in a syllogism.
- ➢ Illegal immigrants are taking many jobs,
- ➢ I need more pay, so we should get rid of all immigrants.

Four terms: illegal immigrants, people who take jobs, I need more pay, getting rid of all immigrants.

Another is that you cannot have an affirmative conclusion from a negative premise:
- ➢ America is not doing well,
- ➢ Doing well requires a Trump election, so:
- ➢ Trump can make America great again.

There are several other deductive fallacies that can make an argument invalid. But this is not a logic class. These are only cited to make people aware of how we are often convinced of something even though it is not logical or true.

BEWARE THE LOGICAL FALLACIES OF POLITICIANS

This book illustrates how modern-day politicians may appeal to every aspect of our mind, from our unthinking, and reacting unconscious mind to our intellect. In the past in America, and today in Europe, it is the appeal to the intellect that politicians usually use. But recently, from George Bush to Brexit to Donald Trump we find an increasing use of irrational appeals to our unconscious minds.

Whether knowingly or unknowingly, politicians are using the psychological motivating insights that advertisers have used for decades. And, as will be shown, many politicians are hiring the same companies that advertisers use. If all is fair in love and war—no problem! But if it is important for you to know the truth before you step into the voting booth, or if it is important to have representatives that are educated and who are able to use the tools of logic-- we had better improve our education.

Two prominent Republicans: Mitch McConnell, the Senate majority leader (member of the Select Committee on Intelligence, and the Agriculture, Nutrition and

Forestry Committee), and Marco Rubio, a major candidate for the presidency and (member of the Select Committee on Intelligence), both said recently relative to their denial of climate change, "I am not a scientist."

The Florida Senator said that proposed policies to curb climate change "will do absolutely nothing" to improve the environment, but will "make America a harder place to create jobs." since he is not a scientist, does he have any evidence for what he says? Or is it just uninformed wishful thinking— promulgated by lobbyists for the fossil fuel industry? There is absolutely no question that climate change exists. That humans have caused it, is affirmed by 98% of climate scientists.

Is it true that legislative policies "will do absolutely nothing?" Some 50 years ago it was found that the ozone layer, which filters out some of the ultraviolet rays of the sun, was increasing. It was due, in large part, because of fluorohydrocarbons, from: refrigerants, like air conditioning units and refrigerators; propellants, like spray cans; and, some solvents. The increased ultraviolet rays were causing skin cancers and cataracts in humans, They also were damaging plants.

According to NASA, ultraviolet rays affect our DNA. This is true for both plants and animals. The United Nations estimated that a 1% decrease of the ozone layer resulted in a 2 to 3% increase in skin cancers. With plants UV radiation interferes with photosynthesis in many species. Among them such crops as: rice, corn, soybeans, winter wheat and cotton.

By reducing the causative agents, the ozone layer is again increasing. It was scientists who discovered the problem and sounded the alarm. It was intelligent legislators that prohibited the manufacture of these culprits.

As serious as this was, it is nothing compared to the effects of climate change, which include: billions of dollars lost because of hurricanes, famines, excess rains, and higher oceans that can flood low-lying cities and farmland. These, of course, are just a few of the factors that result from our human meddling with our air and stratosphere.

With global warming, again it is scientists who discovered the problem and suggested the solutions. In much of the world, legislators have banded together to fight the problem. But this is a much larger problem than the ozone layer. At this time, all we can hope is that legislators will work to slow the damage being done. Perhaps we can speed the development of solar power, wind power, and electric cars. I wonder if Senators McConnell and Rubio have considered developing jobs in these areas. There is more to the industrial output of America than just coal mining!

Kentuckian McConnell also put jobs ahead of climate change and said, in his most scientifically verifiable theory that "I know lots of people who don't believe in climate change." And I wonder, how many are climate scientists. I wonder if he had ever studied logic. He used the **argumentum ad populum**, that-- if some people think so, it must be true!

Do these legislators believe that the world is flat? It certainly looks flat—but I'm no scientist. Scientists found that it is almost round, an oblate spheroid—slightly flattened at the poles. If it were perfectly round we wouldn't have to fly the polar route from Europe to America! Do they believe in evolution? Biologists, anthropologists and geologists are certain it is true. Do they ever fly on airplanes? Do they drive cars? Do they use computers? Scientists developed all of these technologies. I assume that the venerable senators accept the technology developed by some scientists! Maybe they need to listen a bit more to what is empirically verifiable rather than what is politically expedient for some voters in West Virginia and Florida.

CHAPTER 5   UNDERSTANDING VALUES—OURS AND OUR REPRESENTATIVES

Since the major point of this book is to look deeper into how we behave and how we are manipulated, we need to look now at how we base our values. We may value something without understanding the basis for that value. If your society is against capital punishment, as Europe is, you may not look beyond the societal basis for this value. Maybe it has simply grown from the fact that everybody's vote counts equally therefore everybody must be equal. So, everyone has an equal right to life. But this depends on still another assumption, that we are all somehow equal in spite of the fact that it is obvious that no two people in the world are exactly the same--exactly equal.

VALUES

Freud called the seat of our values our "super ego." We are more likely to call it a conscience. But I want to suggest that it is more than just being a conscious choosing between good and evil. Value choosing is done in many areas, like: what kind of car to buy, what color should it be, should I have children, which program shall I watch on TV, etc. However, here I will concentrate on values in the area of ethics and morality.

Our values often come from our backgrounds-- our traditions. Sometimes we think ourselves into new values, such as: a strongly religious person comprehensively analyzing the history, philosophy and possibly archeology of religions or possibly studying various sciences, then becoming an atheist; or, a self-centered criminal who becomes religiously or socially oriented in prison—and possibly starts a half-way house for ex-prisoners or drug addicts, or becomes a minister, after he is released from his incarceration.

Whatever the source of our values, our thinking about values starts with basic assumptions. Basic assumptions are ideas that are basic to our values, but cannot be proven-- so are assumptions.

What values are we talking about? They can be anything from what kind of dress to buy to whether we should allow capital punishment or abortion in our society. Values can also be basic to our political thinking, such as whether we equal or not equal as people. If we are equal, perhaps our incomes should be equal. If we are not equal, it makes sense that those who are at the top economically to make even more money, and forget about those at the bottom of the economic ladder

But on what should we base our thinking about being equal or unequal? Is it because we are all human? If so, what makes human? Most humans have 46 chromosomes, but there are at least 15 other species that have 46 chromosomes. They include:, a couple of kinds of monkeys, a hare, and a couple of kinds of rats, mice, and bats, and various other species. So are these other species equal to humans? In fact, not all humans have 46 chromosomes. Some have 45, some 47, and some 48. So being human must have a different criterion if we are to be somehow special.

Might it be intelligence? There are some zoologists who believe some animals are smarter in some ways than some humans. Whales and dolphins, for example, can talk with each other. On an IQ scale people at the very bottom are often eclipsed by some animals when nonverbally tested.

Many of our values are called "moral values." They relate to how we treat other humans, whether or not we follow the rules that our God has set out in scriptures is a common. A third "morality" is found in how we follow the laws and traditions of our society—or the world society. As mentioned, in James Comey's book "A Higher Loyalty: Truth, Lies, and Leadership," he stated that Donald Trump is not morally capable of leading America.

SCRUTINIZING OUR BELIEFS

The simplest explanation for us is to accept what we have heard and not rely on any contradictory evidence no matter how authoritative it is. This happens with our religious beliefs, our beliefs in democracy, and our beliefs in our selected leaders. When Kin Jong-un tells his people that America has long determined to attack them, most believe it. When Donald Trump tells his flock that Barack Obama hacked his phone line, some believed it. When your mother tells you that the Bible is true, you believe.

A few hundred years ago, nearly everyone believed that the sun went around the Earth. Very few believe that now. Because most of us go to school now, the average person has far more knowledge then did our ancestors 500 years ago. But some of our beliefs are over a thousand years old, yet are so fundamental to our traditions that few of us want to examine them. Often they are so deep that they become "basic assumptions" to our lives. These basic assumptions are often fundamental to what we value, or to what we say we value. While they are only assumptions, they are fundamental--and basic, to what we believe.

When we look at humans as being religious, we often come up with the idea of "soul" as the thing that separates animals and people. Of course, we have no empirical evidence for a soul. When we speak of God or soul, we are into the basic assumption realm.

Values often come to us through traditions. If your mother always fried your dinner in lard, you will probably continue to fry your dinners, possibly using olive oil instead of lard. It doesn't matter that you know that microwave cooking is healthier, cheaper and has far fewer calories.

In the West, we may value our religion or lack of it, democracy, our bank account, our house, our favorite team, etc. Our representatives in government may have some of the same values, but usually have a strong self-centered value to be reelected into their posts as power elites.

In order to understand ourselves, we should understand clearly our values and the basic assumptions on which they rest. In our democratic society, we need to be able to uncover the real values of our representatives. Are they putting their money where their mouths are? Are we looking for people who will make the country better or are we looking for people who will satisfy our self-centered values, even if they are counter to the best possible society?

HONESTY

We shouldn't lie. If we all tell the truth we will be able to trust each other. We will not cheat on our taxes, cheat in business, or in our personal relationships. In campaigns for leadership positions it would be nice to always tell the truth. This would be desirable for many who advocate a society centered moral value. But since acquiring power is the major way to reduce our inferiority complexes, lying may become a means to justify the end desired. So, lying may be desirable to advance our self-centered values.

VALUES FOR NOW—OR THE FUTURE?

Values also come from what we need now or in the future. If I am out of a job or if my pay does not match my financial needs, I will feel a self-centered value to vote for someone who promises me a job or higher pay. Trump promised this very effectively. But can he can deliver on putting miners back in the coal mines or reopening the steel factories when the world has too much steel and China is subsidizing its steel production making Chinese steel very cheap for world buyers. Now that he has applied tariffs to Chinese steel, 2% of our steel imports will cost more—since only 2% of American steel comes from China. The initial reaction to the tariffs was a 700 point drop in the Dow-Jones index.

Values are based on either what the person wants (self-centered), what they think that God wants (God based) or what they think is good for society (society based). Each of these is based on assumptions that are not provable. You may want something today, like a motorcycle, that cripples you tomorrow in an accident. What you thought would be best for you turned out to be wrong. If you do something because you think that is what God wants, there are a couple of problems. You can't prove that God exists and you can't prove what God wants. With the many religious people in the world why do they not agree on what God wants? Society's values also are not clear-cut. Is it the best society that that has the lowest taxes, the greatest happiness, the best economy, that has the best welfare state, or a society that we have long passed—"the good old days?"

This is a subject that requires a very long book. If you are interested in looking at the assumptions of the different bases for values and at how they can be important in a number of questions with which society is wrestling, such as: abortion, capital punishment, torture, etc. (I would suggest reading "On Human Values" which is Book 4 of the popular free e-book series "andgulliverreturns.info.")

Basic assumptions are fundamental to our thinking. Once you understand the deepest grounds for what you will believe, you can amass the evidence relative to the question you are investigating. The evidence will help you to determine what your stance should be on every question of ethics or other values.

If you don't know already, thinking is not for sissies!

TYPES OF BASIC ASSUMPTIONS

Basic assumptions are generally non-provable starting points. They can be grounded on the idea of a God, a version of an ideal society, or on a "self" being most important. They are also fundamental in science, in history and nearly any organized body of thought. However, here we are dealing with the starting points of values, of morality, of ethics.

Basic assumptions can include such ideas as: whether or not there is a God, whether the universe is primarily idea (God) or matter, or whether or not people are equal in the most important sense.

SELF-CENTERED BASIC ASSUMPTIONS

If I use a self-centered basic assumption for developing my values, that "self " is commonly me, but it could be my child, my spouse, or a friend. Still, just as I cannot prove: that there is a God, or that a certain society is always preferable, I cannot prove that I am the most important consideration in the world.

Looking at self-centered basic-assumptions we can easily see how we behave. We may shop well beyond our means and run up our credit card debt to a point to where we cannot pay our bills. This may bring us the bankruptcy court where we let our creditors pay our bills. When we vote, we may vote only for what we want now, without thinking of its effects on us, or our families, later. Choosing to use psychoactive drugs like alcohol, marijuana or OxiContin are obviously examples of self-centered value choices.

Donald Trump, Roy Moore, Harvey Weinstein and a number of other politicians, media moguls, business managers and other men from every walk of life have been accused of sexual harassment or assault. They acted upon their self-centered interests in each case. They wanted to do something and did not consider how the woman felt about it.

The "self" can be larger than a single individual. It could be a family, a corporation, or even a nation, acting as an individual. China has stolen about a trillion dollars in intellectual property. This is "ethical," (has value) if the self-centered values for China are primary. For the US it is unethical, since the United States in its self-centered evaluation of the action, finds that China's stealing does not have value for the "self" of the United States.

For those of you steeped in the study of ethics, Immanuel Kant's dictum that, "We should always treat others as end in themselves, not as means only," would find a serious conflict between acting on pure self-centered values and calling them ethical. But as we mentioned in our discussion on semantics, there can be more than one definition to the concept of "values."

SOCIETY BASED ASSUMPTIONS

Then there are basic assumptions that are applied to societies.

When there are two people or two states, each is concerned with itself. If they want to join a group, such as two people starting a family, or two states joining an international organization like the WTO or the UN, the society assumptions should become primary. The rules of the World Trade Organization or the United Nations should become primary.

When Karl Marx developed his ideas of a communist state, he gave a number of reasons why it would happen. History dictated it, if we could only follow the dialectic of history.

Russia tried through socialism to move toward communism. It never got out of its version of a socialist state. And, the selfishness of the people, in opposition to the state controlled government, hobbled it to its death. Marx assumed that we are unselfish people. There are some, but most of us are somewhat selfish for ourselves and for our families.

Using democratic elections for governments has become almost a basic assumption in forming modern governments. But are the elections really expressing the wills of well-informed voters? China has an effective economy and seems to be making progress in fighting that universal bugaboo of society—corruption. But it's national government is an oligarchy of the heads of the Communist Party. In the US, it seems to be largely a plutocracy of the money elites of both parties. It seems that the closest we are getting to true democratic republics is in Western Europe.

One might advocate communism, monarchy or even democracy as an ideal society and work toward it. If a democratic-republic is to be the preferred method of governing and the people choose to elect politicians whom they know have harassed women, should the democratic process be held superior to the non-ethical treatment of some citizens. Should the democratic process be held superior to the concept of a government of laws?

When Roy Moore ran for the Senate seat of Alabama, he had already been twice removed from the Supreme Court for actions counter to the laws of the country. Donald Trump had been found guilty of violating Federal Fair Housing laws and had admitted to harassing and abusing women. Should there be any ethical requirements for those who want to rule in a representative government? If their behavior is counter to your self-centered values should you vote for them?

Whatever the form of government, the laws should reflect the primary interest of the society. That might be the interests of the king in earlier societies. It might be: the interests of the ruling party, as in China; the ruling plutocracy, as in Russia and Saudi Arabia; a combination or business interest and those of the populace, as in the US; or, with the general public primary, as in the Scandinavian countries.

GOD-BASED ASSUMPTIONS

Sometimes definitions are seen as basic assumptions.

"The world was created by God." This assumes the biblical planet that we call home. But there are other planets in the universe-- about two and a half trillion is the best estimate of astronomers, and they are the people who study the universe. They estimate that there are 300 billion suns (stars) and 120 billion planets in our galaxy and 120 billion other galaxies. Is there a God for each planet? That would be 2,400,000,000,000 gods if there is one for each planet. And of course, by the same logic we must ask the question, "who created God."

When you know nothing but a value that has been forced on you, like a religious or political theory, you are in trouble. Recently an ISIS type school was found in Indonesia. Eight teachers and four students, one only 11 years old, attempted to leave for Syria or Iraq to fight for their cause.

There are many religions, so there are many religious basic assumptions. The Hindus, and some in other religions, are pantheistic. That is, they believe that all is God. The universe and all the beings on it are part of the oneness of the supreme spirit. There are some Jews, Christians, and Muslims who also believe this. Usually they have arrived at this belief through meditation. The Jews, Christians, Muslims, and Baha'is are monotheistic. They believe in one creating and judging God. There are also those who are polytheistic---having more than one god. And some are deists, believing in a creating god who is not concerned with people. So, doing good works would not impress this being at all. So you wouldn't use a deistic god as a basis for choosing values or ethics. Many of our Founding Fathers, like Jefferson, were deists.

HOLY SCRIPTURES TO BACK UP OUR BASIC ASSUMPTIONS

The monotheists usually have sacred scriptures to back up their beliefs. The Bible, the Qur'an, Book of Mormon, and the Tanakh are examples. We will briefly comment on a few of these to illustrate how beliefs are influenced, clarified, and possibly discarded.

Authorities have been reading and trying to date many biblical references. When we have an unseen creator in a world beyond the physical it is easier to believe what our priests and ministers tell us because it is impossible to disprove metaphysical myths—we can only cast doubts about them.

But when we move to the physical world probability can be increased. For example, reading Aristotle's Physics it is obvious that a heavy body will fall faster than a lighter body of the same shape and material. But no one tried to see if it was true. Galileo famously disproved it 2,000 years later. Actually, it was disproved 200 years earlier, without the fanfare, by the two Dutch scientists.

When it is a statement about nature, scientists can test the hypothesis. When it is a statement about something supernatural or mythical, scientists can look at the evidence but it doesn't necessarily disprove a scriptural text for the believer. It falls in line with the nonprovable basic assumptions.

People of the cloth, who preach to us, may have absolutely no religious education. They may have education in their sect only. They may be highly educated in the general history of religion, or may be full-fledged highly educated theologians. Anyone can call himself "reverend" and start a church. There are, however, scholars of the various scriptures, as well as historians and archaeologists who search for in-depth information to verify or question the contents of the various scriptures of the world religions.

The Babylonian texts including the creation story called Enuma Elis was found in 1849 in the ancient city of Nineveh, present-day Mosul, Iraq-- the former stronghold of ISIS. This creation story is generally dated as being from the 16th to 18th Century BCE, but some think that is as late as the 11th Century BCE.

Looking at the Torah and the Old Testament we see the stories of Abraham, who might have lived sometime between 1600 and 1800 BCE and Moses who supposedly lived sometime between 1200 and 1400 BCE. As you remember, the pharaoh had decreed that all Hebrew male babies should be killed, so Moses' mother put him in a basket in the river where he was found by the pharaoh's daughter. What a lucky fella! He later led the Israelites out of Egypt-- and along the way was given the 10 Commandments by God.

Tradition tells us that Moses wrote the first five books of the Bible, the Torah. This was held to be the work of Moses, as dictated by God. But starting with some rabbinic voices in the 11th and 12th Centuries, doubts were raised. Among the details that challenged the notion that Mosaic authorship included historical and language issues that indicated an authorship much later than Moses. Of course, he could have written it then had it edited by later scribes.

Probably the most difficult task for our minds to accomplish is to overcome the traditions with which we were born and raised. Do we know about similar myths that preceded our own scriptures?

The Babylonian Epic of Gilgamesh, from about 2100 BCE, with its story similar to that of the Garden of Eden, with man being tempted by woman by food and then covering his nakedness. The serpent also shows up in Gilgamesh with the secret of immortality. It also has the first known flood story in the Mideast.

There was also a Sumerian creation story from about 1600 BCE with its story of the flood and the ark and that the gods would save the people. These myths validated the basic assumptions of peoples prior to Moses' accounts.

Our written evidence of early Hebrew belief is found primarily in the Dead Sea Scrolls, which contain parts of the Torah and Old Testament, and date from about 300 BCE to 100 AD. There are other manuscripts found nearby that date from the Eighth Century BCE to the 11th century AD.

The point here is not to press a religious story, but to make us think about exploring and questioning our own basic assumptions. The myths and traditions we live by may be open to serious scrutiny. When Darwin presented his evidence that simple animals are always found to have developed earlier than more complicated animals, and well before humanoids, it plunged a fatal dagger into the hearts of all creation myths, not only Genesis.

Theologians have long attempted to find a philosophical argument that would prove that there is a creator. There were several arguments. One of the main ones was that since everything is in motion, there must be a first mover. The major one is that since everything shows design, like the sun coming up every morning or that trees grow from the bottom up, there must be a first designer. The problem with both of these theories is that using the same arguments, to get that creating god there must've been a god that created him, and so forth into infinity.

What about the 'Big Bang?" Astrophysicists have measured the speed at which the universe is expanding and so set a date for when it all began to expand. That was about

13.6 to 13.8 billion years ago. And what created that small mass of material that became the universe? God did. So, we never quit looking for that unprovable assumption!

Let's take a look at Christianity. Jesus lived from about 4 BCE to about 30 AD, or CE, meaning the common era. The earliest writing we have about the life of Jesus is from about 300 years after he lived. There are two books, ancient codexes-- Codex Sinaiticus and Codex Vaticanus, from about 300 years after Jesus lived. These include the gospels of Matthew, Mark, Luke, and John. With Mark written about 70 CE, Matthew and Luke about 90, they relied on Mark to a great extent. Then John was written about 105 CE.

But there is another, the so-called Gospel of Thomas which seems to have been written before the other four. But was not accepted by the Council of Nicea, in 325 AD, so is not accepted by most Christians.

In the earliest codex, written about 300 years after Jesus died, Mark did not mention the stone being rolled away from his sepulcher or the resurrection of Jesus. Matthew did mention this. In many later versions, this resurrection story is now in Mark also. From Mark to John, Jesus becomes more godlike. None ever met Jesus.

The Epistles of Paul were written about 55 CE. Of course, Paul never met Jesus, but became the primary prime missionary and visionary of the new religion.

ISLAM

While the Jews and Christians have a number of inconsistencies and gaps in the history and theology of their beliefs, the Qur'an is much more consistent. This may be because it is more recent. According to Muslim tradition, the Prophet Muhammad received the revelations that form the Qur'an, the scriptures of Islam, from the Angel Gabriel in the 22 years between 610 and 632, the year of his death. A copy of the Qur'an has been discovered in the library at the University of Birmingham. It dates from about 650 CE. This copy of the Qur'an may have been written by a person who had met, and maybe was a friend of, the Prophet.

AFTERLIFE

Every society that I know of has some kind of belief in an afterlife. What happens in that afterlife is often quite different. Why do we have such a belief? Psychologically, we cannot think of our own nonexistence. We can think of as being dead and being at our funeral. We can think of us being buried and the worms eating through our bones-- but we are still thinking of ourselves as existing. We can think of ourselves being cremated and sitting on the fireplace mantle or in a mausoleum, but we are still thinking of ourselves as existing.

Whether it is the happy hunting ground of some Native American tribes, a paradise with God as is a common belief among the followers of the religions of Abraham, a joining with our ancestors, or other beliefs-- most people have the hopeful dream of life beyond life.

THEOLOGIANS DEBATE AND ATTEMPT TO CLARIFY OUR ASSUMPTIONS

A major question is how can a merciful God allow such suffering in the world? How does a merciful God allow such destruction as in hurricanes, floods, forest fires and murders? How does a merciful God allow senseless murders, child abuse, rape, wars, and all the other atrocities that we see? One theological answer is that "they are all varying degrees of good—and all are found in God."

Another question relates to the power of prayer. Scientists predicted hurricanes Harvey and Irma, and all the praying of the faithful could not stop them. How much prayer has been unanswered for the victims of the war in Syria?

FROM EDEN TO EVOLUTION

The age of science we can see beginning in the fourth century BCE primarily with the Greeks and Egyptians. By the Ninth Century the Muslim scientists were primary, this continued until about the mid-13th century. Then the emphasis shifted to Europe. Of course, in Asia they were inventing things like: paper and printing, gunpowder, the compass, and the crossbow—and lots of other inventions well before the Europeans.

As sciences developed they often validated facts like where scripturally referenced cities were. But they also cast certain doubt on the various creation and flood stories.

CHOOSING VALUES FOR TODAY OR TOMORROW?

Value choices can be made with concerns only for the present time, right now, or with the future in mind. Most students go to college with the future in mind—getting me a better job or making me a more intelligent person. Others go for present concerns, I can play more and avoid having to go to work. Using psychoactive substances may be fun now, but what if their use makes me lose a job that I liked, a relationship I enjoyed, or my life in a car accident?

You may vote for a candidate or a cause (like Trump, Bush or Brexit) then find in the future that your life is much worse because of your earlier vote that was based on your previous opinions, but the future had become more negative because of your vote. Would you have voted differently if you had had more knowledge?

THE BASIC ASSUMPTIONS OF SCIENCE AND HISTORY.

Nearly every organized body of knowledge is based on non-provable assumptions. However, some assumptions may be more likely to be true than others. Science is no exception. For example, here are some of them.

> There are natural causes for things that happen in the universe,

> Evidence from the natural world is used to explain natural phenomena,

> There is consistency in the causes of the effects. The same effect will have the same cause.

(If you are interested in a thorough discussion of this, read E.A. Burtt 'Metaphysical Foundations of Modern Science.")

Some assumptions of historians might be:

> That their actual descriptions are true, accurate, and complete,

> That their reasoning and interpretation of why things happened are true,

> That a knowledge of history gives us explanations for the present and directions for the future.

SCIENCE DEALS WITH PROBABILITIES

It is well known that two atoms of hydrogen and one of oxygen make water, H_2O. It has been done millions of times in college chemistry labs. But I heard last week that a chemistry student in Munich put two hydrogens and an oxygen together and they came out beer! Still it is extremely probable that two hydrogen atoms and an oxygen atom will make water. But if you add another atom of oxygen you won't get water. H_2O_2 is peroxide!

So science deals with probabilities. Many of Einstein's theories have been affirmed. Darwin's theories of evolution keep being reaffirmed as earlier geological strata never yield later forms of fauna. Bernoulli's finding that fluids, or air, moving faster have reduced pressure. So it we have an airplane wing that is flat on the bottom and convex on top, the air going over the wing must go faster over the top than under the wing. This creates a lower pressure over the wing and it lifts. So every time a plane takes off it increases the "probability" that Bernoulli's theory is true.

Chemistry and physics are "hard" sciences that work often with single or few variables. The "soft" sciences, like: psychology, sociology, or economics, work with many variables at once. Since each person has billions of brain cells and different brain structures, even a study with a single variable, is being processed by many individuals each with different brains and experiences.

TRADITIONS

If we have believed something all of our lives, we just know is true. The fact is, that traditions come to us as a matter of history and our history is often wrong. Read a history book in Russia about World War II. Then read one in Germany, then one in the UK, then one in the US. You won't really read exactly the same story. An old professor of mine said that "history is the story of things that never happened, written by people who were not there." Can we really believe that all the truth of the Peloponnesian wars can be read in Thucydides?

An effective, comprehensive, and unbiased education usually makes one question his or her beliefs. Long-held beliefs in politics, religion, relationships, or vocational expectations may be scrutinized by people who have learned to question and evaluate effectively. This evaluation may make one more confident in the value of the tradition, may make one revise his or her beliefs, or the evaluation may make one totally reject one's traditions. For many young people in the 1960s it was casting off the puritanical practices of sexual abstinence and of shunning mind altering drugs. What about these traditions:

➤Because your long-lost ancestor voted for Abraham Lincoln, and your relatives have all followed suit as Republicans, perhaps you should evaluate their directions today.

➤Because your great-grandfather voted for Franklin Roosevelt, and you have all been Democrats since then, perhaps you should evaluate your directions today.

➤Because your father and mother divorced, it is no reason to give up on marriage, remember the friends of your cousin who have been happily married for 65 years.

➤"Until death do you part," made some sense 2,000 years ago when people lived only 30 years, but now that we live to 80 we may need different mates at different times in our lives.

➤Your parents have been successful dentists for 39 years and want you to take over their practice, but you would like to become a professor of art history.

➤Your family is intensely religious Muslims, but your intense study of religions urges you to convert to conservative Judaism.

➤Your parents are atheists but you have spent a good time in Egypt and want to convert to Islam.

➤Your family has been Catholic since Saint Patrick landed in Ireland. You have two cousins who are priests, but your study of Catholicism, and religions in general, has pushed you to atheism.

Let's look at some religious beliefs as examples. What about the stories of creation? The Egyptians had the god Aron who created himself, then the world. Some creation stories start with the world being created from chaos.

In others, it was created from nothing. In still others from a god or goddess doing some magical thing that created the world out of clay, wood, ocean, dirt or out of their own being. Wherever we grow up we have ingrained in us the story of creation that has been accepted by our tribe. We do want to know where we came from, so anything sounds good. And the simpler, the better. Do you really want to believe that almost 15,000,000,000 years ago something smaller than a golf ball exploded into our universe?

It is probably the least believable story of creation, but it is the only one that has some evidence to back it up.

Most people only know a little bit about their own religion. But history tells us that most of our modern Western beliefs had their origins in older Egyptian, Babylonian and Assyrian religious beliefs. For example, the Egyptians believed in an afterlife. First it was only the Pharaoh that ascended into the heavens to live among the stars. Later, everyone had an opportunity for paradise. After death, a person's heart (soul) was weighed to see if a good life had been led. So, we have judgment and an afterlife inherited from the Egyptians. They also had a resurrection story. The god Osiris was murdered by his brother. His wife, Isis, resurrected him so that he could have had an heir.

The Egyptians had large temples with statues of the gods. They prayed to their gods, offered sacrifices and sang hymns. While they were polytheistic, with many gods, the pharaoh Akhenaten believed in one god. He died in the mid-14th century BCE so some believe that the Hebrew slaves, or Moses, got the idea of a single god from him. However Israelite relics from as late as the 8th Century BCE show that at least some Hebrews were still polytheistic.

It is probably even more essential knowing where we are going, than knowing where we came from.

Let us take a few basic assumptions that would lead us to Christianity. Given these three assumptions, all of which are not empirically verifiable, we have the assumptions of Christianity. Once these are assumed, we can go off and do all kinds of ideological thinking, such as: is God all-knowing, is God all-powerful, is God all good, was Jesus God or man or half-and-half, is the Bible literally true or only a generalized message?

Luckily for many early Christians this was answered at the Council of Nicea in 325, when Emperor Constantine decided we ought to all believe the same thing. So it was decided to use the gospels of Mathew, Mark, Luke and John and forget the gospels of Thomas, Mary and the others. It was also decided here that Jesus was the same as God the Father. The Nicene Creed was developed and those who disagreed were banished to Albania and excommunicated. So the Christians could now be content in their beliefs that the Jew, Jesus, was really God—the same as the creating God. So the basic assumptions of Christianity are: There is a God. The Bible is true. And, Jesus is God. Not all Christians believe in all three, but most do.

CONFLICTS IN VALUES

In both the governmental questions and our personal lives, if we are to be intelligent we need to understand our basic assumptions and be aware of the knowledge on both sides of every issue.

Conflicts in our value choosing often occur when what we want runs counter to the wishes of God or our society. "I want an abortion now." But my society or my religion may see this as bad. Perhaps my society needs more soldiers, as Russia and Germany did during World War II. So, they need all the babies possible.

Perhaps my society needs more consumers. In either case, my self-centered desire for an abortion runs counter to my society's values. My religion may want more souls born so that they can be saved and go to heaven. But NOW is MY immediate concern.

My use of a psychoactive substance is good for my mood, but most governments have laws against it because many drugs impair driving, decision making, and job performance. Governor Jerry Brown of California said that "we don't need more potheads in California" when opposing the vote on legalizing marijuana. Societies intent on advancing economically, like China and Singapore, are strong anti-drug enforcers. Some societies either want their self-centered citizens more content, or want to reduce the criminal drug involvement and tax the drug—like Uruguay, Canada, and some U.S. state have legalized some drugs. Such legalization is society-based.

Then you have the "self" of a drug or tobacco company wanting to sell products to individual buyers (other "selfs") but the state has to pick up the medical bills for heart attacks, auto accidents, or overdoses. So another self-centered versus state conflict.

While the conflicts between the self-centered values and the values of a society or religion are quite common, there are also conflicts between society values and religious values, or the values of one religion as opposed to another, like we are seeing quite often regarding homosexual marriage or abortion— where some societies and religions are accepting and others vehemently opposed. And there are conflicts between societies, which may end in war or sanctions, as we have seen recently with sanctions on Iran, Russia, and North Korea. Then there are conflicts between religions as we saw between the Catholics and Protestants in the Thirty Years War, between the Christians and the Muslims in the Crusades, and between the Sunni and Shia Muslims today.

USING OUR INTELLECTS TODAY
ABORTION

Generally national laws refer to "personhood" as the beginning of human life. Religions often define it as when the body gets a soul. This of course is impossible to estimate.

When people argue about being pro-life or pro-choice in the abortion question, there are both non-provable definitions and assumptions in the argument. Looking at the definitions, we can start with Aristotle's idea that male embryos got their souls 40 days after conception. Female embryos, or fetuses, got theirs at 90 days. Thomas Aquinas, whom many think was the greatest of theologians, agreed with Aristotle. Then in 1869, Pope Pius IX decided that the soul was infused at conception. So life started then.

In 2004 President George W. Bush signed into law the concept that personhood begins at the implantation of the fertilized ovum on to the uterus, which is about a week after conception. Some medical people think that life begins when there is a heartbeat or other quickening in the fetus. This is a few months later.

The traditional Jewish understanding, which is shared by a number of societies and religions, is that life starts at birth. But we can look at the ancient Spartan society where they put babies on a hill to see who would survive, then only the strongest were seen as potential Spartans. So "life" started several days after birth. There is a small African tribe that feels they are overcrowded so they put firstborn girls into the jungle. Only after the firstborn boy arrives can all ensuing babies from the mother survive.

So, we have quite different religious and societal assumptions on when personhood occurs. These are not only in conflict with each other, but they conflict with a woman, or man, who does not want a child. So we have this self-centered value assumption often in conflict with God-based or society based assumptions.

So, it is not as simple as "pro-life" or "pro-choice." The ethical standard that we use in determining when a fertilized ovum, embryo, fetus, or baby is truly a person varies considerably. In spite of the various opinions or definitions of when life starts, we have people ready to murder or die for their beliefs-- beliefs that are seldom understood by the zealots. But if they used their intellects, they would at least understand some of the issues that should be thoroughly understood for those who are making decisions for or against abortion.

In spite of the fact that there are these different definitions and basic assumptions that are unprovable, we have had "pro-life" people shoot and kill adult doctors who are performing legal abortions. So is the lack of a provable definition enough of a reason to kill a law-abiding adult human? Certainly, the assumptions conflict.

There are other conflicts that may occur in this abortion question. Every unwanted child brought into the society will cost about $120,000 to educate through high school. He will also develop a carbon footprint that increases climate change. It is highly likely also that many unwanted children will run afoul of the law increasing the costs of police, judges, and prisons. In spite of this, five states have very restrictive laws relative to abortion. Louisiana, Mississippi, Kansas, Arkansas, and North Dakota are among the most negative to abortion. They are not among our richest states, in fact Mississippi and Arkansas are the two poorest states. Do they really need more taxation?

So it is not enough to look at a single issue, there are often many other issues relative to the issue being evaluated. It is important for the voters and their representatives to understand the whole picture.

CAPITAL PUNISHMENT

What about capital punishment? Here again we have conflicts of opinions. More often in advanced societies today there is an aversion to killing a human being no matter what he or she has done. In Norway, Anders Breivik the killer of 77 unarmed people, received a 21-year prison sentence. There was no question of his guilt, only whether or not he was sane. He was. His trial cost nearly $2 million and his incarceration costs $1,500,000 a year. The average Norwegian prisoner costs $100,000 a year. But Breivik is in solitary confinement in a three-room suite.

He later went to court to complain that he was being mistreated by not being able to be with other prisoners and that his microwave food was often only warm. The court agreed with him and awarded him court costs of over $13,000. An appeals court overturned the lower court decision. So Breivik appealed to the European Court of Human Rights which deals with potential abuses of the European Convention on Human Rights. He lost in June of 2018. But there must be other things he can complain about—after all, he has "rights."

This Convention is based on the idea that all people are somehow equal and entitled to certain equal human rights. Capital punishment is banned. Prisoners are granted the same rights as non-prisoners generally, although they must stay behind bars. The Convention does not require any duties for the citizens, such as not murdering.

In the United States, 32 states still have the death penalty. Because there is a general feeling of the importance of life, death row inmates are given many opportunities to appeal their sentences. Clinton Duffy, former Warden of California's major prison, San Quentin, told me that it was more expensive to execute a prisoner than to keep him in prison for life. The unlimited court appeals cost the state millions of dollars. He therefore had changed his mind about the efficacy of capital punishment.

Money is certainly a factor in determining whether any program of the government should be allowed. Whether it be primary education, free college tuition, better roads and bridges, hiring lawyers, or imprisoning felons.

In Los Angeles County, it costs $10,000 a day for a criminal court hearing. This includes the salaries of: judges, secretaries, marshals, prosecuting attorneys, and public defenders. The average criminal trial lasts two weeks.

The district attorney of the Los Angeles files over 60,000 criminal cases a year. Most of them are defended by public defenders and 94 to 97% are concluded with a plea bargain. But some of the cases cost over $1 million. The O.J. Simpson trial cost over $9 million. The Charles Manson case cost about three quarters of a million. The Sirhan Sirhan case in the murder of Robert Kennedy cost about $600,000. The mass murderers called the "Hillside Strangler" and the "Night Stalker" had their murder cases costing the taxpayers over $1,500,000 each.

When we have people who are unquestionably guilty, such as: Anders Breivik, Sirhan Sirhan or Charles Manson, just how much money should be spent in the trial or in imprisoning them? Could that money be better spent on primary or secondary education, college tuition for highly intelligent very poor students, on school lunches for impoverished children, or for any other worthwhile goals of society.

There are certainly very good reasons for spending money on criminal and civil trials. Justice it is essential in a government of laws. But we might also argue that "justice" also requires equality of opportunity for all young people and citizens for effective parenting and education to the level of their expected competence.

What would be a societal basis for any expenditure? The safest roads and bridges also could be determined to be based on a societal basic assumption. Isn't it "just" to prevent injuries and death to our citizens by repairing and improving our societal infrastructure?

Denmark's total tax intake is about 50% of its GDP. The U.S. taxation is only about half of that. But Denmark's taxes don't cover all the needs that the people would like. And, they don't even have to build a wall on their southern border to keep the Germans out! No Western society has enough money to meet all of its needs!

On the other hand, lawyers might argue from a self-centered point, of view, that lawyers need to be hired to both prosecute and defend the accused. This is the most fundamental need of a government of laws. The fact that there are so many lawyers elected to governments may prejudice them in making laws guaranteeing defenders some sort of legal representation. Likewise, we might also assume that teachers elected as representatives would be more interested in educational financing, similarly ministers and devout followers of a religion might be interested in advancing the cause of religion in the laws.

There may be a self-centered value that you have not thought about. For example, if it were true-- and it is not always-- that killing a mass murderer is cheaper than keeping him alive, from a self-centered point of view, you might be for capital punishment to save on your taxes. The religions of Abraham certainly allow capital punishment for some crimes.

Societies sometimes use what they think is Christian thinking in abolishing capital punishment. They generally turn to the Sermon on the Mount, where Jesus said "Blessed are the merciful, for they shall obtain mercy." They also use, his saying, "turn the other cheek." (Matt 5:18) But neither of these is a refutation of the death penalty. In Mark, Chapter 7, Jesus is chastising the Pharisees for honoring man-made rules rather than the rules of God. He then cites Moses who said in verse 10, "Honor your father and mother," and "Anyone who speaks disrespectfully of father or mother must be put to death."

In Matthew Chapter 5:17-19, Jesus says he is not really changing the directions of the prophets, so the death penalty would still be "on the books." "Do not think that I have come to abolish the Law or the Prophets; I have not come to abolish them but to fulfill them. For truly I tell you, until heaven and earth disappear, not the smallest letter, not the least stroke of a pen, will by any means disappear from the Law until everything is accomplished. Therefore, anyone who sets aside one of the least of these commands and teaches others accordingly will be called least in the kingdom of heaven, but whoever practices and teaches these commands will be called great in the kingdom of heaven."

In The Acts of the Apostles it says, "If, however, I am guilty of doing anything deserving death, I do not refuse to die. But if the charges brought against me by these Jews are not true, no one has the right to hand me over to them. I appeal to Caesar!" (Acts 25:11) The author has certainly not condemned the death penalty.

One danger we often encounter when citing Scriptures, or even laws, is that we take a text out of its context. When we do this we often have a pretext.

AND SOME OTHER VALUES
Let's look at some nonreligious questions where there are value conflicts.

Donald Trump wants to build a $20 billion wall between Mexico and the US. If he does not build it, he will lose face among his supporters. What programs will be reduced or eliminated to pay for the wall? One thing that can be done, and is being done, is to increase the debt limit of the US. We already owe creditors as much as the US earns from its businesses and services in a year—over $20 trillion. It has become standard procedure to continue in increasing our national debt every year. Is this wise?

The government continues to give tax breaks to all, with the richest benefiting the most. Is this wise?

In denying climate change, with the huge costs that it will generate through hurricanes, fires, and employment losses, is this wise?

The biggest value question conflict we face is in reducing the effects of climate change that are bringing extremely high temperatures to many agricultural areas of the world which then results in crop failures and famines. At the same time, it is bringing severe storms to many places in the northern hemisphere, especially Southeast Asia and the Caribbean area. The ultimate cause is that there are too many people burning wood and fossil fuels. Yet no one in any government attempts to severely limit family size. The value of having children has been essential throughout history—so it must still be essential.

A few areas, such as Europe and Eastern Asia, have reduced their family sizes because they do not want more children. It may be because children cost a great deal of money and will interfere with their parents' pursuit of pleasure. It may be because they realized that they cannot give several children the educational and physical benefits that it can give to just one or two.

As the needs change in business, some employees may need to be laid off because they can no longer contribute to the success of the business. And as President Calvin Coolidge once said, "the business of the American people is business." This is often repeated as, "the business of business is business." While some people want businesses to be social welfare agencies, that is really the responsibility of governments or insurance companies-- assuming that the people bought the appropriate insurance coverage.

CHAPTER 6   THINKIN' AIN'T THAT IMPORTANT!

We all think that we can think. Have you ever made a bad choice? A shrimp that made you sick? A wife or husband that made you unhappy? A vote that you regret? Was our vote for Bush or Brexit or Trump the wisest move we ever made?

The truth is that much of what we believe to be "thinking" is often not a part of our intellect-- the part of the mind that really thinks. Sometimes we are so inundated by our culture that we assume that the customs we have learned must be true. Whether that culture be Catholicism or Confederacy, Parisian or Pakistani, urban or rural--it is so deeply imprinted on our minds that if anyone weaves a thread of doubt into our subconscious cloak of certainty we will attack-- verbally or physically. Try to change the Parisian breakfast from a baguette and coffee. Try to tear down a statue of Robert E Lee in the South. Try to criticize the Pope in Vatican City. In every case, you will meet opposition. The Parisian is not about to switch to a high-protein breakfast. White rednecks in the South have two pillars of personality—their state university football team and Robert E. Lee, the best general to ever lose a war.

If we are to be citizens in a functioning democracy, we had better have an effective education and be able to think logically. If we are to be fully functioning adults, who have an enlightened view of our potentials for our lives, we must have an effective education.

We have seen some questionable outcomes of recent elections in the US and the UK. We have certainly seen questionable ruling techniques in South America and Africa. How do these happen? Are the elections rigged? Are the voters aware of all the issues? Have the candidates aimed their propaganda pistols below our intellects and into our unconscious minds? How are they coaxing us to follow their siren's song into the abyss of fantasy? Are these politicians honestly concerned with us or are they on ego trips--on flying carpets leading us to the den of the 40 thieves.

This is a tall order--to polish our own logical thinking tools, to understand the essential knowledge required today, to be able to see what needs to be done in our world, and to be able to see through the barrage of bullshit that bombards us so often in elections.

We will bounce back and forth between: logical thinking, obstacles to sound thinking, how we have been hoodwinked recently, what we need for an effective democratic society, and some ideas about education that might be helpful. It is a long journey for such a short book!

THE WORLD'S MAJOR PROBLEMS

Let us quickly survey a few of the major problems of the world. How many of these were discussed by your candidates for office?

OVERPOPULATION

The world's major problem is overpopulation. It is the reason for climate change, which is our second biggest planetary problem. As technology advances we need fewer people to produce our foods on the farms or our manufactured items in the factories. Computers, robots, artificial intelligence, and 3D printing have taken over the jobs that were once essential for us humans. This leads us to huge increases in the joblessness of our populations--particularly our young people who often have unemployment rates in the neighborhood of 40%. This affects their self-worth. Commonly they find it in street gangs that look for power in violence and in the trafficking drugs. Others find it in various religions, some even in violent jihadist groups.

With the increased use of plastics throughout the world we see millions of tons cast into the oceans. There will soon be more tons of plastic in the ocean then there are tons of fish. Fish eat the smaller bits of plastic, then we the fish. We find fish choked with plastics. We also find fewer fish in the oceans due to overfishing to feed our overpopulated planet.

Overpopulation increases our need for natural resources, many of which are irreplaceable. It overwhelms the world with garbage and other wastes. So overpopulation significantly affects our physical world and our psychological needs.

CLIMATE CHANGE

With climate change we see increases in famines. We see the oceans warming and expanding. How long will it be before it floods major cities? New York, Mumbai, Shanghai, London and many cities along the coast in the southern states and in Southern California are in danger. We are already seeing low-lying islands having to be evacuated. Northeastern China has had such sea change problems along its coasts.

The warmer oceans increase the evaporation of the water which then rises into the atmosphere. Water is the major greenhouse gas, more of a problem than carbon dioxide. But this water now becomes available for hurricanes, rainstorms, and snow storms. When the air cools it cannot hold so much water vapor so it is rained down into our social and economic lives.

And, it is not only the warmth of the water but also the increasing acidity that is destroying or threatening the ocean's life. As excess carbon dioxide (CO_2) is dissolved into water (H_2O). Some of it becomes carbonic acid (H_2CO_3). This makes the ocean water less conducive to the growing of shells in shellfish and it interferes with the reproductive systems of some fish. About 1/3 of the carbon dioxide that is produced by humans is absorbed into the oceans. This is about 22 million tons of carbon dioxide daily.

LACK OF LOVING PARENTS

The third major problem is children being unloved. The inferiority complexes, that we all have to some degree, develop and result in increased drives for power in most people. It is the major reason for violence, from street gangs, to ISIS, to wars. People tend to look at the rationalizations that antisocial people give for their behaviors. Bullies say "I made fun of him because he is fat." ISIS converts say they are killing blasphemers. Street gang members say "I killed him because he was on my street." Relationship partners may argue or fight over insignificant issues because they have a need to exert power. (In my marriage counseling experience, it is this power drive, that was based on the inferiorities developed in unloving homes, that created most of the domestic problems.) So how do you evaluate your behavior as loving?

One child in eight will be abused. Studies of prisoners indicate that as many as 70% of prisoners were abused as children. The numbers of those who were raised in foster homes show that as many as 80% of males and 90% of females had been abused. The lack of loving parents is obviously critical in our emotional development.

Social-psychologist Erich Fromm, in his classic book "The Art of Loving," wrote that "We learn to love by being loved." Most parents probably think that they love their children, but when we measure the children's ability to love against Ashley Montagu's definition in the Encyclopedia of Mental Health we usually find that what they thought was love was really lacking in that the child was not actually "loved."

You remember that Montagu's definition is that: "Love is the communication to another person of one's deep involvement in that person's welfare, of one's a profound interest in him as a person, demonstrated by acts that support, stimulate, and contribute to the realization of that person's welfare and the fulfillment of their personality."

How many people do you know that have been so nourished psychologically?

The word "love" is tossed around so often, meaning "I approve of," that it often becomes meaningless. If I say, "I love pizza," does it have the same level of approval as when I tell my partner, "I love you." When I said that to my partner is it with the same amount of approval as when I say it to my pizza? And, obviously, approving of somebody is not the same as being deeply concerned about developing their personality, as Montagu defined it. (For a more complete discussion of love you might be interested in reading, "Love: The You, The Me, The Us" by the author.) It is this lack of having been loved that increases one's inferiority complex and the need for power. For those few who really have been "loved" we don't find the psychological need to conquer others—to have power over them.

The more we find out about our universe, our planet, our mammalian brothers, and ourselves, the less we seem to know! Just how intelligent are we? What psychological needs must we have? And where do we find information that may give us verifiable directions on how we should improve our human ecology today,

We can look at the potentials of human sexuality in Desmond Morris's "The Naked Ape," or the instinctual violence of humans in Robert Ardrey's "African Genesis" or the common animal desire for power as seen in their territory and possessions in his "The Territorial Imperative." We can look at the studies of John B. Calhoun with mice and rats and worry about overpopulation and the effects of overcrowding on behavior.

In a recent book by the French academic Olivier Roy, who has studied radicalization and jihadism extensively, he writes that that we are seeing not "the radicalization of Islam but the Islamization of radicalism." It was his finding that radicalization generally occurs in prisons and gyms, not in mosques. Although we certainly do see some radical Muslim preachers preaching the caliphate and encouraging young people to fight the West with the blessings of Allah. And if they do die, they go to paradise-- so it is a "no lose" situation. But the radicalization that Roy talks about I would see as a redirection of the attacking behaviors that landed them in prison. Through radicalized Islam they now had a rationalization for their attacking propensities. They also got a promise of Paradise. What a win-win for a person with serious psychological problems!

My own experience in researching, teaching, and counseling is that generally speaking, the extreme behavior of people who have not been effectively loved, resulted in either attacking or withdrawing from the society. They may attack as: gang members, drug cartel members, school shooters, paramilitary group members, or jihadis. They may also become rapists, sexual harassers, bullies, or pedophiles. Their extreme behavior is then rationalized as: a way to find friends who accept me, a way to make money, a way to save society from itself, or a way to Paradise.

Those whose minds are likely to withdraw, may withdraw into a depression or, quite commonly, into drugs-- particularly the downer drugs like heroin, alcohol, or the cannabinoids. Of course, suicide is the ultimate withdrawal from society and it has increased 30% in the last 18 years—45,000 last year. The suicide rate is increasing in nearly every category—both sexes, every social class, every ethnicity. Male veterans have a 1.3 greater chance of suicide than others their age and female veterans have twice the number of non-veteran females. And only about half of suicides had been diagnosed with a mental illness.

Sometimes the same path can be used by attackers or withdrawers. Religion, for example can be chosen as an ideal form of life, emphasizing charity; or as a method of attacking society as in: ISIS, Al Qaeda, or the Westboro Baptist Church that loudly protested and picketed funerals of American soldiers who were killed in Iraq and Afghanistan because America accepts homosexuality which is against the Bible. They also picketed many churches including: Catholic, Episcopal and other Baptist churches.

Religion can also be used to withdraw from society. Many years ago, women who were not married would join a convent. Deep meditation or contemplation may be used as an escape from reality. It is often very difficult to determine whether or not an aggressive or a withdrawing action is within the normal range of behavior or whether, because of its more extreme manifestations, has entered the neurotic range of behavior. If it reaches a psychotic range, it is much easier to see.

MOST POPULATIONS ARE UNWILLING TO PAY FOR WHAT THEY WANT

Almost everything we want in a society costs money. There are the labor costs to initiate and monitor just about every benefit a society wants. What people don't often understand is that they, or their children, will pay for everything. When Ronald Reagan reached into the Social Security Trust Fund to give everyone tax breaks-- we applauded. But who will pay back the Social Security fund? We do-- and we will! We are paying interest on the money we borrowed from our retirement fund. The interest on what was borrowed to give the rich a big tax break, and us a little one, results in us paying interest on our own money. Meanwhile Congress considers reducing our benefits because paying us back takes 34% of the national budget.

Since the national government borrowed about $3 trillion from The Social Security Trust Fund and other government retirement funds, the yearly Federal budget must include the payouts that the government must make because there is little left in the trust funds. In 2010, there was more money going out in Social Security checks than was coming in from payroll taxes. There is enough interest that we are paying ourselves to cover the outgo until 2025. With people living about 15 years longer, but without an adequate payroll tax to cover it, or without a significant adjustment to the retirement age things will keep getting worse. Some combination of an eight-year increase in the retirement age, not one year as recently enacted, or a 5% increase in payroll taxes would do it. But who would vote for a legislator or executive who wants to raise your taxes or make you wait longer to retire?

So we have to keep raising our national debt limit. That's why every year there is the threat to shut down the government. (It has happened twice so far this year, and is due again soon.)

OUR NATIONAL DEBT—THE ASSAILANT IN THE SHADOW

The US national debt is about $20 trillion. State debts are about $1.2 trillion more and local municipality debts add about $2 trillion. Our national debt is about 105% of our gross domestic product (GDP) that is the value of all the goods and services that the US produces in a year. When you think of $1 trillion here and a trillion dollars there, pretty soon it adds up to real money!

We have to get the money somewhere. We have borrowed about 2 1/2 trillion dollars from China and Japan. We have borrowed more than another trillion dollars from various countries such as Belgium, Ireland and Taiwan. We have even borrowed $150 billion from Russia. A good part of our financing for our debt comes from borrowing from government retirement funds: almost $3 trillion from our Social Security Trust Fund, $670 billion from the Military Retirement Fund, from Office of Personnel Management Retirement another $888 billion, $204 billion from other retirement funds, and $294 billion from Medicare. The rest is held by a number of entities like: The Federal Reserve, banks, mutual funds, insurance companies, and other businesses and individuals.

In regard to borrowing from retirement funds, you may call it borrowing or paper shuffling. All money comes into the federal treasury, treasury bonds are issued to the various pension funds, then all of the money can be used by the government to pay expenses, fight wars, bring us out of recessions, and give us small tax breaks and the rich large tax breaks. Meanwhile the treasury bonds accumulate and will have to be paid back. While some in government don't call it borrowing—I disagree. The laws allow it, so it's legal. But those bonds are going to have to be paid off—by us, or our children. Al Gore wanted to leave federal retirement funds untouched by the government. But who would want an environmentalist to lead the country?

Keeping interest rates low, by the Federal Reserve, means that our interest payments are less. Right now we pay nearly 20% of our total individual income tax revenue on interest payments of $310 billion a year. That is 7.4% of our yearly national federal outlay. Did you ever think about what you could buy with $310 billion a year?

We could print more money. The amount of US dollars in circulation is about $1.5 trillion. So, our national debt is about 13 times more dollars than we have. We could print 13 times more dollars then pay everybody off with that. Of course, the value of our dollar would go down to about eight cents. So, anything we would buy from other countries would cost 13 times more. Vacations in other countries would cost 13 times more. But of course, the things we produce would cost 13 times less for other countries so we might export more goods and help our economy. But then, what if all other countries did the same thing, wiping out all national debts?

We could go bankrupt. Other countries have done this.

We could raise our taxes. But anyone suggesting this in America would never be elected in the US. Keeping taxes low is the Eleventh Commandment!

WOULD YOU BELIEVE THERE ARE EVEN MORE PROBLEMS?

The combination of too many people on the planet, with a huge majority of them being unloved, creates other problems. Unloved people who have risen to power in the political areas may seek more territory or greater control through aggressive wars or developing weapons of mass destruction so that they can use it to increase their political power.

In the financial area it is shown by the importance of amassing huge fortunes for some, with the resulting income inequality of the masses below. This, too, increases the propensity to violence from those on the bottom. Just look at the masses of people aggressively demanding that President Maduro step down in Venezuela. And look at how many African countries have leaders with little public backing, from Egypt and Libya to sub-Saharan Africa.

Do you believe that ISIS members have been loved? If you think so you have no concept of what love is! You would have to go beyond what their parents say, and believe, to what they actually did.

Increased drug use, to forget the unhappiness of one's lack of power or one's general unhappiness with life, is another societal evil. Most people can find a bit of power to sooth their inferiority complexes. Owning your own home, having a nice car, having a great job are all experiences that make us feel better. If that isn't enough, we can attach our egos to a sports team or religion especially an evangelical one. There's nothing like being one with God.

THE BEST GOVERNMENT—DEMOCRACY OR___?

Democracy is in decline around the world according to Freedom House, a think tank. Only 45% of countries are considered free today. Are we witnessing the fact of the dying of democracy while we have nothing with which to replace it? Or is it the death of nationalism rather than globalization, and fascism and monarchy rather than democracy?

Democracy is becoming more dysfunctional. Plato was concerned that if the people voted there would be concern with present day problems rather than looking to the future. Therefore, a representative government would not work well in the long run unless the representatives were truly well-educated and concerned for the future.

Of the 535 members of Congress 20 members of the House of Representatives have only a high school education. 213 have law degrees, so 40% of our representatives are lawyers. Have these people ever studied natural or social science, philosophy of religion, comparative religions, environmental science, macroeconomics? If not, how do they justify their qualifications?

Must we, in the unwashed mob, await a Messiah? But the people with all the answers in Congress are not the prophets of salvation, but rather the Hansels and Gretels dropping an occasional bread crumb to us as they hurry along the path to their banks in Switzerland and the Caymans where they deposit their money and discard our dreams.

What will we require of our representatives? Is it the development of more personal power and the all-important goal of being reelected? Is it in making a better world, a better nation, a better country? How much of their focus is eyeing the future?

Thinking only about pleasure today is not the way to run an effective society. What we call populism today is not very much concerned with the future. Climate change, globalization, free trade, equality of opportunity, advanced education and other such needs of the world's societies take a backseat to having lower personal taxes. If we don't pay today for what we want, it must be paid for by borrowing from other nations and investors. Then our children can pay back, with interest, what we borrowed but were unwilling to pay for. Today, every person in the US owes over $65,000. Shall we just pay it by credit card?

It reminds me of what Benito Mussolini said, "all men of action necessarily move towards catastrophe as their conclusion. They live and end with this aura, either for themselves or for others." So I guess the financial catastrophe will fall on the heads of my children.

THE INTELLIGENT VOTER

Do we only look at the problems of today without an eye to the future? Give me a tax cut today. Give me a job today. Give me cheap electricity today. I am not concerned that climate change will dry out the fields that once yielded my food. I am not concerned that displaced young people will attack me in the city. I am not concerned that there will not be enough water to raise my food, or water my lawn. What is important--is that my team wins on Saturday

How can we get our selfish suffering citizens to recognize and work to solve the problems of the future that will save humanity? Pragmatism trumps idealism and reality in most people's, minds, most of the time. Give me a tax break now by borrowing from my Social Security account. It does not concern me that there will be no money left when I retire.

We must look at several of the problems that are evident in modern day democracies—particularly those of the United States, which is looked up to by many-- but is often corrupt, and often the least efficient of many democratic republics that exist in the West. In fact, it is now ranked as the 24th best democracy—a ranking that puts it into the category of "flawed democracies."

How can we change our beliefs and thinking when our main concern is with our personal economics--both the attainment of riches and the multiplication and conservation of the assets that we have. Making money has become our primary concern, in spite of the fact that accomplishing worthwhile things is more likely to give us real happiness. You can't take either one with you when you depart the planet. So, which would you rather have as your life's companion, a bank account or happy memories?

Pensions are seldom adequately funded in the US. The assumption is often that pension fund investments should earn 7.5 to 8% annually. They seldom do. What happens when the housing bubble breaks or the stock market crashes? In fact, pension funds were only 72% funded in 2015. Several European countries, including Britain, France, and Germany, have pension liabilities of more than 300% of their GDP. How can these problems be handled? I guess we'll just let our kids worry about it!

From 1996 to 2015 office jobs dropped over 20% which eliminated 7 million jobs. In the last century, the number of farmworkers dropped from 38% of all workers to 2%. 45% of today's jobs can be done by computers or robots. Yes, there are some real problems in the job area! When our representatives do not provide quality educations, enough jobs for all, adequate pensions and health insurance, and all the other things that concern us, we are not happy with them. Heading into the 2016 election, Congress had a disapproval rate of 82%. We had better drain the swamp!

The people wanted change. They took Trump as the lesser of evils. Was it intelligently arrived at? If we are going to hope, shouldn't our hope be intelligently directed?

HOPE

We spend our lives hoping for something better-- a happier relationship, well behaved intelligent children, a successful finish to the project on which we are working, a more effective government, and maybe even a happy hereafter! If I only hope, probably nothing will get better. If I hope and plan and work, success may be my reward. When someone else promises me that they can make by life, or my afterlife, better without me doing too much except voting for them or contributing financially to their cause—I am moved. If someone else can give my hopes a boost and I don't have to do much, it is enticing!

Hope gives us an energy, often blind. Its energy increases as our life situation becomes darker. When our goals are realistic it can power our dreams to fulfillment. But when hope is simply wishing—it is merely an opium for our emptiness. It soothes but never solves.

EDUCATION FOR WHAT?

Many thought that when Soviet communism died it would kindle in us a flame and passion for thinking through our lives and governing ourselves by facts and positive probabilities. But we continue to see the rise of tyrants, sometimes through ballots and sometimes through bullets. Unhappily their drives for power are not always accompanied by intelligent thinking or ethical values.

In every type of government, the modern ideal is to have educated people, who are aware of the whole situation: enacting laws, administering them, and adjudicating the issues—if a balance of power is to exist. Commonly, all the voters are convinced that they know all there is to know. The fact is that no person today knows enough to rule effectively—and if they did, they would not have the power of the people behind them.

Education is the key, But, children and teens do not vote. All politicians talk about how important education is, but their allotment of money actually goes to the people who vote—retirees, minorities, businesses, and those who want tax breaks.

Education in the complicated workings of today's globalized world requires a good knowledge of social, biological, and environmental science. Do all voters have sufficient knowledge in these areas and do they have values that are based on developing a better society, rather than satisfying their present-day desires? If so, they might vote with enlightened self-interest.

This may be a psychological impossibility but it is a social necessity. Our opinions should be based on facts, if they are to be effective in moving us in a positive direction. Our values must also be based on facts, rather than blind hope if we are to survive the incredible threats of overpopulation, climate change, the lack of meaningful employment and the senseless violence of non-thinking groups of young men.

Quality education is the key, but it must be universal—and that today is an impossibility. If there is such a thing as "truth," only impartial research can get a glimpse of it, and only quality education can make everyone aware of it. When we have leaders of major countries, like Donald Trump, not believing in human caused climate change we threaten posterity.

A good deal of the next part of the book will deal with how uneducated electorates are easily hoodwinked by hopeful talk rather than by hard facts. Many of the illustrations will come from the Donald Trump, George W. Bush, and Brexit democratic elections.

In the recent US election, the huge majority of journalists and other pundits chose Hillary, they listened to what she said and evaluated whether or not it was possible. But the voters did not evaluate the issues. They were interested in jobs, afraid of violence, upset with their legislators, and wanted change. While Hillary was talking to the top 30% of the IQ scale, Trump was agitating the bottom half, and the businessmen.

But a large number, probably a majority, of voters were also upset with the lack of progress in Washington where they had a president with a 55% positive rating and a Congress with an 18% approval rating. Former House speaker Tip O'Neil said that "all politics are local," and President Bill Clinton said that "it's the economy, stupid."

Trump pushed these buttons hard. Even though unemployment was near record lows at 4.6% and the economy was steaming along, better than most world economies at a healthy 2% growth rate, after having slipped to -2.8% in 2008. The "Bush Crash," caused by sloppy lending regulations, and excessive borrowing for tax cuts and the Iraq war had dropped the world into recession.

When Trump said that the US was paying far more than its share for NATO, it rang a bell with voters. Of course, NATO was buying much of its equipment from the US and keeping another war out of Europe that might save many American lives and NATO cost much less than another war! World Wars I and II were not cheap for America.

Trump talked about auto manufacturing in Mexico taking jobs from the US. He proposed a 30% tariff when those cars were brought back to the states. The obvious conclusion is that Mexico will pay the 30%. The reality is that the 30% will be added to the cost of the car so that Americans will pay his proposed tax.

How many of Trump's voters realized this? Would a more effective education have sharpened their knowledge?

CAN WE MAKE EDUCATION MORE EFFECTIVE?

The United States is probably spending enough money on education at the primary and secondary levels, but it is not being spent effectively. Administrators are multiplying much faster than student body growth and teachers are not being rewarded for their work if they are successful. At the same time the number of pupils in the classroom increases. My experience is that there are a few exceptional administrators, some good ones, but most are overpaid, often incompetent, and certainly not needed.

It is easy for people who have never been in a ghetto or barrio classroom, or even many middle-class classrooms, to understand that handling the discipline of youngsters who do not want to be there is difficult—and often impossible. The classes that are fun, like: art, music, and physical education usually don't have the discipline problems you might find in an English or history class. But even the enjoyable classes may encounter discipline problems. In doing some research on barrio middle school education I taught for three years at Sun Valley Middle School in a gang infested area of the San Fernando Valley in Los Angeles. I reduced my college teaching and taught only evening classes.

My predecessor in a physical education class had been wrapped in a volleyball net and suspended from the ceiling of the gym. He resigned immediately. One day, as I approached my class, I was jumped by about six class members. They pinned me to the ground as I struggled. When I finally threw off my attackers, they laughed and said, "OK coach, now you are in our gang." When asked what gang I was now been "jumped into" they said, "Boys from the Hood."

Some of you middle-class readers may not know about common gang traditions. Quite often gangs require a new member to be "jumped in." If you want to leave you need to be "jumped out." So, several boys will try to beat you up and you have to fight them back. This is also true of many girl gangs. At the same school, one of the counselors had convinced a girl that she had more to offer than being a member of a gang. So the girl decided to be "jumped out." She decided to have it done in front of the school so the counselor could see her sacrifice. (Today, 25 years later, most gangs don't allow you to leave alive.)

At the same school during my first year there I had three of my students shot to death. The realities of ghetto and barrio schools are not grasped by people who have not experienced it—but have all the answers.

But it is not all gangs and guns. The most memorable student I had ever had was in my English class as seventh grader. Her mother and father were divorced. Her mother spoke only Spanish. But there was an intelligence and intensity to this young lady. As an older male teacher, I could not show an interest. But when I moved to Norway, I made contact with her and gave her my computer and had my favorite books, Will Durant's "Age of Civilization" sent to her. With her outstanding academic record from high school she was given a scholarship to UCLA. While a student, she worked 30 hours a week as a hotel receptionist at night to support her mother. After graduation she learned German, went to Europe, worked there, then returned to Georgetown for a law degree. She is now a lawyer in a major Washington DC law office.

There are many young people honestly concerned with learning, but often they are slowed in their ascent by unruly classmates. Oftentimes this changes from middle school to high school because the unruly merely stop going to high school. This makes the job of the teacher and the serious student much easier. Of course society will have to deal with the dropouts later in social welfare spending, job training, or prison.

EDUCATION FOR DEMOCRACY

Can we have an effective democracy when much of the electorate, and our elected representatives, are uninformed of the present and future benefits and costs of the various proposals for laws? Can we have an effective government when the predominant values are personal power and the pursuit of riches? If former President Calvin Coolidge was right that, "The chief business of the American people is business," then we are on the right track. However, if raising loved children, leading socially worthwhile lives, or working towards world peace can be considered worthwhile American objectives—perhaps we need a more thorough examination of our values.

Values held by electorates are varied. To be sufficiently educated we must be able to question the assumptions of ourselves and others, then approve or disagree with them based on the probabilities of truth.

It is sad to say that American democracy which is looked up to by many but is among the most corrupt and often the least efficient of many democratic republics that exist in the West. In fact, it is rated 21st on the latest Economist rankings, and is considered a "flawed democracy". All of the Nordic countries top the list, New Zealand, Australia, and Canada are well above the US. So are most west European countries, and Uruguay. Uruguay?? Wake up Thomas Jefferson and James Madison—we need you now!

In every type of government, the modern ideal is to have educated ethical representatives, who are aware of the whole situation, enacting laws, administering them, and adjudicating the issues—if a balance of power is to exist. But nearly all of our representatives are convinced that they know all there is to know, and what they don't know they will be told by those in the power-positions in their parties.

Leaders must look forward if they are to lead. But any future Pied Piper will have to switch off the electric power to the media before he picks up his flute.

QUALITY EDUCATION

Education in the workings of today's globalized world requires a good knowledge of world history, macroeconomics, philosophy, inductive and deductive logic, natural and biological sciences and environmental science—as well as how to protect yourself from data mining. Would you believe it, Ben Franklin never warned us about data mining!

If all voters had sufficient knowledge in these areas and had values that were based on developing a better society, rather than satisfying their present-day desires, we might vote with enlightened self-interest.

This may be a psychological impossibility but it is a social necessity. Our opinions should be based on facts if they are to be valid opinions. Our values must also be based on facts, rather than blind hopes if we are to survive the incredible threats of overpopulation, climate change, the lack of meaningful employment, and the senseless violence of non-thinking groups of young men.

Quality education is the key, but it must be universal—and that today is an impossibility. If there is such a thing as "truth" only impartial research can get that glimpse of it, and only quality education can make everyone aware of it. When we have leaders of major countries, not believing in human caused climate change or seeking a populist nationalism, when globalism and free trade are the realities of a modern and peaceful world, we must blame our national educational inadequacies. Today education must follow us out of the classroom and lead us day after day as we live lives informed by verifiable facts in our rapidly changing world.

In talking to high school teachers and professors in North America and Europe, I have found a nearly universal concern that the students are not concerned about their education, don't pay attention in class (if they even bother to attend), and they read very little. I was astounded recently in talking to a professor of English literature—even his students didn't read!

It is not enough to vote our opinions. Our world has recently been shaken with major disasters because of voters being swayed by propaganda and impossible promises that truly educated voters would have rejected. Following the propaganda of Bush brought us a leader who devastated Iraq and gave birth to ISIS, which brought more terror than his target, Al Queda.

The vote for Brexit did much more harm than good, because the single-issue voters, voting for sovereignty and Britain for Britons, could not predict the multitude of major problems that should have been evident to a well-educated electorate.

But the fiasco of all farces resulted from the American presidential campaign of 2016 based on untruthful personal attacks and the uninformed promises of reactionary impossibilities for creating jobs where no needs existed and the return of trickle-down economics—which has resulted in very tiny trickles down and huge increases in wealth inequality. And he promised businesses lower taxes, anti-consumer deregulations and tariff protections at home. He also promised to eliminate the national debt in eight years.

He thought he could do everything his base wanted, even though he had no concrete plans to accomplish them. He did increase the coal mining jobs by 500, but he added a trillion dollars to the national debt, and this is before his one and a half trillion dollar tax cut deficits kick in.

A good part of this book will deal with how uneducated electorates are easily hoodwinked by hopeful talk rather than hard facts. Many of the illustrations will come from the Donald Trump, George W. Bush, and Brexit democratic campaigns.

If we are to have an electorate and representatives who are educated in order to have the best results from our democratic republic-- we had better make some significant changes. The realities of psychology, particularly realizing the importance of the unconscious mind and the overwhelming reality of the drive for power, have made advertising what it is and have made modern political manipulation what it is today.

Our first question should be what do we want from our government--low taxes, happiness, free television, more playgrounds, better roads, better education, a lower national debt, universal health insurance, more prisons, or less corruption. Our next question should be how do we know how to get there. Denmark is usually rated the happiest country, but it has the highest taxes. The United States is rated as about the 18th happiest country and has the lowest taxes—and as its taxes are being reduced, its happiness ranking has fallen from the 12th happiest to the 18th happiest country.

In order to make an intelligent appraisal of our desires we really need to understand economics, world history, some sociology, some psychology, a bit about ecology, and a few other areas. In addition, we need to be able to use the tools of logic to evaluate the promises of politicians and our own political views.

In this book we want to evaluate some of these issues, look at how we can determine the most probable outcomes that we desire, illustrate how recent electorates have been fooled by impossible promises that positively reflected their own needs and wants, and finally, look at how our education systems can be made more effective.

Equality of opportunity is an often cited ideal. But how can it be realized when children inherit their parents' wealth—wealth they did not earn. How can it be realized when children in the nation have different curricula in the thousands of local school districts? How can it be realized when the nation's teachers do not have the same minimal standards? How can it be realized when some students are in classes of 20 and others in classes of 45? Ideals are easy to mouth but next to impossible to implement, as long as selfishness is the motivating force of most of the country.

CHAPTER 7 THE PEOPLE HAVE SPOKEN—DO THEY KNOW WHAT THEY MEAN?

When I vote, I speak. But am I speaking with authority and with a broad knowledge of the issues? Did I vote for the same party that my grandfather had adopted? The same that my father had favored? Or was my vote influenced by my neighbor, who was hoping to have his factory job back, after the factory had closed. Was my vote decided entirely on the opinion of a pundit who screams through my car radio? Was I targeted by trolls with fake news. Did my "likes" on Facebook give Cambridge Analytica a way to change my preferences by motivating my unconscious mind?

Was my mind attuned to the issues? Did I listen to the television debates or spend my evening hours with beer, pretzels, and the Pirates? Had I used my mind OR had my mind even been used?

THERE'S MORE TO THE MIND--THAN MEETS THE EYE!

We think we are in total control of our thinking and our actions. Psychologists, neuroscientists and others working with our genes, our neurotransmitters, and our past experiences find that our behavior and our beliefs are not as simply explained as we would like. Our genetics and epigenetics may be responsible for our tendencies, our reactions, or our behavior--behavior that we think we control completely.

People who understand what may be in our minds may be able to control or influence our behavior—and our votes!

Advertisers have been manipulating us for years. They know that we can be influenced to use their cosmetics, drink their beer, or buy their car. We can often be swayed by ads that show us that we can have power in our lives, love and sex in our bedrooms, or special meanings in our daily experiences.

How many men tried Dos Equis beer after seeing 'Most Interesting Man in the World' ads? His adventurous exploits stimulated the drive for power and the need to find increased meaning in our lives. How many women use L'OREAL "because they're worth it"? Again, an affirmation of power over our lives.

These advertisers approached us with the general knowledge of what moves most people's unconscious minds. Modern data mining programs target our individual unconscious minds. Their approach is specific, not general. So the general proven psychological spears designed to conquer a huge audience, are honed into small darts that hit each individual voter in his or her target of primary concern.

Psychological drives, such as for power, and the human need for love, are powerful influences for us to change our behavior. Hurricane Harvey has been occurring for a week as I write. Millions of people have given money for the cause of the displaced. For most of us, doing a loving thing makes us feel good. Being such a "loving person" is one of the highest psychological achievements that one can hope for. But it was not just money. People came from miles around with their boats to rescue their neighbors. Blacks rescued whites and whites rescued blacks. A far cry from the Charlottesville pro-Nazi rally of the previous week.

When we say we want something, do we understand all of the ramifications of what we want? if we want lower taxes, which is the universal cry of Americans, will we take fewer of society's offerings? If we reduce all of our taxes, will we have better roads or schools, better healthcare and retirement pensions, a protective military and adequate government services?

Or will we take a higher national debt or a reduction in the value of our currency? We want lots of goodies, but few are willing to pay for them--except the Scandinavians, the world's happiest people!

What have our voters wanted during the last 15 or 20 years? The desires seem to be rather similar in both the US and the UK. We all want lower taxes and more services. We want to go back to the good old days when we didn't have so many immigrants. The UK has had a number of immigrants, especially since they allowed people of the Commonwealth to be welcomed on their island. The Native Americans have been anti-immigrant for 600 years— and look where it got them!

In the US, many of us can point to our immigrant fathers or grandfathers in the relatively recent past. My parents had to endure the anti-Irish taunts, such as signs of NINA (No Irish Need Apply) or "Irish and Dogs Keep Off the Grass." But having short memories, and a lack of charity, we may want to go back to those nonexistent "good old days" and keep out anybody who wants to come in now.

The Rust Belt and business owners wanted lower taxes, fewer immigrants and the return to the good old days of mostly white America. They don't want to go back to the "good old days" before Columbus. If they wanted to go back to those days, they could drum up a lot of support from the Native Americans in the "swing states.

In the next chapters we will look primarily at the Trump, Bush, and Brexit elections. What did the people want-- and what did they get? Here are just a few of the major promises made by the candidates and the Brexiteers, those who wanted Britain to exit the European Union.

WHAT DID TRUMP'S VOTERS WANt?

- ➢ A wall between the US and Mexico-- with Mexico paying for it
- ➢ Lower taxes, while decreasing the national debt
- ➢ Deportation of illegal Mexicans
- ➢ Repeal and replace Obamacare
- ➢ Jobs in coal mining and steelmaking
- ➢ No more Muslim immigrants

Trump is dismantling Obamacare as much as he can. He signed an executive order to stop paying subsidies for the poorest 6 million Americans many of whom voted for him. It is said that this will save the government $7 billion.

The realities are that health care costs increase annually in every country as people age and need more care, and as new treatments and drugs become available. But America's elected representatives refused to allow Obama's plea for a federal option as an insurer. That socialized idea, and his other ideas to bring America closer to Europe's cheaper but better health coverage, would have cut profits for insurance companies and their stockholders, cut incomes for CEOs and lawyers, and resulted in better healthcare for more Americans. We certainly don't want that—everything good is first thought of in the good US of A! So this welfare state idea must stay where it originated—in Europe. In fact, since we are married to American ideas, we should purge our Federal laws of those European welfare state ideas like: Social Security, Medicare, Medicaid, and the universal education for children. These socialistic programs have no place in a country that demands low taxes and a small government!

The wall at the Mexican border is 1900 miles long and will cost between $1,000,000 and $20,000,000 per mile to build. There was $20 million left in the budget from the last year's budget for border security. Trump has apparently used this to start his wall because Congress will not approve the necessary $20 billion necessary for the wall. Also, since much of the land is owned by private parties, if they do not sell voluntarily, the government will have to take them to court under eminent domain laws. The Republican Party is probably not too happy about having more government, because they have fought for years for less government.

The tax proposal, that Trump proposed, increases the standard deduction on income taxes, but the proposal is about 60% less than what he promised. He proposed eliminating the Alternate Minimum Tax for richer people, but it was just eased a bit. This would have saved him over $3 million on the last Trump tax return we have seen. It also eliminates much of the inheritance tax that only very rich people pay with a $22 million exemption. The richest 5000 people pay $27 billion a year on this. And, of course, because of his tax cuts for the rich--the national debt will increase even faster.

The deportation of Mexicans threat has had several positive results. Crime rate in the Mexican areas near the border has decreased. Fewer illegals have crossed the borders. But there is another side of the coin. 30% more farm workers from Mexico are needed because Americans refused to do the hard labor of harvesting crops.

Most Americans don't realize that nearly half of their fruits and vegetables are grown in the Central Valley of California. About 90% of the almonds and table grapes, and a large amount of wine grapes, are harvested primarily by Mexican labor making less than $13 an hour. Nearly 500,000 laborers are needed during the hot summer months for the harvest. But many are afraid to come to California because of the Trump anti-Mexican actions.

This has farmers worried. Some have bought very expensive equipment to replace the less expensive hand labor. If the equipment was bought from Americans suppliers, it would help America's GDP. If it was bought from foreign suppliers, it would be negative to the American economy. Some farmers are considering moving to Mexico where they do not have to worry about their labor supply.

Another factor that voters may not have considered is the lack of water in the Great Valley. Climate change has reduced the amount of rain considerably from 2013 through much of 2017, when the drought was finally ended by great rainstorms. During the drought, many farmers had to drill very deep for groundwater. The federal government reduced the supply of water in many parts of the Valley. The pumping of the deep groundwater has had the effect in many areas of lowering the ground level. This then has the effect of changing the infrastructure of roads and bridges.

With the policies of Donald Trump reducing inexpensive Mexican labor and possibly increasing climate change, the average voter may find that he or she is paying much more for food.

American steelworkers have lost 400,000 jobs since 1960, from about 550,000 to 140,000. 48,000 of those since 2000. There are now about 150,000 jobs making steel. In spite of the loss of more than 70% of the jobs, output has been reduced only about 20%. Steel production, like most of basic manufacturing, has been affected by technology improvements. Imports and trade deals are not a large part of the problem. In fact, if the US is able to import cheaper steel it reduces the price of steel products that American companies will manufacture. Plumbing pipes, fittings and valves are one illustration. Stainless steel products are another.

Coal mining jobs have also been reduced by technology, but more important, the world is seeking clean energy. The jobs now are in manufacturing and installing solar equipment and efficient batteries. Mercedes-Benz is just building the world's biggest battery plant for car batteries. Oil is heading toward a cardiac infarct and coal is in a hospice.

Did the voters for Trump realize the effects on their pocketbooks of reducing inexpensive farm labor? Did they realize that coal mining has one foot in the grave? Did they realize the reality of global warming and climate change and how it would affect their job possibilities? Did they realize that the economic world is globalized? To think that every country could be talked into buying more American products than they sold to us is more than naïve. Did they realize that a New York businessman who might be very adept at negotiating the lowest price between contractors who want to build his hotel, may not understand the fine points of negotiating international trade deals with Germany or China?

It is certainly easier to talk the talk, than walk the walk!

WHAT DID THE BREXIT VOTERS WANT?

➤ Immigrants deported
➤ Less tax money sent to the EU with more to health care
➤ More money in their pockets with no reduction in
existing services
➤ Deportation of EU citizens from other nations
➤ There will be no change to trading with the EU
➤ The UK to be free to make other trade deals
Surprise, surprise!!

The British voters wanted more money in their pockets, more services, and a return to the good old days when it was just us British here on the island. And why worry about wars? We've already fought "the war to end all wars." We did it in 1918 and again in the 1940s! In fact, we haven't had one since the EU was formed. So, we'll never have another one.

What did they find the day after the election? They had been told that they were sending 350 million pounds to the EU every week and that it could be spent to make the National Health Service better. The day after the election they found that it was not true.

The money they had in their pockets dropped in value as much as 20%. It has recovered somewhat—especially against the dollar as it has dropped about 10%. This made the 40% of their food that they imported cost 10 to 20% more. It will mean their vacations in Greece, Spain and other places will cost up to 10 to 20% more.

The OECD predicts a reduction in the UK's GDP by 2020 of 3.3% which will cost the average household 2200 British pounds. With the pound falling, exports should be increased. As in the US, immigration has dropped somewhat.

A major problem is that UK has very little to bargain with, the EU is holding all his chips. The poorer countries of Europe do not like to see the country, that was contributing economically to them, leave the union. Possibly the best that Britain can hope for is what Norway has. In fact, one of the arguments of the Brexiteers was that UK could have the same arrangement. What they didn't say was that Norway pays about 118 euros per-person per year and has no say in governing the EU. The UK was paying 128 euros per person per year and had a full voting membership.

WHAT DID BUSH'S VOTERS WANT?

➤ Lower taxes
➤ Better healthcare
➤ More prosperity

> Better education in primary and secondary schools
> Reduce the national debt to its lowest level

Glorioski!! Did Americans want more money and less taxes when they voted for Bush? In the first election, versus Al Gore, there was no war in Iraq so some of this might have been possible. But whenever you hear that your taxes will be cut and the national debt will be reduced-- run for the hills! History does not indicate that this has ever, or will ever, happen. But it sounds good when campaigning.

Before intelligent people vote, they should project what will probably happen from the promises of the candidates. Of course, none of us know enough to predict accurately the ramifications of every promise. But we should be able to understand that good things, like healthcare and education, cost money. We had better understand also that tax reductions will result in fewer services and a higher national debt.

A major concern in analyzing political arguments is understanding exactly what they mean. "Let's make America great again." Exactly what is meant by this? America is the greatest economic power, and it has the World Series in baseball and the Super Bowl in "real" football. What more could a country want? We hear words like: democracy, socialism, equality, rights, and many, many more. Do we understand exactly what the speaker means?

Do we understand exactly what we mean when we use the term? Let us come back to the essential nature of semantics in understanding, or refuting, the often pointless, yet seemingly purposeful, speeches of politicians. (But semantic inquiries are not limited to the ramblings of politicians—it's just that their attempts to confuse us all, while gathering our support is their stock in trade!) It is essential to understand what is meant by what we are being told--if we are to be intelligent voters.

OUR CONFUSED SEMANTICS—DO WE KNOW WHAT WE MEAN?

Just a quick reminder—we may think that we know what politician, or even a real person, means when they say: democracy, equality, lower the debt, "I love you," or "I can get it for you wholesale."

Look at the various meanings we give to the idea of democracy. Our democratic ideas have evolved from merely counting the votes of the citizens to determine a political direction, "one man one vote," to including: minority rights, capitalism, equality, liberty, social welfare, graduated income tax, freedom from want, universal education and other such "rights" have made the idea of democracy impossible to define today. Many of these ideas may be essential for a functioning society but they have nothing to do with the idea of "one man, one vote." We must recognize that by espousing ideas about such important areas as: democracy, capitalism, or social welfare, without clearly defining them makes us intellectually blind people in a totally dark room!

WHAT DO WE MEAN BY "RIGHTS?"

What about minority rights? They are only "rights" if they have been affirmed by the congresses and parliaments—otherwise they are only wishes. But how often do we hear people changing the meaning of the term? As an example, an illegal immigrant who has had a child in the country where birth gives citizenship, like the US, may call it a "right" to stay with her child in the child's country of citizenship.

Minorities may get the attention of the governing elites by demonstrations, elections, or revolution. Shortly after Donald Trump assumed office his favorability rating was at a historic low—below 40%. Republican congressmen attending their yearly town meetings were verbally attacked by their constituents for the actions of their president during his first months in office. It seems that the responsibility for determining the path of progress had been turned on its head and the representatives' view became the majority view while the actual majority of voters were seen as the minority-- becoming a strongly vocal minority!

In 1215 King John was forced to give the barons of England certain rights in order to keep his throne. Some rights were also given to freemen, but not to all inhabitants of England-- like the serfs, who were 90% of the population. Through the years rights have trickled down to commoners through common law decisions of judges and acts of Parliament.

Similarly, rights have changed for Americans. For example, in the original Constitutional the right to own guns in 1789 was to maintain an organized militia. And it was important in 1812, when the British and Native Americans invaded again and burned down the White House. How dare they object to America's expressed goal of taking, by force, the lands of the north and west? What's theirs is really ours, and we need our guns to take what's ours. Luckily in 2008 the Supreme Court expanded the rights to own nearly any kind of firearm to nearly everyone. Look out Canada, we may be coming back!

Obviously, laws evolve, and sometimes devolve. What criteria should we use to judge whether we should move in a progressive or reactionary direction. Do the voters, the legislators, or executives, understand all of the ramifications of the promises of a candidate or the purpose of a law and its possible misinterpretation and misuse?

Let us look briefly at a few of the Constitutional Bill of Rights and what they may or may not mean.

THE REASON FOR THE AMERICAN CONSTITUTION

The Preamble to our Constitution gives us the fundamentals of our objectives in establishing the United States. "We the people of the United States, in order to form a more perfect union, **establish justice**, **insure domestic tranquility,** provide for the common defense, **promote the general welfare**, and secure the blessings of liberty to ourselves and our posterity, do ordain and establish this Constitution for the United States of America."

I don't know about you, but it seems to me that our three branches of government often ignore our reasons for our existence. Do the blessings of liberty to own firearms trump promoting the general welfare or insure domestic tranquility? Or, do they merely line the pockets of those who hire the lobbyists?

When we look at how the courts have ruled on weapon possession, corporate contributions to elections, and freedom of speech, we might wonder how their rulings promote the general welfare or insure domestic tranquility. Looking at freedom of speech--in affirming the desires of some anti-social people, intent on showing their perceived power by yelling their hateful diatribes, the Court protects their mental distortions under the guise of unintelligent liberty. Similarly, innocents murdered in schools or clubs have sacrificed more than a bit of their "general welfare." Are the courts killing the forest just to save a poison ivy bush?

Let's look at the Bill of Rights.

THE BILL OF RIGHTS

AMENDMENT I

Congress shall make no law respecting an establishment of religion, or prohibiting the free exercise thereof; or abridging the freedom of speech, or of the press; or the right of the people peaceably to assemble, and to petition the government for a redress of grievances.

FREEDOM OF RELIGION

The freedom of religion has been tested occasionally in the courts. The Constitutional freedom may not allow you to do whatever you want in the name of religion. For example, if you are in a religion that does not believe in medical science, and you refuse treatment for you or your child, the court may overrule your wishes. This is especially true for children. The courts have said that, you can believe whatever you want, but you cannot necessarily practice what you want. There was also the case of the Pentecostal Holiness Sect in Tennessee in which rattlesnakes were handled and strychnine was drunk. The Bible says that the holy people will be able to do these, but the government disallowed it. The government must protect its citizens-- is the legal reason given. So the free exercise of religion is sometimes disallowed.

The free exercise of religion has evolved into huge tax breaks for anyone who calls himself a priest, rabbi, minister, or mullah. Clerics have no requirement for education under federal law. Certainly, many clergymen are educated in some sect of a religion, but this is not a necessity to obtain religious tax exemptions.

As religion became more important in America, and the clergies gained power, tax deductions for contributions became laws as did exemptions from taxation of religious real estate and industrial profits. Consequently, atheists and agnostics pay for the building of churches. Catholics pay for Mormon farms. Muslims and Jews pay for Christian schools and their textbooks. So, while the Constitution did not allow for the establishment of a state religion it did not apparently prohibit the funding of religions through the taxes of the citizens. At least that is what legislators and courts have decided.

In 1977, a man decided to make use of religious tax breaks for himself. He held weekly meetings with a few friends and deducted his home as a church. As you might imagine, the Internal Revenue Service did not take kindly to this tax dodge. They denied his deductions. He went to court and was vindicated because the government has no standards for what is, or is not, a religion.

He then began to sell minister licenses for five dollars. He also sold bishop, pope, mufti and other religious titles for various amounts of money. It seems that he has stopped this source of income, and minister licenses are now sent out free through the Internet. According to the website of the Universal Life Church its ministers include: Paul McCartney, Richard Branson, Stephen Colbert, and Lady Gaga. Once you have this minister license you are entitled to conduct legal weddings.

A large number of these ministers conduct weddings across the country. According to the website, 20,000,000 such minister licenses have been issued. And if you conduct regular meetings of congregation, which might be only two or three people, you are entitled to all of the tax breaks that are given to religions—no property taxes on your house, stop paying Social Security taxes on your income from church related income, and many other tax perks-- if you are a creative minister.

And now another inroad of churches into the states' purses. In the Supreme Court case of 2017, (Trinity Lutheran Church of Columbia, Inc. v. Comer) detonated a massive hole in the wall of separation between church and state. Ostensibly about playground equipment, the case actually dealt with whether religious institutions can be eligible for taxpayer funds. The Supreme Court's split decision opens the door for other sectarian organizations to siphon tax dollars into their churches, temples, and mosques. Four Catholics, two Jews and a Protestant decided the case. One Catholic and one Jew dissented.

Justice Sonia Sotomayor said it bluntly in her dissent: The high court's ruling means our country is now a place "where separation of church and state is a constitutional slogan, not a constitutional commitment."

Should we acknowledge that some religions are not suitable for democracy since either their teachings or their structure is autocratic, such as the Catholic Church. Mormonism, Islam--in some of its jihadist guises, are not compatible to democracy. A God-based theocracy is not compatible with a society-based governmental style, such as democracy.

What about those millionaire mega-church ministers with their state of the art private jets? Shouldn't they be preaching poverty and riding donkeys like the Master? If capitalism and extravagance are ideals in a democracy, as they seem to be, the reverends of revenue are definitely prophets with profits—and their congregations can tithe their way to heaven. This is generally preferable to slaying blasphemers as the preferred path to Paradise.

While a state religion is prohibited, the original Constitution does not sanctify religions. In fact, many of the Founding Fathers were not religious. Washington, Jefferson, John Adams, Thomas Paine and James Madison were all skeptical to religion, especially to Christianity. None could be elected today.

But those men, such as Jefferson, were much influenced by the Enlightenment writers such as Rousseau, Newton and Locke. So, in spite of what many would like to believe, the United States was not founded as a Christian nation. It was rather a nation of people with various beliefs, many of which were Christian such as the Quakers and Anglicans.

Of course, not all of the Founding Fathers were deists or doubters. Samuel Adams and John Jay were very religious.

FREEDOM OF SPEECH

Freedom of speech, at the time of the Constitution's writing, was primarily a concern regarding freedom of political speech. However, the Supreme Court decisions have widened the scope of this freedom far beyond what the Founding Fathers had envisioned. Does freedom of speech have to be true or have evidence behind it or is it merely enough to use it to deflect the arguments on the issue? When President Trump said that Barack Obama had tapped his telephone lines during the election process, without presenting any evidence, is this what the writers of the Constitution meant to include in their "free speech" clause?

Liberal students at some of our best universities are, or should we say still are, protesting against conservative speakers. It has happened at Yale University, Cal Berkeley, and a number of other colleges. Freedom of speech is supposed to only protect your speech, not those with whom you disagree.

Some students are now protesting classes and programs that are not far enough to the left. At one college, a humanities course was disrupted because it was Europe centered. The power-hungry students are probably not aware that every area can have its own course in humanities. Courses in African, Oriental, North American, or Mideast humanities are all possible. They should have been protesting with the Dean of Studies to add other humanities courses. But then perhaps they didn't know that every geographical area has its own humanities--its own music, art, religions and philosophies. But maybe that is what they should be learning in college!

Clark Kerr, president of the University of California until the 1960s said that, "The university is not engaged in making ideas safe for students. It is engaged in making students safe for ideas. Thus, it permits the freest expression of views before students, trusting to their good sense in passing judgment on these views. Only in this way can it best serve American democracy."

In another area of free speech obstacles, we see in the world, is the stoning to death of anyone who utters a blasphemy against the creator or his prophet. How dare anyone blaspheme against the unknowable. How dare anyone use speech and stones to criticize the freedom of someone else who was using his freedom to speak? Oh people!, will thoughtful speech ever be universally permitted--if we find such a common aversion to free speech in both the illiterate and the university students?

How important is free-speech for a democracy?

Most European countries have limitations on saying anything you want—like profanity or extreme political views, like Nazism and racism.

There are two cases that the Supreme Court will decide on after this book is published. Both are actually freedom of religion cases but are being tried on the basis of freedom of speech, since there is a better chance of winning with this approach.

In Cakeshop versus Colorado Civil Rights Commission, in 2018, the Supreme Court decided that people's religious beliefs can allow them to refuse to do something which is required in the state under civil rights laws. In this case, Cakeshop refused to make a wedding cake for a homosexual couple. The Colorado courts had ruled against the cake shop.

The second case is a California issue. In National Institute of Family and Life Advocates v. Becerra, the plaintiff, NIFLA, is a religious antiabortion group which provides pregnancy related information to women. California has a law that states that licensed and unlicensed clinics involved in family-planning must give women information about contraception and abortion. It further states that unlicensed clinics inform their patients of their unlicensed status. The unlicensed clinics do not want to post a sign in the waiting rooms that California offers free contraception and abortion advice and services. NIFLA contends that communicating something that they do not believe in is against their freedom of speech rights. They lost their case in the California courts and in the federal courts of the Ninth District.

FREEDOM OF THE PRESS

Freedom of the press similarly was concerned with political freedom, and we might say, the freedom to criticize the government and its policies. In early 2017 Trump blocked some media outlets from a White House press briefing. They included: the New York Times, the LA Times, and CNN. Was this a violation of this amendment?

These last two ideas, of freedom of speech and freedom of the press, may have been overly stretched in the American presidential campaign of 2016. Fake news, fake history, opinions portrayed as news, the criticism of the legitimate press, as well as the lies and faulty logic that were exhibited certainly took the election far adrift of meaningful intellectual and logical discussions. How much should propaganda be protected in a democratic election?

In April of 2018, the Reporters Without Borders released their latest World Press Freedom Index. The United States fell two places to 45th in the world. Not quite what Jefferson and Madison had envisioned. Who was first? Yes, it was Norway again leading the world. It was followed by: Sweden, the Netherlands, Finland, and Switzerland. Is it merely an accident that the happiest countries are also: the least corrupt, have the greatest press freedom, have the most democratic governments, have students that achieve higher, have inexpensive or free universities, and have less crime? But that isn't really a concern for us Americans. Give us low taxes and let our children pay off the debts we have incurred! Forget promoting the general welfare with a free press, I only want to hear what I want to hear. How else can we out-Fox our opposition?

AMENDMENT II

"A well regulated militia, being necessary to the security of a free state, the right of the people to keep and bear arms, shall not be infringed."

FREEDOM TO OWN AND CARRY FIREARMS

Here again we have the intent of the Constitution writers changed by partisan Supreme Court judges so that now anyone, not associated with a well-regulated militia, can own rapid-fire automatic weapons. As criminals owned more guns, more citizens demanded the same right in order to protect themselves. Meanwhile non-regulated militias proliferated and stood to challenge the laws of the land.

Meanwhile there are daily multiple shootings in America. School shootings and mass shootings, as we saw in Las Vegas, make us wonder if gun ownership promotes the "general welfare" as the Preamble to the Constitution states is the reason for our fundamental law.

AMENDMENT VIII

"Excessive bail shall not be required, nor excessive fines imposed, nor cruel and unusual punishments inflicted."

CRUEL AND UNUSUAL PUNISHMENT

What is cruel and unusual punishment? Capital punishment has been with us since civilization first dawned. Is it now unusual? Under the Bush administration waterboarding (putting a person's head underwater and threatening drowning as a way of getting information) was used. Was it cruel? Definitely! Was it unusual? Yes—It hadn't been done before. "An eye for an eye" or "turn the other check"—which path shall we take?

In colonial America, hangings and other methods to end evil lives quickly were the rule. In fact, sometimes the punishment was the trial. Throw a suspected witch in the river, bound and in her underclothes—if she floats she was guilty, if she sinks she was not.

Some have suggested the same for The Donald, who is always complaining that he is the victim of a witch hunt. Let's bring him to the Potomac, strip him to his underwear, tie him up and let him prove his innocence in the river. That should shut up those fake news people, like those at CNN!

AMENDMENT IX

"The enumeration in the Constitution, of certain rights, shall not be construed to deny or disparage others retained by the people."

STATES' RIGHTS

Since the Founding Fathers did not mention abortion in their Constitution, is it a person's right to rid herself of an unwanted embryo or fetus? Or should this be the right of the states to determine?

What about other "rights?" The Constitution says nothing about crossing the United States borders and living productively or even non-productively on either side of the border. The 14th Amendment does define what is citizen is and the Supreme Court has ruled that the sovereignty of the country allows it to regulate immigration.

The 13 colonies were made up of immigrants and children of immigrants who came to a land populated by the indigenous Native Americans. If "might makes right" were the colonists right? Did the original inhabitants of the land have any rights at all? And it should be noted that the average Mexican is largely related to the original inhabitants of the continent— the average Mexican has a genetic make-up that is about 40% the same as the Native Americans. Does this give the average Mexican non-citizen similar rights to that of Trump's German grandfather who came to California to make money from the Gold Rush? He later became a citizen.

AMENDMENT X

"The powers not delegated to the United States by the Constitution, nor prohibited by it to the states, are reserved to the states respectively, or to the people."

Here again, is the right to allow abortion a right that constitutionally should go to the states or the people? Is it an individual's choice or should the legislatures of the states each decide on limitations to the Supreme Court's decision individually—possibly giving the citizens of the several states varying degrees of freedom?

WHAT DO WE MEAN BY DEMOCRACY?

Look at the countries that call themselves democracies. Are socialistic Norway, supposedly socialistic Venezuela, the United States, Iraq, Turkey and the Philippines identical societies? Of course not. Yet we call them all democracies. Just where does liberty or equality fall in these different countries? What about the varying economic theories that we find in these countries that theoretically use a democratic political theory?

Capitalism, socialism, generous or stingy welfare states, and other aspects of societies-- are often called democratic.

What about freedom of the press? Turkey has the most imprisoned journalists among the "democracies." It was about 80 at last count. But is freedom of the press necessary for a democracy? China is second in imprisoned journalists—but then they don't pretend to be a democracy. Egypt is third. And they pretend!

And freedom of speech? Let's take another look at freedom of speech. The boundaries of freedom of speech vary from country to country. In the US, you can say almost anything and be protected. In other democracies it varies considerably. In Israel you cannot call for a boycott of Israel. In Denmark speech is very free, but you can be called to court if it is not true. In Italy you can say a great deal, but not if it is against the public morality. In the U.S., all speech seems to be OK unless it promotes immanent violence.

Just how much freedom of speech should an individual be allowed when it may be disruptive to the society? What if it is helpful to the society and stimulates it to change?

Several Muslim countries have very strong blasphemy laws that require either long prison terms or capital punishment. Recently a boy in Bangladesh was hanged by his peers because they thought he had blasphemed. He had not. Politicians who have wished to change the laws are often executed. Is it blasphemous to question the divinity of Jesus, the revelations to Mohammed or Joseph Smith, or to question any laws created by people that may go against what someone believes?

Recently in Singapore, a young man named Amos Yee was tried and convicted of the "intention of wounding the religious feelings of Christians," for posting a video of the former prime minister, Lee Kuan Yew, and Jesus. He criticized both. He also posted an image of Lee and Margaret Thatcher having anal sex. Another charge was that he had used threatening, abusive and insulting communication. He was sentenced to several weeks in jail. He eventually was allowed asylum in the U.S., in March of 2017, because he was threatened with more prosecution for his illegal speech in Singapore—speech that would have been allowed in America. Close your eyes and ears America, Amos is on the loose!

How about a trial by your peers? You might think that drug users and dealers should get a fair trial after they are apprehended—innocent until proven guilty, and all that stuff! But in that paragon of Pacific democracies, the Philippines, it has snuffed out 2,500 of them by police actions and another 3,600 by vigilantes. Look at all the money the government has saved in trials and incarcerations. Very frugal!

And freedom of assembly? Spain has banned some demonstrations as have: Egypt, Mexico, Québec, Turkey, Ukraine, and even the U.S. Even though most national constitutions allow for freedom of assembly and it is allowed by the United Nations' Universal Declaration of Human Rights-- we certainly do not want people expressing their points of view in public in a democracy. People should be home watching television and paying attention to the advertising so they can go out and buy things. It's their patriotic duty in today's world.

Democratic term limits just have to go. After all, we elected the best man, let's keep him 'til he dies. Look at all the good that Robert Mugabe did for Zimbabwe and Jacob Zuma for South Africa. What do those citizens who overthrew them know anyhow? Look at all the good Maduro has done for Venezuela! Sri Lanka, Cambodia, and oh! so many more, are following this path—dictatorship is the divine right of the democratically elected!

How far can we move to an extreme and still be considered a democratic country?

BUT WHAT IF WE WANTED TO FOLLOW JEFFERSON AND MADISON?

In spite of the fact that these Founding Fogies were pretty smart for their day, they didn't have a law degree from the University of Mississippi nor the sage advice on how to run the country that the NRA or the pharmaceutical companies can impart. So why follow the Constitution they wrote? If they were around today they would probably insist that:

➤ Representatives should be clear on what they would like to see as policies for the government, then they should make these clear to the voters.

➤ Voters should understand the propensities of candidates to shade the truth, or even lie, to gain the power that comes with a seat in Congress or the parliament. If they promise to cut taxes, what services will be cut or how much will it add to the national debt?

➤ Freedom of speech be limited to statements that can be proven-- or to political theories that might be workable?

➤ If we are going to vote—we had better understand all of the issues and be able to see through the ideological and charismatic smokescreens that voters in democracies are commonly experiencing today.

➤ We should evaluate what the countries with the most effective democracies are doing.

➤ We should evaluate what the happiest countries in the world are doing?

➤ With the knowledge we have today, and with the many ways we have to communicate, voters should be far better educated than they seem to be.

They might question whether:

• Methodists or agnostics should be required to pay taxes to support Catholic, Lutheran, or Jewish schools?

• We should build a wall around America? And believe that someone else will pay for it.

• We have an idea of what brings happiness? A job, high pay, better health care, free education through the university, more vacations, safe neighborhoods, or ___?

• We still need a citizen's militia to ward off Queen Elizabeth's troops.

So with the questions and imperatives of Jefferson and Madison in mind, we will now take a deeper look at modern democracy, hoping to make it a brighter beacon to guide our modern democratic governments.

PART II HOW WE HAVE BEEN MANIPULATED LATELY

Every aware person knows that we are often manipulated. We are often lied to. Advertisers tweak our needs for power, for sexual pleasure, for meaning in our lives, for love. The science of psychology has aided those who want to sell us something. What motivates us? What color is most effective in grabbing our positive attention? This can influence the color of packaging, the cover of a book, the color of a car. But now psychology is aided by neuroscience and incredible technologies. Data mining can discover many of our interests and passions. Once politicians or advertisers have this information they can use it to influence people to vote for their ideas, or to abstain from voting if their psychological proclivities are antithetical to our own. Let's look at a few recent illustrations from recent elections.

Neuroscientists are showing us where in the brain our traditions are buried and how we are resistant to facts that conflict with our traditions and other deeply held beliefs. In late 2017 Fox News anchor, Shepard Smith, contradicted, with facts, a major anti-Hillary charge by Trump that she had engineered sale of a uranium mine to the Russians in exchange for a $140 million donation to the Clinton Foundation. Fox viewers were outraged and demanded his ouster. It is upsetting for most of us to find out we were wrong—and many of us will never accept the facts. People we trust have constructed our realities, and they have often built them on foundations of clouds rather than granite.

In a recent study in a heavy Trump voting district in Pennsylvania, the people realized that he wasn't going to fulfill many of his promises, like opening up the mines or factories or doing much about the opioid crisis that was endemic in their areas. But they still backed him. They liked that he was bombastic and continually attacking people and organizations that they didn't like. His racist defenses were music to their ears. He protected their "white identities" and their "American values." Here is another illustration of how the appeal to the unconscious mind and the drives for power may be even more important than the economic realities. It is clear that Trump merely lives his own feeling of superiority and many in his base can thrive in his shadow--their unconscious needs nursing at his narcissistic nipples

Faith is much easier to be sure of than facts. Faith can be learned in a few minutes—such as faith in a religion or a political party. Understanding or dealing with facts takes years of learning and a knowledge of logic and the continual reevaluation of the facts and their sources.

CHAPTER 8   HOW DID TRUMP MANIPULATE US

DID HE REALLY SAY THAT?

We wonder if he even understands the realities of the world. In attempting to convince Mexico's President Nieto into at least "saying" that Mexico would pay for the wall, he promised to send in US military forces to conquer the drug lords of Mexico.

A few days after President Trump's inauguration, he called President Nieto of Mexico to discuss economic issues. The tape of the conversation was leaked to the Washington Post. Intermixed with his discussion of economic issues, he tried to pressure the Mexican president to not tell the press that Mexico would not pay for the wall. While he said that, "from an economic issue, it is the least important thing we are talking about-- but psychologically it means something…You cannot say that to the press…The press is going to go with that and I cannot live with that." While psychologically it was critical for Trump, because it had been his major promise in the election. But psychologically it was essential for Nieto also, because he would lose face politically if he indicated that Mexico would pay for the wall. Several months later, prior to a planned state visit by Nieto, the issue was raised again—so Nieto cancelled the visit. Trump's one track mind stops others in their tracks.

He also said he didn't take vacations. According to the Wall Street Journal, President Trump has spent 1/3 of his presidency playing golf or at his hotels. He railed against President Obama's numerous golf trips-- which averaged 38 a year, but Trump played more than 95 times his first year. This cost the taxpayers $7 million in airline expenses. But that doesn't count the expenses for Secret Service and Coast Guard protection. The cost of renting golf carts to protect the President while he was playing cost $60,000 for the first ten months, which apparently was income for Trump's hotel. His late-summer, 17-day vacation at his club in New Jersey was interrupted by hurricanes Harvey and Irma. Perhaps he doesn't control the universe!

Perhaps the least surprising upshot of the release of the transcripts of Trump's previously mentioned conversations with Australian Prime Minister Malcolm Turnbull is the confirmation that the President and his administration deliberately misled the public about them. When the Washington Post published an account of the Turnbull conversation in early February, Trump tweeted that it had been a "very civil conversation that the fake news media lied about."

As has happened repeatedly over the course of the administration, the emergence of the facts has upheld the news reports, and shown the Trump denials to be false.

A QUICK LOOK AT DONALD'S RISE

Some have called him a master politician. This may be true but it may also be that his superiority complex, arising from his attempting to cope with his deep feelings of inferiority, have made him not only a braggart but also one who will say anything to enhance his feelings of superiority. It was probably problems of this sort that had his parents send him to a military school to straighten him out when he was young. From a mental health point of view, as mentioned earlier, it is generally agreed that he is narcissistic with a huge superiority complex based on his basic unconscious inferiority feelings which probably go back to his early childhood or to a genetic abnormality.

It is not difficult to tap into the motivations of the man because we are all geared to a large extent to be motivated by things that will reduce our feelings of inferiority. The great majority of us seek power somewhere in our lives. It may be bossing around a spouse or a child. It may be in getting, and doing, a good job. It may be in driving fast. It may be in having a gun. It may be in shooting a deer. It may be in joining ISIS. It may be winning at gambling.

It is usually satisfying to feel superior to others. Trump satisfied many people's need for superiority by castigating Mexicans and China, by threatening to get rid of Muslims, by belittling his primary opponents, by being against Obamacare because insurance premiums were rising—but without having an alternative, by promising to drain the swamp of Washington, and Oh!, so many other threats and promises—but no program policies. Policies come from the intellect, but put-downs usually from the unconscious feelings of inferiority.

We might as well have the Van Pelts in office—Lucy with her bullying and Linus with his blanket and grand plans, and the promises that the Great Pumpkin will deliver—but never does. Not to be outdone, Donald's well-coiffed and beautiful omnipresent Slovenian security blanket prevents opponents from throwing stones. The great pumpkin certainly doesn't want to hide his security blanket.

In a recently released report on Trump supporters, it was found that they agreed that he had not done much of what he had promised. No wall, no Obamacare repeal, no mines opened, no factory jobs, no work on the opioid crisis, but they were excited by his style and his constantly blasting people and groups that they don't like—Congress, the mainstream media, the black football players who knelt during the national anthem. And he supports gun ownership, one of the truly power-providing accouterments that even the poor can afford.

His pro-white stance affirms their identities. Here again, we see the bypassing of the intellect for the power drives stemming from the unconscious mind. Feeling good about yourself is essential, even if it comes from putting down other people

WE MUST REPEAL OBAMACARE!

Trump made a big issue of repealing and replacing Obamacare. What he did not say was that medical costs, like all other costs, generally increase every year. What he also did not say was that because Congress insists on everyone having private health insurance, rather than having a public option, as Obama wanted and as most other advanced countries have, this increases prices even more because the private companies must make profits for their stockholders and the CEOs and other high level administrators who all have seven and eight figure salaries.

It would be poor politics to tell the electorate that we have the worst healthcare of any rich country. We are ranked 38th in the world. Included in this figure is maternal mortality where we are the worst in the developed world with 21 deaths per 100,000 births. Compare this with Singapore and Greece at 3 and Estonia at 2 per hundred thousand. Texas raises the US average a bit since it has 38.5 maternal deaths per hundred thousand births every year.

For this "outstanding" healthcare we pay 40% to 50% more than any other country. Congressmen keep talking about what is best for the American people—so we certainly do not want socialized medicine like they have in Europe. They don't tell us that generally in Europe you have your own doctor, just like in the US. All conditions, such as pre-existing, are always covered. Hospitalization is totally free. But these are facts that might motivate the intellect—and we know that far more people are motivated by prodding their unconscious minds! Is it really that important to show that we are different from, and superior to, Europe—when in this issue of health care, they are far superior to us. But will our power drives allow us admit we are not always the greatest? This is one area where Trump could make America great—but as he said, "who knew that health care could be so complicated."

POPULISM IN THE RUST BELT

Whatever else we may say; Trump's campaign was not "politics as usual!" It seems that his path to the presidency had several factors that probably helped his wins in both the Republican primary and the general election. Donald, himself, was a major factor. Being well-known as an enterprising billionaire and a television performer, he already had a leg up—all he had to do was knock the legs out from under those experienced politicians who opposed him. He did this by putting them down in a very high-handed way. Calling them liars, low energy, sleepy, lazy, crooked, or "parts of the establishment" that must be removed.

By attaching themselves to an outsider, a billionaire businessman, and by joining in with the massive putdowns of his opponents, the lowly educated and unemployed or underemployed could feed their need for pride. It didn't matter that Donald was outright lying 50% of the time and only partially truthful 40% of the time, because they didn't have enough education to sort out the facts. But it really didn't matter because their unconscious minds were being angered even more than they already were. It really didn't matter because he amplified their fears and gave them objects to be angry about and fearful of. And mostly, he gave them hope that he could turn it all around—because he was a successful businessman.

But there were also peripheral forces that reinforced his messages. Fox News was certainly not the only source of real news. Russia was helping in any way that it could with more fake news, ostensibly from legitimate sources, like Facebook. Then there were people who wanted immediate money from their fake news—like the Macedonian teenagers who put out fake news on both sides of the election, but found out that they made more money on the pro-Trump and the anti-Hillary articles.

There was another audience hopefully awaiting his election. Business owners and stock traders were avariciously awaiting the cancelling of regulations that protected the consumers, and would put green in their pockets from the promised tax cuts.

Kellyanne Conway seemed a major part of the campaign. As an experienced pollster, she seemed to be able to find the messages that were right for the section of his base that Trump was addressing. She was probably the best at using what we think of as traditional political techniques. It is hard to say just how much of Trump's rambling messages were orchestrated, at least in part, by Kellyanne.

Billionaires played their part in funding the campaign, and some like Robert Mercer, were able to use their data mining companies, such as Cambridge Analytica, to entice likely Trump voters to the polls, while discouraging likely Hillary voters from voting.

AND THEN THERE WERE THE RUSSIANS-- THE RUSSIAN TROLLS

We know that the Russians were working to influence the 2016 election. US intelligence has found substantial evidence that seven states had their voter rolls compromised by Russians in the election of 2016. Alaska, Arizona, California, Florida, Illinois, Texas, and Wisconsin were definitely compromised. It included even intrusion into voter registration databases. This was found during the last weeks of the Obama administration. There were 14 other states that were probed by the Russians during the 2016 election

We don't know yet all about exactly how they approached the election, but we know that they used fake news, real news that helped them make their point, and paid ads on Facebook and other social media sites. From what we know, they appealed to both the right and left sides of the political spectrum. And we know that it was not just the US that has been targeted. The UK, France, and Germany have been targeted with the objective of electing far right anti-EU candidates. The more they can split the NATO alliance, the happier they will be.

In November of 2017, it was revealed that over 2,500 Russian Twitter accounts were sending false messages that were then picked up and passed on by at least 3,000 global news outlets. Sean Hannity of Fox News, Jake Tapper of CNN, along with people at CNBC and HuffPost Canada, Washington Post, and the Daily Mail were duped. Donald Trump and his son were among the 855 politicians, public figures and other celebrities who were fooled into retweeting, publishing, or broadcasting information they received. One of the many Russian accounts, which went by the name @TEN_GOP on Twitter, had 130 million followers. Donald Trump was one of them.

A recent research article in the journal Science indicated that falsehood travels to other users six times faster than true news. France discovered it in their presidential election—with Russia backing the far-right, anti-EU candidate. Spain found Russian and Venezuelan influences in Catalonia's attempt to secede from Spain. Russia has much to gain if the European Union and NATO can be weakened.

The Russians, using fake social media personas, attempted to depress turnouts among Blacks and Muslims in the 2016 American election. Some of their social media accounts had 100,000 followers.

Russian meddling goes way back. In the 1960s the KGB started the Liberty Book Club. Its first publication was a book asserting that there was a conspiracy to assassinate John Kennedy. In backing the Trump campaign, the Russians used a number of different addresses, each with a number of different URLs. They might be related to activists of some sorts such as:

➤Black activists --@blacktivists

➤They might be related to a geographical area such as--@SouthLoneStar

➤They might be simply a person's name such as: @Pamela_Moore13

➤They might be related to a special interest such as: @WarfareWW.

Some examples of the Russians delivering fake news in tweets:

➤From July 23, 2016, "Hillary Clinton wrote the anti-police and anti-Constitutional policies for Obama."

➤One tweet read, "This vet passed away last month before he could vote for Trump."

➤ "Massive riots happening now in Sweden. Stockholm in flames. Trump was right again." As you know Sweden has a huge number of immigrants and this tweet was supposed to show their violence. And as you know, this tweet was totally false. So, Trump said he read it on Fox News.

➤And this from November 2, 2016, "Voter fraud by counting tens of thousands of ineligible mail-in Hillary votes in Florida."

The top ten countries from which articles, based on the fake news tweets, were published include, in descending order: Russia, the United States, Germany, Australia, Italy, Ukraine, Switzerland, Finland, France and the United Kingdom. Other countries too, have copied the Russian approach to influence citizens for different purposes.

This has prompted former high-level American and German computer scientists to attempt to alert us to the dangers hiding in our computers and phones. The Alliance for

Secure Democracy (securingdemocracy.org) will help to keep us alert to the dangers to an informed democracy.

WHAT IS BEING DONE TO TRIP UP THE TROLLS?

Sweden is developing a national curriculum designed to help students sort out truth from falsity.

Because Germany has large fines on digital suppliers that distribute fake news and hate speech, the platforms are blocking more content than they might need to. Facebook is hiring 20,000 people to monitor abusive content

THE BILLIONAIRES

It was Trump's appeal to the unconscious mind's need for power, not the intellect that was the focus of his diatribes. He may not have known that he was hitting at the unconscious, but the data mining of Robert Mercer's Cambridge Analytica knew full well how to get votes. While Jeb, Ted, and Hillary were generally focused on intellectual arguments, Trump's natural inferiorities and his superiority complex, along with his pollsters' advice, correctly went for the psychological breadbasket of many voters.

Yes, we are being manipulated not only by foreign governments, but also by the selfish interests of some billionaires—especially hedge fund managers and fossil fuel tycoons. There are a number of companies that mine the data on social media sources to pinpoint where their messages can best be instrumental in supporting their interests. For example, the recent tax bill proposed by Donald Trump was touted as a "middle-class miracle." But the major recipients were the richest of the rich.

Voters might be influenced to support it by pinpoint ads developed by information about them that was data mined. Many of these data mining companies are being bought by billionaires. And, as you might guess, they will not take a charitable deduction for their purchases. The charity they have in mind is in their hip pockets!

Peter Thiel is a billionaire who started PayPal and eBay, and is a founder and Chairman of Palantir Technologies. Palantir does data mining for the federal government—for the CIA and others. It now works on controlling immigration. Thiel was the first from Silicon Valley to endorse Donald Trump. No evidence yet that Palamtir was used in the election.

A former vice president of Cambridge Analytica, Steve Bannon, was the CEO of Trump's presidential campaign and senior adviser to President Trump. He is now working hard to get far right, alt-right, congressmen elected.

It should come as no surprise, if you have followed Edward Snowden's revelations and those of others, that we are all being spied on. Our smart phones tell others where we are at any given moment. They can be turned on remotely to listen in on our conversations.

Facebook may be the biggest supplier of information to Big Brother, but so are Google, Twitter, and any number of other Internet eavesdroppers. This, of course, is done to a large degree to keep us safe. But data mining companies can use our information against us.

AND THE NEXT ELECTION!

Artificial intelligence is progressing so fast that it can be the next wave of election meddling. It will be nearly impossible to determine what is true and what is not, according to researchers at Oxford and Cambridge universities, in their paper titled, "The Malicious Use of Artificial Intelligence: Forecasting, Prevention and Mitigation" They mention: the insecurity of our computers; the increased use of otherwise labor-intensive attacks; the use of speech synthesis that may or may not imitate the voices of famous people, like the president or a trusted news commentator, your friends or your family; automated hacking; and through data poisoning.

In addition, artificial intelligence will be able to: data mine then critically analyze mass collected data; personalization through targeted propaganda; deception through manipulation of videos and other means of communication. Artificial intelligence will also be able to more effectively analyze human behaviors, beliefs, and moods. While these are more effectively used in autocratic governmental systems, they will also be used in democratic governmental systems.

It is hoped that artificial intelligence will also be able to aid in the evaluation of both true and untrue communications. It may also be able to assist in ethical evaluations. Can you imagine a presidential debate where a false, or partially false, statement is evaluated as the candidate is speaking, and as the last word is uttered a loud buzzer petrifies the audience and the corrected information appears on a large screen behind the podium. Candidates talking through their teeth would be corrected by an AI search engine. Sort of like gargling with Google.

There are already companies working on algorithms that will interrupt a story you are reading on your internet device and tell you that it is false information.

BUT, WE THINK WE ARE THINKING!

Influencing the electorate is done in many ways. Candidates, or proponents of a proposition, like a referendum, can argue intellectually about its benefits or drawbacks. This type of analysis is good. This is the way that voters should be informed in a democracy.

The major mission of this book, however, is to look at how we are influenced by conscious and unconscious fears, anger, and hope—these are often irrational. These can then be intensified by: the candidate, the supporters, the major news media, fake news, and the targeting of our personality profiles as portrayed by the social media.

We can imagine Trump thinking, "If I can make people feel anger at Muslims or pro-choice people or at the 'do-nothing' people in Washington, I will tap into the anger of a large part of the population. If I say I can get your job back, I can reduce your taxes, or I am for you keeping your guns—I have tapped into many more interests of many more voters."

As a Machiavellian politician, you don't really need facts to back up your positions unless the people you hope to influence can think for themselves. Niccolo is mentioned here because he saw the practical psychology of politics 400 years before the science of psychology was even conceived. That's why his "The Prince" is one of the truly great books of our Western civilization. Unknowing people call sinister politics "Machiavellian," but he was only being an insightful observer of the Renaissance royalty of Florence—and the Medicis!

The real and passionate interest of a large part of Americana is who will win the "big game" today. "Meet the Press" gets about 3,500,000 viewers a week, a little more than "Face the Nation" and about twice as many as "Fox News Sunday." On the other hand, the Army-Navy football game had 8 million viewers, the college basketball regional finals had 10 million and the Super Bowl got 111 million viewers. So "Meet the Press" gets about 1% of Americans watching it, while the Super Bowl gets 33% watching it— almost as many as voted!

The 2016 presidential election topped any election in history for insults, disagreements, personal attacks, propaganda, and lies. Republicans, particularly Donald Trump, relied more on insults than on policy proposals. He set new standards for campaigning by selecting his base of: evangelical Christians, the unemployed or underemployed in the Rust Belt, Tea Party sympathizers, anti-tax Republicans, veterans, and those who did not feel safe because of domestic crime or international terrorism. Of course he had that other base—people in business and stock traders.

FOOLING THE VOTERS

Once you have your voting bases you can figure out how to appeal to each of them. The less intelligent they are, the more you can bypass their intellects and go to their unconscious minds—helping them to feel more angry and powerful. Getting them angry and giving them hope are among the most effective methods for exciting people who are not too smart. With anger and hope you can hit both the intellect and the unconscious—promise to get rid of the immigrants who are taking your jobs, the same immigrants who are inferior to you in ethnicity, religion, or race.

Of course, he did have some business owners who wanted a businessman running the Washington show. For them he could promise fewer regulations, lower corporate taxes, and lower personal taxes. These also warm their intellects while allowing them to climb up the economic ladder and become superior to those with less money and less power.

There are so many ways to try to fool the public. You can use fake news, you can choose your statistics, you can rely on fear, or hope, or anger to stimulate their appetites. You can find out what are their main concerns, then address them with real or false hope.

With his bases identified, he could make vague promises, lie, brag or use whatever means necessary to ensure their votes. It is impossible to know just how much of his successful campaign was due to political strategy and how much was due to his bragging and lying. Were his lies about his opponents fueling the egos of his followers by making them feel superior to each opponent while riding the coattails of the billionaire outsider? Or, did they really believe his lies and promises without understanding the ramifications of them in real life.

Did they know that attaching tariffs to less expensive foreign-made goods would be paid for by them in the eventual higher purchase price for those foreign-made goods, or in the higher prices required to buy the more expensive American made products? If, as he promised, the Keystone and Dakota Access pipelines were to be made of American steel, the cost to American taxpayers would be much greater than if foreign steel were used. However, the steel being used is actually from Russia, India and Italy. Apparently, the gauges of the steel needed were different from what American steel makers could supply, also, most of the steel for the pipelines had already been purchased. But the promise sounded good. Was it a lie, or did he not have the facts?

THE TRUMP BASE

The Trump base seemed to be stimulated by traditional business-oriented interests, such as: low taxes for both individuals and businesses, job creation, fewer regulations that had protected the consumer, and the elimination of undocumented immigrants who might have been holding down wages.

It was clear that Trump's mission was to help business. In his first Asian tour, as in other pronouncements at presidential meetings, he emphasized equalizing trade opportunities. He said that his "America first" idea should be adopted by other countries because each country should put its own interests first. In a speech in Vietnam, he made it clear that "America has things to sell."

His early executive orders, which countermanded Obama's pro-citizen, often business inhibitory executive orders, placed business and stock trading ahead of the interests of the citizens. This often was in contradiction to the interests of the other part of his base, the lower-class white working people— who actually elected him.

To his business base was added people who were traditionally conservative, particularly in religion. These are not mutually exclusive categories and Trump played to them on many fronts. He was particularly effective in appealing to their conscious and subconscious fears and their conscious hopes. He was generally deficient in offering concrete proposals, but rather strongly indicated that his business success was enough to get the job done. He was particularly strong in promising that his negotiating skills would be able to make America great again—even if it weakened other countries.

BELIEFS OF HIS RELIGIOUS BASE

Conservatives and reactionaries are more likely to be religious in a way that is more conservative, that is more biblically oriented, even if their beliefs are not actually specified in the Bible—such beliefs as:

> ➢ Life starting at the instant of conception, rather than at birth;
>
> ➢ Jesus being a Christian rather than being a Jew all of his life;
>
> ➢ Papal pronouncements, such as changing the time of receiving one's soul from

1 to 2 months after conception, as had been the belief for well over a thousand years, to ensoulment at the instant of conception as decreed in 1869 by Pope Pius IX. For some reason, many Protestants adopted this Catholic view.

Of course, under George W. Bush it was determined that life, that is "personhood," didn't start until implantation into the uterus for American human embryos. The fertilized ovum implants in the uterus about a week after conception. In other societies personhood may be believed to occur at any time after conception and until the first breath is taken at birth. A few societies have even practiced infanticide since their beliefs may require that an infant is not a person unless it can eventually contribute to the society.

Americans are far higher in their percentage of believers, who have faith in an unknowable creator, than other First World countries and are far lower in their student and adult academic achievement than other countries.

This blind faith in something "unknowable" may make many Americans less likely, or less able, to critically analyze political promises. Studies have shown that these fundamentalists were far more likely to believe the fake news that inundated the 2016 electoral process.

This leads to the conviction that: if you would like to believe it, it must be true! Fundamentalists are more likely to believe in a biblical interpretation of reality than in scientifically verifiable facts. This is evident in their disbelief: in evolution, in the perils of overpopulation, and in global warming and its human causes. As Kellyanne has informed us—there are "alternative facts" that people can believe. But she didn't say that they were equally true to verifiable facts.

This, of course, is not true of all Christians, just those whose major beliefs come from the single book that tradition tells us was written by Moses, at least the first few books. He wrote about Adam and Eve and Abraham. These stories had been passed down orally for at least six centuries from Abraham--assuming that he actually lived. Then another thousand years elapsed before we had any actual written evidence. This came from the Dead Sea Scrolls.

So, the Old Testament Scriptures were definitely not eyewitness accounts. The Christian scriptures, similarly, were not eyewitness testaments. None were written by people who knew Jesus. The earliest remnants of copies of the New Testament are found in various papyrus fragments, dated by writing samples as being from the second and third centuries, and codexes, complete or nearly complete, from the fourth and fifth centuries

The most famous being the Sinai Codex found in a monastery near Mount Sinai. It was written three to four hundred years after Jesus lived. It has gospels not found in modern versions of the Bible and it is lacking many writings that were included in the "official" version of the Bible which was finally determined after 325 at the Council of Nicaea.

After much argument, it was decided here in Nicaea, by men, that Jesus was, in fact, God. Additionally, there were many corrections and changes throughout the Codex, when compared to the Bible that followed. This casts doubt on the original intention of the writers.

Here is another example of looking a bit deeper at a belief—after examining deeply, follow the evidence. Here we use a religious example, but political and personal beliefs need be examined. As Socrates said, "The unexamined life is not worth living."

So the simplistic traditional beliefs of most evangelicals are not nearly as precise as some ministers would have us believe. Biblical scholars, both Jewish and Christian, have found many more variations in older parchment and papyrus copies that yield the legitimate writings of the prophets and early chroniclers of these "religions of Abraham." The history and philosophy of religions is unbelievably complicated. But simplicity rules in the hearts of us homo sapiens, or should we say "homo fairytalous?"

Two of the major components of American fundamentalist religion are the literal belief in the story of creation in Genesis, along with its rejection of the major scientific finding of evolution. 57% of white evangelicals in the US believe the creation myth of the Bible. A second major belief is that the Bible, as it stands today, is the exact word of God and has not been changed through the generations. They reject biblical scholarship which is generally accepted by the major religions. There is no question that there are huge gaps in the writing of the biblical stories. If Moses lived in the 13th or 14th century before the common era, we have no manuscripts from that time. The earliest writing is from the Dead Sea Scrolls of a thousand years later. There is even a question as to what language the earliest Old Testament writings would have been written. The earliest evidence of Hebrew writing is from about three hundred to six hundred years after Moses supposedly lived. Since he lived in Egypt, were his original writings in Egyptian hieroglyphics? Could they have been written in Phoenician?

But the essence of their religion was not important, what was important is that it was the only true religion so everyone should follow it. Having the true religion puts one above the law and gives one a feeling of ultimate power, which is an effective way of dealing with our nearly universal feelings of inferiority.

It was also critical that we get back to American values for real Americans.

White evangelical Christians want a white evangelical nation. Trump played to that. While he has never been particularly religious, as evidenced by his multiple adulterous relationships starting with his first marriage and continuing through his third, he took a major issue "abortion" and played that card. On the other hand, Hillary was a lifelong Christian who carries her Bible with her continually. But she was pro-choice.

HOW IMPORTANT IS RELIGION IN OTHER COUNTRIES?

We tend to think that everyone thinks like us. Not all have the same idea of democracy, of how to use our leisure time, or on a commitment to a religion. Of the 170 countries, ranked by their commitment to religion, with Sweden the least religious at number one, US is 44th. It is more religious than Israel at 38, Catholic Ireland at number

40, and Spain at number 34. Generally speaking, the less religious countries are the more scientifically trained with Ireland ranked 19th to America's 25th. Japan, ranked as the sixth least religious country, is the second most scientifically literate. The United Kingdom, the eighth least religious country ranks 15th in science ability by the PISA scores.

Fundamentalists in the major monotheistic religions usually have very little evidence for their beliefs. They normally do not know very much about Biblical or Koranic research and do not have a thorough history of their theology. Since there is often no real requirement to be a minister or a preacher, many preach ideas that are not generally accepted by the scholars who study their religion. In general, they do not have high levels of education in biology, philosophy, history, or science. They are therefore more likely to believe unprovable ideas and conspiracy theories. They tend to be more likely to believe in "abstinence only" sex education and a negative relationship between vaccinations and autism. The ideas that Barack Obama was not born in the US and that he is a Muslim had also found fertile ground here.

Americans are consistently optimistic. I wonder if this faith is what brings them to have faith in their unprovable religious beliefs.

Sociologists have found that fundamentally religious people are more likely to be guided by hope. They are externally motivated. They feel that an "other" controls their lives. Studies on people killed by tornadoes found that those who felt responsible for themselves were more likely to seek adequate shelter from a storm and emerge safe. Those who hoped that Providence would protect them were more likely to wind up dead—or in the land of Oz!

Because they may encounter a number of beliefs being forced on them by teachers and others, they may develop an animosity toward those who have an education. This may make them more likely to believe fake news as a way of showing their power and independence. Donald Trump got 81% of the evangelical vote. This was far more than "born again" George Bush got.

But it would be shallow to believe that all Trump voters were only voting their religion. As Newt Gingrich said, "all politics are local." When people are unemployed or underemployed, when they are poor or think they are poor, when they are not content—they want change. Voters nearly always want change. The "ins" have never done enough for me!

Trump was promising a way to escape poverty and to create jobs for the poor and fewer regulations and lower taxes for the rich. Mighty powerful motivators! But even more—he gave them a feeling of power because they were with him—a billionaire who was going to take on Washington and drain the swamp.

You wonder why people in the Southern and the Midwestern states are most likely to be Tea Party members and anti-tax Republicans. The fact is that they are poor and get a greater percent of their state budget from the taxes that others pay to the federal government. In a recent year, Louisiana got 42% of its state budget revenue from the federal government. Louisiana is the poorest state in the nation.

Trump probably did a better job with his base than about anyone ever has. He kept coming back to the same issues. "Make America great again" by employing those who have lost their jobs. It was the illegal Mexicans who took many of them. But jobs that went to Mexico took more. Then the Chinese were selling cheaper than anyone so they were taking American jobs. The other major issue was safety. "Make America safe again." We have to keep out those Muslims because so many are terrorists. You don't want "Lyin'

Ted" or "Crooked Hillary"—they are part of the Washington establishment that we have to get rid of. We must "drain the swamp." We have got to get back to the good old days.

By repeating these charges over and over, we learned them. "I am the only one who can do it." So he had a strong base of voters on steroids—drugs of despair, anger and hope. This was a base that would vote for him rain or shine.

THE TRUMP CAMPAIGN

His approach to campaigning was to pamper the fears of the unemployed and the underemployed and to develop new fears. He could then blame the problems on the previous administration. With fears enflamed he could offer the salve of hope, often impossible hopes, to reduce the fears that he had elicited. He could threaten tariffs which would make it harder for other countries to sell their goods and would make those goods more expensive for Americans.

He did not mention the obvious negatives to the American public for his solutions. For example, sending out undocumented Mexicans who work in slaughterhouses will increase the price of meat if Americans are willing to do the work—which they do not seem to want. Hotel sheets will not be changed or laundered unless Americans are willing to do it at higher wages. This of course increases the costs of hotels. Restaurants will lose cooks, waiters, busboys and dishwashers. Who will do these jobs for the traditionally low pay?

His approach was to:
➢ Criticize, without evidence, the prior administration,
➢ Criticize the media outlets that disagreed with him,
➢ Call real news "fake news,"
➢ If a media outlet agrees, praise them and consult them—InfoWars, Rush Limbaugh, Fox News.

We will take a brief look at the imprecise or undefined terms used in his non-intellectual play for the voters. These are the semantic ambiguities mentioned earlier. Then there are the downright lies or half-lies that he continually paraded before his admiring audiences, as well as an onslaught of inductive fallacies.

MANIPULATION—AND THE MONEY

Pinpointing the message to the voters has become essential in recent elections. Psychology and neuroscience have given the militaries of the rich world tools to manipulate our perceptions and our attitudes—and even what we think of as knowledge. But the methods of these sciences cannot work without information. That information comes, to a large degree, from social media and a large number of other sources.

Google knows where you have been, if you have your tracking turned on. It knows everything you have ever searched and what you have deleted. It has your advertising profile, which includes: your gender, age, career, interests, hobbies, relationship status and your income. It knows all the apps that you use. It has all of your emails to and from your account and even those that have been deleted. It knows all that you have looked at on YouTube. It knows the photos you have taken on your iPhone. The amount of the information that Google has on you would fill millions word documents.

Facebook has a record of every message you have ever sent, or been sent. It can figure out what you are likely to want based on your comments with friends. It recently revealed that as many as 125 million Americans probably viewed Russian ads during the 2016-- without realizing their source.

Once researchers have mined the data and determined what information they wanted, the analysis for the Trump campaign was primarily done by Cambridge Analytica. Then when they knew which people they want to target, and with which messages, the pinpointing of the messages is done by AggregateIQ.

Much of the psychological research, that is aimed at persuading people to do something, has been funded by military budgets. It was first picked up by advertisers and it is now being used to sway elections by those who can profit by a certain outcome. Some billionaires, countries like Russia and North Korea, and other well-connected parties are involved in manipulating our democratic processes

Billionaires are buying up these data mining and "psyop" companies that are geared to manipulate the votes of electors during important elections, just as they have historically given money to the legislators who legislate for them in our republic. We might ask if it is really "our" republic or are we merely puppets of our billionaire plutocratic masters?

We should be worried about how we are manipulated continually. Do we honestly understand the unconscious hypodermic needle thrust into our unconscious minds while we are being entertained or informed by those television commercials we watch five times an hour each night? The advertisers are not doing this out of the goodness of their hearts, they are doing this to increase their riches. And where will those dollars and pounds come from? Our wallets! So, if you want to keep what you have, it is well past time to be vigilant.

The same is true in how Trump's psyop people invaded our unconscious minds with music to our invisible ears. Let's go back to the good old days: when we all had lucrative jobs, when God held our hearts, when America was the international icon, when the people had a real voice in their government, when business was freer to set its own rules.

"Go back to where we wuz!" is the battle cry of the reactionaries. Going back is not necessarily bad. But how much of what we have are we willing to give up? How far to the right shall we go? Henry the 8th might be farther than most of us would like.

Reactionary billionaire Robert Mercer and millionaire Steve Bannon, the key Trump aide who was his chief strategist but is now doing his own alt-right thing, have been thought to be on a mission to replace the mainstream media with far-right media outlets and to increase the use of alternative facts, fake history and reactionary propaganda. If we don't want to don our medieval coat of armor and joust with the black knight— perhaps we should see through the Trumpian attempts to manipulate us.

WAS HE PREPARED FOR THE JOB?

Anyone with any basic knowledge of liberal arts would see that Trump has been an inveterate liar and is ignorant of the facts of history and economics. He said that Andrew Jackson was furious about the Civil War. But Jackson died 16 years before it happened. He said that Frederick Douglass has done an amazing job and is being recognized more and more. Douglass, of course, died over 120 years ago.

His hundred-word tax plan was not even long enough to give a hint as to what might follow. It took ten months before he actually submitted a plan— his "middle class miracle" tax plan—which was actually designed to save the rich millions, and in his case, billions. He said he would pay more under this plan, but if we use his leaked 2006 tax return as an indication, he would have actually paid $86 million less. He tried to eliminate the Alternative Minimum Tax that Ronald Reagan had signed into law. That would have saved him $31 million in 2006. He kept the capital gains tax rate for stock traders and those who buy and sell real estate. It saves them about 50% in taxes. He kept all of the perks for the rich and added more—such as eliminating the inheritance tax, which will save his kids from becoming homeless. They will have $3 billion instead of the $2 billion they would have without the tax break. (His proposals were not accepted in their entirety, but the inheritance taxes were significantly reduced.)

Of course, if he can take it with him, his kids might not get anything! Maybe he can negotiate with St. Peter to cover the Pearly Gates with diamonds!

After railing against the Obama health care plan for months and promising to bring in a better program, when the House program stalled he said "Nobody knew healthcare could be so complicated." He had no idea of what he was criticizing. He was criticizing only for the sake of being critical. It helped to add another incendiary to the feverous fire of anger that was being fueled by the logs of illogic and empty rhetoric.

His outlandish promises, unwanted criticisms, and lack of a knowledge of international politics prompted many people to say he was merely a con man.

WHAT ABOUT THE INCONSISTENCIES IN HIS PROPOSALS?

We see inconsistencies in his solutions to many problems. For example, if abortion is stopped for women who do not want a child, the local tax rates increase because that unwanted child will need 12 years of education paid by local taxes—at about $10,000 per year per child. Will society be improved and will taxes be reduced if unwanted children are born? One of the simplest ways to reduce taxes is to allow for abortions for people who do not want children. Not only does it reduce taxes for education, but it reduces taxes for the judicial and penal systems. Unwanted children are far more likely to seek the power and approval they need in street gangs and criminal activity. You can't have lower taxes while preventing abortions!

He was adamant that he would appoint an anti-abortion Supreme Court judge, which he did. How would he decide on issues like these? We have seen fundamentalist anti-abortion men kill doctors who are performing legal abortions. Is it really possible that an unborn fetus or embryo is more important than the life of an educated doctor? What about sending drafted young men to wars, knowing that many will be killed or maimed—are they less important than a fertilized ovum?

Reactionary thinking tends to want us to declare war on countries that oppose American politics. In bygone days, war was often the first option for royal avarice-- diplomacy was tardily attempted over the losers' carcasses. How novel now to use economic sanctions to bring the parties to the table. Napoleon would never approve. What cowards we are in the shadow of the mushroom cloud! But not fearless Donald! Do you hear that, rocketman?

Too bad we can't settle this like Aaron Burr and Alexander Hamilton did. Two angry politicians don't need to involve thousands of young lads killing others with whom they have no grievance. True reactionaries, as Trump and Kim are, might consider stepping back into the Wild West past, and meet at the OK Corral. Think of the TV beer commercial revenue—enough to feed North Korea for a year and send son Barron to the college of his choice.

What about tacking on tariffs for Mexico and China. These are our third and fourth major export markets. It is true that the trade balance with China is heavily in China's favor, but Mexico's is not nearly as significant. Tariffs are merely added to the price of the goods imported. So we have a hidden federal tax paid for by the American shoppers. Did the "rust belt" anti-China crew know that their TVs and Smartphones would increase in cost to cover the cost of the tariffs? Or, they pay more for American made goods that were protected by the tariffs. Then when the other countries reciprocate with tariffs of their own, those items cost us more and Americans are paying into the treasuries of other countries, essentially paying taxes to China, Canada, the EU and any other country that puts tariffs on American-made products. Way to go Donald!

When things aren't going well for you, you had better strike out at somebody. But with Trump's solutions you are likely to "quick draw" and shoot yourself in the foot. Trump voters will suffer the most from a repeal of Obamacare and with trade wars with Mexico. Canada, the EU, and China.

According to a major exit poll, Trump edged Clinton by 3% in areas where the family income was between $50,000 and $100,000 a year. The Affordable Care Act, Obamacare, gave premium subsidies to incomes of up to $98,000. The suggested Republican replacement healthcare program relies on tax credits, that is a reduction in the income taxes owed, to reimburse the medical expenses. But these people pay little or no income tax, so the Republican replacement of Obamacare is of little or no value to these people. It benefits the rich people who do pay taxes.

My nephew, who teaches high school, pays $1200 a month in medical insurance for his family of three. He pays far less than $14,000 in income tax. He would lose big in the Republican proposal. For example, in a socialized plan he would pay $7,000 to $10,000 more in taxes and nothing for medical insurance—a net savings of $4,000 to $7,000 per year.

If voters want less government, I wonder about their thinking. For every tax dollar from the state, every state gets some money back. For example, for every dollar South Dakota spends in federal taxes it gets back $7.85. North Dakota gets back $5.30. Florida receives $4.50 and Louisiana gets back $3.30, about the same as Alabama. All these are very "red" states that apparently want less Federal input and more "states' rights." Are they shooting themselves in their wallets?

If Trump is serious about reducing taxes and reducing government spending, it seems that a vote for him would be counterproductive in these states, yet they all voted for The Donald. Did they know that they were voting against federal income for their states?

PAID MATERNITY LEAVE

He promised six weeks of paid maternity leave—the US is the only advanced country without it—and that six weeks will be the shortest maternity leave in the OECD. Several countries have close to a year off, and some require that the father take some of the leave time. Other countries have it as a national benefit paid for by federal taxes. Trump plans for it to be part of the state unemployment insurance—paid for by state taxes. So, he makes a magnanimous requirement that somebody else must pay for, and administer. It's kind of like the schoolboy who says "why don't you and him fight." You make the rule, but you have somebody else pay for it and decide how it is to be implemented.

REPEAL AND REPLACE OBAMACARE

On the second promise, to repeal Obamacare, as he said partway through the House negotiations "Nobody knew health care could be so complicated." He didn't know enough about the many provisions of the Affordable Care Act that people really liked. If he wanted to improve it he should have suggested what Obama really wanted:

➤ A federal option (as all advanced countries have) that would have been cheaper for the citizens, but it would have taken much of the profit from the insurance companies—in CEO salaries and of course shareholders profits;

➢ Pre-existing conditions covered (as all other advanced countries have);

➢ Reduce medical malpractice unlimited legal awards (other countries don't allow themselves to be sued);

➢ Nationalized digital medical records (as Norway has). These allow any doctor you see all your medical and drug information. It also allows you to go to any pharmacy to have your prescription filled—since your prescriptions are in the computer, not in your hand.

We must realize that in America private profits are our number one concern. The welfare of the citizens runs a poor third, after the military.

BUILD A BORDER WALL PAID FOR BY MEXICO

The third promise, to build a border wall, and have Mexico pay for it, is so absurd that we won't even comment. But it was his major promise! Now he is attempting to get it as part of an immigration plan.

SUSPEND IMMIGRATION FROM SOME MUSLIM COUNTRIES

He did attempt to suspend immigration from terror-prone countries. Trump suspended the issuing of US visas or travel permits to people from Iran, Iraq, Libya, Somalia, Sudan, Syria and Yemen. The problem is that the countries he barred had sent no terrorists to the US Between 1975 and 2015 not a single American has been killed in the U.S by citizens from any of these countries. But, of course, there were no Trump properties in any of them.

However, of the European terrorist attacks up to mid-2017, two were from Syria, one from Iraq, and one from Libya. So that might be cause for concern if they have a rowboat to paddle to New York! However, of the major terrorist attacks in Europe up to mid-2017: 16 were from Morocco, ten from Algeria, seven from Tunisia, two from Mali, and one each from Afghanistan, Palestine, and Egypt.

Among those countries he allowed to have their citizens visit the US were: Saudi Arabia, Egypt, and the United Arab Emirates. 3,000 Americans were killed by citizens from these countries in the last 40 years—most in the New York City 9 /11 attacks. Yet, people from those three countries are still welcome to apply for US visas and travel permits. This is probably because Trump has business interests in all three countries.

Saudi citizens killed 2,369 Americans between 1975 and 2015. Also, the Saudi government and some of its wealthy citizens have been reported by US intelligence agencies to have funded radical mosques in the US prior to 9/11. Trump registered eight companies in Saudi Arabia in 2015. "They buy apartments from me," he said. "They spend $40 million, $50 million. Am I supposed to dislike them? I like them very much." Then in 2017 the Saudis bought $350 billion worth of military equipment, $110 billion immediately. What's not to like? And, the cost to rebuild the World Trade Center is only about $15 billion. What a deal! We finally have a trade surplus with a country.

In the past 40 years, Egyptian citizens have killed 162 Americans. The State Department discourages tourists from going there since terrorist attacks have been relatively common in Egypt. Trump has business dealings there, such as the Trump Marks Egypt developments. So Egypt is OK. Indonesia and Azerbaijan have ties to Islamic terrorism — yet neither is on his no-travel list.

In the last 40 years, 314 Americans have been killed by UAE citizens. The State Department has warned tourists that there are ISIS and Al-Qaida linked groups there. Trump has a number of projects in or near Dubai, including two golf courses and a luxury villa development. So, let 'em in!

The Supreme Court in June of 2018 upheld the third version of the ban by that traditional overwhelming majority of 5 to 4. And yes, the killer countries are not banned!

RENEGOTIATE NAFTA AND---

It does look like he is going to renegotiate NAFTA with Canada and Mexico and he has exited the Trans-Pacific Partnership. I wonder if China will fill the void? He hasn't shown signs of renegotiating the Iran nuclear deal or appointing a special prosecutor for Hillary. Maybe the same special prosecutor that is investigating him for colluding with the Russians can investigate her! Or maybe they can both be investigated for their Wall Street ties. If she had been elected, maybe she would have appointed more billionaires to the cabinet than he did. Hardly likely!

WAS HE A SMART POLITICIAN?

The smart politician, not the ethical statesman, will do what is necessary to win—not what is necessary to rule well for the good of the citizens. But which citizens? The larger the country the more diverse are the concerns. In the United States if you want to be president you must win a majority of voters in enough states with enough electoral votes. As you well know, Hillary Clinton won the popular vote by almost 3 million votes but lost big in the Electoral College. So becoming the president in the US takes a different kind of planning than it does in France—where presidents are elected democratically.

Naturally, as an individual with a huge inferiority complex, you must do something to elevate yourself in your group. As a politician with an inferiority complex you must project yourself as the best candidate. With an educated population, you can do that with intelligent proposals that are workable.

With lesser aware voters, just tear down your opponents with either a challenge to the truthfulness of their proposals, or the easy way is to bring them down by insults. This does not raise your status, it just lowers theirs. This is what Donald Trump used throughout the primaries then into the general election. Since this is part of his adjustment to his feelings of inferiority, he continues to insult people in the government and in the media—calling any reports that don't agree with his baseless opinions as fake news. If a candidate that I support pushes others down, I can climb on his shoulders and watch others sink around us. What better way to overcome my own inferiority complex.

Criticizing the person rather than the message is a basic inductive fallacy. As mentioned in previous chapters, this was done continually by Donald Trump in the primaries, the general election, and in his rants against the media. Here are some examples:

> Florida Senator Rubio was "Little Marco" who was "dumb."

> Texas Senator Ted Cruz was "Lying Ted," who was "worse than Hillary."

> "How can Ted Cruz be an Evangelical Christian when he lies so much and is so dishonest?"

> Then he attacked Cruz's wife and father.

> "Be careful, Lyin' Ted, or I will spill the beans on your wife!"

> "His father was with Lee Harvey Oswald prior to Oswald's being—you know, shot. I mean, the whole thing is ridiculous,"

> Former Florida Governor Jeb Bush was "low-energy" and "weak."

> Ben Carson, a primary opponent, "He is worse than Jeb; like Ambien for insomnia. We need energy in the White House." Then he appointed him Secretary of Housing and Urban Development. Is this where we need a low energy person when so many jobs are at stake? Or could Donald have been lying?

> Hillary Clinton was "crooked Hillary" and "pretty dumb."

➤ "Hillary Clinton was the worst Secretary of State in the history of the United States,"

➤ Senator Bernie Sanders was "Crazy Bernie: who was "weak and old."

➤ Senator Elizabeth Warren, a potential challenger in 2020, was "weak," "goofy," and "was worse than Hillary." Additionally, she was often referred to as "Pocahontas."

He was an equal opportunity 'insulter." In his own party he said:

➤ Lindsey Graham, the Republican Senator from South Carolina — "What a stiff, what a stiff, Lindsey Graham. By the way he has registered zero in the polls," At a campaign speech in Bluffton, S.C., on July 21, Trump called him "A total lightweight,. . . In the private sector, he couldn't get a job."

➤ Mitt Romney, the Republican nominee of four years earlier, — "Why would anybody listen to Mitt? He lost an election that should have easily been won against Obama. By the way, so did John McCain!"

➤ Senator John McCain of Arizona, — "He's not a war hero." He further said at a rally on July 18, "He was a war hero because he was captured. I like people who weren't captured." This followed a July 16 tweet saying that McCain should be defeated in the primaries and that he graduated last in class at Annapolis, followed by "what a dummy."

These anti-hero statements were made by a man who avoided the military draft for Vietnam by continued student deferments. In late July 1964, he got a student deferment. In December of 1965 he got another one. In November 1966, he was classified 1-A as suitable for the draft. So, in December he got another student deferment. In January 1968 he got another one. Then in July he was classified again as 1-A. In October 1968 he was classified as 1-Y, for service only in time of war. Then in February 1972 he was classified as unfit, 4-F, because of a heel spur. Heel spurs are very common among most populations. When asked, Trump could not remember which foot was affected! He was in college during the major part of the war from 1964 to 1968. Of course, he could have volunteered like McCain and Kerry did!

THE PRESIDENTIAL POPULARITY CONTEST

Once in the presidential race, Trump continued his approach of pushing down his opponent in order to make him feel superior and to make his audience think he was superior. He had only a 40% approval rating, probably because of his: anti-minority, sexist, wealth-flaunting, and crude approach to the election. Hillary had her own problems. While her ratings had been as high as 65% when she was a Senator and Secretary of State, her approval ratings during the election process were around 45%. So both candidates were viewed rather negatively—in fact quite negatively! Why was she viewed so negatively? The reasons given generally were that:

➤ She was highly educated, which increased the feelings of inferiority of uneducated women and men;

➤ She was connected with the Washington establishment which is nearly always a target in elections;

➤ She did not divorce her husband for his affairs (some saw this as a positive);

➤ Her email situation, which Trump continued to charge as being traitorous even though the FBI called it careless and not criminal.

It is true in democracies across the world that the people are always upset with the leadership, but they keep voting them in. Congress has a 20% approval rating yet incumbents generally win. "My guy is a good guy, but those others are all worthless."

But that brings us to the next point. Thomas Hobbes wrote that we are all equal because we are content with our own amount of common sense. In observing people at every age in many cultures for 80 years, I would add that people are content with their own facts and opinions. But this is often counter to what is required for developing an effective society in the 21st century.

After all, if intelligence were as common as people think it is—why is the world in such a mess?

THE TRUMP CAMPAIGN

Normally in modern campaigns there are a number of strategists who tell the candidates what to say and to whom. Trump had this information and the approved message was on his teleprompter, but it seems that he often abandoned the teleprompter and went off on his own. This is probably more effective because he was transmitting his superiority "persona," which masked his own inferiority feelings, to his audiences many of whom had the same feelings of inadequacy. Both longed for power.

His base could feel they had a champion—so it made them feel powerful. If politicians can learn anything from Trump's actions it might well be that there should be more appeals to the psychological side of the people than to their intellects.

Roger Ailes, the founder of Fox News, the only trustworthy source of real news – according to Trump—gave us the winning formula. In his book, "You Are the Message," he wrote that to be successful in media or politics one should be emotional, not intellectual.

This, of course, is the major concern of this book—because we think that democracy needs our intellects, not our unconscious emotions, leading the way. We need the details, but Roger said "just use themes, avoid the details." Trump followed his advice—and won. Ailes used this concept in developing Fox News into a major network.

Trump's approach was to promise much, without any details, and say he could do it because he had built a great business. He did it with big and small lies, fake news, impossible promises, promises that sounded good but actually hurt his constituents, and appeals to their unconscious minds—making his supporters feel superior.

People often mistake faith or hope for thinking. Then they reinforce their hopes with anything they hear, whether it is totally true, partially true, or totally false.

You have lost your job, or are in danger of losing it. Why?

➢ China makes it cheaper.

➢ Mexicans work cheaper than I do.

➢ NAFTA, the North American Free-Trade Agreement, lets people in other countries take my job.

Very simple explanations! Could it be that the widget I was making, or the coal I am mining, is no longer needed? Is it possible that other people are making it cheaper so consumers around the world can buy it cheaper? Is it possible that fewer people need coal—and is it possible that because of technology that fewer people are needed to mine each ton? Is it possible that Internet shopping is outpacing brick and mortar stores? Is it possible that computers, robots, 3D printing, drones and self-driving vehicles are making many people economically disposable?

Am I capable of being retrained for a 21st century job? Employers in the US say they have plenty of jobs open but cannot find qualified people. But for many of the unemployed, complaining is easier than retraining!

THE UNCONSCIOUS MIND—OUR UNFELT SOURCE
OF FEAR AND HOPE

As we have mentioned, the largest part of the mind is unconscious and it controls far more of our actions than we would like to admit. There are very few people, if any, who do not have some remnants of their inferiority feelings directing, some of their behavior. most of us have very large needs for power to overcome our basic inferiorities. Consequently, when we hear an appeal to do something that will make us feel more powerful, we are likely to do it. Trump did this better than any politician I have ever seen. Most have appealed to our intellects, to our selfishness, and to our hopes. Trump appealed to the intellects of some people in business— promising fewer regulations and cuts in business taxes. But for most of us he appealed to our need for power, our fears and our hopes. It worked! The question is, whether in a modern democracy this is the best way to choose our leaders.

Nearly all politicians, all of the effective advertising companies, and all psychologists know what motivates people. Fear, anger, hope, making them feel superior, and making life easier, are among the most common motivators.

The electorate should be smart enough to understand whether a proposal is helping them or hurting them. And it would be nice if we could tell when we are being manipulated by appeals to our power drives in our unconscious minds where our inferiority complexes sit.

SOME MAJOR MOTIVATORS

POWER

He appealed to our power drives by telling us that we have the ability to help him "drain the swamp" in Washington. If we believe in him we can feel better about ourselves because we backed the winner. As Christians, we should make our country Christian again. Let's get rid of the Muslims or at least stop more from coming in. We need to bring back family values and stop abortions. But pussy grabbing is OK—It's all in fun. We are better than those raping, drug dealing Mexicans who are taking our jobs by working harder and for less money.

While we are at it, let's bring back torture. That will put us in a really powerful position. We'll make those guys talk! It doesn't matter that the FBI says it doesn't work. I've seen it work on TV.

PRIDE

Pride goes along with our need for power. If I can do something that reduces my inferiorities I should feel proud about it. Let's make America great again!

The fact is that: Trump did not mention why America is not great. This was always a problem for those who think.

➤ America is the world's greatest economic power. It has the world's largest and most capable military.

➤ Its Summer Olympic team won nearly twice as many medals as the UK or China, the second and third placers.

➤ American teams always win the World Series and the Super Bowl. (Of course, they are the only ones that play in those games!)

➤ Admittedly we are only second to China in global CO_2 emissions, but we are far ahead of Russia and India. Of course, global warming is only a hoax perpetrated by the Chinese. So we are probably really number one here, too!

We are still waiting for The Donald to tell us what we need to do to be great again. Should we have another revolution? It looks like we just did! Do we need more classic Disney cartoons? Do we need more money for education? Should we have more people in college, and should they study there with free tuition? Other countries do this. Should we have better roads and bridges? Should we have better relations with Russia? There are certainly a lot of areas where we can be better. Which ones did he mean?

➢ We are Americans, so we are better than everybody. This helps to give us a feeling of pride—even if we are high school dropouts and unemployed.

➢ Those damn Mexicans are rapists and drug abusers and they are taking our jobs. We have to remove them because we are better than they are.

➢ Those Muslims are all trying to kill us. Heck they kill everybody, even their own kind. We don't need them. They even pray to the wrong God and on the wrong day! And why do they take their shoes off when they pray? Everybody knows that God wants you to pray with your shoes on.

➢ Hillary Clinton is a crook and we should lock her up. We are better than she is because we divorced our spouses when they were unfaithful. The Bible says we can do that.

➢ China is taking our jobs and they are a currency manipulator—whatever that is.

All of these arguments give us feelings of pride and power because we are better than our state in life would indicate.

We should certainly fear Islamic terrorism. 9/11 and the Orlando and San Bernardino shootings show us that. What about hotels in Las Vegas? What about shootings in schools, like: the Sandy Hook Elementary School, Columbine High School, Parkland High School, Virginia Tech University? There have been more than a couple hundred school shootings in America starting even before the Declaration of Independence was signed. Should we outlaw students? Will arming teachers and students increase or decrease this factor? Based on what we know from a psychological perspective, it will increase killing considerably. But one thing we know is that the Supreme Court's 5 to 4 decision in 2008, interpretation of the Constitution gives us that right.

With our fear of terrorism on our minds, let's ban all Muslims. Not only should we ban Muslims from coming into our country, but we should have a registry of those who are already here—all 3.3 million of them.

But there are so many things to be afraid of! Chicago's murder rate is out of control. Let's make America safe again.

Immigrants are taking your jobs and are reducing your pay. Let's get rid of them all. In fact, let's just keep the people who came over on the Mayflower. My own relatives came from Ireland in the 1860s to the 1880s. Let's get rid of me!

Donald Trump's ancestors immigrated a generation later. Actually, his grandfather came to America in 1885, ostensibly to avoid military service in Germany. He opened a restaurant, which apparently doubled as a brothel, in Seattle. (I wonder if avoiding military service and an affection for paid sex is genetic.) Anyway, grandpa returned to Germany, then back to the US, then back to Germany where the authorities found him to be a draft dodger which was against the law. (It seems to run in the Trump family!) He came back to America in 1905 and Donald Trump's father was born that year. So his grandfather was a refugee fleeing from prison in Bavaria. It's a good thing for Donald that Teddy Roosevelt was president and accepted immigrants who had broken the law in their own country. Of course, Germans have no history of starting wars or other terrorist activities. It seems that Donald is not quite ready to send all of us who are descendants of immigrants back to where we came from—and leave the country to the Native Americans.

As Donald has told us, countries that accept Syrian refugees "have great problems just as happened in Sweden." Oops! This was fake news that he had heard on Fox News. Maybe he should have listened to those other fake new outlets, like CNN,

CNBC or read those fake news tabloids, like The New York Times or the Washington Post—but they all missed that Swedish story. Do you think that possibly they check their news sources before publishing them?

YOU HAD BETTER HAVE A GUN

If you are afraid, you'd better have a gun. The Constitution allows it you know!

If you are interested in what the Constitution actually said as opposed to what a majority of one said in that 5 to 4 decision in 2008 (District of Columbia v. Heller, 554 US 570) you may be amazed.

The Court found that the D.C. ban on handgun possession violated the Second Amendment right because it prohibited an entire class of arms favored for the lawful purpose of self-defense in the home. It similarly found that the requirement that lawful firearms be disassembled or bound by a trigger lock made it impossible for citizens to effectively use arms for the lawful purpose of self-defense, and therefore violated the Second Amendment right. The Court also decided that the Second Amendment right applies not only to the Federal Government, but also to states and municipalities. So, this overturned the earlier Cruikshank case.

As will be addressed later, the Supreme Court makes its decisions based primarily on the basic assumptions of the judges—whether they are religious, in which religion, and whether they are more in line with the ideas of the Democratic or Republican parties. They can twist the laws and the Constitution in many ways. For example, in the above-mentioned case, it gave citizens the rights to own guns for their protection and that the gun need not be disassembled nor locked. In this case, the Second Amendment phrase which allows guns states that: "A well regulated Militia, being necessary to the security of a free State, the right of the people to keep and bear Arms, shall not be infringed."

In previous Supreme Court cases, it was the first phrase "a well-regulated militia being necessary," that was considered the primary concern. In the Heller case, it was the second phrase, "the right of the people to keep and bear arms, shall not be infringed," was considered primary. Any person with an English or philosophical background would see it as a totality. However, the judges wishing to give more freedom to gun owners decided to make the phrase which is obviously primary, having a "well-regulated militia," of minor importance. It is very clear that at the time of the Constitution's writing, the threat of being attacked by England or other entities was a real concern. Remember that this new "right" has only been around since 2008. But it was extended to all states in 2010 in McDonald v. City of Chicago. Would you believe that the same five judges that changed the meaning of the original Constitution in the Heller case expanded it to include all the states. Billy the Kid would be so proud of them.

Previous cases had used the original Constitution's meaning as the guide to the decision. In United States v. Miller, 307 US 174 (1939) it was the "well-regulated militia" clause that was primary when Miller brought a sawed-off shotgun across state lines.

In a much earlier case, United States v. Cruikshank 92 US 542, 553 (1875), it was decided that the Second Amendment applied only to the federal government, not to the states.

The Heller Court, however, stated that the right to keep and bear arms is subject to regulation, such as concealed weapons prohibitions, limits on the rights of felons and the mentally ill, laws forbidding the carrying of weapons in certain locations, laws imposing conditions on commercial sales, and prohibitions on the carrying of dangerous and unusual weapons. It stated that this was not an exhaustive list of the regulatory measures that would be presumptively permissible under the Second Amendment. So the "right" is not really unlimited—as the National Rifle Association seems to tell us. In fact, they are suing Florida because it just raised the gun purchasing age from 18 to 21, after the Parkland High School shooting. Now we have a major problem—with the increased age for buying guns, what is a disgruntled student to do? Sling shots, rocks, and cursing are all that is left!

So, while the right to own guns, for most people, is the law of the land, it has only been true since the decisions made in 2008 and 2010. One might suspect that the writers of the Constitution would disagree with the recent court decisions—at least if we can believe Founding Father James Madison's essay in Federalist Papers, Number 46. He tells us of the intention of the "right to bear arms" phrase. It was all about a national guard to protect the nation. It wasn't about hunting or self-defense. But why are we paying Supreme Court Justices if it isn't to change the meaning of the Constitution? At least it keeps them off the welfare rolls!

Has the Heller decision increased or decreased murder rates? Murder rates reached a high of 9.8 murders per 100,000 people in 1992. They then dropped spectacularly to 5.8 in 2007, before the Heller decision. They continued downward to 4.5 in 2014, then rose to 4.9 in 2016.

If the Heller decision slowed murder rates because of homeowners being allowed to use handguns, it is nearly imperceptible because of the steep and continuing decline of the murder rate from 1992. That steep decline has been attributed to the national availability of abortion since the Roe v. Wade decision in 1973. Steven Levitt of the University of Chicago and John Donohue of Yale University made this claim in their 2001 paper "The Impact of Legalized Abortion on Crime." It was popularized In Freakonomics, a book by economist Levitt in 2005. The book has sold more than four million copies.

Their findings were that 19 years after abortions were made legal, murder and many other crime rates, dropped. It doesn't take much sociological and psychological knowledge to conclude that women who didn't want children would most likely not be the most loving and caring parents. And as mountains of sociological research has shown, unloved children are most likely to attempt to satisfy their inferiority complexes and need for power by resorting to the most primitive instincts—physical power. And power is easily utilized in anti-social situations, such as in murder and other crimes.

There are some who do not like to associate the "evil" of abortion with the "good" of reduced crime rates. Some have attempted to reason that the rise in crack cocaine use in the 90s and the ensuing imprisoning of its users is the reason for the drop in murder rates. The evaluation of this idea has not shown this to have a significant effect on murder rates. The availability of abortions seems to be, far and away, the best answer we have today.

If abortion reduces crime rates, but Trump wants to make it illegal while "making America safe again" is he again advocating conflicting ideas for solving a problem? It's similar to his ideas of:

❯ Lowering taxes while lowering the national debt,
❯ Attempting to reduce jihadist terrorism while allowing the most likely terrorist counties to have its citizens allowed into the US (i.e. Saudi Arabia and Egypt),
❯ A middle-class tax cut that mainly benefitted the rich,
❯ Increasing tariffs on China and Mexico that would bring higher consumer costs,
❯ Erecting a wall paid for by Mexico, now being paid with American tax money,
❯ Saving jobs with Carrier paid for with tax credits, made up by local taxes,
❯ Reducing soldiers in Afghanistan, then sending 4,000 more soldiers,

➢ Spending $60 million to bomb an empty airfield after Syrian gas attacks,
➢ And so many more!

ANGER

Anger is one of the best ways to motivate people. Anger may come from either the intellect, when you realize you are somewhat powerless against the forces that control your life, or it may come from deeper down in the mind, in the unconscious mind. The unconscious anger can be developed because of your feelings of inferiority and powerlessness in general. There is much of our behavior that comes from deep down in our minds but we rationalize or become angry without knowing exactly the source of our discontent. We think we know, but we cannot really know the exact source of our anger—because it springs from our unconscious. It is highly likely to come with poor parenting. However, we may blame our government—or whoever our candidate tells us to blame. If you don't have a politician to tell you who to blame, you always have your spouse!

This might be such an example. A person who is unloved as a child, is quite intelligent, but either dropped out of high school or stopped his education at high school graduation. He then works in a factory or in retail and is frustrated because he knows he could've done better. He may blame the government because of his unhappiness, but it is really his parents who should be blamed—and maybe even himself. In politics we know that the government has done a terrible job for us. We need to get rid of that Washington establishment. Or as The Donald promised, he would "drain the swamp." He was going to do this several ways. One was to impose term limits on the legislative branch. This of course could never be done, but we would all like to see it happen. Of course, we can blame Hillary. Let's "lock her up." She is a part of those Washington insiders, so she must be to blame. Let's vote against "lying Ted" and "little Marco." They are all to blame!

The majority of people are never totally happy, they always want to change to something better—and it seldom is. It is really not possible to meet everyone's felt needs and not increase taxes. It's also not possible in the US to fight business interests for the good of the common citizen. The "pull yourself up by your own bootstraps" motto is often as impossible as teaching a fish to talk.

The simplest way is to aim the anger, which is already present, toward your opponent and even your opponent's family. The next level is the Congress. While not all Congressmen are ineffective, it would seem that today a majority are. They are so concerned with protecting their parties that they forget to protect their constituents. Then you can go to the next level, the lobbyists. Those who lobby for what you want are the good guys, those who don't are evil and deserve your anger. Once you have aimed anger at all the possible targets within your borders, look beyond. Have the Europeans cheated us on NATO? Have the Chinese done anything, real or imagined, that we can criticize? What about drugs coming in from Central and South America? We should be angry and do something about it. What about computer engineers from India coming over and taking our jobs? What about outsourcing telecommunications entities to Ireland, India, or the Philippines? They are all taking your jobs, so you should be angry.

Remember, that as a politician your statements do not have to be true, they just must be believed by your potential voters. So what is the way to make other people's anger work for you? Trump did a masterful job—with the help of Fox News, reactionary radio commenters, Russian trolls, fake news from digital sources like InfoWars and some Macedonian teenagers. And we can't forget his major advisors: Steve Bannon, Kellyanne Conway, and Michael Flynn.

You will find that traditional news and the right leaning news often report on different news events. For example, in May of 2017 CNN and MSNBC were emphasizing Trump's problems in Washington, like the Comey firing and the appointment of a special prosecutor to investigate links between Russia and the Trump campaign, while Fox News was reporting on the visit of the Columbian president to Washington and the runaway driver in Times Square. One might wonder if their selections of news were from the same world. So it is not only fake news with which we should be concerned, but with whether or not we are given all the news.

"Muslims hate us," Trump said in the electoral speeches, but he took a very different approach in his speech in Saudi Arabia. Getting elected may require one set of messages. Dealing with other nations may require a somewhat different message. The Middle Eastern Muslims were quite familiar with his ranting about Muslims hating America and with his proposed travel bans on several Muslim countries. Could they really believe his conciliatory speech before over 50 Muslim heads of state—especially when he emphasized the Saudi's buying over $350 billion in armaments from the US? What's his motivation to have more Middle Eastern countries buy more armaments from America, or was it to help fight ISIS—as he said? Quite possibly it was the combination of the two.

POWER OR ANGER AS MOTIVATIONS

It is quite common that our psychological motivations make us react in one way, then we rationalize our actions by what we believe, or what others tell us to believe. Jihadist terrorists attack primarily because of a drive for power that is based on deep-seated feelings of inferiority from their earliest years, or because of anger developed because they have not achieved as high as they would like. Then because of a rabid religious teacher or jihadist' sites on the internet, they become radicalized and act out their frustrations violently. They then rationalize their actions as being for Allah, and because of this they expect to go to Paradise if they are killed.

We see this rationalizing of anger or of inferiority driven power actions in many other groups. Neo-Nazis and other white supremacist organizations have the same motivations. Antifa, a supposedly anti-fascist group which should be approved of by most Americans, often does the same type of senseless violent behavior. We see this violence in street gangs, in pro- and anti-Zionist groups and in many other violent—usually young male—groups.

Such groups are always driven by the need for power, but sometimes it is the need for power to satisfy one's anger, sometimes for power achieved through the acquisition of money—such as drug gangs or extortion.

Violent youth gangs often give rise to adult organized crime. We see this in nearly every country. Murder is quite acceptable in these pursuits. The difference between the youth gang violence and the adult organized crime is primarily that the youth attack by burning cars, looting, smashing store windows, and fighting. These are rationalized by supposedly higher callings, such as: doing it for God, protecting my street and territory, protecting my race or nation, or other such reasons that sound good. The organized crime of the adults is not rationalized. It is unquestionably for money.

HOPE

Fears can be created or enlarged. Anger can be inflamed. Our conscious minds want to be safe so just about every serious politician in every country plants fears in our minds. Your taxes will go up. Immigrants will take your jobs. Your enemy is arming itself for a nuclear war. You have an unhealthy water supply. Your health insurance rates will go up. Global warming will make much of the land uninhabitable. The retirement age will raise. Your pension will be cut. Your tuition will rise. Under my opponent, the prisoners will go free. You can certainly imagine another 50 or 60 fears that may make us consider an alternative to the present.

But the flip side of this is that I can save you. A typical candidate might say, "Your only hope is me. I will reduce your taxes. I will eliminate college tuition. I will repeal Obamacare. I will provide drinkable water, I will reduce the national debt."

"I don't have to tell you how I'm going to do this. I am certainly not going to raise your taxes or increase the national debt. Just trust me!"

Some politicians actually have plans that might work. But those of us in the electorate are not sufficiently knowledgeable about economics, accounting, world affairs, physics or chemistry to be able to understand the proposals and project whether or not they will work.

Rebuilding the infrastructure is certainly necessary. But what infrastructure are we going to rebuild?: roads, bridges, dams, water supply, electricity and renewable energy, or re-pave Wall Street?

Increasing pensions and lowering the retirement age sounds good, but with us all living longer and with the increased cost of healthcare and the lack of qualified people for the technological jobs that are available—how?

Promises are like clouds. Look at them now and they have one form. You look at them now and the form has changed. Change is the constant in all of life. We listen to the promises of our politicians, and we realize that they have as much chance of them being realized as I do of making water into wine.

"I will bring back jobs," Trump said. He emphasized coal and steel producing jobs. The steel industry has lost 48,000 jobs in the last 17 years. The coal industry has lost 65,000 jobs in the last 25 years. Coal is now mined by machines, and driverless trucks move the coal. The jobs are just not there. But hope does not need reality.

He hasn't shown any interest in the 500,000 jobs lost in retail sales since 2001. Maybe that's because it has affected women, youth, and minorities primarily.

In May 2017, the Green Party of Denmark suggested as part of its promises to the voters that it would reduce the workweek from 37 hours to 30. It did not say whether the Danes were expected to work 20% harder during their 30 hours so that production would not fall. It did not project how this might affect their import–export balance. Presently they are practically balanced with about a hundred million dollars more in exports. To make up for fewer exports will they increase taxes?

They are already taxed at about 50% of their gross national product. Will they make up the human labor difference by using robots and 3D printing? What if the Vietnamese use the same labor enhancing technologies and work 40 hours a week? Will the Danes still be able to compete? Promises by politicians should be accompanied by the economic realities. Dream on, realistic citizen!

Bringing manufacturing jobs back to the US is a top priority for President Donald Trump, who has made "Buy American, Hire American" a key element in his pro-business agenda. However, the manufacturing industry is no longer what it used to be. According to the US Bureau of Labor Statistics, 4.9 million manufacturing jobs have disappeared in the past 20 years—in part because of increased automation. Industry executives say today's manufacturing is about collaboration with innovation, and learning to work with robots as partners.

Using modern technologies, American manufacturing may become more competitive with the cheaper labor costs of East and Southeast Asia. But the Asians are not standing still. They too are employing higher levels of technology. So there is a race between the lower labor costs of Asia, with some advanced technology, and the higher labor costs with more advanced technology in the West. Macy's will close 68 of its hundred stores. Payless Shoe Stores will be closing hundreds of stores. The Sports Authority has filed for bankruptcy as have many other retailers in the last year. Trump will have his hands full! But then he never promised to get retail sales jobs back!

He promised jobs in coal and in steel. In an executive order on March 28, 2017 he reversed the Obama regulations to reduce climate change. Trump denies that humans cause climate change in spite of the overwhelming scientific evidence that they do. He also assumes that people will buy coal if the coal miners go back to work. The Clean Air Task Force estimates that 7,500 Americans are killed by breathing coal-produced pollutants in a year. This is down from 13,000 in 2010. The suggested reason is that the number of coal powered plants has been reduced from 523 to 251. This is a result of cheaper fuel being available, such as natural gas and renewable energy. Another factor in the loss of coal mining jobs, from 220,000 in 1980 to 65,000 today is the increased use of higher-level technology and automation that is reducing jobs in most blue-collar occupations.

Trump's plan to put coal miners back to work is about as realistic as bringing back shorthand stenographers, Morse code telegraph operators, and horse and buggy drivers. The realities are that the type of jobs available continue to change. When Neanderthals went hunting bison with spears, it became unnecessary when they domesticated them.

Once people plowed the fields behind bullock and plow, tractors took that job away in the advanced economies. Traditional jobs are being lost in great numbers yet there are many openings for qualified people in engineering, robotics, and computer science. Having a strong arm is seldom required today, what is needed is a strong mind powered by an effective education.

Part of his jobs program might have been to increase the Army to 540,000 active duty soldiers, rebuild the Navy to 350 ships, and increase the Marine Corps to 36 battalions from 23. He also wanted to provide the Air Force with 1,200 fighter aircraft. However, his budget proposal falls quite short of these goals.

The President also ordered a review of foreign-worker visa programs in hopes of encouraging domestic corporations to hire more Americans, though the details of implementation are unclear; effects on the H1-B visa program won't be immediately known, as this year's visa process won't be affected.

Trump has been quick to take credit for the state of the economy, including claiming credit for job gains that came under President Barack Obama. He is also celebrated for the same monthly jobs reports he had suggested were fraudulent under the Obama administration. There have now been 81 straight months of job gains. I don't know how he plans to take credit for the 75 months of gains before his inauguration. Certainly, Barack couldn't have had anything to do with it.

In fact, there probably weren't any job gains then. Trump was emphatic, when in campaigning he said the unemployment rate might be as high as 42%. Then when he was president, the 4.8% unemployment rate was accepted. Then a year later it went to 4.1%. His cutting of regulations and tax cuts may have had something to do with it. The new jobs are in construction, clerical and secretarial areas, and discount retail like Target and Home Depot. His tariffs may increase the steel employment to make up for the 2% of steel that was imported from China. Of course, if Canada and South Korea increase their exports to the US there might not be much of a need for American-made steel. But the tariffs on them in June 2018 will increase the price to American industrial users of steel and aluminum.

In his speech in Saudi Arabia he said he had created 3 million jobs. This was about six times higher than the true number. But who believes "truth" anyway!

What's more, Trump's anecdotal claims of success have repeatedly been found to be exaggerated or had been announced months and sometimes years ahead of his presidency, like when he touted 900 new or saved jobs in Michigan that were part of a larger effort that saw a net loss of 200 jobs, or when he boasted of saving a Ford plant in Indiana from being relocated when it was not up for relocation. He said he saved 1000 jobs at Carrier, promising $7 million in tax credits—which will have to be paid by taxpayers or by borrowing—thereby increasing the national or state debt again. Within a year 700 of those jobs had been lost.

Trump's only action to date on an infrastructure project is his approval of permits for the Keystone XL and Dakota Access pipelines. With that, Trump made good on one campaign promise while reneging on another: The Keystone XL pipeline won't have to use American steel in construction, despite a White House order mandating American made pipes.

Meanwhile there are other pressing job related problems. Retailers lost nearly 30,000 jobs in March of 2017, and nearly 90,000 retail jobs were lost in the preceding six months. This is particularly true of the general retail stores like: Macy's, JCPenney, Sears and Nordstrom. It's been a tough month for the retail industry, with more than 1,000 stores closing their doors for good. Luxury retailer Michael Kors announced it would be closing over 100 locations, and electronics giant Radio Shack closed 1,000 locations across America.

The retail industry, which represents $5 trillion in economic impact, has changed significantly over the past several years. More than 100,000 workers have lost their jobs since October 2016. Hiring has picked up in 2018 and over 12 million are now employed in retail.

Online marketing is a major factor. These will lead to more human job losses. Still companies like: Lowe's, Home Depot, Walmart, and Costco are doing well.

Possibly The Donald will roll back the clock and require horses and buggies for transportation instead of driverless cars and trucks. The big business guys wouldn't like that! They just want fewer regulations and lower taxes. Maybe he can eliminate the robots and computers. However, this might affect his own building programs. If we roll back the clock far enough we will all have to live in Trump-Tents instead of Trump Towers.

It may have dawned on some people that one businessman may not know all about all businesses. Overseeing hotel and golf course buildings may not give one the knowledge to deal with the macroeconomics of the world or the varied agricultural and industrial businesses in the United States.

We sure hope he will get rid of ISIS and all that terrorism. He sure showed 'em when he sent 59 missiles, costing a million dollars each, to ravage an empty airfield. It took the Syrians almost 24 hours to repair the runways. I'll bet they'll think twice before they gas any more kids!

> We hope that he will make America great again. But what are his plans?
> We hope he will make America safe again—but how?

►   We hope that he will eliminate ISIS and other terrorist organizations—but how?

HOPING THERE IS NO CLIMATE CHANGE REASSURES SOME VOTERS

Here are some unbelieving tweets from the Tweeter-in-Chief, showing he doesn't understand the critical difference between weather, which is short-term, and climate, which is long-term:

➤ "The concept of global warming was created by and for the Chinese in order to make US manufacturing non-competitive." (Nov 2012 tweet)

➤ "I did not. I did not. I do not say that." (First Presidential debate versus Clinton, reminding him of what he said in November of 2012))

➤ "This very expensive GLOBAL WARMING bullshit has got to stop. Our planet is freezing, record low temps, and our GW scientists are stuck in ice." (Tweet 2014)

➤ "NBC News just called it the great freeze - coldest weather in years. Is our country still spending money on the GLOBAL WARMING HOAX?" (Tweet 2014)

➤ "Snowing in Texas and Louisiana, record setting freezing temperatures throughout the country and beyond. Global warming is an expensive hoax!" (Tweets in 2013 and 2014)

➤ "Ice storm rolls from Texas to Tennessee - I'm in Los Angeles and it's freezing. Global warming is a total, and very expensive, hoax!" (CNN interview 2015)

➤ "I believe in clean air. Immaculate air.... But I don't believe in climate change." (2014 interview)

➤ "Well, I think the climate change is just a very, very expensive form of tax. A lot of people are making a lot of money. I know much about climate change. I should be receiving environmental awards. And I often joke that this is done for the benefit of China. Obviously, I joke. But this is done for the benefit of China, because China does not do anything to help climate change. They burn everything you could burn; they couldn't care less. They have very—you know, their standards are nothing. But they—in the meantime, they can undercut us on price. So it's very hard on our business." (Interview on Fox and Friends)

➤ "Obama's talking about all of this with the global warming and...a lot of it's a hoax. It's a hoax. I mean, it's a money-making industry, OK? It's a hoax, a lot of it." (2015 rally)

He does not know that geologically we have been in a cooling phase for a few thousand years. But the more than 1000 thermometers throughout the planet, in the oceans and on land, in cities and in the mountains, are all showing us that the world is warming significantly. How many thermometers does Donald Trump have measuring the Earth's temperatures? And how many years has he been measuring it? The thermometers that are used by the official climate agencies have been monitored for at least 50 years and many for over 100 years. Of course, verifiable facts have never been a concern for The Donald. The only facts that are really important are how much is that land going to cost me and what will the buildings cost me.

THE CAUSES OF CLIMATE CHANGE—IF YOU STILL DOUBT

Climate change is caused by a number of "greenhouse gases" that reflect the Earth's heat back to the Earth, thereby warming it more than would be normal without the reflecting gases. We hear most about carbon dioxide (CO_2) from oil and coal burning. Methane is another, largely from intestinal gases and feces from animals and people. These greenhouse gases can affect warming for anywhere from minutes to millennia. It depends on their various half-lives.

The half-life of a compound is how long it takes to break down half of the original amount. As an example, Delta 9 tetrahydrocannabinol (delta 9THC), the major psychoactive ingredient in marijuana, has a half-life of 7 to 10 days, depending on the make-up of the body that smoked it. If no more marijuana was smoked, in a week there would be half of the original amount. In another week, half of that, etc. Alcohol has a half-life of a few hours. But it might do more damage to the body in two hours than the longer acting marijuana. Of course, each body reacts differently to each chemical put into it.

The same situations occur in the atmosphere. The relatively rare greenhouse gas SF_6 (sulfur hexafluoride) has a half-life of 3,000 years. But that gas is nowhere near as important for warming as CO_2 (carbon dioxide) with a half-life of about 50 or more years, or methane with a half-life of 7 years. Other greenhouse gases have half-lives of a few minutes to hundreds of years.

The world releases about 40 billion tons of carbon compounds annually into the atmosphere. 40 billion may not seem like much, but it's more weight than Arnold Schwarzenegger has lifted in his whole life!

The most potent greenhouse gas is water vapor. The amount of water that air can hold depends on the temperature of the air. The warmer the temperature, the more water can be absorbed. This creates drought conditions in the warmer areas. Then when the atmosphere cools, often because of Arctic weather patterns moving south or upper atmospheric jet stream changes, rain or snow storms are much more intense because there is more water vapor in the air that can no longer be held.

The severe storms of the northeast are attributed to the increased water vapor from global warming being released in summer or winter storms—so we call it climate change, since global warming can affect weather patterns in summer or winter. In the century before 2011, the northeastern US states saw their average temperature rise 2 degrees Fahrenheit. In the next 40 years it is expected to rise another 5 to 10 degrees.

One might think that the hot weather in Texas might have sucked up any groundwater and resulted in the serious droughts experienced there. Then the cooling released all the water vapor and flooding occurred. If this had happened in New England or California it would have been recognized as the effects of climate change. Luckily for Texas, the oil industry protects it from the effects of warming and climate change. It is the only place in the world where climate change is not happening. Lucky Longhorns!!

THE PARIS ACCORDS

Trump wants to renegotiate the Paris Accords. Other countries say "No."

Not everything is negotiable internationally. National interests are different from business interests. Trump may have been able to negotiate between several contractors who all wanted to build a hotel for him, but it's different negotiating with a world that wants to save itself—being led by other heads of states.

Thankfully, his intention to exit the Accords cannot begin until after the next presidential election—and he may not be hovering in the Oval Office in 2021.

DRAIN THE SWAMP

It is always a good political idea to blame anyone who has been there before you. Let's get rid of: all the Congressmen by term limits, any people left over from the executive branch, and all the lobbyists. What a great idea, Donald!

But he didn't exactly clean the swamp. He did bring in some people without extensive Washington experience. Lots of rich people who may not have the citizens' interests foremost in their minds. We might expect that being businessmen, they would be primarily interested in business. Whether this will translate into many more jobs in coal mining and steelmaking is yet to be determined—but it is doubtful.

When we look at his appointments to cabinet posts, as he refills the swamp, we see some people who seem to have interests at cross purposes to the departments they are heading.

Rick Perry, when running for the presidential nomination in 2011, wanted to eliminate the Department of Energy. He is now its boss. When he was Governor of Texas, a major concern was oil interests. Because of the reality of carbon monoxide and carbon dioxide spewing into the atmosphere from oil products, regulations were put in place by Obama that reduced the profits of the oil companies. He's out to change that.

Scott Pruitt, Secretary of the Environmental Protection Agency, brought many cases against the agency when he was the Attorney General in Oklahoma, another oil heavy state. He had bragged about the competition he had with the Attorney General from Texas relating to who could file the most cases against the agency he now heads. He vowed to have a "regulatory rollback" to protect certain businesses. It certainly does not matter that global warming is one of the two major problems facing the world. I wonder if he realizes that Americans are part of the world.

Betty DeVos, now the Secretary of Education, would like to reduce the amount of money spent on public schools and deferred to charter and religious schools, many of which are operated for profit. This is in spite of a large number of studies that show that public and charter schools score very similarly on math and reading testing. Also, very few charter schools take students with special needs, both the physically and the mentally impaired. And no unruly kids need apply. Let the public schools take them. She has no experience in teaching or in the public schools. Her experience is primarily in being very very rich!

Ben Carson, now the Secretary of the Department of Housing and Urban Development, is a neurosurgeon with no experience in housing or development. But he lived in the "projects" when he was young. So we see two departments hated by the people who oppose the missions of their departments and two departments headed by people with no experience in the areas they now supervise.

But is it a swamp or a country club swimming pool? Former Veterans Affairs Secretary David Shulkin took a trip to Europe with his family and a security detail, spending more than half of his time sightseeing and attending the Wimbledon tennis tournament on free tickets-- which was illegal.

So far, the Trump department heads have spent over $2 million in unnecessary or illegal charges, including $1 million spent by Tom Price, the former Secretary of Health and Human Services, for various flights including to a resort property he owns and to see relatives. I don't understand why people are upset, he is human and he was providing himself with a service.

The Environmental Protection Agency administrator, Scott Pruitt, has taken a number of charter flights including one to Morocco to promote the use of fossil fuels. This only cost $40,000, but this was added to another $60,000 for other flights. It is not understandable to me that the EPA Inspector General has opened an investigation of these trips. It is my understanding that no fossil fuels were used because he took all of his trips on gliders. But then he did spend $25,000 on a privacy telephone booth for his office. This too seems reasonable. Soundproof telephone booths are necessary for talking with one's girlfriends, political backers, and Russian trolls.

Housing Secretary Ben Carson, spent $31,000 on a dining room table for his office. He fired the secretary who would not approve the expense. All this while contending that the people in federal housing projects were too comfortable. But we can all understand that as Secretary of Housing, he needs a dining room.

There have been many more such expenditures by Trump's appointees. But people don't seem to understand how expensive it is to drain a swamp when the alligators are in charge of the operation.

PRESIDENTIAL TEFLON

When you are the leader, remember that you're always right. You can rationalize, lie, deflect the blame, change the subject or use any number of political techniques that will absolve you of any knowledge of what may have gone wrong. You must be perfect to be in the position you are in, so don't ruin it with ethical behavior. Hillary Clinton was able to take the blame for using the private email server when she was Secretary of State. That admission of negligence was enough to turn many voters against her— even though the FBI didn't find enough wrongdoing to prosecute. Obviously, she was not perfect.

But Donald was as perfect as one can be--what with: grabbing pussies, making false statements in over 70% of the "facts" he stated, being the defendant in about 2,000 legal cases, and being involved in 6 bankruptcies of his businesses.

PRESIDENTS HAVE HAD TO APOLOGIZE IN THE PAST

Barack Obama was ethically strong enough to admit if he made a mistake. But he was already President.

Three weeks after Hurricane Katrina was so mismanaged by the Bush team, Bush apologized saying, "Katrina exposed serious problems in our response capability at all levels of government. And to the extent that the federal government didn't fully do its job right, I take responsibility."

Bill Clinton went the "I'm responsible" route, too, which is essential in presidential apologies—and pretty unavoidable in the case of sex since it's not like he could affix blame for that elsewhere in his administration.

If you must apologize, after everyone knows you did wrong, Reagan's speech was classic:

"Now, what should happen when you make a mistake is this: You take your knocks, you learn your lessons, and then you move on. That's the healthiest way to deal with a problem. ... You know, by the time you reach my age, you've made plenty of mistakes. And if you've lived your life properly— so, you learn. You put things in perspective. You pull your energies together. You change. You go forward."

Nixon, in classic presidential style, denied knowing about Watergate, but at his resignation he apologized to those few who were there. "I'm sorry. I just hope I haven't let you down." Then a few years later in a TV interview he was more candid. "Well, when I said: 'I just hope I haven't let you down,' that said it all. I had: I let down my friends, I let down the country, I let down our system of government and the dreams of all those young people that ought to get into government . . . . Most of all I let down an opportunity I would have had for two and a half more years to proceed on great projects and programs for building a lasting peace."

But their apologies were done by people not afflicted by the narcissistic personality disorder. Getting a severely narcissistic person to apologize is more difficult than getting him to part the Red Sea, or admitting that he has a personality disorder.

MISDIRECTION OF BLAME TO OTHERS

Blame others for your failure.

"I inherited a mess," is frequently repeated by The Donald, as well as that CNN and CNBC are "fake news".

The fact is that the mess he inherited included an economy in which the high unemployment rate had dropped from 10% in 2010 to under 5% when he took over, and an economy that was growing about 18% faster than the economies of Europe. The Dow Jones had nearly tripled under the Obama administration. The number of military troops had been reduced significantly even though the military budget had increased. Where was the mess that Trump inherited? Was it in the unswept streets of Toledo or the problems with his casinos?

Attorney Roy Cohn had worked for Sen. Joseph McCarthy in the 1950 communist "witch hunts" and was introduced to Donald Trump in the early 1970s. He was very close to Trump and defended him in counter-suits against the government for violations of the Fair Housing Act in which he had different rental terms for black and white renters in 39 of his buildings. Cohn countersued the federal government on Trump's behalf for $100 million. Trump lost the case but never admitted guilt.

Cohn's advice was to always attack those who disagree with you. Sue them and never admit guilt. These "rules" Trump has followed continuously. He said he would sue the women who accused him of sexual harassment or abuse, after the election. So far, he has not. When students at Trump University sued him for fraud, he countersued then settled for $25 million, not admitting guilt. Of course, he can deduct the $25 million as a business loss.

Cohn was disbarred in 1986 for several illegal actions including: professional misconduct, witness tampering, and perjury. It is conceivable that Trump will eventually follow his mentor's exact illegalities.

DIVERSIONARY TECHNIQUES

At the debate in St. Louis he said that if it were up to him Clinton would "be in jail." This became a rallying cry of his supporters to "lock her up."

Ten days later, Trump insisted at the Las Vegas debate that allegations made against him by nine women of groping and other unwelcome physical contact were baseless. He said he would sue them.

On the campaign trail, he said that he would appoint a special prosecutor to investigate Hillary Clinton. But when a special prosecutor was appointed to investigate his campaign's contacts with Russia, he called it a "witch hunt." Mueller hasn't yet found his warlock, but he has found several spooks and ghostly behavior among them—including making money invisible. Several have admitted their wrongdoing. One might think that these breadcrumbs of guilt might lead to the witch's house.

RELAX LIBEL LAWS TO BE ABLE TO SUE THE PRESS

Libel means "to publish in print (including pictures), writing or broadcast through radio, television or film, an untruth about another which will do harm to that person or his/her reputation, by tending to bring the target into ridicule, hatred, scorn or contempt of others."

"Libel is the written or broadcast form of defamation, distinguished from slander, which is oral defamation. It is a tort (civil wrong) making the person or entity (like a newspaper, magazine or political organization) open to a lawsuit for damages by the person who can prove the statement about him/her was a lie…"

If Trump were to be able to change the free speech guarantees of the Constitution as the Supreme Court has amended it, there are many who could sue him—all his rivals in the primaries as well as Hillary, for instance.

He said, "there was zero growth in the GDP, in fact it was below zero." This of course was false. Since the third quarter of 2014 there had been positive growth every quarter, ranging from 0.5% to 5.2%. In 2014, the GDP growth was 2.6%; in 2015, it was 2.9%; in 2016, 1.5%; and in 2017, 2.3%. The first quarter of 2018 is projected to be 1.6%.

In 2014, the dollar had dropped to about $0.70 against the euro, then it increased in value to about $0.96 at the end of Obama's term in December of 2016. Under Trump it then began a consistent drop to $0.80 in April of 2018, a 16% drop. As of this writing (June 2018) it is down 10%;

The stock market rose 6000 points from January 2017 to early March 2018, a 30% rise. Then in March of 2018, Trump's association with Cambridge Analytica, which had used Facebook in his election campaign, dropped Facebook's value; his imposing tariffs threatening a trade war; then his challenge to the major online shopping outlet—dropped the market to under 24,000. So, as of April 2018, the Dow-Jones had risen 20% while the dollar had dropped 10%, a 4% rise in 15 months--so the rise in buying power against the euro was an annualized 3%.

Meanwhile Argentina's market rose 77%, Nigeria's rose 48% and Turkey's 42%.

And, he said, that we might have had 42% unemployment under Obama. We never know if he is purposely lying to the audiences or if he is lying to himself. Does he really care if what he says is not factual?

He talked about China killing us on trade deals. There are no such deals. We are both members of the World Trade Organization.

He said the reason for the Trans-Pacific Partnership was to aid China, when the exact opposite was the reason for the partnership. Among other things, it would prohibit child labor and give workers collective bargaining rights.

He said he could get the economy to a 4% growth rate. The first quarter of 2017 was 1.2%, the worst in three years. The second quarter was about 3% and the year of 2017 ended with 2.3% growth—which is very good, particularly for a Republican administration. Since World War II, the average growth rate has been 4.4% under Democratic administrations and 2.5% under Republicans.

TRUMP AND CHARLOTTESVILLE

President Trump used his freedom of speech guarantee to express some truths about the confrontations of the right and the left in mid-August of 2017 in Charlottesville, Virginia. What he said was true. Why was there such an outcry from nearly everyone about his press conference blaming both sides? He said that white supremacists and Nazis had a permit to demonstrate and the counter-protesters did not. He said there were violent people on both sides. He said that there were nonviolent people on both sides. All of this is true. Why the outcry?

The "Unite the Right" group of Nazis, KKKers, and their sympathizers had a permit to demonstrate. Their right to free speech was guaranteed by the Supreme Court in Brandenburg v. Ohio in 1969. Brandenburg, a KKK member, who had advocated violence against "niggers and Jews," was represented by the American Civil Liberties Union which had four Jews on its nine-member board. The Supreme Court's unanimous decision affirming his right to free speech included Justice Thurgood Marshall, an African-American.

Not all states allow a person to carry a firearm in public. Virginia does. California does not. This was protested in June of 2017 in Peruta v. California, but the Supreme Court refused to hear the case so California, or any state, can prevent the "open carry" option for firearms. Two judges protested it not being heard, John Gorsuch, the Trump appointee to the Court, and the Black conservative Justice, Clarence Thomas.

So what the alt-right, Nazi, and KKK and their sympathizers were originally doing was legal. Of course, there is a difference between what is legal and what is ethical! I can't think of any other country that would allow the open carrying of guns and the hate expressed against Jews and African-Americans. But then, the ethics of the society are normally incorporated in its laws. So, I guess it is ethical in America—only in America!

After this "legal" demonstration began, counter demonstrators emerged. Some demonstrators were also prepared to fight. Some alt-right demonstrators attacked some unarmed black youths and beat them up. As the alt-right marchers paraded down the streets they chanted, "You will not replace us," "Jews will not replace us," and "Blood and soil"—a Nazi phrase indicating pure blood and the tradition of our land. It is not difficult to understand that such phrases go against American and Western democratic ideals.

It is easy to see how the inferiority complexes of the marchers were empowered by the thousands of other power-seeking comrades. And of course, as Christians, the Jews have traditionally been an object of envy, and the Blacks are conveniently the antithesis of whites.

It is easy to see how a tough "patriot" like James Fields, even though he wasn't capable of qualifying for the Army, so was released, was tough enough to beat up his mother at home and later ram his car into a group of people who were protesting his Nazi ideas. The one dead woman and the 19 injured by him deserved it! How could they protest against the white Christian ideal? How could they protest against the thousands of people who needed their togetherness in order to assuage their inferiority feelings?

Trump, as in so many other cases, saw only what he wanted to see. He felt that truth is in the eye of the beholder. What he did not see was that his eye had a serious astigmatism, or was blind. There is an objective reality out there—too bad he is blind to it. If it is OK to form a large legal gathering to chant hate slogans at other citizens, and the Supreme Court says it is, maybe a Constitutional amendment is necessary to require the Court to make its decisions based on the legislative intent of the writers of the laws being interpreted.

MAKE AMERICA SAFE

He harped on the violence in Chicago which is certainly a problem. Chicago was possibly selected because it was the residence of Barack Obama, his predecessor, and the birthplace of Hillary Clinton, his opponent in the election. He bragged about his Mar-a-Lago golf course in Florida where he played nearly every week in his early presidency. But the nearby town of West Palm Beach in Florida had a higher rate of crime than did Chicago. Here are the rates per 10,000 per year.

	VIOLENT CRIME	PROPERTY CRIME
WEST PALM BEACH	67.6	61.4
CHICAGO	58.9	52.1
USA	31.1	38.1

It is a matter of selecting which facts you will present, or you can just use "alternative facts!"

HIRE AMERICAN, BUY AMERICAN

But he hires foreign workers at Mira Lago and his other businesses because he can't find Americans to do the jobs. And Ivanka has much of her merchandise made in Mexico and China. But it's all you other people who should hire Americans.

Politicians know that you must be pragmatic to win. Statements and charges that help you win an election may not help you at the negotiating table with other nations. While ethical statesmen may keep their promises, they may even change their positions as new evidence emerges, but the consummate politician is not averse to changing positions often and abruptly. Trump did this a number of times in his first four months.

FBI director, James Comey, was praised because he investigated Hillary Clinton's emails, then was fired supposedly for not doing enough investigative work on those emails. But it was clear that the real reason was that the FBI was investigating the links between Russia and Trump and his close associates.

During the presidential campaign, Trump repeatedly criticized China for taking American jobs and for manipulating its currency. After meeting with their president and realizing the potential harm that North Korea could do with its missile and nuclear programs, he realized that China could be an asset. It was no longer a currency manipulator nor an economic threat. There was a bigger shark in the fish bowl.

As mentioned earlier, NATO was now an important ally, especially as he found himself on the other side of the bombs from Putin in Syria.

Russia, which he had courted during the campaign, was now an adversary in the Mideast. But Russia should not be left out in the cold if doing so might anger its leader. Consequently, as mentioned, when he got upset with the Syrian bombing with poison gas and sent missiles to destroy the airport that housed the bombers, he alerted Putin, so there were no planes there when the $60 million in missiles blew up the dirt airstrip. But what a show of force!! It would be enough to scare any spineless dictator. But it seems that neither Assad nor Putin are cowardly lions.

"We have wasted an enormous amount of blood and treasure in Afghanistan," Trump tweeted in 2013, just one of many such broadsides. In an earlier interview with Fox News' Bill O'Reilly, Trump insisted that "money should be spent in our country, we should rebuild our country. ... Let's get with it, get out of Afghanistan."

Then in September of 2017 he sent more than 3,000 additional troops to Afghanistan, which his military advisors strongly suggested. We all have the problem of thinking that we know more than we actually do. Once we are in a position to act we generally have more information and more insight. This happens in our own relationships as well as in decision making at every level. Trump may have learned, as we should, that criticism without all the facts is often absurd. You know the old Native American saying, "Don't judge a person until you have walked a mile in his moccasins."

It is difficult to know just how much Trump is an uninformed liar and, how much he is a skillful politician or negotiator. When he talked to the President of Taiwan he said that he might not continue the "one China policy." His campaign promise of tariffs for Chinese made goods and his calling of China a "currency manipulator" sounded very anti-China. He now had three chips he could play in his negotiations with Chinese leader Xi Jinping. But it seems that now that he is buddies with Xi, he doesn't have to play them.

POSSIBILITY OF IMPEACHMENT

Because of his continual lying and many of his stated policies, legislators on both sides of the aisle, and apparently more than fifty percent of the electorate, are seriously talking about impeaching him.

There are a number of ways that a United States government official can be impeached. Impeachment means accusing an official of wrongdoing. If a person is impeached by the House of Representatives, which takes a majority vote, the trial is held in the Senate with the Chief Justice of the Supreme Court presiding. To be found guilty, the Senate must have two-thirds of the Senators (67 votes) affirming the guilt of the accused official.

At the present time, with Republicans controlling both Houses, bringing articles of impeachment now would probably be a waste of time—although the way President Trump "tweets" policies and angers Congressmen, it could be possible in the next year or so. However in January 2019, if the Democrats control the House, as is probable, based on the historical precedent of off-year elections and the low ratings of the President, it is almost certain that they will pass articles of impeachment. While it is likely that the Democrats will pick up some seats in the Senate, it is impossible to gain a two-thirds majority.

In the 2018 election, 34 Senate seats will be contested. 25 are already held by Democrats. If they keep all 25 and pick up all the Republican seats, they would have 57. If this were to happen in an impeachment trial, they would need all Democrats and ten Republicans to convict. Anti-Trump Republicans Flack and Corker will not run for re-election, and Senator McCain might die of his brain cancer by that time.

It is becoming more likely that more Republicans will break ranks with Trump because they: disagree with his policies, are afraid that they might not be re-elected if they support him, or are threatened by the Trump or Bannon approaches that seem to be attempting to split the Republican Party—making it more reactionary and less conservative. If the few elections in November of 2017 are any indication, threatened senators may trek from Trump.

CONSTITUTIONAL REQUIREMENTS FOR IMPEACHMENT

Many are looking forward to Trump's impeachment, but so far there is only some evidence of actions or inactions that might be considered "high crimes or misdemeanors," which Article II of the Constitution requires for impeachment.

"Article II, Section 4. The President, Vice President and all civil officers of the United States, shall be removed from office on impeachment for, and conviction of, treason, bribery, or other high crimes and misdemeanors."

But what are "high crimes and misdemeanors?"

HIGH CRIMES AND MISDEMEANORS

"High crimes and misdemeanors" means misconduct, be it criminal or public, committed by people high in the government. The "high" does not indicate a special type of crime but rather indicates the position of the one committing the misconduct as an official. Officials serve the public interest, and if they commit an offense that heaps mistrust on them, even if the offense is not a crime or under criminal law, the official may be guilty of high crimes and misdemeanors.

It was first used in the late 14th century in England when the King's Chancellor broke several promises to Parliament. He had not followed the advice of a parliamentary committee on how to improve the kingdom. In the mid-15th century this charge was also levied against an English Duke for obstructing justice, cronyism, wasting public money, and treason. In the early 18th century it was used again and included charges of: negligence, abuse of power, abusive trust and using his position to make financial profits.

According to the Supreme Court, as early as John Marshall's tenure, it was decided that such terms of law as "high crimes and misdemeanors," should be used in their original intent and not in a modern version.

In the United States, "high crimes and misdemeanors" has been used against judges for: chronic intoxication, soliciting a bribe, tax evasion and/or perjury. In Bill Clinton's case, it was perjury before a grand jury dealing with his sexual misconduct and a related obstruction of justice charge. The vote was along party lines with Republicans being in the majority in the House of Representatives. He was accused by majority vote on two of the four charges brought against him. Being accused (impeached) he was then tried in the Senate which also had a Republican majority. However, although you need only a simple majority vote in the House to impeach, you need a two thirds majority vote in the Senate to convict. He was not convicted.

IMPEACHABLE OFFENSES

With these possibilities in mind, what acts of misconduct can be said to be impeachable offenses? President Ford probably said it best when he said that, "impeachable offenses are whatever Congress says they are."

Because the United States, like England, uses what is called "common-law", laws set by judicial precedent, we can go back hundreds of years to other countries to find cases that back up our contentions. Most countries use the laws as they are written, often called Napoleonic law, to determine guilt or innocence. But with common-law, clever attorneys or House of Representatives members, can often find precedents in other states or countries to back up their position.

Under Napoleonic law, as is common in Europe, the letter of the law would be upheld, so there might be no impeachment possible.

CATEGORIES OF HIGH CRIMES AND MISDEMEANORS

Here are some ideas on high crimes and misdemeanors that some academics gave to the House of Representatives before the Clinton impeachment. They included:

Political crimes: crimes that affect the nation, not all crimes qualify. So if the person takes a bribe to sign a law, that would be a political crime. If he has sex with someone or shoplifts a tuxedo for the Inauguration Ball, that would not be a political crime. Obstruction of justice might be a political crime, depending on the total circumstances.

Offending the sensibilities and values of the public: public drunkenness and or browbeating a witness have been found to be impeachable offenses for judges. It is possible that illicit sexual encounters, as with Clinton, or sharing secrets with the Soviets, as with Trump, might be impeachable under this category.

Other categories might include breaking international treaties and agreements, which may or may not be laws or include an action by a national leader that runs counter to the interests of the citizens of the United States— such as withdrawing from the Paris Accords.

A question is whether any crimes committed by people in "high" places must be equal in severity to treason or bribery. How severe to the national interests must an action be before being impeachable? It would appear that Clinton's sexual activities would not be severe enough, but was his perjury in front of the grand jury about the activities of a high enough order?

The other impeached president, Andrew Johnson, was impeached for having fired his Secretary of War, whom Congress had approved and strongly supported. Johnson, Lincoln's vice president, was more sympathetic to the South than his hostile Congress The hostile legislators in both cases were Republican majority Congresses. In both cases the Senate did not convict them. Clinton was 17 votes clear of being guilty, Johnson only one.

Richard Nixon would have been impeached by the Democratic Congress but resigned before it happened.

POSSIBLE HIGH CRIMES

There are many possible crimes committed by people high in the government that might lead to impeachment such as: treason, obstructing justice, bribery or colluding with Russia. One might wonder if Trump's pulling out of the Paris Accords is against international law—but it isn't. It does not have to be, however. Was it in the best interests of the citizens of the US or the world? If not, is it a high crime? Is lying to the citizens after being elected a high crime?

A number of different interpretations have been used to try to explain what is meant by "High Crimes or Misdemeanors." From Madison's papers to modern legal research we might find that these qualify:

A serious injury to the constitutional system-- (Would appointing cabinet members whose past experience was counter to the duties of the department they headed qualify?)

Would his impeding the pursuit of the truth in the investigations of Russian involvement in the election tampering qualify? (Would any obstruction of justice qualify? Richard Painter, ethics lawyer under George W Bush, says the president's involvement in Trump Jr.'s comments to Mueller, suggests an "obstruction of justice.")

Democratic Representative Al Green submitted to the House a list of factors that he thought were impeachable offenses. These included: a demonstrable record inciting white supremacy, sexism, bigotry, hatred, Islamophobia, and the decision for stopping transgender soldiers from serving in the military. Here is his introductory paragraph:

"Donald John Trump, President of the United States of America, unmindful of the high duties of his high office and the dignity and proprieties thereof, and of the harmony, respect, and courtesies which ought to exist and be maintained in American society, has under the inane pretext of dispensing with political correctness, produced a demonstrable record of inciting white supremacy, sexism, bigotry, hatred, xenophobia, race-baiting, and racism by demeaning, defaming, disrespecting, and disparaging women and certain minorities. In so doing, Donald John Trump, President of the United States of America, has fueled and is fueling an alt-right hate machine and its worldwide covert sympathizers engendering racial antipathy, LGBTQ enmity, religious anxiety, stealthy sexism, and dreadful xenophobia, perfidiously causing immediate injury to American society."

A SERIOUS BREACH OF DUTY

Madison doesn't mention whether a breach of duty needs to be against the US only. In our globalized society, could that breach of duty be against the world? If so, leaving the Paris Accord climate change agreement could be against the world.

Is lying on the campaign trail a misdemeanor? When voters are told absolute lies and vote for you because of them? Is this a high crime or misdemeanor?

Is lying about opponents a misdemeanor? It may be robbing the electorate of an honest candidate.

Endangering the freedom of the citizens may qualify. Would his attacks on the free press qualify? How about his rants against Muslims and Mexicans and endangering their freedom? In Portland, Oregon, two men died protecting two Muslim women who were being harassed by a ranting white supremacist.

Abusing the powers of the presidency may qualify. Would excluding countries where his company held properties from his "Muslim ban" be a consideration? What if those countries had provided terrorists who had attacked America? Saudi Arabia, the

United Arab Emirates and Egypt accounted for 94.1 percent of all American deaths in terrorist attacks on US soil committed by the foreign-born.

OBSTRUCTION OF JUSTICE

Obstruction of justice is defined in the omnibus clause of 18 USC. § 1503, which provides that "whoever . . . . corruptly or by threats or force, or by any threatening letter or communication, influences, obstructs, or impedes, or endeavors to influence, obstruct, or impede, the due administration of justice, shall be (guilty of an offense)." Persons are charged under this statute based on allegations that a defendant intended to interfere with an official proceeding, by doing things such as destroying evidence, or interfering with the duties of jurors or court officers.

A person obstructs justice when they have a specific intent to obstruct or interfere with a judicial proceeding. For a person to be convicted of obstructing justice, they must not only have the specific intent to obstruct the proceeding, but the person must know (1) that a proceeding was actually pending at the time; and (2) there must be a nexus between the defendant's endeavor to obstruct justice and the proceeding, and the defendant must have knowledge of this nexus. (18 USC. § 1503)

Here is Title 18, Part I, Chapter 73 of the US Code, noting the most likely paragraphs that could lead to an impeachment for an "obstruction of justice" charge.

- 1505 - Obstruction of proceedings before departments, agencies, and committees
- 1506 - Theft or alteration of record or process
- 1510 - Obstruction of criminal investigations
- 1511 - Obstruction of State or local law enforcement
- 1512 - Tampering with a witness, victim, or an informant
- 1513 - Retaliating against a witness, victim, or an informant

wa1515 - Definitions for certain provisions; general provision

- 1521 - Retaliating against a Federal judge or Federal law enforcement officer by false claim or slander of title.

Under § 1505 a defendant can be convicted of obstruction of justice by obstructing a pending proceeding before Congress or a federal agency. A pending proceeding could include an informal investigation by an executive agency.

The special prosecutor, Bob Mueller, has indicted several close Trump associates and is apparently trying to include the President in the list of people who have been proven to have some link, such as conversations, with Russians. So far, he has: Trump's former campaign manager and Chief of Staff, his son, his son-in-law, his former National Security Advisor, and a number of other people. Trump himself may be investigated for obstruction of justice because he fired James Comey who was investigating the Russian involvement in the 2016 election.

NOT PROMOTING THE GENERAL WELFARE OF THE PEOPLE

In looking at the Preamble to the Constitution "We the People of the United States, in Order to form a more perfect Union, establish Justice, insure domestic Tranquility, provide for the common defence, promote the general Welfare, and secure the Blessings of Liberty to ourselves and our Posterity, do ordain and establish this Constitution for the United States of America."

Does it promote the general welfare of the United States to take us out of the Paris Accords? Does it promote the general welfare when global warming changes the climate and causes or compounds such devastation as Hurricane Katrina, Hurricane Harvey,

Hurricane Irma, Hurricane Sandy? These were all made considerably worse by global warming.

The oceans are warmer so evaporation is easier. Since the air temperature is warmer, evaporation is easier from the oceans and other bodies of water, and because of the warmer temperature of the air, more water can be held in the atmosphere as water vapor, which is then released as heavy rain when the atmospheric temperature is reduced. Because of the water temperature, the ocean volume is higher so the storm surge could move higher into the land, as happened in the Gulf Coast states. Fossil fuel use and the operation of many manufacturing sites, such as cement manufacturing, all increase the release of greenhouse gases. Trump is promoting their use.

TREASON AND COMMON LAW

In April of 2017 a convoy of cars carrying the main opposition leader of the Zambian president did not stop to allow the president's motorcade to pass. Two days later the opposition leader was arrested and jailed on a charge of treason—he supposedly had put the president's life in danger. So there might be varying definitions of treason, under common law. This might be an avenue for enterprising lawyers to pursue. Treason under this concept might be putting citizens' lives in danger by withdrawing from the Paris Accords. If citizens are the de facto rulers in a democracy, then killing a "ruler" might be considered treason.

But Trump's own definition of treason is much less. The draft dodging Trump, as Senator McCain labeled him, called Sergeant Bowe Bergdahl "a traitor who should be hanged." Bergdahl left his post in Afghanistan to walk to another military post to report what he believed to be incompetent leadership at his station. He was captured by the Taliban and caged and tortured for 5 years. He did leave his post, which was illegal, but he was not deserting. Ask yourself—where would you go if you were going to desert your post in Afghanistan? Disneyland?

In a preliminary hearing, the Army's chief investigator, Maj. Gen. Kenneth Dahl, testified that he had found no evidence that any soldiers had been killed while specifically searching for Sergeant Bergdahl. Neither was there evidence that the sergeant intended to desert and join the Taliban. General Dahl also testified that he found Sergeant Bergdahl to be truthful, albeit naïve and delusional, and that jailing the sergeant would be "inappropriate."

Mr. Trump should make himself aware of the US definition of treason, found in US Code 18, paragraph 2381: "Whoever, owing allegiance to the United States, levies war against them or adheres to their enemies, giving them aid and comfort within the United States or elsewhere, is guilty of treason and shall suffer death, or shall be imprisoned not less than five years and fined under this title but not less than $10,000; and shall be incapable of holding any office under the United States." The US was not in a declared war in Afghanistan, and Sgt. Bergdahl had no intention of giving comfort to the enemy.

Treason is defined even more narrowly in the Constitution in Article 3, Section 3, "Treason against the United States shall consist only in levying war against them, or in adhering to their enemies, giving them aid and comfort."

Would giving classified information to Russians, while visiting him in the White House, be giving aid and comfort to an enemy? No. We had not declared war on Russia, for one thing. And when a president gives out information that was previously considered "classified," it is no longer classified. When he tweets previously classified information, similarly, it is no longer classified. Therefore, treason would not be grounds for impeaching Trump.

But the US uses common law concepts, so it might be possible to see an enemy of the United States in such people as: the Koch brothers, or organizations such as the Petroleum Institute, or the coal company Southern Company—since global warming has been a factor in such weather incidents as the heavy rain and snow storms in the Northeast, the droughts and subsequent floods in Texas and California, the stronger than normal hurricanes in the Caribbean and Gulf of Mexico, and not to mention the severe increase in forest fires often due to excess drying of the trees and brush in the West due to warming. These are estimated to have cost the US $300 billion so far plus hundreds of lives lost.

Is it possible that people inside or outside the US who spend large amounts of money denying climate change because it will hurt their businesses, like the Koch brothers, actually are "enemies of the United States?" And those, like Trump, who follow those people are treasonous because by not fighting the causes of global warming and climate change it will damage the US and the world far more than any war of muskets and cannons.

USING THESE IDEAS HOW MIGHT TRUMP BE IMPEACHED?

Treason and bribery are, so far, highly unlikely grounds for Trump's impeachment. If it is eventually shown that he was bribed by the Russians to put them in a better light and to remove the US economic sanctions against them for their help in the election—that would clearly be bribery. And, although they definitely helped in getting him elected, there is no evidence that he promised anything in return—so far. It undoubtedly will be dependent on the findings of the Mueller investigation.

On the other hand, if the Russians have information on him, such as video tapes, that prompted him to be bribed into working for Russian causes—as is widely surmised— this could be an impeachable offense. His advocacy for readmitting Russia into the G7, his advocacy of populist parties that seek to break down the European Union or NATO, and his releasing previously classified information and revealing their source as intelligence gathered by allies—all indicate preferential treatment for a nominal political foe.

OBSTRUCTION OF JUSTICE

At the present time, this looks like the most viable option.

Sally Yates, a veteran of 27 years in the Justice Department, became the acting Attorney General on Inauguration Day when her superior resigned. She was fired 10 days later after she instructed the Department of Justice not to defend Trump's executive order of January 27, 2017 which barred immigration from seven predominantly Muslim countries. She believed that it violated Constitutional requirements. This order was later stopped in the courts. She also warned Trump that the White House was being misled by General Flynn about his calls with the Russian ambassador before the inauguration. She also told the White House that there was a possibility that Russia would be able to blackmail Flynn.

The White House said in a statement that Sally Yates "betrayed the Department of Justice by refusing to enforce a legal order designed to protect the citizens of the United States." (The order was subsequently found to be illegal.)

James Comey was dismissed as the Director of the FBI for several reasons. One was that he would not pledge loyalty to Trump. Another was the FBI's investigation of possible Russian meddling in the 2016 presidential election. Another was that the President thought that removing Comey would make it easier to negotiate with Russia if there were no investigation on the Russian interference. The President had also asked him to stop the investigation into former National Security Advisor Michael Flynn. If Trump were to fire Robert Mueller, that would be a major factor in an obstruction of justice charge. (As of June, 2018, Mueller reported that Russia was still attempting to manipulate American elections.)

Trump also noted in his letter of dismissal that Comey could no longer effectively lead the FBI. In another letter in the case it was said that he had lost the support of members of the Bureau. This was later denied by members of the Bureau. Others have said that Trump was angry with Comey because he would not back up his story that Obama had wiretapped his office during the election period and that he refused to stop the Russian investigation. There may be questions about whether some of these actions were merely inappropriate, as House Speaker Paul Ryan mused, or whether they were obstructions of justice.

Relative to the potential testimony of Donald Jr. before Congress, there has been information leaked that Donald Sr. had a hand in turning some of the phrases to less incriminating statements.

The firing of Comey may qualify, especially if Robert Mueller's investigation and grand jury indictments yield evidence that Trump actually knew of, or approved of, the Russian meddling in the election. As more establishment Republicans strongly disapprove of Trump's behavior or as they fear the Bannon-Trump reactionary threats to their Congressional seats, this type of evidence could tip the scales.

HAS THE HOTELIER-IN-CHIEF VIOLATED THE CONSTITUTION"

The District of Columbia and the State of Maryland have filed suits claiming that Trump's hotel, just down the street from the White House is siphoning off profits from other hotels and convention centers because lobbyists and other groups and people are hoping to curry favor with the president by using his hotel. This is corruption, according to the complainants, and is against the Constitution. The cases will undoubtedly end in the Supreme Court.

UNKEPT PROMISES TO THE CITIZENS

If unkept promises to Parliament were sufficient to impeach in pre-democratic England, might promises made to the people in a democracy also be impeachable? Trump made nearly 700 promises on the campaign trail. In his first 100 days he had broken 80 of them. He had said that he would keep 34 of his promises on the first day in office. He did fulfill two. In his first month in office he kept seven promises but broke 64.

Among his un-kept promises are:

➢ Getting funding for his wall between Mexico and the US

➢ Mexico would pay for the wall. (Mexico absolutely refuses to pay, and would consider such a wall a hostile act.)

➢ Imposing a mandatory two-year prison sentence for those entering the US illegally. (No bill yet introduced.)

➢ Repealing and replacing the Affordable Care Act (Not done)

➢ Restoring National Security Act, and rebuilding military (bill introduced, no budget action)

➢ Drafting a bill to reduce unemployment of Americans when companies move offshore. (No bill yet.)

➢ Middle class tax relief (His proposals benefit the rich primarily.)

➢ Restoring Community Safety Act (None introduced).

There are many more, but unless the Supreme Court changes its mind, lies and libel are expected in campaigns, so are not usually actionable. In Susan B. Anthony List v. Driehaus (573 US ___[2014]) the Supreme Court unanimously overruled Ohio District

Court decisions based on Ohio law that made it illegal to knowingly use false information against a candidate in an election. The Ohio law was overturned on free speech grounds. Where there are false statements made, the aggrieved person has the opportunity to answer the charged based on his own free speech rights—"then let the voters decide." (This assumes that the voters will hear the offended candidate and that the candidate has the appropriate amount of time to answer and that the same channels will be available to the wronged candidate as to the liar.)

However, since the decision addressed only lies about a candidate with whom an organization disagreed and not with promises to future constituents— post-election false promises may be actionable. Among his State of the Union promises were:

"Dying industries will come roaring back to life; heroic veterans will get the care they so desperately need. Our military will be given the resources its brave warriors so richly deserve." No evidence of this yet.

"Crumbling infrastructure will be replaced with new roads, bridges, tunnels, airports, and railways, gleaming across our very beautiful land. Our terrible drug epidemic will slow down and ultimately stop, and our neglected inner cities will see a rebirth of hope, safety, and opportunity." No evidence of any of this yet.

"Above all else, we will keep our promises to the American people. It has been a little over a month since my inauguration, and I want to take this moment to update the nation on the progress I have made in keeping those promises." This may retroactively make his campaign promises actionable in an impeachment hearing.

"And I have issued a new directive that new American pipelines be made with American steel." (No directive was made, only a request to the Secretary of Commerce to come up with a plan. It would appear to be against the non-discrimination international treaties of the GATT (General Agreement on Tariff and Trade) and the WTO (World Trade Organization.) Article 1 of WTO and Article 3 of GATT. There is a direct comparison between the Trump proposals and the case that the US brought against Canada in 1984. The United States has brought more cases against countries using their own products than has any other country.

"We will stop the drugs from pouring into our country and poisoning our youth, and we will expand treatment for those who have become so badly addicted. (No action so far. In October, nine months after this promise he moved to appoint Representative Tom Marino as the drug czar, but when it was learned that he had sponsored a bill that was aimed at undercutting enforcement efforts to stop the opioid abuse, he withdrew from the nomination.)

Relative to his promise to expand treatment for those who are addicted, in October 2017 he eliminated the cost-sharing reduction payments of the Affordable Care Act which would affect 6 million low and moderate income Americans. His executive order was designed to stop the Federal financial assistance to individuals earning less than $30,000 a year or families earning less than $60,000 per year. This would eliminate or lessen the previous action in which the government might pay $3,200 of a $3600 yearly health insurance premium.

Later in October he declared the opioid epidemic to be a national "public health emergency." This allowed about $64,000 dollars of public health funds to be spent of the problem. That's about $1300 per state. With that much money to work with, we should probably expect the opioid crisis to be eliminated by next Wednesday! Had he called it a "national emergency," billions of dollars would have been available.

He also said, "According to data provided by the Department of Justice, the vast majority of individuals convicted of terrorism and terrorism-related offense since 9/11 came here from outside of our country. (According to data from New America, all 12 jihadists who have committed fatal terrorist attacks in the United States since 9/11 have been either native-born citizens or legal permanent residents.)

"To launch our national rebuilding, I will be asking the Congress to approve legislation that produces a $1 trillion investment in the infrastructure of the United States, financed through both public and private capital, creating millions of new jobs."

TRUMP'S CLIMATE CHANGE PROGRAMS ARE DANGEROUS TO CITIZENS

Trump signed an executive order to curb the federal government's enforcement of climate change regulations on February 14, 2017. The order rescinded six executive orders of President Obama that required the government to prepare for climate change, and outlined the "growing threat to national security" that climate change poses. Trump's policies reduced federal aid for creating jobs and safeguards to protect America.

It allows corporate polluters to have free reign. It increases the danger to the health of Americans and the citizens of the world.

His appointment of Scott Pruitt as EPA administrator brings a person who denied that carbon dioxide is a primary contributor to climate change (from a CNBC interview in early February, 2017). As Attorney General for Oklahoma he had brought a number of suits against the EPA. Rick Perry of the Department of Energy, and Ryan Zinke, as Secretary of the Interior, are others who want to increase fossil fuel production.

HEALTH COVERAGE FOR THE NATION

Tom Price, his Department of Health and Human Services Secretary, fought against the Affordable Care Act for mandatory health insurance, which was often subsidized by the federal government. He supported a voucher program for Medicare, which would slash Medicare and Medicaid federal costs and require the purchasing of health insurance by those who would be covered—with some federal subsidies and tax credits or vouchers. He has now resigned for having used several hundred thousand federal dollars for private jet flights.

Is reducing health care for Americans unconstitutional in that it does not "promote the general welfare" of the citizens? The same reasoning might be used in his executive orders that eliminated health protections of citizens while eliminating regulations to aid business.

NATIONAL SECURITY

Giving classified information to the Russians, that was obtained from Israel, might cause national security problems. Once he gave the classified information, it was no longer classified because he has the power to classify or declassify information. Israel was not happy about the disclosure because it could indicate some of their sources of information. This could result in their not giving further information to the US. It might well also reduce the supply of information from other allies because of the fear that such information and sources would be leaked.

MAKING *SPEECHES WITH THE INTENT OF DISRESPECTING CONGRESS*

President Andrew Johnson was impeached on 11 charges. The first 10 were related to his dismissal of the Secretary of War, whom the Senate had approved. Under the Tenure of Office Act, which has been repealed, the President could not fire appointees which the Senate had approved. But the tenth charge was "Making three speeches with intent to show disrespect for the Congress among the citizens of the United States."

President Trump has "tweeted" and commented negatively on Congress, in general, and on individual members of Congress many times. Here are a few of his tweets (his grammatic errors are not corrected here):

➢ Congress now has 6 months to legalize DACA (something the Obama Administration was unable to do). If they can't, I will revisit this issue!

➢ Corker dropped out of the race in Tennessee when I refused to endorse him, and now is only negative on anything Trump. Look at his record!

➢ Sen. Corker is the incompetent head of the Foreign Relations Committee, & look how poorly the US has done. He doesn't have a clue as.....

➢ Wacky Congresswoman Wilson is the gift that keeps on giving for the Republican Party, a disaster for Dems. You watch her in action & vote R!

➢ The Fake News is going crazy with wacky Congresswoman Wilson (D), who was SECRETLY on a very personal call, and gave a total lie on content!

➢ Democrat Congresswoman totally fabricated what I said to the wife of a soldier who died in action (and I have proof). Sad!

➢ Rand Paul, or whoever votes against our Healthcare Bill, will forever (future political campaigns) be known as "the Republican who saved Obamacare."

➢ Rand Paul is a friend of mine but he is such a negative force when it comes to fixing healthcare. Graham-Cassidy Bill is GREAT! Ends Ocare!

➢ Bernie Sanders is pushing hard for a single payer healthcare plan - a curse on the US & its people...

➢ Republicans, sorry, but I've been hearing about Repeal & Replace for 7 years, didn't happen! Even worse, the Senate Filibuster Rule will

➢ Congress, get ready to do your job - DACA!

➢ The only problem I have with Mitch McConnell is that, after hearing Repeal & Replace for 7 years, he failed! That should NEVER have happened!

➢ ...didn't do it so now we have a big deal with Dems holding them up (as usual) on Debt Ceiling approval. Could have been so easy-now a mess!

➢ If Republican Senate doesn't get rid of the Filibuster Rule & go to a simple majority, which the Dems would do, they are just wasting time.

➢ Obstructionist Democrats use the courts ...the entire World WAS laughing and taking advantage of us.

➢ People like liddle' Bob Corker have set the US way back. Now we move forward!

➢ Isn't it sad that lightweight Senator Bob Corker, who couldn't get re-elected in the Great State of Tennessee, will now fight Tax Cuts plus!

➢ And I think Senator Blumenthal should take a nice long vacation in Vietnam, where he lied about his service, so he can at least say he was there associated delay at all times.

➢ Must stop! Interesting to watch Senator Richard Blumenthal of Connecticut talking about hoax Russian collusion when he was a phony Vietnam con artist!

➢ 3 Republicans and 48 Democrats let the American people down. As I said from the beginning, let Obamacare implode, then deal. Watch!

THE CHANCES OF IMPEACHMENT AND CONVICTION HAPPENING?

There are many charges on which he can be impeached, but you need enough Democrats in the House for a majority to impeach. To impeach means to formally accuse.

I would guess, with 99% certainty, that there will be a Democratic majority in the House on January 1, 2019. History is on the side of this happening. In 19 of the last 21 mid-term elections, the President's party has lost seats in Congress—an average of 30 House seats and 4 Senate seats. Add to that 38 House Republicans deciding not to run and 17 Democrats not running, as of mid-April 2018, and you have an overwhelming chance for a Democratic House. So I am confident of impeachment, but conviction is much more difficult to accomplish—in fact it has never happened. You must have a 2/3 majority in the Senate to convict.

Two presidents have been impeached, but neither was convicted. In the Andrew Johnson trial, some senators voted not to convict because it would soil the office of President.

To impeach Trump two things must happen. More Democratic senators must be elected in 2018, and more important, the non-Trump Republicans must be made anti-Trump and pro-American. This may be done through educating them about what is good for the country, or making them fearful of losing their seats in a future election.

Some have thought that Section 4 of the 25th Amendment to the Constitution might be an option. The section reads:

Whenever the Vice President and a majority of either the principal officers of the executive departments or of such other body as Congress may by law provide, transmit to the President pro tempore of the Senate and the Speaker of the House of Representatives their written declaration that the President is unable to discharge the powers and duties of his office, the Vice President shall immediately assume the powers and duties of the office as Acting President.

Because of the loyalty he demands, the use of the section is highly unlikely.

UNDOING OBAMA

Trump immediately on election:

➢ Reduced regulations for manufacturing,

➢ Approved the pipelines Keystone XL and Dakota access to Canadian oil sands which threatened the contamination of Canadian drinking water—while providing over 20,000 American construction jobs plus steel jobs since only American steel should be used,

➢ Eliminated restrictions on the production of $50 trillion worth of energy potential such as: shale, oil, coal and natural gas,

➢ Forbad Americans, working abroad for the government, from discussing abortion,

➢ Ordered a review of any major tax regulations set last year,

➢ Signed his intention to withdraw from the Trans-Pacific Partnership,

➢ Signed his intention to repeal the Affordable Care Act,

➢ Undid climate change policies—with the hope of putting more coal miners back to work.

But the jobs available are not going to be in coal, but to a lesser extent will be in steel. As times change, jobs change. We don't need the printing press of Gutenberg because we have immediate printing from our computers. We don't need blacksmiths, harness makers, or livery stables since most of us don't ride horses to work anymore.

It was not enough to undo Barack's executive orders, he had to undo Michelle's good works for children. Children are the least important of all— they don't vote, they are expensive, and they often talk back! So we can understand why Donald Trump froze regulations that Michelle Obama championed for school lunches. He allowed an increase in salt and a decrease in whole-grain products. She was trying to reduce childhood obesity through healthy school lunches, among other interventions.

She also criticized the Trump administration's delaying putting the calorie count on foods in supermarkets and restaurants. She thinks that you should know what you are eating. Is Trump so busy undoing Obama's programs that he will hurt more of the citizens in the process?

PROMISES

➢ Make America safe again—nothing done so far.

➢ Make America great again—stock market up considerably, so it's good for capitalist stock traders.

➢ Cancel billions of dollars to UN climate change programs and use it to increase the American water and environmental infrastructure.

➢ Bring mining jobs back.

After six months in office he bragged that he had brought back 45,000 mining jobs. The correct figure for coal mining was 800 jobs. 500 fewer than Obama had created in his last six months on the job. Oh well, just another falsification of the facts—so what else is new?

The Trump budget reduces the Department of Labor budget by 19.8%, the Department of the Interior by 10.9%, the Department of State and international aid by 29.1%, the Department of Justice by 3.8%, Department of Housing and Urban Development by 13.2%, the Department of Education by 13.5%, the Corps of Engineers by 16.3%, Environmental Protection Agency by 31.4%, the Department of Transportation by 12.7%. But it increases the Department of Defense by 10.1%, over $50 billion, the Department of Veterans Affairs by 5.2%, and Homeland Security by 6.8 %.

Additionally, there are a number of organizations and programs under the above-mentioned departments that will be cut or combined with the existing services.

CUT PERSONAL TAXES

Mick Mulvaney, the White House Budget Director said, " I think, the first time in a long time the administration has written a budget through the eyes of the people paying the taxes." The unemployed people in Trump's base pay little if any income tax. It's the rich guys at the top who pay most of the income tax. These are the ones with which Trump is really concerned. But governments don't need taxes, it is enough that they are fueled by promises!

With that in mind, the proposed budget showed significant increases in military spending and significant decreases in spending on entitlement programs for low income Americans—many of which were his supporters— while Congressmen have said that his proposals were, "dead on arrival," because Congress knows that voters want entitlement programs. Still, it gives us an idea of where Trump is, as opposed to what Trump said.

His proposals varied considerably from what he had promised his base. He predicts a $250 billion savings in healthcare with his proposals. While this may be high, the fact is that only people who pay income taxes will be able to deduct, as tax credits, their expenses. Reforming the tax code in favor of high taxpayers, by lowering the tax rates, eliminating the alternative minimum tax, and eliminating inheritance taxes—helps Trump and the other super-rich people like those in his cabinet.

The Trump budget proposal will increase defense spending from $594 billion a year to $722 billion a year in the next ten years, non-defense spending, such as domestic programs will be reduced from $619 billion a year to $429 billion a year for the next ten years. It would cut $616 billion over 10 years from Medicaid for low income and disabled

Americans and the Children's Health Insurance Program. He promised to leave Medicaid untouched during his campaign. There is no chance that his proposals will pass in total, but it gives you an idea as to where his priorities are.

Let me play the devil's advocate here for a moment. What have each of us given to our society and taken from our society? Trump has certainly employed many people in building his golf courses and hotels, so the rich people can play and stay. Does that counterbalance his illogical, and possibly illegal, way of gaining the presidency and his trashing of the expectations of the office in the minds of most Americans and a majority of our allies?

But back to his budget. Is it fanciful or grounded in sound economic theory and societal needs? His rosy expectations come from a projection of 6% growth, which most economists think is totally impossible. It would require nearly doubling growth during the time when historically we should be the end of our growth phase Also, the aging populations apply some brakes to nearly all societies today. Their pension benefits, increased spending on health care, and the lack of productivity because of their retirements from work—all make them economic negatives in a modern society.

All these are beyond the control of the White House. Perhaps if he raised the retirement age to 75 and increased the required contributions to Social Security and Medicare it would help. But we still have the expected downturn in the business cycle. It is actually quite rare to have a growth cycle as long as the one we are in. If this cycle lasts until 2019 it will break many records.

Cutting non-defense discretionary spending would save, according to Trump, $1.4 trillion over the next 10 years. This is at a time when spending requirements are actually increasing. Spending on education, environment and medicine will be hit very hard. He promised not to cut Social Security but plans to cut disability coverage under Social Security which benefits 10 million people today. This would save over $7 billion per year. according to Trump's thinking, the disability insurance part of Social Security is not part of Social Security.

Mulvaney said, "If you ask 990 people out of a thousand, they'd tell you Social Security disability is not part of Social Security." Trump could not have said it better himself. But there is absolutely no evidence for that profound statement of "fact" that 990 of a thousand would answer the way Mulvaney said they would. In fact, ten million people receive Social Security disability insurance payments for such disabilities as blindness and work injuries. Since there are 125 million households in the US we might assume that the members of those families might be aware of the insurance payments to a family member. So if no one else in the country was aware of that type of insurance, it would be more than 25% of the population who would know it. That's a bit more than the 1% cited in the Mulvaney guess. Definitely a "post-truth" pronouncement. Definitely an inductive fallacy!

Since the election, his promise of lower taxes has produced a plan to cut taxes for the richest Americans, including the elimination of the inheritance tax which only one in 500 estates actually pay. This is because a single person's estate must be worth over 5 1/2 million dollars before it is taxed. Obviously, these rich people cannot afford to pay more taxes. The estate must be left to those who have not earned it. That is the American way!

The tax plan, as proposed and signed, looks something like Ronald Reagan's plan that was supposed to have trickle-down effects from the wealthy to the poor. But it didn't work out that way. It also created a huge national debt because Reagan had to borrow to pay for the taxes that did not cover the American budgetary expenses. Where will Trump borrow? From Social Security, like Reagan? From China or Japan? How much will China lend if it is in a trade war? Or will he print more money making the dollar worth less and increasing the cost of imported goods? It's one of the questions that should be asked. And when legitimate news media ask these questions they are regarded as coming from fake news reports.

THE NATIONAL DEBT

We have mentioned the national debt earlier. Should we pay for what we want? Never in the USA! Norway and Denmark may be willing to do it but not us capitalistic countries. As mentioned, we could print more money, declare bankruptcy, or raise our taxes. Trump has another suggestion. He wants to talk to the American creditors and see if they will take less than they loaned us, thereby reducing our debt. He did not say whether he would ask the Social Security administration and the Military Retirement Fund trustees to take less than what was borrowed from them.

Are you willing to reduce your pension? He doesn't say whether the Federal Reserve Board will be asked to take less money in return than it lent. As of now, the USA's percentage of debt to its gross domestic product is the sixth greatest in the world, behind only: Japan, Belgium, and the well-known problems of Greece, Italy, and Portugal. Rating agencies, like Standard & Poor, have slightly downgraded American debt from AAA to AA+. The only AAA countries are: Australia, Canada, Germany, Norway, Sweden, and Denmark. The higher the national debt goes, the lower will be the ratings. And the lower the ratings, the more interest that will be charged by countries or people who lend to us. And now, as the recession has eased, interest rates in general are going up. All this portends that more interest will be charged and the tax rates will increase--- unless we continue to increase our national debt. Then, of course, we will increase the speed of the debtor's snowball. And we thought that Greece's austerity program was smothering!

MORE PROMISES

- ➢ Spend on the infrastructure
- ➢ Increase the number of people in the Armed Forces
- ➢ Eliminate competition of the Mexicans and China
- ➢ Hire Americans first
- ➢ Place 35 to 45% tariffs on Chinese goods. (This may be renegotiated)
- ➢   Keep jobs in America.

CUT BUSINESS TAXES

He signed the tax bill to significantly lower corporate taxes.

His proposals were estimated to add $5 trillion to the national debt. Almost 27 times as much as Hillary Clinton's proposals. If this were true, it would increase the national debt to over $25 trillion, while our GDP would probably continue upward at about the same pace it has since 2009. With a debt to GDP ratio of about 135% it would put us in a league with Italy and Portugal in the five most debt leveraged countries.

CUT REGULATIONS

Trump has ordered most departments to cut two regulations for every one that they impose. He has made more cuts in regulations than anyone since Reagan. In both cases the new regulations were pro-stockholder and pro-business rules that were negative for workers or the citizenry in general.

He canceled the "Fair Play and Safe Workplaces" rule that barred companies from government contracts if they had a history of violating workplace safety, wage or labor laws. This was called the "blacklisting" rule which has been found to be legal in the courts. The original regulation was signed by President Obama in 2014.

A land management rule gave the federal government more power over land-use decisions. The energy companies did not like this because they wanted to be able to drill for oil in more places.

He said that eliminating these rules will increase the number of jobs available. He did not say how.

THE TRADE DEFICIT

The American trade deficit is the largest in the world. And China is the major beneficiary. Look at the amount of trade and the US deficit in these countries.

- China - $535 billion traded with a $375 billion deficit
- Canada - $582 billion trade with a $18 billion deficit
- Mexico - $557 billion traded with a $71 billion deficit
- Japan - $204 billion traded with a $69 billion deficit
- Germany - $171 billion traded with a $65 billion deficit

The average wage of an American worker is over $23 an hour, for a German worker $26 an hour, and for a Chinese worker $3.60. The average American worker works 8.6 hours a day, the German 8.1 hours per day, and the Chinese 8 hours a day. The American worker, with the help of automation, produces about three times his salary per hour. But the Chinese worker produces far in excess of his low salary.

If America is to compete in factory work, pay has to be significantly reduced. This, of course, will never happen. The other way would be to significantly increase the automation. This, then, will put the American workers on the bread line.

In an ill-thought-out attempt to partially remedy this, Trump has imposed some tariffs.

TARIFFS

He has enacted a tariff on Canadian lumber. He has also put tariffs on solar products and washing machines. In early March of 2018 he proposed a 25% tariff on imported steel and 10% on aluminum. This went into effect on June 1.

He imposed a tariff on steel, because Chinese steel is flooding the market. But there are at least ten other countries from which we import more steel. Canada is number one. We import 17% of our steel from Canada, 13% from Brazil, 10% from South Korea, and 9% from Mexico and Russia. Only 2% of steel imports are from China. Over half of our aluminum imports are from Canada. China, rather than being an exporter of aluminum, is the world's top importer of it—over 50% of all aluminum imports.

So the Trump tariffs would hurt our northern neighbor almost as much as the American consumer, who will pay higher prices for American made products of American or foreign steel or aluminum. Canada, Mexico, and the EU plan tit for tat tariffs. Naturally Trumps sees these as being "stabbed in the back." He is a great fighter as long as his opponent has his hands tied behind his back.

Tariffs, as you know, put money in the federal coffers and is eventually paid for by American consumers because the price is higher—because the price is increased on foreign goods because of the tariffs or because the American made goods were more expensive to produce. The idea is to increase American job opportunities and reduce the jobs in other countries. So, we have the interests of the financial costs to consumers played against the interests of business and the possible increase of jobs in America.

Of course, for every tariff he enacts, other countries will undoubtedly retaliate. They can put tariffs on US agricultural products and services, or they can choose to buy products from other countries, like airplanes from Airbus instead of Boeing. Three weeks after imposing the tariffs on China, the Chinese imposed tariffs on 128 products from the

US. This included tariffs on pork, raised primarily in states that supported Trump; fruits and nuts, wines, steel pipes and other such items.

Trump's trade policy is reminiscent of George W. Bush's. Bush's tariffs on steel resulted in European Union tariffs of its own. The World Trade Organization ruled that the US had violated international trade agreements. The EU targeted tariffs on goods made in the swing states, which hurt Republican election chances. So, Bush then reversed the tariffs in 2003.

The 20% tariff on Canadian lumber will be paid by Americans as they buy the lumber for construction. So we should save American lumber jobs by making American consumers pay more for wood!

He's blasted Canadian dairy farmers as a "disgrace" because their government-subsidized farms are charging low prices that undercut some American farmers in certain milk products, and he declared that the Canadian government's protection of its dairy industry through import tariffs and other measures is unfair. His America first battle cry seems to be in conflict with Canada's "weird" idea of Canada First. As it stands, America has a $400 million surplus in the cross-border dairy trade in all dairy products. But, it seems that Canada has not fully understood that it is their duty to make America first!

Actually, through 2016, the US subsidized its dairy farmers, but Trump is removing many of the subsidies that farmers have long enjoyed.

TRADE—NAFTA AND TRANS PACIFIC PARTNERSHIP

He has pulled out of the TPP and has given notice that he will renegotiate NAFTA. His "America First" promise and ideal, is actually making "America alone." His narrow and shallow ideals appeal to narrow and shallow minds. It is difficult to continually expand our horizons—from family, to community, to national and finally to international concerns and possibilities. Populism, in the US and other parts of the world, views progress as moving backward from international ideals and peaceful progress into the comfortable walls of national sovereignty and its attendant disagreements. But who shall we trade with if we all live behind these impregnable national walls? As reactionaries, we should make war on the people behind those other walls. As President Macron warned us—nationalism means wars.

CLIMATE CHANGE—REMOVE US FROM PARIS ACCORDS

He has done this. The US now is the only country that apparently doesn't believe in climate change being caused by humans. The only other country that has not signed the Accords is Nicaragua. They have not signed because they do not think the terms are strong enough!

A few doubters have looked at partial geological records of the temperatures of the Earth and say that warming is normal. While this is true, it is not so for the period we are now in. Geologically we are now in a cooling period. But humans have significantly reversed the cooling with their use of fossil fuels.

This is like when we believed in the tooth fairy, but as more evidence accumulated, the tooth fairy disappeared from our knowledge of history—and only Santa Claus remains! But the problem with the deniers is that while they think that Santa Claus is still around, the knowledgeable people know that it is only the Grinch and the "ghost of Christmas past" that are the realities today.

The shortsighted quest for increasing coal mining jobs blinds Trump to the realities of the trillions of dollars lost because of the climate change that has already occurred. Does he realize that his golf courses in Florida, California and Dubai will soon be too hot for players? Los Angeles temperatures broke all temperature records this week.

State officials in Florida, as the federal government mandates, have ordered that the term "climate change" can no longer be used in official documents. While the national and Floridian governmental heads are in the hot sand, temperatures are rising, the ocean is rising and the hurricanes are getting stronger. I wonder if President Trump of the United States realizes that the president and CEO of Trump Enterprises is going to be losing money because the uncomfortably hot weather, as well as the increase in both droughts and hurricanes, will cost his company millions.

REVISITING SOME FACTS ABOUT CLIMATE CHANGE

Let us revisit climate change because the deniers usually use partial truths that they weave into gross distortions of fact.

Our world goes through warming and cooling cycles about every hundred thousand years. We should now be entering a cooling cycle which would've started in about 1970. From 1940 through 1970 our Earth had cooled about 3/10 of a degree Celsius. In 1967, a Russian climatologist Mikhail Budyko, wrote a paper saying that the Earth would begin to warm because of the human emissions of carbon dioxide. Another paper in 1975 suggested that chlorofluorocarbons, which were 200 times more heat retaining than carbon dioxide, would warm the earth even more. They were outlawed in 1989 because they were damaging the Earth's ozone layer.

The hundred thousand year cycles are divided into approximately 80,000 to 90,000 years of ice age and 10,000 to 20,000 years of warming. Normally the warming comes before the CO_2 is increased. In the naturally recurring warming and cooling cycles, the climate changes were related to the Earth's distance from the sun and various other factors, like the tilt of the earth and increases of solar activity.

Frozen tundra then thaws and carbon dioxide is released from the carbon containing flora and fauna buried in its icy shroud. This will then increase the warming even more due to its greenhouse effect. We are already seeing this now in northern Russia and Canada. So present-day warming began with fossil fuel burning and is now being increased by the thawing of the tundras. Clearly today's climate change is human caused, not caused by the Earth's distance from the sun.

During the last 250 years, it has been CO_2 that is leading the climate change warming. The last cycle of warmth ended around 10,000 years ago. So, we have had a cooling trend since then. This cooling trend would have continued for thousands of years if there were no people. But since 1750 the carbon dioxide content of the atmosphere has deviated from the normal cycle.

Instead of the temperature decreasing as expected, it increased because of fossil fuel burning. Methane and nitrous oxide have also increased because of agriculture, with methane being produced by cattle and fertilizer.

The climate change denying politicians have told us that for millions of years the Earth's temperature has risen and reduced. This is true, but what they do not tell us, in fact it is doubtful that they even know, is that we should be in a cooling period but our temperatures are spiking, giving us record-breaking hot years nearly every year. So, this is what the politicians do not tell us, either because of ignorance or deception.

Evidence from coring into the last 5 million years of sediments in the oceans and the polar regions shows that, prior to 3 million years ago, even with the hundred thousand year variations, the average temperatures were higher than during the last 3 million years. They were higher still in the previous 60 million years. And now we are entering another cooling period but our temperatures are increasing faster than any time in the past. And

CO_2 is leading the way. (Normal for the last 10,000 years has been is in the area of 280 parts of carbon dioxide per million parts of air.) In the last 45 years, it has increased to over 400 parts per million. This is a rise of over 70%.

The previously mentioned hundred-thousand-year cycle is due to the fact that the Earth's orbit around the sun is elliptical, not circular, and the orbit is elongated about every hundred thousand years. This makes the time that the Earth is near the sun shorter and the huge distances from the sun longer, resulting in longer cold periods.

But there are other cycles within this hundred-thousand-year cycle. About every 41,000 years the landmass of the northern hemisphere tilts more toward the sun, and then more away from the sun. Every 26,000 years there is a polar wobble that also exposes the landmass to or away from the sun.

So we have a number of factors that change the climate and increase or decrease the amount of landmass that faces the sun or is farther from the sun. Then within these cycles the sun often gives off extra heat through sunspots or irradiance. This can cause more heat to reach the earth. So there is more to explain the Earth's warming and cooling than just looking at a single temperature chart showing the last 60 million years. The West Virginia coal miners would probably appreciate this more complete explanation as to why most people want alternative and renewable sources of energy.

If you don't understand this brief explanation, ask Donald Trump, Steve Bannon or the Koch brothers to explain it more fully!

MAKE AMERICA SAFE AGAIN CONTROL IMMIGRATION

We have already mentioned the fact that countries with Trump properties, like Saudi Arabia and Egypt, which have sent more terrorists in the US, are now safe because Trump has a financial stake there with his hotels and other business interests. These are the countries that might be hiding potential terrorists, although they have never attacked within America. Iraqi and Yemeni citizens cannot be allowed into the US yet. However, their citizens might become less jihadist after they allow Trump hotels in their countries.

DOMESTIC CRIME

The Donald made a big thing about Chicago's crime rate, after all it was Obama's hometown. Perhaps now our president should start cleaning up crime in his home city, Washington, DC. It equals Chicago's murder rate at 24 per 100,000 people, and exceeds it in the total of violent crime by 30%. But those are almost paltry numbers compared to St. Louis, Missouri with 52 murders and 83 rapes or New Orleans with 42 murders and 104 rapes per 1,000. Where and how should he start?

He is trying to do something about crime by encouraging people to follow the NRA guidelines and have guns in their homes. Certainly, the best way to decrease crime is to have more guns available. In addition, it keeps more people working making guns and ammunition! While he hasn't done anything yet to reduce domestic violence, I'm sure it will come—possibly in his second term!

BIRTHRIGHT CITIZENSHIP

He called for an end to birthright citizenship, where illegal immigrants or visitors to the country can have a baby and that baby would be a US citizen. A bill has been introduced into the House of Representatives to do this. However, in the 14th Amendment of the Constitution it says that "All persons born or naturalized in the United States, and subject to the jurisdiction thereof, are citizens of the United States and of the State wherein they reside." This, of course, was enacted primarily to give slaves citizenship.

It has been tested once in court. In United States v. Wong Kim Ark, 169 US 649 (1898) a man born to Chinese parents who were working legally in the United States was denied entrance to the US after returning from China. Immigration from China was heavily restricted in the late 1800s. The Supreme Court ruled that he was a natural born citizen under the Constitution and was entitled to all of its rights under the 14th Amendment. Part of the decision follows:

"A child born in the United States, of parents of Chinese descent, who, at the time of his birth, are subjects of the Emperor of China, but have a permanent domicile and residence in the United States, and are there carrying on business, and are not employed in any diplomatic or official capacity under the Emperor of China, becomes at the time of his birth a citizen of the United States, by virtue of the first clause of the Fourteenth Amendment of the Constitution."

Because that decision includes the terms "permanent domicile" of the parents and also "carrying on business", there may be loopholes for a new Supreme Court to eliminate some anchor babies in the future. For women who come from another country to have their babies in the United States, where they can have dual citizenship, it might be made illegal. But outlawing the right might be more difficult for women who are undocumented but have been in the country for some years and are working. Their babies might be legal under the 14th Amendment.

It appears that for Trump to carry out this promise he needs either a Supreme Court decision or a Constitutional amendment.

In the "olden days" we needed workers to build railroads, farm, or work in the factories. Both of my grandfathers came to America as laborers.

DOMESTIC ISSUES

HEALTHCARE

"Obamacare is responsible for the high health insurance premiums you pay." This was the message of Trump and many Republicans.

"It's going to be fantastic health care," the president said, referring to the House Republicans' American Health Care Act. Then turning to the visiting Prime Minister of Australia, he said, "I shouldn't say this to this great gentleman and my friend from Australia, because you have better health care than we do."

The World Health Organization ranks Australia's health care as the 32nd best in the world, while the US system ranks 37th. But Trump should be proud. America's health care is the most expensive in the world. That is because health insurance CEOs make eight figure salaries and the stockholders make good profits—and many Congressmen are stockholders in health industry stocks.

According to an analysis by the Congressional Budget Office and policy experts, the American Health Care Act, the House bill his Republican caucus proposed, and Trump endorsed, is a way to repeal much of the Affordable Care Act and replace it. But it would have broken all of those campaign promises. The CBO estimated that more people would lose their insurance under the GOP's proposed replacement than if he simply repealed Obamacare, and moderate Republicans in the House refused to support it, in part because the cuts to Medicaid were too deep. More conservative Republicans, meanwhile, were frustrated that it didn't repeal the law in its entirety. With Democrats united in their opposition and Republicans divided in their support, GOP leaders pulled the bill from consideration.

This situation is an example of the different basic assumptions of the far-right Republicans and the far-left Democrats. The far-right Republicans generally hold liberty primary, while the far-left Democrats hold equality primary. People may slide along the liberty-equality scale with each different issue, so a far-left Democrat might be to the left in the health care issue, but far right in his thinking of owning firearms. But let's look at health care now.

The far-right citizen would likely want care for himself, and would be willing to pay for it, but not be willing to pay for insurance for those who have not worked hard enough to escape poverty. Those people had the freedom to succeed and didn't—so why should I take care of them. The far-left people assume that all people are equal so their needs are equal, and all citizens should share in the costs to equalize.

My guess is that Obama wanted socialized medicine because in other countries people get better care for about half the price that Americans pay. But Americans have been sold a bill of goods that private enterprise is always better than a government controlled entity. With the high-priced lawyers, hospitals, and health insurance CEOs, it is the American way to have every business done through private enterprise. The rationalization is that competition will lower the price, but in actual practice this is not always the case. It is definitely the case in health care.

If Obama had had his way there would have been a federal option for insurance companies to compete against. The proposals that he wanted would have significantly reduced the price of medical insurance. However, the fact that the American government finally entered into a program that would make insurance possible, or even mandatory for most, sets the stage for what Obama really wanted in the first place but could not but get. But, the foot of national health insurance had finally been put in the door—and with a liberal Congress that is not beholden to lobbyists, a European-style national health program could later be in place.

But can the special interests that the lobbyists represent be quieted? Not while Americans are not educated to the realities, and not while America remains corrupt—with lobbyists' money more important to our representatives then we are!

Since 2010 when Obama's Affordable Care Act was passed, the Dow Jones industrial average had increased 252%. The major health insurance companies have far surpassed the average with: Humana increasing 1010%, Cigna 1113%, Aetna "only" 628%, WellCare 1410%, and Anthem 469%. Wall Street banks, Congressional Health Committee members, and other holders of health insurers have reaped the benefits in stock appreciation and dividends.

The CEOs do reasonably well financially. UnitedHealth's CEO earned $66 million in 2014—over $5 million in salary, and most of the rest in stock options. Investors make out pretty well too.

While America is the number one country in many areas, it is far down the list in terms of healthcare. If Donald Trump were serious about making America great again, he would concentrate on healthcare and education. But as everyone knows, he believes that Obamacare was a failure. However, he cannot seem to suggest anything better.

As you remember, Obama wanted a federal option for insurance. This would've been much cheaper for the citizens, but the insurance lobbies and the doctor lobbies contributed enough money to the Congressmen that they did not give him that. So, America remains the only major country without a single-payer or tax-paid health program. Since business lobbies, such as the insurance lobby, contribute a great deal to the election campaigns of our representatives, we expect to have business interests getting what they want in most areas of legislation. This is particularly true of the Trump administration.

It is true that a socialized medical system reduces business profits and jobs. The paperwork is so simple when there is one payer and everybody works for the same department of the state. But the American idea, which is pro-business and often anti-citizen, has such a long tradition that it may not be easily changed. You will probably need government paid elections with no campaign contributions allowed from anyone—but that is a long way from happening because of our traditions.

Here is a chart showing a percent of gross domestic product that countries spend on health care and the rankings of several countries in terms of their World Health Organization evaluations as to the quality of service.

WHO ranking of health care systems and the % of GDP spent on health care:

France	1st	11.5%
USA	37th	17.1
Australia	32nd	9.4
Italy	2nd	9.2
Canada	30th	10.4
Mexico	61st	4.8
Israel	28th	7.8
Norway	11th	9.7
Denmark	34th	10.8

Looking at the healthcare delivery rankings, it does not mean that America has the 37th ranked doctors. American doctors are exceptional. Much of the best research in medicine is done in America. But making money ranks very high among many doctors. Part of this is because they have often amassed about $400,000 in educational loans before they begin to practice. In most countries, college education, such as medical education, is free.

Also in America, with all the insurance billing that every doctor must do, it takes a good deal of secretarial time to complete this work. This is not necessary in socialized medicine programs. So doctors here are usually caught in the capitalistic net and must charge enough for their services to include the secretaries and the malpractice insurances that are required so that lawyers, too, can be employed in suing doctors for real or imagined malpractice.

I am surprised that there are not more coal miners going to medical school or secretarial school or even law school—oops!—Our need for more lawyers is even less than for coal miners! You must go where the jobs are.

The federal government and the state governments are the major funders of private insurance companies (Medicare, Medicaid, and Obamacare subsidies); one might wonder why the federal government doesn't take over all of the healthcare insurance. I guess the answer is that if the federal government handled all the insurance there would not be the many multi-million dollar salaries or the stock dividends for the stock traders. So they would be out of jobs.

And if the experience in other countries is any indication, the doctors who would be employees of the national government would not be sued. But of course, that goes against everything Americans really believe in, such as that nothing is our fault and so we must blame somebody—and collect money, because money is the most important element in our capitalistic lives.

Europeans commonly believe that the doctors are doing the best they can and mistakes sometimes happen. The Europeans, being more socialistic tend to be more loving, forgiving, and empathetic. When a severe case of malpractice does occur, it is generally settled in mediation. In Germany only 6% of the cases are litigated. But we might surmise that if European countries began to produce lawyers at the rate of the US, one per 300 people, rather than at the rate of France, one per 1,403 people—the EU might develop its own army of ambulance chasers.

BUILD INFRASTRUCTURE

He has yet to embark on this need. His plan was to give tax breaks to private companies to stimulate infrastructure construction. Might this mean toll roads and toll bridges so that the construction companies could recoup their investments? Or would the federal or state governments finance the projects with local tax dollars?

SCHOOL VOUCHERS

School vouchers sound good. Trump pledged $20 million from other parts of his budget to allow poorer parents more school choice.

The first question to ask is whether every parent knows how to choose the best education for their children. Just what are the elements of an educational experience that will make a child or teenager better citizens and more likely to be successful in their vocations? It is highly likely that most poor parents do not have the educational or vocational experience to make such decisions. The philosopher Josiah Royce said that, "Education is learning to use the tools that the race has found to be indispensable."

While there is no guarantee that professors in universities and professionals in the field of education will have all the answers to the key needs of children in the 21st century, particularly in the future needs for jobs--the probabilities certainly lie with the education professionals, rather than poor parents! But here again, you see the call for liberty, for the freedom to choose even if you are not particularly qualified. It's almost as if you should allow a patient with a brain tumor to decide on every step of the operation to remove it. Most of us trust the surgeon's education, training, and experience.

Do they choose a school because it will give their children a religious education? Do they choose it because of commercial advertising? (Religious and for-profit schools are the major options for charter school enrollment.) Do they choose it because it is a "charter school?" Studies of the effectiveness of charter schools are mixed. They do not show a superiority of the typical charter school over the typical public school.

The quality of the teachers employed is critical. States often allow non-certified people to teach in religious and other private schools. This may or may not be an important criterion.

Public schools must take all students except those very few who have been expelled from the school district. Discipline problems aren't the major, obstacle to effective teaching. It is much more likely to be a problem in the lower social class schools. However, discipline problems are likely to occur in nearly every school, especially in the 12 to 15 age group.

Some school districts, like Los Angeles, have created charter schools from primary through the secondary levels. Magnet schools as separate schools, or as a division of a public high school may offer advanced experience in math, science, business, medical and other related subjects. These have become very attractive and effective areas of focus for schools. Of course, they are public, not private, schools.

REPEAL OF COMMON CORE

Common Core sets up national standards in education that should put us back on track to compete more effectively with other countries in reading, math, and science. It is not a federal program so Trump cannot repeal it! He prefers state or local standards. But following these varying standards, America now ranks 24th in reading, 40th in math and 25th in science among the 72 countries tested.

Trump seems to be intent on undoing anything that was done in the previous eight years, whether in the White House or the state houses, and cast them into the outhouse. One might hope that people with newfound power might read and understand what has gone on before—but that would be an intellectual approach, and as you understand most of us are directed by the feelings emitting from our unconscious minds.

Building on the best of existing state standards, the Common Core State Standards provide clear and consistent learning goals to help prepare students for college, career, and life. The standards clearly demonstrate what students are expected to learn at each grade level, so that every parent and teacher can understand and support their learning. Such standards do not help business today—we would have to wait for a few years before it benefits American business and we can't wait! In case you are interested, the standards are based on being:

> ➢Research and evidence based,
> ➢Clear, understandable, and consistent,
> ➢Aligned with college and career expectations,
> ➢Based on rigorous content and the application of knowledge through higher-order thinking skills,
> ➢Built upon the strengths and the lessons of current state standards,
> ➢Informed by other top-performing countries to prepare all students for success in our global economy and society.

But nowhere in the standards is there a mention of the necessity of input from impoverished parents with primary school educations. How can this be democratic? How do these standards prepare future coal miners? How do they prepare students to ignore verifiable facts in election campaigning? Why do they assume that these standards are good for our democracy, when the students are not allowed to determine their whole curriculum? Too bad Trump can't repeal them!

On the other hand, they do inform parents, students and teachers about the expected learning objectives—the necessary skills found to be essential in various state and international curricula. Facts and skills are necessary for educated and employable citizens for our future society. But if we are going to make America great again, how do we do it if we are looking at the curricula and teaching methods employed by non-Americans? Will looking at what highly rated educational systems do, like: Singapore, Shanghai, Estonia, and Finland, make us better? After all we are the greatest!

But if we truly educate a majority of the population, how can they be easily manipulated by future unscrupulous office seekers—like we have been recently? Never fear, the states and the local districts can continue to save money on teachers' salaries and continue to hire teachers from the bottom 20% of college graduates from low ranking universities. This is the opposite approach to that taken in the high-ranking countries.

MATERNITY LEAVE

Ivanka talked her father into promising paid maternity leave for 6 weeks. While Scandinavian social welfare countries give about a year of paid family leave, Trump's program would have at least made some dent in the problem. However, it is estimated that this would cost about $680 billion. He did not mention how this would be paid for by the Federal government while he is reducing taxes. So he planned to make the states pay for it!

ANTI-ABORTION

He promised to:

> ➢ To nominate pro-life justices to the US Supreme Court. This he has done

➢ To sign into law the 20-week ban, aka the Pain-Capable Unborn Child Protection Act, to, as Trump put it, "end painful late-term abortions nation-wide."

➢ To defund the largest abortion provider in the country, Planned Parenthood, and reallocate those funds to community healthcare centers that provide comprehensive care to women.

This is in his budget.

To make the Hyde Amendment permanent law, protecting Americans from having to pay taxes to pay for most abortions. (But they will eventually pay $120,000 per unwanted child to educate them through high school.)

Although he did not promise to appoint anti-abortion and anti-contraception people to posts in the Department of Health, he did just that. One of the women appointed was Teresa Manning, who had said in a National Public Radio interview in 2003: "Of course, contraception doesn't work, Its efficacy is very low especially when you consider over years, which you know a lot of contraception health advocates want, to start women in their adolescent years when they're extremely fertile, incidentally. And continue for 10, 20, 30 years, over that span of time the prospect that contraception would always prevent the conception of a child is preposterous."

But according to the Center for Disease Control of the United States Department of Health, in which she will now work, the use of the contraceptives does work. The department's research on the efficiencies of different contraceptives if used by 100 women for one year show their "failure rates" per 100 women in a year.

➢For those choosing no contraceptive method (85% failure) 6 of every 7 women will be pregnant by the end of the year;

➢Of those using the calendar method, which is acceptable to the Catholic Church, 76% will be at pregnant at the end of the year;

➢The most effective contraceptives are the intrauterine devices (IUDs) and sterilization which would have about five pregnancies per 10,000 women in a year. A failure rate 0.05 per year);

➢Those choosing pills, patches and diaphragms would have about six pregnancies per hundred women in the year. (Failure rate 0.1 to 6%)

➢Male and female condoms and withdrawal would leave about 20 of the hundred women pregnant in the year.

So her knowledge of the area was totally wrong.

When people are appointed to high level government posts we would expect that they would be knowledgeable about the proven facts. But then Kellyanne Conway has told me that there are alternative facts. But she hasn't told me where, or if, these facts are proven. There must be some alternate universities somewhere on Earth—or on Mars!

Then of course, there is to the legality of abortion. As shown by the Supreme Court decision in Roe versus Wade, abortion is legal. But Manning has referred to it as a crime. So her opinion runs counter to the law of the land. And she is a lawyer! But then, "don't confuse me with the laws, when Donald and I know better!"

As part of the role Manning will help manage the $286 million Title X federal family planning program. Without Title X, rates of teen pregnancy would have been 30 percent higher across the US in 2014, according to a 2016 study by the Guttmacher Institute, a nonpartisan health policy think tank. Rates of unintended pregnancy, unplanned birth, and abortion would have been 33 percent higher without publicly funded family planning from Title X centers, the study found. Created in 1970 by President Richard Nixon, the program helps low-income or uninsured Americans access to family planning counseling, contraceptives, and tests and treatment for sexually transmitted diseases.

As we mentioned, economists have pointed out that aborting unwanted embryos or fetuses cuts down on crime twenty years later. So if Trump is serious about cutting taxes and reducing crime, aborting unwanted embryos or fetuses is a necessity. If getting the Catholic and evangelical vote is primary— stop abortions. Maybe contraception too— we do need more unwanted and unloved people in our overpopulated world.

CHANGE LIBEL LAWS

At a campaign rally, Trump promised, "I'm going to open up our libel laws so when they write purposely negative and horrible and false articles, we can sue them and win lots of money."

What is libel? Libel means "to publish in print (including pictures), writing or broadcast through radio, television or film, an untruth about another which will do harm to that person or his/her reputation, by tending to bring the target into ridicule, hatred, scorn or contempt of others. Libel is the written or broadcast form of defamation, distinguished from slander, which is oral defamation. It is a tort (civil wrong) making the person or entity (like a newspaper, magazine or political organization) open to a lawsuit for damages by the person who can prove the statement about him/her was a lie…"

If Trump were to be able to change the free speech guarantees as the Supreme Court has amended the Constitution, there are many who could sue him. Jeb Bush was called "a basket case." Ted Cruz was called "a liar." Ben Carson was said to have a "pathological disease." And Trump said about Senator John McCain: "He's not a war hero. He was a war hero because he was captured. I like people who weren't captured." Of course, he had no proof for his libelous rants.

Under American law, telling lies about a political opponent is perfectly fine according to the Constitution as interpreted by the Supreme Court. Here are two recent illustrations of many examples.

In New York Times v. Sullivan (1964), the Court, in a 9-0 decision, extended First Amendment protection to false statements of fact in a defamation suit. The New York Times had carried an advertisement in which public sympathy for the arrest of Martin Luther King was a topic and erroneously stated that he had been arrested by the Alabama State Police seven times. In fact, it had only been four times. Sullivan, the Montgomery Public Safety commissioner sued because of the error. The court stated that in public discussions of political actions there must be "breathing room" otherwise people might be afraid to express what they thought was true. The Times had printed a retraction in response to a request of the Governor of Alabama. The Court stated that the publication could not be sued unless "actual malice" of the newspaper could be shown.

In truth, extreme freedom of speech rulings by the Supreme Court give the US the freest speech in the world, especially for public figures. This makes his threats to change libel laws impossible without a series of Supreme Court decisions that would undo almost two

The European Parliament is considering eliminating racist comments and hateful comments from their debates. How far should political correctness go? If a person complains about ISIS being a Muslim terrorist organization, is this anti-religion? Is this blasphemous, even if it is true. If a person says that there are relatively more black men in prison than whites, is this a racist statement even though it is true?

ETHICS

Hillary Clinton repeatedly told us what Michelle Obama had told her, "when they go low we go high." The idea was to appeal to the higher level of ethics that some people subscribe to. But it was the lower psychological levels of inferiority and finding an identity that brought out the votes. So the political advice for the future might be "to appeal to the basest level of the voter.

At one of the debates with Hillary, Trump brought three women who said they had been sexually assaulted by Bill Clinton. The idea seemed to be that if your spouse had an affair, you were not fit to be president. Of course, all well-informed people knew that Trump had had a long affair with the actress Marla Maples during his first marriage. He divorced his first wife and married Marla. So it is apparently okay if you have affairs, the problem is if your opponent's spouse has had an affair.

Clinton tried to talk about the real issues (such as: a fair tax system, drug addiction, and campaign reform) and how she would solve them, but enough voters in the swing states did not care about the issues she talked about. They were interested in getting jobs, building a wall, stopping abortions, cleaning the swamp, and making America great again.

I wonder about the ethical questions revolving around those Republicans who were lied about in public, then supported Trump. Does Ted Cruz think he is a liar? If so, it is easy to understand how he supported Trump, who was merely stating a fact. On the other hand, if he does not lie, or lies only occasionally, why would he support a liar for his party's presidential bid? Is party loyalty more important than personal ethics?

Because of Trump's avoidance of the issues while continually tearing down his opponents he managed to sway enough voters to believe that he would somehow do the things he promised while lowering taxes—because he was so successful at building hotels.

The message for politicians seems to be to develop some catch phrases that the voters can repeat, and believe, and make them feel superior by tearing down your opposition. This gives them the hope and the faith that their desires will be realized and they will feel good because they are now smarter than all of your opposition.

AND THE LIES CONTINUE

In March of 2018, on a visit to California, President Trump tweeted, "The state of California is begging us to build walls in certain areas. They don't tell you that." But in actuality, California had sued to stop the building of the wall on its side of the Mexican border.

The same week, also in California, Attorney General. Jeff Sessions had accused the Oakland Mayor of warning 800 illegal immigrants of a coming raid. James Schwab, Immigration and Custom Enforcement spokesman, said that this was not true. He confronted the government officials and was told "deflect" the Sessions' statement. He refused and resigned. It appears that there are still some honest patriots out there!

OTHER PROMISES

RELEASE TAX RETURNS

He said he would release his returns after the IRS audit was completed. But now the he has no intention of releasing his tax returns.

LOCK HER UP!

One of his more successful promises, as a campaigner, was to promise to appoint a special prosecutor to investigate Hillary Clinton's emails. The FBI did this and found no criminal intent. Still the vocal followers continued to chant "Lock her up," at every rally.

They certainly could feel superior to Hillary because their emails were never questioned. FBI Director Comey said "She was careless but lacked intent."

WILL SUE HIS ACCUSERS

His followers were able to overlook any possible sins of their saint. He called his pussy grabbing conversation merely locker room talk. However, people who have really been in locker rooms disagreed with his ideas of what goes on in locker rooms—where the conversation is more likely to be about the practice or the game.

He said, "When you are a star, they let you do it." A number of women came forward accusing him of molesting them. He said he would sue them after the election. He has not.

I can understand how men with huge inferiority complexes can see themselves as superior to all women. What I cannot understand is that women could accept a candidate who would put down their sex so irresponsibly. Was it because they really feel inferior and should be treated as he did? Was it that their inferiority made them so complacent that they would vote for whoever their husbands said to vote for? Was it that they wished to be groped by a billionaire? I can't figure it out.

But looking at interviews with women who voted for Trump I can find several reasons why his attitude and behavior in terms of women was sublimated to other more important needs.

Interviews with women around the country showed a range of reasons for their pro-Trump or anti-Clinton votes. The cost of healthcare was increasing far too fast. Although they did not know what would replace it they voted for its repeal. Had they known the legislative history of Obama's Affordable Care Act and that Obama wanted a federal option which would've been much cheaper than what the legislators voted in, they might have voted out their lobbyist-controlled senators. The House wanted a federal option, the Senate didn't.

Fears about immigration and terrorism were also high on the list, as was the opposition to abortion.

Many women were actually voting against Hillary Clinton because of Trump's claims that she was hiding emails and was responsible for the death of her friend, the ambassador to Libya. Investigations showed that she was absolved of any guilt in these two situations. Nevertheless, his continued harping on these issues made people believe that they were unsettled or should be re-opened.

There were women who believed that under Obama there was not the support for the police or the military that there should have been. Here are some comments of female Trump voters:

➤"And if I refused to vote for any man who objectified women, I couldn't vote for any man. Actually, Donald Trump is a good man down deep and I believe he cares about our country and wants to help everyone. He was just the better choice."

➤"I am very concerned with getting our manufacturing plants back. He knows how to build things. I believe he can do it."

➤"I think there is too much immigration. We must take care of ourselves first."

➤"We must run America like a business. Don't spend more than you make."

➤"I felt like once you got past the bluster, he really was interested in helping everyone."

So Trump's message was louder than his locker room talk and his proven sexual advances to underlings on his television show and in his Miss Universe pageant. His superiority complex and his riches made him an icon whose ethical behavior, while in question, could be overlooked as long as he promised things that female voters prized more than his sexual and legal depravities, such as economics and safety.

THE COMMON POLITICAL TRUMPIAN TECHNIQUES
ATTACK WHEN QUESTIONED OR ATTACKED.

As his friend and adviser, the disbarred Roy Cohn had continually advised him, "When you are attacked, attack back with greater force." Threaten them. Sue them. Never admit guilt.

DENY AND DEFLECT

Among the common ways that people deflect blame are:

➤Denying that it happened (Trump denied losing the popular vote),

➤Blaming somebody else ("I inherited a mess"),

➤Generalizations that may or may not have some truth in them
(Mexicans are drug dealers),

➤Personal attacks on the opponent ("Lying Ted"),

➤Comparing a person to another who is less than stalwart, then denigrating the existing person ("Ben Carson's pathological disease),

➤Changing the subject (criticizing a moderator when asked a question he couldn't answer in a TV debate),

➤Smearing the opponent (as he did with Hillary's emails and charitable work),

➤Put downs that he laughs at as if they were jokes ("Jeb Bush is a basket case.),

➤Acting superior, and possibly sarcastically, to belittle your adversary and make his arguments less believable (as he did with Lyin' Ted Cruz)

➤Saying that someone else is worse—if you catch them in a lie or an unethical situation. (While running against Hillary Clinton he said that his "pussy grabbing" bragging was not as bad as Bill Clinton's sexual experiences).

Deflecting is a nearly universal political technique for people who have been rightly blamed for something, from four-year-olds to 94-year-olds denying and blaming others is a built-in defense mechanism. Politicians, of course, have much more to lose by being wrong, so their denials and deflections are louder and more elaborate than that of a four-year-old. And when you are in contention for being the world's greatest liar, as Trump is, your blames and deflections can reach gargantuan proportions. If Trump had the same nasal affliction as Pinocchio, his proboscis would be approaching Pittsburg, while he's standing in Washington!

He blamed "the generals" for a raid that led to the death of a Navy SEAL in Yemen. He accused former president, Barack Obama, of fomenting protests against him and leaks within his administration. He blamed the judiciary for future terrorist attacks against the United States, and the media for the firing of his first National Security Adviser. He even blamed the weather for his smaller-than-desired inauguration crowd. He has blamed the media for the fact that his son, son-in-law, and campaign manager met with some Russians to get information on Hillary. He blamed Obama for tapping his phones—when they weren't tapped. Then there is the all-purpose deflector—the charge of voter fraud in his election. As the first year passed, he even blamed his daughter and son-in-law for things beyond their control. The one person President Trump never seems to blame is himself.

Deflecting questions and avoiding answers is as common among politicians as gray hair. But Trump and his press secretaries, along with Kellyanne, have taken it to a whole new level. I guess that with the preponderance of fantasies and fallacies there has never been the need for such an avalanche of alternative facts. The White House has never been so aptly named—since we have been "snowed" so often.

When his press secretary was thought to be losing his job because he could not adequately explain the inexplicable behavior of Trump and could not clearly explain his policies to the press corps—he was fired.. When pressed for an answer about Spicer's potential firing, or his intentions relative to Sean Spicer keeping his job, Trump said, "He is a wonderful human being and a nice man" and "He has been with me since the beginning," He didn't answer the question asked. More deflection!

For a businessman, the world is a series of wins and losses. Donald either wins or whines.

The fake news of the New York Times does not take into account the alternative facts that cloud the catastrophes he has created. There are so many targets to blame—Hillary, Bill, Barack, CNN, CNBC, The Washington Post, China, Mexico. There is whole universe of unsuspecting targets out there!

Oh, but his wins! Leaving the Paris Accords showed the world that America doesn't need the rest of them. Who needs science when we have Fox News? Why believe empirical evidence when you have energy lobbyists funding your campaigns? Winners win, losers vote. Who cares how you got there, or how you stay there, when you are THE king of the mountain!

Trump tells us that "This administration is running like a fine-tuned machine." Yet internationally it is a disaster. Citizens of all other countries, except Israel and Russia, have negative views of him and the US.

Trump's contention, after he had been elected, that he actually won the popular vote and that there was voter fraud is another oft-repeated lie. Why? He's in the Oval Office—maybe he should study up on healthcare instead of making excuses. His continual arguments that his was the most attended presidential inauguration ever, are totally false—as shown by the photographs, but it keeps attention on things that are not really important. As long as he could keep attention on other things he didn't have to work on his promise of producing coal mining jobs.

It really doesn't matter if there was fraud because he was elected. For the same reason, it doesn't matter how many people were at the inauguration, because he was elected.

He said he would seek a major investigation into voter fraud by illegal aliens who are dead people. No one I know saw any sombrero wearing zombies at the polls.

Deflecting issues is not a singular trait of Trump, although he is the leading candidate for the record in the Guinness's book! In Russia, because Russians are getting poorer since the oil price dropped, Putin had to keep feeding them news about Ukraine and the Syrian conflict. Dishonest or immature leaders around the world will usually make false claims about the others whom they blame.

Trump's tweets do the same thing. Deflect the public from the real issues. And by all means—keep blaming Obama and Hillary.

The FBI director, James Comey, asked the Justice Department for more resources for his investigation into the Russian inquiry just days before he was fired.

Comey's abrupt dismissal shook Washington and exposed fears that America is facing its biggest constitutional crisis since the Watergate scandal.

HE HAS A WORK ETHIC—NO GOLF

He said he will be too busy to play golf like Obama. "I will be too busy to play golf." But in the first 100 days, Trump played 19 times—compared to Bill Clinton's 7, Obama's 1, and Bush's 0. As of his first year, it was 95 rounds. So far in 2018 it is 110 rounds at a cost to taxpayers of $97 million. (He must take security and they must follow him in rented golf carts.)

HIS FIRST EUROPEAN TOUR

Our Donald has brought the epithet "The Ugly American" to its lowest level. Pushing the Prime Minister of Montenegro out of the way so that he could preen in front of the camera at a major photo shoot for NATO was a major dash of despicable demeanor. Obviously, protocol is for sissies—not for Americans, who are the greatest. Let's hope the world leaders are suitably impressed. However, Harry Potter's biographer J.K. Rowling was only minimally impressed according to her tweet labelling him "You tiny, tiny, tiny little man."

BUT NOW NORTH KOREA IS AT THE TABLE

Whether Kim came to Singapore because of being out-bullied, because of the severe UN sanctions (done at Trump's behest), because his bomb-testing mountain had collapsed, because he could get some concessions from an eager president, because he wanted to try a Singapore Sling, or because he needed to get more Tiger Balm—he got more than he expected. This sadistic, unethical, regime inheriting man has now risen to a paragon player in the world. He now clearly overshadows such lightweights as: Trudeau, Merkel, Macron, May, and Shinzo Abe—at least in the current mind of the headline seeking tweeter-in-chief.

Kim's tough negotiating stance had him give up his missile engine building factory and release three prisoners. For that he got the cessation if the American-Korean defense exercises and the probable reduction of American forces in Korea. That makes he an Xi happy little Munchkins, "cuz" the Wicked Witch of the West gave up one of her prized silver slippers which she had borrowed from the witches of the East, Moon and Abe, leaving them with pairs of worn-out bamboo sandals. But it was certainly worth it for the red carpets, the TV coverage, and the heaps of hopes that were generated.

The former "rocketman" put pen to parchment and promised less than his father had done in the six-party talks of 2005 in which North Korea agreed that: "The Democratic People's Republic of Korea committed to abandoning all nuclear weapons and existing nuclear programs and returning at an early date to the treaty on the nonproliferation of nuclear weapons and to International Atomic Energy Agency safeguards."

Of course his father soon reneged on that promise just like he had in his agreement with President Clinton in 1994. The tradition of signing treaties to stop their nuclear research and development, then reneging goes back to Kim Jong Un's grandfather in 1985. Nearly every year since there have been talks and promises, still their nuclear program progressed.

Clinton's jubilant speech, in October of 1994, included: "This agreement is good for the United States, good for our allies, and good for the safety of the entire world," he assured the nation. "The agreed framework was designed to put the brakes on North Korea's nuclear program, and it promised to put an end to years of increasing nuclear tension, including a near war, to a halt. . . This agreement represents the first step on the road to a nuclear-free Korean Peninsula, . . .It does not rely on trust." So, the United States agreed to normalize relations with the nation—and both agreed to pursue "formal assurances" not to nuke each other.

In a joint statement, in 2005, after the six-party talks among the U.S., South Korea, North Korea, Russia, Japan, and China they called denuclearization as "verifiable" then established a process for the verification to occur. Since 1985 North Korea has agreed several times to denuclearize and to allow inspections. Each time they got money, needed products, assurances for the continuing of their regime, and promises of peace and normal relations. Is this just another stall? Or is Kim ready to sample the good life and maybe get an NBA franchise? Will he let his captive citizens have a taste of the good life? Will he allow any freedom of speech? Dream on, O'Connor! But at least we can keep our fingers crossed that we will not be double crossed again!

Kim has already got more that he gave. The great negotiator may have overstepped. Oh well, just another Trump bankruptcy. But what if he's successful? The time may have been right to bully Kim into fame and riches. Let's hope so.

CHAPTER 9   HOW WE WERE MANIPULATED IN THE BREXIT CAMPAIGN

In June of 2016, voters in Britain voted to exit the European Union. This "Brexit" has not gone as smoothly as the voters were told. In fact, the bumps in the road threaten to derail the whole train. The "little engine that could"—can't!

As with Trump's election and the Brexit referendum, the voters were not told the whole story. This is normal in democracies—but it is far from the ideal! Those who want to be elected at any cost will lie and try to confuse opposing forces. In voting for referenda, those who can gain from one position will similarly lie and confuse the issues. If these unscrupulous people have their way, the voters will be kept in the dark. They must be made aware of and taught how to call opposing arguments ridiculous.

Those who voted to leave were told that they could:
- Get rid of the immigrants,
- Take back the European court decisions and decide them based on British law,
- Bathe in British sovereignty, behind their secure borders,
- Trade with the European countries as they had been doing, and,
- Be richer because they would save on the EU dues.

The reality is that if they were to trade with the EU, they needed to follow the EU rules on immigration and laws and that it would require annual dues nearly equivalent to what they were paying—but they would have no say in formulating EU rules.

If they did this it would be a "soft" Brexit. If they decided to separate totally from the EU, with no trade possibilities, it would be a "hard" Brexit. The EU is not happy with the UK leaving. They are not making it as simple as the pro-leave politicians said it would be!

When a member of an exclusive golf club quits because he doesn't like the rules, but wants to play free, the chances are not too good that the club members will look kindly on him. Not only do they not like him anymore, they are not willing to give an inch in what he wants. When an enemy has all the marbles and you have none, but you want some, and are not willing to buy them—good luck!

Three major proponents of leaving the UK were: Michael Gove, who said, "the day after we vote, we will hold all the cards and we can choose the path we want." David Davis said to "be under no doubt, we can do deals with our trading partners and we can do them quickly." And Boris Johnson, the former Mayor of London, said, "there will continue to be free trade and access to the single market." All were lies, but spoken forcefully and with conviction by influential politicians.

AND SO NOW IT'S DONE!

Both the leavers and the stayers believe in the advantages of trade with the EU. A major problem is that the European Union does not want Britain to leave. Certainly, the Eastern European countries that have been benefiting from the large contributions of the richer countries, like Germany and the UK, do not want a major contributor to leave.

The former mayor of New York and billionaire Michael Bloomberg said in late 2017 that voting for Brexit was the stupidest thing a country has ever done—except for the election of Donald Trump.

"THE POPULISTS ARE COMING! THE POPULISTS ARE COMING!"
Where is Paul Revere—we need him again.

The Pied Piper of Trump Tower led many Americans out of the mainstream and into the swamp. Brits followed the pipes of Farage and Johnson into Westminster, and then into the Thames.

Many Britons voted to reduce immigration and increase their national sovereignty, it is doubtful that any voted to become poorer. As you will soon realize, if you didn't already, much of the money that pinpointed the attacks on our unconscious minds came from the same American billionaire who did the same for Trump campaign.

Meanwhile populist movements have been proliferating, such as: Catalonia wanting independence from Spain; rumblings of Lombardi leaving Italy; the Flemish leaving Belgium; and the Basque separatist movement. Each group seeking to split from their home country, then join the EU. But since acceptance into the EU requires a unanimous vote, would Spain vote for Catalonia or the Basque region to join? Would Belgium vote for a new Flemish nation? Probably not!

Along with these separatist movements, we see an increase in far-right parties in: Germany, Austria, France, Netherlands, Sweden, Hungary, Poland, Norway, and some others. These parties might want to leave the EU. Globalization and the reduction in national sovereignties, along with increased immigration, give many people the urge to return to the comfortable cocoon of their national past—when intra-European wars were the rule, rather than the exception.

But as President Macron, of France, reminds us—"nationalism means war." But how many people today were involved in World War I or World War II? How many have seen in person the ravages in Syria, Serbia, and Iraq? We dream of more local control, but we haven't experienced the nightmares of the major reality of history—WAR. And the next world war will leave terrifying images for any who survive—if any do!

The populists are pragmatists. "Let's do what we think will work for now." This American philosophical tradition sometimes works. It was the banner of the Brexiteers in June of 2016. But in June of 2018, with little agreement on the expected exit, Jean-Claude Juncker, the President of the European Commission told the Irish Parliament, "that with pragmatism comes realism." What some people think is pie in the sky, may only be an eagle relieving himself on your picnic blanket!

INFLUENCING OUR VOTE BY APPEALING TO OUR UNCONSCIOUS MOTIVATIONS

The campaign to have Britain exit the European Union (Brexit) was a prelude to the Trump campaign. It even had some of the same players and it used the same tactics:

FEAR

➤Fear that the immigrants were taking jobs from Britons,

➤Fear that we are losing our sovereignty,

➤Fear of that unknown globalized world.

ANGER

➤Anger that the European Court of Equal Justice was overturning British High Court decisions,

➤Anger that the UK was paying more to the EU than it was receiving.

➤Anger at the immigrants,

➤Anger that we weren't becoming richer,

➤Anger that wages were not increasing.

HOPE

➤Hope that the money saved by leaving could be used by the National Health Service,

➢Hope that the British economy would do better alone and without the EU regulations,

➢Hope that my personal economy will be better.

➢Hope that Britain can again be the center of the world.

But "hope" is neither a strategy nor a tactic. It is merely a dream.

Intelligent hope requires a plan—and the proposals of the UK to the EU in the last 20 months does not indicate that it does. It seems now that a permeable border between Northern Ireland and the republic to the south is a primary concern for the British negotiators. This key issue was never addressed by the Brexiteers. It might well be solved if the UK would stay in the customs union of the EU—but this would require the free flow of EU citizens into the UK, which is precisely what the "leavers" didn't want.

INFERIORITIES FELT IN THE CONSCIOUS OR SUBCONSCIOUS MIND

Here is our previously used chart including factors relative to the Brexit conditions. You will note that the basic inferiorities from childhood may still influence adult behavior.

➢ Adulthood—Poor job situation or no job, poor personal economy, ineffective personal social network, threats to one's status

➢ High School—Poor grades, poor physical skills, few or no friends

➢ Elementary school--Can't master subjects, few or no friends, poor athletic ability

➢ Infants—Can't walk, talk, feed themselves

These inferiorities give rise to fears, angers and hopes at every age. As infants, we hope we can soon walk. In elementary school we hope that we can become important. In high school we continue our drive for importance, identity, and success. As adults we want a prestige job, successful relationships, and money. But we are frustrated by the status quo.

➢ FEAR—that things will not improve for the UK without leaving, immigrants cost more than they contribute, a loss of sovereignty to the EU.

➢ ANGER—that things are not better, European Court of Justice decisions are often negative for the UK.

➢ HOPE—that things will improve without the EU, new positive trade agreements will be possible, more money for National Health Service.

Before the Brexit referendum in the United Kingdom in 2016 the people who wanted to remain felt that things were fine as they were. They were not. Those who wanted to leave the European Union felt that all problems would be solved by leaving. They will not.

People in Britain were not all doing as well as they would like. Of course, this is true in every country—and for many people. With more people than needed, because of: overpopulation, automation, computerization, globalization, artificial intelligence, and 3-D printing—every country is facing problems. The rich people get richer and the poor get poorer, and there is no end in sight.

Coal mining, previously absolutely essential, is now rapidly becoming a societal evil—being a highly polluting and non-renewable source of energy as well as being relatively expensive. People in other nations, who are willing to work for less money, can produce steel, and many other essentials, for much less than the workers in the West. The "good old days" are well behind us if we are blue collar workers or even middle management white collared personnel. Consequently, a vote for "the good old days" is unrealistic. Wishes don't make reality!

Just what issues were used by the people who wanted to leave the European Union? Some were legitimate, others were lies or merely unrealistic. As in the case of many elections, what appears to be true may not be. Here are some arguments from those who wanted to leave—and the answers from those who wanted to stay. But often neither side had the complete information needed, so we have added additional information to show the incompleteness of both arguments.

If the UK leaves the EU it can be done as a hard Brexit or a soft Brexit. A hard Brexit would allow for the stopping of immigration from Eastern Europe but would put Britain on the outside, forced to negotiate everything with the EU. This would undoubtedly include tariffs for British goods. Obviously, the other countries in the EU are not happy that Britain has decided to leave and will not negotiate kindly with them.

On the other hand, a soft Brexit would require the UK to accept the same immigration regulations that many of those who wanted to leave saw as the major problem. Consequently, since the "leavers" major concern was immigration, a hard Brexit was the only real alternative. So Britain would be forced to negotiate with the EU that was angry with them and who had all of the marbles.

There is a big difference between "hard realistic politics" and "playing nice." The EU certainly does not want anyone to leave the union. If they make it easy on the UK to leave, others may leave. They must make it as tough as possible for the UK—and they can do it. This will discourage others like Italy or Greece from leaving.

As you will notice, when there is a projected negative outcome for one's position, the shrewd politicians do not mention it. This was true of the value of the pound being projected to drop and the attendant increased cost of imports and traveling. The pound dropped about 10% immediately and is now down 14% against the euro. It dropped 10% against the dollar, but the weakening dollar has erased half of that drop.

Just what issues were used by the people who wanted to leave the European Union? Some were legitimate, others were lies or merely unrealistic. As in the case of many elections, what appears to be true, may not be. We have cited some arguments from those who wanted to leave—and the answers from those who wanted to stay. But often neither side had the complete information so we have added additional information to show the incompleteness of both arguments.

HERE ARE THE MAJOR BREXIT ARGUMENTS FOR (STAY) AND AGAINST (LEAVE)

IMMIGRATION

LEAVE: Britain can never control immigration until it leaves the European Union, because freedom of movement gives other EU citizens an automatic right to live here.

STAY: Leaving will not solve the migration crisis but bring it to Britain's doorstep, because the border is controlled from the European continent, and holding areas for illegal migrants will move from Calais in France to Dover in the UK.

The "leavers" blamed many of Britain's woes on immigration. Poor pay, fewer jobs, more crime and a loss of Britishness were all factors. Britain cannot regain control over immigration until it leaves the European Union But, if the border between Northern Ireland and the south is not closed, EU immigrants might still have an easy entrance to the UK.

The "stayers" answered that leaving the EU would bring more asylum-seekers to Britain. At the time, they were being stopped in Calais, which is in northern France. If Britain were to leave the EU those asylum-seekers would just arrive at Dover. The "stayers" also argued that the UK's economy was increasing—even though British wages were not keeping pace because Eastern Europeans were working for less money than the Brits were willing to do.

SOVEREIGNTY

LEAVE: The British Parliament is no longer sovereign. With the EU hell-bent on an "ever closer union" and further economic integration likely after the economic crisis, it is best to call it quits before more sovereignty is lost. Leavers said that an independent UK would have more influence on the world. But they didn't say how or where. We want to control our own borders and destiny. Additionally, the people of the UK, in general, have never felt a part of the rest of the continent. Sovereignty therefore is an easier sell than it might be in the Netherlands.

Contributions to EU can be better spent at home. The UK is the third-largest contributor to the EU after Germany and France. It is also third from the last in terms of the percentage of its contributions that come back to it, after Germany and France. Much of the money contributed by the major contributors goes to help develop the economies of Eastern Europe. The hope is that eventually these economies will grow and possibly become larger markets for the exports of the other EU countries.

A nation's contribution to the EU is a percentage of their gross national income and a percent of their value-added taxes (VAT—a national sales tax on goods and services, usually at a 20 to 25% rate) from the prior year. Occasionally a country is temporarily given a reduction in the contributions owed. Denmark, Sweden, Austria, and Germany have occasionally been given a temporary reduction in their annual dues. Only the UK, because of Margaret Thatcher's negotiations, has been given a permanent rebate. That rebate varies from year to year depending on its contributions.

Since the UK's agricultural interests are handled differently than the rest of the EU's Margaret Thatcher negotiated a permanent rebate of contributions from the EU. It is something like this, from the UK contributions subtract the amount of money the EU gives back to the UK. Take 66% of the difference and that will be the rebate from the EU to the UK. So if the UK contributed 15 billion euros to the EU and received back €10 billion, the difference would be €5 billion. The next year's rebate would be two thirds of that 5 billion or approximately 3,333,333 euros. So if the next year the contribution was again €15 billion, the UK could subtract the 3+ billion euros from their expected contribution and would actually pay around 11 1/2 billion euros for their contribution for the next year.

Because of this rebate, the per person contribution of UK citizens is only the eighth highest in the EU, even though theoretically the UK is the third highest country in its gross amount owed—before what it receives money back and its rebate.

STAY-- In a globalized world, every country must work closer with others if they want to flourish economically. Retreating behind the beach borders of Britain will be sticking the national head in the sand of the 18th Century past--while the 21st Century wind of globalization will merely tickle the rump of the cowardly British lion.

If the U.K. leaves the EU, its citizens could end up needing visas to travel to continental Europe. Even the Brexiteers concede this.

Then there are the hundred thousand, plus, Brits who live in Spain, France and Greece who could be evicted or who could lose their guaranteed EU health care and public services.

The U.K.'s college students also could lose out, as they have benefited from EU freedom of movement rules, using them to study at universities on the Continent — some of which have lower or no tuition fees.

A look at history may make one wonder about the advantages of sovereignty. Two thousand years ago the Romans occupied much of the island. Nearly a thousand years later the Normans took it over. Then France had its way with the island. And in 1918 and the 1940s if America had not come to the aid of the British they might be all speaking German.

The two constants of human history are war and religion—often going hand in hand supporting each other. Sovereignty for any nation is therefore not guaranteed by Providence.

The UK's relationship with Europe has never been simple nor static. It took the country years to join what was then the European Community and, even then, when it was last put to the vote in 1975 many backed it grudgingly or for narrow economic reasons. Many of those have since changed their minds, with their earlier ambivalence turning into outright hostility. There have been decades of skepticism towards the EU among politicians and in large parts of the UK media.

What appears clear from the campaign is that the vote to leave was as much a statement about the country's national identity, and all that involves, as it was about its economic and political future.

A caution: If the border between Northern Ireland and the south is not closed, EU immigrants might still have an easy entrance to the UK.

INTERNATIONAL INFLUENCE

LEAVE—Britain does not need the EU to prosper internationally. By re-engaging with the Commonwealth, the UK can have just as much clout as it does from inside the EU.

STAY—It is said that Britain will be "drifting off into the mid-Atlantic" if it leaves the EU. In a globalized world, the UK's interests are best protected by remaining part of the EU block. This was the opinion of both American and Chinese leaders.

LAW

LEAVE—Too many of Britain's laws are made overseas by dictates passed down from Brussels and rulings upheld by the European Court of Justice. The UK courts must become sovereign again. Occasionally the European Court of Equal Justice overrules British courts—and their giving all rights to individuals sometimes runs counter to the good of our society. Decisions that allowed a life-sentenced murderer to sire a child, and a decision to let a known terrorist re-enter the UK were largely viewed with excessive negativism by Brits.

Britain wanted to escape the European Court of Justice, but it won't be possible for any business it does with the EU. All EU related grievances must go through that court.

STAY—The exit campaign has over-exaggerated how many laws are determined by the European Commission. It is better to shape EU-wide laws from the inside rather than walking away.

CRIME

LEAVE—The European Arrest Warrant allows British citizens to be sent abroad and charged for crimes in foreign courts, often for minor offences. Exit would stop this.

STAY—Rapists, murderers and other serious criminals who commit offences in Britain can be returned to face British justice thanks to the European Arrest Warrant. Exit would stop justice from being done.

TRADE

LEAVE—Britain's links with the EU are holding back its focus on emerging markets – there is no major trade deal with China or India, for example. Leaving would allow the UK to diversify its international links. There were too many regulations that did not allow Britain to pursue other markets. There are many emerging markets that the UK could pursue. So there were few benefits to staying in the EU.

STAY—44 percent of Britain's exports go to other EU countries. Putting up barriers with the countries that Britain trades with the most, would be counterproductive. If they leave they will undoubtedly face stiff tariffs. Putting up barriers with one's major trading partner is counterproductive. Trade deals that are profitable for the UK may be difficult to find. For the last 20 years, Britain has been a net importer.

The first quarter of 2017, six months after the Brexit vote, showed that the UK had increased its GDP only 0.2%, the slowest of any of the 28 EU countries. The others had averaged a 0.6% increase. The UK slump was surprising because there had been a strong second half of 2016 after the Brexit vote. Actually in 2016, the UK did slightly better than the Eurozone, increasing 2.1% compared to 1.9% for the Eurozone. The fall of the pound and the fact that wages have not kept up with inflation is to blame. Meanwhile, the rest of the Eurozone is doing quite well. The UK was also trailing the world's most advanced economies in increasing GDP. Canada, with all its immigrants, was leading the advanced nations in increasing its economy. Perhaps the UK could become a province of Canada and get the existing trade arrangements as perks!!

Something the "stayers" didn't mention was the required queuing of cars and trucks at the borders. This has been estimated to add one billion British pounds to the cost of doing business. Will this financial cost be paid in increased taxes? It should provide more jobs in border control, in both the UK and abroad. It will certainly add to the inconvenience for the drivers, whether they are hauling goods or on their way to vacation.

JOBS

LEAVE—The danger to jobs has been over-exaggerated. By incentivizing investment through low corporation tax and other perks Britain can flourish like Norway outside the EU.

Those who wanted to leave said that jobs will stay in Britain and that Britain could be better off if they follow the approach of Norway. What they did not say, or possibly did not know, was that Norway paid €118 per person to the EU but had no input into EU legislation while it had to take in immigrants. The UK was paying about €128 and had a full say in making the laws.

The "leavers" argue that if they can reduce corporate taxes companies will keep workers in Britain. The "stayers" wonder about the 3 million jobs in the UK that are linked to the EU that now exist, and how many might move to the continent. (This has already begun with banks moving to Dublin, Paris and Frankfurt.)

The cheap and plentiful labor from Eastern Europe does not require the owners of the companies to invest in production technologies and in research and development. Many British laborers have not had an increase in wages for eight years. They blamed the immigrants who would work cheaper. They blamed the money going to the EU, and they blamed the regulations put in by the European Union. They feel that they have lost because of the EU rules. You may surmise that people who feel they've lost want to gamble to break even. This is why they backed Brexit.

As an aside, Norway is an example of a country profiting from the low wages paid in Eastern Europe, since it takes in many college graduates from Poland to do housecleaning work. Among my own house cleaners, I have had young ladies with master's degrees in economics, history, and microbiology. It seems that Poland's anti-abortion stance does not take into consideration that they cannot employ the number of qualified citizens they now have. This is an example of national legislators and administrators not seeing all of the ramifications of a policy position. This is becoming more and more obvious to post-Brexit Brits and to the post-Trump-election Americans.

STAY—Around three million jobs are linked to the EU and will be plunged into uncertainty if voters go for exit, as businesses would be less likely to invest if the country was outside the EU.

Those who wanted to stay argued that with Brexit, jobs would leave the UK, and banking could leave for the continent, as it has since the UK will no longer be the banking center for the EU. Frankfurt, Paris, Brussels, Luxembourg, or Dublin will be the new banking capitals. All of the UK's leading banks have plans to either move their headquarters to an EU country or to open major branches out of England. Manufacturers from vodka makers in Scotland, clothing makers in Leeds and IT service companies from Microsoft to gaming developers are moving to where their major continental market exists.

AGRICULTURE

LEAVERS—Since the UK pays over 12.3 billion British Pounds to the EU annually, there should be plenty of money saved to subsidize farmers and fishermen. They should receive just what they had received for at least five years.

STAYERS—55% of farm income comes from European Union subsidies. At present Britain is growing about 60% of the food it uses, and this percentage is dropping.

Between 70% and 97% of the country's food and drink exports will be at risk from Brexit with no agreed trade deals, says a report from the House of Lords. The agricultural industry has overwhelming dependence on the EU. According to the report, leaving the European Union without a trade deal in place could put up to 97% of British food and drink exports at risk that the latest House of Lords report on the implications of Brexit exposes particularly high dependency on the single market and associated EU trade deals among British farmers and food manufacturers

In 2013, EU farm subsidies were worth €200 a hectare (£58 an acre) and made up 35-50% of total gross farm income. Most farmers have thin margins, if they have any at all. The DEFRA (Department of Environment, Food and Rural Affairs) figures for 2013-2014 show that 20% of cereal and grazing livestock farms failed to make a profit, and this was before the latest move downward in global commodity prices. Average cereal farms earn around £100,000, and £55,000 of this comes from the EU single farm payment.

Evidence of the House of Lords EU Energy and Environment Subcommittee revealed the interconnected nature of much food and drink production that would be threatened by non-tariff barriers. Ian Wright, director general of the Food and Drink Federation said, "If you take one example—a bottle of Baileys Irish Cream . . . if you are a Northern Irish cow, your milk crosses the border five times before it goes into the bottle . . . The idea that that would be subject to tariffs hither and yon is really very scary." A similar example would be baked foods since raw ingredients, such as wheat and flour cross EU borders several times before cakes and cookies find their way to market shelves.

Instead, the only access guaranteed in the event of no new trade deals being struck would stem from Britain's membership of the World Trade Organization, which has particularly punitive tariffs for many agricultural goods—rising to 30% for much of the dairy industry.

58% of British farmers voted to leave the EU, even though those advocating leaving the EU are promising lower food prices for the UK. This might now be more possible with separate agricultural treaties with the US, Brazil, and African countries such as South Africa. These, of course, would reduce the profits of UK farmers. In fact, without a special agreement with the EU, many think that British sheep and cattle farmers may have their days numbered.

Farmland prices in the UK have risen 150% in 10 years. Some young farmers thought that ending the EU subsidy would drop land prices and allow more young people to get into farming.

During the referendum, Michael Gove promised cheaper food if the UK would vote to leave. Recently, when confronted by farmers, he said that their subsidies would continue for at least five years. However, the farmers have been accused by government economists as being "subsidy addicted." They not only get subsidies per acre, but also free red diesel for their tractors, no inheritance tax on passing down their property, and several other perks. Now farmers are realizing that once the subsidy requirements are removed from the EU, farmers will be competing for funding with other UK interests such as: health service, education, and social care.

Depending on how "hard" the Brexit is, farmers may not get the "tariff-free" trade agreement that they had expected. The World Trade Organization rules might require a 60% tariff. That, with the UK importing 80% of its fresh vegetables and 40% of fresh fruit, a falling pound, and potential tariffs and costs from customs delays--there could be significant price rises.

NATIONAL FINANCE

LEAVE—Talk of capital flight is nonsense. London will remain a leading financial center outside the EU and banks will still want to be headquartered in Britain due to low tax rates.

The United Kingdom pays 4.7 billion euros more than it contributes, so that can be used at home. This was a major argument for leaving the EU. It was said that the 350 million pounds a week could be spent on the national health service. But the EU contributions were actually less than half of that after rebates in 2016—156 million pounds per week. And, as we noted earlier, the promise that it would go to the National Health Service was refuted the day after the referendum.

STAY—"Prosperity is necessarily the first theme of a political campaign," said Woodrow Wilson, and for the Remainers it should have been the first, second and third. They predicted that the banks would flee the UK and the City of London might collapse if Britain votes for exit, because the trading advantages of being inside the EU help boost banks' profits. This, of course, is already happening—and some estimate that 70,000 banking jobs may be lost.

Several negative employment predictions were also made, one was that while the average inflation rate will be 2.3% and the average pay rise will be 1%. So, the worker would get poorer. When the chapter was first written, in March of 2017, the inflation rate is 3.0% and pay increases generally varied from 0.1 to 1.3%. As I am doing the final edits, in June of 2018, UK pay has been rising as fast as inflation.

Inflation is rising because imports are now more expensive with the devalued pound. And with 442 billion British pounds of goods exported and 617 billion British pounds of goods imported you see a 40% gap between the two. This, of course, will increase as more exporting companies relocate.

Also, it looks like there will be increasing unemployment as well as falling real pay. The unemployment rate is expected to grow, but it has stayed steady at 4.3% so far, probably because the weakened pound lifted exports. It is expected to rise to 5.8% next year. The Bank of England also warned that Brexit would damage living standards. But so far it hasn't happened.

On this issue, the Remainers had the status quo on their side (with an economy predicted to be the fastest-growing in the developed world prior to the Brexit vote.); they had a prime minister who had presided over record job creation, and opponents who could only offer vague "John Bull" optimism.

Don't underestimate how much the U.K. needs the rest of the EU, warned The Economist, a U.K. magazine that opposed a departure. "The Brexit camp's claim that Europe needs Britain more than the other way round is fanciful: the EU takes almost half of Britain's exports, whereas Britain takes less than 10% of the EU's," the magazine said.

The Brexit vote has already resulted in higher costs for imported goods because the British pound has lost close to 12% against the euro. It had lost more against the dollar, but with Trump's tax cuts for the rich, the dollar has weakened significantly, so the pound is down only 5% against the dollar.

And while the bank's interest rate of 0.25% is extremely low it is expected to rise soon in order to keep inflation controlled. Inflation was estimated to be about 3.0% while economic growth rate will be about 1.5%, according to the International Monetary Fund compared with 2.7% for the US and 2.2% for the Eurozone.

These combined factors translate to real wage reduction of 0.8%. But Suren Thiru, head of economics at the British Chambers of Commerce, said the Bank was too optimistic about the UK's near-term growth prospects. He said that the weakness in the pound made imports much more expensive and will reflect in the economic output. This may be borne out by the fact that the first two quarters of 2017 showed that the UK had dropped to the bottom of all EU countries, after outperforming them in the two quarters after the Brexit referendum. If it were a horse race, not many would bet on Britain!

PERSONAL FINANCES

LEAVE—Didn't mention what might happen to the Consumer Price Index.

REMAIN—After Brexit, the U.K. economy could be around 6% smaller by 2030 — and that would mean a loss of income equivalent to about £4,300 (or $6,100) a year for every British household, according to a report by Treasury chief Osborne, about a year after the vote.

House prices will fall, was the prediction. What has happened so far is that the annual rise in prices of 4.5% has slowed to 0.6%. So the remainers seem to have overstated the problem. Others were predicting stagnant prices for London property after Brexit is finalized. As of March 2018, London house prices in some areas had dropped 15%. On the other hand, the northwest was booming. Blackburn's home prices were up 16%.

U.K. shoppers save 350 pounds a year, or about $511, thanks to lower prices that come from being part of the EU. That's according to the remain campaign, which cites London School of Economics data.

Michael O'Sullivan, chief investment officer in Credit Suisse's wealth management arm said, "The impact of the Brexit vote is widely thought of in terms of GDP but the impact on household wealth bears watching. Since the Brexit vote, UK household wealth has fallen by $1.5 trillion. Wealth per adult has already dropped by $33,000 to $289,000 since the end of June. In fact, in US dollar terms, 406,000 people in the UK are no longer millionaires."

VALUE OF THE POUND

Those wanting to leave the EU did not mention the possible devaluation of the pound. Economists had suggested that there would be about a 15% drop in the pound if the vote went to leave and about a 10% increase in the value of the pound if the vote went to stay. Immediately on the tallying of the vote, the pound dropped about 15%. This made selling British made goods more attractive to buyers and it made importing goods and travel more expensive for the Brits. As mentioned, it is down about 12% against the euro and 5% against the falling dollar at this writing. Immediately after Brexit it fell 15% against the stronger dollar.

Most investors expected that the Remain camp would prevail. As soon as the first results were in, they dumped their holdings of sterling. A weaker pound is, in essence, a sign that international investors are less keen to buy British assets and need to be enticed by a lower price. The result has helped British exporters, but has also pushed up inflation and squeezed real wages as imported goods became more expensive. That may explain why the British economy, which performed well in the second half of 2016, has recently shown increased signs of slowing.

Consumer prices were up 3%, average weekly earnings were down 2%, Sterling has reduced over 10%, government bond consumer yields have reduced 33%. In stocks the FTSE 250 share price index has increased by 25%. So it helped businesses involved in exporting but hurt workers and retired people. This was just the opposite of what workers and retired people expected in voting for leaving the EU.

DEFENCE

LEAVE—The leavers suggested that Britain could soon be asked to contribute to an EU Army, with reports suggesting Angela Merkel may demand the Prime Minister's approval in return for other concessions. That would erode the UK's independent military force and should be opposed. There was no evidence of such a proposal, it was merely a hypothetical fear generator.

STAY—European countries together are facing the threats from ISIS and a resurgent Russia. Working together to combat these challenges is best— an effort that would be undermined if Britain turns its back on the EU.

While it is possible that an EU Army might be developed, it is not a certainty. NATO is already in place and that might be stronger than an EU Army.

HEALTH

LEAVERS— Britain can save 350 million pounds each week which can go into the National Health Service. This was denied immediately after the vote.

STAYERS—While the "stayers" did not make much of an issue of this, a few newspapers and economists criticized it. It was not 350 million pounds per week but actually 248 million pounds per week, as mentioned earlier. The actual amount sent, on a weekly average, varies from about 136 million pounds to 165 million a week—after the rebates and the money sent back to UK for various worthwhile purposes.

Boris Johnson, the Mayor of London, campaigned using this false message. Click"
https://vimeo.com/285601581/ac6676f5f6

Nigel Farage, after the vote, was criticized for allowing this fabrication to continue to influence voters. He recanted the day after the vote. Here are two TV interviews. Click:

https://vimeo.com/285533998/ae67ec4058

The stayers also brought up the fact that it is easier to bring in trained doctors, nurses, laboratory technicians and "carers" from Eastern Europe than to train them ourselves.

With the current consumption of natural resources and the pollution of the air, land, oceans and freshwaters—it is easier to tackle these problems from a European-wide and global response

There are some areas of improvement possible, as seen in these comparisons.

	US	UK	Japan	Fra	Germ.	Czech
Hospital beds per thousand people	3.26	2.95	13.4	6.37	8.27	6.84
Physicians per 1000	1.8	1.6	1.7	3.6	3.8	3.6
Health spending % GDP	17.1	9.1	10.2	11.5	11.3	7.4

BORDER BETWEEN NORTHERN IRELAND AND THE REPUBLIC OF IRELAND

This was not really an issue in the lead up to the referendum vote. But it has now become a major issue. The Democratic Unionist Party, the Northern Irish group that props up Teresa May's thin majority in Westminster is adamant that there can be no hard border between Northern Ireland and the Republic of Ireland. But if there is not, EU citizens can come to Ireland, walk across the invisible border and be in the UK. Then it is only a short flight to London.

Similarly, goods could come from the UK, cross the border to the Republic of Ireland, then make their way to the continent. This could not be done for all goods, but is certainly possible for some.

Boris Johnson said in February 2017 that the Irish border was being used to frustrate the Brexit negotiations. But in fact, the serious issues of the border should have been discussed by both sides prior to the vote. It is, and was, a very important issue—but as with so many other issues it had either not entered the minds of the leaders of the opposing sides, or they had kept it from the voters.

The LEAVERS said little and when they did, whitewashed it. In April of 2017, Theresa Villiers, Secretary of State for Northern Ireland said, "I think that the land border we share with Ireland can be as free-flowing after a Brexit vote as it is today." The same month Lord Lawson, of the Vote Leave campaign, said, "There would have to be border controls but not a prevention of genuine Irish from coming in across the border."

After the vote, David Davis, the Brexit secretary, said, "It should be relatively easy to maintain a soft border in Ireland as long as there is a zero-tariff trade deal with the EU." But if there are tariffs on trade between the UK and the EU, then "we've got a real problem".

The REMAINERS were also generally not concerned, although a month before the vote, Phil Hogan, European Commissioner for Agriculture, said, "The fear in Dublin is that our border towns would become a backdoor into the UK. In that instance, what sort of fortress would the Northern Ireland border have to become to close that backdoor?"

Meanwhile Theresa May has pledged not to put a hard border separating the two Irelands. But she said the EU might want it. French farmers certainly want it. They don't want cheaper UK farm products entering the EU when Brexit finalizes.

OPINIONS OF WORLD LEADERS

David Cameron argued vociferously to stay in the EU. Christine Lagarde defended the International Monetary Fund's stark warnings about what would happen to the UK if it left the European Union. President Obama said that if UK left the EU it would go to the back of the queue in terms of trade relations. Of course, it was at the end of his tenure and there is no guess as to what President Trump's "America first" idea will bring to the UK.

Her Majesty's Treasury released a report claiming that a "Leave" vote in the referendum on whether the United Kingdom should leave the European Union would plunge the British economy, which had been growing modestly for the past couple of years, into a slump. The report said that, in the event of "Brexit," the unemployment rate would jump, while GDP, house prices, the stock market, and the value of the pound sterling would all be hit hard. To emphasize this message, the Treasury posted a big headline on the home page of its website: "UK economy would fall into RECESSION if Britain leaves the EU." In case the message wasn't clear, the word "RECESSION" was printed in red, with cracks in the letters.

The warning was generally true, except for the stock market, which has risen like most of the other world markets.

But since we are all are certain that we know just about everything, these warnings of world leaders could not shake our resolve.

As in the other elections being discussed herein, we do not yet know what will happen to the UK in the post-Brexit years. Doesn't look good so far! We don't know whether or not Donald Trump's ideas and programs will do well for America. Doesn't look good so far! We do have an assessment on George W. Bush's presidency. His unethical politicking has landed him among the three worst presidents in the history of the United States. He will soon be fourth, because there is no question that Donald Trump will soon take over first place—as the very worst!

A HEALTHY MAJORITY VOTED FOR BREXIT

The vote to leave the European Union was 52% to 48%. While so far things look rather negative because of the vote, we might wonder if people might have changed their minds. Because of the false promises and the use of data to manipulate voters, one wonders if people had a change of heart. They probably haven't. In a poll by The Economist, a year after the vote, only 3% of those who voted to leave have changed their minds. Other polls have slightly different results. One major poll had it 51 to 49 to stay. The same poll had only 36% believing that their economy would be better if they left.

Perhaps we see here the same unconscious concerns, the craving for identity, that the previously mentioned National Academy of Sciences report pointed out—that other issues than the economy are of prime concern, for instance: sovereignty, and related issues such as law, crime, and immigration.

As is common in elections, people are given promises, often false promises, and not told what the eventual realities are. After the unexpected win for those who wanted to leave, the Brexiteers, the realities of the options became clearer. It was not just a matter of stopping immigration or recapturing British sovereignty, there were real decisions that had to be made. Was it to be a hard Brexit, a 100% breaking of all ties. Or, was it to be some sort of a soft Brexit where some of the ties that the EU has developed are retained? Here are some of the options that other countries have negotiated. The options now:

> Stay in the European Union—assuming a new referendum.

> European Economic Area (EEA) —Norway, Iceland and Lichtenstein have chosen this option. This option allows the trading of goods with some exceptions, like fish and agriculture. This may cost nearly as much as EU membership and may require other things like taking in refugees and allowing the free flow of EU citizens.

> European Free Trade Association (EFTA) Switzerland joins Norway, Iceland and Lichtenstein in this. This may also require the free movement of UK citizens

> An individual customs agreement with the EU.

The second and third options require some of the premises of full membership in the EU. The free movement of people, goods, services, and capital are required. They also must abide by European Union rules which the UK would not have a say in developing. All require some payment to the EU.

LOOKING AT THE ARGUMENTS—WE WONDER WHY THE VOTE TO LEAVE

Since before Aristotle and well into our future, thinkers have realized that most of us can be manipulated and that we are not too smart. Machiavelli developed some rules on how we can be controlled, but we don't like to think that he was right. In fact, he was so evil to think such thoughts that when politicians manipulate us we call it Machiavellian!

Today, in the age of mass data, thinking politicians have many means by which they can select for their electorate and manage their thinking. Data mining, fake news, fake history, wild promises, wilder guesses, and other propaganda techniques have come to the forefront. We in the "herd" have enough problems and wishes, that we are fair game for anyone we might look up to.

It is like a religious leader promising Paradise if we will only do his bidding. If we will only contribute 10% of our wages to him, kill whoever he says, be charitable, pray daily, bring more people to the altar—if we will only BELIEVE!

Whether it is in the hereafter or in the now, we need only believe our prophets. And who are these prophets? They preach to us every day—on TV, on Facebook, and on blogs. Believe in me and I will:

> get rid of the immigrants,

> get you to heaven,

> increase your pension,

> bring you happiness, or

> lower your taxes.

There is no end to the desires we have-- and the promises we will believe. Give me faith that my hopes will be fulfilled!

But the recent elections in the US and the UK have manipulated us to do the bidding of billionaires. Of course, we didn't realize it, but when powerful capitalists control somewhat-honest legislators it is a cause for concern. Putting in pro-citizen regulations, like the US and the EU have done, makes it harder for capitalists and other business people to make a dishonest dollar, or rather, an unethical dollar. When the citizens of the country are losing because of business practices that hurt the citizenry while enriching the billionaires—legislators who are interested in the common good make laws that place hurdles in the lanes where the capitalists wanted a flat track—something needed to be done. And who has the money? The billionaires!

In using the term "capitalists" I am using it in its purest Marxian definition, "People who make money on their money." Not all people making money fit into this definition of capitalism. Marx certainly included business owners who had employees making them money. Banks and stock traders are obviously pure capitalists. I don't know what Marx would say, but I don't believe that entrepreneurs are capitalists, certainly not in the developmental stages. When Bill Gates and Steve Jobs were fiddling in their garages with revolutionary ideas for the Internet age, I don't see how such work is capitalistic, although in modern parlance it seems that everyone who wants to make money is called a capitalist.

A BIT ABOUT THOSE WORKING TO MANIPULATE THE "LEAVE" VOTE

After the financial crisis in 2008, the EU began a tighter regulation of speculators, such as hedge funds. It is said that the major stock speculators wanted revenge. According to T.J Coles, there were a number of hedge fund managers and others who did not like the European Union's regulations on speculation on stocks and other entities. It was decided to use the dissatisfaction of many in the UK to seek to escape the shackles of Brussels.

Patrick Barbour, founder of the Barbour Index, donated £500,000 to "Vote Leave." Michael Farmer, of the Red Kite group donated £200,000 to Vote Leave. Hedge fund manager Crispin Odey had put 870,000 pounds into the leave campaign. He assumed that the stock market would crash by 80% after Brexit. It did for a day or so but then rebounded somewhat. A year later his net loss was 125 million pounds.

The FTSE index of stocks rose from about 6,200 to well over 7,500. Is this what the hedge fund managers expected due to the drop in the British pound sterling? Did they also expect that inflation would increase for the general population? Did they care? I would guess, No.

USES OF PSYCHOLOGY IN MILITARY CONFLICTS

As we have noted before, going through the conscious mind to elicit stronger unconscious motivations has been used before, but as the science of psychology becomes more verifiable, particularly applied to psychological techniques of motivation, we are better able to select susceptible people then motivate them in the direction that we want them to move.

The various militaries have attempted to increase the killing efficiency of their own soldiers while attempting to demoralize their enemies by psychological techniques. Replacing round targets with more human looking targets is one way to slightly desensitize soldiers to killing.

In World War II the Japanese were portrayed as, "yellow bellied slant-eyed devils." Because of this the American soldiers could feel vastly superior, which appealed to their drives for power. Killing them was not killing real people.

Attempting to demoralize the enemy is another. In World War II the Japanese used "Tokyo Rose" to broadcast her daily or weekly diatribes telling American GIs that their wives or girlfriends were untrue to them—as a way of lowering their morale.

The US drops leaflets in Taliban territory to influence them to surrender. Not to be outdone, ISIS sends nearly 100,000 messages a day attempting to recruit fighters and potential wives for them, as well as spreading positive propaganda for their cause.

INFLENCING ELECTIONS

So psychological techniques, when properly applied to susceptible individuals, very often change behavior. We know how important this is an advertising. We know how important it is in war. And, for the last several years we are finding how important it is in elections.

Today, there are huge amounts of data on people in much of the world because of social media, particularly Facebook. This is then developed and reworked with our greater knowledge of applied psychology. It can result in effective targeted advertising to both proponents and opponents of a candidate or proposition. Companies such as AggregateIQ, which was extremely important in the Brexit outcome, and Cambridge Analytica, which was essential in the Trump campaign, are only two examples.

According to the Guardian, Christopher Wiley worked for Cambridge Analytica before the Trump election. He said that they spent over $1 million harvesting Facebook profiles for the election. In 2014, Bannon and Wiley sought to study personality by quantifying it.

How Cambridge Analytica acquired the data has been the subject of internal reviews at Cambridge University, of many news articles, and much speculation and rumor.

When Alexander Nix, CEO of Cambridge Analytica was interviewed by members of Parliament in early 2018, he denied that Global Science Research had worked with him since 2014. However, Christopher Wiley has a copy of a contract between the parent company of Cambridge Analytica and Global Science Research (GSR). GSR is owned by Aleksandr Kogan, a researcher who was associated with both Cambridge University and St. Petersburg University. Wiley also has receipts for $1 million spent with GSR, a total of $7 million to amass the data.

Kogan, through a series of manipulations and contacts, was able to access peoples' Facebook profiles. This yielded 320,000 profiles. And each of these yielded an average of 160 other people. Kogan did have permission to pull Facebook data, but only for academic purposes. Under British law, it is illegal to sell such a data without the consent of the third-party. Facebook was alerted because of the vast amount of information being downloaded, but was told it was for academic purposes.

Kogen, it is now known, had received grants from the Russian government to research "Stress, health and psychological wellbeing in social networks." The Russians had already begun to research how to disrupt American elections as early as 2014. Cambridge Analytica had, Wiley said, given a great deal of information to the head of a Russian oil company, who had used it to spread rumors in a Nigerian election. The company had oil interests in Nigeria. It was said that the Russian oil company, Lukoil, had strong ties to Putin.

While Cambridge Analytica had apparently not been paid by Russia or its companies, Lukoil was well aware of techniques of micro-targeting data mining, and election disruption. In 2016, it was revealed that an advisor to the Czech president, who is strongly pro-Russian, was being paid by Lukoil.

The various "Leave" organizations are said to have spent over 4.5 million pounds with AggregateIQ. This was about 40% of their total budget.

Both campaigns, for Brexit and Trump, were geared to find issues that a majority would vote for--while primarily fostering the interests of business people and stock manipulators. The major interests for the most generous donors to Trump and/or Brexit included:

> Fewer regulations affecting business interests,
> Fewer regulations regarding hedge fund managing,
> Lower business taxes
> Lower personal taxes,
> Lower inheritance taxes.

The voters, however, were told that they were voting for:

➢ National sovereignty,

➢ Fewer immigrants,

➢ More jobs, and

➢ A safer and better life.

We must remember that the concerns of those who manipulate many of us are about self-centered financial interests, not with bettering society. Money, not morality, is generally the objective. And we, the citizens, usually end up with the bill.

The modern data firms are reasonably effective in finding the interests of varying clumps of voters. They can often determine which groups of people will vote for a proposal, and which groups may be influenced to vote for a proposition. They also try to identify which opposing voters may be likely to be dissuaded from voting by using varying findings and tactics.

A large part of their work may be fashioning the appropriate propaganda for the varying voting blocs. Propaganda can be true or false—it is merely geared to "propagating" an idea or behavior.

For example, if crimes by immigrants or losing jobs to immigrants are factors, the anti-immigrant propaganda can be utilized on those voters. If health is a major concern, as it might be with seniors, then increasing money for the National Health Service is a natural "hook." If people want to live in Spain, with all the free health perks of the EU, the "stayers" would have a powerful voting bloc, if they could convince them to get out of their sunbeds and vote. But if you have lived abroad for over 15 years you would have to return to the UK to vote.

Zack Massingham, the 34-year-old founder of AggregateIQ, told the Canadian newspaper The Globe and Mail that, "Coming from the technology and business world, I saw that the way campaigns were being run was wildly inefficient," He explained his philosophy like this: "You always want to try and reduce everything down to the simplest form of the argument and then repeat those simple lines again and again and again--and that becomes your brand." The continued calls to "Lock her up." made many believe that Hillary deserved it. The objective truth was that she had never been found guilty of anything in a court of law. The Donald however had actually been found guilty of breaking federal laws. But the truth is not important in modern "democratic" elections where the intellect is by-passed and the deeper conscious and unconscious needs and drives are manipulated.

Winning is the only outcome to applaud—the only ethical standard for demagogues. If you want to beat the odds at the race course, bet on the steroid stimulated stallions. If you want to win the election stimulate the conscious and unconscious minds of likely voters and use whatever techniques necessary to keep the naysayers at home. Maybe you can rig some polls to show that their vote is not needed. Maybe you can create enough doubt in their minds that they even questioned their previous decision on the candidate or the proposition. The ethical basic assumption here is self-centered for the person pulling the strings. We would hope that in a democratic election the ethical assumption of the politicians would be society-based.

To give you an idea of what AggregateIQ advertises, here is part of its website.

DISCOVER WHAT WE CAN DO FOR YOU PLAN BIG & DON'T SWEAT
THE SMALL STUFF
AggregateIQ delivers proven technologies and data driven strategies that help you make timely decisions, reach new audiences and ultimately achieve your goals.

Persuasion—Message Testing—Public Opinion Polling—Direct Door-To-Door
Contact—Online Engagement & Intervention—Data Management—
Software Development—Audience Analysis—
Clear Reporting—Measurable Results

Finding "persuadable" voters is key for any campaign, and with its treasure trove of data, Cambridge Analytica could target people high in neuroticism, for example, with images of immigrants "swamping" the country. The key is finding emotional triggers for each individual voter.

A small number of people they identified as "persuadable" were bombarded with a huge number of ads, often on Facebook. It has been estimated that there were over a billion total views, with the targeted populations receiving many such messages.

WHERE DID THE MONEY COME FROM?

Transparency International found that 95 percent of all money raised during the referendum campaign came from just 100 donors—a tiny fraction of the millions who voted on June 23, 2016.

Although all the donations were entirely legal, Transparency International's own polling found that 76 percent of the public now think wealthy individuals are using their influence on government to benefit their own interests.

Commenting on the EU referendum campaign, Duncan Hames, the director of policy at Transparency International UK, said: "The debate around the biggest question we have faced in a generation was financed by an astonishingly small group of exceptionally wealthy donors. That's a dangerous situation for any democracy. It illustrates the general dependency of our country's political parties on a millionaires' club of some 50 donors."

The top 10 donors during the EU referendum campaign. Six were for leaving.

To leave the EU (in British pounds):

➢ Peter Hargreaves (financier) 3,200,000

➢ Better for the Country (Arron Banks, investor) 2,060,375

➢ Jeremy Hosking (investor) 1,691,296

➢ Diana Van Nievelt (conservative businesswoman) 1,000,000

➢ International Motors LTD (automotive imports, etc.,) 850,000

➢ JC Bamford 670,000

To stay in EU

➢ David Sainsbury (Super markets) 4,223,234

➢ Trailfinders (travel industry) 1,000,000

➢ David Harding (financier) 1,000,000

➢ Mark Coombs (financier) 750,000

RUSSIAN INFLUENCE IN THE UK

When beginning this book, I realized only that politicians were bypassing our intellects to motivate us through our unconscious minds. The data mining that pinpointed our unconscious desires and the fake news that played to this theme were unknown to me. As the book was being written, the influence of the Russians and other countries on the Brexit and Trump campaigns began to be realized. We don't know yet all of the factors, but we also find that their meddling did not stop in the UK and the US. They were influential in stirring up Catalonian independence desires as well as anti-immigrant and anti-EU feelings in France, Germany, and the Netherlands. And, Robert Mueller, who was appointed to investigate Russian interference in the 2017 American election, affirmed in June of 2018., that the Russians were still hard at work--trying to influence the 2018 mid-term elections.

"Russia is seeking to undermine the international system. That much is clear—international order as we know it is in danger of being eroded," said Teresa May in a November 2017 speech. Russia is obviously intent on reducing the integrity of the European Union and of the threat of NATO. It also wants to have the monetary sanctions against it eliminated. They have much to gain, and little to lose, from their free Facebook, Twitter, and Google messages and inexpensive advertising. Naturally, as astute politicians, the Russians deny any knowledge of the extensive campaigns.

Academics at the City University in London found that 13,000 twitter accounts that were pro-Brexit disappeared after the referendum. UK academics had already established that at least 419 Twitter accounts operating from the Kremlin-linked Russian Internet Research Agency (IRA) tweeted about Brexit and that thousands of other Russia-based Twitter accounts posted more than 45,000 messages about Brexit in one 48 hour period during the referendum.

One of the accounts, run from the Kremlin-linked operation, attempted to stir anti-Islamic sentiment during the Westminster Bridge terror attack in March of 2017 in a bogus post claiming that a Muslim woman ignored the injured victims. But it is more than just the elections that are being infiltrated. "I can confirm that Russian interference, seen by the National Cyber Security Centre over the past year, has included attacks on the UK media, telecommunication and energy sectors," said Ciaran Martin, the founding chief executive of the NCSC (National Cyber Security Center of the UK).

DON'T CONFUSE ME WITH FACTS—MY MIND'S MADE UP!

Loud mouths, rather than reasoned evidence analysis, seem to connect better with our unconscious minds and our need to feel power. Donald Trump is a prime example. In Brexit, Boris Johnson, Michael Gove, and Nigel Farage were the reactionary front men seeking to move back to the good old days of jolly old England. Did they steer us wrong?

A common tactic of politicians is to call those who disagree bemoaners, needless worriers, or uninformed. If we are to vote intelligently, we need to evaluate the evidence on both sides of the argument.

When people have had their minds made up on an issue, such as that immigration is bad for the country or that we must take our borders back, all the other arguments may be rejected. For example, there were stark warnings about the effect on the country's economic system and on the personal finances of individuals. When President Obama said that the UK would have to go to the back of the queue if they left the European Union. He meant that there are many existing trade agreements with other countries, and even though there has been a close relationship between the US and UK, the US would not therefore give priority to the UK over other treaties.

But these fell on deaf ears. The Bank of England, the OECD, the International Monetary Fund and a number of other knowledgeable institutions and people warned of the negative financial consequences of Brexit. The Bank of England warned of recession and the Treasury warned of increased taxes, and the necessity to cut the budget for schools and the National Health Service.

The leavers responded that the remainers were over-using fear tactics, they called it Project Fear, and they charged that the remainers were wealthy unaccountable elites advocating their own vested interests. It was a case of two rich pots, each calling the other black!

But the fact that the public discounted so readily the advice of experts points to something more than just a revolt against the establishment. It suggested that far more people felt left behind and untouched by the peaceful and economic benefits of five decades of EU involvement.

It is the self-centered desires of the present that cause most of us to act and to vote. Recession, depression, or war will never again be felt. History should not warn us for the future. My hopes are the only guideposts I need.

DENYING THE TRUTH

It is always an effective strategy to deny whatever arguments your opponents present—however factual or probable they may be. Trump did this repeatedly both denying the facts, criticizing the purveyors of the facts, and deflecting any arguments against his position.

When Michael Gove was the Environment Secretary in Cameron's cabinet he criticized the nearly universal views of economists who predicted a fall in the British economy. He said "People in this country have had enough of experts," Gove argued, "experts from organizations with acronyms, saying they know what is best and getting it consistently wrong." So after six months he was partially right because the experts at the Bank of England worked to minimize the problems. But after six months it was found that consumer confidence was at the lowest level in four years, new car sales were down for four consecutive months, and the Bank of England forecast that investment in business would be down by 20%.

ALMOST TWO YEARS AFTER THE VOTE

It's taken well over a year, but as Britain's economy slumps and inflation bites, the warnings about the costs of the vote to leave the EU are coming true.

Britain is officially the worst performer among the G7 so far this year. It is held back by high inflation that is putting consumers under pressure. Since the pound dropped 10% to 12%, it has made imports much more expensive. So inflation has arrived with a thud. The average household now spends $100 more a year on food. Energy, holidays, and airfare are all up in the neighborhood of 15%.

Unions now blame the government for the problems. You certainly don't want to blame those who voted to leave! Always blame the government, then vote them out in the next election—after you disbelieve their promises.

Just as in the American election, the unconscious fears were pandered to and the electorate was not sufficiently academically astute in the realities of economics. There are certainly well grounded reasons for some of the leavers concerns, like some of the Court of Equal Justice decisions, but as an American political observer once said, "It's the economy stupid."

When you expect to negotiate to get what you want, and your adversary doesn't like you, and has all the marbles—your hopes for what you want are likely to be dashed like Mother Goose's Humpty Dumpty after he fell from the wall.

On the other hand, Alice's Humpty Dumpty, whose semantics changed with his mood, might have explained the British economic concerns of the "remainers" as uninformed, then anti-Britain, then unpredictable, then probably short term, then . . . correct?

Who could have predicted that the UK economy could have fallen to last place in the G-7 and that the pound would have fallen to its lowest point in 30 years? Who would have believed that living standards would fall and inflation increase? Probably would have happened anyway, Brexit or no Brexit. The majority of voters believed Farage instead of

Cameron, and Johnson instead or Obama. Oops! Fairytales win again over evidence. So sad!

Who could have predicted higher energy and food bills, more expensive vacations, and the possibility of 190,000 British ex-pats being forced to return to England—putting additional strain on the NHS—to the tune of a half billion pounds a year, while lessening the Spanish responsibility for taking care of Britishers' health needs? Oh my! Who would have "thunk" there could be so many repercussions! Then there is the possibility of a shortfall of 20,000 nurses and 30,000 other health carers if immigration from East Europe is curtailed.

Voters who think of only one pet issue while burying their heads in the sand of ignorance, relative to the impact of all the issues in a complex election, should expect that reality may be different than expected when the sand is washed from their blinded eyes.

A little over a year ago, David Davis was confident that Brexit Britain would soon strike new trade deals across the world. They could be negotiated and agreed without the difficulties and the delays of which the Remainers had warned. All parts of the global trade jigsaw would fall quickly and neatly into place. "So be under no doubt," the Brexit secretary wrote for the website ConservativeHome, three weeks after the vote, "we can do deals with our trading partners, and we can do them quickly . . . . I would expect that the negotiation phase of most of them to be concluded within between 12 and 24 months. Trade deals with the US and China alone will give us a trade area almost twice the size of the EU, and of course we will also be seeking deals with Hong Kong, Canada, Australia, India, Japan, the UAE, Indonesia – and many others."

About the same time, international trade secretary Liam Fox predicted that a free-trade deal with the EU, giving continued access to EU markets after Brexit, "should be one of the easiest in human history." His fellow Tory, the hardline Eurosceptic John Redwood, also saw no problems in "realizing this great reconfiguration of British interests around the world." He declared, "Getting out of the EU can be quick and easy – the UK holds most of the cards in any negotiation." But the cards the UK held were not from a poker deck but from an "Old Maid" deck!

Now, 24 months after the referendum, the talk is no longer of quick deals, or smooth routes out. Instead, Theresa May and her cabinet are preparing the country for the possibility of "no deal" at all being reached with Brussels before the UK leaves at the end of March 2019. No deal might also mean only a 21-month transition of the kind that May said would be so important in her recent Florence speech.

Many of the hardline Brexiteers now champion "no deal" as the only way to become independent again. None of the trade deals they argued would be "so simple" have been realized and none are in sight. (It is not possible to enter into them until they leave the customs union).

The EU is refusing even to begin to talk about post-Brexit trade arrangements with the UK because other issues, like the multi-billion euro EU agreements that the UK is balking at paying. So "no deal" is looking more and more possible. And, parting as enemies may make future deals more difficult.

Right now, 43% of UK exports go to the EU. That is £240 billion of their total exports of £550 billion. 54% of the imports into the UK came from the EU. About 80% of UK exports are in services such as banking and IT. If 70,000 banking jobs were to leave the UK, as has been predicted, their export balance would be significantly affected. Presently the UK runs an £80 million deficit with the EU.

If there is no UK–EU deal before March 2019, the consequences will be nasty. They could be huge and immediate. The return of customs checks would mean a return to the hard border between Northern Ireland and the republic. For trade, the UK would default to WTO rules, meaning tariffs would be imposed on goods leaving the UK for the EU and on those sold to the UK market by the remaining 27 member states.

The government has said it wants the continuation of "frictionless" trade with EU countries. But a WTO regime would mean, by contrast, tariffs of between 2% and 3% on many industrial goods, 10% for cars and 20% to 40% for many agricultural products. Some British companies have moved, and many others are considering relocating. This certainly doesn't help the economy. But I guess it's worth it to take back our borders!

Naturally, those who were the strong Brexiteers are blaming the EU or those who voted against leaving. They seem to be using the traditional tried and true political excuses. They are learning from Donald Trump, the master deflector.

MANIPULATING THE VOTERS

As we become more aware of how to manipulate people by finding the conscious and unconscious interests then hitting them with verbal or visual messages aimed at their basic motivations, advertising becomes more effective and political messaging becomes more deeply ingrained. We become more effective in manipulating people, especially the less informed. Whether we are trying to sell cigarettes, scotch, or perfume we appeal to the drives that Freud and Adler postulated over a century ago—pleasure, sex, and power. We poor, deprived mortals fear that we may not have enough of them or are losing them, and we hope to again satisfy them.

Some people don't associate the idea of disapproving of, or hating, the present government with their unconscious drives for power. For example, when Prime Minister Cameron and President Obama along with Christine Lagarde of the International Monetary Fund tell you that leaving the EU will be disastrous for the economy, but you are interested in getting rid of immigrants, you can gain a strong feeling of power because you are superior to those well-informed people in powerful positions whose opinions vary from yours.

It's not just in politics that these drives and needs raise their perennial heads. When you win at gambling, and you know the odds are against you, you feel really good—and powerful in your conquest. If you can join others who want to "drain the swamp," you can feel superior to all those in the swamp. When you can criticize your boss, along with your fellow unhappy colleagues, you can feel superior because of your high level of intelligence and your superior knowledge of the business. When you and your same-sex friends can criticize your spouses because of their ignorance, incompetence, or bossiness, you feel superior. (And why was it that you chose that person to be in your partner in a relationship? Who is the dumb one?)

In the referendum for Britain to exit the European Union (Brexit) big money and loud voices pandered to the fear that native Brits were losing out to EU immigrants and that too many British pounds sterling were being sent to Brussels with not enough coming back. When 52% of the voters agreed with the arguments of the Brexiteers, led by reactionary politicians Nigel Farage and the mayor of London, Boris Johnson, did they realize the ramifications of their votes?

THE MONEY BEHIND THE MANIPULATION

Robert Mercer was a major factor in the Brexit vote and then in Trump's victory. He was a major contributor financially to both. Mercer is a computer genius who has amassed a billion-dollar fortune as a hedge fund manager. He is a reactionary thinker who professes ideas from conservative through reactionary. His funding often goes to propagandizing reactionary political thinking. He certainly wants less government. Mercer gave Trump $13.5 million for his campaign.

He funds the libertarian Heartland Fund which denies global warming and has denied the link between cigarettes and cancer. The fund has utilized a number of messages that are logical fallacies in its propaganda campaigns— such as since the Unabomber believes in climate change so climate change must be untrue. You remember the *ad hominem* fallacy in which one criticizes a person then concludes that his argument is false. So if Hitler believed that the Earth was round—it must not be round!

Mercer funded Breitbart media with $10 million that enabled them to establish the far-right wing media organization.

Arron Banks, the second largest contributor to the Brexit campaign, and Nigel Farage, a primary politician in the campaign, had a meeting with Russian ambassador. It is said that he was offered a stake in Russian gold mines. He is being investigated for possible pro-Russian advocacy in working to have the UK leave the EU— a strong desire of Putin.

FEW PEOPLE ARE ALWAYS CONTENT WITH HOW THINGS ARE

People generally want change since there are always actions or inactions of the government that they are not happy with. I want lower taxes. I want a higher pension. I want quicker access to better doctors. I want free college education for my kids. I am tired of this saber rattling—I don't want another war. I want cheaper restaurant prices and hotel room rates—but I don't want immigrants here even though they are the reason for the lower prices. I want cheaper gasoline and less traffic. I guess the only way to get all this is to throw out the scoundrels in Washington and Westminster.

There were people in Britain who were not doing as well as they would have liked. Of course, this is true in every country. With more people than needed because of overpopulation, automation, computerization, globalization and 3-D printing—every country is facing problems. The rich get richer and the poor get poorer, and there is no end in sight. Coal mining, previously absolutely essential, is now rapidly becoming a societal evil, being highly polluting and a non-renewable resource of energy as well as being relatively expensive. People who are willing to work for less money can produce steel, and many other essentials, for much less than the workers in the West. The "good old days" are well behind us if we are blue collar workers or even middle management white collared personnel. Consequently, a vote for "the good old days" is unrealistic. Wishes don't make reality!

THE ICEBURG COMETH

As frightening as this is, it's just the tip of the iceberg. The post-communist era of stable Western democracies (i.e., liberal democracy) seems to be collapsing under the weight of its own contradictions and corruption, barely 25 years after certain political theorists were declaring the "end of history." Far-right demagogues, like Trump, are rising across Europe by scapegoating immigrants and strongly opposing the European experiment, while the authoritarian government of Russia may very well have tipped America's own presidential election. Illiberal populists are threatening the status quo.

NEGOTIATIONS WITH THE EU

When challenged about the costs of Brexit, leading "Leave" figures continue to argue that the UK can enjoy all of the benefits of membership, such as frictionless, tariff-free access to the single market, while bearing none of the burdens. When asked about the challenges, they respond with false reassurances that everything will be fine. And nostalgia for our past glory days is essential, as if this is a prescription for the future. It is both because the Leave campaign was so deceitful and the real policy cupboard is so bare that many Brexiteers have attempted to shut down all debate about Britain's future since the referendum result was declared.

If the UK leaves the EU will it be a hard Brexit or a soft Brexit. A hard Brexit would allow for the stopping of immigration from Eastern Europe but would put Britain on the outside and forced to negotiate everything with the EU. This would undoubtedly include tariffs. Obviously, the other countries in the EU would not be happy that Britain had left and would not negotiate kindly with them. The UK was a net donor to the union. Most countries are net recipients. They certainly do not want a donor to leave.

On the other hand, a soft Brexit would require the same immigration regulations that many of those who wanted to leave saw as the major problem and the major reason for voting to leave. Consequently, since the "leavers" major concern was immigration, a hard Brexit was the only real alternative. So Britain would be forced to negotiate with someone who was angry with them and who had all of the cards—so different from what the leavers had promised.

As you will notice, when there is a projected negative outcome for one's position, you do not mention it. This was true of the value of the pound projected to drop and the increased cost of imports and traveling.

Brexiteers were unhappy with the "now," but had no programs. This is a problem with populism—it acknowledges some problems but has no realistic programs for the rapidly changing future. Then, when the populists are in power, their voters bemoan them. If you can't solve the problem, find a scapegoat. Theresa May was the girl! Having been against Brexit, but eager to pick up the power pom-poms when Cameron withdrew, she was to be the irresistible force that could mow down the EU immovable object.

But low and behold, the EU prince had all the jewels and the departing pauper could merely plead for "fairness," fairness as defined by the underdog. The starting point was the over 60 billion pounds that the UK had already promised for projects in the EU. 60 billion pounds is enough to keep the citizens of Liverpool and Manchester in soccer players and fish and chips for over a year! Since all of the EU countries have a vote on the final agreement, and the East European countries will lose a lot of the EU subsidies that Britain was financing, you can be certain of at least one "nay" vote. Additionally, most of the members of the EU do not want members to leave, it therefore behooves them to give nothing more than is absolutely necessary.

Naturally the "leavers" will blame whoever is in power for not negotiating a cornucopia contract with an unfriendly neighbor. They expect all of their "I wants" granted by the wicked witch while only giving up a few breadcrumbs. A very Grimm possibility!

THEN THERE WAS THE VOTE!

Older people remembered the realities of the past. They voted. Younger people looked more at a dreamy idealistic future. Since only good things will happen, why vote. The answer, of course, is—if you don't vote you may get a Bush, a Trump, or a Brexit. In a democracy, the votes count—not the more hopeful dreams for pleasant outcomes.

Wishes don't win elections!

Did all UK voters thoroughly analyze every argument and every possibility that might ensue from either a "vote leave" or a "vote stay"? As they say, "You don't know what you have until you lose it," and "The grass always looks greener on the other side of the street." But will your vote get you safely across?

THERE'S STILL A REAL CHANCE FOR A SECOND BREXIT REFERENDUM

The key is timing. The people may well want a rethink once the clock runs out in March 2019—when the disaster will be clear. Former Prime Ministers Tony Blair and John Major are strong voices for a "do-over."

As the Labour Party has advanced in the polls, and since it is more friendly to a soft Brexit idea, another referendum might be asked to clarify whether the people want to proceed with leaving the European Union, and if so, whether they want a hard or soft Brexit. But the UK does not want to accept the EU requirements for a softer Brexit at this time. The Guardian conducted a poll of those who were certain of how they would vote in a second referendum, ignoring the undecided voters, and found a 16% majority for having a second referendum.

BUT—a large survey UK survey on happiness showed that people in England were slightly happier a year after the vote while the people of Scotland, Northern Ireland, and Wales had not improved in their happiness feelings. So, who knows?

CHAPTER 10.   HOW DID GEORGE W. BUSH MANIPULATE US –
AND WHERE DO WE GO FROM HERE?

Vice-President Cheney said, "that by voting for Kerry, Americans would be inviting another terrorist attack." Kerry did not respond to such charges except in saying that they were lies. He could have rightfully attacked Bush's avoiding the Vietnam War by joining the Air National Guard in Texas and not following orders while in that organization. His service records showed such problems as not taking his physical exam and not showing up for required flying.

Bush lost his authorization to pilot Air National Guard planes and the records show that he did not attend any drills between mid-April and the end of October in 1972. He was however discharged honorably.

Does this ring a Kipling bell?

> I could not dig; I dared not rob:
> Therefore I lied to please the mob.
> Now all my lies are proved untrue
> And I must face the men I slew.
> What tale shall serve me here among
> Mine angry and defrauded young?

(From the Epitaphs of War 1914-18, "The Statesman.")

THE PROMISES OF POLITICIANS

George Bush promised to bring affordable healthcare for the 43 million uninsured citizens. During his first two years, this number of uninsured increased by 4 million and health insurance premiums had risen by an average of 12 1/2% per year. Adopting his proposals would have driven them up even higher.

He promised a $500 million fund over five years to address targeted health risks such as childhood diabetes. This was never done.

He promised that the federal government would comply with all environmental laws. The Department of Defense could not meet these legal rules.

He said he would fully fund Pell grants for the first year of college by more than 50% to $5100. In actuality, he cut the budget for Pell grants to $4050 and for three years reduced this amount.

He promised assistance for lower income people with energy assistance costing up to $1 billion over 10 years. In practice, he actually cut the budget for it and the number receiving assistance-- in spite of a colder winter and more unemployment.

He promised to attack pork-barrel spending. But did not veto a single bill with enormous amounts of pork-barrel projects.

The majority of his tax cuts were to go to the bottom end of the spectrum. In actuality 70% of the cuts went to the top 20% of the population.

He promised that he would reduce the national debt to a historically low level. It actually finished at an historically high level of over $7,000,000,000.

He said that Social Security surplus must be locked away only for the recipients. But he spent $159 billion of the Social Security funds in increasing the national debt because of the Iraq War and his tax cuts.

THE GORE CAMPAIGN

In the 2000 election, we had the traditional battle of political innuendos and associations. A major point of the Bush strategy was to paint Al Gore into the sexually immoral actions of the previous president. Gore, of course, had been the vice president. "Bring back dignity and honor to the White House," was a major thrust. Early in the race, Bush was seen as more likable and a better leader. After all he had owned a pro baseball team and had been Governor of Texas. What's not to like?

Guilt by association is often a good political tactic. But as the campaign rolled on, the race was pretty much of a dead heat. Consequently, Bush's team started attacking on the issues, often painting the proposals of Gore in negative terms that were far from reality. Of course, this is not a new political strategy. It is as common as harassment in Hollywood.

"Al Gore's prescription plan forces seniors into a government-run H.M.O.," said one commercial. "Governor Bush gives seniors a choice. Gore says he's for school accountability, but requires no real testing. Governor Bush requires tests and holds schools accountable for results."

It was decided that the Bush campaign had to change the way the public thought about the issues. Just as the Republicans had negatively attacked the Clinton universal healthcare coverage by stating that it was the government trying to intrude on people's private lives. The plan died in 1994 when the Republicans won control of Congress.

As the campaign rolled on, Gore was able to separate himself from the Clintons and show his leadership abilities. Bush criticized Gore's idea to create a prescription drug benefit inside Medicare. He said it would create price controls. Three years later Bush signed legislation to do exactly that. Was this a dishonest criticism?

THE KERRY CAMPAIGN

Kerry was portrayed as an extremely liberal Northeastern elitist. He was also labeled as a flip flopper because he would vote for one aspect of the bill, then vote against it in another form.

He was portrayed as one who was out of touch with middle America being a rich New Englander. The Bush ads were more anti-Kerry than pro-Bush. On the other hand, Bush was painted as an ordinary American. While both candidates were very rich, Bush was a "good ol' boy" driving around his ranch in a pickup and hunting rabbits. Kerry was high society. But their political positions were quite different with Kerry espousing liberal causes for the common man and Bush backing the conservative causes of the rich— although some of his programs, such as "No Child Left Behind" were theoretically forward steps in education. But this is open to question. For all the fanfare, it didn't make much difference in high school graduates' knowledge.

In my own case I had taught English in two colleges, a middle school and a high school, had a California teaching credential that allowed me to teach it, and had published more than twenty books, but English was not my college major so I was not allowed to teach English in a ghetto high school where I was the football coach.

Kerry's twenty-year service in Congress necessarily showed some changes in positions sometimes because of compromises needed to pass certain legislation. Such changes of ideas are not compatible with a steadfast commander-in-chief. Criticizing, or at least questioning why, legislators' change their views is certainly reasonable in elections. Did the representative change because of new knowledge, because of a lobbyist's contribution, because of a compromise needed to get a more important bill passed?

Kerry didn't answer these criticisms effectively. And if he had, he should have done it at half-time of a Cowboys-49er game, since so few young voters watch the news. Younger people are much more likely to get their news online—and this is where fake news flourishes. Republicans are much more likely to solidify their opinions by watching Fox Views-- sorry I mean Fox News! 40% of Republicans watch Fox. On the other hand, the under-50 group get much of their "news" from Steven Colbert and the Daily Show!

As a liberal, Kerry was for tax increases to help pay for the war and social expenses. But Americans are not for tax increases at any time. This tradition goes back to the Boston Tea Party.

Bush's most effective knife thrust was the highly questionable Swiftboat Veterans for Truth. It was an organization designed to discredit Kerry's battle experience. It was, by far, Bush's most effective lie. Kerry was a legitimate hero in Vietnam and had three purple hearts awarded for injuries— and a silver star and bronze star for outstanding bravery.

In 1971, he spoke to a congressional committee concerning the conduct of the war, which he thought was unethical or illegal. The Swiftboat Veterans for Truth criticized Kerry's testimony as unpatriotic. This group had no one who had actually served in battle with Kerry. Those who had served with him backed his story and his heroism. It was later found that the group was largely funded by three major Republican donors from Texas and its postal address was registered to Susan Arceneaux, the treasurer of the Majority Leader's Fund, a PAC closely tied to the former Congressional leader, Republican Dick Armey.

The accusations of the group have been criticized because none had served with Kerry in battle. From 2004 until the final evaluation of the group in 2016 it was clear that the group was a politically motivated pro-Bush group that had amassed a group of total lies. While Republican Senator John McCain denounced the Swift boat campaign, no one brought up the fact that George Bush had avoided service by joining the Texas Air National Guard, where he didn't perform all of his requirements.

Kerry, like Gore before and Clinton later, had not effectively countered the political lies that drowned them. Each was highly ethical and believed that the voters thought like them. They were wrong!

PLAYING TO OUR CONSCIOUS AND UNCONSCIOUS MINDS

HOPE—that things will improve (better job or marriage, go to heaven)

FEARS—that things will not improve

ANGER—that things are not better

The Swiftboat Veterans group had a two-pronged psychological attack. One was fostering "anger" against Kerry because his testimony to the congressional committee was anti-American to most gun-toting Texans. In retrospect, experts wholeheartedly agree with his testimony, but at the time it was seen by some Texans as being traitorous—the "good ol' US of A" should never be criticized. The group's other psychological push was to develop fear—a common and effective political tool.

While Bush pushed the idea that America was more in danger of terrorism and even of nuclear war if Kerry was elected, Kerry started a mass fear offensive of his own. He portrayed Bush as a headstrong leader whose rush to war in Iraq had isolated the U.S from the world community, enraged the Arab world, and permitted Osama bin Laden to remain free. Kerry said that, "This president has made, I regret to say, a colossal error of judgment, and judgment is what we look for in the President of the United States of America." Kerry criticized Bush for failing to enlist the help of the United Nations and other allies before going into Iraq, saying that as a result the United States was enduring a disproportionate number of casualties and costs.

Fear is a very potent moderator because it enlarges our inferiority feelings and lessens whatever feeling of power we possess.

Naturally, you don't leave your voters feeling only fear and anger, you must give them hope. So, promise them anything!

While we expect some lies and misinterpretations of the opponent's programs and policies, we may also expect some "guilt by association" claims, but outright lies about an opponent have not been traditional. In the Gore campaign, we had the expected misinterpretations that we often find in political campaigns. In the Kerry campaign, Bush went to great lengths to discredit John Kerry, as an American war hero. He was not only a hero, but he was for the common man. He was a formidable foe.

It was required to criticize his policies and programs, but it was essential to discredit him as a hero while George Bush had avoided active service by joining the reserves. How could a reservist, who did not even do all of his required reserve duties, compare with a real war hero? He had to make Kerry look like he had not deserved his honors. This required some far out thinking and probably was the beginning of the downfall of Republican honesty in politics. A few years later Republican John McCain returned to honest politics—and lost.

During the McCain versus Obama campaign. McCain pushed people to understand that Obama did not have the experience needed. He continually said, "you don't understand," to Obama in the debates. Obama kept pushing for long-term goals. It was generally a high-level campaign on both sides, more of what one would prefer in an American presidential election.

It appears that the elections involving Trump, Bush, and Brexit were not decided on the best interests of the voters, even though, of course, the voters decided. It appears that using the psychological techniques that pinpoint and agitate the voters through fear, anger, and hope are more effective than logical arguments. It appears that we voters are more psychological than logical. But who of us will admit it?

ALL MAJOR CANDIDATES USE DATA MINING

Every major candidate in a political race in America uses data mining. How they use it can vary. it can be used to: connect with your base, to try to find and flip independent voters, to discourage opponents from voting, and how to use the information you have to best influence the voters. (on emails, TV, radio, newspaper ads, billboards, etc.).

It appears that Hillary Clinton's data mining was geared to a large degree toward the types of television advertising that should be done. Trump, as in the Brexit election, used emails considerably. This kept the cost of advertising down. All major parties will use both emails and television ads. Effective data mining should be geared not only to advertising but in gauging not just whom to talk to, how to talk to them, and what to say — but also when to say it (six months before the election, three months, two days, etc.).

When Michelle Obama told Hillary Clinton that "When they go low, we go high," it would work well in campaigns that were traditional. But when the opposition is playing dirty, you must get down in the dirt too. If you don't do it, important aides must do it. When, in a debate, Trump left his podium and followed closely behind Clinton, she should have turned around and tried to humiliate him. "Get back behind your podium, you are acting like my puppy." Or, "What are you doing so close behind me? Are you trying to read my mind so you get some good ideas on how to debate, or what to say next."?

It is a sad state when the people we expect to be statesmen are barroom brawlers. If we are using intelligent arguments and they are shooting us down with verbal AK-47s, then if we are going to win we must attack them with our own AK-47s, or even rocket launchers!

It is the weaker, less informed, and unethical people who are most likely to use these psychological techniques. But if the well-informed and ethical people are to win, they need to attack fire with fire. Can you imagine Donald Trump calling Joe Biden or Cory Booker "little Cory," "a liar," or "crooked Joe?" Biden would have probably popped him in the nose and left him crying. Booker, as a major college tight end from Stanford, would be imposing to any sarcastic coward—as Trump is. Happily, we are on an evolutionary path from physical fisticuffs to informed logical arguments as the way to a better government. But we are not there yet. The psychological Neanderthals must be quieted by weapons bigger than the stones and spears they brought to the fight.

In the Kerry-Bush campaign it was not Bush who called Kerry a coward. It was some people friendly to the Bush campaign who enlisted some people, who didn't know Kerry, to say things that were not true. While Kerry called them lies, that was not really enough. He did have the people who served with him speak out. But that was not enough either. There should have been a pro-Kerry group that called Bush a coward for not enlisting in the war and for not performing his duties in his Air National Guard unit.

As a political technique, attacks or threats of attacks, are the most primitive methods—but they are tried and true through the centuries. But the stronger warrior today uses digital daggers and deadly comebacks to the false claims of his or her challengers. When they go low, we go for the groin! And when they are doubled over in psychological pain, we deliver an uppercut of truth while rendering their vocal fallacies numb by challenging them at a logical level.

At the same time their probes into our unconscious minds— through anger, fear, and hope—must be challenged with even more anger, more fears, and more hope. The shallow narcissists and the henchmen of billionaires must be psychologically slaughtered with their own weapons—by exposing their logical fallacies and challenging them as to how, exactly, they will implement their policies—then going one better in their appeals to the conscious and unconscious fears and angers and outdoing their hopes with greater and more realistic hopes. The Brexiteers, Bush, and Trump don't really stand out in the intellectual areas—even if their daddies did get them into Oxford, Yale and Penn.

Hillary Clinton should have attacked Trump directly when she was called "crooked." She should have pointed out all the crooked things he had done, the legal cases he had lost, the actions against him by contractors, his breaking of federal laws, etc. She should've pointed out that she had never been found guilty in a court of law—but he had. So, who was crooked?

Trump has railed against political correctness. So his opponents, unfortunately, need to move down to his level and slug it out in the mud. As a basic coward, he would be forced to change his tactics because it would be catastrophic for his narcissistic ego and his superiority complex.

In the Brexit referendum, there really needed to be face to face debates with the "leavers" forced to produce evidence for their idea that it would be easy to negotiate with the European Union. There was no reason why the UK should get a better deal than Norway, which was paying almost as much as the UK in dues per person, and was taking in immigrants from Eastern Europe. Some of the "leavers" had suggested that the UK could have the same deal as Norway. But Norway's "deal" was really not that ideal for those who wanted no immigrants and closed borders.

In the future, when one side of a proposition or an opposing candidate either does not tell the truth or is psychologically pugnacious, the other side must tear down the arguments while making better arguments for their own cause—and above all, attack at the psychological level. As we said before, "people are far more psychological than logical." Successful campaigns must rely on both levels of our minds—only the intelligent can be persuaded by valid, fallacy-free, arguments. But sadly, many poorly educated express their anger is the voting booth—without having thought through the total impact of their Xs.

HOW TO WIN ELECTIONS

As long as most of us are psychologically motivated, and hopefully a little bit logical, it seems that candidates who want the best chance of winning should not forget to appeal to our psychological sides. Fear, anger, and hopes require some planned subconscious appeals-- along with making us feel more powerful to assuage our inferiority feelings.

FEAR

If one were running against Trump, he or she could play up:

> How he let Russia establish a strong foothold in the eastern Mediterranean.
> How has he minimized Russia's new nuclear missiles?
> How can we be defended against a nuclear attack from Russia?
> Why he is so pro-Russian.
> How his tariffs are increasing consumer prices.
> How the reciprocal tariffs are hurting our profits.

ANGER

He promised a better and cheaper health insurance, but did not deliver. And, many of his voters lost the federal subsidies that they needed to help pay for their health insurance.

Would some of his supporters be a bit disappointed if they found out that the reason he is soft on Putin is that he has plans for building a Putin Palace across the street from his proposed Trump Tower in Moscow? Vladimir could stifle those plans quicker than he executes a journalist or does away with a presidential challenger in a Siberian gulag?

How about an opponent surmising that he is weak on Russia because Putin has films of him cavorting in many unseemly activities with Russian prostitutes during his trips to Moscow. My guess is that it is 99.99% sure that Putin has some sexually unseemly films to hold over his head.

When I was first in Russia in 1962 it was well known that all hotel rooms and student dorms were bugged with hidden microphones. Just connect the dots—hidden cameras in all hotel rooms, with cinemascope visuals and high fidelity sound in the suites. Eager voluptuous Putin pussycats indulging your every fantasy—it's a dream film worthy of the Golden Porn award for the "Most Surprised John" flick at the annual Adult Film Awards at the Mustang Ranch—where every filly is a winner.

His Teflon mattress that bounced with Playboy bunnies and porn stars might be tossed from Trump Tower if his sexual adventures in St. Petersburg held his country hostage. But no—The Donald is far too smart for that. He would just have his lawyer pay them off—or he could sue them. So no sense of getting angry. It was Hillary or Barack who framed him!

HOPE

Every politician promises some hopes-- a job, a better job, higher pay, inexpensive health insurance, peace, smaller government, better education, free college tuition, less immigration, more immigration, tax reduction, and whatever the local voters want in the rally he or she is speaking to.

REFERENDA FOR SOVEREIGNTY

If your government is asking for a referendum to become separate from the European Union, NATO, or another group with similar interests, you can certainly play on the fear card. Europe has never gone so long without a war. Having the European Union and NATO standing by to stop any future Napoleons, Kaisers, Stalins, and Maria Theresas from attacking their neighbors or their countrymen-- is certainly a strong reason for a realistic alliance.

Commonly, an alliance between two or a few countries, is as strong as a lattice roof against a hurricane. However, the multi-country alliances of the EU and NATO have worked effectively since they were forged after the second "war to end all wars" was settled in 1945,

But of course, there will never be a war in your country. England has never been attacked. Germany has never been attacked. France has never been attacked. So why worry? But as the French President Emmanuel Macron observed, "nationalism means war." But, of course, he was only looking at the realities of history, not the fairytales of dreams. Wars will never happen in today's world, just ask the Syrians, Iraqis, and Afghans.

The UK wanted sovereignty. Why pay the European Union millions of pounds a week just for a significantly increased chance for peace, open borders for tariff-free trade, increased access to workers, access to millions of pounds of research grants, advanced university opportunities for your students, extensive retiree opportunities for living abroad for healthcare, and a number of other perks.

That referendum tweaked the interests of: Catalonians to leave Spain, Lombardy to secede from Italy, Poland and Hungary to flaunt the rules of refugee protection, of Greece to secede. But generally cooler heads prevailed and realized that the peace and advantages of a strong union outweighed the inconveniences of unwanted immigrants and of a distant Supreme Court that could overrule local jurisdictions.

Look at the UK, bargaining with Brussels and having no bargaining chips other than asking for pity. More far thinking heads could see that leaving the EU is chopping off your wallet, along with your hips and your legs. When only one EU country can prevent whatever you were bargaining for, it seems best to stay the course. You know any agreement hammered out will have to be approved by all EU members. They can't stop the UK from leaving, but they can stop any future participation with the EU.

Talk about fear and hope, the Catalans were voting with their dreams, rather than their realities. If they separated from Spain, who would they trade with? Europe could be beyond their reach.

So, when advocating a position, the wise politician will appeal to the intellect while jabbing at the unconscious. Anger and fear may stir the soul— but well-conceived hope must lead it in the direction you want the population to go.

GIVING THE VOTERS A FEELING OF POWER

This is more difficult for people in government to do than those challenging from the outside. If you are one of those in the swamp, it's difficult to call for draining the swamp. Of course, you can always call for draining those on the other side of the aisle! But now, The Donald is in middle of the swamp, so if you are hunting alligators or water moccasins, you know where to look. The Oval Office is crawling with them! In fact, a challenger to Trump could easily call for the tearing up of Wall Street and whittling the billionaires down to size. This might be done with the call to 100% tax on inheritances in order to pay for college tuition for all.

People with money are probably as good a target as the Washington insiders.

When C. Wright Mills developed his "power elites" concepts, he looked at political, economic, and military elites. It would probably be unwise to attack the military. But the other two are fair game.

WHAT IF THE VOTERS WERE RIGHT?

But what if history finds that the voters were right? What if Trump's policies for North Korea prevented them from developing their nuclear capabilities? That would be good for the world. What if putting tariffs on Chinese made goods magically increases American jobs and the American consumers don't have to pay more for the things made in China? What if American consumers paid so much more for the tariffed goods that we could pay down on the national debt—or give even bigger tax breaks to the billionaires?

But what if his policies start a nuclear war that wipes out most of the northern hemisphere? What if his tariffs start a worldwide trade war?

The nuclear holocaust might be even better! Since overpopulation is our major problem and it is directly related to the very negative factor of climate change. A nuclear war would wipe out most of the polluting countries and their spewing of noxious gases into the atmosphere and their casting of plastic into the oceans. Such a war might incinerate all of the ISIS and Al Qaeda threats. Another plus! Then will the Antarctic penguins rule the world?

What if Brexit's populist leadership entices other nations to follow? It is true that the United Nations, the European Union, and NATO have reduced the wars that used to occupy humanity's time before television and smart phones were invented. Why not go back to the good old days when men were men and women were women? Don't we really miss Attila, Hitler, and the Vikings?

And what is a positive potential outcome of the Bush administration? He did shake up the Middle East, even though he attacked Iraq instead of Saudi Arabia, where the 9/11 attackers were from. He only missed the proper target by a thousand miles.nHis leadership brought us to understand what should have been obvious to everyone—that being a person begins when the fertilized ovum attaches to the uterus. He had that idea made into law. And of course, there was our huge increase in the national debt. But without that, we probably would've frittered away that money on healthcare, education, or on reducing global warming.

History may speak to us of many things, but why listen? What happened yesterday is no gauge of what will happen today or tomorrow. Keep those history books closed because we don't have time to read them—we have to invent the wheel today. Tomorrow we are going to be occupied inventing fire.

OR—Do we care?

➤   Do we care if we are dumbed down, manipulated, and treated as means to some billionaire's avarice?

➤   Do we care if our sons and brothers are maimed or killed in a trumped up military action?

➤   Do we care if our bank is robbed by the financial elites while we are handed a few silver coins to look the other way?

➢ Do we care if our progeny will be impoverished by our pandering to the promises of politicians—and their lack of concern for education from pre-school through the PhD?

If not, we must learn to think, using the facts and theories that are available to us. We must educate ourselves and demand that our schools produce thinking citizens. We must rise above our subconscious selves and the digital data that seems to define us in our modern world. If we are to govern ourselves, we must become our own Founding Fathers and understand the problems that face us today, then with the method of science, work toward the best solutions.

With today's knowledge of psychology and the tools of manipulation available to those who would have an economic plutocracy, if we are to slay Big Brother, we need more than a sling shot and a couple of stones. We need a comprehensive education, the tools of logic, a belief in democracy, and the passion of David.

PART III. WHAT KIND OF GOVERNMENT DO WE WANT?

TRUST IN OUR GOVERNMENT

In the 2018 Edelman Trust Barometer, of the 28 countries evaluated, using both college-educated citizens and the general population within each country, China was the most trusted, followed by India, Singapore, Indonesia and the United Arab Emirates. European countries were far down the list with America dead last, below Russia and South Africa. It is unusual that this lack of trust in the US is happening at a time of economic prosperity--with the stock market up and the unemployment rate very low.

The analysis is that the cause is a lack of rational discussions and the absence of verifiable facts in any discussions. Only a few people high in government are readily acceptive of "alternate facts." There is a huge lack of faith in government.

The collapse of trust in the US is driven by a staggering lack of faith in government, which fell 14 points to 33 percent among the general population, and was down 30 points to 33 percent among the informed public. The trust of NGOs, business, and media also dropped significantly. This drop in trust in American government and other institutions is reflected increasingly across the world as problems with immigration, terrorism, the penchant for dictatorial impulses oozing from democratically elected presidents, and with the acquisitive and selfish capitalistic abilities of the "haves" propelling them farther and farther from their economic "have not" inferiors. The ideal of the comfortable national family has devolved into grumbling groups of avaricious avatars striving to be the fittest who survive.

ARE WE SATISFIED WITH THE PRESENT—AND ARE WE PREPARING FOR THE FUTURE?

There are very few citizens who do not want an honest government, but corruption is the rule of most economic systems. Sometimes it is obvious--like when business owners give money to legislators. Sometimes it is overlooked, as with Putin and his oligarchs. But mostly it is frowned upon by the citizens who are powerless to change things.

In Third World countries, you will often have to bribe a clerk to get a driver's license, a permit to build a house, or to rent an apartment. In the developed world, cities give tax breaks to businesses to locate there, and lobbyists contribute to legislators who do their bidding. And, have you ever noticed that in a Las Vegas showroom, the more you tip the maitre'd the closer you get to the stage? But that's another world!

Most of us would probably like honest, competent, ethical, and knowledgeable leaders, but they are in short supply. In fact, they may be practically nonexistent.

JUST LOOK AT OUR WORLD

The world is so complicated today that it is impossible to predict the future. Will climate change make the equatorial countries uninhabitable? Will it destroy much of the farming potentials in the temperate zones? Will you soon take your winter vacations on the warm sunny beaches of Scandinavia?

Will overpopulation continue its destruction of natural resources and of our abilities to care for our people? How much will illegal immigration continue to strain the economic and social boundaries of advanced countries?

Should we attempt to limit population, or do we need more workers to support the retirees? Eight workers to support each retiree today, then in 40 years 64 workers to support today's eight, then in another forty years 512 workers to support the 64? Dream on! Think only about today, tomorrow may never come! Or maybe the robots will pay Social Security taxes.

Do we want some kind of liberal democracy when more authoritarian democratic regimes like Singapore, Rwanda, and China are advancing economically faster in many areas than other countries?

Do we want more of a socialized democracy such as in Denmark or Norway, where the taxes are high but the people are the happiest on earth?

So many questions!

CHAPTER 11 NO OTHER COUNTRY HAS SUCH LEGALIZED CORRUPTION AS THE U.S.

IF IT'S BROKE SHALL WE FIX IT?

Let's look first at some of the obvious problems in our American democracy. With some exceptions, the American system is quite corrupt and undemocratic.

If it is true, as Winston Churchill opined, that "Democracy is a terrible form of government—but it's better than all the others," we may question its merit—especially the American brand of representation that has legalized corruption that would be felonious in China and many other countries.

LOBBYING

One important concern for American democracy, and increasingly in Europe, is the often corrupt practice of lobbying by special interest groups. For example, energy firms spent $3 billion to convince legislators to deny climate change and its human causes—such as burning fossil fuels.

There are about 13,000 lobbyists in Washington DC. At least ten make over a million dollars a year. The total spent on lobbying in Washington is about $29 billion a year with financial and bank interests and health interests (pharmaceuticals, hospitals, physicians, etc.) spending over $4 billion each. Of course, there is also lobbying in each state. In California, "only" a bit over $300 million is spent on lobbyists.

Not all lobbyists are paid. Some paid lobbyists work free (pro bono) for causes they support, and some are supported by their jobs, being called "public relations advisors" or other such titles. Lobbyists for religions and other social causes may fit into this group.

Because for many congressmen, staying in power is more important than running a good government for the people, and because it costs a lot of money to run for a congressional seat, it is easiest to sell your vote. It costs on average a million dollars for a successful campaign for the House of Representatives where the terms are only two years.

A special election for a congressional seat for Georgia, in June of 2017, saw $50 million spent in the traditionally Republican district. Democrats hoped to start a Democratic snowball there for the 2018 election. The Republicans wanted to show solidarity with Trump and keep the congressional majority.

The average Senate seat costs about $6 million to campaign for a six year term. For the four-year term of president in 2016 the Democrats spent over $1.3 billion and the Republicans over $900 million, and while most of this went for the presidential race some was spent on other important congressional races.

On April 24, 2018, Mick Mulvaney, President Donald Trump's budget director and the acting head of a top consumer watchdog group, related his policy when he was a member of the House of Representatives. He said, "We had a hierarchy in my office in Congress . . . If you're a lobbyist who never gave us money, I didn't talk to you. If you're a lobbyist who gave us money, I might talk to you." He encouraged industry to lobby lawmakers. Lobbying is one of the "fundamental underpinnings of our representative democracy. And you have to continue to do it."

The Republicans in the House Committee on Science, Space, and Technology were led by a man who has received a total of about $700,000 in campaign contributions from the fossil fuel industry since 2008. He dutifully and publicly shared misinformation denying global warming and its resulting effects on climate change, which has an overwhelming scientific consensus.

Former Republican Virginia Governor Bob McDonnell was convicted of 11 counts of corruption in federal court, for accepting gifts of $175,000 from a company that wanted him to have the Virginia universities do studies on a new product—a dietary supplement based on tobacco. The Supreme Court by an 8-0 decision reversed the conviction then narrowed the definition of bribery for public officials. This new definition has allowed several indicted officials to go free.

Democratic Senator Robert Menendez from New Jersey, was charged with corruption because he was asked by a doctor to have the $9 million fraudulent overbilling for Medicare services dropped by the federal government. The doctor had treated the senator to several trips abroad in lavish hotels and had contributed $750,000 to support his reelection and had given $20,000 to pay legal bills necessitated by his recall election. The earlier McDonnell decision was pivotal in the hung jury which resulted in a mistrial. All's fair in American politics.

Trump has criticized the lobbying of the pharmaceutical industry and has set some rules on hiring lobbyists in his administration. Yet, many have found their ways into his administration, often working in departments handling business in the fields for which they recently lobbied.

POSSIBLE SOLUTIONS

1. Have publicly funded elections with no contributions allowed. This would of course upset those who are already in power.

2. Use of public service requirements of radio and television stations to broadcast debates between the top 10 candidates of each party. The primaries would allow the candidates from each party to debate each other. There could be three such series of debates: Democratic Party, Republican Party, and other parties.

3. Television and radio debates in the final election period. This is done in several countries, Norway, particularly, comes to mind.

4. Lobbying may be essential for the democratic process, but it should not be influential in the electoral process.

5. Lobbyists could fully fund a government office that would present all of the issues, pro and con, on proposed legislation and on legislation being debated. The government office would, working with both sides of the issue, develop both a comprehensive and abbreviated version of the points pro and con. When the lobbyists on each side agree on their own arguments, the reports would be circulated to every legislator.

GERRYMANDERING

The party in power in a state can reorganize its voting districts so that areas with large opposition voting blocs are put into one irregularly shaped district while the surrounding districts give the party in power majority districts. This is called gerrymandering, after Governor Gerry, in the early 1800s in Massachusetts, who first designed such irregular boundaries for congressional districts. In fair elections, the voters choose the politicians. In gerrymandering the politicians choose the voters.

A few weeks after the 2016 presidential election a federal court in Wisconsin ruled, in a 2 to 1 decision, that the Republicans had unconstitutionally drawn partisan gerrymandered districts to take away legitimate voting rights of Democrats. The decision is being appealed to the US Supreme Court. The Supreme Court of Pennsylvania ruled that the Republican gerrymandered districts were unconstitutional. In February of 2018 the US Supreme Court let the ruling stand.

The Supreme Court has ruled a number of ways in gerrymandering cases. In 1964, in Reynolds v. Sims and Wesberry v. Sanders by 8 to 1 majorities, the courts ruled that states were required to draw their districts in equal measure according to population. None of this, however, prevented districts from being drawn along partisan lines. In cases in which black voters were gerrymandered to reduce their voting clout, the Supreme Court generally protected them—but not always!

To give you an idea of some extreme differences in state and federal elections, a few years ago:

—Connecticut had one house district with 191 people; another had 81,000.

—In New Hampshire one township with three people had a state assemblyman; the same as another district with 3,244 people. The vote of a resident of the first township might therefore seem to be about 1,000 times more powerful in deciding state issues.

—In Vermont the smallest district had 36 people, the largest had 35,000, again a voting-power ratio of almost 1,000 to 1.

—In Utah the smallest district had 165 people, the largest 32,380 (196 times the population of the other).

—In the 2012 national election for the House of Representatives, more than a million more Democrats voted, but the Republicans won more seats, 234 to 201.

—In the same year in Wisconsin's state elections, 51% voted Democratic, but the Republicans won 60 of the 99 State Assembly seats—60%.

On May 22, 2017, in Cooper v. Harris, the Supreme Court ruled in a 5–3 decision that the 14th Amendment's Equal Protection Clause had been violated in North Carolina's racially based gerrymandering in two Congressional districts. In January of 2018, a three-judge federal court ruled that the Republican gerrymandering of the districts was unconstitutional. While Republicans represent about 50% of the voters, to the Democrats 46% to 48%, their gerrymandered districts give them 10 of the 13 House of Representative seats—77%. Here is North Carolina's 12th District—which is safe for Democrats.

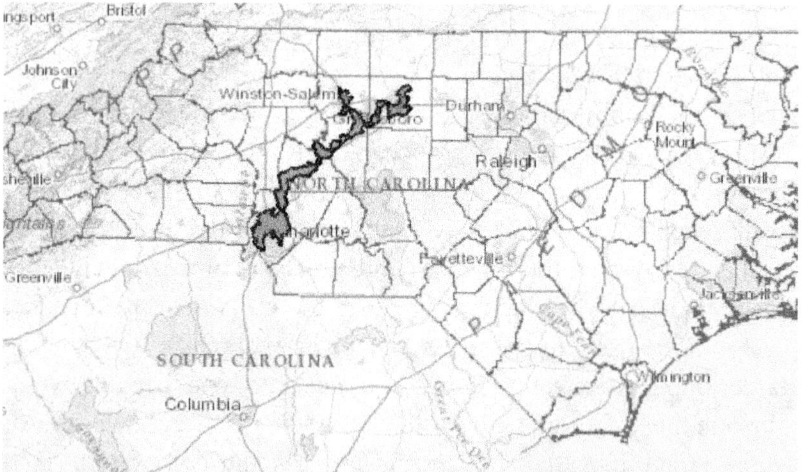

If "one person, one vote" means anything and the legislators ignore it, an impartial Supreme Court should rule on this principle. But there's the rub! Supreme Court justices are nominated based on their points of view. They are confirmed based on their points of view. So the checks and balances envisioned by the Founding Fathers is often a rubber stamp for the other two parts of the ruling Washington triangle. The triangle sometimes looks like a straight line— as it does in 2018.

Recent Republican redistricting in Wisconsin and obvious racial redistricting in North Carolina have convinced the Supreme Court to take another look at this political power- building practice. But the prime concern for any government is building a power base for its interests. Democracy? Ha!

The Supreme Court, in another Republican gerrymandering case, *Gill v. Whitford*, which is based, not on race but on political party preference, will examine the issue in its 2017–18 session. With a Republican majority on the Court of 5 to 4, will the right to gerrymander win?

The Supreme Court, in June of 2018, kicked two cases back to the lower courts. One was the Wisconsin case in which the Republicans had gerrymandered the districts so that while 53% of the votes cast for Democrats that only received 40% of the state assembly. The other case was in Maryland, where the GOP won 41% of the vote and got 12% of the seats in Congress. The Maryland governor admitted that the intent of the redistricting was to ensure that Democrats would be elected.

14 years ago, in a dissenting opinion, Supreme Court Justice David Souter warned that with new technology incumbents would be able to redistrict their states so that there were great dangers to representative democracy. The justices on the Court could not agree as to what was legal and illegal redistricting.

A POSSIBLE SOLUTION

Voters of both California and Arizona, through the initiative process, forced a popular vote on the method of redistricting. Naturally the leading political parties were against the proposed methods. What right do the voters in a democracy think they have, anyway! Legislators should have the ultimate authority to rig elections. It's like the divine right of kings. If God didn't want them to gerrymander districts She wouldn't have let them be elected!

The Arizona solution for federal and state representation is to have two Democrats, two Republicans, and one independent chair as the basic deciding group. Their general criteria are:

☐ That they are in compliance with the US Constitution and

the Voting Rights Act, that districts are roughly equal in population,

☐ That they appear compact and contiguous,

☐ That they respect communities of interest,

☐ That they incorporate visible geographic features; city,

town, and county boundaries; and undivided census tracts,

☐ That they are electorally competitive as long as the

aforementioned criteria are satisfied.

California's anti-gerrymandering law applies only to state offices. The legislature still draws the federal districts. There are three groups of commissioners: five representatives from each of the two major parties and four from neither party. A solution must have three positive votes from each group.

Another possibility that we might consider would be to utilize a computer program which would develop nearly square districts within the state that would be based on the population of the last census, and with the most populous district having no more than 5% of the number of voters in the least populous district. Arizona's requirements would be a good start for developing an efficient and fair program.

OTHER COUNTRIES ARE MORE BRAZEN THAN JUST CHANGING DISTRICTS

Other countries use other means to sway elections and the direction of the government. Shooting judges in South America or journalists in Russia is one way. Stuffing ballot boxes in Zimbabwe is another. Russia often arrests viable candidates, such as Aleksei Navalny recently. A trumped-up charge with a guilty verdict makes a potential candidate ineligible to run. Denying permission for rallies is another obstacle for those who would redirect the "Putin-ocracy."

THE SUPREME COURT

The Supreme Court is peopled by competent judges, but their interpretation of the Constitution usually depends on their political and social values. Presidents nominate judges who fit their mold for a like-minded jurist. Donald Trump promised to appoint justices who would be pro-life—probably because it is in the interest of society to have children born to parents who do not want them. If Hillary Clinton had been elected she promised to do just the opposite.

As mentioned, having a Supreme Court that is selected by political interests, certainly weakens the checks and balances that the Constitution provided.

If the judges looked at the Constitution or the laws and looked at the legislative intent that went into forming those laws, our Supreme Court decisions would probably be 9–0 or maybe 8–1. But they are often 5–4. So one person in the country decides the constitutionality of an important issue, whether it be: abortion (Roe v Wade, 1973) by a 7–2 decision; gun control (District of Columbia v Heller, 2008) by a 5–4 decision allowing firearms as individual rights; or uncapping donations in elections (Citizens United v Federal Election Commission, 2010) by a 5–4 decision, which allowed corporations and unions to spend unlimited money in media advocacy for running candidates, probably indebting the Congressional recipients to favor them in legislation.

Since McDonnell v. United States (2016) by a unanimous decision, it is extremely difficult to prosecute a public official for bribery. Chief Justice Roberts' rationalization, I mean reasoning, was to prevent a "pall of potential prosecution" that could disrupt the healthy functioning of "democratic discourse." He warned that some former White House lawyers were worried that the "breathtaking expansion of public-corruption law would likely chill federal officials' interactions with the people."

McDonnell's conviction was vacated on the grounds that the meaning of "official act" does not include merely setting up a meeting, calling another public official, or hosting an event. If these are not official acts, I would guess that "official acts" are limited to state dinners, so the only legitimate bribery action might be asking for a second dessert!

I might remind you that you should certainly be aware of the essential nature of bribery in a maximally functioning democracy! Heck, if the Congressional palms aren't crossed with silver, Congress would get nothing done! Looking at Congress the last several sessions, it looks like there isn't enough "green" stuffing their wallets to get them to do anything!

The Heller decision changed two centuries worth of Supreme Court decisions that generally adhered to the original Second Amendment which allowed guns for a well-regulated militia. Citizens United overturned the long line of decisions that disallowed large contributions from unions and corporations that might influence the legislators or the executives to act on behalf of the more generous donors.

Drastically changing the meaning of the original Constitution is not new. Judges have changed the meaning of the document since the earliest days. James Madison in writing his Federalist Papers was very clear that civil laws that were passed after a citizen's action could not be used by the government in pursuing a case. These are called *ex post facto* laws. An early Supreme Court case, Calder v. Bull (1798) ruled the exact opposite of what the writers had intended when they wrote that *ex post facto* laws applied only to criminal proceedings. Madison was very, very clear that *ex post facto* was prohibited for civil cases while bills of attainder applied to criminal cases. (To be "attained" means an act of legislature finding a person guilty of treason or felony without a trial.) The separation of powers that the writers of the Constitution desired is highly unlikely when judges are political appointees as they are in federal courts and of course, in the Supreme Court.

President Trump's Supreme Court nominee, Neil Gorsuch, in his doctoral writings and his book said "human life is fundamentally and inherently valuable." He has not said why he believes this, unless it has to do with his religion. He says that his personal philosophy will not influence is judgment. However, we might wonder about his ideas on abortion, assisted suicide, euthanasia, capital punishment, etc. He has written that "our entire political system" and our Declaration of Independence and Constitution reflect the founders' belief in "self-evident human rights and truths."

I don't know where he found this idea in the Constitution? It is in the Declaration of Independence. But a message being advocated when readying a revolution is significantly different from the concepts used in forming a constitutional government. If we used Jefferson's logic from the Declaration as the soul of the guiding principles of a government we might well have a theocracy. This would be diametrically opposed to Jefferson's deistic beliefs in which a creating supernatural being would not be one bit concerned with what we little earthlings believe or do.

Amazing how we are so adept at taking a text out of its context—making a pretext for influencing others. It is certainly essential that when God doesn't point us in the right direction with revelations, we can certainly fill in the scriptural blanks with our universal knowledge—and die, if need be, for the genie we released from the bottle. Where in our scriptures is abortion definitely proscribed or capital punishment condemned? But five people on the Court can determine our conduct.

WHAT MIGHT BE DONE TO MAKE THE COURT LESS POLITICAL?

It would appear that without a constitutional amendment, appointments to the Supreme Court will still be largely political. Although there have been a few appointments that surprised those who appointed them. When President Eisenhower nominated Earl Warren to the court he expected a conservative but got one of the most liberal judges in history. Likewise, when conservative President George H.W. Bush appointed David Souter, he got a fairly liberal justice. Naturally the political parties want a say in who is on the Court so that their agenda can be affirmed as constitutional. But here are a couple of thoughts as to what might be done:

Congress can increase or decrease the number of justices. The number has ranged from 6 to 10. It can also impeach justices. Although the appointment of a Supreme Court justice is a lifetime appointment, the Constitution at Article 3 Section 1 states, "The Judges, both of the supreme and inferior Courts, shall hold their Offices during good Behaviour..." Federal judges have been removed under this section, and one Supreme Court Justice has been impeached by the House of Representatives but not convicted by the Senate. Article 2, Section 4 states that, "The president, vice president and all civil officers of the United States, shall be removed from office on impeachment for, and conviction of, treason, bribery, or other high crimes and misdemeanors." Because federal judges are considered civil officers, they are subject to this rule. Congress has not limited "crimes" to mean only criminal acts.

In the impeachment of Justice Samuel Chase in 1804, decisions and prejudicial tactics
in which the majority of the House members disagreed, were not sufficiently impressive for

the Senate to affirm.

A justice might be impeached if a decision, or a series of decisions, did not "promote the general welfare" of the country—as is required in the Constitution's Preamble. For example, requiring a woman to give birth to an infant, then nourish it for 20 years certainly does not promote her personal welfare. The increased taxes required for educating the child and the highly probable increased police and judicial costs for a number of unwanted young adults certainly does not promote the general welfare of the nation. The House has many options for impeachment. But conviction in the Senate would probably be very difficult.

What if the court were expected to reflect the makeup of the population? With nine judges, a group of citizens would need 11% of its population to be represented. Of course, there is no reason to limit the court to nine judges. The European Court of Human Rights has five sections, each with nine or ten justices.

If we use the 11% number: at least one judge would have to be black, the gender ratio would require at least four women, at least one judge would have to be Hispanic, two or three would have to be Catholic (before Justice Scalia died in 2015 there were six Catholics and three Jews on the Court).

If we were to consider religion as a factor in choosing judges, the 68 million Catholics would be entitled to two judges and the 6.8 million Jews would be unrepresented. But one to two judges would have to be "unbelievers." And about four would be Protestants. Of course, this will never happen, but perhaps competent judges should be nominated by the justices in the federal courts with some sort of representational equivalence on the courts.

Possibly judges could be nominated by "independent federal judges"— judges with no political party affiliation. Article II, Section 2, Number 2 of the Constitution gives the President the power to nominate Supreme Court justices "by and with the Advice and Consent of the Senate." The Senate, if it decided to act in the interest of the nation, could make rules to de-politicize the appointment of all federal judges.

There is no question that nearly all of us base our opinions on basic assumptions, that are unprovable, as well as on our traditions and experiences. Just as people can use their scriptures and the writings of various theologians, to be for or against nearly any ethical position, common law allows judges to find cases somewhere in the world that back up their prejudices. What is needed is competent minds that interpret the law as it was meant to be enforced at the time it was written. Legislative intent, rather than judicial activism, should be the function of the court systems. It should be up to the legislators to determine and write the laws.

Maybe we should just renounce the "common law" judicial system we inherited from England and use the Napoleonic interpretation of law that is common in most other countries. Just look at the law, understand its intent, then make the decision. This would certainly reduce the legislation by the judiciary that is so common today. As I remember, laws were supposed to be made by the legislature. If we don't like what they legislate, we can drain the swamp. But Supreme Court judges are with us "until death do us part." And "irreconcilable differences" are not enough for a divorce.

ELIMINATING OUR LITIGIOUS SOCIETY

Being litigious makes us even more selfish than most other countries. America is the most litigious society in the world—by far. The reason is that we produce far more attorneys than any adequately functioning society needs.

Lawyers are needed in every society. We have to be able to understand and apply the laws. The problem in the United States is that there are too many lawyers for the necessary jobs that are needed for the society. You can have too many qualified people in almost any job. There are far too many administrators in our schools. There are too many coal miners for what we need. And, there are too many lawyers. There are not enough jobs in Congress to fill with additional lawyers. There are not that many additional judicial jobs available. What is left? Ambulance chasing is a popular route. Taking cases at a 30% to 40% contingency makes lawyering relatively lucrative for a number of law school graduates.

What other professions work on contingencies? Does your brain surgeon say "$20,000 now or $40,000 if you live." Do teachers get a percentage of what their students earn throughout their lives? Do they even have that option? No. Certainly contingency fees make it possible for anyone to sue anyone. Often insurance companies are afraid of what juries will award even if their client is totally innocent. So they settle and the attorney collects 30% to 40% of the settlement. And you wonder why your health or homeowner's insurance premiums are so high!

There is an old saying among lawyers that "if your client is innocent go to a judge. If your client is guilty, go to a jury." Another old saying is that, "Anyone not smart enough to get out of jury duty is easily swayed by their emotions." The famous O.J. Simpson murder case is an example. The evidence was quite clear that he had done it, but in downtown Los Angeles it was essential to have African-American jurors. The African-American community was rightly incensed that over the years that they had been treated unequally by society and by the courts. Any African-American who voted for "guilty" would not have been welcomed back in his neighborhood! If O.J. had been a normal member of the community who was actually guilty of murder, and was being defended by a public defender, he would have been given a life sentence. But the millionaire football player paid $5 million to his attorneys for the eight month criminal trial. In a civil trial later, by the parents of one of his victims, he was unanimously found guilty.

Smart lawyers know the ropes. Some years ago, in the San Fernando Valley of Los Angeles there were two lower-level judges who handled almost all the divorce cases. In one courtroom sat a middle-aged Jewish woman. In the other courtroom was a middle-aged Jewish man. The local attorneys knew that if you are defending a man you would go to the female judge. If you were defending a woman who would go to the male judge. The woman took all the odd-numbered cases. The male judge took all the even-numbered cases. So the lawyer's assistant who would file the case with the clerk would wait until the appropriate case number would come up, then submit his papers. He would merely ask the court what number would be next. If there was an odd number and his boss was defending a man he would file immediately. If not, he would wait until someone else filed a divorce case, then would file his case, which would be an odd numbered case. Here was a situation where a knowledgeable lawyer might be worth the money.

One case with which I am familiar involved a lawyer who was divorcing his wife. When the judge asked her how long they had been married, she answered "30 years." So she got lifelong spousal support and half of their community property which had been accumulated during those 30 years. But the arrow of Cupid was not long in its quiver when they began to date again. A few months later they decided to remarry. Another few months and he decided he wanted a divorce. They arrived in court and the judge asked her how long they had been married. She answered "30 years." The judge said, "I only see three months here." She got no spousal support and only half of what he had earned in the last three months as her share of the community property. That was one smart and unethical California attorney!

☐ Attempt to determine the actual amount of damage done to the victim and add fair attorney's fees to that amount.

☐ If the offending organization or person is to be taught a lesson by a very high financial penalty, give the rest of the award to the state or the board of education.

☐ If it is a state organization to be punished, such as the police department, the award could be given to other state departments.

☐ Million-dollar rewards by juries primarily line the pockets of the lawyers, who are working on a 40% contingency.

Many of you are familiar with the Rodney King case. Rodney had robbed a store in Southern California, threatened the Korean store owner with being hit by an iron pipe, but he did hit him with a wooden club. He stole $200. He was caught, convicted and sentenced to two years in prison. He was released on parole after one year.

While still on parole a California Highway Patrol unit found him to be driving erratically in the wee hours of the morning. He had been drinking with two friends, was legally drunk, and was afraid that he would be sent back to prison for violating his parole. He led police and the Highway Patrol on a high-speed chase for 8 miles, at speeds up to 80 miles an hour, with several police cars and the helicopter in pursuit. When his car was finally cornered and stopped, the three men were ordered out of the car. His friends obeyed but were still hit by the police. Rodney finally emerged from the car and while police attempted to handcuff him, he fought back. The police were then ordered to hit him with batons to subdue him. It was a rather savage beating. About this time, a neighbor began to video the action. The next day he went to the police to give them the video but no one was interested so we went to a TV channel which publicized it.

Rodney sued the City of Los Angeles and was awarded $3.8 million and $1.7 million in attorneys' fees. The US Department of Justice charged the police with civil rights violations and two of the four police were sentenced to 30 months in prison.

King continued to have trouble with the law, especially driving while under the influence of alcohol, cocaine, and marijuana. He also attempted to run down one of his three wives with his car. He eventually drowned in his swimming pool while under the influence of alcohol, cocaine, and marijuana.

A question that many ask is whether his $5 million from the City of Los Angeles was excessive and primarily aimed at punishing the police. Certainly, King should have been awarded something for his injuries—and for his pain and suffering. But his injuries may not have been worth the settlement of the $5 million. It did not straighten out his life.

Might the punishing part of the judgment award have been given from the City of Los Angeles to the Board of Education, the State of California, or a charity like the Red Cross or the Salvation Army? There is no question that he was severely injured, but he was resisting arrest violently. So where was the best use of the money that was punishment for the police? Buying drugs and cars for Rodney might not have been the best use of taxpayer dollars!

Another example, when a person dies from smoking cigarettes and his life is considered to be worth $200,000, but the cigarette company is to be punished with a $50 million judgment—give $200 thousand to the plaintiff, fair fees to the lawyer for the award to the plaintiff, and the rest to the state or federal governments. But the lawyers' lobbies and the lawyers in Congress and state legislatures would never let this happen. Take care of your attorney amigos—if you don't win re-election you may be joining them soon!

THE ELECTORAL COLLEGE

The Electoral College is undemocratic, and it gave us Bush and Trump. But keeping it makes it a bit easier for political parties to plan election victories by ignoring the states that are more partisan and concentrating on the swing states needed to win the 270 electoral votes. And political power, not the wishes of the nation, should certainly be primary. Just wait until my party controls Washington—we'll really take care of you guys!

The four presidents who lost the popular vote but were elected by the college are all ranked in the bottom half of presidents in terms of their performance, as determined by presidential historians and political scientists. If we count the 43 presidents through George W. Bush we find that Benjamin Harrison had an average rank of 29th and Rutherford B Hayes averages about 25th in the 25 most authoritative rankings. George W. Bush ranks about 35th of the seven surveys that include him.

So, they were all in the bottom half of all presidents. We are yet to see where Donald Trump will rank. But it is clear that the Electoral College idea has not been particularly effective in choosing presidents. It made sense in the 1700s, but not now.

Another Electoral College situation happened in the 1824 election. Not all states had a popular vote but each sent electors. Andrew Jackson got the most popular and electoral votes but did not have a majority in the Electoral College, so the House of Representatives had to hold a contingent election. They voted for John Quincy Adams. Adams ranks as about the 15th best president while Jackson, who was elected for the next two terms, ranks about 10th. So again, the popular vote picked the better man.

And now we have Donald Trump, loser of the popular vote by over 2,300,000 votes. Clinton had 1.7% more votes by the people. But she had 25% fewer Electoral College votes than he did—227 to 304.

From Plato and Aristotle to today, political observers have been worried about "the mob" taking over a democracy with ill thought-out ideas. Alexander Hamilton, in the Federalist Papers, believed that the people should have a say in choosing the electors but the electors should be free to choose the best candidates for president and vice president. He wrote: "Men most capable of analyzing the qualities adapted to the station and acting under circumstances favorable to deliberation, and to a judicious combination of all the reasons and inducements which were proper to govern their choice."

In Federalist 68, Hamilton, cautions us that being electable does not make one presidential. He wrote that "the person who will become president will have to be a person who possesses the faculties necessary to be a president. He may be elected because he possesses: Talents for low intrigue, and the little arts of popularity, may alone suffice to elevate a man to the first honors in a single State . . . ." But to fill the job, he said "it will require other talents, and a different kind of merit, to establish him in the esteem and confidence of the whole Union, or of so considerable a portion of it as would be necessary to make him a successful candidate for the distinguished office of President of the United States." Oh my! What have we wrought today?

Over the years these original ideas have been changed by the political parties and the states. Twenty-nine states and the District of Columbia bind their electors to the candidate who won the most votes in that state. The legality of this has been affirmed by the Supreme Court. In other states an elector might become "faithless" and either not vote or vote for a different candidate. This occasionally happens.

In the 2016 election, if a total of 107,000 people voting for Trump had not voted in Pennsylvania, Michigan and Wisconsin, Clinton would have had enough electoral votes to win. So you might say that 0.09% of the voters decided the election.

If we are to have a true democratic republic we must eliminate the Electoral College. In 1789 it was a better idea than the alternative, which was to have the president chosen by the House of Representatives. Dealing the responsibility to the states was much more democratic. In 1789, there were not many telephones or computers to relay information—and the government didn't have the money to set up polling booths around the country and, even if they did, in most cases the voters couldn't even read the ballots. So Article 2 of the Constitution allowed for each state to choose electors for the president and vice president. A great idea for 1789!

The political parties generally approve of the Electoral College because it makes it easier to campaign in states where they have a better chance of making good use of their money. California, Oregon, Washington and Wisconsin are so safe for Democrats that they don't need to campaign much to win heavily there. Did I say Wisconsin? Oops! Maybe the Democrats should have spent a dollar or two there in 2016!

Anyway, now that most of us can read and the states have the ability to effectively count the votes of all those who wish to vote, maybe we should propose a constitutional amendment to advance our national elections 200 years and get a little closer to truly democratic elections.

In the last 200 years, more than 700 proposals to eliminate or reform the Electoral College have been made. About 70% of lawyers and 80% of Americans favor eliminating it. There are some who think that third-party candidates may be hurt by eliminating the college, but in 1992 Ross Perot won 19% of the popular vote but got no electoral votes.

WE HAVE ONLY TWO VIABLE POLITICAL PARTIES

Here is another off-the-wall idea. Tradition in America is to have two political parties. Is it really rational to have two parties each representing: all the farmers, billionaires, coal miners, auto workers, teachers, communists, socialists, libertarians, all ethnic groups, all races, all religions, all college students and everybody else? Even little Norway with its 5.2 million population has a 169-seat parliament with eight parties occupying seats and another 12 parties with too few votes for representation. Compare that to the 8 parties, including independents, in the US with a 320 million population where only 2 parties hold all the 535 legislative posts except for the four held by independents. Theoretically there are about 30 more parties in the US but they have such limited appeal that they have very few members. The Tom and Jerry Party, for example, has only one cat and one mouse.

The two-party system poses two reasonably identifiable platforms which limit the options for expressing opinions. When other parties exist, like the Libertarians and Greens in 2016, they have no chance of winning, but the protest votes they earn may take the vote from the more desirable major party candidate in the election.

George Bush won Florida by 537 votes. Ralph Nader, the Green Party nominee, had more than 97,000 votes there. His position was to the left of Al Gore and far from the conservative position of George Bush. If 600 of those votes for Nader had gone to Gore he would've been the president and we would probably not have had the Iraq war, the rise of ISIS, or the several trillion dollars added to the national debt. Of course, if the omniscient and conservative Supreme Court had allowed a recount, as was possible under Florida law and a Florida Supreme Court decision, it might have been different and Saddam Hussein and his family might still be ruling Iraq, fewer Iraqis and Americans would be dead and America would have at least a trillion dollars less of a national debt.

When you have multiple political parties, as is common in Europe, more options are on the voter's ballot. In the US, you have two viable parties for 330 million people. Norway's three major parties generally range between 12% and 38% favorability. Another four parties are in the 4% to 7% approval rating zone. Then there are a couple of parties in the 1% to 2% range. To get a majority of the legislature it generally takes 2 to 4 parties forming a coalition. Then in major issues, the coalition may split and the government might fall. The Norwegian administration, like the UK's, is done by the prime minister with the help of ministers from the various coalition parties. It is easier to flirt with a couple of parties, then date one for the election. In America there are too many voters married to one party for life—"for better or worse."

In the US election of 2016 the two major parties got 97% of the votes, but all of the seats in the House of Representatives.

What about other countries? In the UK, UKIP got 12.6% of the votes and one seat of the 650 seats in parliament. Should it have been 82 seats? In Norway, the Green party got 83,000 votes and one seat, the Christian party got 123,000 votes and eight seats in the 169-seat parliament. What do we mean by "democracy" anyway? In Turkmenistan, which now has a multiparty system since 2012, the incumbent got 98% of the vote. One wonders!

And more! In Cambodia, the leading contender for the presidency was arrested for treason by a hundred police. His crime was a four-year-old video of a speech in which he said he received American advice about how to be a responsible opposition party. Dozens of activists and politicians have found themselves behind bars there. In spite of this, in the election, the opposition parties won 46% of the vote. The press is now being controlled, and pro-democracy NGOs have been closed.

UNREPRESENTATIVE REPRESENTATION

Then there is the "democratic" idea that Wyoming should get one senator for each 290,000 people and California should get one for each 20 million people. The Great Compromise of 1787 was necessary to make our union, but does it make sense today? -- Certainly, not democratic sense!

CONFLICTING DEMANDS OF THE SAME LEGISLATOR

Conservatives generally want both low taxes and no abortion possibilities. If unwanted children are born they will each be expected to complete 12 years of education, with each year costing an average of $10,000 per student. Additionally, if those children are born to poor parents there will be additional expenses for welfare costs. Also, since it is highly likely that the unwanted children will not be as loved as much as children who are desired, their chances of running afoul of the law increase. This increases the need for police, judges, public defenders and prisons. Each of these, of course, increases government spending.

Liberals, on the other hand, realize that the social welfare perks that they want will cost a great deal of money, for which they know that Americans are not willing to be taxed. Universal healthcare, free college education, longer vacations, realistic maternity leaves, livable pensions, and inexpensive public transportation are not attainable without a total tax burden of over 45%. This is about 15% to 20% more than what most Americans have been told they are willing to pay.

There are other inconsistencies that we see. Having the separation of church and state, yet giving churches nearly unlimited tax breaks which increase the tax burden for everyone else, may be questioned. This tax burden has been estimated to be over 70 billion dollars per year for the federal, state, and local levels. This does not include the deductions from income taxes of contributions to churches. Of lesser concern may be the various court decisions which have allowed parochial schools to be given free school books and other perks. And now there are the proposed school voucher programs that allow full or part payment of tuition to religious schools.

In Trinity Lutheran v. Comer (2017) a church applied for state money to safely cover its playground. The state's constitution forbade this. In a 7-2 decision, the Supreme Court decided that the First Amendment's right to freedom of religion ("Congress shall make no law respecting an establishment of religion, or prohibiting the free exercise thereof;. . . ") trumped states' rights. They apparently concluded that exercising on a church owned state-funded playground was covered under the "free exercise of religion" phrase in the Constitution!

HEALTH CARE

Obamacare was a big issue in the 2016 election campaigns. Americans spend 30 to 60 percent more than any other country on medical care and their medical care is rated as the 38th best in the world. Obama tried to reduce the costs by having a federal option for insurance rather than having everything private—where the CEOs of health insurance firms are making over $7 million a year. This was scrapped by the lobbyists for the health insurance industry and by hiring the spouses of members of the important congressional committees to be on the insurance companies' boards of directors.

Obama tried to limit medical malpractice insurance awards to $250,000 because a major expense for doctors is their malpractice insurance. Their high insurance premiums are reflected in their bills. The lawyers' lobby and the insurance companies' lobbies defeated this. So the cost of health insurance went up for the citizens as the legislators took their payoffs and health insurance companies prospered, as did their stockholders. It is no wonder that insurance premiums are so high. In nearly all other advanced countries health care is a government obligation paid for by taxes. All countries also have a private system for those who want it.

Let me repeat some comparisons of World Health Organization's health care efficiency and the per-person spending as a percent of GDP: U.S. spends $9024 per person and its health care system is rated the 38th best in the world, Canada $4500 ($30^{th}$), Germany $5100 ($25^{th}$), Sweden $5000 ($23^{rd}$), Switzerland $6800 ($20^{th}$), the UK $4000 ($18^{th}$), Italy $3200 ($2^{nd}$), France $4407 (best in the world).

Both socialism and social welfare are dirty words in America. It doesn't matter that Social Security is a welfare program for most of us, because we live too long for our contributions to support us. On the average, if we retire at 67 we will use up our contributions by about 73 or 74, but the average person lives to be over 80 so the government must make up the difference. Medicare is even worse. The average person uses up their contributions even earlier. Medicaid is even more of a social welfare benefit because you do not pay into it.

As mentioned earlier, by definition, Medicare and Medicaid are communistic—"From each according to his abilities, to each according to his needs," according to Karl Marx. And Social Security is socialistic—"From each according to his abilities, to each according to his work," according to Vladimir Lenin. Most of our education through high school is a social welfare benefit. It is paid for by the general population in taxes. But in the US, healthcare should not be a social welfare benefit, according to most legislators and millionaires, even though it is such a benefit in all the advanced countries. Only the US, Mexico, and Turkey do not have tax paid universal healthcare.

Here are some examples of medical charges:

►   An MRI (magnetic resonance imaging) costs $2,600 in the USA. The cost in Norway is $25 with prescription at a state hospital or $400 at a private clinic.

►   Cost of a knee replacement in Kansas is $29,000, in Colorado $40,000, in Norway free.

►   Cataract removal surgery in Alaska is $8000, in Florida $2300, and in Norway free.

►   Pacemaker for heart, $50,000 in Indiana, Norway free.

You can see why Americans pay 30% to 60% more for medical care than any other country. The costs, of course, increase as the population ages and as new treatments and pharmaceuticals are developed. For example, a new genetic treatment for blindness costs $850,000. How many people can society support with such near-million-dollar treatments? Medicare pays $50 billion annually to doctors, hospital, and insurance companies for medical bills for dying people during their last two months of life. The amount spent may be close to $10,000 a day for a terminally ill patient.

When we hear President Trump or Congressional leaders talk about healthcare they are clear that it is for "the good of the American people." They assume that healthcare for the nation must be provided by insurance companies who have highly paid CEOs and are responsible to their stockholders to make profits. While Medicare is partially government paid and Medicaid is totally government paid, ObamaCare pays insurance companies directly for those who cannot afford the coverage. So insurance companies are making money from both the premiums paid by the people or their employers and from the federal government.

To hear our leaders talk, there is no other way. They often criticize the socialized medical systems is Europe, without citing any evidence that they are problematic. In fact, all European health systems are rated better than America's except for a few Eastern European countries--Hungary, Poland and Slovakia.

It is no secret why Congress derides the better and less expensive healthcare systems in the West. It is about Wall Street, donations of lobbyists, their relatives in highly paid positions on the boards of health insurance and pharmaceutical companies, and their own health insurance stock holdings. They are certainly concerned with the American people!

But we lead the world in billionaires and in economic output. Of course, all Americans know that business is more important than the health or happiness of the citizens. That's why Congress votes the way it does.

IS TRUTH IMPORTANT? AND WHO DETERMINES WHAT IS TRUE?

After Bush, Brexit, and Trump, might society be better off if the voters heard only the truth? If it were possible to allow only objective truth in campaigns and in national and international decision making, we might have had Gore or Kerry rather than Bush. We might not have had the false information that Saddam Hussein had weapons of mass destruction. Then we would not have had the Iraq war, many thousands of deaths and injuries, and a trillion dollars or more in national debt.

If the truth were told and the opponents in an issue were limited to rational arguments, not influencing our unconscious minds, perhaps the Brexit vote would not have been successful.

If the "alternative facts" of Donald Trump and the Russians had not been believed, we might now have Jeb Bush or Hillary Clinton as president.

At the Davos World Economic Forum, Trump said that the stock market had risen 50% since he had taken office. Actually, the S&P had gone up 23% and the Dow Jones 29%. At the same time the dollar had lost over 10% of its value—19% against the euro. So the actual rise in the value of the market was somewhere between 7% to 19%, depending on which stock market average you use. He forgot to mention that the German and Japanese stock markets performed better than ours during that time. In fact, nearly all the world's stock markets were rising as the world economies were finally recovering from the recession that started ten years earlier.

At the turn of the century, 90 cents bought one euro. The Iraq war reduced the value of the dollar so it took $1.60 to buy one euro. By 2016 the dollar had increased in value so that $1.20 bought one euro. In January 2017 $1.05 bought one euro. In January 2018 $1.24 bought one euro. So the dollar has lost about 19% of its value against the euro in the last year.

We might note that from 2010 to January 2017 the stock market rose from 8,000 to 21,000—an average increase of 14.7% per year. The dollar increased about 1.6% per year. So if we use the Dow Jones Industrial as an indication of how the economy is going (and that's a bit of a stretch), we can assume that the value of the Dow was advancing healthily under Obama.

As of this writing the Dow has increased about 1% per month during Trump's first 18 months of his term. But the dollar has lost about 0.50% per month. So, investors didn't make as much money as they thought they had. So overall the gain in the value of the stock market in Trump's first year was nowhere near as profitable as it was under Obama. So much for a businessman running the economy! His tariffs certainly pressured the Dow down. On the other hand, the upward business cycle is expected to lose steam within two years, and he can't be held completely responsible for that.

Another way to look at the Dow would be in the percentage increase. So, a gain from 8,000 to 9,000 would be a gain of 12.5%, while a gain from 25,000 to 26,000 would be a 4% gain. As we have oft repeated, we must go beyond the obvious or a simple statement in order to understand the whole—whether it be in political rhetoric, religious pronouncements, moral imperatives, romancing, electioneering, or economics. If someone is trying to convince you of something, they may have their own interests in mind, not yours!

AND MAYBE SOME ETHICAL BEHAVIOR MIGHT BE NICE!
We hear the joke that "all's fair in love and war," and we think it is an ethical precept. How often has this rationalization been given by politicians when they lie or make promises they can't keep? But, all is not fair even in war. Poison gas has been outlawed—except for Assad and Putin.

As a mental health therapist, I have heard a number of cases where couples had a great sexual relationship before marriage, then on the return from the honeymoon it either ended or was severely limited. One patient related that after a fantastic sexual courtship, on returning from the honeymoon his new wife said "we are married now, so I don't have to do that anymore." That was supposedly "love" and it wasn't fair. The woman in this case had knowingly grossly misrepresented her future actions in order to get married to an attorney who was quite well off financially.

There are a couple of elements necessary to behaving ethically. One is Immanuel Kant's dictum that "we should treat everyone as ends in themselves and not as means only." We might also include honesty here, although it is implied in Kant's maxim.

A problem with ethics in politics generally, and in American politics specifically, is that the basis for ethical behavior can be grounded in any of the three major assumptions: self, God or society. Every value decision that anyone makes is based on one of these basic assumptions. But it is not quite as simple as that. The God on which you are basing your belief may vary considerably from others who use a "God based" assumption. The society that you think is ideal may be quite different from others' views of an ideal society. And self-centered values might be based on what I want right now or on what I want for myself in ten years. My actions, then, would be quite different. Here are a few examples.

God-based ethics can vary depending the scriptures used:

➤If a Jew—on the tradition of Moses and the Torah,

➤If a Catholic Christian—on the pronouncements of the Vatican,

➤If a Protestant Christian—on Martin Luther's freer interpretation of the Bible,

➤If a Mormon Christian—on the Bible and the Book of Mormon,

➤If a Muslim—on the Quran and hadiths,

➤If a Hindu—on the Upanishads and Bhagavad Gita.

For societal ethics:

➤If a monarchist—on what the king desires for the country,

➤If a communist—on a dictatorship of the proletariat and distribution of goods and services based on need,

➤If a socialist—on the elimination of capitalists and the distribution of goods based on how much people work,

➤If a capitalist—on the freedom of people with money to control the economic system,

➤If a welfare state advocate—on a combination of capitalism and communism, with equality of opportunity being a major desire,

➤If the goal is a democratic republic—equality of opportunity might be a goal, representation based on the interests of the various groups that elect a representative,

➤If desiring a true democracy—all of the legislative decisions would be done by the people,

➤If following Jeremy Bentham's idea for society—on "the greatest good for the greatest number," the ethical precept would be achieving the greatest amount of physical or mental pleasure possible,

➤If following John Stuart Mill's ideas, the greatest good would be based on higher human values, so the quality of the good would be important: "To suppose that life has no higher end than pleasure—no better and nobler object of desire and pursuit they designate as utterly mean and groveling; as a doctrine worthy only of swine."

If for self-centered ethics:

➤If totally selfish, and only today counts, it is ethical to do exactly what I want,

➤If self-centered with the future in mind, ethics would depend on what will help me get what I want in the future,

➤If my family is primary in my life, what will advance my family's interests;

➤I want to understand my true self, so I will meditate continually.

Obviously, it is highly unlikely that anyone would base their entire life's behavior on any one of these ideas. For example, a woman may have a self-centered desire to become a member of the US Congress. At the same time, she may be a devout Methodist who has socialistic ideals. One may have devout Catholic ideals, become a priest, then in self-centered moments, sexually abuse children.

Certainly, not all of our behavior is ethical—even according to these broad categories. A person may love his family very much, but in a fit of rage, possibly not related to the family, may physically strike out at a child. Child abuse is commonly caused by inferiority feelings in the unconscious mind. Abusing the child gives one a feeling of power. Often, we act out of anger—not ethics.

Since we are talking about government here, we can understand how a person can want to be re-elected in a Catholic district, while believing that women should have a choice for terminating a pregnancy in an ideal society. Does he hide his abortion views in order to be elected? He must choose between his self-centered and society-based values. Another self-versus-society situation could be a congresswoman who disapproves of the president, who is in her own party. She can take a society-first position and criticize the president on national television but this might force his party to stop supporting her as a candidate. This might negatively affect her self-centered desires for re-election.

We could look at former House Speaker Dennis Hastert, who apparently did not have enough power in his life many years ago, so he sexually abused some boys in his care. We don't have any evidence that he did this while in Congress. Perhaps being a congressman satisfied his inferiority complexes.

If we look at Donald Trump, we see his superiority complex that has developed to make up for his feelings of inferiority. His pussy-grabbing, insults to his opponents, and unwillingness to listen to factual arguments, such as the reality of climate change, have made him an international political buffoon. Some are already touting him as the worst president in history. But being president may be enough to reduce some of his inferiority feelings. Several of his appointees have been forced to resign because of their corruption.

Should our society be based on self-centered values? The US elected Donald Trump even though multiple women accused him of sexual harassment and sexual assault. They elected him even though he had violated federal laws, such as fair housing laws and fraud with his "university."

Should Roy Moore have even been considered for a major public office when his views of what God wants conflict with what American law has declared, such as with abortion or LGBTQ rights? Obviously, Moore realized that God had made mistakes in not specifically saying that abortion is a sin— and in his evangelical fervor he criticized lesbian, gay, bisexual, transgender, and queer humans.

Fundamentalist Muslims, as fundamentalist Christians, want a society based on their scriptures and on the voluminous commentaries and hadiths, which are often contradictory-- and written since the original revelations and prophecies.

Or should a just society be pragmatic in solving problems, adjusting, and eliminating directives in its constitution?

A major caution! Most people are self-centered all or most of the time but will commonly rationalize their behavior as being based on scriptures or a vision of a better society—a society that can be as small as a family, a social group, or a gang.

Examples of irrational self-centered actions to make up for our deep feelings of inferiority are common. A young Muslim man, who has not achieved in society to a point where he feels some power over his situation, may kill people (which is the ultimate action of power) and say it is for Allah. A white man who has not achieved enough to satisfy his drive for power, may, in the name of God, kill a doctor who performs abortions. A young black man may shoot a police officer and say it is a punishment for the black lives that policemen have taken. This would be a rationalization based on what he thinks is a better society.

These conflicting value decisions confuse not only our legislative representatives, but they also confuse us in the voting booths and in our personal lives. Seeing some people act on what they think are their ethical values and others acting on their unconscious needs and their need for power to overcome their inferiority feelings, makes it extremely difficult for us to evaluate our own beliefs and actions—but also the beliefs and actions of others.

We may be able to evaluate our representatives from afar, based on their actions and their voting records. Are their actions in accord with what we want as citizens? If not, what can we do about it? A serious debate should be ongoing, but that would tax our intellects and our value systems—and would take us away from our videogames.

WEALTH INEQUALITY

Another problem is inequality between households. In the OECD countries in the 1980s, the gap between the richest and poorest in society accelerated rapidly. It continues at a dizzying pace. The richest 10% of US households have incomes that are 11 times those of the poorest 10%; in France and Germany, the difference is sevenfold, and in Denmark it is fivefold. These differences accumulate over time, meaning that the differences in annual income nearly always translate to increased differences in wealth as the years roll on. Across the globe, the richest 1% own slightly more wealth than the rest of the world put together, according to Oxfam. (Some economists doubt the statistics used.) But it is pretty well agreed that the richest 62 people are richer than the bottom three billion people. In the UK, the top 1% richest people own 24% of the nation's wealth. In the US, the top 1% own 40% of the nation's wealth. The bottom 80% owns 7% of the nation's wealth.

Some groups believe that the huge gap between rich and poor is "undermining economies, destabilizing societies and holding back the fight against poverty." Over two millennia ago, Plato wrote that the gap should be no more than four times. A little over a hundred years ago the legendary banker and financier John Pierpont Morgan thought that a multiple of twenty was appropriate. According to the SEC, the Security and Exchange Commission, the multiple for CEOs of billion dollar companies in the U.S. is 130—with the single highest ratio for one oil company being over 9000 to one. But in reality, these enormous salaries are necessary. It costs much more to operate a 50-room mansion than it does to operate a one bedroom apartment. And all those vacation homes don't run themselves. And if you have to contribute a hundred million to a major university to ensure that your first-born will be accepted in the freshman class—what could be more important?

Certainly, some people are worth more to a business, a governmental facility or a school than others—but how much more? Were the teachers of Bill Gates or Sergey Brin somewhat responsible for the ideas and enthusiasm of their students? If so, were they paid in cash or pride for a job well done?

HOW MUCH FINANCIAL INEQUALITY CAN A SOCIETY TOLERATE?

We have here the perennial conflict between *liberty* and *equality*. Should people have the freedom to keep the money they earn or inherit? Or, is there something that makes people equal and entitled to share the wealth that others have accumulated? If so, what is that factor that makes people equal? If we are equal how much should we curb the liberty of others to keep all or part of the money they have earned because of their intelligence, knowledge, hard work—or their rich parents?

Should we abolish all rights to inheritance in an effort to equalize opportunities with each new generation? Should we merely attempt to reduce income inequality to allow for a better functioning and more content society, as philosopher John Dewey proposed? Or should we wait a bit longer and let a revolution and guillotine do the job? I think that happened once before!

The world is producing a new billionaire every two days. One out of three billionaires inherited their wealth. Born with a bulging green wallet—so to speak! In the next twenty years 500 of the world's richest people will line their progenies' play pens with $2.4 trillion—a sum greater than the GDP of India, with its billion plus population.

Should justice be based on absolute economic equality, total freedom to keep what you earn, or something in between?

AND SO

Trying to make the elected officials honest, eliminate gerrymandering, make the Supreme Court impartial, doom the Electoral College, and initiate other intelligently democratic ideas have little real interest among the voters in the US. These political anomalies are only seen as unjust in most other democracies, where intelligence and civility are deemed important.

Who cares anyway! 28% of British voters didn't think that voting in the Brexit referendum was worth their time. 44% of Americans didn't care who governed them in the 2016 election—in fact for the last 50 years 45% to 50% of voters haven't cared who governs them. But that's democracy!

Perhaps a king appointed by God would be better. Of course, he might tax your tea—but who cares!

CHAPTER 12. DO WE HONESTLY WANT OUR PRESENT-DAY DEMOCRACY?

If you had your choice, which would you choose?

- Happiness or low taxes
- Liberty or equality
- Freedom of speech
- Freedom of the press
- Freedom of religion
- A republic or autocracy
- Consideration for minorities
- Capitalism or socialism

➢ When politicians in a democracy lie,

▪—should we be concerned?

➢ When politicians state, as facts, ideas for which there is no evidence,

▪—should we be concerned?

➢ When politicians make us afraid of inconsequential things,

▪—should we be concerned?

➢ When politicians give us hopes that can never be realized,

▪—should we be concerned?

➢ When politicians appeal to our unconscious motivations rather than our intellects,

• —should we be concerned?

➢ When a politician advocates diametrically opposed positions,

• —should we be concerned?

➢ When every voter doesn't have a far-reaching vision of what is important for the nation and the world,

• —should we be concerned?

➢ When our school systems are delivering students who rank between 24th and 36th in subjects such as reading, mathematics, and problem-solving,

• —should we be concerned?

➢ When students do not learn the basics of logical thinking,

• —should we be concerned?

If you are not concerned, there is no sense in reading any further!

SO MANY OPTIONS—SO MANY QUESTIONS

As mentioned, Churchill told us that "Democracy is a terrible form of government. It's just better than all the others."

Einstein told us that "The measure of intelligence is the ability to change."

From the divine right of the king to the divine right of the mob—is it always a step upward? From Aristotle to today, political thinkers have abhorred the king, but also the mob. The Electoral College was established to allow the mob's choice of a qualified and ethical elector to be able to think beyond the present-day desires of his or her electors and choose the best president, The Supreme Court, of course, has disallowed this intention of the Founding Fathers in half of the states so that the mob still speaks loudly. The shrill of the unwashed and uneducated is constantly heard in the halls of Congress, and very often it generates a presidency that cannot see the forest for the trees of voters.

DO WE WANT HAPPINESS OR LOW TAXES?

Many people do not think very deeply about what is important in their lives. In the U.S., we hear so often about reducing taxes that we often think that that is the major concern of government. In many countries in Europe they start with what will make people happier throughout their lives. They then decide how much money that will cost and they attempt to adjust their tax rates to those needs. However all but Norway usually have to borrow additional money to make this goal of happiness a reality.

Are we willing to pay for what we want (health care, pensions, infrastructure, education, prisons, military)?

Not many countries want to pay their way. The electorate believes the promises of the candidates for leadership. No one wants to hear anything bad. They want to hear that: they can have free health insurance cradle-to-grave; they can have free education through the university; they can have extensive prison systems to lock up all the bad guys; the problem of global warming will be solved without having to do anything about it; food will be cheap and the roads will be better; and they can retire earlier with a huge pension. But, they want to do this with lower taxes.

OUR NATIONAL DEBT

At the end of 2017 the US national debt was estimated to be $23.29 trillion, including federal $20.24 trillion, state $1.17 trillion, and local $1.88 trillion.

There is often confusion about how much money the government has borrowed. This may be figured as public debt (debt owed to other countries or individuals), and the intra-governmental debt, which could include the money borrowed from other departments of the government, such as Social Security and other government retirement funds, Normally, the national debt is quoted as the combination of public debt and intra-governmental debt.

If we figure only the interest on the public debt, it will be lower than the interest on the total national debt and the debt on bonds issued by states and cities. Since not everyone agrees on the definition of the national debt, we may find different estimates as to its total amount, and of the interest owed on it.

According to the Office of the Management and the Budget, interest paid on the public debt has risen from $220 billion in 2012, when the debt was lower and the interest rate was at 1.8% to the current level of $310 billion at a 2.6% interest rate. This takes about 8.2% of the national budget. However, interest rates will soon rise to over 3.5% so the interest paid in 2024 will be about $658 million and will take about 12.4% of the national budget.

The government has borrowed trillions of dollars from governmental pension funds. Since it has promised to pay the agreed-on pensions when they come due, interest is not a factor. What is the factor is whether the government will be able to make those payments when they are contractually due. Some are afraid that the legislature will adjust pension payouts, or increase the retirement age, at different levels than were true when the worker began to contribute to the retirement system. Remember, that there was real money in the pension funds at one time. It's not there now!

When we look at taxes and debts, we usually estimate them based on the gross domestic product, the GDP. Here are a few examples of national debts of countries, as a percent of GDP, and the total taxes they pay as a percent of GDP.

	Debt as % of GDP	Total tax rate
Japan	250%	28.3%
Greece	185%	39%
Italy	133%	43.5%
Portugal	126%	37%
United States	104%	26%
Denmark	44%	50.8%
Norway	30%	43.6%

From these figures, we can make a few assumptions, based on other facts that we know. From Greece and Italy, we can assume that their high level of corruption has been a factor in their national debts. (They are ranked as the most corrupt and second most corrupt countries in Europe.) Quite commonly shop and restaurant owners will require cash payments so that they need not pay taxes on the transaction.

In Japan, we see an unrealistic retirement plan with the government having to pay retirees for 20 to 30 years after they have stopped working. The average lifespan for women in Japan is 87 and for men 81. This is the longest lifespan in the world. Until recently, retirement was at 55. Then it was raised to 60. Now it is 61 and will be inching up to 65 in 2025. Social welfare payments to the elderly are a major part of Japan's debt problem. Japan does not have enough workers but allows retirees to collect pensions for 20 to 30 years. Such a program is popular among workers, especially the retirees, but places the country in a precarious situation. Japan's national debt is generally listed at 250% of its gross domestic product. But since much of it is owed by one government department to another, the true external debt is probably about 135% of its GDP. This could easily be handled by raising the retirement age and/or increasing taxes to the common European level. But every country has traditions and it is very difficult to make such unpopular changes.

In the US, we see a very low tax rate for the size of the military it desires. We also see an unreasonably early retirement scheme because the government pays out about eight years more in pensions than the workers have actually contributed towards.

In Saudi Arabia, we see the benefit of abundant oil to keep the borrowing and taxation very low. Norway also has an abundant oil supply but it also has a social welfare system second to none. This requires a relatively high total tax revenue of about 44%. Norway has traditionally invested at least 95% of its oil money in its pension fund, which is now worth a trillion dollars. It is the largest stockholder in Europe and has bought or leased a great deal of real estate in other countries.

Denmark has an extremely high tax rate which has been used to reduce foreign debt and to fund a social welfare system that makes the Danes the happiest people in the world in most annual surveys. This year they dropped to third, behind Finland and Norway. But conservative rumblings are indicating a move toward lower taxes and a later retirement age, perhaps 67 or later, along with requiring student loans rather than giving tuition grants from the government.

The United States pays $266 billion a year, 6% of the federal budget, on the interest of the debts that it owes. And it still owes more than $20 trillion ($20,000,000,000,000). Just think how fancy a car you could buy with that $20 trillion! President Reagan borrowed over a trillion dollars from the Social Security fund to fund his tax cuts. Cut people's taxes today and let their children pay, with interest, twenty or thirty years from now. Sounds dishonest to me! It's like if you bought a present for yourself then billed it to my credit card. But that's the American way!

In eight years, the national debt will rise $1.5 trillion from Trump's tax cuts, and more if the infrastructure spending and military spending are increased. With the Trump budget proposals of 2017, the Congressional Budget Office predicts an additional ten trillion dollars added to the national debt by 2027. Interest on that debt will probably be well over 12% of the national budget,

The interest rate is expected to rise to 3.6% or even 4%. So the picture gets bleaker while the politicians promise us more—while cutting our taxes. Thirty years ago the interest rate on our national debt was 8.8%; recently it has been as low at 2.3%. It will begin rising soon; the expectation is for three interest increases in 2018.

Today there is $1.61 trillion in circulation, including the Federal Reserve notes. So if the government were to issue $20 trillion new dollars to pay off the $20 trillion present debt, your dollar would be worth about ten cents on the international market. Your Japanese or Korean television set would cost ten times as much.

So, printing more money is an approach that America could take. If we doubled our currency, foreign debtors like China and Japan would be paid back at only half of the value they have loaned us. Our exports would be cheaper for others to buy. Our imports would cost twice as much for us to buy.

Since the Social Security Fund is the major lender to the US, it would still be able to pay pensions. But for those people who are expats, living in Mexico or Europe, their pension would be worth only half as much in buying power. And for those who planned on foreign travel after retiring—forget it!

For those countries whose currency is pegged to the dollar, like Iraq and Vietnam, prices wouldn't rise, but you can be sure that they would unpeg their currencies in minutes if the US devalued to that extreme. What is more likely to happen is that the US would have to undergo an extreme austerity program, as Greece has been forced to do for the last several years—and believe me, it ain't fun! Prior governments promised much, without taxes, so their present government is stuck with the grim consequences. And you can imagine that the citizens blame everyone but themselves.

Whenever a president does not balance the budget because of tax reductions (usually with the rich as the major beneficiaries—because they contribute the most to political campaigns) and spending for: wars, anti-terrorism, the military, bailouts of industries and financial organizations (like the Wall Street bailout and the General Motors bailout—which were both repaid), Medicaid, federal pensions, and etc.—he must ask Congress to increase the debt limit, then borrow to cover it. This was done twice in the first two months of 2018. Because the presidents seldom balance their budgets, our debt keeps increasing. Raising taxes on ourselves to reduce the negative financial consequences for our children is seldom an option. So our children will live with: devalued dollars that will buy less, if we print more money; or, if the legislators decide—on severe austerity, like Greece, with reduced government pay and pensions and less infrastructure spending. Sounds like a lose-lose situation!

Government bonds help finance America's spending. Japan is now our biggest creditor, with China second. But many countries have lent us money, as have many individual investors at home and abroad, but we still go on believing that our taxes can be cut and there are no repercussions. When was the last time you heard a politician saying he would raise your taxes—and you voted for him?

The total debt of the world's countries is about $53 trillion, so the United States only owes about 36% of all of the debt of all the world's countries. Conservative politicians generally say that they want a balanced budget. This is good, but the last time we had one was in Bill Clinton's last term—and even then, our national debt was already $5.7 trillion.

Social Security taxes are collected by the government. They are put into a fund. If the government runs a deficit, which is every year now, the government needs to borrow. It can borrow from individuals, nations, or the Social Security and other federal pension funds. The government now owes $2.8 trillion to Social Security, $888 billion to Personnel Management Retirement, $670 billion to the Military Retirement Fund, and a few hundred billion to other government retirement funds.

HOW MUCH IS THE INTEREST ON OUR DEBT?

About 20% of the personal income taxes that we pay, a total of $1.6 trillion, goes toward the payment of interest on the debt. The revenue from corporate income taxes paid, $292 billion, wouldn't cover it. But why worry, our kids will have to pay it.

INCREASING OUR DEBT IS A BAD HABIT—SHOULD WE CALL IT A NATIONAL ADDICTION?

The highest percentage increase in the national debt was by Franklin Roosevelt who increased the debt by over 1,000% in his 12 years in office. This was due to a combination of social spending because of the Great Depression and the expenses of World War II. The actual amount was about $236 billion which would be about $4 trillion in today's currency. Woodrow Wilson increased the debt by over a thousand percent during World War I. His $3 billion increase in the debt would be equivalent to about $48 billion today.

Ronald Reagan added $1.85 trillion to the debt. GHW Bush added a little over $1.5 trillion in his four years, His son added nearly $6 trillion. Clinton had added $1.4 trillion in eight years. Barack Obama increased the debt by $7.9. Part of this was used in extending employment benefits for the unemployed and reducing taxes to get the country out of the "Great Recession" of 2008. Both Bush and Obama had to increase their budgets to take care of higher spending for Social Security and Medicare. To reemphasize, because we are living longer we do not contribute near enough to pay for our retirements and our medical expenses.

Earlier presidents who were operating before Social Security and medical benefits increased our federal spending, were able to produce surpluses in the budget. Calvin Coolidge left a $1 billion surplus every year, Warren Harding also left surpluses of $1 billion a year, and Woodrow Wilson left $3 billion in his last two years.

Without wars and "entitlements"—and with no interest on the national debt, it is relatively easy to have surpluses. But the necessity of wars, and the desires of the people for welfare benefits, as well as $266 billion for interest on the national debt, increases the debt.

There are a number of ways that we can look at how bad the debt is. The common way is to look at the national debt versus the national production of goods and services, our GDP. We could also look at it as the national debt versus the taxing ability of the country. America now has a debt of about 105% of its gross domestic product. That is very bad. It is one of the worst ratios in the world. If we look at it relative to our taxing ability it is even worse because the total tax rate of America is only about 26%. That includes income tax, sales or value added taxes (VAT), corporate taxes, excise taxes, tariffs, etc. When we look at Norway, with no real debt (its invested pension fund is about equal to its borrowing), we see a country that taxes itself at almost 44%. When we look at Denmark, commonly ranked as the happiest country in the world, we have a total tax rate of almost 52%.

What can we do? We either raise our taxes to pay for what we want or we will have to default on our loans. We can either print twenty times as much money as we have in circulation or we can declare ourselves insolvent. Some of our municipalities have already gone bankrupt, several of our states are in financial positions that make them candidates for bankruptcy.

Bankruptcy, or insolvency, of nations is not new. There have been more than 200 sovereign bankruptcies in the last 200 years. It is common in Central and South America and Africa, but it has also occurred in Europe.

AMERICA'S BUDGET PRIORITIES

America's budget is a shade over 50% for pensions and healthcare, Medicare and Medicaid. Then it is about 17% for military and 17% for nearly everything else. There are additional mandatory programs, such as food stamps and unemployment compensation which amount to about 12% of the budget. Then there is 6.6% for the interest on the national debt. Expenditures are classified as mandatory—with payments required by specific laws, or discretionary—with payment amounts renewed annually as part of the budget process.

If you were to read from the CIA's annual World Factbook you would see that the US debt-to-GDP ratio is about 77.4%. But that includes only the debt owed to foreign governments and individuals, not to government programs such as the Social Security Trust Fund. When we add the intergovernmental borrowing would come up to 104% to 106% of the GDP. Using this figure, we realize that every person in America owes about $65,000 as their share of the national debt.

But there is more. Social Security payments exceeded income in 2010. Medicare Part A, hospital insurance, payouts also exceed the income. To fix Medicare, the government should either increase the tax or take over the payments by eliminating insurance companies. But that would not be capitalistic!

The estimates of the future payouts, if the Social Security and Medicare taxes are not increased, is over $7 trillion for Social Security and over $38 trillion for Medicare and Medicaid. Medicaid is a federal program aiding the states in providing medical care for people who cannot afford it. So it is not provided for by a special tax, it comes from the general fund.

We might wonder today whether survival is more important than the form of government. Patrick Henry did say "give me liberty or give me death," but it may not be quite that simple. There are realities that many seem to overlook or not even know about. Here are a few.

PLANETARY PROBLEMS—OVERPOPULATION AND CLIMATE CHANGE

Overpopulation is the major problem of the world according to the environmental science department at one of the leading New York universities. Certainly, overpopulation is responsible for climate change which is in turn responsible for famines in some areas and hurricanes, heavy snowstorms and inundating rains in others. Forest fires, due to the lack of rain and the overheated air have raged out of control in the US and Europe.

Some don't understand why. To repeat--the carbon dioxide emitted by fires, coal-burning, oil-burning, cement plants, vehicles, energy production and many other carbon producing entities heat the air. (They remain in the atmosphere for 30 to 90 years—

depending on how much is absorbed by the oceans.) When air is heated, it is able to absorb more water from the oceans, rivers and lakes. This water vapor is the most potent greenhouse gas. But when the air is cooled, it cannot hold the excess moisture it has picked up. If the air is relatively warm the water vapor is released as heavy rain or hurricanes. If the air is relatively cold the water vapor creates great snow storms.

As increased populations eat more meat, the problem compounds. Methane from grass eating animals, like cows and chickens, finds its way into the atmosphere from the manure and gases emitted from the animals. About 15% of the greenhouse gases come from animals and about two thirds of that comes from beef. Methane remains as a greenhouse gas for 12 to 15 years.

As population increases people are more likely to move to the cities in their native countries or to migrate to other countries. More cement is therefore needed to house and employ the new city dwellers. The migration of people from poor or war-torn countries is initially welcomed by unselfish populations but as more migrants populate a country with starkly different traditions, the economic burden and the social diversification makes many of the previously unselfish people selfish. We see that in countries that are developing the reactionary (populist) parties and attitudes. The United States under President Trump, the UK, the Netherlands, France, Poland, Sweden and Germany are among the nations that are developing small but often effective "populist" parties.

The earlier humanitarian empathy of the countries with low fertility rates eventually dissipates and the impoverished fertile families of the south and east, with their markedly different traditions and their reticence to totally integrate, are less likely to be welcomed. Immigration is more likely to be open to the educated engineers and trained medical personnel. The assent of acceptance is evolving from "what can we do for you," to "what can you do for us."

Overpopulation and the rapid rise of technology give us a combination of more people but fewer jobs. The technology is increasing so rapidly, but we can all think of the better days of our youth when there were plenty of jobs. Yes, there are plenty of high-level jobs for mathematicians, physicists, engineers and information technology specialists but the countries producing these skilled people are quite different from the countries with the high birth rates. How many major universities can you think of in Mali, Congo, or Afghanistan?

OVERPOPULATION CAUSES CLIMATE CHANGE—AND EVEN MORE PROBLEMS

Without the opportunity to find a satisfying life situation, people (especially men) need to fulfill their drives for power. We see this in most countries. In some it has become attached to a religion, such as Islam. So we have the Islamists acting out their drive for power then rationalizing it as a tenet of their religion. We also see it in gang membership which is often associated with drug distribution and human slavery. In the less organized parts of a society we may see gang violence merely for the sake of violence—so the perpetrators can feel more power and therefore less inferior. Other times the violence is attached to making money through intimidation, protection, or human trafficking. Here again we see the acquisition of power—but through riches, not gang-banging.

In the more advanced societies youth sport often makes inroads into this need for standing in the community. In the most primitive societies, working in the fields may satisfy the youth. It is in that great middle area of developing nations where societies are developing somewhat but cannot provide the physiological or psychological necessities for the young, where most of the problems occur.

WE NEED INTELLIGENCE, EDUCATION, AND MONEY

Norway has its oil and fish to allow funding for education and employment, so it is easy to find a secure place in the society. Some of the oil-rich Arab countries have plenty of money for their natives but import many workers to handle the economic needs of their countries. But when we have countries like India, Pakistan, Iraq and most of the South American, African and Asian countries—we often can't provide for their economic, physical, educational, or psychological needs.

CAN DEMOCRACY RISE TO THE CHALLENGE?

We like to think that democracy will handle all situations, but this is unrealistic. There are too many people and not enough education, not enough meaningful employment opportunities, and too many power-hungry despots— many of whom have come to power through the ballot box. Assad, Zuma, Erdogan Putin, Maduro, and Mugabe are just a few of the recent power-hungry rulers who have mishandled their populations while amassing great personal wealth.

How far can we move to an extreme and still be considered a democratic country?

We have expanded the meaning of "democracy" from the one-person-one-vote idea to a government that allows liberty—such as freedom of the press, a number of human rights— and has some semblance of an equality of opportunity. We might even include the idea of reducing income inequality.

There are people in the US, such as many in the Tea Party, who look down upon the Scandinavian countries because there is more social welfare in those countries. But these countries are far happier than people in the US according to the annual global polls on happiness. Tea Partiers seem to think that laissez-faire capitalism is a major element of democracy. In Scandinavia, they would see social welfare as a major element of democracy. Understanding what we mean by a word (semantics) is essential in any political discussion.

WHAT DO WE MEAN BY DEMOCRACY?

Before we decide to keep or change our democracy we must understand what we mean by the word. Each of us has different significations for the word. For some it means one person one vote. For others, "capitalism." For others, "socialism." For others, it includes freedom of speech which may or may not be tolerant of fake news, propaganda or other lies. For some it includes freedom of religion which may mean freedom to believe what one believes or wants to believe, for others it includes practicing what they want in the name of religion even if it means: handling poisonous snakes, taking illegal drugs, or preventing your child from lifesaving blood transfusions.

So many authoritarian or libertarian ideas have become associated with the word democracy that what we are discussing must be clearly defined before we talk about it. Generally, all meanings of democracy include political, economic, and social elements to large degrees.

DOES DEMOCRACY REQUIRE CAPITALISM?

The same is true of economic systems that many include in their idea of democracy—like capitalism. Do you mean what Karl Marx meant—that it was making money on your money? If so Warren Buffet is a capitalist as is anyone who makes money on stock trading. But that is only one way to make money; how about the entrepreneurial way of Bill Gates and Mark Zuckerberg? We might also define capitalism as an economic system in which the individuals own and control industry and trade.

But that is not what we have now. Governments do quite a bit to control trade. They even control much of industry in that the government usually buys many things from private companies-- like airplanes, artillery, and furniture. So maybe we need to look at the ways that people make money.

➢ Capitalists make money on their money, such as: stock trading, banking, real estate manipulation, and absentee ownership of companies,

➢ Entrepreneurship would be the method that creative people would choose to develop new products and services,

➢ Owners of businesses and factories,

➢ Other free enterprise options,

➢ Private-sector employees would do the work assigned to them by private companies,

➢ Government employees can include everyone from the king, president or prime minister to the lowest paid file clerk,

➢ Self-employed, like an independent farmer or subsistence farmer,

➢ Indentured servants,

➢ Slaves.

There would probably be many more such categories. Many of these categories will be found in socialistic as well as in free enterprise societies. European countries would tend to be more socialistic, with more welfare programs, and with more government employees. But they have plenty of free enterprise. In the United States, it is theoretically a free enterprise economy, but there are large-scale socialistic and communistic aspects to the government.

So, we cannot really list most Western economies as being only socialistic or only free enterprise. However, they tend to have a guiding primary theory of either, the Scandinavian idea of making the people happy or the American idea of making as much money as possible.

HUMAN RIGHTS, HUMAN DESIRES, AND HUMAN DUTIES

Often what we call human rights are only our desires. When a foreign national comes to the US and has a baby, that baby is a citizen of the US. When the parents of the baby want to join the baby in the US they may cry and plead for their "human rights" and attempt to elicit sympathy for their cause. Their desire they think is a human right!

The European Union has a list of human rights that does not require any duties of the citizen. Terrorists and prisoners on life sentences have been given rights from the European Court of Equal Justice. The United Nations has a list of rights but they have one section on duties.

Among the normal human rights, depending on the country, are such things as: freedom of speech, freedom of religion, freedom of assembly, and freedom of the press. Not all countries have these typically democratic rights. And when they have them, there may be other laws that are held superior in a court of law. For example, the late Liu Xiaobo was a Chinese activist, writer, and professor who served four prison terms for violating a law of China. He won the Nobel Peace Prize while in prison. The law he violated was Article 105, Paragraph 2, 1997 of the Criminal Code of the People's Republic of China which states that:

"Anyone who uses rumor, slander or other means to encourage subversion of the political power of the State or to overthrow the socialist system, shall be sentenced to a fixed-term of imprisonment of not more than five years. However, the ringleaders and anyone whose crime is monstrous shall be sentenced to a fixed-term imprisonment of not less than five years."

One might think that this law would run counter to Article 33 of the Chinese Constitution which protects human rights or Article 35 which allows for freedom of speech, of the press, of association, etc. China is also a signatory to the Universal Declaration of Human Rights of the United Nations. Article 18 states that:

"Everyone has the right to freedom of thought, conscience and religion; this right includes freedom to change his religion or belief, and freedom, either alone or in community with others and in public or private, to manifest his religion or belief in teaching, practice, worship and observance."

Article 19 states that:

"Everyone has the right to freedom of opinion and expression; this right includes freedom to hold opinions without interference and to seek, receive and impart information and ideas through any media and regardless of frontiers."

Article 20 states that:

1. Everyone has the right to freedom of peaceful assembly and association.

2. No one may be compelled to belong to an association.

China is certainly not alone in denying what many would consider our human rights, under their Constitution.

Singapore has laws against selling chewing gum, spitting on the street, forgetting to flush the toilet, presenting obscene music or other content, taking illegal drugs, and jaywalking. Certainly, these run counter to American ideas of freedom. But Singapore is not the United States—and it runs much more smoothly than does the US. Too few rules certainly encourage anarchy!

WHAT ABOUT EQUALITY?

And what about "equality"? Equality means exactly equal. So 2=2 or 2.001=2.001. No two people are equal. Some are taller than others, some are younger than others, some are faster than others, some are more intelligent than others, some have more of a drive for power than others, and some have more of the capacity to love unselfishly than others.

So what do we mean by "equality" in the political sphere? We usually mean some kind of equal rights. We may want equal pay no matter what we do. Or we may want equal pay for equal work. Under communism, Karl Marx said "from each according to his ability to each according to his needs." So here equal pay is based more on need than on the work done. Lenin said "socialism is from each according to his ability to each according to his work." So you would get paid more if you worked more effectively.

In many societies, the idea of equality includes the right to life. So, no matter how poorly you have treated others, no matter how many people you have killed, you have the right to life, so there is no capital punishment. The previously mentioned Norwegian case of Anders Breivik who admitted killing 77 defenseless young people so was given the maximum sentence for murder— 21 years. In Texas, he would have been executed. Still, he is pursuing a human rights violation case against Norway in the European Court of Human Rights. He might well win there because European Union citizens have no responsibilities to their societies—they only have rights.

The European Convention on Human Rights gives almost every type of right to the citizens including freedom from the death penalty. It does not mention any responsibilities of the citizen to the European Union. The only exception is a mention of responsibilities between a husband and wife. This is a bit different from the United Nations Convention on Human Rights because in Article 29:

"Everyone has duties to the community in which alone the free and full development of his personality is possible.

(2) In the exercise of his rights and freedoms, everyone shall be subject only to such limitations as are determined by law solely for the purpose of securing due recognition and respect for the rights and freedoms of others and of meeting the just requirements of morality, public order and the general welfare in a democratic society.

(3) These rights and freedoms may in no case be exercised contrary to the purposes and principles of the United Nations."

DOES THE EQUAL RIGHT TO VOTE MEAN THAT ALL PEOPLE ARE EQUAL IN ALL THEIR DESIRES?

The idea of "one person one vote"—that is, an equal voice in choosing representatives or initiatives—has been translated into a nearly universal allotment of equal rights without any listed responsibilities. Theoretically one may choose not to work and expect that the government will take care of him. Sometimes a responsibility is implied, such as when one spouse is given equal rights to the other spouse. So if one spouse treated the other unequally, the offending spouse has abrogated his or her responsibility to ensure equal rights in the relationship.

For example, take the case of Kirk Dickson who, serving a life sentence for murder in the UK, married a fellow prisoner. After her release, he applied to have a child with her by artificial insemination. All of the British courts turned down his application. One might guess that if genetics may be responsible for half of our behavior, the child might have some social problems. Another factor might have been that the father was in prison for life, or at least for a number of years if he were paroled, so the child would be fatherless for at least that time. This child might also have been in danger of physical abuse since the father had kicked a man to death because he wouldn't give him a cigarette.

The child would cost the UK for education. There is also the likelihood of welfare expenses and possibly judicial and penal expenses. But the European Convention on Human Rights gives the right of everyone to marry and start a family. So, this was the overriding determinant in the case.

With values being based on non-provable assumptions of either: self-centered, God-based, or society-based ideas-- the Convention on Human Rights emphasizes the self-centered aspect of all governmental decisions and it neglects to consider what might be good for society. And so, the democratic idea of one-person, one-vote has evolved into an arena that might sublimate the good of the overall society to the wishes of each citizen.

Let us look at equal pay or minimum pay for a job. If I am paid $10 an hour for a job but I have three children so I need more money, should I be paid more? What if another person can do the job at least as well for eight dollars an hour? The owner of the company would prefer this. And perhaps he will reduce the price of the widget that I was making so that every person who wants a widget will pay less. This is a benefit to the owner of the business, the society of widget buyers, and the new employee. But my own self-centered desires are totally frustrated because I lost my $10-an-hour job. Of course, now I will go on unemployment insurance so this costs the society money.

When we talk about democracy we are often talking about liberty and equality. Political philosophers know that these are very often antithetical positions or values. If we are to look at equality, it is obvious that we are not equal. As we said, no two people on the earth are equal. As we indicated, we are unequal in terms of: height, weight, age, educational background, intelligence, work incentive, riches, and every other area of human potential. The conservatives generally want to emphasize the fact that we are unequal and that because of this we should have the liberty to achieve. It doesn't matter that some people start with millions of dollars from their parents. It doesn't matter that some people went to the best universities because their parents had connections and the money for tuition. What matters is where you are and what you have. You should be free to make as much money as possible with the lowest taxes possible.

On the other side, we have those who want to give equal pay to all because we are all equal. We have equal rights to education even if we are poor. Should we have equal rights to equal wages because we are equally human.

TAXPAYER-PAID BUSINESSES

Walt Disney, Marriott, and Lockheed Martin are just a handful of companies aided by sweet deals, by state and local governments, at taxpayer expense. Businesses employ people. People pay taxes. But—are the taxes collected at least equal to the tax breaks given?

FREEDOM OF SPEECH

The Danish philosopher Søren Kierkegaard wrote that, "People demand freedom of speech as a compensation for the freedom of thought which they seldom use." Looking at Twitter and Facebook, as well as comments to news stories on the Internet, we can see that his observation is even more true today than when he wrote it—almost 200 years ago.

Free speech is never absolute. When it advocates the immediate killing of a person or group—the US Supreme Court may object. If it violates community standards in vulgarity—the Supreme Court may object. If a student in high school uses vulgarity or hate speech and thinks that this freedom protects him or her, and the school stops it, the speech may not be protected because the school acts as a parent (*in loco parentis*). But the same speech given by an adult would probably be protected. But are there limits to hate speech? When does absolute freedom of speech endanger democracy?

While freedom of speech was originally meant to allow for honest differences in political opinions, it has come to include such areas as vulgarity and hate speech. Decisions from 100 years ago, such as anti-war protests during World War I (Schenck v. United States in 1919 and Abrams v. United State in 1919) and pro-communist sympathizers after the war (McKinley v. California in 1927 and Dennis v. United States in 1951) were found to be in favor of limiting free speech during wartime and also denying free speech for communists, who advocated violent overthrow of the government.

The Court has changed its emphasis on what is not allowed as free speech from being "a bad tendency," as in McKinley and Abrams, to a "clear and present danger" as in Schenk, to an "imminent lawless action, that is likely to incite and produce such lawless action," in Brandenburg v. Ohio (1969). At a Ku Klux Klan meeting in Brandenburg, rural Ohio, one of the speeches referred to "revengeance" against "niggers", "Jews", and those who supported them. (If "revengeance" doesn't sound like a word to you, it really isn't— but you can believe that it has a powerful meaning to some uneducated white Christians with huge inferiority feelings. And the mantra that "we is better than them," is an easy way to develop a feeling of power.)

The Court, in its infinite wisdom, decided that the speakers didn't mean to go out right now to do the dirty deed, so it developed its new theory of "imminent lawless action." So we might conclude that if you say, "Let's kill all the Jews and niggers tomorrow," it is probably okay. But if you say, "let's kill all the Jews and niggers now," it is probably a violation of the Constitutional guarantee of free speech. It might also violate the Christian "turn the other cheek" doctrine! And it would certainly violate the "Golden Rule" of

Christianity and the ethical precept of Kant—to always treat people as ends in themselves, and not as means to your own desires.

The boundaries of free speech vary from country to country. America's are the most permissive.

Just how much freedom of speech should an individual be allowed when it may be disruptive to the society? What if it is helpful to the society and stimulates it to change? Several Muslim countries have very strong blasphemy laws that require either long prison terms or capital punishment. Recently a boy in Bangladesh was hanged by his peers because they thought he had blasphemed. He had not. Politicians, in Muslim countries, who have wished to change the blasphemy laws are often executed. Is it blasphemous to question the divinity of Jesus, the revelations to Mohammed or Joseph Smith, or to question any laws created by men that may go against what someone believes?

➤Should child pornography be allowed? It isn't.

➤How about terrorist propaganda?

➤What about communist information and appeals?

➤What about hate speech targeting religions?

➤Would atheistic or agnostic programs be allowed if they are against your religion?

If freedom of speech was meant for only political speech, should we eliminate freedoms for other questionable speeches? There are a number of laws in Europe that prohibit hate speech of any kind.

WHAT ABOUT THE FREEDOM TO LIE TO THE PUBLIC IN AN ELECTION CAMPAIGNS?

You would think that this is a no-brainer, but not in America. In the US v. Alvarez (2012), a candidate for the local water board had introduced himself as a 21-year retired Marine who had received the Congressional Medal of Honor. None of this was true. He was found to be in violation of the federal Stolen Valor Act of 2005 which makes it a crime to falsely claim that one has military honors. The false claim to have won the Congressional Medal of Honor carries even greater penalties.

The Supreme Court found the decision of the lower court to be unconstitutional by a 6 to 3 vote. They concluded that: the act was overly broad, false statements can be protected by the First Amendment, and we must look at the proportionality of the violation of the act—does the punishment fit the crime?

Justices Alito, Scalia, and Thomas, dissented from the decision because the ruling had "[broken] sharply from a long line of cases recognizing that the right to free speech does not protect false factual statements that inflict real harm and serve no legitimate interest . . . . The act presents no threat to freedom of expression."

A 2007 case, Rickert v Washington, which resulted in a 5 to 4 decision of the Washington State Supreme Court, considered whether a political candidate could be punished for telling deliberate lies about her opponent in a political campaign. Such a lie was in violation of a state law which included the lines: "It is a violation of this chapter for a person to sponsor with actual malice: (a) Political advertising or an electioneering communication that contains a false statement of material fact about a candidate for public office. However, this subsection does not apply to statements made by a candidate about the candidate himself or herself . . . ."

In running for a state senator position Ms. Rickert had sponsored a brochure that said that Senator Sheldon, "voted to close a facility for the developmentally challenged in his district." This was not true and the Sheldon supporters attempted to correct the falsehood. Sheldon complained to the Public Disclosure Commission and Ms. Rickert was fined $1,000. Sheldon won the election and Ms. Rickert filed suit alleging that the state abridged free speech.

The court's majority opinion stated that it was up to the public, not the state, to determine the truth or falsity of a statement: "every person must be his own watchman for truth, because the forefathers did not trust any government to separate the truth from the false for us." The dissent argued that "the majority's decision is an invitation to lie with impunity." The dissent argued that because the law required that punishable speech requires 'actual malice' it was not protected under the Constitution.

So again, we see highly knowledgeable justices disagreeing and a one judge majority setting the law.

In another case, Susan B. Anthony List v. Driehaus (2014), the List organization purchased ads, including billboard space, saying that Congressman Driehaus had voted to support taxpayer-funded abortions because he had voted for the Affirmative Care Act. The fact that the act did not require government funding of abortions was affirmed by a judge. Driehaus complained to the election commission of Ohio that the ads were falsehoods. The commission agreed. The Supreme Court disagreed unanimously saying, "We do not want the government (i.e., the Ohio Elections Commission) deciding what is political truth — for fear that the government might persecute those who criticize it. Instead, in a democracy, the voters should decide."

I wonder whether the voters would have sufficient knowledge of the Affordable Care Act, which did not mention government paid abortions, to make a rational decision on this, or will they merely believe what they see in print? I also wonder if the people who read the false statement would all see the opposing statement, which was true.

It would appear that the Court would support the fake news that appeared to influence the 2016 presidential election, and they would certainly support the innumerable falsehoods of President Trump. The Court seems to allow anyone to say anything, even if knowingly lying.

If the population is supposed to separate alternative facts from verifiable facts, perhaps we must require an additional ten years of schooling.

AND CHINA'S IDEAS ABOUT FREE SPEECH

In early 2013, a movement developed among reformers to enforce the provisions of the constitution. China, like most "democracies," has a constitution that allows free speech, free religious expression, and other common rights. But in Article 28 of the Constitution it is stated that:

"The State maintains public order and suppresses treasonable and other criminal activities that endanger State security; it penalizes criminal activities that endanger public security and disrupt the socialist economy as well as other criminal activities; and it punishes and reforms criminals."

You remember, Xiaobo, the Chinese university lecturer and Nobel Peace Prize winner. He argued that his verdicts were against China's Constitution and the Universal Declaration of Human Rights. And they were. But governments have a way of suppressing free speech when it rattles the cage of power. Article 28 of the Constitution of China clearly protects the government from such anti-government rhetoric.

Looking at these two very successful economic countries, China and Singapore, the lives of the people in general have significantly improved with the authoritarian democracies under which they live. Perhaps as long as the economic needs of the populace is improving, something has to give.

When we compare the rapid increase of income in China with the rapid decrease in income in the US, we may wonder about the balance of freedom versus finances. The same might be true in education. Singapore leads the world in all three categories of the PISA scores—reading, math, and science. China is far ahead of the US in both math and science scores. The US is 30th in math, 23rd in science, and 20th in reading. If America is to be great again, perhaps we should start with education rather than coal mining.

FREE SPEECH IN OTHER COUNTRIES

It is quite common for governments to suppress the free speech of opponents by using blasphemy, libel, or defamation laws to punish and imprison them. In Myanmar, a Facebook poet got six months in jail for criticizing the president. Defamation laws are commonly used in most countries, other than the US, to tame those critical to the people running the government. In Russia, being found guilty of a crime, such as defamation, can make it illegal to run for office.

Recently Stella Nyanzi of Uganda was convicted of belittling the president and his wife and using obscene words to enhance her call for free sanitary pads for girls in school in Uganda—where the average girl must miss a week of school each month because of her menstrual period. She is also an activist for LGBT rights and a strong feminist in a patriarchal society. She also used obscene language in her quest and is said to have undressed herself on live television to make her point. She was placed in a maximum-security prison.

At the same time that these were happening, a referendum in Turkey gave dictatorial powers to the president where he could quash free speech and any opposition, or imagined opposition. In Venezuela, massive protests against the president calling for elections now were violently countered by the military.

The point is that even though most countries have constitutional guarantees of free speech and the freedom of assembly, the government has great power to control those who are exercising their constitutional rights. Free-speech is most free in the United States—it is so free that companies like Info-Wars or Fox News, or individuals like Rush Limbaugh, can continually lie and have their inflammatory lies protected by free speech. Other countries, in fact all other countries, have some limits on speaking freely.

For those who wish to speak up against political power it would be wise to keep the speeches free of obscene, meaningless language. Obscene language, while it may be used to shown one's strong feelings, always brings the message to a lower level and may be seen as blasphemous in a legal sense outside the US.

HATE SPEECH

The First Amendment to the US Constitution provides no exceptions for hate speech, although many states and municipalities have laws against hate speech. But the Supreme Court has recently found that they may be unconstitutional.

An Asian band wanted to use "Slants" as their name but was refused by the Patent and Trademark Office as being demeaning to Asians. In Matal v. Tom (2017) by an 8-0 decision, the band was allowed the name. Justice Alioto wrote, "The idea that the government may restrict speech expressing ideas that offend . . . strikes at the heart of the First Amendment. Speech that demeans on the basis of race, ethnicity, gender, religion, age, disability, or any other similar ground is hateful; but the proudest boast of our free speech jurisprudence is that we protect the freedom to express "the thought that we hate."

Justice Anthony Kennedy wrote, "A law found to discriminate based on viewpoint is an 'egregious form of content discrimination,' which is 'presumptively unconstitutional.' A law that can be directed against speech found offensive to some portion of the public can be turned against minority and dissenting views to the detriment of all. The First Amendment does not entrust that power to the government's benevolence. Instead, our reliance must be on the substantial safeguards of free and open discussion in a democratic society."

My guess is that we have not heard the end of this issue. In the Matal case the band wanted to call themselves what others thought was a derogatory name. But what if in another case, the victim doesn't like what she is called and can show actual mental injury?

On the other hand, a violent hate crime in which the victim is chosen because of his race is illegal according to the unanimous decision in Wisconsin v. Mitchell (1993).

In August of 2017, white nationalists, including the KKK, paraded in protest to the removal of a statue of the Confederate general and hero Robert E. Lee at Emancipation Park, formerly Lee Park, near the University of Virginia. Naturally counter-protesters to the march arrived and some fist fights erupted. The right to protest and the right to protest the protesters were both legal. The violence was not. Paul Ryan, Speaker of the House of Representatives, and First Lady Melania Trump promptly tweeted their disapproval of the violence. It does not take a psychologist to see the need for power exemplified in the alt-right group. If you haven't accomplished much in your life you can certainly feel superior to all non-whites and non-Christians—and it is obvious that attaching your allegiance to a war that was lost 150 years ago may be rather illogical!

In a tweet, Representative Don Beyer wrote, "White supremacists chanting Nazi slogans aren't Virginia or America. They are weak, ignorant, fearful people with citronella tiki torches." Shortly after he wrote this, a car driven by one of the alt-right protesters plowed into a group of counter-protesters, killing one. Very courageous! Fitting for a coward with a huge inferiority complex!

Does hate speech "insure domestic tranquility" as the preamble to our Constitution requires? Does it "promote the general welfare?" If these precepts are meaningful, it is difficult to see how hate speech is protected under the Constitution. Whether it demeans or otherwise harms people because of their ethnicity, race, gender, religion, or gender identification—it does not insure domestic tranquility. Maybe our court should look at the big picture of what the reason for the Constitution is, rather than examining the toes of one of its legs.

I heard a naïve mental health therapist say once that you can say what you want, and it is up to the listener to determine how they take it. This idea is so false and unrealistic that no informed person could possibly believe it. When a person makes a derogatory remark about another person's appearance, beliefs, or behavior, it is intended to hurt—and it usually does. As we have mentioned often in this book, the inferiority of most people needs venting or they must find another outlet to make them feel the power that they lack. Priding oneself on one's political party, religion, gender, ethnicity, or sport team can give one a false pride. But these connections do not necessarily put an end to someone else's hateful venting. Just look at the Westboro Baptist Church's demonstrations against American soldiers killed in Iraq because America had allowed homosexuals to serve in their army. The grieving families of both homosexual and heterosexual military heroes were forced to endure the unpatriotic and imbecilic ranting of uneducated and narrow minded religious bigots. (Nebraska enacted a law to prevent protests within 500 feet of a cemetery. The Supreme Court refused to review it—so it stands.)

Most legislatures are now comfortable passing laws against racial, religious, age, and ethnic hate crimes. The sticking point for some is when it comes to gender identification situations. South Carolina recently refused to pass a law on gender hate crimes. Indiana, Wyoming, Arkansas, and Georgia are also dragging their heels. Meanwhile, 15 states do not cover homosexuals and 28 do not cover gender identity or transgender individuals in their hate crime laws.

The problem is generally Christian fundamentalists who object to God's decision to create such people. Perhaps they generalize the verse of Matthew 18:18 in which Jesus says to Peter, "whatever you shall bind on earth shall be bound in heaven." While Catholics think this applies only to Peter and his successors, the popes, it appears that fundamentalists assume it applies to them, as individuals, also—they seem to hope that if they change the Scriptures, God will approve. God certainly did make a lot of mistakes, so somebody must correct them! And, heavens to Betsy, we don't want those preachers, who are bellowing about the evils of homosexuality or abortion, being arrested for violating hate crime laws!

John Stuart Mill wrote, "there are many acts which . . . if done publicly, are a violation of good manners and, coming thus within the category of *offenses* against others, may rightfully be prohibited." He then concluded that, "Acts of whatever kind, which, without justifiable cause, do harm to others, may be, and in the more important cases absolutely require to be, controlled by the unfavorable sentiments, and, when needful, by the active interference of mankind. The liberty of the individual must be thus far limited; he must not make himself a nuisance." It is regrettable that he doesn't sit on our Supreme Court!

Both the physical and mental well-being of our citizens needs to be a concern. Just as we make both murder and assault crimes for protecting the physical body-- depression and anxiety, and even suicide, can result from verbal statements. We see so many suicides, particularly with youth, that are caused by verbal harassment or hate speech. And it is getting more common in the social media.

Is free speech, or free political speech, the ultimate democratic value, or are there other values that are equally important? If so, we may have to evaluate which value is superior when values conflict in any given case.

TOLERANCE
Tolerance is certainly a valuable attitude in today's globalized multi-ethnic world. But when tolerance is abused, the society can be overcome by the intolerant. When we see this in drug addiction cases we call the tolerant person an enabler. Such tolerance in the enabler allowed the sick person to continue in their illness.

This can also be done in a society. There are limits to what a functioning society can tolerate. There is an old saying in politics that "the surest way to conciliate a tiger is to be devoured by him." So there must be a balance between intolerance and over-tolerance for a society to be healthy.

This tolerance–intolerance continuum applies to most ideas relative to the freedoms guaranteed by the Constitution, the United Nation's Declaration of Human Rights, and the European Union's Convention on Human Rights. Any liberty can be overdone. One person exercising his or her right in some area might take away an equally valuable right of another. The freedom to lie in a political contest may affect the general welfare of the country. The right of a parent to keep a loaded and unlocked pistol may result in the death of another who doesn't understand the danger of the weapon. (A middle school student of mine killed himself with an "unloaded" rifle. Two childhood friends of mine, neighbors in South-Central Los Angeles, accidentally killed themselves while playing with their parent's "unloaded" pistols—before any of us had reached the 7th grade.

Oh well, life isn't nearly as important as owning a gun! But did the right to own a gun, in these cases, "insure domestic tranquility" which was one of the major reasons for the Constitution?

Similarly, one exercising a right might negatively, or potentially negatively, affect the society. Back to the Second Amendment. With all the mass shootings in the US, which is America's way of controlling the population boom, society might have been very negatively affected by the loss of one of those students at Virginia Tech, the University of Texas, or even Sandy Hook Elementary School, Parkland High, or Columbine High School-- who might have discovered a better way to harness the energy of the sun, grow drought-resistant food, or become effective legislators.

Another illustration would be the exercising the Court's allowing us the right to lie in a political contest. Exercising this right might reward us with ineffective, or possibly harmful, legislators or presidents. But *NO,* that could never happen in America!

Freedom of speech and advancing the social benefit of the society are both essential, but some positions advocated in the expression of free speech may be contradictory to the social benefit of society. The recent alt-right demonstrations of racial and religious hatred in Charlottesville, Virginia saw one dead and many injured. Was the demonstration, or the injuries and death, in the best interests of society?

SEPARATION OF CHURCH AND STATE

Churches and nations have had a long history. The influence of the Catholic Church in France was one of the major reasons for their revolution. Kings and cardinals wielded nearly all of the power. The people wanted theirs. Consequently, after the revolution the church was separated from the new republic. In the early 19th century Napoleon brought some influence of the church back—knowing how religions can be used to influence the population. Putin is doing the same thing in Russia.

In America, the separation was to be complete. People like Thomas Jefferson, George Washington, James Madison, Thomas Paine and Ben Franklin were atheists or deists and did not see value in religion. The British philosopher John Locke was clearly influential in their thinking. It is often difficult to see in their writings the differences between the deists, who believe in a creating being that is not involved in the workings of the world and cannot be prayed to, and the theists, who believe that the creating being is involved in the world and can be prayed to. Both use the word "God" but have very different meanings for it. It's like using the word dog. One person may be thinking of a Saint Bernard and another of a toy poodle.

There was a deep suspicion of the Catholic religion by many Founding Fathers even though Charles Carroll of Maryland, one of the signatories to the Constitution, was a Catholic. However, in the 18th century, as even today in the US, religion is quite important in America.

Some countries still have state religions. Lutheranism is the state religion of Norway even though there are very few believers. Only 5% go to church weekly and only 20% say that religion is somewhat important in their lives. Islam is more often found as a state religion today, especially in the Mideast.

In the more advanced economic and educated countries religion is less and less important. 68% of people in the Netherlands are not religious. In Vietnam, it is 63%. In Denmark 61%, in Japan 52%, in China 51%, and in the United Kingdom it is 38%. But in the US only 23% are not religious. On the other hand, Bangladesh is only 0.1% nonreligious, Thailand 0.27%, and in Iran only 1.1% are not religious. As education becomes more advanced, religion tends to dwindle.

Various polls show that atheism is increasing about 1% to 4% per year in the educated countries. France and the Czech Republic have 30% atheists, traditional Catholic countries like Spain and Ireland are now 20% and 10% atheistic. It seems that the reality that there is so much misery in the world and that prayers don't seem to help, may be factors. How can a merciful God allow continuous wars that are more and more brutal; street gangs that rape and kill thousands; and, climate change that destroys life through forest fires, hurricanes, tornadoes, famines, and snowstorms? It has also been suggested that the immensity of the universe makes the god that created the Earth 6,000 years ago, according to Bishop Ussher's calculations, too insignificant to have created the Big Bang nearly 14,000,000,000 years earlier.

Nevertheless, the fact that fifty or more years ago people were generally religious influenced governments to give churches, especially the powerful churches governmental perks. Today the Catholics, the Mormons, and the rich, evangelical mega-churches have been potent lobbyists for the state giving more financial breaks to churches and to clerics.

HOW MUCH ARE CHURCH AND STATE SEPARATED?

Two hundred years ago they were separate. Freedom of religious belief was clearly allowed, but the churches were not given tax-breaks. Tariffs and excise taxes provided the bulk of federal income. As income taxes and property taxes became realities, businesses and other organizations, like churches, sought deductions for contributions to them or exemptions from being taxed.

In 1913, the US Tax Code was only about 400 pages. This was actually quite long. In 26 years, it grew 25% to 500 pages. During the 1930s it was under a thousand pages. World War II increased the need for tax changes, so it increased to 8,000 pages. It is now over 75,000 pages. More and more tax breaks for more and more organizations!

Lobbyists for special interest groups continue to work to allow their clients special privileges. Farmers get unbelievable gifts from the government. Business, being the lifeblood of America, gets nearly unlimited deductions for their expenses. Churches and charity groups, educational enterprises, literary and scientific organizations, and groups that work for the betterment of the world ordination—all get significant concessions from the government. Federal, state, and local tax agencies all give similar breaks. But no group gets the tax benefits as much as churches. While businesses get tax deductions for the buildings and the taxes they pay, churches are tax-exempt. So, while businesses have their taxes reduced through deductions on property expenses, religions are totally exempt from taxes on most of their holdings. They are only required to pay taxes when they are actually in business to make money, such as in farming or tourism.

If religion is separated from the state, why does the state give religions so many tax benefits? Numerous in-depth articles have been written questioning: why do they allow Mormon farming interests, which are tax-free, to compete with farmers of other religions who must pay taxes; why are Catholic business properties either not taxed or are taxed at a low rate; and why are the private jets and mansions of mega-church ministers not taxed? Such tax breaks increase the taxes of everyone else while increasing the national debt.

Currently Americans give more than twice as much in tax deductible contributions to churches than they do to education. Might this have anything to do with our very poor international education rankings?

CHURCH TAX EXEMPTIONS

To understand a bit about how church exemptions wormed their way into American tax law, we might start by looking at England. In Tudor, England the church was part of the state and so was exempt from taxes. There have also been English exemptions from taxes for charitable organizations such as hospitals and churches. In the US, the Wilson Tariff Act of 1894 provided exemptions for religions, but this law was found to be unconstitutional in Pollack v Farmers Loan & Trust (1895); however, the same exemptions found their way into the Payne-Aldrich Tariff Act of 1909.

The US Tax Code (501 [C][3]) allows for tax-exempt, nonprofit organizations if they are operated exclusively for: religious, charitable, scientific, literary and some public safety and amateur sports organizations, and organizations that work to prevent cruelty to children or animals. No part of the net earnings may benefit an individual and no substantial part of the earnings can be used in lobbying or propaganda.

Are individuals, like bishops and mega-ministers benefitting when they live in a church-owned mansion or private house? Are they being benefited when their vacations are paid for by the church? Are they benefitted when they fly where they want in their church-owned private jet?

How about lobbying? What does the Tax Code define as a "substantial part of the earnings" that can be used for lobbying or propaganda? It doesn't.

Today there are more than 200 lobbying organizations in Washington DC, of which more than 80% are tax-exempt organizations under IRS code 501(c)(3). According to a Pew analysis, they employ about a thousand people and spend more than $390 million a year. Almost 20% of these are Roman Catholic advocates and about the same number are evangelical Protestant groups. About 7% are mainline Protestant lobbyists with an equal number of Muslim groups, and 12% are Jewish. The number of lobbyists for religious causes has doubled in the last 30 years.

The Mormons have an 180-person Public Affairs Department based in its World Headquarters in Salt Lake City. This group handles public relations, which can include lobbying and propaganda. Of course, it isn't propaganda if it is true—and this is the true religion.

Certainly gay-rights have no place in any "true" religion. When California's Proposition 8, which would have disallowed gay marriage, was being argued, the Mormon Church reportedly gave more than $200,000 to pass it, and a reported $30 million was contributed by members of the church for its defeat.

In 2016, the New York Daily News reported that the Catholic Church had spent $2.1 million in lobbying to block legislation that would make it easier for victims of child abuse by priests to sue the church. About the same time, Catholic churches in Pennsylvania were advising their parishioners of the evil legislators who had voted for bills that would protect abused children.

These lobbying expenses seem to be illegal according to the Tax Code, but who wants to sue God? The question seems to be just how much these "true" religions can influence the legislators so they can protect their worldly fortunes in their pursuit of salvation for the masses. The Supreme Court has given us a reason for their tax exemptions. In Regan v. Taxation With Representation (1983) the Court found that exemptions for tax purposes are justified if they perform a social benefit. In the case of churches, this is normally meant that they give instruction in morality. But what kind of morality should be taught? For example:

➣ Are homosexuality and other gender identifications God's work—or are the traditional American gender roles based on one's sex at birth the only moral option?

➣ Is abortion good because it prevents unwanted children from s being born and it reduces overpopulation and climate change, or is it that only God who can determine which embryos or fetuses to miscarry or abort. As mentioned, God is actually the greatest cause of abortions, since He causes more spontaneous abortions (miscarriages) than all human doctors combined.

> Is it possible to enter Paradise if you don't belong to the true religion?

> If we are all made in the image of God, do we need physicians to cure ourselves or our children when we are diseased?

We might wonder about whether the previously mentioned Westboro Baptist Church fulfills the social benefit needs of society when it pickets the funerals of US soldiers because the US military allows homosexuals to serve. The Supreme Court says that they have the freedom of speech to do this (Snyder v. Phelps, 2011), but from the point of view of "providing a social benefit for society" we might question their religious exemption from taxation.

The same might be said about allowing tax exemptions to organizations and churches that actively protest against abortions by picketing the premises and harassing the potential patients as they enter a clinic. Roe v. Wade (1971) allowed for abortions in the United States. Are tax exempt religious groups providing a benefit to society when their actions are against clinics and patients who are availing themselves of rights that have been affirmed by the Supreme Court?

CAN, AND SHOULD, CHURCHES LOSE THEIR TAX EXEMPTIONS?

A tax exemption can be revoked by the government, such as the Internal Revenue Service. In Bob Jones University v. United States (1983) the Supreme Court upheld the revocation of its tax exempt status because the university's practices, such as racial discrimination, are contrary to a compelling government public policy.

CRU, formerly the Campus Crusade for Christ, is an evangelical Protestant group that brings in over a half billion dollars a year while supporting 25,000 missionaries and working to advance Christianity in 190 countries. Is this a social benefit for America? What about for American Jews or Catholics or Muslims or atheists?

Two years ago, the 2.3 million member Missouri Synod of the Lutheran Church ousted a minister, who was also a theology professor, from its church because he raised questions about the church's conservative stance on such things as the ordination of women and of the teaching of creationism. Certainly, he had First Amendment rights to raise these questions. He raised questions about the equality of women and the conflict between the scientifically provable theory of evolution and the Biblical account of creation. Is it in the public interest to advocate equal rights for women and the provable findings of science? If so, and the church has violated these socially valuable ideas, should the church lose its tax exemption?

If we are to use the "social benefit" theory for tax exemptions for churches, and they are expected to teach morality, should they all agree on what morality should be taught? If they teach different moralities—some must be wrong. Shouldn't they have to agree on: abortion, teaching creationism versus evolution, the equality of women for all posts in the church, whether or not child abuse is acceptable, homosexuality, the legitimacy of transsexual operations, etc.?

Might it be more effective and less expensive if the government eliminated all tax exemptions and tax deductions for religions, education, literary, athletic, and other groups and let the individuals interested in any of the tax exempt groups fund their own interest areas—without tax deductions for their contributions.

IF WE TAXED TAX EXEMPT ORGANIZATIONS

According to a Tampa University study, religious exemptions add up to at least $71 billion a year. The Washington Post estimated it as $82.5 billion a year.

The latest numbers I could find on the Mormon Church were from twenty years ago. The value of their tax exemptions then was at least $30 billion. Some have estimated its worth at a trillion dollars. Among the assets owned are: the Beneficial Finance Group, worth over $3 billion, the Hawaiian Reserve which includes the Polynesian Cultural Center (Hawaii's major tourist attraction), Brigham Young University Hawaii, Brigham Young University in Utah, and the Farmland Reserve Inc. which holds over 220,000 acres in Nebraska and 670,000 acres in Florida.

Some would like to say that churches are charitable organizations. The Mormon church gives 0.7% of its income to charity, but it does take care of its own members. The Economist estimated that in 2010 the Catholic Church gave 2.7% of its $171 billion to charity--about $4.6 billion. Some other churches give nothing. But the Salvation Army gives 82% of what it raises. The Red Cross gives 91%, the American Cancer Society returns 79% of its contributions. Meanwhile, Walmart gave $1.75 billion to charities; of course, it took a deduction for these.

Because of the long tradition of religion's importance in the world and the power of the principle religion in each country, religions have been able to exert a great deal of power to leave their financial holdings untouched by the taxman. As religious influence wanes because of rising secularism in the West, we see more movements to downplay the power of the pulpit and require them to pay taxes-- at least on their non-church holdings.

In Norway, nominally a country with a state religion, the government pays an annual payment to every belief system. So humanist organizations get the same per person payment as members of the Lutheran Church, Catholic Church, or Muslim mosques. The kicker is that since it is traditional to be baptized in the Lutheran Church, all baptized children are considered Lutheran unless they file papers to withdraw from the church. If they wish, they can associate with another church or with a humanist organization.

About 20% of Americans do not identify with a religion. As a minority are they being prejudiced against since they are having to pay more taxes because of the religious tax exemptions? But the same argument can be made by pacifists who must pay taxes to support the military.

The United States is much more lenient in allowing both church charitable deductions from one's income taxes and in allowing for church exemptions from taxes. This was tested in Walz v Tax Commission of the City of New York in 1969, a 7-1 majority decided that the tax exception to churches was not in violation of the First Amendment even though nonbelievers must pay additional taxes because of the tax exemption for the churches. Justice William O. Douglas wrote in his dissenting opinion that "If believers are entitled to public financial support, so are nonbelievers. A believer and nonbeliever under the present law are treated differently because of the articles of their faith... I conclude that this tax exemption is unconstitutional."

The Catholic Church is the third largest real estate holder in the world after the Queen of England and the King of Saudi Arabia. It is impossible to determine the wealth of the church because it is found in church property, business property, stocks and bonds, and other areas. While we can't yet tax the king and queen, the church might be within reach.

THE EUROPEAN APPROACH

Several countries in Europe require church taxes, among them are: Sweden, Finland, Iceland, Denmark, Germany, Italy, Austria, Spain and Portugal. The requirements for taxes vary considerably. Countries like Norway and Croatia support churches out of the general taxation proceeds. Croatia supports the Catholic Church, Norway supports all churches according to the number of members, of course the state church is Lutheran so it gets most of the money. Italy has a required church tax but allows the individual to direct that tax to one of several churches allowed by the government. In Germany and Finland a person is allowed to opt out of the church tax if he or she is not a member of the church. Spain allows for taxpayers to allocate a percentage of their taxes to the Catholic Church, but not to other churches. In Denmark, the church receives about 15% of its budget from the state taxes.

SHOULD TAX EXEMPT ORGANIZATIONS BE REQUIRED TO FOLLOW NATIONAL LAW?

Religions that take positions counter to the Supreme Court's decisions are: The Roman Catholic Church, the Church of Jesus Christ of Latter-day Saints (Mormons), Hindus, the Lutheran Church (Missouri Synod), Southern Baptist Convention, Assemblies of God, and the African Methodist Episcopal Church. Should they keep their tax exemptions? What about those who want some limits on abortion, like: the Episcopal Church, the Evangelical Lutheran Church of America, and the United Methodist Church. Muslims generally vary from allowing abortions up to four months to allowing abortion without restrictions. Since the state gives tax deductions and tax exemptions, should it require any groups supporting contrary views to the law of the nation to follow national law if they want tax exemptions?

TAXING CHURCH BUSINESSES

While the Tax Code requires church sponsored businesses to file and pay income taxes, often they are disguised as church-related expenses and incomes. Italy, which has a huge national debt, has recently begun to tax business property owned by churches. This was done after an Internet survey showed overwhelming support for such taxation, and even removing its tax-exempt status. Italy's Catholic Church owned 110,000 properties—including residential property and shopping complexes, worth about 12 billion dollars, all of which were untaxed.

In the US, if municipalities taxed churches it could net them from $650 million to $2.6 billion according to the New York Times.

The European Commission instituted an inquiry in 2010 into whether tax exemption for churches equaled illegal state aid and stifled competition. In 2017, the Court of Justice of the European Union ruled that tax exemptions for a church may constitute state aid for the church, and this is prohibited by the European Union. Prior to Spain entering the European Union it had an agreement with the Vatican to exempt many non-religious activities from taxation.

LET'S TAKE A LOOK AT TAXES

It is conceivable that America's taxes could be revised and not have income and Social Security taxes as the primary sources of revenue. So let's take a look at some options.

Taxes commonly come from: personal income tax, corporate profits, social security taxes (including pensions and healthcare), property taxes, goods and services taxes, excise taxes, and wealth and inheritance taxes. The percent and types of each tax vary considerably from country to country. For example, in New Zealand and Australia there are no Social Security taxes, they are included in the income tax.

The US gets 40% of its revenue from personal income taxes, and another 9% or 10% from corporate taxes. Under Trump's tax cuts these will be reduced. The average sales and service taxes is 34% for OECD countries, which includes the United States, but they are much higher in most of the world. In the US, Social Security taxes amount to about 24% of revenue. In the OECD, the average is 26%. Some Eastern European countries and Japan are in the 40% range.

Sales taxes, such as value added taxes (VAT) in the US are only about 25% to 35% of what is common in the rest of the world.

Property taxes are much higher in the US, about 10% of total revenue, compared to 6% in the OECD countries.

Revenue from different sources in the OECD countries includes taxes for the national government as well as for municipalities and states. The amount of taxes collected as a percent of the federal budget for other OECD countries and the US are:

Type of tax	OECD	US
Personal income tax	24%	39%
Social insurance Social Security	26 %	24%
Corporation taxes	9%	8%
Consumption taxes (VAT)	33%	17%
Property taxes	6%	11%
Other taxes	3%	1%

Recently in the US, the top 1% of earners earned 17% of all income and paid almost 37% of all income taxes. Their average tax rate was 24%. For the top 1/10 of 1% of earners, almost 140,000 people, their average income was $4.4 million and their average tax bill was over a million dollars. The total revenue earned was nearly $150 billion. This does not seem fair to me since about 45% of Americans don't pay any income tax. However, if we look at how the rich made their money, many of them made it because of the government, through contracts, favorable tax breaks, and so forth.

While the personal exemption has been doubled under Trump's tax plan, many popular deductions are reduced or eliminated like: state and local income tax, casualty losses, unreimbursed employer expenses, home equity loan interest, etc. But the child care credit is increased to $2000. In addition, home mortgage interest has been adjusted to cover only the first $750,000 of home value. If you are rich, your estate and gift taxes will be exempt to a large degree.

While the rich will still pay most of the taxes on incomes, they can pass on to their children just about all of their wealth. Some of the new tax provisions are smoke and mirrors. For example, take the child tax credit. It would be deducted from the taxes you owed. But 45% of Americans don't pay income taxes, so it does them no good. And what is the point of giving a credit for children, when the world has too many of them!

As with democratic republics throughout the world, the people who have been elected to pass the laws usually have more than the normal amount of money—and are not likely to pass laws that negatively affect their financial status. Self-centered values win out over comprehensive societal values. Secondly, the major corporations, whose financial oxen would be gored by equitable taxation. consistently bribe the legislators through financial gifts for other promises. Be that as it may, let us suggest some ideas for possible just taxation.

Many billionaires today have made their own fortunes through their own entrepreneurship. Jeff Bezos—with online shopping, Bill Gates—with Microsoft, Warren Buffett—with his business enterprises, Sergey Brin and Larry Page— with Google and Alphabet, Carlos Slim—with his extensive businesses in Mexico, and Oprah Winfrey—with her many ventures, have all made huge fortunes through their intelligence, work ethics, and senses of purpose. Why not keep their taxes relatively low while they live, then taxed heavily when they die?

SUGGESTED PRINCIPLES OF FAIR TAXATION

1. Everyone should earn the money that they have as their own "wealth," so eliminate inheritances. This is essential to realize the ideal of "equality of opportunity." Equality of opportunity requires that no one start life with significant advantages over other people. This would eliminate any inheritance tax breaks.

2. People shouldn't have children until they can afford them. We might tax pregnancy, then return full tax, plus interest, when the child starts school.

3.Taxes should be based, as much as possible, on how they are used. (For example: roads and bridges from auto and gasoline taxes, business taxes on trade and similar expenses, consumer taxes on schools, income taxes on general government expenses, etc.)

4. Corporations should be taxed at as low a level as possible to bring more corporations into the country to create jobs and to increase revenue broadly. International corporate tax rates, that are actually paid after all business deductions are taken, are generally within a 3% to 4% range of each other. Deductions are often so liberal that major companies do not pay any corporate taxes. There should be a very low flat corporation tax rate based on gross profit.

A flat rate on the business done in each country, rather than a tax in the home country of the corporation—which might be a tax haven or a low tax country, would be fairer.

5. There should be no deductions or exemptions to a flat tax—which should be much lower than today's rates.

6. Sales and value added taxes should be paid to the municipalities or states where the buyer shops. In 1992, the Supreme Court exempted Internet sales from many such taxes. The loss of tax revenue is estimated at $34 billion. The Court is revisiting this issue this year.

7. Pensions must be fully funded by workers' and employers' payroll taxes.

8. All income should be taxed at the same rate: no capital gains, all stock trade gains, gambling winnings, etc. with no deductions for losses or expenses. Whatever way we make money there are almost always negative factors. If you work ten miles from home, you drive your car or take the bus. You use your time to travel, but don't get paid for it. This negative, which is an essential for your economy can certainly be compared with other negatives people encounter when making money: like selling stocks at a loss or picking the wrong horse at the racetrack. And capital gains tax rates on stock trading or the selling of property, at half the rate of tax that a worker pays—is a special advantage to the wealthy. Possibly we should reverse it and have people who earned money from the sweat of their brow pay half the tax that a capitalist pays! Only kidding! But why shouldn't all income be taxed the same?

9. Any institution collecting money, including schools, colleges, churches and charities would pay 10% in taxes. Since numerous studies have shown that some charities are far more efficient than others in their use of donations, a non-partisan committee could

award the tax income from all charities to the most efficient and worthwhile charities or educational institutions. All charities will still have 90% of their pre-tax income to use as they will.

10. Tax greenhouse gas producers to aid in reducing global warming. Tax plastic and other products that increase global garbage or products, like paper, that reduce global forests. Taxing greenhouse gas use would apply to many users, such as: gasoline and coal use, cement (a major polluter), electricity produced by polluting fuels, beef and other animal foods and dairy products, since they emit methane and use water, etc. With the amount of plastic in the oceans equaling the weight of the fish—non-biodegradable plastic should be taxed high.

11. When infrastructure is needed, or repairs are needed, tax those who get the benefit of the facilities. So, gasoline and diesel taxes and automobile or truck excise taxes and registration fees would be the sole source of funds for road repair and building, bridges, etc. Electric vehicles, while good for the environment, still use roads and bridges so appropriate taxes on car registration, batteries or electricity need to be found. These should be less expensive than fossil fuel taxes.

If new airports are needed or personnel are needed to handle aviation, tax new airplanes, the yearly registration of the planes, etc. and tax the tickets. The same would be true of railroad and public transportation means.

12. Unhealthy substances or activities might be taxed higher, such as: sugary drinks (as in UK), tanning salons, tobacco, alcohol, other psychoactive drugs, some entertainment,

TAX AVOIDANCE—TAX EVASION

Tax avoidance or tax evasion. Tax evasion is illegally not paying taxes or failing to report income. Tax avoidance is taking legal means to not pay taxes, such as legitimate deductions or even using tax havens to hide income or to pay a lower rate to another country. Tax havens should be eliminated or forced out of business by international agreements.

RIGHTS AND RESPONSIBILITIES

Rights and responsibilities often conflict. The relatively recent right of rich people to hide their incomes and avoid or evade taxes conflicts with their responsibilities to be productive citizens in their countries. Some rights may have to be altered or eliminated in the interest of justice. It is true that the ideas of both liberty and equality have followed, or even preceded, our ideas of democracy. Because of this, more rights have been given to underlings as more power has been demanded to be shared. In the Magna Carta (1215), it was the barons who wanted some of the king's power. Little power flowed to the common citizens.

Looking at another right, the right to reduce one's taxes, should be eliminated although sanctified in a Supreme Court decision in Gregory v. Helvering (1935) which affirmed the Second Circuit's decision that was based on Judge Learned Hand's oft-quoted opinion that legally avoiding taxes may be acceptable, but evading taxes by sham business manipulations is not within the intent of the tax law.

An abbreviated version of Hand's opinion is that: "a transaction . . . does not lose its immunity, because it is actuated by a desire to avoid, or, if one choose, to evade, taxation. Anyone may so arrange his affairs that his taxes shall be as low as possible; he is not bound to choose that pattern which will best pay the Treasury; there is not even a patriotic duty to increase one's taxes . . . . Nevertheless, it does not follow that Congress meant to cover such a transaction, not even though the facts answer the dictionary definitions of which term used in the statutory definition . . . . the meaning of a sentence may be more than that of the separate words, . . . and no degree of particularity can ever obviate recourse to the setting in which all appear, and which all collectively create. The purpose of the section is plain enough; men engaged in enterprises . . . might wish to consolidate . . . their holdings. . . . But the underlying presupposition is plain that the readjustment shall be undertaken for reasons germane to the conduct of the venture in hand. . . . To dodge the shareholders' taxes is not one of the transactions contemplated as corporate 'reorganizations.'"

Tax havens should be eliminated or forced out of business by international agreements. Governments can do this, but the power of the rich to control governments, especially in democratic republics like the US, makes it very difficult. More recent affiliations of government, like the OECD (Organization for Economic Co-operation and Development), which was founded in 1961, are a step in the right direction. Its goals are to increase democracy and aid in the development of the economies of the members. It has developed provisions against unfair taxation shielding and tax havens. The problem is that countries are not required to follow the OECD recommendations. So, the rich who control the individual nations are free to reject or adhere to recommendations.

Laws could be passed that would require corporations and individuals to bank their profits in the country where the profit was earned. This, of course, would bring screams for freedom from all those attempting to avoid or evade taxes.

It might be possible to have international treaties to require this. Strong penalties for corporation chiefs who will avoid this, like life sentences in prisons, might go a long way in developing adherence to such laws.

The US has a law requiring American earnings in other countries to be reported to the US tax authorities. On the other hand, it doesn't allow the US to report to other countries on funds held by US institutions. This, according to authorities such as Bloomberg, makes the US a major tax haven for many people around the world—in fact it is THE major tax haven! The Tax Justice Network ranks it as the third most secretive tax haven after Switzerland and Hong Kong, and it is more secretive than the Cayman Islands and Luxembourg

In spite of hiding accounts for other countries, US firms are often better served by non-US havens. The Public Interest Research Group has reported that the pharmaceutical company Pfizer paid no income tax from 2010 to 2012 on $43 billion in earnings. Microsoft had five tax-haven units holding over $76 billion, and so saved over $24 billion in taxes. Citigroup had 21 tax-haven subsidies in 2013 so saved almost $12 billion in taxes.

Oh well, all's fair in tax avoidance and evasion!

LET US TAKE A QUICK LOOK AT PENSIONS IN THE DEVELOPED COUNTRIES.

Most people have a combination of their state retirement program, like Social Security, and a private plan through an insurance company or tax-deferred plans, like a 401(k).

In the United Kingdom, retirees receive about 29% of what they made when they were working as their pensions from the state (equivalent to Social Security in the US). This puts many of the over-75s into then poverty class. That 29% pension compares with an average of 63% of in-state pensions in other OECD countries, which range as high as 80% in Italy and the Netherlands. United Kingdom workers and other Europeans rely often on privately purchased retirement insurance. In the UK, the private pension assets are $2.2 trillion, which is equal to about 95% of their GDP. Some countries are even higher in the amount of pension fund insurance, such as: the US, Switzerland, the Netherlands, and Denmark. Once the UK's private pensions are added to the state pension, the average income in retirement for UK pensioners rises to just over 60% of their former career earnings, just below the OECD average. In the US, the average Social Security pension is 45% of what the retirees were earning. The average for the OECD countries is 63% of what they had been earning.

Had they contributed 9% of their income to a private pension fund annually, the US retirees would have total pensions of about 82% of what they had been earning. Many more Americans are working well past retirement age. This eliminates their reliance on Social Security, while it funds their trust account so that when they do retire it will be at a higher level. In some countries, this is not possible for state workers who must retire by age 70.

Retirees in the US are more often living in poverty than any other OECD country. It is about 22% in the US. Compare that with the Netherlands at 2%, France at 4%, Canada at 7%, Germany at 9%, and the OECD average of 13%. In other countries, the pension contributions are higher and are generally supplemented by higher taxes.

As you know, Social Security retirement now starts at age 67, but people are expected to live past 80. (When Social Security started, retirement was at 65 and the lifespan was 64. (The government made money on that!) Because the government continues to borrow from Social Security to finance tax-cuts, it owes a great deal of money to the potential retirees.

The revenue exceeded the payments until 2010. That year $74 billion more was paid out than was deposited. The interest that the federal government owed the Social Security Trust Fund made up the difference. This will be true until about 2020 when the Social Security payments will exceed its revenue and the interest that it is owed by the federal government. By about 2035 the present pension payouts are expected to decrease by about 25%.

A campaign promise made by Al Gore when running for president was that he would not allow the government to borrow from the Social Security Trust Fund. But he lost, and his opponent borrowed $1.7 trillion from the fund to finance tax cuts for the rich and the war in Iraq.

In the US, because of the aversion to higher taxes, retirement is commonly underfunded. But luckily, we have low taxes! The current combined Social Security contribution is 12.4%, equally shared by the worker and the employer. If we assume you earned an average salary of $60,000 for 45 years, and assume 3% interest on your contributions, then add the interest and it would total about $343,000. If you were to live at your average salary it would last about 7 years. But if you averaged $60,000 a year, your final salary was undoubtedly over $100,0000 per year, so the savings would last less than four years.

Let's continue with the above figures. Assume that you were born in 1950, worked 45 years, have a salary of $100,000 a year and will retire this year. Your monthly Social Security retirement check would be about $2,434, or $29,000 per year—just 29% of what you had been earning. You are now 68 and are expected to live 15 more years if you are a male and 17.5 if female. Your contributions will last about 12 or 13 years (since your unused contributions will still be earning interest). The government will have to pay you $30,000 to $100,000 more than you contributed.

If your final yearly salary was $50,000, your contributions plus interest would be about $175,000. Your monthly check would be about $1,515—or $18,180 per year—36%

of what you had been earning. Your contributions plus interest will last about nine and a half years, so the government will have to reach into its pocket and pay you $100,000 more than you contributed if you are male and $145,000 more if you are female.

As you can see, the way Social Security payments are determined gives lower income workers a higher percentage of their contributions than is true for the higher income workers. Do you think you might need retirement insurance—or should you work more years?

AN EXAMPLE OF HOW ADEQUATE PENSIONS MIGHT BE FUNDED

If you worked 45 years and you and your employer contributed a total of 30% of your gross earnings, and if you started with a salary of $20,000 forty-five years ago and finished with the salary of $100,000, we will assume that your average income was $60,000. We will assume that the interest earned from the government was 3%. (We will not assume compounding interest because that would be far more complicated than this simple illustration is meant to convey.) So, 3% of that average salary of $60,000 would be $1,800 multiplied by the 45 years that you worked. So, the total interest for the 45 years would be about $81,000. So, your total contributions would've been about $18,000 per year for 45 years which would equal about $810,000 plus the interest of about $81,000. Your total nest egg will close to $900,000. If you to live 13 more years, until you are 80, you would have almost $70,000 a year to live on in retirement.

If the typical 12.4% contribution worker mentioned above were to have the same retirement income as the 30% contributor, it would last about 4 years and eight months.

Neither of these calculations include spousal benefits, so if a person wanted to cover the spouse the contributions would have to be increased or other insurance would need to be purchased.

A LITTLE FUN WITH TAX IDEAS
UNREPORTED INCOME

There are a large number of transactions that are either trades of services or under the table non-tax reported payments and income. (A large number of people collect unemployment insurance, get food stamps, etc. while doing undeclared work. House cleaning, day care, and construction work are common examples.) It is commonly called "under the table pay" in the US, "moonlighting" in the UK, and "working black" in Scandinavia.

The estimate of such work in America is $210 billion in untaxed wages. A UCLA study found that about two million workers in California had unreported income, often full-time employment, such as in restaurants or construction.

THE FEDERAL BUDGET

In 2017, before the tax cut bill was passed, the US government was estimated to collect $3.37 trillion in tax revenues and spend a total of $3.76 trillion in its 2018 budget, resulting in a deficit of $392 billion. The deficit was expected to be 2.3% of the total estimated GDP of $17.4 trillion that year. However, since the tax cuts, varying estimates of the revenue shortfall have increased. The recent estimates give us an average yearly cost of $230 billion per year or $2.3 trillion over ten years. As citizens, we might keep in mind that for every trillion the national debt increases, every man, woman, and child in the US owes another $3,000. And, as of now, we each owe over $60,000. In ten years, if the annual budget is balanced—a highly unlikely possibility, we will each owe $67,000. Don't worry! Just put it on your credit card—then declare bankruptcy. Problem solved!

All joking aside, if you can smile through your tears, how could we fund this budget? It should be noted that this year, all of the federal departments took budget cuts except for Defense and Homeland Security. You might argue for your favorite items that are missing from Trump's proposed national budget, such as: Planned Parenthood contributions, education, the State Department, environmental protection, etc. But let us to just look at funding the budget proposed. We might rethink the levels of taxation that we already have. If the balanced budget amendment finally passes, we will have to.

The new budget will put many Americans to work building planes, battleships, and guns. And there will be more positions for soldiers and sailors—so more people will be working.

POSSIBLE TAXES

There are many possible taxes that the u.s. doesn't use or are undertaxed. Let's look at a few possibilities.

First let's bring down the income tax to a flat tax of 10% on gross income for all people and corporations. No deductions for anyone. For corporations, that now have a 20% rate and a lot of deductions, the average amount paid on their profits is now averaging slightly under 15%. So, the 10% rate should make the honest CEOs and stockholders happy. It might even bring in other corporations to the country because of the lower tax rate.

My idea is to have everyone become a taxpayer and be able to enjoy the money they earn while they are still alive.

The top income tax rate in the United States is now 39.6 percent. That ranked 33rd highest on a list of the top rates in 116 nations compiled this year by KPMG, an international tax advisory corporation. A survey by tradingeconomics.com ranks the US top income tax rate 38th highest among 155 nations and territories. The highest brackets were 60% in some African countries.

The bottom income tax rate in the US is 10 percent. Forty-one countries have higher bottom rates, according to data on 157 nations and territories compiled by Ernst & Young, an international accounting corporation.

a. The total amount brought in by a flat 10% personal income tax would be about $874 billion. Presently, personal income tax receipts are about $1.8 trillion—so somebody should be happy, but not that 45% that pay no taxes.

b. The total amount brought in by corporate taxes at the 10% rate would be $230 billion. It is about $419 billion now, so some should be happy.

So that's $1.1 trillion—only $2.6 trillion to go.

c. A value added tax (a sales tax on goods and services) of 20% on the $5.3 trillion now sold would add $1.05 trillion. European VATs range up to 25% and often include taxes on food.

Still need $1.6 trillion!

d. A $3 tax on the 143 billion gallons of gasoline would bring in $430 billion. (The tax now is 18 cents federal and averages 28 cents for states.) The $3 tax would put the US about equal to Europe. (This tax would be part for infrastructure and part for CO_2 production.)

e. A $3 tax on the 35 billion gallons of diesel fuel would yield $105 billion. (Federal tax now is 24 cents.)

While we are on cars, what about a $200 annual fee for the 250 million cars available? That would yield about $25 billion. In Norway, they have all kinds of taxes on new cars such as: the weight, the horsepower, and a carbon dioxide tax. Taxes on new cars in Norway more than double the cost of a car. I can see General Motors and all of his soldiers trying to shoot this idea down. So we won't play with this pregnant option just now.

In February of 2018, the OECD issued a call for far more taxes on harmful emissions: "Greater reliance on energy taxation is needed to strengthen efforts to tackle the principal source of both greenhouse gas emissions and air pollution." Their data shows that energy taxes "remain poorly aligned with the negative side effects of energy use. Taxes provide only limited incentives to reduce energy use, improve energy efficiency and drive a shift towards less harmful forms of energy. Emissions trading systems are having little impact on this broad picture."

In 2015, outside of road transport, 81% of emissions were untaxed, according to the report. Tax rates were below the low-end estimate of climate costs—30 euros ($40) per ton of carbon dioxide.

e. Taxes to reverse the impact of global warming from these activities:

Tax gasoline and diesel are already covered. 729 million tons of coal are mined. Coal is the largest CO_2 producer— more than transportation. Coal-use for energy production is reducing as natural gas is more frequently used. A $10 per ton coal would yield $7.3 billion per 30 million BTUs used. But natural gas is only half as polluting as coal so the $10 tax would be on every 30,000 cubic feet of natural gas.

Emissions from electricity generation account for the largest share of US greenhouse gases, 38.9% of the US production of carbon dioxide in 2006 (with transportation emissions close behind, at 31%). Although coal power only accounted for 49% of the US electricity production in 2006, it was responsible for 83% of CO_2 emissions caused by electricity generation that year.

Meanwhile, tax credits could be given for photovoltaic electricity-producing and water heating installations.

Other taxes:

- On cement plants.
- On methane producing beef, milk, dairy products, and sheep.
- Tax on paper to help develop forests.
- Taxes on non-biodegradable plastic and packing materials to develop projects to re-use these products and not deposit them in the ocean or other bodies of water or in garbage dumps.

Now we need to find another trillion dollars.

Current tax revenue from alcohol is $9.6 billion and on tobacco it is $14.5 billion. They could be increased. Then there is marijuana that could be taxed. Even pets could be taxed. The UK taxes sugary drinks—increasing tax income while reducing health care costs for obesity and diabetes.

We could put a high, and refundable, tax on plastic bottles.

I've got it! Let's have a 100% tax on inheritance! Wait! I hear the screams of those rich kids who want the millions or billions that they didn't earn. I don't hear anything from their parents—they are 6 feet under. They are on the other side of the grass, and could care less. They did complain a bunch when they first heard about the tax, but even though they had heard rumors, they still believed that they could take it with them.

Oh! And remember we still have to pay for retirement and Medicare. So now we have more than a $1 trillion surplus. Should we pay down a bit and the national debt?

Should we offer free tuition in all the community colleges and state universities? Should we improve the infrastructure of the country? Should we fund a national education system and eliminate the expensive and often ineffective state and local control of education? More on this idea in the next section of the book.

CHAPTER 13. CAN JUST ANYONE RUN A COUNTRY IN TODAY'S COMPLICATED WORLD?

THE REALITIES OF RULING
BEWARE THE TYRANT WHO HAS ALL THE ANSWERS!

For most of civilization we have been ruled by chiefs and kings who gained their power by being outstanding warriors. But then their children inherited the kingdom and had to rely on other means to continue the power. The church is a major player in this power-continuing game. From the earliest days, shamans and medicine men claimed the power of the Spirits as their source of power. We gullible people, without enough knowledge to criticize, believed what they said. As the years rolled on the shamans became bishops, popes, and caliphs. Their connection with the Almighty, or almighties, allowed them to bless the temporal rulers who often fought their battles for them.

While Greece had experimented with a democracy of male citizens and Rome had used a non-elected senate to advise its rulers, it was not until the Age of Enlightenment that enticed men of education to rule themselves or at least choose their rulers. The American and French revolutions started the ball rolling toward a true democracy. Some people voted in were real statesmen and concerned with their societies. Others reflected the urge for power that has traditionally enticed people to rule. With parliaments and courts wielding a great deal of power it has become more difficult for a tyrant to rule a modern developed nation.

We can look to Hitler to see how a tyrant can best take over a country. One of the first things that needs to be done is to convince the country that the election, no matter how small the majority, gave the aspiring tyrant a mandate to rule as he sees fit. Naturally you cannot have a free press because intelligent reporters will warn the populace. There can be only one truth—the propaganda machine will tell you what it is! Since the basis for such a self-centered ethic is the rule of the tyrant and his cohorts, rather than the good of society (society-based ethics) or the word of God (God-based ethics)—lies and other propaganda in every form are moral, that is, have value for the tyrant. His Nietzschean morality is the method of the "overman," that has been used to control us, the herd, since societies emerged from the caves of the Neanderthals.

If there are problems, they were not caused by the tyrant. Identifiable minorities, whether religious, racial, ethnic, gender-based, or political are to blame. Tyrants generally aim to amass great fortunes stolen from the general population. African rulers are quite famous for their huge deposits in Swiss bank accounts. Vladimir Putin is considered by some to be the richest man in the world, although he denies this. Along with a tyrant's personal selfishness, his family may be brought into the inner circle as long as they do not try to usurp the power, like the assassinated half-brother of Kim, the tyrant of North Korea.

Tyranny seems to be the simplest and most natural state of our species. Tell us that we will be among the chosen few--if we will follow. Tell us that paradise is ours—if we will follow. Tell us that we will have more food and luxuries—if we will follow. Tell us that our tribe will lead the world—if we will follow. Tell us that we will be nobles and generals—if we will follow. Tell us that we will be murdered—if we do not follow. Why did it take so long for a Machiavelli to tell us the truth?

DO WE UNDERSTAND OUR VALUES–AND DO WE LIVE THEM OR MOUTH THEM

Then we learned to read—and sometimes to think. Locke, Mill, Rousseau, Jefferson and many others enticed us to value ourselves. They challenged us to even rule ourselves. But I was happy with my flask of wine, watching the gladiators provided by Sulla and Caesar. I am now happy with my can of beer, watching gladiators perform on my computer.

Should I be expected to be concerned with my present or my future? Should I be concerned that rich congressmen may cut my pension? Should I be concerned that a senator increases his health benefits while decreasing mine? Should I be concerned that some of my representatives break the laws, while I will be imprisoned if I follow their lead?

ETHICS CONCERNS WITH ELECTED REPRESENTATIVES

Just hours before the 115th Congress opened, the House Republicans voted to weaken the independent ethics office that investigates House lawmakers and staff accused of misconduct. Passing by a vote of 119 to 74, House Republicans defied their leadership to adopt an amendment by Representative Bob Goodlatte, a West Virginia Republican, to place the independent Office of Congressional Ethics, under the jurisdiction of the House Ethics Committee. This action would effectively give the ethics oversight to the lawmakers themselves and prevent information about investigations from being released to the public. This obviously put the self-centered values of unethical Congressmen ahead of the good of society. Social outrage stopped it from becoming a law, when voting in favor of the bill was reversed the next day.

Would it be ethical to:

o   Require elected officials to be honest,

o   Eliminate gerrymandering,

o   Make the Supreme Court impartial,

o   Doom the Electoral College,

o   Effectively educate the voters so that they can tell real news from fake news and have some idea of science and logic,

o   Have government-paid campaign expenses—with no outside contributions?

Special interest funding, whether from individuals or corporations, would not be allowed. This has been shown to increase the number of candidates but is generally opposed by the major parties and major contributors to the parties. Consequently, where free elections have been legalized, they have sometimes been reversed by statute or referenda.

Who cares anyway! 28% of British voters didn't think that the Brexit referendum was worth their time. 44% of Americans didn't care who governed them in the 2016 election—in fact, for the last 50 years 45% to 50% of voters haven't cared who governs them. But that's democracy.

Perhaps a king appointed by God, like George III, would be better. Of course, he might tax your tea—but who cares!

IS IT TRUE THAT ALL'S FAIR IN LOVE AND WAR?

"All is fair in love and war" is an often heard rationalization for being unethical. If it is true that Immanuel Kant's dictum that "always treat people as ends in themselves, not as means only," is considered to be the major pillar of ethical behavior, then honesty, rather than desired outcomes, should be the standard of behavior that we should expect.

Unfortunately, most of us are self-centered so we do what we think will give us what we want. In love, we often use sex or gifts to melt the heart of the one that we want—the object of our infatuation. The daily sex of our dating time may soon, or even immediately, be lost in the fog of excuses after marriage.

But this "All's fair" idea we find oozing through all societies. However, as we become more advanced, or at least we think we are more advanced, our citizens should be better educated, our businesses and politics should be less corrupt, and the nation or the world should become more responsive to the legitimate concerns of their citizens.

In the opera Cosi Fan Tutte, often translated "women are like that," Despina tells the two other girls, whose fiancés supposedly had been called back to war, that if they die it is better for the girls because there are far more fish in the sea. In fact, they should not be faithful because men are never faithful. So:

So rather than
Wasting your time in idle tears, think about enjoying yourselves. Making love
furiously, as your
Dear gentlemen will be doing on active service! You look for fidelity
In men, in soldiers? *laughing*
Don't tell me that, for pity's sake!
All of them
Are made of the same stuff; The quivering leaves,
The inconstant breezes Have more stability Than men.
Crocodile tears, Lying looks, Deceiving words, False endearments Are the basis
Of their tricks.
In us they only prize Their own pleasure;
Then they despise us, Deny us affection, And from such tyrants
There's no mercy to be had.
We women should pay out This hurtful,
Impudent breed In their own coin; Let's love them
To suit our convenience and our vanity!

So relationships may be flimsy, and we should each enjoy ourselves to the maximum. While there is no question that the relationships should be friendly, fast, and faithful—our divorce rate and the number of unhappy non-divorced couples indicate that love may not be fair and forever! Does this make the "All's fair in love," a necessary strategy or is it really a major cause of eventual misery? Does our dishonesty, once found out, destroy the relationship that was built on the immorality of the "All's fair" principle?

War, of course, although called "the ultimate extension of politics" is totally unethical in that thousands of young people, who may or may not want to fight, become the means for the ends of some middle-aged or elderly leader who wants more territory than he currently possesses. This would be an unjust war. But those who chose resist may have the goal to preserve what is now theirs and be willing to fight and die for their cause.

American politicians want to accuse China of such things as human rights violations, probably to throw suspicion off themselves as they take millions of dollars from lobbyists and special interest groups to fund their elections. Meanwhile China has arrested over 100,000 for corruption—from low-level politicians to high-level public figures and businessmen. Xi Jinping, the General Secretary of the Communist Party has spearheaded this drive. Possibly not all ethical behavior is enclosed by one's national boundaries.

Since many politicians throughout recorded history have apparently cast ethics aside in their pursuit of lust, land, and dominance we know that this is nothing new, but should it be changed? As we move toward a globalized society in which several of the players have the nuclear potential to destroy the planet, should international societal values be clarified and agreed to? We have lists of individual freedoms, should we also clarify the responsibilities of governments and their leaders? The corruption of leaders is the perennial problem. But too few governments are courageous enough to tackle it. Are we ethical when we allow this?

Corruption is not only about becoming richer. When the Biblical King David placed Bathsheba's husband in the front row of his attacking army, knowing he would be killed so that David could marry Bathsheba, was this ethical? When the citizens in the Agora found Socrates traitorous, because he taught people to think for themselves, was this ethical? When Hitler blamed the Jews, homosexuals and Catholics for the depression in Germany, was it ethical? When Trump, Bush and the Brexiteers knowingly lied in order to accomplish their goals—was it ethical?

If we are to have some control over our government, must we insist on honesty in their public debates and private speeches or shall we continue to be dumb lambs content to be slaughtered both physically and economically? Perhaps a non-partisan, government funded but independent group, such as PolitiFact, could be established to check the statements of the politicians for accuracy—and perhaps even bring them up to date on scientific findings, such as global warming. But in our world of fake news and alternative facts—who would believe them? I guess we are going to have to start with real education, but it seems that many influential politicians are more in favor of minds receptive to their opinions than to verified facts and highly probable predictions and policies.

JUSTICE—IS IT LIBERTY OR EQUALITY, YOU CAN'T HAVE ALL OF BOTH

When a millionaire has the freedom to make as much money as possible and is able to keep his taxes low while the person living in poverty wants some bread, a TV, or a smartphone because he wants to have "some equality"—we have a conflict in the ideas of justice. Most Westerners who currently write treatises on justice assume that the equality of all humans is the pervading value. Karl Marx wrote that the economics of a society should be "from each according to his ability to each according to his needs." This would result in an "ending equality," where all human needs are equally valuable.

But what if we had equality of economic opportunity and someone comes out at the bottom of the economic pile, should they be given a guaranteed annual wage? If there is a serial killer, should he have the right to life?

But what about the person who wants the liberty to produce more and see the results of his creativity and industry in his bank account? Our natural selfishness is not yet honed to accept lower rewards for higher level work.

Vladimir Lenin, who led the Communist Revolution in Russia acknowledged that the USSR was socialistic, not communistic. His ideal for the socialist government was "from each according to his ability to each according to his work." This may sound better than Marx's idea, but Lenin's central planning yielded a highly inefficient economy. So, Lenin recognized the unequal contributions of individuals to a society and believed in a comparable unequal reward for unequal production.

The American philosopher, John Dewey, acknowledged that people are not equal, but believed that for the good of society there must be some economic equality in order to keep the people content and the society functioning effectively.

OVERPOPULATION IS THE MAJOR PROBLEM

Thomas Piketty author of the mega-selling 2013 "Capital in the Twenty-First Century" wrote that, "Rising inequality is largely to blame for this (Trump's) electoral upset. Continuing with business as usual is not an option."

Thomas Piketty sees the world as being challenged by two major problems, global warming and wealth inequality. Both of these are results of the bigger problem of overpopulation. (See: Book 1 "Reversing Overpopulation— The Planet's Doomsday Threat" at andgulliverreturns.info)

Tradition and selfishness will never allow the suggestions of the "Reducing Population" book to become law. Requiring parents to be qualified to have children goes against tradition. Limiting families to one child is not possible in a democracy. China's "one child policy" worked because of an authoritarian government. But even with its "one child policy" it dropped its birthrate only to that of Norway's, about 1.6 children per woman. But China's program reduced the number of births by 400,000,000; so it was then possible to use the money that would have been spent on their educations to be funneled into higher education for many, for reducing poverty, and for better economic options for the country.

So what happened next? China's economy ranked 12th in the world in the 1970s in terms of its GDP growth, behind such powers as Mexico and Spain. By the early 1990s it had moved to fourth. Now for several years it has been first in growth, with the US third behind the EU. From 1980 to 2017, the per capita GDP of China has increased 60-fold while the US has increased five-fold.

There is no question that the "one child" policy was a major contributor. Was this ethical? Yes, from a society-based morality. Was it possibly unethical? Sometimes yes, based on whether a religion is against contraception or abortion. And yes, from the self-centered views of those Chinese who wanted more children. It took away some liberties of people who wanted children, but it added liberty for those who wanted higher education or for those who wanted to succeed in a business. It also added more economic equality for all, including universal health care. Equality of educational opportunity exists—but city dwellers are more likely to be blessed than people on the farms. But to paraphrase George Orwell, "Some people are more equal than others." But, of course, that is a societal universal!

Now with the increased allowance of two children, because the number of old people needed to be supported by new bodies working, it is possible that growth might slow. With women retiring at 50 and men at 55 and with 40% of the population expected to be over 60 by 2050, realities must be confronted. Can the economy continue to expand and pay for all the social welfare needs? Should people contribute more for their retirements? (Chinese workers now contribute 8% and the employers 20%.) Should the retirement age be raised to the now untenable 65, an age that made sense in 1936 when it was inscribed as the indelible mandate—which has been long-since shown to be many years too early. (But nobody wants to work longer than necessary.) Should China, and other countries, import temporary workers to shoulder some of the brunt? How will economic equality be fostered? Or will it?

China's first decision on reducing children was directed at long-term realities. The second decision, allowing more than one child, was based on short-term pragmatic thinking.

It is impossible for most to see the causative factors of problems in our globalized world. We look at carbon dioxide as being the main problem of global warming, but who is it that puts the carbon dioxide into the air? It is the people driving their cars, the trucks driving goods to the increased number of people, the cement manufacturing companies that must produce more for the increased number of city dwellers, the coal-fired plants that must produce energy for the increased number of inhabitants.

By 2050, the number of Africans will have doubled to more than 2 billion and could double again in another 50 years. In 2020 or 2030 Nigeria is expected to pass the U.S. population level, making them the third largest country in the world. We already see the effects of overpopulation there. Huge numbers of economic migrants attempting to flow into Europe create massive problems on both sides of the Mediterranean. Some of the migrants, from sub-Saharan Africa have been caught in Libya and sold as slaves. There are not enough jobs in Africa now—imagine what doubling or tripling the population will do.

The lack of opportunities in Africa results in meaningless lives for many, so they join jihadist organizations such as Boko Haram in north-east Nigeria or al-Shabab in Somalia. There are over thirty such groups, many are offshoots of Al-Qaeda, ISIS, or the Muslim Brotherhood. The need for power over their lives is increasingly evident among the male unemployed youth of the continent.

THE REALITY OF POPULISM—THE "HAVE NOTS" WANT SOME

Then there is the modern reality that we need fewer people to provide our economic desires because of robotics, computerization, and more effective manufacturing. Many call for more equitable and fair distribution of jobs and wealth. But the "haves" who run the world will not permit it.

People and their governments must go beyond the obvious to explain the realities. It is not enough to say "democracy," you must understand exactly what it means. It is not enough to say "equality" without knowing exactly what we mean by the term. It is not enough to say "more equitable distribution of wealth," without knowing all of the pluses and minuses that might occur should it happen.

Trump's Electoral College victory is primarily due to the explosion in economic and geographic inequality in the United States over several decades and the inability of successive governments to deal with it. This inequality is not unique to the United States.

THE GINI COEFFICIENT

The most common way to measure inequalities is with what is called the Gini coefficient. This can be used to measure income, wealth, availability of education, or a number of other factors in which economists might be interested.

We will look here at just income and wealth inequality. Income is measured both as gross income and as income that is reduced by taxes or increased by welfare and other income equalizers.

The Gini Coefficient is a measure of inequality. A measure of 1.00 would be complete inequality. For simplicity, it is often multiplied by 100, so a score of 0.1614 is often reported as 16.14. A measure of 0.00 would be complete equality.

In terms of gross income, a Gini coefficient of 1.00 would indicate that one person got all the income in the society. A score of 0.00 indicates that everyone in the society received the same income. The score is figured this way: % of income minus the % of the population that receives it.

According to the World Bank Gini indices of 158 countries, Ukraine is the most equal at 25.50 at number 158th. Of course, they are in a war right now. That may have something to do with it. Iceland is next at 25.60 and is ranked 157. Norway and Finland are at 26.80 and are ranked at 150th. These are the two happiest countries in the world in

2018. Sweden is 27.20. Denmark is the 144th ranked country with the Gini index of 28.50. The least equal country is South Africa with a score of 63.40. A number of other African countries are on the list as being the least equal in terms of income inequality. Several South American countries are also high on the list with Brazil at 51.30. The United States is number 59 with a score of 41.0. The United Kingdom is 105th with a score of 34.10.

But income does not measure total wealth. You will see that the wealth held in the country is far more unequal than the income. In the US and Denmark, a great deal of wealth is concentrated among relatively few people. The billionaires or multimillionaires may make "only" a few million dollars a year in income but may hold billions in real estate, commercial properties, stocks, bonds and in tax-free havens like the Cayman Islands. In addition, the wealth is relative—not absolute. So owning 50% of the wealth in Zimbabwe is not the same as owning 50% of the wealth in Switzerland.

Looking at it from a global perspective, half of the world's wealth is held by one percent of the people. The top 10% of people own 85% of the wealth. And the top 30% own 97% of the world's wealth. Incomes are also developing in a more unequal direction. Looking at the last 200 years, we see increasing inequality in income and total wealth.

Here is the Gini wealth index for some countries: USA 80.56, Sweden 79.90, UK 75.72, Indonesia 73.61, Austria 73.59, Germany 73.34, Columbia 73.18, Chile 73.17, Brazil 72.56, Mexico 70.00. As you can see from the wealth index of Sweden, welfare-state billionaires are not entirely altruistic!

The distribution of wealth (cash, property, stocks, etc.) is clearly the greatest in America. It is surprising to see socialistic Sweden second on the list. Socialistic countries generally have a wealth tax as part of their income tax. In Sweden a center-right party came into power in 2007 and abolished the wealth tax. A similar party in Norway reduced the wealth tax in 2016.

Since people believe themselves to be at least equal to everyone else in their own self-worth, and as Thomas Hobbes observed, people believe they are equal "in their own amount of common sense" and even superior in terms of their desires, it is not surprising that people are a bit grumpy. The *status quo* is not acceptable. I want more. Whoever will promise me a bigger share of the pie will get my vote.

So, what is just?

➢A God appointed king who makes all the rules,

➢A communistic approach where needs are primary and everyone's needs are equal,

➢A society based on economic liberty, where wealth can be passed to succeeding generations,

➢A society based on equality of opportunity, where each generation starts as close to equal as possible, with physical, emotional, and educational needs primary,

➢An economic system based on laissez-faire free enterprise,

➢A welfare state where the basic needs of individuals are provided for by high taxes.

➢Some combination of the above?

CHAPTER 14. WHERE DO YOU AND YOUR REPRESENTATIVES SIT ON THE OLD AND NEW POLITICAL SPECTRA?

What we think is "just" has a great deal to do with where we sit on the political spectrum.

Our old friend Aristotle thought that the rule of the mob, which he called democracy, was bad. But another form of rule, by intelligent and virtuous people, he thought was good. He called this polity. We might call it an ethical and enlightened republic. Plato's version of the best government was to have philosopher-kings, who were the wisest to rule. We might see it as the type of republic that we seek.

Some wonder if it is the mob or the intelligent and virtuous that elected Donald Trump, Robert Mugabe in Zimbabwe, George W. Bush, Jacob Zuma in South Africa, and voted for Brexit.

As we have moved through the book, semantics has been emphasized. We cannot think if we do not know exactly the meaning of the concepts with which we are dealing. If a Dane and an American are talking about how they agree on democracy, the Dane is probably thinking about the economic benefits of the welfare state and that they see the government's primary duty is to work for the happiness of the governed. The American is probably talking about the advantages of what he thinks of as capitalism and that it is the government's duty to keep taxes low.

WHICH PATH?-- TO YOUR IDEA OF JUSTICE—OR TO HAPPINESS?

Objectively we can see that surveys indicate that Denmark is usually the happiest country in the world, never lower than third, while the US is about 12th to 18th every year. But the US is far lower in the amount of taxes paid--being at about 25%, the third lowest of the OECD countries, while Denmark tops them all at over 49%. Denmark ranks 13th in the world in terms of the quality of the infrastructure, while the US is ranked 25th.

What do you want? Justice or happiness? Are they mutually exclusive? Is it fair that non-contributors reap the same benefits as the contributors to a society? Does having the 46 human chromosomes give you special rights? But what if the genes on those chromosomes are very, very different? Should that alter one's rights?

So, what has all this to do with democracy?

THE POLITICAL SPECTRUM

The political spectrum was originally designed to label and differentiate between the different views we have of justice and what will make us happy. They are:

➤Those who wanted to go back to the past, or what was thought of as the past—the reactionaries;

➤Those who wanted to go slowly and conserve the values they had grown up with--the conservatives;

➤Those who wanted to move slowly in what they thought was the right direction--the moderates;

➤Those who wanted to move more rapidly toward what they thought was the right direction, toward a social welfare state--the liberals;

➤And those who wanted to move very quickly toward a welfare state, even using violence if necessary--the radicals.

We like to think that people have thought their way into their political views. In some cases this may be true. But often, they have reacted into their positions based on their inferiority complexes and need for power or even because they have been loved effectively as children into a liberal position. We would hope that wherever one is on the five positions on the spectrum, it is based on: understood basic assumptions, sound semantic understandings, strong probable evidence, and sound logical reasoning. But such a hope is seldom a reality.

When people have arrived at a position because of their psychological makeup, their inferiority complexes and need for power or their ability to love unconditionally, they may rationalize their beliefs on the spectrum rather than having reached their positions thoughtfully through understanding their primary ideas and looking at the probability that their ideas may work.

My idea is to take the existing five elements of the political spectrum and limit them to rational opinions and sound logic. Each of the positions can be postulated by verifiable facts and potential projections. However, people often become so enamored by their beliefs that they may resort to psychological or physically violent means to obtain their desired ends. I therefore propose two additional categories on each end of the spectrum. The first addition to the spectrum would be propaganda, such as: fake news, fake history and false promises. The farthest level on each end would be physical violence.

So the original five category spectrum might look something like this:

Radicals<Liberals<Moderates>Conservatives>Reactionaries

Let's look at the traditional spectrum.

Starting from the far right, the reactionaries may want to go back to monarchy, to slavery, to irrational prejudices, to pure capitalism (in a Marxian sense), to what they believe to be a return to fundamental religion, to fascism, etc.

People typically call all those to the right of center "conservatives" and all those to the left of center "liberals." This is oversimplifying the possibilities and range of beliefs. It would be like merely calling all Olympic champions or NFL quarterbacks athletes. Yes, they are athletes but there are a few major differences between a champion walker, a champion sprinter, and a champion quarterback. Simplifying their prowess as merely "athletes" is equivalent to calling a king and a slave equally "images of God." We need to be more precise in our thinking.

I suggest that we use the traditional five categories and assume that they are logical and based on facts. For example, on the far right reactionary end, it is factual that people are not equal. No two people are exactly equal. They differ in age, height, weight, intelligence, knowledge, traditions, beliefs, work ethics, and family backgrounds. Should unequal people be given equal rights? Might this reactionary belief be then used to advocate serfdom or slavery? Might it be used to advocate monarchy? If we take an earlier idea of God, a vengeful God, an all-knowing and all-powerful God who is intimately involved in human affairs (and who gives to popes and kings the divine right to rule)—we have reactionary thinking.

THE TRADITIONAL POLITICAL SPECTRUM

So on the extreme right we have the reactionaries who want to go back to a previous time, based on their religions or other traditions or because they profit by being the "haves." (People on the top of the economic, social, political and religious hierarchies have a lot to lose when the common people want equal rights or a larger share of the profits or decision making.) When we move from left to right, one of the major trends we see is a movement from equality to liberty (freedom)—and perhaps, inequality. Those who have the power and the money are already unequal monetarily to those who don't.

Typically, they want to share neither their power nor their cash. They want the freedom to keep what they have.

Among the reactionary positions are: monarchy, fascism, neoliberalism, and alt-right ideologies like Neo-Nazism, and the KKK.

This reactionary approach may be based on the fact that people are not equal. No two people in the world are equal to each other. To add a few more areas of inequality to the above list, we vary in: education, race, intelligence, religions, ethnicity, social status, industriousness, athletic ability, physical health, mental health, and a number of other factors. These differences may influence some people to want to return to an earlier time when some people were serfs or slaves or when women were chattels or otherwise inferior. They may want us to return to monarchy or to a time when national interests were settled by war.

Trump's plan to change Obamacare health insurance is to give tax credits for health insurance buying. The Tax Policy Center estimates that 45% of Americans pay no income tax. Would they be able to afford insurance— especially if there were serious pre-conditions that might not be insurable? But they are not equal, so who cares?

Data from the British Election Study on the Brexit referendum shows that support for the reactionary position on the death penalty was a more reliable predictor of voting behavior than any standard demographic measure of age, income or social class. 56% of those over 60 voted to leave. We generally expect older people to be more reactionary and want the "good old days." Being reactionary is not necessarily wrong. Even though liberals will use it as a derogatory term, oftentimes the past was really better. There are numerous reasons why the death penalty may be good or bad. (See: andgulliverreturns.info in Book 4 "On Human Values, in the chapter on the death penalty.). The death penalty can be good or bad from a self-centered point of view, a God based point of view, or a society based point of view. It depends on your basic assumptions and on the evidence that you attach to those assumptions.

There are a number of factors that may influence a person to be somewhere on the spectrum. Family or social traditions, especially conservative religions, may put one on the right. Very often, experience with other people of different social classes or different nations may put one more on the left. Quite often a strong belief in equal rights will put one more on the left. Being on the right is often more comfortable because of the traditions it protects. Liberty (freedom) is often found on the right especially when one inherits money, prestige or social standing.

Equality of opportunity is often advocated by people on both sides of the middle. However, the tools necessary for real opportunity are usually lacking. While the children of the richer parents may attend private schools, children in the ghettos and barrios may be in larger classes in schools, have less competent teachers, and fewer opportunities for supplementary education like foreign travel or computer summer camps. Additionally, teachers in the lower social class schools are much more likely to spend a great deal of time in disciplinary action because a major way for teenage children to achieve power in the lower social class setting is to disrupt the class.

Reactionaries might approve of any number of methods of execution: hanging, crucifixion, firing squads, electric chair, injection of poison—are all possible. But where the old traditions of violent executions used to exist, like hanging or the electric chair, in the US the liberal influence has made the death penalty less painful.

People on the right see people as unequal, usually with:

➤Unequal rights to life, if they are criminals (President Trump has proposed the death penalty for drug traffickers. Malaysia, China, Vietnam, Iran, Thailand, Thailand, Saudi Arabia, Singapore, and the Philippines already have such laws.);

➤Unequal right to health insurance if they can't pay for it;

➤Unequal need for eldercare if they have not paid into an insurance account;

➤Unequal right for a job if they have not prepared themselves educationally;

➤Unequal right to a top university if they cannot pay for it;

➤Unequal right to the top legal representation if they are poor and can only rely on public defenders; etc.

The feeling of equality on the left often includes the idea of Immanuel Kant and some religions that teach that every human life is precious no matter what the person has done. Consequently, a mass murderer like Anders Breivik in Norway has the same rights in Norway as any other person—well almost! Many of those people killed were or would become contributing members to the Norwegian society. This was certainly an economic negative for Norway because of the killing of its politically interested young people. Then the state had to tear down the government building Breivik had partially destroyed with a bomb. Then the state had to go to great expense to prosecute and defend him in the courts. Then they needed to hire extra guards to make sure he wouldn't kill himself in his three-room prison cell. Then a few years later he again went to court against the state, with the state paying the expenses, while he contended that he was treated inhumanely because he could not talk to other prisoners. At the lower court level, he won because everyone has equally valuable human rights, according to the European Union's granting of rights.

"The prohibition of inhuman and degrading treatment represents a fundamental value in a democratic society. This applies no matter what — also in the treatment of terrorists and killers," wrote judge Helen Andenaes Sekulic in her ruling. The ruling also said that the Norwegian state had not violated Breivik's right to a private and family life.

While just being "human" gave Breivik many rights, in spite of his lack of any showing of responsibility, the UN Declaration of Human Rights requires some responsibilities toward others in the society. After 28 articles granting rights, Article 29 states:

1. Everyone has duties to the community in which alone the free and full development of his personality is possible.

2. In the exercise of his rights and freedoms, everyone shall be subject only to such limitations as are determined by law solely for the purpose of securing due recognition and respect for the rights and freedoms of others and of meeting the just requirements of morality, public order and the general welfare in a democratic society.

3. These rights and freedoms may in no case be exercised contrary to the purposes and principles of the United Nations.

THE MODERN EMPHASIS ON EQUALITY

Equality, usually enunciated as equal rights, has emerged as superior to liberty in many instances in Europe. What they do not seem to acknowledge is that equality of opportunity is often denied to worthy people because so much money is being spent to enforce equal rights for antisocial people. If we take the millions of dollars that are being spent on Breivik, we wonder if it could be better spent in Norwegian schools and colleges. And if they don't need the money might it be better spent in education for deserving people in Africa, India, Afghanistan, or even Scotland?

It is obvious that many people will flip back and forth between liberal, moderate, and conservative on different issues. For example, they may be for capital punishment, which puts them on the right, and for free college education, which would put them on the left. Quite commonly in the UK and Norway the conservative or reactionary idea of monarchy is cherished while a liberal welfare state is equally loved.

A person may be against the wearing any religious symbolism such as: a hijab or burqa, a cross, or a yarmulke—which would put them on the far left but also deny climate change which would put them on the far right, in the "reactionary" category. They may be for free public education, which would be a liberal position, but also for school vouchers, which would be a conservative position. They may be willing to take up arms to fight communism any place in the world, a far-right position, and also willing to go to war against oppressive dictators in the Middle East, a far-left position.

The reactionaries, as mentioned, want to go back to a real or imagined past. They may also deny science, since it rattles our modern minds with possibilities we could never imagine. It's just not emotionally comfortable.

The conservatives tend to want to keep the values of their religious upbringing and other traditions. This gave the churches more power. China and Russia eliminated the churches, now they have returned. In France and the U.S., they had to be content with marginalizing the churches. But with liberty came a number of freedoms, including freedom of religion, that gave the churches a foothold.

As we have cautioned throughout the book we must understand the meaning of a term. For example, we often hear the term "neoliberalism" and may mistakenly believe that it is a position on the left, a new kind of equalitarian thinking. Actually, it is generally used in a reactionary sense meaning: privatization, deregulation, fiscal austerity and the 19th century capitalist ideas that pre-dated the welfare state and other liberal ideas.

Other social changes, such as gender identification and vocational possibilities in the digital age, are difficult or impossible to live with. How can people have sex with people of the same gender? Marriage can only be between a man and a woman, like mine is. When I go to the market, I want a human checker—not a robot scanning my groceries.

The moderates recognize that the world and society are changing and we must keep up with the changes. For example, climate change is a reality. There are genetic, epigenetic, and environmental influences that can influence our gender identities. The moderates recognize the need to preserve the world, but that it is changing. Information technology and robotics are factors that significantly change the way that employment in developed countries will evolve. Services, rather than manufacturing, are essential in developed countries.

Liberals are more likely to want to move faster than the moderates in anticipating changes. They usually are interested in developing more equality in the society. They tend to be against kings. The Magna Carta was such an equalitarian exercise. It was really between nobles and the king—but at least it took some of the power from the top and spread it around to others near the top—like the freemen. But 90% of the population, the serfs, were not included. However, during the last 800 years, more equal rights have seeped to the bottom of English society, still much of the land is owned by royalty. But why not? God gave the land to the kings and nobles in Medieval days—and God does not go back on His word. But wait a minute! What makes us believe in a God? Why should people inherit anything, titles or wealth, when they didn't earn it? We should all start as close to the same starting line as possible. And if some of us lag behind the average we need to give them a helping hand. The homeless, the drug dependent, the prisoners, and the otherwise needy must have our help.

The radicals want change faster. They might use violence to achieve their ends. The leaders of the revolutions in America, France, Russia, and China are prime examples of radicals who wanted to replace the traditional leaders of the society with a more democratic government of the people. But there are always leaders who want their ideas followed—and maybe everybody wants power! In Russia and China, it was concentrated in the Communist Party. In America and France, the idea was to get more liberty to those who could wield it.

BUT FIRST—A LOOK AT THE PSYCHOLOGICAL SPECTRUM

Another continuum that is somewhat akin to the political spectrum is the psychological spectrum of selfishness to the ability to love humanity. There is a similarity in this spectrum to where a person, or a society, sits politically and psychologically.

Here the continuum would be read from right to left.

HUMANITARIAN << ABILITY TO LOVE A FEW<< SELFISHNESS/
LOVE   NEED FOR
POWER

Infants are totally self-centered. Their only concerns are: being fed, changed, played with, and cuddled. If they are cuddled enough they may be on their way to what Erich Fromm called the stage of self-love, which might come somewhere after age four. In this stage they realize that others are also important, so selfishness dwindles somewhat. Eventually, according to Fromm, we might be able to develop the general ability to love— and the highest form of that is humanitarian love. Not many reach this stage.

As a nation, the U.S. tends to be on the selfish end of the spectrum. The concerns are for making money and saving on taxes, while demanding things like Social Security and Medicare that we only minimally finance. So, let the government borrow from Japan and let our children pay back the loans. This is not to say that there are not people who are individually humanitarian. We see that when there are tragedies that require charity—with many Americans giving both money and time.

Nationally, on the other end of the psychological spectrum, we could see the Scandinavian countries where they are much more equalitarian and are quite willing to pay high taxes for the good of the general welfare. The national consciences of the Scandinavians tend to be very liberal—and loving.

The political spectrum can often, but not always, be seen as the societal applications of the psychological continuum of selfishness to love. Here are two recent situations in which the three types of ethical, or value, assumptions can be seen where they are complicated by the empathetic attitude of humanitarian love. Then let's throw in some intellectual questions to complicate the matter.

Let us briefly look at two recent situations. People from Honduras were escaping the high murder rate of their country. They traveled across Mexico with the idea of finding refuge in the United States. At the border, the adults were arrested and the children were taken from the adults-- because they were not allowed to be taken to prison. Priests and ministers, using the passages of the Bible that require charity frequented the media outlets.

Here we have the self-centered desires of the potential immigrants played against the society-based values and laws of the United States. But the outcry of the cruelty of taking children from their parents was deafening. The Attorney General cited the Bible, where St. Paul tells the Christians in Rome to obey Roman law. So, we have the three basic assumptions of ethics used in this battle.

In a parallel situation in Europe, migrants from a number of countries in the Mideast and southern Africa attempted to land in Italy. They were turned back and allowed to land in Spain. Italy has huge economic problems and has already taken in more than 100,000 migrants this year. Their newly elected government was elected largely to control and even reverse immigration. Again, we see the self-centered desires of the migrants in conflict with the needs and laws of the society. The God based ethical assumptions were not much of a factor in this situation.

So we have a group of people who are not highly educated, often of a different religion, nearly always from traditions that are different from the countries they want to accept them. The ethical and legal assumptions are clear that they have no rights. BUT, our psychological propensities for empathy cloud the legal aspects. We see crying children. We see mothers nursing their infants. What human being cannot feel sorry for them?

But are the non-accepting countries ultimately to blame? Should the refugee parents have brought children into such a terrible world? Should the governments of the emigrants have protected all of their citizens? Should the government have enacted laws that would have protected babies from being born into such a lawless or non-economically fertile environment? In Honduras should the president have followed the idea of President Duterte of the Philippines and had police and vigilantes shoot the violent gang members without a trial? Should the ideals of a government of the laws and of fair trials be seen as superior to a society that might live in peace and prosperity? Yes, we have the assumptions of the far far far right against the assumptions of the liberal left.

And who said that ruling would be easy?

Now let us look at the expanded political spectrum.

A WIDER SPECTRUM

It seems to me that the political spectrum that we commonly use is too limited for a complete description of the possibilities of politics. I propose a nine-category spectrum.

We will assume that the middle five of the traditional categories are nonviolent and logical, based on facts as well as on preferences. The categories, from right to left are:

1. Violent Reactionaries
2. Reactionaries who lie and use propaganda to achieve their goals
3. Honest thoughtful reactionaries
4. Conservatives
5. Moderates
6. Liberals
7. Radicals
8. Radicals who lie and use propaganda to achieve their goals
9. Violent radicals

These can be laid as a continuum 9< 8 <7< 6< **5**> 4> 3 >2 >1

WE SHOULD BE ABLE TO TALK TO EACH OTHER

The various categories along the spectrum may contain adherents who fell into their beliefs by tradition or by listening to others. They may also contain adherents who climbed into their beliefs by thinking, researching, and discussing. So far, no one has all the answers to all the problems facing our world.

In May 2017, Vice President Pence was giving the commencement address at the University of Notre Dame. About a hundred graduates got up and walked out. Why? Was it because he had left the Catholic Church to become an evangelical, since he calls himself "an evangelical Catholic." Was it because of his opposition to abortion? But this is the same position that the Catholic Church takes. Was it because he was a reactionary and they were liberals? But might they have learned something from him? Were they afraid that their minds, which they had made up before or during their university experience, might be changed?

It is often said that we should not argue about politics or religion. This is because every religious point of view and every political point of view usually rests, at least in part, on basic assumptions which cannot be proven.

How can you prove there is a God or heaven? How can you prove that people are equal or unequal? How can you prove whether liberty or equality is the more important basis for our government?

But there are other areas in religion or government that may be provable.

• Do Mormons break fewer laws than other religious people or

nonreligious people? Here we could just look at the percentage of prison inmates of the various religions and the nonreligious.

• Does climate change really exist? Here we can look at: the measured temperatures over the last hundred years in over a thousand worldwide temperature stations; the temperatures from the last 2,000 years as shown in coring research in the oceans or in Antarctica; the number of major hurricanes, rainstorms, and snowstorms over the last 50 years.

• Can we find jobs for the huge number of unemployed young people? Here we can look at the incredible increase in population and the various types of technology that do the work that humans used to do.

So here are the categories for the expanded nine category political spectrum. Where do you fit on this political spectrum? And do different issues have you in different categories? What about: capital punishment, minimum wage laws, the use of DNA links to identify criminals, equality between men and women, euthanasia, abortion, data mining for electioneering?

VIOLENT REACTIONARY ACTIONS-- THE FAR-FAR-FAR RIGHT

Moving back to a supposedly earlier time, whether real or imaginary, is a great political technique. When it involves killing as its political technique, it delivers a forceful message from its often cowardly messengers.

Hitler called for the extermination of Jews and other undesirables in order to bring Germany back to its pre-Depression state. The alt-right's pro-Confederacy march in Charlottesville, Virginia in August of 2017, the Ku Klux Klan's violent actions, the shootings of abortion-performing doctors, Dylann Roof's shooting of nine black churchgoers, and Canadian Alexandre Bissonnette's murdering of 6 praying Muslims in Quebec—are examples of this belief. Perhaps the most violent individual action in this regard was done by the aforementioned Norwegian neo-Nazi Anders Breivik in 2011 when he killed 77 people and injured hundreds through his bomb and his automatic weapons. He didn't like the left-leaning government of his country. Recently a group of Bulgarian vigilantes, both men and women, has been hunting immigrants and refugees with the purpose of killing them.

The terror of Al Qaeda, ISIS, and the many allied groups is a major reactionary goal. Going back to setting up a caliphate from Europe to Asia, and possibly for the whole world, is reactionary. A thousand years ago such a caliphate existed from Spain, across North Africa, up to Turkey, and across the Mideast and India. These were the glory days of a dominant intellectual Muslim conquest. Seeking to return to this, and an even more extensive caliphate, is the stated goal of many Muslim terrorists. Calling them "radical Islamic terrorists," is actually not semantically correct They are not seeking a new and equalitarian caliphate, they should be called "reactionary Islamic terrorists," because they are trying to go back to what once was—or what they imagined once was.

The President of the Philippines, Rodrigo Duterte, has given the police orders to kill drug suppliers and he brags that he has done such killings himself.

The killing of former Russian spies in England recently is such a violent reactionary act—if they were ordered by the Kremlin, as is generally believed in the West.

In Dylann Roof's killing of the nine black people praying in 2016, we always wonder if his animosity toward blacks and his thought that a race war was coming was psychotic, merely an illustration of a severe inferiority complex, or whether he really thought his way into this irrational behavior. As we have repeatedly indicated, it is common for people to believe what a person says or does without searching for the underlying subconscious motivations.

There is always a question as to whether some of these people were psychotic and using reactionary thinking to stimulate their irrational behavior or whether they had really thought their way into their killings. And if so, exactly what positive results did they expect would emerge from their murderous behaviors?

In Singapore possession of 15 grams of heroin is a capital offense—and you can expect to be hanged if you violate this law. While the number of hangings has decreased, recently two immigrants were hanged under this law. Malaysia and Indonesia have similar laws. In the Philippines, after President Duterte's 2016 ordered executions of drug dealers and drug users, over 6,000 suspected drug users have been executed without trials. (Trials are more likely to be held when governments are moderate or liberal.)

Such violence, in law enforcement, is more common in Asia than in the West, where individual lives are held to be sacred and where individual desires are often excused even when they disrupt an orderly society. In Asia the society, as a whole, is more likely to be the overriding concern.

The funds spent on the drug problems take money from other valuable societal duties such as paying for education through the graduate level of the universities. There is only so much money to run a society. Singapore's home minister, when asked why his country used such forceful methods to curb drug use said, "show us a better model, a model that is as effective in reducing drug use." Some U.S. states have gone the other direction—taking the radical route of recognizing individual desires as rights and hoping to reduce criminality by legalizing some drugs.

This is, indeed, a question for modern society. Should individual desires that are counter-productive for a society be allowed because of a notion of "human rights," or should the rights of others in the society, who are not drug dependent, be at least as important as those of the addict or the habituated person? Should society's money be spent to attempt to rehabilitate the drug addict or should it be used to fund the college education of someone who has avoided the lure of chemical happiness and who might be an important contributor to the society?

Another action that may be viewed as unjust is the imprisonment of suspected terrorists. The US has imprisoned a number of men whom they call dangerous terrorists. They are quite certain of their evaluations but do not have enough evidence to bring them to trial. So the speedy trial promised by the Constitution does not apply to these non-citizens who are suspected terrorists, during what the government calls "a time of war."

China recently jailed, beat, and killed a human rights advocate who worked in a high position in the government. In Turkey after the failed coup attempt, thousands were jailed on suspicion of being sympathizers. Imprisoning such foes has a long history for both reactionaries and radicals.

Assassinations are almost the rule rather than the exceptions in our political worlds. They go back at least to the 11th century BCE in Egypt with the assassination of Ramses III, to the third century BCE in Rome, and to the seventh century in Greece. Known assassinations reach into the hundreds throughout the world. They are perpetrated by both far right and far left murderers. In the US, the assassination of President Abraham Lincoln is a prime example of the far-far-far right's determination for a return to the past.

President Erdogan of Turkey used imprisonment and worse after a failed coup in 2016.

Dictators must continually eliminate, either verbally or physically, those who oppose them. The Chinese Constitution makes this legal. While many basic freedoms are guaranteed by their constitution, such as freedom of speech and freedom of the press, citizens must realize the sovereignty of the state, as shown by these elements:

Article 51.

The exercise by citizens of the People's Republic of China of their freedoms and

rights may not infringe upon the interests of the state, of society and of the collective, or upon the lawful freedoms and rights of other citizens.

Article 52.

It is the duty of citizens of the People's Republic of China to safeguard the unity of the country and the unity of all its nationalities.

Article 53.

Citizens of the People's Republic of China must abide by the Constitution and the law, keep state secrets, protect public property and observe labor discipline and public order and respect social ethics.

An official at the Israeli Embassy, in January of 2017, was caught saying that the members of Parliament in England who opposed Israel should be "taken down." When it was revealed what he had said, he was released from his embassy job and his remarks were countered by official statements from the Embassy. But it should come as no surprise that the Israelis, as many other countries, use lethal and other techniques to silence their critics.

Fascists commonly use both violence and propaganda to gain their power. As you remember from our discussion of semantics, fascism was defined and expanded in the essay titled, "The Doctrine of Fascism" by Giovanni Gentile in 1935. Benito Mussolini added a bit to the end of the essay. Gentile rejected democracy, liberalism, and Marxism. People are not equal, so they should not have an equal say in governing. In fact, the state is primary. Mussolini told us that you gain power by plucking the chicken one feather at a time. Pluck too fast, and the people will know what you are doing. Toward the end of his career he plucked too fast and the people skewered him and hung him upside down in a square in Milan—sort of a *pollo alla Milanese*!

THE REACTIONARY PROPAGANDISTS—THE FAR-FAR RIGHT

This is the major topic of this book. As illustrated it was used by George W. Bush in his campaigns, particularly when trying to minimize John Kerry's heroism in Vietnam.

It was used to a greater extent by the Brexiteers, and was probably used more than anyone else in history by Donald Trump in his primary and presidential quests and in his early presidency. Fake news, fake history, and alternative facts were the overwhelming rhetoric. Russia seems to be involved in this area now in both the American and the German elections, as it was in Brexit and in the Trump campaign.

But this falsification of facts is not new. Backers of Thomas Jefferson called John Adams an hermaphrodite in their presidential contest. Joseph Goebbels was the Minister of Propaganda for the Nazis during World War II. Tokyo Rose used her wily ways to try to influence American soldiers in the Pacific Theater to be concerned about the unfaithfulness of their wives and girlfriends back home, and that they should stop attacking the Japanese.

Trump violated the rules of formal logic hundreds of times in his Democratic Primary advance and hundreds of times more in his presidential quest versus Hillary Clinton. He was aided by far-far-right wing radio, television and newspaper commentators. In her recent book, Hillary talked about the unnerving technique that Trump used during the second debate. He would follow her around the stage in close proximity, making faces while she was trying to make legitimate points. His uncouth antics made the audience focus on him, as a superior man toying with a woman. It was a non-verbal propaganda message.

He continued to use such techniques to convince the American people, particularly his base voters, that the previous administration had used illegal wiretaps against him. There was no evidence that this had ever happened and the director of the FBI and others said that his charge was untrue.

Another example of propaganda is the Trump denial of climate change because it is bad for the fossil fuel industries—and some of his major contributors. This has resulted in government agencies having to use the term "weather extremes" instead of "climate change." They have also been told to use the term "resilience to weather extremes" rather than "climate change adaptation." Other meaningless phrases have been inserted in place of terms like "sequester carbon" and "reduce greenhouse gases."

The infamous Nunes memo was declassified by President Trump and publicized worldwide. The four-page memo was an abridgment of about 100 pages of secret testimony before the House of Representatives Intelligence Committee. The Nunes staff members who compiled the memo eliminated essential information that would have been a more complete picture of what happened in this very small chunk of testimony before the committee. The memo was opposed by all of the Democrats and some of the Republicans but was deemed essential to show the political motivations of the investigation into the possible involvement of the Russians in the 2016 presidential election. The memo was classified, but was declassified by President Trump and released to the media.

There is an old saying that "a text taken from its context is a pretext." A pretext, of course, is a ruse or ploy that is removed from truth. For those who believe in the Bible, they should understand that the Bible says, "there is no God." That is a very powerful text. But if we look at the full context, the full verse says, "The fool says in his heart, 'There is no God.' They are corrupt, they do abominable deeds; there is none who does good." (Psalm 14:1)

Objective analysis might consider such a political technique, of using a pretext to be an objective truth, to be a "corrupt and abominable deed."

In early 2018, a huge outcry erupted from many Republicans, or right leaning public servants, such as: former FBI director James Comey, present FBI director and Trump appointee Christopher Wray, Rob Rosenstein of the Department of Justice who is ultimately in charge of the investigation, Robert Mueller, who is conducting the investigation, and former presidential candidate and Senator John McCain. They believe that the declassification and release of the memo was counter to the interests of the American people by revealing sources of intelligence.

Such a release for political purposes might very well inhibit future informants from aiding in American intelligence gathering. The Democrats concurred with this breach of confidential intelligence gathering and added that the report was incomplete, having edited out essential information. This made it a political ploy, rather than an essential release of classified intelligence, according to Democrats. If so, it was therefore propaganda. The consensus of opinion was that it was geared to give a reason for the President to fire the Department of Justice personnel who were investigating possible Russian involvement in the 2016 election.

In early February of 2017, the front page of the official Vatican newspaper had a fake interview with Pope Francis. Reactionaries in the Vatican have given the liberal Pope a great deal of trouble. But rumors and lies are not new to the Vatican. Pope Paul VI, Pope John II and Pope Benedict XVI have all had false rumors foisted against them by foes on the other end of the sacred political spectrum. It seems that using the power of propaganda is as often the motivating force in church circles as it is in secular squares and plazas. Getting what we want is more important than ethical behavior—even in religions.

The alt-right is that far-right group which is associated with Islamophobia and anti-Semitism, right-wing populism, neo-reactionary movements, etc. The Ku Klux Klan would be a small part of this group. Neo-Nazis and some men's rights advocates (anti-feminists) could also be included, but there are far more individuals and splinter groups. Depending on the situation, they may or may not use violence.

Reactionary propagandists in Europe and America today are more likely to focus on immigrants who are racially identifiable and who profess a different religious belief. The Mexicans and Muslims in America have been major targets for President Donald Trump. Moroccans have been the major target of Geert Wilders in the Netherlands. The Brexit vote seemed to target most immigrants whether from the EU or from other countries.

Some of these reactionary groups are occasionally violent. But, as with all people, they may shift a bit along the spectrum depending on the issues involved.

The reactionary groups that use propaganda to influence the voters have been very visible in recent years. Donald Trump's promise that he can bring back coal mining and steel production and make it pay are totally unrealistic. However, such promises got him elected.

Once he was in office he did follow through on his promises of eliminating the climate change ideas of President Obama--and the rest of the world. He attempted to undo the healthcare act that Obama had sanctioned. He struck at the airfield that had been used to bomb helpless citizens with gas. All of these would be reactionary actions which were approved by his supporters.

While a person may get into office using propaganda, if he or she follows the promises made it is a rational reactionary development.

Some rather comical attempts at reactionary propaganda were recorded it 2017.

Reactionary commentators, Ann Coulter and Rush Limbaugh, said that hurricane Irma would be a light rain and that the media were exaggerating the severity of the storm to increase the fears of climate change. They said that it was only to advance the liberal political agenda. Then a few days later, Limbaugh had to cancel his program because his home in Palm Beach, Florida was being severely lashed by the imaginary storm.

A few weeks earlier after Hurricane Harvey had hit Texas, Coulter tweeted that "I don't believe Hurricane Harvey is God's punishment for Houston electing a lesbian mayor. But that is a more credible theory than that it was caused by 'climate change'."

THE REACTIONARIES—THE FAR RIGHT

Many whom we call conservatives are actually reactionaries. Here we will discuss briefly both rational and irrational, yet honestly held, views that are reactionary.

Every ethical, religious, and political view is based on either non-provable basic assumptions, on tradition, on observation, or on what we have heard or seen.

Let us briefly look at these sources of religions, ethical theories, and political views. Each of these is generally grounded in what we call "basic assumptions." Basic assumptions cannot be proved. When one assumes that there is a supreme being this is a basic assumption which is not provable. You may say that it says so in the Bible, the Koran, the Upanishads, or any other set of scriptures. For example, if a person says "I believe in God," because it says in the Bible that God exists. And who wrote the Bible? God did. So we have a circular argument that doesn't prove a supreme being.

In political theories, many begin with the assumption that people are either equal or unequal. Of course, in our physical bodies we are obviously not equal. But is there something deeper and more meaningful than the body? Do we have a soul or a life force? Here again we get into basic assumptions— assumptions that are non-provable.

Other beliefs may come from personal experience. My job was taken by a Polish immigrant who worked cheaper than me. (He may also have worked better than me!) But the fact is, I lost my job and I don't like it. I may also observe that people who have come to my country do not share the same values as I do. They may wear hijabs or burkas, yarmulkes or black broad brimmed hats shading their full beards, they may wear a colored turban and a beard.

Beyond their looks, they may not work as hard and they may want to collect welfare money without having contributed much. When this is true, the native taxpayers have a legitimate gripe. Of course, it is not always true. The Somalians in the US are said to be the highest achieving immigrants from sub-Saharan Africa. But in Norway they are found to be the lowest achieving group, often with large families who are given financial aid for every child born.

There are two terms that sound contradictory that are both conservative approaches to economics. "Neo-conservatism" and "neoliberalism" are different but still in the same area of the spectrum. Neo-conservatism is concerned with honoring and living the past through traditional religious morality and the traditional "might makes right" military approach to safety and security.

NEOCONSERVATISM

Neo-conservatism looks to history to see that the strongest country survives. They also look to history for morality. And American morality, they think, stems from Israel. For this reason, they want to protect Israel as the founding religion of the Western world.

Morality is often black-and-white. It is found in the Bible or what people think is in the Bible, like abortion prevention and homophobia. Divorce is evil; so is gay marriage.

In military terms the United States should use its power to democratize the world. Certainly, communism should be fought and social welfare programs should be chastised. Ronald Reagan's tough stance on communism brought the wall in East Berlin down. National security is paramount.

NEOLIBERALISM

Neoliberalism is a different kind of conservative approach to economics. It espouses economic freedom. Reagan and Thatcher used this theory to try to reduce state interference in economics while deregulating and privatizing state businesses. This approach to libertarianism will accept aspects of the liberal welfare state when they are really needed.

ILLUSTRATIONS OF POWER IN REACTIONARY GOVERNING

In 2017 President Erdogan won a referendum that gave him much more power in his pro-Muslim leadership. It undid many of the democratic reforms put into place by Ataturk many years before. He controlled the press so that potential challengers in the presidential elections had weakened voices in their "democratic" elections. Maduro in Venezuela is currently attempting to do the same thing. Donald Trump can't silence the free press so he treats it sarcastically as "fake news," unless it sings his praises, as does Fox News.

PREJUDICE CAN BE POSITIVE OR NEGATIVE, RATIONAL OR IRRATIONAL

Prejudice means pre-judging. I have a positive prejudice for Italian restaurants and negative prejudice against Japanese restaurants. But the worst meal I've ever had was in an Italian restaurant in London, and I've had some of my very best meals in Japanese restaurants in Kyoto.

A number of years ago in France there was a positive prejudice for Blacks and a negative prejudice against Algerians, who are Caucasians. The Blacks were generally in business or were college students, and their ebony-like skin was so beautiful. Some Algerians, on the other hand, were more likely to be antisocial and criminal.

We generally think of prejudice in terms of racial or religious ideas. If an American were prejudiced against Colin Powell or Condoleezza Rice because they were Republicans or were Black, that would be a very irrational prejudice because both are extremely intelligent and have provided great services to the country. I would place them in the top 25 of all Americans.

Racial prejudice can also be experienced within the race. Two of my good friends, from my coaching days in the ghetto of Los Angeles, are Black. One time they related how they were walking down the street in Beverly Hills and heard steps behind them. They turned and saw that there were two white guys, so they were relieved. They, too, were prejudiced against young Black men. One of those friends had two brothers who were members of the Bloods. The last time we coached together in Compton, he warned me about wearing either red or blue clothes. Wearing red could get you shot by a Crip, while wearing blue could get you shot by a Blood. So there is a rational prejudice for wearing neutral colors.

Naturally the ideal is to take everyone as an individual and judge him or her by their ethical standards. Martin Luther King reportedly said, "don't hate me until I have earned it." The reactionaries often hate or distrust those who are not like them. It is psychologically comforting to want to keep what you have. It didn't do King Louis XVI much good in the French Revolution. Muammar Gaddafi met a similar fate.

Prejudice against those who are different is not always directed downward toward immigrants of lower social classes. In Malaysia there is often prejudice against the higher social class Chinese and Indians. One area where this happens is in higher education where Malays are often given preference over higher achieving Chinese. This also happens in the US universities, where the higher grades of Chinese students are often disregarded so that other races or athletes can balance the ethnic makeup of the student bodies.

In California, no race or ethnic group has ever received negative irrational prejudice like the Chinese and Japanese. In the 1850s "hanging a Chinaman" was great sport for a Saturday night. During World War II the Japanese were interned in camps to separate them from the general population. Germans and Italians, with whom we were also at war, were not so separated. But these Asians have had the last laugh! The Chinese have risen in society and now have achieved at a higher level than any other group—about two and half times higher than the Caucasians. And Japanese have achieved at about twice the level of the Caucasians.

BUT IT IS COMFORTABLE BEING A REACTIONARY

Because of our universal inferiority feelings, we must put people down to feel better. Inferior men must keep all women down. Non-educated people must find objects for their power drives to be nurtured. Consequently, anyone who is different can be looked down upon. Catholics can look down on Protestants because they do not have the true Christian religion. Protestants can look down on Catholics because they are not allowed to make up their own minds on theological issues. Of course, both can look down on Jews because they didn't come along with the new teachings of Jesus. They forget that Jesus was always a Jew and there is no evidence that he would have ever have approved of a new religion in his name. Muslims, have the latest revelation from God, so they are better than any others. In fact, if you don't believe as they do, you are an infidel—a nonbeliever. Then of course the Mormons have an even later revelation so that makes them even more knowledgeable.

And so the story goes: let's go back to an earlier time when "we" were the dominant people and didn't have all these other people bothering us.

But how far back should we go? 600 years ago the Native Americans owned the Western hemisphere. About 200 years ago California belonged to Mexico. 2,000 years ago Palestine belonged to the Romans and 4,000 years ago it belonged to the Canaanites, many of whose descendants now inhabit Lebanon. Just how far back should thinking reactionaries go?

Small parties in many countries want to move backward in time to the earlier periods when there were few or no immigrants. Geert Wilders in the Netherlands, Marine Le Pen in France, the Alternative for Germany Party, the Golden Dawn Party in Greece and the Future Party in Norway are illustrations of nationalistic reactionary parties that oppose immigration. Nearly every European country has such movements, which vary from 5% to 30% in approval rates. The populist movement toward national sovereignty and against immigrants and those of very different religious beliefs has had recent success in America and the UK.

American reactionaries want to eliminate the conservatively tailored medical insurance bill (Affordable Care Act or "Obama Care") that Obama had suggested, which was actually not a very liberal approach, compared to the existing approaches to single payer plans or socialized medicine in all other advanced countries. Eliminating the federal option that President Obama proposed moved the president's moderate proposal (moderate in that it followed the existing plans of all other advanced nations) to an American reactionary (or conservative) capitalistic plan that was designed to enrich health insurance companies and their stockholders—among which were many of the Congressmen on the committees that changed the originally proposed, more socialized, health plan.

Here are another couple of instances! In March of 2007 Poland's delegate to the EU Parliament said that women are not entitled to equal pay because they are shorter, weaker, and less intelligent than men. Two years earlier he was sanctioned for giving a Nazi salute in parliament. This type of behavior is, of course, completely irrational—and reactionary.

Reactionaries also are likely to hold religious views that may or may not reflect the current views of a religion. Recently over 10,000 Norwegian Lutherans left their church because the church had decided to allow homosexuals to marry. In the US some Catholics want to return to the Latin mass rather than hearing it in English.

In India, the leader of Upper Pradesh, Uttar Adityanath, is a 44-year-old Hindu priest. The 220 million people in his state generally agree with him. He was India's youngest member of parliament when he was elected at 25. Adityanath is a high priest and wants to undo many of the laws that have changed Hindu history in India. For example, he wants to ban cow slaughtering. He wants to erect a Hindu temple to the Lord Ram on the site where he believes that God was born. One problem is that the sacred site is now covered with a Muslim mosque. Among his other reactionary ideas are that women are weak and are liable to turn into demons when they take jobs traditionally given to men. He also wants to eliminate the threat of Muslims converting Hindu Girls to the Western faith. Enough? Not yet!

In many parts of the world, religion would be reactionary belief. But in America and in the developing countries, religion is a moderate belief. Religion certainly has tradition in its favor.

Abortion, as a method of birth control, is opposed by people who think that it is prohibited in their Bible, Actually, the Jewish tradition saw life as beginning at birth, not at conception. The Catholic view traditionally had had life starting 1 to 2 months after conception—until 1869 when Pope Pius IX decided that life starts at conception. Many Protestants seem to have picked up the idea that life begins at conception or at implantation. They seem to relish the idea that there is a sanctity of life that begins well before any biblical verse determines it. They condemn humans for stopping a pregnancy— but don't condemn God. And, as we have said, it is God who is responsible for the greatest number of miscarriages and spontaneous abortions, which by far outnumber human initiated abortions.

CONSERVATIVES—THE RIGHT

The conservatives in America would be more likely to uphold the values of liberty over equality. They should support equality of opportunity in education and in employment. Sadly, they do not often do this. However, such ideas as age discrimination and racial or ethnic discrimination are now the law of the land and should be upheld by conservatives. These laws were passed by Congresses that were overwhelmingly Democratic and liberal.

However, because of America's deep tradition in the importance of religion and the freedom of religion, dating back from the earliest colonists, unprovable faith commonly is more important than provable facts. America trails most of the world in the percentages of people who do not believe in global warming—especially that it is human caused. America also leads the developed world with the number of people who believe in religion. The true conservatives in America are therefore overwhelmingly protective of religions, or at least give lip service to these beliefs.

Unhappily—faith is more important than facts. Look at Trump's policies—the fact of climate change is denied but the minority religious idea of the unproven soul entering the unseen microscopic ovum is affirmed and protected by legislation and by the appointment of judges that know the truth of a political promise. Blind belief is generally protected by our laws. Faith in any religion is sacred—and the closer your faith is to mine, the more sacred it is.

Recently, in Europe, the right-wing parties have been pushing more for welfare. This is unusual in that right-wing parties tend to be for liberty and more traditionally conservative values. It may be that now in Europe, the values that we are used to, such as with the welfare state, are being touted by right-wing parties, such as: in Poland, Hungary and in the opposition parties of France's National Front and the Netherlands' Freedom Party. It may not be so strange in that in Europe welfare issues, like health and pensions, which were very liberal ideas originally-- are now so ingrained in the tradition that the conservative parties want to conserve them.

MODERATES –THE MIDDLE

The moderates in America are often called liberal. The true moderate is willing to look at what is working in the world and work slowly and effectively to make it work in America. By many criteria, President Obama was really largely a moderate. But he had many liberal ideas, ideas which would be considered moderate in Europe.

LIBERALS—THE LEFT

The liberals in America would be quite moderate, and even often conservative compared to European values. Liberals tend to move toward both equal rights (which are essential to liberty) and the actual equality of the citizens.

The slogan that "Black lives matter," illustrates a plea for universal equality. The fact that many of the blacks killed were breaking the law is often forgotten. But does the penalty fit the crime when someone is attempting to avoid arrest and is therefore killed? A question is how might laws be enforced if suspects are allowed to run away. Should there be less lethal weapons, like Tasers, that might be more often used? But Billy the Kid didn't use Tasers and America still is guided by the spirit of what they mistakenly believe happened in the Wild West! Thank goodness, we have television to give us a true picture of yesterday and today. But the various CSI series may not portray accurately what went on in your neighborhood this morning!

In America, the movements toward Social Security, Medicaid, and Medicare are all liberal movements. Affirmative action and universal free education are liberal ideas. The equality of opportunity is a goal of all liberals and moderates and many conservatives. It is frustrated by the fact that the Constitution gives the states the rights to education and the states allow for many local school districts to decide much of the curriculum—which is often far from the verifiable facts and aesthetic appreciations necessary for a real education.

Historically liberals have been for liberty, advocating for equal rights in freedom of speech, freedom of the press, freedom of religion, a democratic society, a secular government (separation of church and state), gender equality, and a cooperative globalization. Rights for homosexuals and transsexuals have recently been adopted. Once these values have found their way into society they are often adopted by the conservatives, so freedom of speech and of the press are accepted by most of those in the middle three categories of this spectrum. Those who don't want such freedoms for all, fall into the reactionary camp

Absolute monarchy, a state religion, and the privileges of heredity are frowned upon by liberals. However. the hereditary privilege of inheritance may be accepted by liberals just as it is fundamental to the beliefs of reactionaries and conservatives. Liberals can be selfish, too!

RADICALS—THE FAR LEFT

Franklin Roosevelt's liberal, if not radical, actions to pull the US out of the Great Depression through government funding of infrastructure, and the development of the beginnings of Social Security, put America on a welfare-state path. Then World War II brought it back effectively into the reactionary-capitalistic realm.

Radicals in our newer spectrum want faster change but are nonviolent. Martin Luther King in the US and Mohandas Gandhi in India would be examples of people who wanted progressive social change to happen faster. Much of the racial equality movement in America began in 1955 when Rosa Parks of Montgomery, Alabama refused to get up and give her bus seat to a white person. The second-class treatment of Blacks in the South angered them along with many whites. Rosa said that "I have learned over the years that when one's mind is made up, this diminishes fear; knowing what must be done does away with fear." It was that type of courage along with the non-violent resistance championed by King that changed the laws of the South—and the nation.

Many people, Black and white, were subjected to police maltreatment— cattle prods and dogs, as well as jail. Nine years after Rosa's heroic deed, The Civil Rights Act of 1964 was passed—and non-violence won the day.

THE RADICAL PROPAGANDISTS—THE FAR-FAR LEFT

These people use propaganda, fake news and other non-violent, non-rational methods to convert others to their ideas.

PETA, People for the Ethical Treatment of Animals, has a videogame in which the player can punch animal-experimenting scientists. They have publicized to children that their parents are evil because they feed them animals.

The umbrella revolution in Hong Kong in 2014 was a peaceful protest against China's heavy hand in ruling their recently acquired province.

Because the far right tends to be ruled by tradition, such as religion and laissez-faire capitalistic beliefs, it is often attacked by the liberals for being unscientific, in the case of religion and being unloving and unjust, in the case of capitalism. Consequently their "propaganda" is likely to be based on science and on humanitarian ethics.

Conservatives complain that media coverage has a liberal bias about such things as: the theory of evolution of humans; the existence of climate change, especially that caused by humans (such as Al Gore's "An Inconvenient Truth" promoting environmentalism), and the left's acceptance of non-traditional sexualities as shown in Disney's "Friends for Change", which shows homosexuals and transgender people as normal.

VIOLENT RADICAL ACTIONS—THE FAR-FAR-FAR LEFT

Among the most violent radical actions have been the American and French revolutions—fighting the over-controlling king in both cases, and the controlling Church in the case of the French.

Revolutions and uprisings have been recorded since early in Egyptian history. There have been hundreds, some were reactionary, others were radical— like the Cuban revolution in the late 1950s and the English Revolution in the mid-17th century. Lenin's revolution, and that of Mao, also qualify.

Antifa is a militant leftist organization that traces its roots to the 1920s and '30s, when militant leftists battled fascists in the streets of Germany, Italy, and Spain. It was involved in the violence in Charlottesville when it encountered the neo-Nazis. They popped up again in San Francisco and were both praised as being anti-racist and condemned as being thugs.

PETA has also done some violent actions to advance their cause. Buckets of blood or green paint have been thrown on people wearing fur coats. Although the official line is that they do not cause violence, members of the organization often get carried away with their mission and resort to violence. Similarly, ALF, the Animal Liberation Front, ostensibly nonviolent, has had a number of violent clashes with scientists and has destroyed laboratories.

While not physically violent, economic sanctions may also be seen here. The US-led United Nations sanctioning of Russia, Iran, and North Korea are examples. The sanctions in Iran were certainly effective in forcing Iran to stop its nuclear arms buildup. They haven't yet had an effect on Russia in stopping its incursions into Ukraine or Syria, and they first seemed to have made North Korea more belligerent—but after the summit, we will see.

A recent lone wolf example of this far-left violence is the 66-year-old white man who shot at Republican Congressmen in June of 2017 while they practiced for a charity baseball game near Washington D.C. He had approached them earlier and asked which ones were Republicans.

As a reactionary parent (sic) you may withhold a week's allowance rather than bruising your hand spanking your less than perfect child. Either action might fit in this category—as economic violence!

AND SO

Those who have the power and the money are already unequal. Typically, they want to share neither their power nor their cash. They want the freedom to keep what they have.

So, throughout our spectrum we have many conundrums:

☐ Should we have absolute equality for every person no matter how they choose to live (i.e. equal pay for everyone whether or not they work),

☐ Only equal rights for every person (should that include free education to whatever level a person can profit intellectually?)

☐ The liberty to achieve based on one's intelligence and work ethic, or on one's inheritance,

☐ To the degree that liberty and equality are often in conflict, which should we choose?

And—elected officials always charge their new communities to work together in their acceptance speeches. Is it really possible to expect all the people to reject their political views and accept the ideas of the victor.

CHAPTER 15.   WHAT DO WE WANT FROM OUR SOCIETY?

There are a number of questions that need to be answered for an ideal society. In this chapter we will look at just a few of them. Any proposed solutions will have at least as many opponents as proponents. But let's play with them for a few minutes. What we want will probably include is the question about how will we pay for these proposals? And about who will oppose us—and why?

In developing our ideal society there are at least two major considerations. One is whether liberty or equality will be primary, and to what degree will equality of opportunity will be a major factor. The other is which value system will be primary: self-centered values, society-based values, or God-based values. Most societies in the West use a combination of all of these considerations, but they are often contradictory. The human rights emphasis in recent years is primarily based on self-centered values. Some countries, such as Saudi Arabia in the recent past, were God-based to a large degree. Others like China and Singapore are society-based to a large degree. Every government must have a major concern for the society, but individual rights, or desires, often conflict with the smooth running of a society. The hope is that with more individual rights the society will function better and will have a stronger commitment to what many people consider to be fair—justice.

There are societies in which societal values are more important than individual values. In the West, individual values—that is, self-centered values— are considered extremely important. Some, such as freedom of speech and freedom of the press may even be geared at making the society better. Some desires, like drug use and the urge to enrich oneself through corrupt practices, may make the society less functional.

So where do we want to put our emphasis? Today, China and Singapore are well ahead of countries in the West in terms of economic output, the general peacefulness of their societies, and in their education. But to do this they have clamped down on some freedoms that the West would often tolerate. Singapore's laws are geared more to not offending one another while China's laws are geared more toward supporting the single rule of the Communist Party as it improves the general life of the citizens. I can think of no society that has risen economically and politically as fast as that of China in the last 50 years. And, the Edelman study shows that the Chinese people trust their government more than any other government is trusted by its citizens.

In China or Singapore, an action that would be considered merely offbeat or even innocuous, in the West, might well result in severe punishment, such as being whipped or imprisoned.

In deciding on what type of government you would like to have, you might consider the vastly improving economies and educational achievements of China or Singapore, as well as their peaceful gun-free societies in which illegal drug use is fairly well controlled. Against these advantages, there are freedoms that are taken for granted in the often violent West that you may not want to give up. You probably cannot have both—those fundamentals that we call "human rights" or a calm and rapidly improving peaceful society.

What a choice! It's like wanting a scoop if chocolate ice cream, and one of vanilla—but you can afford only one.

Here are a few of Singapore's laws that you might find disconcerting. The country has laws against littering, graffiti, jaywalking, spitting, expelling "mucus from the nose," and urinating anywhere but in a toilet. Even not flushing a public toilet is a crime. If you walk around your home naked and the curtains are not drawn, it is a crime. If you sing obscene songs or distribute obscene literature you are in trouble. Disturbing someone by playing a musical instrument could cost you a $1,000 fine. Homosexual sex can land you in jail for two years. (There is some effort to change this law.) Many of these laws may interfere with what you would like to do—what you might call your "rights."

China's laws tend to be for perpetuating the Communist Party's rule as well as for keeping the society peaceful. While freedom of speech is guaranteed in the Constitution, it has to be done in certain areas and those areas may be closed to speakers. Freedom of the press is not a fact. Free access to the Internet may find anti-government items blocked by Chinese censors. And China is now increasing the surveillance of its citizens through algorithms that evaluate their Internet usage, and whether or not it adheres to what the government thinks is appropriate for model citizens. Also, China does not allow free association with non-approved groups such as unions.

In China, there are civil rights movements: against the death penalty, the suppression of Falun Gong and other religious groups, the jailing of human rights lawyers, and others protesting for "rights" that are freely given in the West. In Hong Kong there was a large protest seeking free elections. The peaceful "umbrella protest" resulted in the jailing of three leaders. They were released by the court a few months later with the strong warning that if they did it again their minimum sentence would be six months. So much for free speech! Meanwhile the Chinese economy seems to be steaming at at least twice the speed of that of the West. So what is important? Would you give up free speech and free association for better education and a better economy?

SOME HUMAN RIGHTS DECLARATIONS

Since the American Constitution (1787) and the French Declaration of the Rights of Man and the Citizen (1789) were written, many suggested rights have been proposed, such as those by the United Nations' in their Declaration of Human Rights (1948) and the European Union's Convention of Human Rights (1953). Here are some of the rights asserted for citizens with the notation as to which declarations have expressed those rights. Some of those "rights" are supreme laws, like those in the American Constitution. Some of the European Union's Convention's provisions have not been ratified or signed by all Council of Europe members. The United Nations Declaration is also not unanimously ratified and signed.

Let's start with the UN Declaration of Human Rights Preamble: "Whereas recognition of the inherent dignity and of the equal and inalienable rights of all members of the human family is the foundation of freedom, justice and peace in the world," these rights are necessary to prevent the necessity of men revolting against tyranny and oppression.

☐ "All men are born free and equal in dignity and rights. They are endowed with reason and conscience and should act towards one another in the spirit of brotherhood." (UN Article 1)

COMMENT: This certainly sounds good, but are we really all born in dignity? When a child in Mali is quickly sold as a slave, does he or she really have any dignity? One of the later rights is to be free of servitude, but what right does this actual child have?

☐ Everyone is entitled to all the rights and freedoms set forth in this Declaration, without distinction of any kind, such as race, colour, sex, language, religion, political or other opinion, national or social origin, property, birth or other status. Furthermore, no distinction shall be made on the basis of the political, jurisdictional or international status of the country or territory to which a person belongs, whether it be independent, trust, non-self-governing or under any other limitation of sovereignty. (UN Art 2)

LIFE AND LIBERTY

☐ Everyone has the right to life, liberty and security of person. (UN Art 3, EU Art   2, 5)

☐ The European Union goes farther in requiring a positive duty to prevent foreseeable loss of life.

COMMENT: When we have the number of mass shootings in the United States, should something be done about the proliferation of firearms? Here the Supreme Court's allowance of firearms runs counter to the United Nations' right to life and to the security of one's person. Does it also run counter to the Preamble to the US Constitution to: "establish justice, insure domestic tranquility, . . . promote the general welfare," In other Western nations one seldom is confronted with a threat of death by another individual. But the number of firearms is the US perhaps requires that all have guns for their security.

☐ No one shall be held in slavery or servitude; slavery and the slave trade shall be prohibited in all their forms. (UN Art 4, EU Art 4; US Const Am 14)

COMMENT: But several surveys indicate that there are more slaves today than at any time in history. The estimate is 30 million.

☐ No one shall be subjected to arbitrary interference with his privacy, family, home or correspondence, nor to attacks upon his honour and reputation. Everyone has the right to the protection of the law against such interference or attacks. (UN Art 12, EU Art 8)

COMMENT: If Donald Trump were to abide by the United Nations Declaration of Rights, he would not have made the attacks on the honor and reputations of his primary challengers or his presidential challenger. He would also not impugn his predecessor, nor foreign dignitaries.

➢ Rights cannot be abused by asserting other rights. (EU Art 17)

☐ Freedom of movement within his own country, and the right to leave and return to his country. (UN Art 13, EU Prot 4, Art 2)

☐ Prohibition against discrimination. (EU Art 14)

PERSONAL LIFE AND RELATIONSHIPS

☐ Adults can marry and found a family without any limitation due to race, nationality or religion. It must be freely agreed upon by the partners. The partners are entitled to equal rights through the marriage and its dissolution. It is entitled to protection by society and the State. (UN Art 16, EU Art 12, Prot 7, Art 5)

☐ The EU does not yet recognize same-sex marriage in these rights, although many countries in Europe do.

☐ Everyone has the right to a standard of living adequate for the health and well-being of himself and of his family, including food, clothing, housing and medical care and necessary social services, and the right to security in the event of unemployment, sickness, disability, widowhood, old age or other lack of livelihood in circumstances beyond his control. (UN Art 25)

COMMENT: This sounds good, but billions of people don't have these essentials. Who is supposed to pay for them? Whether they are the poor in Africa, India, or the homeless in America or the UK, this is, at present, impossible to do. So how is it a right? Perhaps these rights should be realistic rather than idealistic.

□ Motherhood and childhood are entitled to special care and assistance. All children, whether born in or out of wedlock, shall enjoy the same social protection. (UN Art 25)

COMMENT: Is this to be the duty of the government or of the parents? And if it is the parent's responsibility, should the government ensure that the parents are financially, emotionally, and educationally capable?

□ Everyone has the right to education. Education shall be free, at least in the elementary and fundamental stages. Elementary education shall be compulsory. Technical and professional education shall be made generally available and higher education shall be equally accessible to all on the basis of merit.

□ Education shall be directed to the full development of the human personality and to the strengthening of respect for human rights and fundamental freedoms. It shall promote understanding, tolerance and friendship among all nations, racial or religious groups, and shall further the activities of the United Nations for the maintenance of peace. Parents have a prior right to choose the kind of education that shall be given to their children. (UN Art 26, EU Prot 1, Art 3)

COMMENT: In today's world, it is conceivable that not all parents are aware of the educational and psychological needs of children, or the potential needs to be a citizen in the modern world and to be able to contribute economically to the needs of society in the future, and to be able to have job skills that will be employable in the future. Perhaps we need pre-pregnancy education for parenthood! And why are the rights of parents superior to the rights of children?

□ Everyone has the right freely to participate in the cultural life of the community, to enjoy the arts and to share in scientific advancement and its benefits. (UN Art 27)

□ Anyone can own property and cannot be arbitrarily deprived of his property. (UN Art 17, EU Protocol 1, Art 1)

FREEDOM OF THOUGHT AND BELIEF

□ Everyone has the right to freedom of thought, conscience and religion; this right includes freedom to change his religion or belief, and freedom, either alone or in community with others and in public or private, to manifest his religion or belief in teaching, practice, worship and observance. (UN Art 18, EU Art 9; US Const Am 1)

□ Everyone has the right to freedom of opinion and expression; this right includes freedom to hold opinions without interference and to seek, receive and impart information and ideas through any media and regardless of frontiers. (UN Art 19, EU Art 9, 10; US Const Am 1)

□ The EU allows for restrictions of expression in: interests of national security; territorial integrity; safety; prevention of disorder or crime; protection of health or morals; protection of the reputation or rights of others; preventing disclosure of information received in confidence; maintaining the authority and impartiality of the justice system.

COMMENT: If opinions are to be held, it would appear that those opinions should be based on verifiable facts and conclusions adhering to the rules of logic—rather than being merely rationalizations for behavior.

□ Right to bear arms (US Const, Am 2)

COMMENT: It would seem that this right has become counterproductive in terms of guaranteeing life and the pursuit of happiness central to all expressed declarations of rights. The reason for the right, originally, was to protect against King George taking back the colonies. It has evolved to allowing people to hunt unarmed animals. This was also necessary for hunters to seek food. And it was also necessary to assuage the inferiority complexes of the citizens who wanted to show off the mounted heads of unarmed deer, moose, and lions in the living rooms of these brave trophy hunters. It has been suggested that a fairer approach to trophy hunting would be to have the hunters hunt each other. Both sides would be armed. Then, when exhibiting the head of one's prey in the living rooms, the admiring guests would know that the prey was also armed so that the hunting experience was fair and just.

FREEDOM OF SPEECH AND ASSEMBLY

☐ Everyone has the right to peaceable assembly and association and no one can be compelled to belong to an association. (UN Art 20, EU Art 11; US Const Am 1)

COMMENT: Except China, Russia, Venezuela, and a whole bunch of other places.

GOVERNMENT AND SOCIETY

☐ Everyone, as a member of society, has the right to social security and is entitled to realization, through national effort and international co-operation and in accordance with the organization and resources of each State, of the economic, social and cultural rights indispensable for his dignity and the free development of his personality. (UN ART 22)

☐ Everyone is entitled to a social and international order in which the rights and freedoms set forth in this Declaration can be fully realized. (UN Art 28)

☐ Nothing in this Declaration may be interpreted as implying for any State, group or person any right to engage in any activity or to perform any act aimed at the destruction of any of the rights and freedoms set forth herein. (UN Art 30)

PUNISHMENT, DEGRADING TREATMENT

☐ No one shall be subjected to torture or to cruel, inhuman or degrading treatment or punishment. (UN ART 5, EU Art 3)

COMMENT: George Bush and Donald Trump didn't read this far!

☐ Death penalty prohibited (EU Prot 6, 13)

COMMENT: But what if he is really a bad guy, I mean really, really bad—and is costing a lot of money to be imprisoned?

EQUAL PROTECTION OF LAW

☐ Everyone has the right to recognition everywhere as a person before the law. (UN Art 6)

☐ No one shall be subjected to arbitrary arrest, detention or exile. (UN Art 9, US Const Amend 4)

☐ All are equal before the law and are entitled without any discrimination to equal protection of the law. (UN Art 7)

COMMENT: but some animals are more equal than others, especially if they have attorneys who can make the jury cry!

☐ Right to a hearing in a competent tribunal (UN Art 8, 10, EU Art 6, 7, Prot 7, Art 1-4; US Const AM 7)

☐ Right to not incriminate oneself (US Const Amend 5)

COMMENT: You might think that this would be proof of guilt! Is it more important for a society to be concerned with justice or protecting a criminal from prison? Most countries allow a person to not incriminate himself, but strangely, in England where it was originated, the silence of the accused may be a consideration relative to his guilt, but it cannot be the sole consideration for guilt. Related protections that may interfere with justice being served are: attorney-client privilege, the privacy of the confessional or of therapist-patient privilege, or asylum in a church or embassy.

☐ Innocent until proven guilty and no crime if law passed after the action (ex post facto) (UN Art 11, EU)

☐ Right to seek asylum in other countries from political persecution, but not from non-political crimes or for crimes contrary to the purposes and principles of the United Nations. (UN Art 14)

RIGHT TO WORK AND REST

☐ Everyone has the right to work, to free choice of employment, to just and favourable conditions of work and to protection against unemployment. Everyone, without any discrimination, has the right to equal pay for equal work. (UN Art 23, 24)

COMMENT: And where will these jobs come from in an overpopulated world with computers, robotics, self-driving cars, 3D printing, and artificial intelligence?

☐ Everyone who works has the right to just and favourable remuneration ensuring for himself and his family an existence worthy of human dignity, and supplemented, if necessary, by other means of social protection. Everyone has the right to form and to join trade unions for the protection of his interests. (UN Art 23)

☐ Everyone has the right to the protection of the moral and material interests resulting from any scientific, literary or artistic production of which he is the author. (UN Art 27)

COMMENT: No wonder China hasn't signed it!

☐ Everyone has the right to rest and leisure, including reasonable limitation of working hours and periodic holidays with pay. (UN Art 24)

DUTIES OF THE CITIZEN

☐ Everyone has duties to the community in which alone the free and full development of his personality is possible.

☐ In the exercise of his rights and freedoms, everyone shall be subject only to such limitations as are determined by law solely for the purpose of securing due recognition and respect for the rights and freedoms of others and of meeting the just requirements of morality, public order and the general welfare in a democratic society.

☐ These rights and freedoms may in no case be exercised contrary to the purposes and principles of the United Nations. (UN Art 29)

COMMENT: President John Kennedy once said, "ask not what your country can do for you, but what can you do for your country." It seems that a huge majority of us are concerned with what we can get from our governments while giving as little as possible. Welcoming a tax break while the country is going broke is a very selfish act. Retiring on a "disability," when you are not really disabled, is not just.

There are too many of us whose only concerns seem to be with our self-centered values. But our nation cannot survive when so many are not pulling their weight. It appears that in the last year, many more people are becoming interested in running for government offices. This is a plus if their concern is with their duties rather than their self-aggrandizement or enrichment. We have many who want to be the best teachers, police officers, environmental researchers, farmers, and legislators that they can be. These are the necessary backbones of a fully functioning society that is moving forward.

On the other hand, there are those whose only concern is with amassing fortunes or exercising their power—to the detriment of their fellow citizens. What can be done to focus more of our community actions toward the betterment of our nation?

RELATED QUESTIONS TO BE CONSIDERED FOR OUR IDEAL SOCIETY

DO WE WANT TO LIVE?

Living today may be problematic! With Donald Trump and Kim Jong-un arguing about who has the biggest nuclear button, and terrorists tinkering with biological and chemical weapons--maybe we have to head to New Zealand or southern Chile for a chance at safety! Then, of course, we live in a hell of our own making—climate change. But we don't need to worry about that unless we:

➢lost our houses to hurricanes in Texas, Florida, or Puerto Rico, or

➢lost our homes to massive fires in California or Portugal, or

➢are starving to death in the area south of the Sahara because we have had no rain for crops, or

➢live on islands sinking into the rising oceans, like: the Maldives, Tuvalu, or Kiribati.

THE ENVIRONMENT—HOW IMPORTANT IS IT? HOW TO CONTROL CLIMATE CHANGE

Climate change is out of control. We see it in the extra strength and occurrences of floods, fires, hurricanes, droughts, and the heavy rain and snowstorms. The greenhouse gases we have emitted will last for years, some for hundreds of years. Probably the first thing we need to do in the US is to fight the denier's erroneous opinions with facts. The oil money, that funds many politicians, blinds them with hoods of greenbacks. We need to start electing statesmen and stateswomen instead of politicians whose only concern is being reelected. We have a real problem. Pandora's box has been opened and we don't seem to be willing enough to find and solve all those troubles that were released.

Our environment is where we live! It's that cozy wood-burning fireplace releasing carbon monoxide and dioxide into the atmosphere. It is taking the family on a well-deserved vacation in our fossil fueled SUV. It's having a pleasant breakfast while reading our newspaper, which is made from carbon dioxide absorbing trees. It is that romantic dinner with the flickering candles, releasing that small bit of carbon gas that contributes to our planetary problem.

But the major cause of all those greenhouse gases is the 7 billion people driving cars, building with cement, burning their fires, and eating their steaks— which, when they were alive as cattle, used a great deal of water and grains and released almost 125 pounds of methane each year, through both ends of their digestive tracts. Dairy cows emit twice as much as beef cows. One dairy cow emits as much methane per year as: 14 sheep, 22 goats, or 74 pigs.

This methane (otherwise known as "natural gas") is responsible for about 25% of global warming. But don't blame the cows for all of it, most comes from processing oil and gasoline.

Much of methane is removed from the atmosphere within 10 to 20 years, but while it is there, it is more than 80 times more warming than CO_2. Carbon dioxide, on the other hand, may take hundreds or even thousands of years to dissipate, so it is a very large problem. Much of it has been dissolved in the ocean, making it more acidic. This is why so many of the coral reefs are dying.

Other greenhouse gases, such as fluorocarbons and nitrous oxide, last from a few years to thousands of years. Nitrous oxide lasts 114 years. Nitrous oxide comes primarily from natural soils and the ocean, but some comes from manufacturing and cultivated soils. So, there is not as much that we can do about *this* greenhouse gas.

A recent report of Scripps Institute may clarify the multiplying problems of CO_2. At present over 9 billion tons of carbon is released annually. The ocean has absorbed 26% of all carbon released from the various emitters of the gas. About 28% was absorbed by plants and 47% went into the atmosphere. The amount of carbon dioxide that the oceans can absorb is limited. At the beginning of the Industrial Revolution the ocean was able to absorb a higher percentage of the greenhouse gas. Every year the ocean is less able to absorb what it absorbed the year before. This is complicated even more by the fact that as the oceans warm from the carbon dioxide and other greenhouse gases reflecting heat back to the oceans, the surface of the ocean, which is the warmest, has absorbed more of the carbon dioxide, so is closer to its maximum absorption level. The deeper colder water in the ocean could absorb more, but it is protected by the warmer layer at the surface of the ocean.

This lack of ability to absorb carbon dioxide is complicated by the destruction of rain forests for lumber. Rain forests were a major absorber of carbon dioxide.

On a brighter note, as the world lowers emissions and as fossil fuels are reduced, the oceans may be able to absorb a higher percentage of the carbon dioxide emissions. But this will take some time, and the world will heat up quite a bit before this can happen.

We are already starting to use solar energy to heat water and produce electricity. We are already planting more trees and bushes to absorb CO_2. Not nearly enough in either case. We are developing electric cars and trucks. But where do we get the electricity to power them? Is it by burning fossil fuels to make electricity? If it is photovoltaic (converting sunlight into electrical voltage) it is ideal. If the electricity comes from hydroelectric plants, that is also very good. But if it comes from fossil fuels, like oil and coal, it is counterproductive. And if it is from nuclear sources, it may be cleaner, but the radioactive waste might be a problem in the future.

Then, as we have mentioned, it is all those people needing electrical or gas power that is the real problem. But nobody wants to talk about that because having children is a human right and a long-held tradition—and even a religious commandment.

HOW TO CONTROL OVERPOPULATION

Overpopulation is the major problem that the world faces. It is responsible for these factors:

☐ Climate change, because more people are using fossil fuels and other chemicals that produce greenhouse gases. If we only had a million people on the earth they could use as many fossil fuels as they wanted we would not have a global warming problem.

☐ Combined with the increased use of computers, robots, artificial intelligence, self-driving vehicles, 3D printing and mechanization of farming, we need fewer people to produce the food and goods that we need.

☐ Because of the increased population in Africa, South America, and the Mideast, we have millions of people seeking jobs and benefits in Europe and North America.

☐ Because of the mechanization of agriculture and manufacturing, there are fewer jobs available for the workforce, particularly for the younger people. We therefore have unemployment rates for youth in the 20% to 40% range.

□ Because of the above-mentioned facts, more farmland is being desolated by erosion and pollution, and normal rainfall in many areas is not adequate for farming.

□ With fewer jobs available for the youth, they have less status and more time on their hands for crime and terrorism.

While many have recognized this problem during the last 50 years, people and nations have not responded by attempting to limit family size. The United States tries to reduce population by allowing nearly unlimited gun ownership. But since only 33,000 people are killed by guns annually, 45,000 by suicide, and 35,000 by car accidents some other approaches to population reduction should be tried. We are still increasing by two million per year.

Let me suggest two possibilities. One would be to license parents to have babies or to limit every family to only one child, as was done in China from 1980 to 2015. The other suggestion is to give everyone in the world a smart phone. Smart phones, with their internet connections, are so much more interesting than people. You may have noticed in restaurants where conversation is eliminated as the adults and children engage with their phones. Who needs sex today when touch screens are so responsive and don't get pregnant.

(If you are interested in an in-depth study of overpopulation and some possible solutions to it, including licensing parents, I would suggest again the free e-book series available at: andgulliverreturns.info. As you can imagine, there are many psychological and ethical questions related to controlling population. This series of 10 books, in a combination of fictional and nonfictional books, delves deeper into areas such as: climate change, family-planning, psychological impediments to limiting families, and a complete examination of values and how they are used in a number of societal problems. The books are also available in print.)

SHOULD PARENTS BE LICENSED NATIONALLY OR INTERNATIONALLY?

If population is to be reduced, which is highly unlikely given the poverty and traditions of most of the world, either limiting parents to one child or licensing parents to have children would be ways to go about it. In Europe, because of the higher standard of living and the entire level of education of women, fertility rates have dropped significantly— well under the 2.1 children that has been traditionally used as the replacement requirement for a population.

In China, since the one-child requirement was lifted to create more workers to support the aging population of workers; relatively few parents opt for a second child because of the expense and the time and effort required to see the child through the educational process. Since the year 2000 the fertility rate in China has ranged from 1.55 to 1.7 per woman. The one child requirement was lifted in 2015, but the fertility rate in 2017 was 1.6. Less than half of the babies were second children. Potential parents in China recognize the emotional and financial cost of having a second child.

If we were to license parents they would probably need: an educational background in nutrition, physiology, normal and abnormal psychology, and child psychology. It would also be important, in fact essential, to make sure that they had positive experiences with loving—in childcare experiences, in homes for the aged, or in a loving home of their own.

Should we think about the children—or only the potential parents?

HOW TO CONTROL TERRORISM

As we have attempted to do through the book, we must look deeper into why people become violent. It is usually because they have not been raised in loving homes.

The type of violence that they will exhibit because of the inferiority feelings they develop can come from the media, the pulpit, acquaintances, or other influential groups. But it is love and the ability to understand that other people are also worthy of respect, that is the key to reducing violence, harassment, and bullying.

(I would suggest here that you read Erich Fromm's "The Art of Loving." It is a masterful presentation of how the ability to love develops from infancy to adulthood—if a person is loved effectively. Ashley Montague gives us the essence of love in his treatise on love in the Encyclopedia of Mental Health. His definition of love is that: "Love is the communication to another person of one's deep involvement in that person's welfare—of one's profound interest in him as a person demonstrated by acts that support, stimulate, and contribute to the realization of that person's potential and to the fulfillment of that person's personality.")

You can understand that loving someone is more than just feeding them and saying "I love you." Developing the ability to love in a child is one of the most difficult occupations in the world.

An additional essential to reducing any impulse to terrorism is a high level of education where competing values and traditions are exposed and scrutinized. This can minimize the impulse to rationalize terrorism through religious or political beliefs—beliefs which do not withstand academic scrutiny.

WHAT WOULD BE A "JUST" SOCIETY?

☐ A democratic-republic like we have in the United States or Europe—with either a two-party system as in the US or with multiple important parties as in Europe, where coalitions must generally be formed in order to have a functioning government.

☐ A limited term republic, where representatives would serve only one, two, or three terms—or where they might be drawn by lots, such as in ancient Greece.

☐ Philosopher kings, such as Plato suggested, where the most educated people would rule the Republic.

☐ Democracy or a democratic republic by proven knowledge of the voters. In this form of government everyone would get one vote, but those with more proven knowledge in areas such as: economics, world history, natural science, environmental science, etc. would get more votes—possibly 2 to 10 more votes than the uninformed.

☐ Direct internet democracy where the pros and cons for each proposed law are given during a newscast, and the people would vote immediately by Internet.

☐ Hereditary monarchy. This has been attempted most often in our human history—it occasionally works. But maybe we should ask someone who ran afoul of the monarch, like Anne Boleyn or Thomas More, because there may be some downsides to absolute rule.

☐ One party rule as in China, where the ruling party works to make the society, as a whole, better.

☐ OR?

So how will we determine what is best?

HOW SHOULD WE USE THE DEMOCRATIC PROCESS?

☐ Should legalized bribery be allowed through lobbyists' contributions to governmental legislators and administrators? Should all elections be financed by the government, and the government only—with no individual or corporate contributions allowed?

    ☐ Should there be a real separation of powers between the legislative, executive, and judicial branches of government?

    ☐ How should conflicts between this nation and others be handled?

    ☐ A major question is how equally should we treat those of us who are unequal. We all are unequal because we are not identical. Should we reward with pay, power, or recognition and respect those who contribute by: being effective legislators or administrators; being inventors or entrepreneurs who advance our society in some ways; being outstanding educators.

    ☐ With more people living longer, should the government provide for old age homes? If we are all equal, why not? If so, what will it cost and for how many years should it be provided?

    ➢   Which "human rights" should we allow our citizens?

    ➢   What responsibilities should we require of citizens?

    ☐ Since everybody in a society is not unanimous in their approval of their government, how much free speech or how many demonstrations should be allowed? Both Singapore and China, who have highly efficient functioning economies, have many laws that would be considered harsh anti-freedom laws in the West. How much dissent can a functioning society allow?

    ☐ Will we have a happier and more effective society if we have true equality of opportunity? If so we need to start anew with each new generation. One of the best ways to do this is to eliminate the possibility of inheriting from one's parents or relatives. Making it impossible to hide money in foreign accounts and having 100% tax on one's wealth at death, are necessities. But since big money runs most countries, this is highly unlikely to happen. If there were a grassroots movement to have a constitutional amendment, it might be possible.

    •   It would not be the first time in history that this was tried. Julius Caesar had such a rule for kings. On their death, their property was handed over to Rome.

    ☐ In legal civil cases, should financial awards be massive in order to punish the offender, such as the government, corporations, or individuals? If so should the aggrieved person be given all of the money or only a portion which was commensurate with the injury—and the rest being given to another entity, like: the government or charities?

    ☐ In criminal cases which is the more important aspect of justice—punishing a severely guilty person or ignoring the actual crime because of a technicality? We have continually seen very guilty people being released because of legal technicalities. One of the major cases was Miranda v. Arizona in 1966, in which the Supreme Court, by a 5-4 majority ruled that suspected criminals who are arrested must be apprised of their right to remain silent and their right to an attorney. It is amazing how many times one person determines the law of the nation! In this case, Miranda who had been judged guilty of kidnapping and rape, was allowed to go free. But he probably didn't know that kidnapping and rape are both unethical—even illegal! So I guess it was OK.

ONCE YOU MAKE THE LAWS--HOW SHOULD THEY BE ENFORCED?

Hanging a drug trafficker, as they do in Singapore, goes a long way in reducing drug trafficking. A heavier penalty can force the criminal to move to a society with a more merciful, or lackadaisical, system of disciplining criminals. Donald Trump enacted a harsher method of discouraging asylum-seekers and economic migrants at the Mexican border. In June of 2018 he enacted a policy to separate children from their parents for any families who came across the border. This discouraged many parents from attempting to enter the United States, even if they were asylum-seekers.

IMMIGRATION

This brings us to another issue that has become more pressing as overpopulation continues to explode and as advanced technological options make many traditional jobs either scarce or obsolete. There are fewer low-level jobs, yet more people. This is a cause for increased economic migration—escaping poverty. But while the home country may not be able to supply jobs, the accepting country may not have jobs to offer.

Combine this with the wars that are a fact of perennial human discontentment and of terrorism which is aided by advanced weapons. Whether the terrorism is religious based and international or homemade gang violence, many people seek peace as refugees.

But empathy for the plight of both categories of potential immigrants is not infinite. It has given rise to the far-right parties who do not want change and to severe government chaos as we have seen in the Brexit and Trump's election aftermaths.

WHOSE LAND IS IT ANYWAY?

Why is the accident of birth the major determinant of life? If my father was a farmer in Senegal will I have the same opportunities as if by father was a billionaire Wall Street investor? My parents and their homeland determine 99.999999% of my opportunities in life.

If I had been born in San Francisco in the year 2000, why do I have more rights to the land than the Mexicans who had owned it before 1850 or the Native Americans who had owned it for 10,000 years before that. If I was a Jew born in Jerusalem, why do I have more rights than the Arabs who had populated Palestine for over a thousand years, the Romans who had owned it before that, the Egyptians, the Canaanites or any other group that has owned or controlled the area before and after it was an Israelite kingdom. The political answer is that "might makes right." But how does that comport with Kant's dictum that "we should treat everyone as ends in themselves, not a means only." To that we may add the nearly universal highly esteemed emotion of "empathy."

YOUR NEED vs. MY EMPATHY—
A NEARLY IRRESISTABLE FORCE vs. AN ALMOST IMMOVABLE OBJECT

The conflict between the psychological reality of empathy, for many of the immigrants, and the economic and political realities that face them in their hoped-for new homes are increasingly incompatible. The rapidly increasing poor populations of Africa and Latin America cannot expect the U.S. and the EU to continue to welcome the eager, but impoverished, under-educated economic migrants. On the other hand, university educated engineers, doctors, IT specialists, and nurses may be welcomed.

Then there are those fleeing wars, terrorists, or violent gangs. Empathy for their plights may be even greater. But even a temporary refugee status is increasingly difficult to gain because of the total number of potential immigrants. An ideal solution to these conflicting desires is not yet possible.

The relative poverty of the home nations with frightened, impoverished, or uneducated citizens, or those without opportunities for the unemployed, or without opportunities for their eager and talented citizens to prosper—is a factor.

But why are they impoverished? What part does corruption play? Whose pockets are being filled with gold? Are there any natural resources that can be utilized to enrich the country? Is there enough money to educate people through the secondary level? Are there universities that can train the talented citizens for the jobs of the 21st century? Has family planning been attempted? To what degree wasn't it successful? And why?

Sometimes it is the mother or father who gain pride by having large families. Should the state emphasize pride in smaller families or childless marriages? Is it the government's job to provide for its present and future citizens? What about the religions, like the Catholics and Mormons, who advocate or require more births? Both churches are extremely rich.

There are about 160 million Catholics in Africa. In Latin America the percentage of Catholics in the varying countries ranges from 55 to 95%. Since the Catholic Church advocates large families, perhaps there should be pressure put on the Church by the national governments to subsidize children in Catholic families and to provide schools and colleges for the countries. Of course, this will never happen because the Church wants to keep its riches.

It is impossible to determine the exact worth of the church but it is estimated at over $200 billion. It owns in excess of 170,000 properties including the Vatican, embassies, businesses, and churches. At first one might think that if an entity is to make a rule, it should be financially responsible for the carrying out of that rule. For example, if a government requires young people to attend school, it should supply the schools. If a government wants you to stop at a street corner, it should supply the stop sign. Similarly, if a government wants you to have a child that you do not want, by prohibiting abortion, it should pay all the expenses of this child, as it does in education-- and sometimes through welfare payments and food stamps. It might also raise the child itself in orphanages—all this, while lowering everyone's taxes.

Then there are the swords of violence jabbing us to escape the anarchy of our corrupted countries. Both poverty and plenty can increase crime. The impoverished seek to survive, so may steal. Having plenty of people usually limits the opportunities for societally useful positions—so our inferiorities may push us to the welcoming arms of street gangs or Jihadis. How better to show our power than to kill another person—for territory or traditions.

ARE THERE ANY SOLUTIONS?

When boatloads of people embark from Libya on their way to Italy, should they be accepted? The newly elected government, backed by 59% of the citizens, refused to allow them to dock. They were accepted by Spain. Amnesty International blames the European Union for their non-acceptance of refugees and migrants. But Amnesty International is sitting on the outside of the conflict and are taking the side of the immigrants and the attitude of empathy as the controlling concern. But people in the desired destination countries have a different criterion for evaluating their plight.

The Brexit vote was, to a large degree, a vote against immigrants from other countries in Eastern Europe. The difference in religion and race, that conflict with UK traditions, was not nearly as extreme as those of the Middle Eastern and African émigrés who were attempting to enter Greece, Italy, and Spain.

We have recently seen countries less willing to accept war refugees and economic migrants. Hungary and Poland have been adamant that they will not take immigrants.

Across the waters in the United States, refugees from violent areas such as are often found in nations like Honduras, El Salvador, Guatemala, and Nicaragua trudged across Mexico and illegally entered the United States. The Trump administration enacted a "get tough" and "zero tolerance" enforcement policy. In the past, families would be caught and released, only to try again. His unpopular policy of separating parents from children was soon reversed—but some children had been scattered around the country, and have not yet been reunited with their parents. The policy of "get tough" still stands, but families may not be separated in the future.

What are some options to these immigration problems? These might be considered singly or in combination.

> **To reduce the need to emigrate:**
* Pay young people to be sterilized in the Third World countries.
* Set up assembly plants in Third World to provide jobs.
* Encourage family-planning in Third World countries.
* Advanced countries could send in police and military to eliminate the criminal elements of the country or to take down the dictatorial government that allows cruelty to its citizens.
> **Allow the self-centered desires of the potential immigrants to supersede the society-based values of the potential host countries.**
> **To lessen the financial and political strain on the accepting country:**
* Allow only sterilized people to enter the country.
* Allow all immigrants to enter if they have a sponsor who guarantees to employ them and to pay all their expenses, including legal expenses if needed. A posted bond would be required.
* Accept only highly educated people such as: doctors, nurses, and engineers.
* Reduce the desires of potential immigrants to enter the country.

Few of these are palatable for a majority of potential immigrants, their governments, or the hoped-for host countries. Such actions will often cost the potential receiving country a great deal of money which they would rather spend on domestic programs—and armaments. In some of the options, the United Nations would be preferable to an individual country in attempting to eliminate the cause of the problems in the home countries.

According to an OECD migration report in June of 2018, the US has 43.7 million people born in other countries. This is 13.7% of the population. Mexico accounts for 26%, India for 5.6%, and China for 29%. Germany has 22% of its population with a foreign background, and has taken in 3 million immigrants in the last two years. Italy had 5 million foreign nationals registered in an increase of 21,000 in the year. 8.3% of the population one in five was under 19 and 40% were under 29.

CHAPTER 16   THE IMPOSSIBLE QUESTIONS FOR SOCIETY—AND THE UNPALATABLE ANSWERS

We are such creatures of tradition that thinking our way out of the paper bag is generally well-nigh impossible. But let's look or "re-look" at a few necessary ideas, such as those mentioned in the previous chapters.

SHOULD WE ADMIT THE REALITY OF THE DRIVE FOR POWER?

Power, based on our inferiorities, is an almost universal plague. It may be disguised by clerics and terrorists as religious. It may be disguised by political leaders as patriotism. It may be disguised by business leaders as free enterprise. It may be disguised by the generals as the need for security.

Developing the power to do socially useful things is essential to a person's psychological maturity, Sadly, too few develop this level of maturity, Many, if not most, of us are stuck with the need to show power over others, rather than moving on to our fullest potential, that which Abraham Maslow called "self-actualization" or meeting our "meta" (higher level) needs.

Some people evaluate just what they see as the cause of a problem. For example, with ISIS and Al Qaeda it is religion that is the cause of the terrorism. In spousal beatings, it is the person who was beaten who caused the situation. In bullying it is the immaturity of the bully that is the cause.

But the rationalizations that perpetrators give as the reasons for their actions are not enough of an explanation. Often, we can go beyond the obvious with philosophical or scientific tools to find the ultimate cause.

Most knowledgeable people will look a little deeper to find that exerting one's power is the reason. Street gang members obviously want to be superior to their rivals. Coaches want power over their teams. Business owners or managers want power over their employees. We see it in every criminal activity. Can you get away with shoplifting a dress? Can you get away with robbing a bank? Can you get away with picking a pocket? Can you get away with hacking a bank's financial records and take a million or so dollars for yourself?

But is the recognition that power is behind the religious, business, or criminal activities enough? Can we find the reasons for the drive for power? While we have talked about this before, it is so central to the theme of the book that we must do it again. Possibly in a more succinct form. Yes, the need to have power in our lives comes from the insecurities we felt as infants and toddlers—and even our inabilities to cooperate successfully with our world in many areas today. Do we have the job we want? The relationship we want? Are our children as successful as we had wanted to be?

As Alfred Adler told us, our inferiorities began in infancy when we could not walk, or talk, or even eat without assistance. It followed us through high school and even college when we found that we were not in control of our world. Still we remember making some progress. We had a job. We had a car. We were successful in sports. We were successful in educational pursuits. We were socially successful. But maybe there were some chinks in our armor! Perhaps we were not successful in all of these areas.

It all starts with parenting, and possibly even before that—in our genes! Parenting is probably the most difficult occupation in the world, yet we have no preparation for it other than our traditions and maybe a bit of common sense—a less than common blessing!

Perhaps we have dwelt too much on the negatives of power. Our drive for power over ourselves, our society, or our world, has produced the geniuses of our civilization. Power and the drive to escape our inferiorities is a necessity for our own positive psychological and educational potentials. Can you attend the university then learn and think your way toward enlightenment? Can you learn the skills necessary to accomplish the goals you set for yourself? Can you invent a better way to harness solar power? Can you invent a better operating system for computers? Can you think your way to a better form of government? Can you entice people to follow your ideas? (I recommend the video book "Finding Yourself in the Town of Geniuses" by Valentina Knurova. I suggest the e-book version.)

As we have earlier indicated, the cause of most power manifestations can be found in ineffective parenting, ineffective education, and a society that inhibits the equality of opportunity. This includes traditions that stifle or stimulate one's effort to succeed. When we look at the Chinese, Japanese, and Jewish youth we are more likely to find parental and traditional pressures to succeed academically. Sometimes these pressures and inferiorities result in suicide, but far more often they result in academic and professional success. This success is often denigrated by those whose parents expected little—and were rewarded by having their expectations fulfilled.

There are undoubtedly also genetic limits and potentials to overcoming our natural inferiorities.

MONEY IS THE SIMPLEST THING TO MEASURE AS A GAUGE FOR SUCCESS!

We can't measure courage. We can measure some kinds of intelligence reasonably well, but not as precisely as we can measure wealth or income. We cannot measure ethical behavior easily. We cannot measure happiness objectively. We cannot measure one's ability to be an effective parent. We can measure educational achievement somewhat, but not all supposedly educated people have the same amount of knowledge. We cannot measure one's ability to love. But we can look at their paychecks, their real estate, their securities, their jewels. And since it is measurable it must be of ultimate importance! Tax reductions must be good because they are measurable in terms of our wealth.

Wealth must be more important than happiness or love—because it is measurable.

SHOULD WE BELIEVE EMPIRICAL SCIENCE?

As we move from primitive people with our myths and traditions as the fog that clouds our spectacles, it is often difficult to look to the probabilities of science when they conflict with the certainties of our illusions. Yes, science deals with probabilities. A thousand years ago it was highly probable that the earth was flat and that the sun circled the Earth. As we developed more accurate measuring devices and intelligent curiosity we discovered that the earth was round. Then as we learned more we found that the earth is flattened at the poles. So the Earth is not round, but an oblate spheroid. As science developed our ability to fly, science found that flying nearer the pole is shorter than drawing a line on a globe from Paris to Los Angeles and following that path. The polar route was actually shorter.

By measuring the speed at which the universe is expanding, science could pinpoint the approximate date of the Big Bang. About 14 billion years ago, for the start of our universe. This is a bit different from the 6,000 years ago that Bishop Ussher determined as the time of creation. Of course, Bishop Ussher was calculating from the

Bible while the scientists were calculating from radio telescopes and other advanced instruments.

Science has given us nearly all the things we use today—cars and computers, satellites and smartphones, refrigerators and railroads, gaming and Google! Perhaps we should submit our long-held traditions to the same standard—of verifiable facts over unprovable faith.

WHAT ABOUT RELIGION?

Every society has its creation stories, its afterlife hopes, and its version of morality. Some, like the original teachings of the Buddha, are very simple and peaceful. Among the monotheistic religions, we can only give a pass to the Baha'i faith as being peaceful. The Catholics started the Crusades against the Muslims, with popes often giving indulgences to the Crusaders so that they would go directly to heaven if they were killed. Does this sound like the jihadists today?

Can you imagine Mohammed telling the Sunnis that it is okay to kill the Shias, or vice versa? Can you imagine Jesus telling the Catholics and Protestants that it was okay to kill each other in the 30 Years War? The prophets had quite different ideals than the popes, potentates and mega-church ministers.

Viktor Frankl believed that our most basic psychological need is to find meaning in our lives. Finding meaning in our lives would be most likely to be applied to the founders of those religions. Adler's and Nietzsche's ideas of power would be more likely to be found among the eventual leaders of the religions. Looking at ISIS and Al Qaeda we find the most repugnant uses of religious power that we have seen since the Catholic Crusades and the Inquisition. Having *THE* true religion, which seems to infect only the monotheists, excites the passions of power in those whose limited knowledge knows only what their mothers told them.

EQUALITY—ARE WE EQUAL?

From our "one-person, one-vote" democratic idea we have internalized the assumption that all people are somehow equal and deserving of equal rights. What is the basis for this idea? We are not the same size, sex, or color. We do not have the same level of intelligence, education, or work ethic.

We don't all have 46 chromosomes. We don't all have highly effective parenting. We don't all have equality of opportunity from the start of our lives.

Some, in the Western religions, would say that we have equal souls. And that is enough. But who has seen a soul? And not all theologians who believe in souls believe that they are equal. And no one can define "soul" so that it has a universally accepted meaning.

And certainly, no one has been able to produce a soul for us to examine. Is the Harvard mathematics graduate, with a doctorate from the University of Michigan, who became the youngest professor at the University of California at Berkeley, the equal to Sergey Brin who dropped out of the Stanford PhD program? Sergey, of course, was a co-founder of Google and is now worth over $45 billion. The Harvard graduate, Ted Kaczynski, is now serving a life sentence in prison for killing three people and injuring 23 others with this letter bombs. He is the "Unabomber."

Is Anders Breivik, who killed over 70 unarmed youth in Norway, the equal of Mother Teresa who saved thousands of orphans in Kolkata? Is Donald Trump the equal of Thomas Jefferson?

Remember that equal means exactly the same: 2=2, not 2.1. But since no two people are exactly equal, how much equality difference would you have in your ideal society?

Are all voters equally aware of the significant issues that they will be deciding? If not, might a better democracy weigh the votes differently? Should the Nobel prize-winning economist have more votes than the high school dropout? But that's not democracy!

This idea of a universal equality of people often brings us the ideas that:

☐ There should be no capital punishment,

☐ When prejudice exists, we should have affirmative action to remedy it,

☐ All potential parents will love their children equally,

☐ Fetuses with severe genetic defects should be born, even though their care will cost society millions of dollars---and their parents may not want them,

☐ If provided free education all children will have equally competent teachers and equally small classes,

☐ Everyone's opinion is valid even if it is counter to the facts,

☐ One's personal beliefs, however counter to empirical facts, are deserving of protection even if they run counter to the goals of a society.

EQUALITY VERSUS LIBERTY—WHAT ABOUT THE LAW?

Americans often think that because the Declaration of Independence says that "all men are created equal" that this is fundamental to American law. But the Declaration of Independence is not a law, it is merely a call to revolution against the King of England. Whenever people want to revolt, they always use the call that we are all equal. However, after the revolution it is liberty that is the fundamental of their constitutions.

In the original Constitution, the equality of people is not mentioned. "Equal" is only mentioned relative to voting by Congressmen and those in the Electoral College. It is not until the 14th Amendment that "equal" is mentioned relative to people, and there it speaks only to citizens of the United States having equal protection of the laws—not being actually equal in every sense.

It is one thing to say that we have equal rights, another to say that we should aim for equality of opportunity—but the actual quality of life of people is never addressed by modern governments. If we are not actually equal, do we have the right to expect wages beyond our value to a company? Do we have the right to:

➢ Subsidized housing,

➢ Food stamps,

➢ Avoid capital punishment,

➢ Collect retirement benefits beyond what we have contributed,

➢ Medical care if we have not paid for it?

If we are equal, what is it that makes us equal? It is not our genes. It is not our accomplishments. It is not our intelligence.

We return to those religious people who say that we have equal souls. But of course, we can't see a soul, so should that non-verifiable belief be a basis for law in a society that theoretically has a separation of church and state? Do we take the view that—in order to keep the society functioning efficiently, we should not let the economic inequalities become too diverse.

When economic inequalities become too great, and the differences in power become too extreme, you have the essential ingredients for revolution. While in earlier days it might be against the king, today it may be against the self-perpetuating legislators and executives—we see this in the populist movements today in many democratic countries. Perhaps tomorrow it will be against those who perch atop our monetary mountains.

In the French Declaration of the Rights of Man and the Citizen, "equal" is mentioned three times, but only in terms of equal rights. Here are Articles 1 and 6:

1. Men are born free and remain free and equal in rights. Social distinctions can be based only on public utility.

6. Law is the expression of the general will. All citizens have the right to take part personally, or by their representatives, and its formation. It must be the same for all, whether it protects or punishes. All citizens, being equal in its eyes, are equally eligible to all public dignities, places, and employments, according to their capacities, and without other distinction than that of their virtues and talents.

The West has moved considerably toward the idea that we are equal or at least have equal needs. Universal healthcare, the abolition of capital punishment, the right to assisted suicide, minimum wages, adequate pensions, food stamps, subsidized housing and other programs indicate at least some essence of equality permeating our societies.

On the other hand, liberty, even if it runs counter to the best interests of society, has brought us: gun rights, unlimited free speech rights, legalized alcohol and marijuana, huge tax breaks for the rich, the elimination of inheritance taxes, and many other perks for our individual freedom.

HOW IMPORTANT SHOULD A LIFE BE?

We generally hold our own lives as being all-important, except for the one million who have chosen suicide every year in our world. We who are mentally and physically healthy and enjoying our lives may think that everyone should be like us. It is a human trait to assume that everyone thinks like me. But what about: those who want to die such as: the terminally ill, those living with excruciating pain, prisoners serving life sentences who would prefer death, martyrs who want paradise now?

Very few of us will be remembered a thousand years from now. Possibly Einstein and Hitler will make the list. Possibly Neil Armstrong. But at the rate that we are making weapons of mass destruction and power-driven depots, our civilization may not make another millennium. I wonder what the odds in Vegas are for us ending our non-thinking run as *homo sapiens.* We certainly wouldn't be the first species to bite the dust!

I like being around, but should my desire for life be extended to those who want to die or to those who make life miserable for others, like: serial killers, slave traders, political despots, tax dodgers, burglars, or members of my favorite team who lost the big game?

SHOULD WE ALLOW CAPITAL PUNISHMENT?

Most Western societies frown on capital punishment because everyone has a right to life. In 2016, the US executed twenty men. But we don't universally oppose death to our other citizens. We allow our soldiers to be put in harm's way to be injured or killed in foreign countries, even if there is no declaration of war. We may even draft people who do not want to fight and send them off to possibly be killed. We allow nearly unlimited gun ownership even though guns are used in over 21,000 suicide deaths, 3,800 more died of accidental shootings, and 11,000 more in homicides. But in America we won't outlaw guns. Apparently, convicted murderers are more valuable to society than those citizens who don't want to die!

Should we outlaw skydiving? Forty-two skydivers died last year. Should we outlaw high school sports? Ten or twelve athletes in the various sports are killed annually. Should we outlaw motorcycles? More than 4,000 motorcycle deaths occurred last year. Motorcycles comprise 1% of the vehicles but cause 15% of the deaths. Last year we had more than 50,000 drug overdose deaths—but golly!, we already outlawed many of those drugs.

The best argument I have heard for outlawing capital punishment was from Clinton Duffy, the retired warden of San Quentin Prison in California. He said that the legal appeals offered to death row inmates was more expensive than keeping them locked up for life. The question, of course, then is—are the appeal expenses worth the cost to society? So every answer brings a new question. Where are you Socrates, now that we need you?

SHOULD THE REALITY OF OVERPOPULATION BE A CONCERN?

As mentioned several times before, overpopulation is the major problem of the world. It is the cause of global warming, with more people using air and water polluting substances. It is the cause of the plastic garbage that fills our seas. It is the cause of the rapid depletion of irreplaceable natural resources. It is the scourge of planet Earth. But it is more than the destruction of land, water and air. It affects our humanity and our societies.

The fact that with more people and fewer jobs there are more social problems, especially with men, who cannot find acceptable means to positively express their drives for power. We see the war refugees and economic and political emigrants boarding overcrowded boats in Turkey and Libya hoping that the welfare states of the European Union will welcome them, and they did. But with over a half million per year seeking asylum, and with the overwhelming numbers being Muslim, the Christian and non-religious Europeans encountered people with widely different traditions. Prejudice by the natives often followed. Resentment by the newcomers was the normal reaction. Educated immigrants often found themselves in low level jobs, if they could even find jobs. And an infinitesimal number became major terrorists.

In the US, we see this in youth gangs, where the Crips and Bloods, numbering about 35,000 members nationally each, and the MS-13's numbering about 10,000 nationally, create huge societal problems. All these started in Los Angeles. Then of course you have Hispanic gangs and Southeast Asian gangs and of course, white gangs including such groups as Aryan Nation and various alt-right groups like the neo-Nazis and the KKK. Recent estimates are that 40% of gang members are white. Looking internationally, we have a number of jihadist groups like: Boko Haram, ISIS, Al Qaeda, Salafia and about a hundred more. But these are only some of the big groups. Boys and girls, men and women need something to show they are worthwhile and accepted.

With the major gangs, it is not only the violence of murder and rape that gives them power, it is the pursuit of money. Prostitution, drug manufacturing and sales, extortion and protection, robbery, and now even cyber-crime, bring cash and flash—the nearly universally prized accoutrements of power.

There seems to be no way to find a legal, economically satisfactory, and psychologically rewarding place in society for every male and female in the world—or in our country. Artificial intelligence, robots and other inventions are replacing humans while humans are reproducing like rabbits.

What to do?

SHOULD WE PREPARE POTENTIAL PARENTS FOR PARENTING?

Parenting is simple! If you believe that, I have a Caribbean island paradise I can sell you for $10. Parenting may even be thought to be easier than conceiving, but maybe not as much fun!

But looking around, there seem to be some people in the world who did not receive the love and understanding, the proper food, the proper education, or many of the other things that make a parent successful and the child feel adequate.

In other important jobs, like being president, there are lots of experts at your beck and call. As a parent, you may have neighbors to confer with, but they probably are no more aware than you of the necessary physical and mental needs of your infants, toddlers, teenagers—or thirty-somethings! You may be lucky enough to have your parents to rely on, but they raised you—and you don't have all the answers!

If we are going to have the best society possible, should parents be prepared for the inevitable? Can they recognize physical and mental illness? Can they feed their children properly? Do they know the essential developmental tasks that each of us needs to master at every age in order to be fully functioning adults?

(See: Erik Erikson's "Childhood and Society" in which he lists a set of necessary tasks we must confront and conquer. Then have a look at Robert Havighurst's summary tasks of developing maturity at: https://www.psychologynoteshq.com/development-tasks/)

Or should we just leave it to chance?

PART IV WHAT CAN BE DONE

For every problem, education seems to be the solution. If a person is a skeptic on climate change, maybe their opinion can be changed if they are exposed to all of the facts. If there are problems with our government, perhaps more people should be made aware of the problems and possibly help to find solutions to them. There is so much to know today but we are handicapped by our tradition of education developed 200 years ago by people who were not educated in modern science, world history, logic, or the possibilities of the Internet and other modern necessities.

We have gone beyond the days when the maxims of education were:
> It doesn't matter what they learn--as long as they don't like it!
> Latin and geometry discipline the mind.
> Spare the rod and spoil the child!

Let us take a quick look at what is and what could be--in terms of education for the 21st-century.

Education, as important as it is, sits pretty close to the back burner— when we compare it with the areas in our lives that are really essential to our lives. Tax reduction and pro football are much more important. Then there are the other essentials of our society, such as preventing abortion. Every society needs more unloved children. They add significantly to the existing drug abusers, bullies, criminals and future child abusers. And while the Scriptures don't mention abortion—it is merely an oversight, and God will correct it as soon as He re-reads what His prophets have written.

School children and college students cannot afford lobbyists, so they will lose out to business interests, religious interests, and the American Association of Retired People! Another reason to keep spending on education low is that if we really educate our children, few current legislators would be voted in.

But if any modern government is to succeed and survive, it will need an educated population. Most of the developed world is ahead of our American and British pillars of democracy in their education achievement. You can see the disastrous results in our recent elections.

We must make quality education available to all. Each of us should have been educated for citizenry and for understanding and appreciation our world and what it has to offer. Recently we have tended to focus only on our vocational education needs—medicine, plumbing, teaching, auto mechanics, business, apparel design, engineering and IT, and lawyering. Our vocational education is much more complicated than it was a few years ago, what with computerization, new technologies—such as lasers, 3D printing, and artificial intelligence. Likewise, our world is being expanded in both problems and knowledge.

We need to rethink our school curricula, our methodology, our school organization models, the extension of the school day and year, and the number of years needed. Four years of college was once the standard. Many universities in Europe have decreased it to three. Learning about the world and how to function intelligently in it was pretty much the extent of higher education two centuries ago. Today, with few exceptions, the focus of higher education is to produce adults who can work effectively in a small slice of one section of the world's myriad of vocations and jobs.

We will now take a look at what is, both the many minuses and the few plusses of modern education, then we will look at some suggested ways to go in our future educational planning for an effective democracy.

THREATS TO DEMOCRACY

People who want to lead a nation or to vote intelligently for representatives need much more information today than ever before. We need an extensive knowledge of world history, macroeconomics, natural science, biological science, the theory of science, philosophy of religion, comparative religions, political science, along with some knowledge of psychology and sociology and an understanding of ethics and logic. Armed with a strong background in basic knowledge we can then effectively criticize or agree with propositions that are proposed to us by candidates want to run our governments. ***BUT WHERE ARE WE IN AMERICA?***

We have already mentioned the poor showing of American high school students in the international PISA testing. American adults are at least as poorly educated. In a number of recent studies United States adults have been found to be on the bottom, or near the bottom, of advanced countries in both their literacy and in their mathematic abilities. In a major OPEC study, summarized by US Department of Education in "Adult Education and Assessment Scores: a Cross-national Comparison," (2017) there were various comparisons between high school dropouts, high school graduates, and those with two years of college, in 22 countries ranging from: Japan, Korea, and Australia to Western Europe, Canada and the US. The US rated very low. It was 14th in problem-solving, 19th in literacy, 19th in numeracy. The US was behind England and Russia in all three measurements but it was ahead of Turkey and Israel in all three.

On the literacy scale used in this survey, with a perfect score being 350--Japan was 296, US was 270. On the numeracy scale with a top possible score of 350 Japan was 288, the US was 253. On the problem-solving scale with a top of 75 Japan was 36, Sweden and New Zealand were at 44, the US was at 31. A study from 2012 with the same participating countries, showed US was 21st in literacy and last in numeracy. The UK was also near the bottom. Korea was number one and Japan and the Netherlands. were second and third.

Americans with two years of college were about equal to other countries participants who also had two years of college.

In a survey of countries relative to college graduation rates, Russia had the highest percentage with 58 percent. Switzerland had 49%, the UK 42% and the US 36%.

The relatively low rates of literacy, numeracy, and problem solving, coupled with the low college graduation rate gives us a pretty good indication of why Americans are such easy targets for trolls and bots, fake news, and propaganda. Americans must learn that, just because you hear it or see it--it does not have to be true. Purported facts need to be checked for validity, how does it correspond with truth. It must be evaluated in terms of its semantic signification-- exactly what do the words in the message actually mean.

So the real problem is not what Twitter or Facebook did or did not do, the problem is that the United States is one of the least intelligent and informed nations in the developed world. We aren't good at processing and analyzing information. If America is to be made great again, wouldn't education be the logical place to start? If Donald Trump thinks that making steel and aluminum is a national security issue, what about having educated soldiers and sailors? What about having the best engineers and information technology specialists?

This poor level of education is seen as being responsible for Americans often believing in the information in bots (web robots) that automatically repeat the message many times, or trolls (people who attempt to influence behavior or thinking, often through fake news or untruths).

➢Because so many Americans are very low in their educational achievement, they are prime candidates for unsubstantiated opinions and non-verified information, such as is found in: fake news, fake history, and the opinions of pundits on the media.

➢Varying studies and polls have found that in 14 states there are some schools still teaching creationism, while they collect tax dollars for their curricula.

➢34% of Americans do not believe in evolution, and believe that humans have existed since the earth was formed. (A Pew survey.)

➢Slightly over half of Republicans, and also viewers of Fox News, believe that Americans found weapons of mass destruction in Iraq after their invasion.

➢11% of Clinton voters thought that Barack Obama was born in Kenya,

➢18% of her voters believed that vaccines cause autism,

➢More Americans can name the Three Stooges (a 1940s comedy team), than can identify the three branches of government,

➢77% of Americans could name two of the seven dwarves in Snow White, but only 24% could name two Supreme Court judges,

➢Only 25% can name more than one of the five freedoms in the First Amendment to the Constitution. Only one in a thousand could name them all, but 22% could name all five of the Simpson family members.

Might you assume that their elementary or secondary school citizenship lessons were somewhat lacking? And what about general knowledge? The Rumanian troll's message that the Pope had endorsed Donald Trump in the presidential election, was retweeted nearly a million times. What intelligent person could have believed such a ridiculous story?

But it is more than elections that we need to worry about. In Texas, a Russian troll generated turnouts on both sides of an issue and attempted to have both sides resort to violence.

Whether our lack of ability to discern truth from falsity comes from: our poor educations, our scant attention to legitimate media, the opinions of friends, or wishful thinking-- if democracy is to survive, we need intelligent voters. If the avalanche of evidence is clear that we are woefully lacking in the knowledge of the issues and the ability to discern truth from falsity.

There are so many questions, we can't address them all—so we will list some in the next chapters. You take it from there!

CHAPTER 17.   WHERE ARE WE TODAY IN EDUCATION? WHO CONTROLS EDUCATION IN THE US

As everyone knows universal education was not even thought of in the days that the Constitution's writers toiled in Philadelphia. The education for most "y'ung uns" was in learning how to farm or in apprenticeships in the various trades that were necessary in colonial America. However, in the 1630s in Massachusetts a few schools were formed-- and at least one was public and supported by local taxes. Harvard College was also started at this time. Early education was primarily about learning how to read, especially the Bible, and learning arithmetic. The colleges were largely religiously owned and were often for training ministers. Doctors were generally trained in apprenticeships.

Education was nearly always privately financed, so was not available to everyone. Universal public education received great impetus when Horace Mann, the Secretary of Education for Massachusetts in 1837, desired to pursue free public education like the Germans were doing. By 1900 thirty of the 45 states had laws requiring primary education. Only four southern states were among them. By 1918 every state required children to complete elementary school.

Education has always been a state and local responsibility in the US. This is because the 10th Amendment to the Constitution gives power to the states for all activities not granted to the federal government by the Constitution. Each state sets curriculum standards for its students. Each local district determines what will be taught and who will teach it within the curriculum of the state. A school district may be so small that it contains only one elementary school or it can be as large as New York or Los Angeles and control hundreds of schools.

There are many factors that seem to come into play when we look at what is wrong with education at the different levels.

LOCAL AND STATE GOVERNANCE INCREASES EXPENSES AND COMMONLY DECREASES QUALITY

Local, and even state-level, politically appointed boards of education may not be competent to determine curriculum in all grades and in every course. County, state, and local control, needlessly increase and duplicate overlapping services. Curriculum and financial specialists at every level needlessly increase the administrative costs.

California provides instruction and support services for roughly six million students in grades kindergarten through twelve in more than 10,000 schools throughout the state. The total system includes: of 58 county offices of education, more than 1,000 local school districts, and more than 1,000 charter schools. What are the chances that the student in Palo Alto, in the heart of Silicon Valley will have the same educational opportunities as a student in the ghetto of Watts?

CHARTER SCHOOLS

There has been a great deal of advocacy for charter schools. It seems to be the only concern of the Secretary of Education of the United States under Donald Trump, Betsy De Vos. But she is not alone in her position. A former Los Angeles mayor and candidate for Governor of California was backed by many millions of dollars from pro-charter school interests. Who were opposed by the teachers' unions of California. Congress, however, has not followed these ideas.

The pros and cons of charter schools are extensive. The existing private schools, particularly the Catholic and other religious schools, would like to be funded by state tax money. In the case of religious schools, there is always the question of how much of a separation between church and state is required under Constitution. (Congress shall make no law respecting an establishment of religion or prohibiting the free exercise thereof, . . .)

But with the Supreme Court having five Roman Catholics and one who was raised Catholic and is now an Episcopalian, the Catholic Church has strong allies on the Court. The three Jews on the court might also be persuaded to vote for religious charter schools since there are nearly a thousand Jewish schools in the US, accounting for about 6% of all private schools. About 40% of private schools are Catholic and another 40% are operated by other religions. A little over 20% are nondenominational private schools.

Sharing the tax money collected for the public schools with religious or private charter schools, and perhaps even with people who are home-schooling their children, will either greatly increase the taxes needed to support all of the schools or will result in far less money for the public schools. (Trump has pledged, but not budgeted, for $20 million for school vouchers from federal funds.) This would average 40 cents per student. This would not go too far in reducing the $10,000 to $12,000 per year cost per student. Would state tax money be required to make up the difference? If so, it would require $50 to $60 billion in additional state taxes to help to fund schools to which parents voluntarily send their children.

There are 50 million students from kindergarten through high school. Five million are in private schools. If school vouchers are approved, state taxes for education will have to be raised 10% or public schools will have their budgets cut by 10%.

The public schools will be forced to continue to take nearly all of the special needs students, who are more expensive to educate. Few private schools will take students with special needs. Additionally, the more highly trained and more experienced teachers will be in the public schools and not available to the students of the private schools. Teachers in private schools are less likely to have a teaching credential, which is essential for teaching in public schools.

Since there are no requirements in most states for credentialing of home-school teachers or private school teachers, a parent may not be aware of the differences in teaching abilities. The private school teacher in an elementary school might have a high school diploma and some college. But it would not be necessary. On the other hand, in the high school, the teachers may have master's degrees or even doctorates. What they may not have are the teaching methods courses that increase their ability to get across the information that they have. Additionally, without courses in educational psychology, it is unlikely that they would understand the various psychological stages that students must traverse toward mature adulthood.

<u>For the students</u>, the needs are not only the academic background necessary for: an intelligent life, an adequate social life, and a life that is purposeful and societally useful. This should result in a happy lifetime. While the modern requirements for language, math, and science are essential to the curriculum of any school, extracurricular activities, including athletics, can go a long way to developing a confident, socially competent, and well-rounded citizen. Some private schools have athletic programs, often limited to: soccer, volleyball, basketball, tennis, and softball.

<u>For the parents</u>, the goal of a college education is often primary, but the development of a happy and confident child is important. Not everyone will profit from a

college education. Bill Gates, Richard Branson, and Mark Zuckerberg, seem to be living happy and productive lives without a college diploma!

Since in the US, the parents are ultimately in charge of the education of their children, they will have the final say on where their kids go to school. But who is a real winner in this charter school battle? The existing private and religious schools and the mult-millionaire capitalists who would like a mouthful of that tax money. Some of the federal tax credits for charter schools were cut with the Trump tax bill, but they are still available in many states.

STATE AND FEDERAL FUNDING FOR EDUCATION

In spite of the remarkable comeback of the economy after the recession of 2008, most states have not restored the funding that was cut to fight the recession. During the last 10 years, elementary and secondary school funding has significantly decreased.

Arizona is down over 36%, Florida and Alabama down over 20%, in fact about 30 of the states are below their prior funding. According to the OECD figures, the US is down 4% since the recession while other countries have averaged a 5% per student increase. In Turkey the spending rose by 76%, in Israel by 36%, in the UK by 32%.

The same is true for public higher education, which is down $9 billion from its 2008 level. Only two states spend more on higher education now than they did before the recession in 2007. North Dakota is up 38% and Alaska 6%. All others were between zero and Louisiana's minus 41%, Alabama is down 39% (not counting their football coach who makes over $11 million a year), Pennsylvania is down 37% (and their football coach earns only $4.6 million), and South Carolina down 36% (and their football coach makes $8.5 million). We Americans know what is important!

We must have our circuses. The ringmasters of college football and basketball coaches, pro athletes and their coaches, actors, and video game developers all should be paid more than our governors, our teachers, or even our president. Who cares about how we are governed—as long as we are entertained!

Well I guess that spending on prisons, football coaches, and making tax cuts will have more positive effects for the country than spending on quality elementary, secondary, and university education. The people who run the top businesses of America already have enough money to send their kids to the best schools-- so why worry?

In California, the budget for higher education, the highly-rated University of California and the state university system, has been reduced from 15% to 9% while prison spending has increased from 3% to 10%. To keep a prisoner for a year costs $75,000. Tuition at Stanford or Harvard is about $45,000 per year. Tuition and all living expenses at the University of California is a shade over $30,000. For the good of society, where is the money better spent?

PRISONS OR SCHOOLS—WHAT DO WE NEED MORE?

Prison guards must have a high school education. Prison guard salaries are from $51,600 to $84,000 plus overtime at time and a half. Retirement is 2.5% of the final salary times the number of years worked at 57, or later.

California teachers must have 4 to 5 years of college education. Starting salaries are about $41,000 with top salaries at around $90,000 if they have a master's degree and a large number of additional college courses and have been employed 10 to 13 years. At age 65 they multiply the number of years they have taught by 2.4.

So prison guards do not need a college education, can start their careers at an earlier age, start at a higher salary than a teacher, can work a great deal of overtime, and can retire eight years earlier with a higher multiple for each year worked. Way to go, California!

As it stands now, if teachers want more salary and a higher retirement they need to go into the administration of the schools. If we want to get greater learning in the classroom, perhaps we should have pay scales in which teachers can make as much or more than administrators. And perhaps we should look at the pay scales of other public occupations to determine whether or not teachers should be paid more than Highway Patrol officers, correctional officers, sanitation workers and other necessary public servants. The question is: do we want quality education, and if so, how are we willing to pay for it.

When you have political appointees controlling curriculum at the state level, and elections for boards of education at the local level, you may not have qualified people with broad experience in education making the decisions.

Some years ago, I moved to a rural area in California. One of my friends there was a longtime member of the board of education and often its president. When I first moved there, the district had only one elementary school. By the time I left, it had six elementary schools, two middle schools and two high schools. The population had changed from a rural middle class population to a suburban upper social class population. There were some rich people, too. Three neighbors were Ronald Reagan, and actors Charlie Sheen and Kelsey Grammer (Fraser).

My friend, the school board member, was a high school graduate who worked in construction and got all of his news and political views from Rush Limbaugh. Because he was a longtime stalwart of the community he could continually be elected to the school board. Was he qualified?

A few years ago, the Texas Board of Education required that creationism be taught along with evolutionary theory in biology classes. The science teachers fought it. In April of 2017 the Board finally eliminated the requirement to "evaluate" competing theories of science and evolution. Science teachers are now allowed to teach science.

Only the United States has local control of education through the secondary level. There is a better way, but it wasn't known at the time that the Constitution was written.

MIGHT THERE BE A BETTER WAY?

As mentioned earlier, Singapore's educational system finds its PISA (Program for International Student Assessment) scores for: science, reading and mathematics number one in the world in all three categories for 15 year olds--in the 72 countries measured. The US was: 25th in science, 24th in reading, and 40th in math. The UK was: 15th, 22nd, and 27th. This should tell us something. If Vietnam was 8th in science and Estonia was 9th in math and 6th in reading—then the US and UK are doing a lot of things wrong, or ineffectively. But in the US to modernize education it requires a constitutional amendment—or individual states could opt to join a federal system—if Congress would allow it.

Among the other countries that did better than the US were:

In reading: Singapore was first, Estonia was 6th, Slovenia was 14th, and the United Kingdom was 22nd.

In mathematics: Singapore was number one, Estonia 9th, Finland 13th and the UK 27th.

In science: Estonia was third, Finland 5th, Vietnam was 8th. China 10th, the UK was 15th.

If America is to be made great again, as President Trump has promised, we need to start with better education, not with opening more coal mines.

DEVELOP NATIONAL CURRICULA AND REDUCE LOCAL CONTROL

Nationwide curricula in most countries seems to be more effective. Professionals are generally far more knowledgeable about the present and future needs of society than are local politicians.

As it is, each school district needs to hire curriculum specialists to suggest and oversee the educational potential of the local students. With a national program, specialists could be hired for each level of education, such as fifth grade history or introductory chemistry in high school. These specialists could provide detailed lesson plans as well as audio and visual aids to supplement the lessons. This would make it easier for the teacher, who would not have to develop comprehensive lesson plans but could add to or delete portions that might not be appropriate for his or her students.

Naturally, the old self-centered values creep in, and the top-flight schools are concerned about being brought down to a lower level. This is a legitimate concern. While it would be impossible to bring every school in the country up to the academic level that we find in some schools in California, Massachusetts, and New York, there are undoubtedly students in other school districts with extremely high potentials who are being held back by the lack of local money which often results in poorer quality teachers, poorer quality technology, and larger class sizes.

If we had federal financing of all education it might be possible to allow local financial input into schools to supplement the federal financing.

ELEMENTARY SCHOOL TEACHER EDUCATION

Presently, a university student studying elementary education would often major in "multidisciplinary studies" while taking some courses in teaching methods. They would probably take: one class in how to teach mathematics, one class in how to teach health, one class in how to teach music, one class and how to teach English, one class in how to teach reading, etc. A problem is that teaching math in the first grade requires quite different skills and competencies than teaching math in the fifth grade. The same is true for teaching: health, physical science, biological science, reading, history, geography, physical education, etc.

The local nature of the school districts also crimps school budgets holding teacher salaries lower thereby reducing the attractiveness of the vocation. In the US, the average teacher comes from the lower 20% of college graduates. In Finland, they come from the top 10%. America also has a way of increasing administrative bureaucrats in the schools and in the district offices, giving them higher wages, more months of paid work, far higher pensions--thus making administration financially far more desirable for those who have been effective, or even ineffective, teachers.

As it now exists, there are curriculum specialists in nearly every district. Large districts will have a number of such specialists. Each state, and most counties, will have its own set of curriculum specialists as well as its own Board of Education. So, there is a huge amount of duplication in terms of both the curriculum to be offered and the curriculum specialists who are supposed to help the teachers. My own experience was that when teaching in high school or middle school I never saw a curriculum specialist, nor had any communication from them.

So, using a national curriculum with national curriculum specialists, a higher level of assistance for the teacher would be possible. Additionally, since there is so much overlap, the local and county, and even the state, curriculum specialists of today could be sent back to the classrooms which would reduce class sizes. So there are numerous advantages to a national education program. As we have seen of late, some appointees to the national executive branch of our government want to impose their own simplistic ideas to a very complicated national priority. The education system should therefore be separate from both the administrative and legislative branches in order to avoid the often irrational political motives of those who are temporarily in power.

CLASS SIZES MAY BE TOO LARGE

There is an old saying in education that real education would be Horace Mann sitting on one end of the log with the student at the other end. This one-to-one fantasy may work with your own children, but is seldom practical in our education system below the doctoral level.

I remember talking to a high school history teacher at one of the two "worst" gang infested high schools in the Los Angeles District. I said, "It must be terrible." "Not all," he said, "25 of the 35 students registered in the class cut every class. It is a great teaching situation. I have only eager students in every class."

Class size in Los Angeles is about 26 students in primary school and 35 to 40 in high school. Rich districts usually have fewer. Singapore by contrast has about 20 students per teacher at both levels.

TEACHERS MAY NOT BE WELL PREPARED

When we take our average teachers from the lowest quarter of their graduating class holding only a bachelor's degree, while the Finns take theirs from the top 10%--and require a masters' degree, we may have cause to worry.

We have all sorts of education programs in America. Most universities will offer majors in education. We have very low ranked colleges producing teachers and we have the very top level colleges and universities offering education majors. In some cases, prospective elementary teachers take a major in "multidisciplinary studies." This gives them a little bit of each area that they might teach, but does not really prepare them for teaching in every grade level effectively.

Some universities do not take education majors until we have graduated from a university in some major. UCLA does this. It has a two-year master's program. So we might expect graduates of such programs to be exceptionally well-trained. While in Finland, a person holding a master's degree has five years of university studies. In schools like UCLA, the teacher would have six years. Graduates of the top schools, such as: Harvard, Stanford, UCLA, University of Wisconsin, University of Pennsylvania, and Columbia are probably several cuts above their European peers. Consequently, we have a huge range in competencies of the students, and of the universities, in America.

Tuition at the top universities generally costs $16-$50,000 per year. When beginning teachers make well under $50,000 you can understand why many cannot avail themselves of this higher level of education. And many would not be qualified even if they had the money. If America wants better education, perhaps we should grant scholarships to the most promising teachers. If we want better healthcare, perhaps we should grant scholarships to promising medical students. But this is not the way that our "business-oriented society" generally operates. There is certainly something to be said for free college education. Many countries have it.

The State of California requires a test for all new teachers, the CBEST. It is a very simple test for prospective teachers in the areas of math, reading, and writing. And some of them fail! Here is a sample question from the math test:

Which of the following is the most appropriate unit for expressing the length of a pencil?

__inches __feet__yards __miles__meters

I'll bet that didn't take more than an hour to figure out!

Here's one from the writing test:

_____ James had a lot of experience in HR, he hadn't actually done any firing before.

Choose the best word to fill in the blank.

1. Despite

2. When

3. Although

4. Because

My goodness you're smart! Wanna teach in California?

Just kidding California teachers—I was one of you for forty years. And I have seen far more outstanding teachers than incompetents! But there are some who shouldn't be allowed in a classroom. And I recently learned that there are now exceptions for those who fail the CBEST---many are still allowed to teach.

TEACHERS ARE NOT RESPECTED

We have some real problems in American education. Teachers are not respected like they are in most other countries. In Finland, South Korea, Japan and Singapore a teacher is held in high regard. This is worth something! Money isn't everything! You remember the concern for overcoming our inferiority complexes in Part I of this work—esteem is critical.

TEACHERS ARE OFTEN UNDERPAID

New York spends over $20,000 per student, California about $12,000, Mississippi about $9000, and Utah about $7000. The average is about $12,500 per student per year. This translates to beginning teachers' salaries of $25,000 to $40,000 and average salaries of $40,000 to $75,000. The same as for plumbers and firefighters—which don't require five years of university.

We should give a little thought to what should be valued in our society—education, plumbing, prisoner guarding, or firefighting.

MERIT PAY

Since all teachers are exactly equal in their abilities to educate students, they should all be paid exactly the same. This seems to be the position of teacher unions. But we all know that teachers are not the same. The question is should they be paid better if there are better teachers?

Singapore, which leads the world in the international PISA scores, does give merit pay. The question is, who is to decide? Traditionally the principal or college president decides. But often this is based on the teacher's relationship to the boss.

In college, students often evaluate a professor after the semester. The problem here seems to be that the teachers who are easy graders or funny are most likely to be given the highest evaluations. Perhaps if major evaluations were done 10 or 15 years after the experience with the teacher, a more objective evaluation could be secured. The teacher who was the hard taskmaster may have proved to be more valuable in the student's adult life.

There should probably be some kind of merit pay for teachers and administrators in which the great teacher can make a higher salary than a mediocre administrator. Is this blasphemy for teacher unions—because all teachers are equal? You probably noticed that equality in your own education. Every teacher was exactly the same, and you learned exactly the same amount from every teacher you ever had.

TEACHER RECRUITMENT

Various recent reports indicate that while Singapore, Finland, and South Korea hire teachers from the top third of the graduating classes, US gets only 23% of its teachers from the top 30% of graduates. Poverty schools get only 14% from the top 30% of graduates.

In addition to this, teacher training schools can vary from extremely low quality to extremely high quality in the hundreds of universities in the US. The entrance requirements to a university can also vary from nonexistent to a high SAT score and outstanding grades from high school. Probably no other discipline has such wide variations in both the quality of the applying student--and the quality of the academic major.

In New York City, a beginning teacher starts at $45,000 while a beginning lawyer starts at $160,000. Nationally teacher salaries average about $39,000 raising to an average maximum of $67,000. In South Korea the salaries range from $55,000 beginning to a maximum of $155,000. In Singapore teacher pay ranges from $24,000 to $96,000, then they can receive $3,000 to $23,000 additional in bonuses. I guess in teaching, as in other fields, you get what you pay for! Do we really want to make America great again?

The combination of low pay and questionable academic credentials often results in low prestige for many teachers, particularly at the elementary level. By contrast, in Finland teachers are held in high regard, as they should be since they are from the top 10% of college graduates and all have at least a master's degree. Additionally, only 10% who apply for teaching positions are accepted. In prestige, teachers are held in higher regard than doctors or lawyers.

Several factors are necessary to recruit people for necessary jobs. Not necessarily in order are: prestige, initial salary, top salary, working conditions, and peripheral positives. These possible positives might include: a pleasant working environment, more vacation time, sabbatical leaves, a substantial pension, smaller class sizes, supportive administrators, a pleasant classroom atmosphere without disruptive students, adequate teaching supplies (computers, tablets, books, audiovisual aids, etc.).

Prestige will not come until it is earned. Some of the other perks cost money. Still others, such as the removal of disruptive students, require administrative courage and the option to transfer students. Two administrators transferring their most disruptive students will generally find that the positives outweigh the negatives. The disruptive student finds himself in an unfamiliar environment with no friends to appreciate his disruptive antics.

There is a big teaching shortage in the US. Many districts are going outside the country, such as the Philippines, to staff their schools. Might more students be interested in teaching if college were free for future teachers? Might more quality students be enticed into the field if their workplaces were more enjoyable and they had the best tools with which to teach? Today, many are lacking textbooks!

IMPROVING THE LEVEL OF PROSPECTIVE TEACHERS

One major report laid out a way to attract a number of high level graduates to enter the teaching profession at the elementary and secondary levels. While 14% of the top third of college graduates now go into teaching in poverty school, it is proposed that the number could be increased to 34%, by raising pay. This would cost about $66 million for each state. Giving scholarships or forgiving loans would be another way. Providing performance bonuses of up to 20% would be another way.

The report suggests that 68% of new teachers could come from the top third of college graduates if they would raise the starting pay to $68,000 per year, while offering a maximum pay of $150,000.

In the US, teacher education has been largely spent in college classroom instruction, but in many industrialized countries teachers are given more time to work with other teachers in apprenticeships.

It is difficult, if not impossible, to compare countries. Singapore has 23,000 teachers while America has 3.3 million. There are also far more differences in the United States when we compare impoverished rural students in Alabama with the largely urban areas of Singapore. There are also huge differences in the ethnic makeup of Americans, as well as in the educational background of the parents.

TEACHER RETENTION

Because of the aforementioned negatives for American teachers, 14% drop out of the profession every year in the US—with a 20% drop out rate in high-poverty schools. Teacher attrition in Singapore is 3% and it is 1% in South Korea.

While it would be nice if we took our teachers from the highest levels of our universities as is done in so many of the higher achieving countries. The number of administrators at every level of school and college in America is far more than what is needed to do the job. This is a major, major problem in nearly every school and college.

What is needed is highly paid respected competent knowledgeable people in the classroom who honestly like to teach. The issues should not be charter or private schools versus public schools, it should be staffing the schools with competent teachers. This is true at every level from kindergarten to the graduate school. Universities are usually stocked with PhD's who are competent researchers, but may or may not have any idea of how to teach.

THERE ARE USUALLY TOO MANY ADMINISTRATORS

Here are a few illustrations from my own experience. When I was in high school we had a principal, two vice-principals and a couple of teachers were given extra money to run the attendance office, the counseling office, or to coach. My high school had 3500 students. At the end of my college teaching career I taught at a barrio middle school and a city high school in the same school district that I had attended. Both the middle school and the high school had about a thousand students. They each had a principal, four vice-principles, and a couple of deans.

In 2016, the Los Angeles Board of Education increased its administrative staff by 22% while its teaching staff had dropped 9% in the same year. The number of students had decreased by 100,000 from 2003 to 2015--to about 600,000 today. The downtown headquarters of the district employed 3400 people, most of whom were administrators making $85,000 to $110,000. The district is so large that it has been divided into six smaller regions, each with its own set of administrators some of whom are called "coaches" because there were so many "administrators," that they appeared top-heavy, which they are! Originally each of these regions had an administrator and a secretary, now they house both necessary workers and an unnecessary duplication of non-teaching personnel. There are 3200 additional administrators outside of the head office.

Meanwhile, the average salary for an LAUSD teacher is $70,000. About the same as the average household income in Los Angeles County. The average secondary school principal earns about $140,000 a year.

With over 100 middle and high schools, if we were to go back to the number of administrators employed in 1950, per school, this would make about 200 to 400 administrators free to teach. If we do this, it would save about $20 million which could be spent on increasing teacher salaries or adding more teachers to the classrooms thereby reducing class size.

In 2017, an independent report concluded that in Los Angeles 10,000 administrative positions should be eliminated. So, 1600 administrators were notified that they might lose their positions. 115 were actually reassigned. None of these were administrators working in actual schools. All were non-school personnel.

The Los Angeles district has 640000 students and 26,500 teachers. This equals 24.1 students per teacher. If the 10,000 surplus administrators were returned to the classroom the average class size would drop to 17.5. And it would cost less because the administrators pay would drop to that of teachers.

In 1965, my college had 20,000 students. We had a president, four deans and an assistant dean. When I left, we had 22,000 students, an increase of 10%. But our administration had increased to: a president, four vice presidents, four deans and four assistant deans. Naturally the secretarial pool increased along with the administrative mushroom, since every dean needed a secretary. All this happened while the extracurricular activities were severely reduced. The athletic program was cut in half. There were no school dances. Outside speakers were eliminated. So the students were getting shortchanged while non-teaching administrators increased geometrically!

At the same time at the college, full-time faculty were being decreased and replaced with part-time hourly-paid instructors. Part-time instructors generally are paid about half of what a full-time instructor would receive. They usually have no retirement benefits and no health benefits. So if money is the factor, let's bring in all hourly teachers so that we can increase the number and salaries of the burgeoning administrative force. (Or maybe we should make all administrators part-time and the professors full time!)

As this began to be more common, the state legislature determined that for every 10 full-time professors that left, at least five full-timers had to be hired. The others could be hourly instructors. You can easily see that within about 30 years there could be very few full-time instructors at the college. It may seem to be an uninformed and antiquated view, but I used to think that the function of a college was to educate students. If this is true, we need more qualified full-time instructors at every level.

One more unbelievable fact from my college. Guess who the highest paid employee on the campus was. You probably guessed the president, as I did when first asked! Would you believe that it was the school carpenter? He made union wages and got lots of overtime pay at time and a half. The academic staff, including the president, are "professionals" so they get no overtime pay. Meanwhile today's rates for a carpenter are $42 and hour plus $18 in fringe benefits. So, $2400 a week for a year is $125,000 per year, plus overtime. A professor with a doctorate and 15 years' experience makes the same base salary—but gets no opportunity for overtime. But the president has now outdistanced the carpenter. The carpenter would now have to work 5 hours of overtime a day to match the president. So the president is now the top dog! But it looks like the teachers' unions need to take a page out of the carpenter union's book. Maybe they can require the carpenters to earn a PhD before they work in a college!

DISRUPTIVE STUDENTS

Disruptive students often interfere with effective learning in the classrooms and may not need to face repercussions. With the idea of human rights entering the schools, older methods of punishment are now forbidden.

The realities are that in some schools, usually middle schools, there will be a number of potentially disruptive young people. They will all have needs to show their superiority because of their inferiority complexes. These commonly develop because of: their lack of love at home, their drug use or addiction, their lack of interest in academic pursuits, or their abusive family life-- including sexual violence.

There is no single solution. If the parents are truly loving, they may be involved in their child's therapy. If the parents are drug addicted, such as alcoholics, the solution may be to remove the child from the home or to find other possible therapies in the school or in the community. Sports programs with a competent coach may be able to redirect the behavior. Vocational programs, such as auto mechanics or gardening, may also be valuable.

By the time a child is in middle school, the peer group is probably more important than the family-- or the school. Gang membership is a powerful motivating force for many young people, especially in the ghettos and barrios. And today, it is impossible to leave most gangs. Death is often the only out.

As mentioned, one method that is occasionally used is to transfer a disruptive student to another school where the friends or the gang are not available for showing off.

TECHNOLOGY FOR TODAY'S EDUCATION

Tablets or computers are essential, but are too expensive for many schools. More money is the obvious cure. In upper class schools students can bring their own. But not all schools are upper class. With every student having a computer or tablet, textbooks, lessons, and tests can be delivered to each individual.

TEXTBOOKS

The cost of textbooks enriches the publishers while the students read books that are often far out of date. Elementary school textbooks will generally cost about $80. Each subject area requires another textbook. These books will last a few years. If homework books are bought by the district they will cost about $15 each and will probably be used only one year.

WHY THE HIGH COST OF BOOKS?

The cost of printing the book will probably be about two dollars. But then there are costs for: storage, transportation, the sales force (because each publisher is trying to get its books adopted by every school district). The author will make about 10 to 15% on the profit of each copy sold and the sales force adds about 12% of the cost of the book. Many books today are written at the publishers' offices by recent college graduates, then checked for accuracy by the listed author, who is paid less than the aforementioned royalty.

Authors used to be in charge of their books, but many publishers today put price, publication date, and other factors ahead of a quality book, and a fair price for the school district or student.

Should the states publish their own books at an 80% reduction of costs? Definitely not! The primary job of American education is to enrich publishers!

A DIGITAL AND E-BOOK SOLUTION

Textbooks cost about $100 each and publishers profit to the tune of $4 billion a year on selling them. Three publishers have 85% of the textbook market. The printed books are soon out of date in many subject areas. They are heavy for the students to carry. They sustain damage.

In secondary schools you may need a full-time clerk to handle all books. In large districts, you may need a separate section to store all the elementary school books and to check them in at semester's end and checked back out in September. They may also have a book repair section to rehabilitate damaged books. All of these negatives for print books are eliminated for digital books. However, data repair people will be needed to handle problems with school owned digital devices. Lost or damaged devices may be a problem, particularly in impoverished districts. Still the advantages lay with digital books.

E-books offer far more intellectually stimulating options than does a printed textbook.

Videos, interactive options, and other bells and whistles make the digital offerings more enticing for students. In addition, e-books can be updated annually, or even semi-annually, compared with the normal seven-year cycle of print textbook adoptions.

Since all books started as digital pages, then when they are copy-edited and pictures and graphs inserted, they can be printed and bound. So even the most primitive e-books will be equivalent to a printed book.

There are groups, such as Wikibooks, that offer free elementary school textbooks in many areas. Some individuals, as well as some official organizations, are working to cut the exorbitant publisher profits. If states, or ideally the federal government, would begin to publish school textbooks they could significantly decrease textbook expenses. Outstanding teachers could be enlisted to write the books in their areas. They could be paid more than the publishers pay, now usually a 10 to 12% royalty. Of course, this could redirect school budgetary items from the private sector stockholders to the teachers' salaries. This would be un-American! Private sector workers and stockholders should be able to capture more of the governmental funds. Public-sector employees should be happy to work for much less money than those in the private sector!

Publishers naturally want to stay ahead of the flow and be able to offer more services with their expensive books. They may offer many selected Internet articles and YouTube or publisher produced videos. Of course, states could do the same thing. Publishers may offer digital testing with automatic answering, the score going directly into the teacher's digital roll book. But then, the state could also do this. Publishers have not yet figured out how to automatically grade essay testing-- which is an essential in modern education. We must learn to write. Multiple choice or "multiple guess" questions may give you an idea of subject mastery, but don't give you an idea of how people can think about, or apply, the knowledge they have.

There can be some minuses with using tablets connected to the Internet. Students may opt for games or other distracting possibilities. This could be eliminated if there were special tablets for school use only. These could not connect to the Internet but would be able to connect to programs selected by the teacher.

The cheapest tablets cost less than a single textbook. A special elementary school tablet, without Internet possibilities but with connections to the teacher's master files or with thumb drives for each device, with the curriculum of the teacher and all reading material included would be a way to keep the students' attention directed at the concepts and goals of the areas to be learned.

So, somewhere down the line we must decide whether enriching stockholders should be a primary goal of education. Or, should we even consider the novel idea of putting the money into the classroom and the educational experiences of our future citizens?

PRIMARY AND SECONDARY SCHOOLS IN THE US

Many countries allow for both public and private schools. They usually require that the private schools fulfill state requirements. Obviously, the majority of private schools are religiously based. The Catholics have the most by far. The Lutherans have a number of schools. The Jews have some, as do some other sects. Home-schooling is legal in the US and in about half of the countries of the world. Usually there are requirements for those who want to home-school their children.

Public schools are required to take all children, including the mentally and physically disabled. Charter schools have developed over the last several years and offer many parents an option to the traditional public school. Many of these charter schools are financed by the public-school system, in fact they may be an integral part of the public-school system. Others are private and are for profit. Teachers may hold teaching credentials, especially if they are teaching academic classes. The rule and credentialing varies from state to state. The research is not conclusive about whether charter schools are superior to the regular public schools.

Some larger school districts have secondary magnet schools which may emphasize: math and science, medical professions, business interests, performing arts, college prep, etc. Naturally there will always be required courses in every school--in such areas as: English, math, history, political science, etc.

PUBLIC SUPPORT FOR RELIGIOUS EDUCATION

There have been several Supreme Court cases where Catholic schools have benefited from public money such as: reimbursed bus payments to and from school; the loaning of public school books to Catholic schools; and that a public university was required to finance the publication of an evangelical religious newspaper just as it funded secular papers. Generally, these decisions are 5 to 4, and sometimes 6 to 3. The question is often, does it actually establish a religion for the state, or is it helping children.

Some people think that charter schools or parochial schools are always better than the public schools. This is not necessarily true. Studies reported by the US Department of Education have found no particular advantage to charter schools. The social class of the students is usually the critical factor—upper class parents are able to provide more help with homework and more extracurricular advantages—such as travel, special summer camps, and museum visits.

There has been a great amount of publicity for charter schools. Some of these are public, many are private. Some in the federal government are pushing for school vouchers to allow parents to choose which school their children will attend and have the government pay all or part of the tuition. Betsy deVos, the Secretary of Education under Donald Trump, advocates charter schools. Naturally, religious schools would benefit greatly from a voucher system. The question is always whether this would violate the separation of church and state.

In Zelman v. Simmons-Harris, 536 <u>US 639</u> (2002), in another 5 to 4 decision (3 Catholics, a Lutheran and an Episcopalian as the majority) it was decided that a school voucher program in which 96% of those who had school vouchers chose parochial schools did not violate the First Amendment clause relative to establishing a religion.

UNIVERSITY EDUCATION TODAY

We are now in an age where many, if not most, jobs require some specialized training or education. The best jobs generally require the most education. You just don't pick up a knowledge of advanced coding for software by watching reruns of "CSI." Effective education takes more years, and if we are to develop citizens who are broadly versed in the liberal arts and are highly educated in a field which is a needed service for the society, it is going to take more than four years of university study.

Since highly technical jobs generally do not require blue-collar type labor, people can work well past 65. With our lifespans slightly over 80, and increasing yearly, there is no problem with having people work many more years than they do today, before thinking of retirement. Society would undoubtedly profit if its citizens studied for more years and worked more years before retiring.

A bachelor's degree should give you some competence in your major area of study. In Europe, primary and secondary education takes a total of 13 years. A bachelor's degree is another three. In the US, primary and secondary education take 12 years and the bachelor's degree is another four.

The European bachelor's tends to be relatively narrows Typically a student takes 60 credits a year. One common breakdown of these over the three-year period is: 80 credits in the major, 40 in the minor, possibly 20 in required general education, and the remaining 40 in any number of options.

The American program is more likely to be at least 50% of required courses, 35% in the major and perhaps 15% in the minor. The remainder in elective courses and required general education studies.

UNIVERSITIES USUALLY HIRE RESEARCHERS—NOT TEACHERS

The European and similar bachelors' degrees tend to be oriented toward a vocation. The masters' and doctoral studies usually require very little coursework with a heavy emphasis on research. At the doctoral level, it is often required that the student publish 3 to 4 articles in respected academic journals. They usually have the option to write a dissertation monograph. They may or may not be required to take any coursework. Consequently, their education narrows considerably. You have heard the definition of an expert-- a person who knows more and more about less and less until he knows everything about nothing. Because of the emphasis on research and the narrow base of knowledge, many PhD's are not qualified to teach in any area except in their own very limited expertise. Still most PhDs will teach in the universities.

As we mentioned earlier, it is easier to measure a person's bank account than that person's intelligence, morality, courage, empathy or any number of important attributes. If you have a huge bank account, you must be hugely (or shall we say "bigly") wise, moral, and socially concerned. In hiring college instructors, it is easier to evaluate their research than their potential teaching ability, the breadth of their knowledge, their concern for their students, their willingness to help students with personal problems, or to guide them academically.

The research emphasis at the doctoral level and in the hiring of professors further complicates and reduces the importance of teaching abilities. Universities are commonly ranked by the quantity, and quality, of the research they produce. The quality may be considered, especially if a professor has won a Nobel prize.

Research is also evaluated by the quality of the academic journal that publishes it. A medical research project published in the Journal of the American Medical Association would be held in much higher regard than an article published in a start-up online journal on educational psychology in Zimbabwe. Journals carry ratings from academic societies.

Another factor that makes the authorship of journal articles difficult to evaluate in terms of the contributions of an author is the number of authors on a paper. Quite commonly in medicine and the biological sciences you may find ten to twenty authors on a paper. In other fields, you may find only one or two. So if you were to employ a physiologist, she might claim authorship on a hundred papers, but may have done less total research in terms of time spent than a psychologist who has published only five papers, but had done all the research. Having more papers published makes one more employable and more likely to gain professorships. It's good to have friends who will include you in their research projects. Another ploy to increase one's number of published research articles is for the professor to attach his name to a research project done by one of his master's or doctoral level students.

While in some top-flight universities in Europe, the requirements might be only a 3 to 10 credit course for the master's and possibly no additional courses for the doctorate. In the U.S., a master's degree is likely to require 30 to 60 units of lecture courses, equivalent to 60 to 120 European credits-- and for a doctorate possibly another 30 to 60 units. A master's thesis and doctoral dissertation are generally required for the advanced degrees in both the USA and Europe.

A great many doctoral students wish to pursue teaching and researching at the university level. As you might guess, graduates with more coursework should be able to be better teachers because of their broader knowledge. If the graduate, who does not have a broad educational background, is expected to teach several courses (as is common in America) one might expect a low level of subject matter expertise. I have experienced this in my European teaching. Often a person is required to put together a course, so will find several people who will teach their own area of expertise in a course that does not have a coherent framework. Effective courses must have a "point of view" and not just be about adding a few facts to some hopefully eager brains.

In bygone days, research output was only one of the criteria for employment or promotion. Teaching quality, professional society membership and leadership, community activity (like membership in the chamber of commerce, Lions, etc.), and their research, might all be given significant consideration.

WHAT ABOUT THE STUDENTS?

Over the years, I have listened to fellow professors bemoan the fact that students read less, come to class less often, and have become increasingly rude. They work less, but demand higher grades. In earlier days, the grades were generally distributed on a "bell curve" with standard deviations allowing for 5 to 7% As and Fs, about 15 to 20% Bs and Ds and about 50% Cs.

I was recently invited to teach for a year at a California state university where I had previously taught. The first week I was cautioned that I couldn't give more that 50% As and Bs. Grade inflation is out of control! I gave one very intelligent young man a Fail because he had copied his term paper, unchanged, from an Internet academic article. He complained strenuously to the dean.

RESEARCH UNIVERSITIES
As you may know, some of the major universities in America are considered to be "research universities," and the research takes precedence over the teaching for many of

the professors. In fact, professors are generally hired based on their published research, not their teaching abilities. This is not true in the liberal arts colleges or community colleges. Here generally the professors are true academics, with broad knowledges-- and hopefully skillful teaching abilities. This is not to say that there are not excellent teachers in the research universities, but where research is king, the students may be paupers.

I remember a colleague at a major university who was the preeminent researcher in several areas in his discipline. He was assigned to teach a beginning course in the area-- and was an abysmal flop. But in a graduate level class, he was exciting, stimulating, and peerless.

Today we seem to need several types of specific education. We are all going to join the workforce at some level. We will need vocational education to be plumbers, astro-physicists, engineers, or elected representatives of the people. If we plan to be in a romantic relationship of some sort, we need information about how relationships may work. If we are to be effective citizens of our nations, we need a great deal of information and an understanding of the various elements of logical thinking in order to think and vote intelligently.

Recent elections, such as those discussed earlier, clearly indicate that the electorate did not have clear ideas of the results of their voting. Often, like in the US, one's political party affiliation or the illogical populist rantings of a demagogue, filled the intellectual and educational vacuums in the voters' minds.

University education is now primarily directed at becoming knowledgeable and successful in our chosen vocational path. Many secondary schools and universities offer us course choices to be able to understand how we can feel successful in our personal lives and whether or not you want to be in relationships, and even be parents. What is often lacking is a concerted effort to make us knowledgeable citizens. This requires some background in world history, political science, macroeconomics, psychology, sociology, the theory of science, and a thorough understanding of semantics and the other components of logic.

Years ago, university education dealt with understanding the world and how to effectively work within it and work to change it. Rousseau, Locke, Plato, Aristotle, Hume, Bentham, and many others made us look at some potential ideas for societies and how they might be accomplished. But today the "hard" sciences of chemistry and physics along with the "soft" sciences of psychology, sociology, and economics give us an expanded view of the universe, our planet, and ourselves.

It is not easy to be a thoughtful and realistic citizen today. No one can know all about everything. But if we are to begin to hone our potentials, we certainly need a more liberal arts education. Perhaps we should look back to better prepare for our future.

LIBERAL ARTS COLLEGES

I would suggest that interested people read a book or two on the content and the advantages of a liberal education. Fareed Zakaria's recent book titled "In Defense of a Liberal Education" is the best I have seen.

In the US, we have a number of liberal arts colleges where students spend their four years in just such pursuits. From Pomona College on the West Coast to Smith College on the East Coast, we have a large number of such schools. It is the purpose of these liberal arts schools to develop a person more fully and as a result to make them more discerning citizens.

The liberal arts have been under attack. Three southern governors have said they will not spend money on liberal arts education in their state universities. Who needs thinking citizens, anyhow?

Traditionally, a liberal arts major specialized in humanities. This is the college major most associated with critical thinking. The popularity of this major has reduced 20% recently. In 2015 only 12% of all degrees from colleges were in the humanities.

HOW ABOUT EIGHT YEARS OF COLLEGE?

Perhaps the ideal tertiary level of education should be expanded to include several years of education to make the students more grounded in their cultures and more qualified to be thinking citizens. Of course, we would then need four or more years of vocational education. So, the ideal would significantly increase the number of years of university work. Of course, education can, and should, continue after that first four-year degree. But eight years of fraternity-sorority life would be way too much!

I understand the problems with this proposal. Students already want to go to work and start making decent salaries. Parents are tired of paying tuition, and room and board for their little darlings! Nevertheless, if we are to protect ourselves and our progeny from the scourges of overpopulation and climate change, we had better educate some intelligent citizens.

Just look at the professed ignorance of some of our leaders! When America has 182 climate deniers in Congress we have a major confrontation with reality and a major hurdle for the future of the human race. These deniers include the Senate majority leader and a Senator who was a strong contender for the presidency for the Republican Party.

I guess we have to remember that America is a capitalistic society where making money (capital) is the most important factor in the nation's progress and in developing one's individual self-esteem and feeling of self-worth.

In contrast, the happiest countries are socialistic-- society is more important than money. But strangely, even in those countries the pragmatic need to get a job is more important than being a thinking citizen. However, people in Europe do read more newspapers and watch news programs and debate programs more often than their counterparts in America. But maybe if we can teach the Europeans about baseball and American football they will have more interesting things to do than to think.

Top American universities like: Princeton, Stanford, and UCLA, emphasize the importance of a general education (GE) for their graduates. Here is an excerpt from the UCLA catalog:

"Courses in the GE curriculum offer diverse perspectives on how human beings think and feel, solve problems, express ideas, and create and discover new knowledge. These courses also help students acquire the skills essential to university-level learning: they challenge students to assess information critically; frame and deliver reasoned and persuasive arguments orally and in writing; and identify, acquire, and use the knowledge necessary to solve problems. GE is the foundation of a UCLA education.

Students follow a general education curriculum that is grouped into three foundational areas:

➤ Foundations of Arts and Humanities
- Literary and Cultural Analysis
- Philosophical and Linguistic Analysis
- Visual and Performance Arts

➤ Foundation Society and Culture

•Historical Analysis

•Social Analysis

➤   Foundations of Scientific Inquiry

•Life Sciences

•Physical Sciences

There are many courses that can be taken under each category.

Princeton, as UCLA, also requires writing competency and a foreign language. As most top-level universities, it also requires proficiency in scientific thinking and logic. Princeton requires:

•Epistemology and Cognition

•Ethical Thought and Moral Values

•Historical Analysis

•Literature and the Arts

•Social Analysis

•Quantitative Reasoning

•Science and Technology

An example of academic requirements can be seen in the SAT scores. Princeton students, for example, are usually in the 1500 to 1600 range. 1600 is a perfect score. The University of California is generally between 1450 and 1600. Liberty University's students are around 1150, and Barry's near 1000. The top-ranked liberal arts colleges are generally in the range of Princeton and the University of California. But others may not require SAT scores at all, such as Allen University.

(You are undoubtedly familiar with the several college and university ranking systems, such as: US News, the oldest and most complete; Princeton; and Times Higher Education. Forbes also has one, but it is inundated with ads for very low ranked schools, so it is easy to be fooled.)

BEST UNIVERSITIES

When we look at the best universities in the USA we find schools like: Princeton and Harvard at or near the top, with public universities such as The University of California very near the top. National rankings, done by such organizations as US News, rank the best 200 universities then have a list of those who did not make the top 200.

Then they rank the top liberal arts colleges. Williams, Amherst, and Pomona are in the top 10. After 200 ranked colleges, there are a number of unranked schools. You might correctly assume that graduates from the highest ranked schools generally will be far more competent than those of the lowest ranked or the unranked schools. So, one college degree does not equal another college degree! Graduates from high level high schools can be far more educated than those with bachelor's degrees from low-level colleges.

UNIVERSITY QUALITY VARIES CONSIDERABLY

High schools and colleges may or may not be accredited by approved accrediting agencies. For example, for many years in California any person could deposit a $10,000 bond, which cost $1000 per year, and start a university. Because it was certified by the State of California, students were able to apply for federal loans for these very expensive private "universities." These supposed schools could give bachelor's, master's and doctor's degrees. Because they were certified by the state, their graduates in psychology could apply for licenses in clinical psychology and other mental therapy areas.

The legitimate holders of these licenses from accredited schools began to be upset with this practice, once they were aware of what was going on. First, they suggested written exams for the licenses through the Board of Behavioral Science Examiners. Soon they required oral exams in addition. Finally, the state realized the absurdity of their law and changed it. However, I have seen several situations in which people have opened such "universities," and given themselves doctor's degrees, then advertised themselves as having received a PhD degree.

Resumes are often padded, and some of those pads may be filled with hot air. One of Donald Trump's high level nominees had written that he had graduated from Dartmouth, when in fact he had graduated from the University of Northern Iowa. Dartmouth is ranked 11th to 38th in the USA by the various ranking systems. Northern Iowa is unranked nationally but is only 30th among Midwestern colleges—so it is way down the national list.

One acquaintance, a certified public accountant who was a fundamentalist Christian and a believer in creationism, showed me proof that people had walked with dinosaurs. There was a man standing in a dinosaur footprint which he offered as proof. He had also written a story to go along with the photo. He signed it as Dr. _____ I checked on his credentials and found that he had started one of those California universities and had given himself a doctorate. He was the only graduate of his university!

One of the first colleges at which I taught, a trade-technical community college, had a small academic faculty. The trade teachers needed at least seven years in their trade before they could apply to teach there. They were quite competent in their fields. On the academic faculty only two of us had doctor's degrees. Others had master's degrees. Only one administrator called himself "doctor." The librarian, who had a master's degree from Harvard, doubted the doctorate claimed by Dr. Adams, a vice-president. The librarian asked where "Doctor" Adams had received his doctorate and was told the University of Illinois. The librarian checked and found no record at that university. He asked again and was told Oregon State University. Contact with that university found no records of Dr. Adams ever being a student there. One vocational teacher, without a bachelor degree, had a former student who was teaching at a Catholic college in Hawaii. Somehow, he got the college, which was not accredited to give an advanced degree, to give him an honorary doctorate. He came back from Hawaii and promptly had his parking place renamed to Dr. Jones. He insisted that people call him Doctor.

Some years ago, it was legal to sell facsimile diplomas from any university and with any degree you desired. These cost about $25. A friend of mine who had gone to Cal Poly for a year, bought a facsimile degree that showed he had graduated from Notre Dame. For him it was a joke. Many of these schemes are now outlawed. However knowledgeable school systems, colleges and businesses now require certified transcripts from all universities claimed to have been attended by a prospective employee.

There are still many supposedly accredited universities advertising for students. They may advertise that they are accredited, but the accreditation is nearly always by accrediting agencies formed by low level schools that are not recognized by any legitimate accrediting organization. So, if you are in doubt about a school, check the internet under unaccredited universities. Their fees are usually high and the requirements for entrance often very low. Many will give credit for "life experiences."

Obviously, we must be concerned with the quality of education from kindergarten through the doctoral level.

ACCREDITING AND RANKING UNIVERSITIES

In the United States, there are several accrediting agencies for higher education institutions. The major ones are regional. There are also subject-specific evaluation organizations. (These can be found under the Department of Education on the Internet. There is also a very long list of unaccepted accrediting groups.)

Being accredited by a recognized agency does not mean that all the colleges are equal. It only means that they have all passed the minimum standards for accreditation.

As mentioned, universities are also ranked unofficially by groups such as: US News, Times Higher Education, Forbes, and a number of others. Since the criteria used are different, the rankings vary somewhat. Check the Internet under "ranking of US universities."

However, there is a great deal of difference between one of the top ten, universities, such as: Massachusetts Institute of Technology, Harvard University, Stanford University, the University of California at both Berkeley and Los Angeles and a degree from an unranked university-- lower than the top 200.

PROFESSOR PREPARATION

You can imagine that a person with a PhD in zoology knows quite a bit about animals. And if her doctoral research was on the Monarch butterfly, she would know a great deal about them. But could she teach a general biology course, a course in equine technology, a course in vertebrate zoology? If her education was in Europe, she would probably have a three-year education in zoology and one other subject. But she would probably not have any coursework beyond the three-year bachelor's degree. So if you are looking for someone to research butterflies, she would probably be outstanding. But if you were looking for someone to teach several different courses in zoology and biology, she might not qualify.

The major American universities are usually research universities. They do a great deal of important research for the government and for business. But if you think that part of the function of a university is to educate undergraduate students, you may find that there are not a great many outstanding teaching professors. Many undergraduate courses at major universities are taught by graduate students, who are busy completing their own advanced degrees.

Competent teachers are more likely to be found in liberal arts colleges and two-year community colleges. The professors here specialize in teaching, and it may be their major interest, since research competence is usually not required.

POSSIBLE SOLUTION TO INCREASING COLLEGE TEACHING EXPERTISE

People who want to teach in a university, particularly at the undergraduate level, should have a broad background in their own field as well as a background in related fields. This would require a doctoral background with broad coursework. Included in the coursework would be educational methods courses. While lecturing is common, and is often an outstanding way to stimulate students, there are other ways of teaching, such as leading discussion groups and supervising students working in the community. Teaching can be merely transferring knowledge, but ideally it should stimulate attitudes in the students to expand their knowledge and possibly to influence them to travel the world. The most effective teacher will probably: impart knowledge, develop inquisitive attitudes, and change the behavior of the students.

One professor, of my acquaintance, was hired based on his publications in another language and on one lecture he gave as part of his interview process. Once hired, the students complained about his poor teaching, the doctoral students who began with him switched to other professors. He was removed from the classroom. So for 15 years he worked diligently on something, nobody knew just what! No one knows if he had any articles published. But he was always hard at work in his office doing something!

It seems to me that teachers who can't teach should be able to be released—but with unions and lifetime tenure, this is difficult to do and usually costs many thousands of dollars in court costs.

This unfairness principle cuts both ways. During the Depression of the 1930s, the school boards of two California districts, Santa Monica and Oxnard, made an agreement that every three years they would trade teachers so that they could keep teaching salaries down. The law at the time was that if you were to begin your fourth year of teaching in the district, you would have tenure and would make more money each year as you moved up the salary schedule. Naturally, administrators were not included-- they could move up the salary scale automatically each year.

As mentioned, the extensive hiring of hourly paid college instructors is a similar way to keep college teaching costs down, while short-changing the students. Full-time instructors would be on campus full time for assisting students. Part-timers are driving to their next job.

So we have a dilemma, incompetent teachers and even sexual predators can be protected by the teacher's unions, but good teachers have been unfairly treated-- and the best teachers cannot be rewarded financially.

Universities are often ranked by the number of scientific papers that their professors have published, and the number of PhD students they have produced. It is too bad that the rankings don't necessarily reflect the quality of teaching, too.

COLLEGE CLASSES MAY VARY IN SIZE

While this may be an often undesirable ideal, real education can be done in large classes with outstanding instructors. The college class that I learned the most in, by far, had 200 students and a lecturer. I got an A in the class, then I took it six more times, without credit-- learning more the sixth-time than I did in most of my other college classes the first time.

I have seen some MOOC (Massive Open Online Classes) lectures that were outstanding. Knowledgeable educators from Harvard, Stanford, and a number of other top universities, lecturing in their areas of competency gives many people a chance to learn from the best. Some of these can easily be included in advanced high school courses and college work. Ted Talks (ted.com) is another source for interesting lectures by knowledgeable people. Both of these sources might be used extensively to broaden the minds of students.

ACADEMIC FREEDOM

Let me remind you again of what the former president of the University of California, Clark Kerr, said, "The mission of the university is not to make ideas save for students, but to make students safe for ideas." This piece of advice is fundamental to the mission of education, but it runs counter to our own thinking--because each of us knows the truth, and we don't want anyone rattling our ivory towers. Consequently, no one who disagrees with me should be able to teach in a university, and no one who disagrees with me should be allowed to speak to these impressionable students.

We are quite willing to censor those who disagree with us, but are not willing to have our own ideas censored.

Recently a conservative instructor at Marquette University, John McAdams, has been under fire. The conservatives on the faculty are crying for academic freedom. The liberals want to justify the administration's action to let him go. At the University of Toronto, Professor Jordan Peterson frequently rattles his liberal colleagues.

Since university professors tend to be left-leaning, it is not surprising that they attack those on the right side of the political spectrum. I remember a former high school teacher of mine, Tom Devine, who later taught at a college where I was teaching. His right-leaning views angered the sociology department and they developed enough clout to have him removed from teaching. When I got to the college he was in charge of the audiovisual section. Sometime later, a conservative leaning Board of Trustees was elected and he was put back into the classroom.

A number of years ago, Angela Davis, a brilliant philosophy student and a lifelong Marxist was appointed as an assistant professor at UCLA. Gov. Ronald Reagan sought to have her appointment canceled. The University Board of Regents followed his lead. She later became a professor at another branch of the University, at Santa Cruz. She also taught at Rutgers.

FREEDOM OF SPEECH ON CAMPUS

America is very lucky that there are so many students who know everything. We can't wait until they graduate and move into the world and solve all of our problems. They are certainly right in disallowing people they see as right-wing fascists from speaking on their campuses. They are also right in keeping left-wing radicals off of their free speech podiums. What students need is to have people who will affirm exactly what they already believe. That way they can feel even smarter.

On the other hand, might it be possible that someone with a different idea might spark a new direction in the student's life? Is it possible that the student might, through questioning the speaker, change the speakers mind? Usually the people invited to speak at college campuses have some experience and have done some thinking about the areas that they will discuss.

They are not quite the same quality of speaker as you often find in Hyde Park in London at the Speakers Corner. I remember standing at the foot of one of the perennial orators at the "corner." Olie was telling us how stray animals were the cause of smog. I had never heard that before, but being curious, I spent the next six months researching his theory. I found no evidence. But at least, Olie got me thinking!

My research has shown that the real cause of smog is the blustering hot air filled haranguing for our national interest when politicians plead for our votes—promising each audience what it wants to hear. I can't wait to get back to Hyde Park and challenge Olie and his well-thought-out theories.

PROTESTS FROM THE RIGHT

I can understand why the seminary associated with the Catholic University of America would revoke an invitation to Father James Martin to speak on their campus. He has written about how the Catholic Church should find ways to interact with homosexuals. He wrote some of his ideas in his book "Building a Bridge." He should acknowledge, with the good conservative Catholics, that when God makes a mistake in some of His creations, the Church must do what you can to correct those Supernatural slip-ups.

Liberal Chelsea Manning, served seven years in military prison for sharing classified documents with Wikileaks. At the sentencing hearing, she apologized for "hurting the US" and said she had mistakenly believed she could "change the world for the better." President Obama commuted her sentence. She had been invited to Harvard for a week of lecturing and meeting with students and faculty. Harvard rescinded her invitation after conservative groups complained.

PROTESTS FROM THE LEFT

Trump supporter <u>Milo Yiannopoulos</u> was scheduled to give a speech at the University of California at Berkeley. Protests by left leaning groups cancelled his speech. Conservative writers, such as Ann Coulter, were also discouraged from speaking.

Eventually the university spent $600,000 on security to assure that Ben Shapiro, a conservative writer, could speak on the campus without being disrupted. I can't think of a better use of the money, unless it were used to hire six more assistant professors for a year!

POSSIBLE SOLUTIONS

If people are going to be effective teachers they need several types of skills. First, they need a broad knowledge of their own subject area, then they need a broad view of how that subject area fits into the totality of knowledge. Then they need to know how people learn, this is educational psychology. They should understand how a curriculum is developed and what methods can be used to most effectively develop a thorough understanding of the validation and the potentials of that academic area into the life of the student and the development of the society.

With the number of electronic tools available today, a thorough understanding of how these tools can be used effectively in developing the knowledge, attitudes, and behavioral changes that are essential in today's world.

As in every profession today, annual or biannual updates are necessary. Video or in person classes, with the passing of comprehensive tests, are necessary.

Whether it is kindergarten, middle school, or the university, if students are to learn most effectively, their instructors need to have the knowledge of the subjects and the methodology to be able to impart that knowledge to their students. How else can we develop thinking citizens? Or shall we stay dumbed down?

Knowledge is only the starting point.

WHAT ABOUT THE STUDENTS?

Well, we have talked about the professors, what about the students? Certainly, we have a large number of students who are intensely interested in learning. However, the experience of many of my colleagues in the US and Europe is that the average student doesn't study as much as was true years ago, reads less, and expects higher grades. Many are working in order to support their studies. Many others seem to be attending college to avoid becoming adults, learning to drink and to toke, and learn to talk to, and use, the opposite sex.

FREE TUITION

Free college tuition would be a blessing to many. Those who have been academically successful will probably remain as energetic and eager students. Those who are coming from impoverished backgrounds can often obtain scholarships for tuition. But there are so many other expenses that are not covered--such as books, lodging, and food. The comprehensive college experience is more than just going to class and doing homework. Nearly all colleges will have outstanding speakers, performances, and social activities that are geared at developing the whole person. For that reason, the on-campus experience is highly valuable.

It seems that somewhere along the line, students should prove their academic interests and proficiency. This may be in high school or in community colleges.

Free college tuition is a universal student desire. But if it is society that taxes itself for this necessity, perhaps some parameters should be established. Should a student who was not academically successful in high school receive full tuition to a low-ranked private college? Should an academically successful personable potential doctor or teacher, who promises to work for 5 or 10 years for the government that provides the academic scholarship, be given a full tuition and living stipend? If a poverty student qualifies for a full academic scholarship at a university, should the government pay the living expenses of the student?

COLLEGE TEXTBOOKS

College textbooks have increased in price 1040% in the last 40 years. The cost-of-living has gone up 406% during that time.

The publishers make an initial profit on the sale of the book, but 80% of the books sold are sold the first semester that the book is available. From that time, the college bookstore is the primary financial beneficiary. It may buy the book back for 50% after the first semester, then sell it at 75%. Then buy it back at 50% and sell it again at 65 to 75%. If the revision schedule of the book is every three years, the bookstore makes a profit all six semesters, starting with 20 to 30% of the list price the first semester, then about 25% of the list price for the next five semesters. And you thought that the students were the primary concern of the college!

In earlier days, books were revised every four or five years. Now it is every one to three years. A part of one chapter may be rewritten and you have a new edition of the book. Publishers are now attempting to collect money on every used book sold by requiring an e-book supplement which must be purchased. So every year the publishers will make something extra.

Publishers do offer perks to the instructors who require that their students purchase the book. Free ancillaries to the textbook are useful. This may be a full box of material including a thousand test questions, lesson plans, video presentations, etc. They may also offer free, a service by which students take quizzes and examinations online and the results are automatically transferred to the professor's electronic roll book. So you can see the advantages of teachers selecting textbooks from the major publishers.

There are options that are much cheaper, if the professors are willing to use them. The problem is that they do not usually include all of the bells and whistles that the major companies offer. A number of smaller companies, with no sales forces, offer very inexpensive books on all the sales channels. A program developed at Rice University, and supported by several major charities, including Bill Gates, offers free e-books in a number of introductory college classes. The same books can be bought in print for about $30. There are also programs that allow teachers to accept existing books, particularly e-books, and have the opportunity to customize them, if they wish. The State of California is one of the leaders in this approach.

THE NEED FOR HIGH LEVEL VOCATIONAL EDUCATION

Often we think of vocational education as merely education for the trades-- such as carpenters, mechanics, and plumbers. But today's college education is in a large part vocational. Physicians, dentists, accountants, engineers, teachers and lawyers are all part of the modern vocational education mission of the colleges.

Things have changed since the 1700s. In the days of the American and French revolutions, concerns were primarily local. In the 1800s and early 1900s concerns became more national. International wars actually brought people together. Now we have a globalized world. The metamorphosis of societies has emphasized the differences and many now wish to return to the comfort of their national and even local interests. So we see the rise in populism as a reaction to globalism. Tip O'Neil, the former speaker of the House of Representatives, said that all politics are local. But:

➢Our economies are to a large degree global. Southeast Asia does much of the manufacturing for the world.

➢The West provides much of the service industries to the world.

➢The realities are that high-level technology is making low-level jobs obsolete.

Self-driving vehicles will soon replace most taxis and most freight trucking jobs. There is little chance that former truckers will become high level coders for artificial intelligence. There will be very few high school dropouts who will be able to do the work of graduate engineers. And college graduation will not guarantee a lifetime job. With scientific discoveries pulling technology ever more rapidly into an unpredictable future, lifetime learning is essential.

Singapore probably leads the way in this regard by giving each of its citizens $350 annually toward additional learning.

We have already reduced the knowledge necessary to do some jobs. Barcodes reduce the knowledge that super-market cashiers once had to have in their heads. And self-checkout is reducing the need for the existing cashiers. Financial institutions have long used computer-generated voice services to obtain information that receptionists once were required to do. Your bank balance is similarly relayed to you by a talking computer. So first we make it easier for humans to do a relatively simple job, then we assign this simple job to a computer or robot.

UNIVERSITY TEACHING

In most universities, an academic doctorate is required. Doctorates may be of several sorts. There are research doctorates which can be in many areas. A PhD (Doctor of Philosophy) can be awarded in almost any field. It is the most common type of doctorate. But equivalent academic research degrees can be in many areas. A Doctor of Science (D.Sc. or Sc.D) is given by some universities. Others would give a PhD in science. Both could be exact equivalents. A Doctor of Education (EdD) would be a specific doctorate in the field of education. Some schools would give a PhD in education. The EdD might also be a research degree. Some of the other academic degrees include: Doctor of Fine Arts (D.F.A.), Doctor of Business Administration (D.B.A.) and there are about 15 other various types of research doctorates.

While the degrees are theoretically equivalent, the quality of the degree varies considerably depending on the university granting it. Several ranking agencies rank the general level of the universities annually. There are rankings for each geographical area and for the world. In the United States a doctorate from one of the top hundred universities would be a quality doctorate.

Other doctoral degrees are called "professional," such as an MD degree for physicians and doctoral degrees for pharmacy, dentistry, and law.

Still other doctorates are honorary. A competent person might be awarded an honorary PhD, EdD, or DD (Doctor of Divinity) by a university. Honorary degrees might be awarded for outstanding contributions to scholarship, outstanding leadership in government or in NGOs (Non-governmental organizations), service to the university as a graduation speaker or, as a financial contributor to the university.

Doctoral degrees can vary considerably between institutions and between countries. Many European doctorates require no coursework, only a thesis. This is even true for some master's degrees. You might imagine that a student who has taken a number of courses and seminars might be more versed in the knowledge necessary to teach several college courses, as is common in the US. The number of college units taken by a student from the bachelor degree to the doctorate may vary from none to more than 70. Each course would generally be a 2 or 3 unit lecture course or graduate seminar and would require 15 to 20 hours lectures or seminar discussions per unit. American universities commonly require both a major and a minor area of study, with comprehensive examinations in each. The major would require 20 to 40 units, and the minor 10 to 20.

So if you are hiring a college professor to teach, it might be wise to hire one with an extensive background in graduate coursework rather than one who has only researching experience. But since the researcher may well have more published articles in academic journals, he or she will likely be hired, rather than the teacher. So what is the major job of a university-- research for the government or educating the young? Both are necessary, but how often can they be found in a single individual?

So that's where we are. Where do we want to go?

CHAPTER 18.   CAN WE DEVELOP A FUNCTIONAL AND EFFECTIVE SYSTEM OF EDUCATION?

Success can be measured by the amount of money one has. You cannot measure courage effectively except by action. Arnaud Beltrame, a French police officer, volunteered to take the place of an ISIS held hostage in France in March of 2018. He knew he would probably be killed—and he was. That's courage! But you can't measure it by a paper and pencil test or a bank statement.

You can measure intelligence to a degree, but intelligence does not always guarantee success-- you must have meaningful ideas and an effective work ethic. How do you measure goodness? When Roy Moore ran for the Senate seat in Alabama in 2017, he was an accused pedophile and had been twice removed from the Supreme Court of the state for violating federal constitutional provisions. Still he claimed to be a man of God. Nearly 50% of the voters voted for him. Apparently, success in Alabama is measured either by one's Republican Party affiliation or by one's professed belief in God.

Regarding riches, people know that "you can't take it with you" but having it now is important and being able to leave it to your children is a right. Having money in the US brings you prestige. It even gives you the means to significantly influence "democratic" elections. Is this what will give us the most effective type of government? One might wonder, however, if having money makes you a knowledgeable concerned citizen? If not, how can we improve our education for citizenship in a modern democracy?

WHAT IS NEEDED FOR AN EDUCATED ELECTORATE

If America is to be made great again, as Trump has promised, we need to start with better education.

As we have indicated throughout the book, in order to make intelligent decisions in our democracies, we need much more knowledge today than has ever been needed before. We need to be able to understand the concepts being presented and the projection of them into the future, if they are passed. We need a good knowledge of logic, particularly of semantics and induction, which we should be able to apply to political and economic theories as well as to scientific principles that may be proposed or are often accepted.

We need to be able to evaluate the knowledge that is accepted and determine whether or not something is highly probable. For example, when we have measurements from over a thousand thermometers, scattered around the Earth that have been monitored daily for 50 to 100 years showing that the Earth's temperature is skyrocketing, is that superior to the statement of an oil company owner who denies the existence of global warming with no evidence? When scientists can predict exactly when and where a total eclipse of the sun would occur, as it did in August of 2017, we applaud. But when science explains what is currently happening, and it threatens our income or the oil lobbyists' contributions for our next election campaign, we deny it—without evidence, but with prayerful hope.

We should be able to look at basic assumptions and see whether or not they are still believable assumptions today as they were 200 years ago. What is the evidence that praying will stop a war or a terrorist act? Since the evidence for evolution and the Big Bang strongly contradict the story in Genesis, are we willing to escape from the prison of tradition? Changing course is always difficult. We may even lose friends and family if we follow the truthful path of verified knowledge.

While the idea of God has always been an unprovable basic assumption, it seems that today we are assuming that democracy is the best form of government and that people are somehow equal. While believing in an unseen and unknowable God will probably always remain an assumption, the beliefs in democracy and equality can be examined. They can be accepted as is, modified, or trashed. We have already amended our Constitution 27 times—17 times since passing the Bill of Rights.

People should understand their non-provable basic assumptions. But in politics often false assumptions are paraded as truths. For example, in July of 2017, there was a vote in the US Senate to repeal Obamacare. After losing the vote, the Republican majority leader Mitch McConnell said that the American people deserve better healthcare and we don't want something like the socialized medicine that they have in Europe.

While this is not really a basic assumption, it is said with such force that it had the appearance of being factual. We have looked at what Obama wanted and what he got, Obamacare. Old Mitch was right that Americans deserve better, but America's healthcare system rates poorer than all of Europe's, and several Asian, countries. The US ranks last in healthcare among the world's richest countries.

We don't know whether McConnell was grossly misinformed, in the pocket of health insurance companies, or just had the typical Republican pro-business point of view. Often when the uninformed hear the word "socialism" they believe it is undemocratic or somehow anti-human. But, as we mentioned in the first chapter, Americans are enamored of their communistic health programs, Medicare and Medicaid. They fit Marx's ideal for communism which he said is, "from each according to his ability to each according to his needs." And Americans love their Social Security which is socialistic according to Lenin, who said, "socialism is from each according to his ability to each according to his work."

Actually, there are a number of different healthcare programs in Europe, all cheaper and more effective than America's. There is tax paid insurance, single-payer insurance, combinations of tax paid and privately paid programs. And they all cost less than the American programs and all are more effective in terms of the World Health Organization's evaluation of health services.

So, when politicians say "for the good of the American people," can we actually see whether it is for our good or the good of that politician. We had better have a good bit of verifiable knowledge—and a knowledge of practical politics so that we can see when we are being hoodwinked.

DO WE WANT OUR FORM OF DEMOCRACY?

We may even wonder if our present form of democracy is the best we can have-- or even if democracy is the best way to run an efficient modern government which works for safer and happier people. Certainly slightly more than 50% of the people are happier with their choices, at least until the promises don't pan out!

We know we are not really for communism because most of us are too selfish to work as hard as we can and not realize the fruits of our labors.

Socialism, according to Lenin, doesn't sound too bad except that it requires central planning which has usually been a disaster.

So what do we want? When we look at the most democratic countries in the world, the five Nordic countries come out in the top five places. If we want to look at economic growth and comfort, look at Singapore, which ranks variously between 40th and 70th of the countries of the world in being an effective democracy. And China, which has had phenomenal economic growth, ranks about number 120 of the world's nearly 200 countries in being an effective democracy. The most recent ranking has the UK at 14th and the U.S. at 16th, as being effective democracies. Tom Jefferson would undoubtedly be disappointed in us.

So what do the Nordic countries have that others do not? They have a welfare system that is comprehensive, high taxes, low corruption, free or inexpensive university education, many freedoms, and the happiest people in the world. Is this what we want? If so, we would need a major overhaul of the American ideas of capitalism. Making a few people filthy rich seems to leave most of us far behind. But is that bad? Just because I want to be equal to them doesn't mean that I am!

Certainly, business is essential. But in which ways does providing for business hurt the populace? There are some pluses and there are some minuses.

It is in our educational opportunities that we can evaluate what we have, and what it can be. These opportunities include the required education through the secondary level, the voluntary level of university education, and the purposeful further education that we afford ourselves in our free time.

You may never have studied Plato's Republic, but you can read it in your spare time. You may never have read a book on justice, but you can do it in your spare time. You may never have listened to one of the free outstanding lectures on the Internet, such as the Ted Talks series (https://www.ted.com/talks) but you can do it in your spare time. Since there are more than 2500 outstanding lectures, you can fill a lot of spare time.

Here are some ideas for formal education, self-study, or discussion groups.

THE CURRICULUM

EDUCATION MUST BE ABLE TO HELP US UNDERSTAND WHERE WE ARE—AND SEEK WAYS TO IMPROVE OURSELVES

We have so many beliefs that have been handed down to us from our parents, our preachers, or even strangers. These can be confusing because they may conflict with what we have heard in school, in the media, or from other strangers. We might assume that many people would like to know the truth— but it may not be as psychologically comfortable as the myths that mother taught us. What if there is no God—is there still an enjoyable afterlife? If some rulers are psychotic in their drive for power—might we be eradicated by nuclear, bacterial, or chemical methods of mass destruction.

WHAT KIND OF KNOWLEDGE DO WE NEED?

As a legislator or a citizen in our globalized world we need much more knowledge than at any time in the past. We need to know a great deal about world history. Every country sees the world through the eyes of its past. We must know about religions.

STUDYING WORLD HISTORY

World history is vitally important as a subject to be studied. But it has been said that history is written about things that never happened by people who were not there. That is of course sometimes true. Homer composed the Iliad hundreds of years after the battle supposedly happened. Some things seem to have been true, some things are obviously fantasy.

The study of history has been variously defined as being the study of war and religion or of being the study of great people. In either case, we must be aware that the psychological motivations of people have probably not changed a great deal in the last 5,000 or 10,000 years. That is why history so often repeats itself.

If reading a history textbook during the early 1940s in Germany or in the US, you would be reading about two different wars being fought. History is easily fabricated by the rulers of the country. Even recently in the United States in some school districts, the biblical story of creation was held to be superior to the theory of evolution.

We must realize that in studying history we are not studying a highly verifiable science, like physics. Historians are often influenced by the rulers of their country, their own political or religious prejudices and assumptions, and the limitation of knowledge in the area being studied. For example, in studying early Egyptian history we are limited to a very small number of written documents and those may have been influenced by the rulers at the time.

Studying World War II is a little easier because we have both historical records of those who were there, and a number of films. But we don't have all of the records of Hitler, Mussolini, or Tojo to complete the historical analysis. Even today, we have Donald Trump's analysis of the world and the predictions of the Brexiteers. How will historians judge this period of democratically determined chaos? Did "one person, one vote" lead us upward or downward in our path toward utopia?

STUDYING RELIGIONS

Religion has been a major motivator and mesmerizer of humans. We want to know where we came from and where we are going. It also gives us a basis for our ethical behavior, even though our societies had generally put down the ethical-legal rules earlier:

> ➢ Don't murder each other
> ➢ Don't steal from each other
> ➢ Don't lie to each other
> ➢ Don't worship gods from another tribe
> ➢ Don't sleep with another person's mate without permission
> ➢ Honor your elders

These are general, but not universal, ideas of how to run a society. Stealing, sharing the wife, even lying, may be found to be ethical in a society or two. And there are times when finding a new supernatural is looked upon as a miracle—so is highly desirable.

While both the primitive and the modern religions should be studied, in the West there is plenty to learn and question about the monotheistic religions that trace to Abraham. Religions have been primary motivators for rulers, rebellions, and wars.

What about the Bible? If Moses actually lived it is estimated that it was around 1400 to 1200 BCE. He wrote the first five books of the Bible which included the story of creation, which Bishop Usher estimated to be in 4004 BCE. The one God that Jews, Christians and Muslims believe in was first revealed to Abraham who was supposed to have lived around 1800 BCE. Moses then went up to Mount Sinai and God gave him the 10 Commandments.

These might be interesting discussions:

• What language was the Bible written in?

• Is the Old Testament true?

•   Is it true that the Koran allows the beheading of unbelievers? What did it really say?

• How has Christianity developed?

Since Jesus and the Greek god Dionysus (the Roman god Bacchus) were both conceived by a god with a human female, both turned water into wine, both died and were resurrected after three days—could there be a relationship in their importance?

• Did Jesus want to start a new religion?

• Is Buddhism, as conceived by the Buddha, a religion or merely a philosophy of life?

While the answers may seem simple, they may not be. For example, if Moses wrote the first five books of the Bible, and he lived between 1200 and 1450 BCE, but written Hebrew first appears in about 800 to 900 BCE—would Moses have written the Bible in Egyptian hieroglyphics or Phoenician? If he was raised as an important person in the house of the pharaoh he probably knew both languages. The ancient alphabets of the eastern Mediterranean area seem to have been developed from hieroglyphics. Phoenician was probably the first. But, of course, we haven't discovered everything that was ever written in that region three or four millennia ago—so it can only be an educated guess!

Our earliest copies of the Old Testament of the Christian Bible, the Tanakh of the Jews, are from a thousand years after Moses lived.

What about the New Testament? None of the writers of the Gospels ever saw Jesus. Paul, who was the major voice in the development of Christianity had never seen Jesus. It was at the Council of Nicaea in 325 AD that it was decided on the nature of Jesus, that he was God, and the true history of his actual life. Not all gospels were accepted. Those of Thomas, Mary, and Judas were dropped from consideration.

The monotheistic religions, where there is only one God, are generally highly intolerant to other belief systems. It is not only the major religions, such as the Christians and Muslims, but also the sects within the religions that accept different points of view. Why doesn't God allow just one true story?

In the Thirty Years War, it was actually Catholics against the Protestants. Recently it has been the Sunni against the Shia. And throughout history we have seen major confrontations between the major religions. This intolerant bias, in religion or in politics, makes it generally impossible to agree on the basic assumptions or the issues involved in a disagreement.

You don't have Buddhist or Hindu wars, where the adherents to the religion attempt to convert others. In Hinduism, all is God so they believe that all beliefs can be accepted within their pantheistic basic assumption. With pure Buddhism, it is not a religion but rather a philosophy of life. This does not mean that Hindus and Buddhists will not be involved in wars. They will be involved in political wars, but not wars to advance their religious ideologies.

The situation in Myanmar is not a war to convert Muslims, but rather a political move to keep the population homogeneous. Siddhartha would be ashamed!

Intolerance, by definition, disallows competing points of view. For that reason, religions should be studied, in terms of--their philosophies, their histories, their places in history, and the comparison of their political implications.

LET'S LOOK AT A FEW QUESTIONS THAT MAY RATTLE SOME BELIEFS

If we are to be educated, we must examine our basic assumptions and the facts and values that we have long held. Examining our beliefs in:

➢ Our religion,

➢ Our political assumptions: -- for example, that democracy is the best method of government today,

➢ Our economic assumptions, especially related to socialism and capitalism,

➢ Our ethical beliefs

As Socrates said, "the unexamined life is not worth living."

ECONOMICS

Another important area to understand is macroeconomics. The realities of local, national, and international economies are changing at breakneck speeds. Overpopulation, the lack of education, the unrealistic low ages for retirement based on our increased lifespans, the increased use of computer programs, the use of robots, artificial intelligence, and 3-D printing all affect the kinds of jobs that are, or soon will be, available.

Knowing a bit about currency valuation, inflation, stock markets, growth domestic products and other such economic concerns can help us to see beyond what our leaders tell us about the economy. For example, President Donald Trump took credit for the increased stock market, employment increases, and business success. These were actually already underway for several years before he took office. However, they may have been speeded up by his corporate tax breaks and his eliminating of regulations that protected the consumer at the expense of businesses and stockholders. We'll see.

Relative to the stock market success of 2017, the Dow Jones industrials increased 25%, the S&P 500 increased 19%, and NASDAQ increased 20%. These were all outstanding increases, but of the 73 worldwide stock markets, 64 showed gains in 2017. In fact, $9 trillion was added to the worth of world stock markets. A number of countries did much better than the US. The Argentina Merval index increased by 77%, the Nigerian All-Share index increased 42%, Turkey's stock market increased 48 percent, and Hong Kong's increased by 36%. In fact, the world stock markets increased by about 24.6% in 2017, and emerging markets increased by 37.75%. So by world standards, America's increase was not really that great. But then perhaps when Trump trumpeted his influence on the stock market, he may not have known all about the world.

The American Dow-Jones index more than tripled under Obama's administration from 6000 to 20,000. Under Trump's pro-business approach (low taxes and the cutting of pro-consumer regulations) it went over 26,000. Then, under Trump's anti-business approach (trade-war inciting tariffs) it had lost about 2,000 points—as of this writing. Still, not bad. Another factor was the value of the dollar, decreasing 12% against the euro in 2017, which made American exports cheaper. Trump wanted a weaker dollar to stimulate exports. His tax cuts were a factor in its weakening. As the national debt goes up, interest on our debt increases, and the dollar goes down—generally!

When Obama took over it cost $1.47 to buy one euro. By the end of his term it only cost $1.13. As of this writing it varies between $1.17 and $1.20. This is all academic drivel, unless you want to: vacation out of the country, buy a foreign made car, or like Norwegian salmon.

The value of the British pound also reduced, which made British exports cheaper. Of course, when a currency weakens it also increases the cost of imports which may raise the cost of living. In the UK during the year that they voted for Brexit, the inflation rate was 0.7%. One and a half years later it was 3.1%. In the US inflation had bottomed out at about 0% in 2015 and 2016, then it went up, then down to about 1.6% in the summer of 2017. It then moved up to 2.7% at the end of 2017. There are many reasons for inflation to go up and down, wars and recessions have huge impacts. The UK has had inflation rates in the 20% range in the 1970s, and the US has had rates over 10% at various times in its recent history.

If pay keeps up with inflation, there is no real problem. But in the UK since Brexit, wages have increased about 1%, while inflation has increased to 3.1%. So there was a net loss in purchasing power.

In the US, according to Bloomberg, the lower income earners have increased wages above the inflation level, but the middle-income earners are slightly below the inflation level in their wages, and the highest wage earners' pay increases are quite a bit below the inflation rate.

When the American dollar lost 12% of its value, against the euro, during 2017. This was equivalent to $175.5 billion for the year. Compare this with the near $5.5 trillion dollar increase in the value of American stocks and you see that on average, investors gained 30 times more than they lost. But if you are not an investor you lost 12% of the value of your dollar on imported goods and foreign travel. And if you are buying from China, things will cost more, since their currency has gained 3% against the dollar.

With tax cuts increasing the national debt by $1.5 trillion, the dollar continues to lose value and investors in treasury bills are less likely to be interested in buying. The Chinese, for example, are shying away from further financing the debt of the United States. If they decided to sell some of their $1.2 trillion treasury bills, interest rates could rise on our national debt and the dollar could lose more value.

While some knowledge of economics may help us understand a bit about our finances and how we fit into the world economy, the social science of economics has far too many millions of variables to be even close to the natural sciences in its ability to predict outcomes. Many are predicting a drop in the stock market. But no one can predict exactly when or how much.

No one knows exactly how much national debt can be safely handled, but many think that the US has long passed that measure of safety. Spending our way out of the next recession, as Obama did; spending our way to more wars, as Bush did and Trump may; or spending our way to more tax cuts, as Trump, the Bushes, and Reagan did—will soon take its toll. The austerity requirements of Greece and Portugal were nearly intolerable to their citizens. My guess is that they will be totally intolerable to American citizens. So what is the alternative? Does anybody know?

There are a few findings of economics that seem to be generally true, such as when you spend more than you earn, you will have trouble. Whether it is our individual credit card debts or our collective national debt, we can't live beyond our means without eventually having to pay the piper. Personal bankruptcy means a loss of money for our creditors. National bankruptcy or insolvency means the same thing.

Puerto Rico recently defaulted on its debt. Belarus, Argentina, Jamaica, Belize, and Venezuela are all near bankruptcy. Greece has been fighting bankruptcy for several years by restructuring its debts and undergoing national austerity. But the country most in danger of bankruptcy today is Ukraine. Fighting a war with Russia while its agriculture and other possible exports are diminished by the war, is not an ideal way to balance a budget!

Many countries have defaulted on their debts throughout the last few centuries. France defaulted in 1812 due to Napoleon's military expenses. Sweden did it the same year for the same reason. In the next few years Denmark and Netherlands defaulted. 50 years later it was Egypt. Germany had several problems in 1932. Through the years, Austria, Russia, and Spain have defaulted. Most African and South American countries have also experienced defaults in payments. United States and the UK have also defaulted at different times.

When a country defaults, it may try to restructure loans and enter a period of austerity with high taxes and reduced government services. It may reduce the value of its currency, as the US. did soon after the Declaration of Independence. It may simply walk away from their debts, as Germany did after World War I, saying that they are issuing a moratorium on debt repayment. As you might expect, the creditor nations that will not be repaid may think unkindly of the debtors, and may not be ready to loan money in the future.

Another concern. Jobs popular in the past are significantly reduced or eliminated. For example, farming occupied about half of all workers two hundred years ago. Today it is about 1%. The railroads needed workers to build them. But few are needed today. Manufacturing occupied many as the Industrial Revolution developed. But robots, as well as the cheaper labor in Africa and Asia reduced the call for manufacturing in the West. The call today is for service industries: medical, banking, IT, engineering and other jobs that require a high level of education. But with the booming population and the impossibility of educating all the people of the world to the level that they can achieve, unemployment continues to increase and economic migration surges.

The idealistic and empathetic urge of many is to open the gates of the West to those escaping war or poverty, but this may pinch the wallets of the natives and incite the populism that reactionary leaders like: Trump, Le Pen in France, Orban in Hungary, Petry in Germany, Strache in Austria, Wilders in the Netherlands, Farage in the UK, and many others--who voice their discontent. And many more voters heed their calls.

The love-filled liberals may be lowering the potential of their own welfare states—unless they limit their refugees to physicians, engineers, and mathematicians. It is a Catch 22. Being a humane and sympathetic person to another human being who is in dire need, may reduce my own financial fortunes and bring me closer to neediness.

Got it? Lots of problems, few solutions. That's why they call economics "the dismal science." Maybe we shouldn't study economics at all! There may be no way out-- with our propensity to procreate, our inclination to invade, and our concern for the present rather than the future-- can we really look intelligently at our economic realities? And if we look, will we act? And if we act, will we be moving in the right direction? And if we are moving in the right direction, will we have followers? And if we have followers, how committed will they be?

(For more on the problems of overpopulation, let me again suggest reading Book 1 "Reducing Overpopulation" in the free e-book series andgulliverreturns.info.)

SOCIOLOGY AND PSYCHOLOGY

Immigration is a major concern for much of the world. To begin to understand it we must know something about psychology and sociology. Here are some illustrations of how these social sciences may aid us in understanding some social problems.

While in the United States, Canada, and Australia, immigrants may commit fewer crimes than the native population, in Europe various studies show increases in crimes by immigrants at 3 to 450% depending on the country and the type of crime reported. (Although Germany's latest crime statistics show a 30-year low, in spite of taking in more than two million refugees.) The incidence of rape and robbery are often much higher for immigrants. European immigrants from the US, Canada, China, and Japan tend to be much lower than the average of the native population in crime rates. But countries such as: Lebanon, Pakistan, Tunisia, Morocco, and sub-Saharan Africa tend to be much higher. This is particularly true of young men between the ages of 15 and 45.

Norway found that the rate of immigrant crime was much higher for second-generation youth than for first generation youth. Italy found that it was the undocumented (illegal) immigrants who were the vast majority of criminals. In Switzerland 70% of the prison population were noncitizens, but noncitizens were only 22% of the total population.

In Ireland immigrants are under-represented in the prisons. This is probably due to the homelands of the refugees and the amount of work available for the immigrants.

Sociologists point out that socioeconomic factors such as: unemployment, poverty, inability to speak the language and other such factors may be the real causes of the crime rate discrepancies. While these are undoubtedly factors, it is generally the lower socioeconomic class of the refugees and immigrants combined with the traditions of ethical and legal traditions of the countries of their births.

For example, in countries where multiple brides can be purchased-- like South Sudan, Somalia and a number of other sub-Saharan and Mideast countries-- women are like chattel. A fetching 15-year-old may be worth 15 to 300 cows. Not many young Somalians can afford such a price. Consequently, stealing cattle is a viable option. The newspapers of the area frequently note how many people and how many cows were killed in a raid. When young men enter a country where women are equal, they may not be able to understand that rape is not acceptable. Societal realities, including values, are learned early— and may be difficult to unlearn.

Understanding such economic and social realities may be intellectually possible, but it is difficult to grasp the real situation. I can't remember the last time I heard of a Denver lad paying 300 cows for the love of his life! It may have been enough to take his future in-laws to Dairy Queen for a chocolate milk shake!

We tend to think that everyone thinks like we do. How can anyone be a Methodist, an atheist, a socialist, or a Democrat-- when I am a capitalistic Lutheran Republican?

SCIENCE

Science also has to be studied. It is not enough to know something about some sciences, like: chemistry, physics, biology, zoology, psychology, sociology, economics, etc. Intelligent citizens should know something about the foundations of science and that not all sciences are equally probable. Chemistry and physics are far more probable than the life sciences of biology, botany, and zoology. Then when we get into the social sciences of psychology, sociology, and economics, we are in areas that have an immense number of variables so the probability of their findings is much lower than in chemistry or physics.

HISTORY

When we look at the field of history we have even more variables. Who witnessed the parting of the Red Sea or the battles between the attacking Achaeans and the Trojans. There are serious questions about whether Moses actually existed. And what about Achilles or Hector? Even today we can read many different accounts of the Civil War in America in different history books. So history is nowhere near as probable or as verifiable as chemistry. What can we believe in the history books? Still we need some concept of the past, so Herodotus and Caesar have at least given us a glimpse-- even if through clouded lenses.

What about "our land"—America? As we all know, the Native Americans have inhabited North and South America for over 10,000 years. After Columbus, the British, Spanish, Dutch, French and Portuguese claimed all of the Western Hemisphere. Spain claimed most of South America, all of Central America and what we now know as the Southwest United States from Texas to California.

Not all Americans are aware that in 1845 President Polk offered to buy what is now the southwestern United States. Mexico refused. So in a gesture of democratic compromise, the United States attacked Mexico and went as far as Mexico City. To end the war, Mexico signed the Treaty of Guadalupe Hidalgo in 1848. It ceded much of its northern land to the US. This included California, Nevada, Utah, most of Arizona, about half of New Mexico around 25% of Colorado and little bit of Wyoming. Texas was already a state through what some consider a dubious acquisition of Mexican lands. Ah, democracy!

This might not have happened if Mexico had only had a Trump-like president in the early 1800s, a man who threw out all of the illegal undocumented "gringos" who had crossed the borders of Mexico without permission, then built a wall to keep them out. And maybe they could have had the US pay for the wall!

PHILOSOPHY

And what about philosophy? Is it valuable to understand: our basic assumptions, how we think, what is good, what is beautiful, and what is ethical?

Then we come back to our oft-pondered perplexity--do we want lower taxes or more happiness? And if happiness, what is the stuff of happiness, a job, high pay, more vacations, safe neighborhoods?

EVEN MORE KNOWLEDGE

But we need much more knowledge today. How can we understand the complexities of climate change without some knowledge of chemistry, geography and ecology?

How can we understand the legalities of our world without some knowledge of international law?

How can we understand the people in our societies without understanding psychology, cultural anthropology, and sociology?

How can we separate fact from fiction when we hear political proposals or religious ideas, unless we understand the essentials of logic?

People say that we are all entitled to our opinions but we are not entitled to our own facts. Our opinions should be based on probable truths and sound logic. No one is entitled to be ignorant, and still be called a citizen, in our modern democracy.

Can artificial intelligence help us to see the way? The US has more AI companies, but China may have more data. Should we cooperate or compete? AI may be able to filter out fake news. It may be able to give immediate feedback on politicians' statements during debates and on their pronouncements to the press. AI can do such things as aiding traffic flow by controlling traffic signals immediately when there is congestion.

But who has control of the algorithms that run much of today's society? If the billionaire puppeteers have control, we are in even more trouble than we are now-- Big Brother and his father may have almost complete control over our data.

According to a study from Oxford University, 47% of American jobs are at risk from new technologies, including artificial intelligence. Changes in technology are happening at a rate of about 3000 times faster than happened in the Industrial Revolution. People like the late Stephen Hawking, the physicist, and Elon Musk, the entrepreneur, are concerned that artificial intelligence might take over the world of humans.

And what about our personal lives? In the singles world, it won't be long before people will check the database of their prospective dates before going out with them. I can imagine online dating services with a wealth of information on every client. My gosh, I would never get a date!

Maybe we won't even need to date. Artificial intelligence will probably be able to select that perfect mate for me from the three and a half billion people of the opposite sex in the world. Or if I don't want someone of the opposite sex, there are still three and a half billion of my sex for my perfect match. And If I want to be a hermit, it can match me with all the available caves in the climate zone of my choice. And we were worried about the future!

LOOKING DEEPER INTO ALL OF OUR BELIEFS

Since Hurricane Harvey is battering Houston and Rockport as I write the first draft of this book, we might look at the causes of the catastrophe. It could be that God is not happy with Texas, the US, or President Trump. After Hurricane Katrina, the Reverend Pat Robertson said that the reason for the storm was that God was unhappy with America because of its legalized abortion. He did not say why God was not unhappy with the legalized abortions in Europe.

If God had planned Hurricane Harvey, certainly no human prayers could change His mind. But lots of Texans were praying.

Another theory of why Harvey happened is that global warming that has increased the temperatures of the Gulf of Mexico to 3 to 7° higher than normal. The hot weather in the area has invited storms for hundreds of years. However, the increased temperature of the air and water has amplified the amount of water that the air can hold as water vapor. When the atmosphere is cooled a bit, it can't hold as much water vapor so the water is released as heavy rain or snow. 20 to 50 inches of rain, and even more in some areas-- more than any city can handle.

So choose your explanation-- should it be the traditions of the last 3000 years, sanctified by what your mother and your preacher have told you, or should it be based on the empirical evidence and the analyses of the scientists who study the environment?

In either case, both science and religion should be studied in the curriculum. We cannot understand human history without understanding how it has been, and still is, influenced by religion. We need to know about the differences between religions, their varying basic assumptions, and the many questions relative to the philosophies and the history of religions.

THE LIBERAL ARTS

All of these areas of study have a place in the education of the intelligent citizen. And of course, no one can know everything. The last Westerner to supposedly know everything was Francis Bacon, a contemporary of Shakespeare in the late 17th century. Of course he knew nothing about the knowledge that existed in India, China, Japan, Iran, Peru, Mexico, and other non-European civilizations.

So all we can do, if we want an education, is to scratch the surface of some of the important areas of knowledge that a citizen should know. And we should be able to use the tools of logic to separate fact from fiction, knowledge from opinion, and unsubstantiated belief from probability. It is critical to be able to separate uncomfortable provable empirical facts from comfortable unprovable faith and our unexamined traditions.

It isn't enough to examine our long-held traditions to catch a glimpse of the truth. Today with every gradient on the political spectrum having media voices that may give us some truths and some untruths—how do we determine what is true? Is the loudest voice the most authoritative? Are the voices merely mouthing the messages that the millionaire owners of the media outlets want us to ingest? Are the voices purposely outlandish conspiracy mongers, trusting that their different views will bring them more listeners, and therefore more dollars?

Shall we devour the garbage cast before us swine, or shall we dissect it with our scalpels of semantics, then examine it with our knowledge on inductive logic and our verifiable knowledge of the world?

Will we use the same mental tools to eviscerate the propaganda of the bots and trolls that are fabricated in: the Kremlin paid troll holes of Saint Petersburg, the enterprising but dishonest teenagers in Macedonia, or the offices of the Venezuelan president? The propaganda pellets on our digital devices are more difficult to dodge than a snowflake in a winter storm.

DARE WE BECOME TRUE *HOMO SAPIENS?*

Dare we intellectually challenge the voices on the radio, the personalities on the television, the President of the United States? Dare we swat the bots that bombard us on our phones and tablets? Dare we challenge our representatives to make us great again through education?

The less educated among us are far more likely to hold onto traditional values—conservative orthodoxy is easier to hold in religion for Jews, Christians, and Muslims. It is also easier to hold in politics. Why bother to think when your ancestors have already done it—and commanded you to follow?

Moving to the left requires examining one's values. Remaining on the conservative side also requires studying and re-examining one's values. Educated thoughtful people are found from the right to the left—what is essential is that you have thought your way into your belief. Espousing a value just because it will make you more money, or because it is based on a wish, is not worthy of an educated person.

SOME IDEAS WE SHOULD THINK ABOUT

Following are a number or questions that might be discussed in a liberal arts program in college or high school. Engaging students in discussions on issues has been found to be a highly effective method of education. Lectures often give a high quality of information, but forcing people to think is critical to a deeper learning experience. A quality instructor is necessary to make certain that the various ramifications of the issues are addressed.

These questions and ideas might also be food for thought in adult discussion groups—or even over the family dinner table. Most people will have an opinion on most of them—but opinions without factual foundations, or deeply reflective thought, are not worthy of a true *homo sapiens.*

HERE ARE SOME REALITIES

➤We are all going to die, so how important is it to protest capital punishment or donate to starving children in other countries? How about euthanasia? If we are going to die someday but want to die now—what's the problem? I will have less pain, society saves many thousands of dollars, and my grieving relatives can get back to their computer games instead of having to visit me at the hospital.

➤The world is overpopulated, so are the humanitarian efforts to save everybody today counterproductive to saving the planet for our grandchildren?

➤There is not enough money in the world to supply everything that everyone wants.

➤Healthcare must get more expensive. Diseases of old age, like Alzheimer's and stroke and heart attacks and cancer, increase the price of health care internationally.

➤The only way to get lower costs for healthcare is to eliminate insurance company profits and the high salaries of their managers. It must be done as a state sponsored healthcare program.

➤We must choose between happiness and low taxes. It seems impossible to have both. Which do you prefer, and why?

➢It seems that tax rates from 45 to 50% are necessary to finance the needs that most people want.

➢The national debt, which is increasing by leaps and bounds, will have to be paid off by us or our children. How and when shall it be done?

➢Many of the ideas that people are willing to die for are unprovable: a supreme being, a communist society, a current government.

➢Our sub-conscious minds are major influences on our behavior, including our values.

➢The drive for power, to overcome our inferiority feelings, is nearly universal.

➢The ability to love unselfishly is not as prevalent as many liberals seem to think—in fact it is quite rare!

➢Women have great abilities in the academic and political areas, but to allow them access to the hallowed halls steps on the toes of those men who are their inferiors.

➢The "Me too" recognition of the sexual harassment and abuse by unethical men with huge feelings of inferiority—seems to be increasing gender equality.

➢Most people in the world base their lives on faith and hope—not on empirically verified facts.

WHAT ABOUT THESE DILEMMAS?

➢In the UK about 25% of a person's lifetime medical bills occur during the last month of life. With limited funding, where is society better served: in primary and secondary education, in free college tuition, in treating severely deformed infants, in building up the military, in promoting business, in building better roads and bridges, in lowering retirement ages, in increasing pensions, OR?

➢With separation of church and state, should churches be taxed? Should church schools be supported by tax funds?

HERE ARE SOME QUESTIONABLE BELIEFS

➢Tax breaks for the rich will make them richer and their profits will trickle down to the social classes below. It sounds good—but doesn't happen.

➢Tomorrow will be a better day.

➢Democracy is the best form of government.

➢Every country should be ruled by shariah law.

➢All our legislators are primarily concerned with us, not with being re-elected.

**A LIBERALLY EDUCATED PERSON WOULD HAVE THOUGHT
ABOUT MANY OF THESE QUESTIONS**
SOME ESSENTIAL QUESTIONS ABOUT OUR WORLD

➢ Since overpopulation is a major problem of the world, with too many people using fossil fuels and building fires and too many people using irreplaceable natural resources, why is everyone afraid to mention it? Is it because having children has been so important throughout human history that we cannot challenge it now?

➢ With a population heading toward 9 billion people, if we educate a billion to be farmers, shopkeepers, doctors, and teachers-- do we really need 8 billion computer engineers and videogame programmers?

➢ Why don't foods that are so good for you, like broccoli, taste so bad?

➢ Why don't we elect more women to important posts? Since they don't seem to be nearly as power driven as most men? Maybe we could get something important done.

➢ Why can't we teach people to say exactly what they mean? Using the same four letter adjective to modify every noun is not very intelligent-- but then maybe we don't need to talk while our mind is on the game.

➢ In ethics, many people subscribe to Kant's rule "to always treat people as ends in themselves—and not as means to my own success or pleasure." Or the Golden Rule of religions, "to do unto others as you would have done unto you." But many economically or politically successful people use the observation of Herbert Spencer, applying Darwinian observations, that in society it is the "survival of the fittest." Should we use only one, or both, of these diametrically opposed ethical directions?

➢ What should be appropriate punishments for: illegal drug sales, murder of a family member, serial murder, treason, bank robbery, rape, sexual harassment in the workplace.

➢ When there are refugees from a war, such as in Syria or Sudan, should your country take in refugees? How many? What will it cost?

➢ Why don't 40% of Americans care who governs them? They average only about 60% voter turnout for major elections.

➢ Why don't Black athletes get white tattoos?

THE ENDURING QUESTIONS AND OUR EDUCATION

Should we introduce questions that the world must answer into our liberal arts curriculum?

ETHICS

➢ How do we determine what is ethical? Should we look at self-centered, society based, and God based reasons for determining our ethics?

➢ When what I believe cannot be examined scientifically, such as religions or political parties' points of view, how much credence should be given to unprovable faith?

SELF CENTERED VALUES

➢ If I can't take it with me, why am I so concerned with getting so much more?

➢ If I earned it myself, and I'm happy with myself, will my children be more mature and happy if they don't have to earn anything?

➢ What would make me truly happy?

➢ Why am I so much more important than anyone else?

➢ How much money do I really need? Europeans are more likely to take more vacations, travel more, and read more. Would my life be more satisfying if I followed their lead?

➢ Have I considered what The Buddha said about achieving happiness? He said, "eliminate your desires and you will have all you want."

➢ Why am I concerned more with the pain in my little finger than with that person who has had his leg blown off by a landmine?

➢ Why am I more concerned with the price of my stock portfolio than with the hundreds of thousands of people who are starving and impoverished from a war?

SOCIETY BASED VALUES

➢ When people get themselves into problems, should society help them out? What about the homeless, the mentally ill, drug addicts?

➢ How can population be reduced other than by war?

➢ What if people smoke and get emphysema or heart disease, how much should the government pay to treat them?

➢ What if people have children that they could not afford when they had them or they were not capable of providing for them physically or emotionally? Should society take over the children with foster families, orphanages, etc.

➢ Leaders such as Merkel in Germany, May in the UK, Modi in India, Abe in Japan, and Macron in France do not have children. It gives them more time to succeed in life. What about this?

➢ What shall we do about global warming and climate change?

➢ What can be done about cleaning up our oceans so that the fish are not filled with plastic?

➢ Should we tax inheritances? Or should the government merely take all of the assets when a person or couple has died?

➢ In what situations should the US go to war to save other countries for democracy?

➢ Should war be the first political action considered or should we look for other means to entice countries to act ethically?

➢ Should religious holdings, like land and buildings, be taxed as either personal income or taxed as property?

➢ Should we eliminate the capital gains tax, which gives a much lower tax rate to stock traders and other property owners than to workers?

➢ Should there be a flat tax on all income, with no deductions?

➢ Should there be a flat tax on all income of a corporations, with no deductions?

Should fines, like traffic fines, be a percentage of one's yearly income, or total wealth, rather than a flat fee—so that the rich are inconvenienced as much as the poor when they break traffic laws?

➢ Should society pay for all education from preschool through the doctoral level? If so, how will it be financed?

➢ Should society pay for all adult education whether vocational or recreational?

➢ Should youth sport be directed by youth or by their parents?

➢ Where should the money that we have be spent?

On school children at every level? At $12,000 per year in school,

On free college tuition, at $20,000 per year?

On serial killers at $70,000 per year in prison?

GOD BASED VALUES

➢ If the objective of religion is to get people to heaven—and if a very good person is severely injured in an accident, rather than life-saving surgery, should the person be allowed to die, thereby saving money for the society and hastening salvation.

➢ When people say "God gives and God takes away," paraphrasing Job 1:21, how does that personal observation of Job equate with prohibiting a suffering person who wants to die through euthanasia, or preventing the abortion of an unwanted child?

➢ In 2017 when evangelical Christian Judge Roy Moore was running for the US Senate and had been accused of dating and the sexual abuse of young teenagers, one of his defenders said that the Virgin Mary was only a teenager when the adult carpenter from Nazareth, Joseph, married her-- so when the 30-year-old assistant district attorney dated a 14 or 16-year-old, it was approved by the Bible. What would you say?

--If the leader of your religion, or sect, orders you to: kill infidels, burn witches, torture non-believers, or go to war to recapture the Holy Land, what would be your reaction?

--If the leader of your religion asked you to give all your wealth and possessions to disaster relief in Haiti, what would be your reaction?

QUESTIONS ABOUT JUSTICE

Justice Is often demanded, but seldom understood. "Justice is what I want." But you may have noticed that people have very different ideas of what fairness is. The rich want more money, and it is only fair-- because they have earned it. The poor want more money and what it can buy, especially for housing and food. The recent college graduates want jobs. They are qualified but no one will hire them. Immigrants want what the natives have. Conquerors want what the conquered possess. Might makes right! Do unto others. . .! Walk a mile in his moccasins!

Modern writers on justice usually assume that some sort of equality, especially equality of opportunity and the equality of human rights, are clearly the stuff of which justice is made. But look at the super rich and their acquisitiveness. What is fair for them is lower taxes and no inheritance taxes. Liberty is primary.

So we have the ideal of equality on one hand and of liberty, which is the product of various types of inequality, on the other.

Then we have the idea that citizens have a duty to behave ethically. The United Nations Declaration of Human Rights is clear that citizens have a duty to their countries. China's Constitution is also very clear on the duties of citizens. But the European Union in its declaration of rights does not require any duties of a citizen. However, we will assume that citizens have some duties.

EQUALITY

When you want the government to pay for a program—How much will it cost, and where do you think the money should come from?

➤How much should government pay for the living or health expenses for poor people?

➤Should there be a guaranteed annual salary for all citizens, whether they work or not? If so, from whence comes the cash?

➤Should people who have greater expertise in a critical area of world or national problems have more than one vote in a democracy? If so, how might the number of additional votes be determined?

➤Do equality concerns stop at our borders? If not, what are you willing to do for the children of Haiti, or refugees from Nigeria who have been raped, beaten, or sold into slavery

LIBERTY

➤If politicians lie, should there be a penalty for that, and if so what? (The Supreme Court says "No.")

➤Should there be a way to take away the riches that were acquired by corruption? If so how?

DUTY

➤Do you have a duty to your parents? If so, how can you exercise it?

➤Do you have a duty to your country? If so, how can you exercise it?

➤Do you have a duty to treat every person as an end in himself or herself?

➤Do you have a duty to work to prevent sexual harassment and abuse?

➤Would you report sexual harassment or abuse if you saw it happen?

EQUALITY OF OPPORTUNITY

➤How should equality of opportunity in education be enhanced? Or should it?

➢Should there be a 100% tax on inheritance so that all young people start closer to equal financially?

➢How can education be made more effective?

➢But if education were effective, few of our politicians would be elected!

➢Which ones do you think are not qualified to legislate or lead?

DANGERS TO DEMOCRACY

➢Is there a chance that America can be taken over by an authoritarian tyrant? Some of our presidents would probably have liked this. I can certainly think of one right off the bat!

➢It is so tempting that when once in power to throttle the free press, cast your opponents into prison for treason, and write a new constitution. Which democratically elected presidents have done any of these recently?

➢On the right side of the spectrum, with societal traditions and the Almighty, on your side, where this is most likely to happen. Or is it?

➢There are a number of anti-government private militias ready to take on the central government. Should they be encouraged or outlawed?

➢In today's globalized world, the modes of prediction and the realities of economics clearly show that it is education, not brute strength, that drive's the wheel of progress.

➢Whether we like it or not, the world is globalized. The Boeing Dreamliner is a case in point. Over 30% of its costs are paid to manufacturers in foreign countries. So why are there so many populist movements for sovereignty?

➢Opening coal mines, when people are switching to solar power and wind power, is definitely closing the barn door after the horse escaped. How should we anticipate, and prepare for, jobs for the future?

➢Should a presidential election be merely a popularity contest? If not, what accomplishments should be required? (TV personality? Business success? PhD in political science? Having held a high state or federal office? Or?)

➢Should there be knowledge requirements to be qualified to be a member of Congress or the administration? If so, what areas should be tested? This would require a Constitutional amendment.

SHOULD THE EDUCATED PEOPLE BE ABLE TO QUESTION LONG HELD TRADITIONS?

What about the idea of democracy being the best method of government? Of course, democracy is seldom used in government. Usually we have popular elections of the representatives we want to rule us, so we have democratic republics. Occasionally in referenda, as in Brexit, the people actually have a voice in what will happen in their country.

In the United States the popular vote of the people in 2000 and 2016 did not matter because of a 200-year-old provision in the Constitution that required that the people could only elect electors. In 2000 people voted for the nationally experienced and outspoken environmentalist, Al Gore. They got George W. Bush, a shoot first and ask questions later Texas cowboy. How would Gore have handled the 9-11 New York bombing? How did George Bush handle it? He attacked Iraq, telling everyone that they had weapons of mass destruction. But that was not true. The negative outcomes of his actions cost nearly 5000 American lives and more than triple that in Iraqi lives. In fact, the total body count is well over 110,000 and some estimates are over 450,000. Certainly, not just a quick skirmish!

It developed ISIS which created many more problems for the Mideast and the West. It cost the American taxpayers almost $6 trillion --which raised the national debt several trillion dollars. There were 4500 US military deaths and 32,000 wounded in action out of the estimated totals of 110,000 to 600,000 total deaths in the war.

Since our days in the caves, adults and teenagers, even children, have been able to have babies. In the past, large families have been hailed. Those babies will soon become adults. Have they been loved? Have they been fed properly? Have they been educated to their fullest potential? Should they have had the rights to these? Whose rights should be primary, the potential parent or the potential child?

WHAT ABOUT EDUCATION FOR PEACE?

If everybody in the world could be raised by loving families, free of genes that may lead to violence, have satisfying jobs and be able to communicate effectively, maybe we could reduce the perennial pastime of *Homo non-sapiens*--WAR. Until then, we can expect more and bigger wars and more terrorism. How else can we control our overpopulation problem unless we use more accurate firepower, develop more powerful nuclear bombs, and more effective chemical and biological weapons. How else can we keep killing off many of the brightest young minds of our societies?

How often are we left with people with only enough courage to join the military reserves, or only enough cowardice to avoid the Armed Forces. But since they avoided the wars, after we have elected them to lead—they become great warriors. Their newly found courage toppled Hussein and rattled the cages of Iran and North Korea. We must keep our instinct to violence honed. Peace is for sissies! We need more draft dodgers with their thumbs massaging the nuclear button—and threatening "fire and fury."

PART V WHERE DO WE GO FROM HERE?

Well, we can continue with our apathetic contentment with our Netflix, smart phones, and beer-- but history shows us that this is the direction of doom. Societies die from within. It may not happen during our lifetimes, or those of our children-- but the horrors of history dictate that we are sliding downward with our selfish overspending and our refusal to take responsibility for what we want.

The comfort of our couch, along with our wireless TV channel changers, numb us now. And soon our robots will be able to fetch our beer and chips. What a life! And we thought the Roman orgies were degenerate! Luckily there are some who still want to accomplish important things. But will their discoveries and work ethics be greater than those of the intellectually hungry young people of China, Vietnam, or India?

We are not dead yet. The threat of autocratic rule, of late, has stimulated many to run for elective office. There is energy yet in this old bald eagle! Are you part of the solution-- or part of the problem?

If you recognize that our world is changing far faster than ever before, you are on the left side of the political spectrum and are probably ready to work with the changes you recognize-- globalization, changes in the gender roles, changes in the relationship roles, changes in the need for education-- yes, and even changes in our sacred Constitution.

So, let us examine a few possibilities that may save us, at least temporarily, from the fates of the pharaohs, the Caesars, the medieval kings, Soviet communism, the British and Spanish Western empires, and so many of the lesser autocratic societies of the past. Intelligence, a high level of comprehensive knowledge, a humanitarian spirit, the ability to cooperate with others for the greater good, and a tireless work ethic-- are needed. Are you ready?

CHAPTER 19. WHAT THE HELL!—JUST GIVE 'EM BREAD AND CIRCUSES

What is important is to be able to sit on my sofa and watch my favorite teams win. After all, life is about winning. When my team wins, I win. Who cares what they teach in schools!

My team winning--is what life is about! And they better win! Alabama should win in football, their coach makes over $11 million a year. So he must be worth it. I will watch Real Madrid when I can. Cristiano Ronaldo makes $82 million a year. He must be a winner. Lionel Messi from Barcelona only makes $77 million a year. What a loser!

Would celebrities play games or act in movies if they were paid as much as a plumber? Of course they would! They are employed in their hobbies! And celebrity is more important in fulfilling our drives for power. Is it essential for society that all celebrities also be millionaires?

Since winning is all-important, I don't care if Tiger Woods, Floyd Mayweather, and Michael Jordan have each surpassed one billion dollars in income. But if my toilet is stopped up, a plumber becomes more important than any of them.

Ever wonder who pays for these guys? Obviously, it is ticket sales and the advertisers. So, if I drink a beer that is advertised on television, the beer has been increased in price to help pay those salaries. If I buy a car advertised during the game, part of the price of the car was in advertising. Then you pay a bit more in taxes because the owners of the professional sports teams depreciate their players over many years. This gives them huge tax deductions, which you must make up.

And now computer gaming is attracting billions of people. Many are dropping out of school to be amateur or professional gamers.

Let's see---what do games and professional sports contribute to a better world?

Reduce the wage gaps?----NO.

Reduce climate change?----NO.

Reduce overpopulation?----NO.

Make parenting more effective?----NO.

Reduce taxes?----NO.

Eliminate wars?----NO.

But they must do something! They give us something to relate to so we can increase our drive for power. If my team wins, I am more powerful and my feelings of inferiority are reduced. Hooray for me!

If money is king, we should just have our children pick up computers, golf clubs, baseball gloves, or footballs rather than books.

But why fight it? Soothing and controlling the minds of us common people lets the elites run the world.

Since the glory days of Rome when Juvenal observed how the citizens were made docile by the imperial imperative of giving them "bread and circuses." What more could be desired than food and entertainment for Romulus the Roman? As today, with Arnie American, human nature seems to move too few people to energize their full humanness. We are mesmerized by the media and our digital worlds.

Then as the power people pulled the strings of their politician puppets, taxation sleight of hand made the rich richer. This made the Roman poet wonder about who was watching the watchers. In America there is supposedly a system of checks and balances with the legislative, administrative, and judicial bodies each overseeing the other, this was supposed to solve the problems. What the Founding Fathers did not anticipate was that there would be the superrich bankrolling the first two branches of government-- and that they controlled the third. So the overseers are watching from the inside, not from a distant mountain.

Buying votes with lobbyist's dollars and with the legislative bribery of pork-barrel incentives, unhindered by a line item veto, puts Congress in the catbird seat. The Supreme Court, appointed for their partisan views, twist and turn their arguments to further their political agenda. When we do elect an intelligent and ethical president, a wise program may be stalled by the Congress. By the same token, an unconcerned president may stall the legislation of a forward-looking Congress. Our checks and balances often become stumbling blocks and hurdles too high to vault.

We don't need a revolution, but we need some important revisions and redirecting if we want an effective democratic republic. We are not in a "virtual" world, but in a real world. And real changes are difficult. Should we think deeply and work hard for positive change. Or should we just slouch back on the sofa, pop a brew, open some pretzels, and criticize the quarterback. Somebody else is running the government for me—so why worry?

CHAPTER 20. WELL!, IF YOU REALLY WANT OUR DEMOCRACY TO SURVIVE!

The power elites have always ruled. The military, the business interests, and the politicians have the power to make, or not to make, decisions that will preserve and improve our democracy and the survival of our society—in fact, the society of the world. The generals, the CEOs, the big money guys, and the senators and presidents don't have all the answers. Nobody does! In fact, those who think they know all the answers don't understand the questions. Just look at "The Donald," who said that, "only he could fix it." When it came to the health care bill he didn't even understand it. He said, "Who knew health care could be so complicated." His thinking required only: a large army, more nuclear bombs, and a belligerent mouth. That worked fine a few hundred years ago. It didn't work for Hitler or Mussolini!

We have enough bombs to destroy Earth and most of the solar system. Mass destruction is just a button push away. The obvious intelligent action is detente and diplomacy.

According to sociologist C. Wright Mills, the "power elites" are those who occupy the dominant positions, in the dominant institutions (military, economic, and political) of a dominant country, and their decisions (or lack of decisions) have international consequences, not only for the US population but often for the world. These elite very often come from the most prestigious universities in the West, such as: Cambridge, Harvard, Oxford, Yale, Stanford, and the University of California. Quite often today, they find themselves in positions of power because of their dominance in digital technologies and the media. Of course, those who enter politics have a chance at being primary elites, as do those who rise to the top of the military.

WHAT ABOUT PEOPLE-POWER IN OUR DEMOCRACY?

Theoretically, democracy is a government of the people. Of course, that has not yet been possible to achieve in large societies. So, we must abdicate our wishes to those we elect to run our republic. But as our republic has evolved, we have seen the rise of two parties that control our destinies. And, the economic elites and the political powerhouses have usurped the will of the people.

➢ 90% of Americans do not realize that the huge consensus of scientists (97%) is that global warming is human caused. Is our national education at fault? Is it the gifts of the lobbyists that have our president and many representatives denying the truth?

➢ 60% of Americans believe that humans cause climate change. Are the politicians responsive to the opinions of their constituencies or to the financial gifts of the fossil fuel industries? But then 50% think the threat is so distant that it will not hurt them—or even their grandchildren.

➢ With our educational achievements so low, are our representatives doing anything to increase our educational efficiency? 60% of Americans want national objectives for elementary and secondary education. 60% want free college tuition. Are the politicians responding to these wishes? No!

➢ 85% of Americans want a balanced budget. But every year we increase our national debt to cover our unbalanced budgets.

➢ 60% of the people want government paid health insurance or a combination of government and private insurance.

➢ More than 50% of Americans want tighter gun controls and over 90% want stricter background checks.

It would appear that our representatives are not enacting laws that reflect the wishes of the American people. This is because the cashier's checks from the lobbyists for their clients: the insurance companies, fossil fuel companies, lawyers, the NRA and many others, speak more loudly than the wishes of the populace.

We, the people, do have a way to make gigantic changes, but it would take gigantic efforts to overcome the gigantic power of the elites and the gigantic entrenchment of our two gigantic parties. Does that sound like a "gigantic" task? Making massive changes in a society requires huge efforts from many citizens.

We saw the Freedom Riders, both white and black, in the South in the 60s. We saw protesters being arrested, attacked by dogs, tortured by electric cattle prods, and even killed. But their efforts resulted in the Civil Rights Act and less of the subhuman treatment that many African-Americans still endure. It was a giant step that required superhuman commitment to the peaceful process led by Martin Luther King.

Are we ready to shout from the rooftops, "I'm mad as hell, and I am not going to take it anymore!"

Possibly, many of you readers have not seen the 1976 Academy award winning film "Network," in which a TV anchorman on a low rated station explodes with indignation and anger and stimulates an' entire city to open their windows and shout, with him, "I am mad as hell, and I'm not going to take it anymore!" The echoes of his speech still resound in the memories of those of us entranced by his passion. Here is his soliloquy.

"I don't have to tell you that things are bad. Everybody knows things are bad. It's a depression. Everybody's out of work or scared of losing their job. The dollar buys a nickel's worth. Banks are going bust. Shopkeepers keep a gun under the counter. Punks are running wild in the street and there's nobody anywhere who seems to know what to do, and there's no end to it. We know the air is unfit to breathe and our food is unfit to eat, and we sit watching our TVs while some local newscaster tells us that today we had fifteen homicides and sixty-three violent crimes, as if that's the way it's supposed to be.

We know things are bad – worse than bad. They're crazy. It's like everything everywhere is going crazy, so we don't go out anymore. We sit in the house, and slowly the world we are living in is getting smaller, and all we say is: 'Please, at least leave us alone in our living rooms. Let me have my toaster and my TV and my steel-belted radials and I won't say anything. Just leave us alone.'

Well, I'm not gonna leave you alone. I want you to get MAD! I don't want you to protest. I don't want you to riot – I don't want you to write to your congressman, because I wouldn't know what to tell you to write. I don't know what to do about the depression and the inflation and the Russians and the crime in the street. All I know is that first you've got to get mad. (shouting) You've got to say: 'I'm a human being, god-dammit! My life has value!'

So, I want you to get up now. I want all of you to get up out of your chairs. I want you to get up right now and go to the window. Open it, and stick your head out, and yell: 'I'm as mad as hell, and I'm not gonna take this anymore!'

And the city responded. Every window flew open. Disgusted and depressed citizens filled the open windows and shouted their displeasure with their world. If we are not happy with our society and our government, we should be angry. The promises of hope have reached too few of us. And the elites are getting "eliter?"

This is not to deride those who have prospered while boosting our potentials. Bill Gates, Steve Jobs, Jeff Bezos, Sergey Brin and Larry Page are American heroes. They should join the pantheon of Washington, Jefferson, Lincoln, Edison, and FDR. But their children should begin at the same starting line that they did.

So what are you willing to work for?

➢Do you want better medical care at half the cost? Then you had better think about a national health insurance rather than a private profit –making company where the stockholders and CEOs are bleeding us dry—and many legitimate claims are denied.

➢Do you want your children saddled with a national debt in the $20 to $30 trillion range with each citizen owing more than $100,000 on that debt? We each now owe "only" $64,000 on that debt today.

➢Do you want your schoolchildren subject to attacks by psychotics wielding automatic weapons? What about your own safety-- going to the theater, a concert, or to work?

➢Do you want to continue to endure the draughts, flooding, fires and increased heat caused by global warming?

➢Do you want your fellow citizens and their children to be at, or near, the bottom of the developed countries in their abilities to read, think, and count?

➢Would you be willing to increase your taxes by 80% in order to have free health coverage, better schools, free tuition, free maternity leave for a year, longer vacations, and a more generous pension? If so, you may need to change the Constitution.

DO YOU WANT TO CHANGE THE CONSTITUTION?

It is essential to change the Constitution so that a few years down the road the political party elites and big business don't pull us back into the quicksand of the big-money boys, and drown us in the lake of the lobbyists' special interests.

Article V of our Constitution lays out two ways to amend it. One way has been used 17 times since the Bill of Rights was ratified in 1791.

So far, these 27 amendments have originated in Congress and been sent to the states for approval. Once three-quarters of the individual states ratify an amendment, it becomes the law.

The second method has never been used. It involves petitions from at least 34 states to call for a constitutional convention, where one or several amendments are proposed. The amendment or amendments are then sent on to the states, where 38 states are needed for ratification.

The method that I think we need now is to use the referendum or initiative method in each state. This way, the barrier of the career politicians and the two-party system can be bypassed. There are a couple of groups that are doing that just now. The Balanced Budget Task Force has passed 27 states of the 34 necessary to call a convention. It has done this with practically no financing—just a determined group of citizens trying to save the nation. They are hoping that by 2019 they will have the 34 states in hand.

The other group, the Convention of States, has been funded and has over 2 million volunteers working for it. It also wants a balanced budget, but it also wants a limitation on the federal government's power, and on establishing term limits for members of Congress.

It is a big deal to try to get enough states to sign on to a constitutional convention. It has been tried over 500 times in the last 200 years.

The fact that in the last 200 years the various branches of government have often veered from the intent of the general principles of the Constitution and that the needs of the American society have changed—some possible amendments to the Constitution might be considered.

DO WE WANT POWER FOR THE PEOPLE—OR TO CONTINUE WITH POWER
TO THE POLITICIANS?

History is replete with the power people running our world. Kings and bishops, the Rothschilds and Rockefellers, Napoleons and Charlemagnes, have sought to control us-- today and into posterity. Whether they inherited their throne or had them bestowed by God, they have not always been on the right side of the political spectrum, and the self-centered side of the ethical roadway.

In the olden days, we peasants and serfs were illiterate and thankful for whatever crumbs or promises we were given. But today many of us can think as well, or even better, than our "betters." Today, many of us can see a light at the end of the tunnel. And it is not a train intent on running us over! It is a beacon beckoning us to enter the full light of day. It is the spark that stimulated Gandhi. It is the spirit that guided Martin Luther King. It is the hope and the courage that spurred Barack Obama, Emmanuel Macron, Colin Powell, Thomas Edison, Frederick Chopin and many others. It tells us that, "We can." But are there enough of us to do what is necessary to save our nation?

Modern-day parliaments and congresses are elected. But it is the political parties that usually control the finances necessary for their elections. A girl I went to high school with, Roz Weiner, set her sights on being elected to the Los Angeles City Council after she graduated from college. She knocked on nearly every door in her district and introduced yourself. No money, but lots of work, got her elected. While on the Council, she was instrumental in bringing the Dodgers to LA from Brooklyn. For Brooklyn, it was tantamount to a capital crime.

It is still possible today. Last year a Black, former refugee from Liberia, was elected mayor of the capitol of Montana, St. Helena. (St. Helena has a 1% Black population.) He defeated a popular four term mayor by knocking on doors, attending all the forums—and having ideas that could make the voters' lives better. Although a university graduate in Liberia, he became a school janitor in St. Helena. He worked his way up to being a child protection specialist in the Montana Department of Health and Human Services. Wilmot Collins was lucky to enter the country before the borders were closed—as was Donald Trump's grandfather.

THINGS ARE A-CHANGIN'

The election of Donald Trump, and the referendum for Brexit, stimulated many people to arise from their sofas and get involved in the political process. The hundreds of "marches of women," stimulated many women to run for office.

The publishing of the sexual assaults of Harvey Weinstein set off the "Me, too" movement around the world. There have been many thousands of women who were just "not going to take it anymore."

Women in Iran cast off their hijabs. Women in Saudi Arabia began to drive their cars, illegally at first. Citizens in Venezuela, Zimbabwe, and South Africa erupted in violence against their elected leaders.

There is a threshold for each of us that will stimulate us to act--to act with our whole selves. Many cry and complain after each school shooting where innocent children and teenagers are killed with automatic weapons. How many will run for office or work to elect those who will to call for a constitutional convention to undo the 5 to 4 decisions of the Supreme Court that have totally reversed the thinking of the Founding Fathers on the right to own firearms. The single shot muskets and pistols of the 18th Century, that were needed to repel a future invasion from the Continent, have been replaced by automatic weapons with armor piercing capabilities.

The Supreme Court allows guns for protection at home. It allows stun guns, but not automatic assault weapons. However, you can buy automatic weapons easily. At gun shows you will probably not be required to have your identity checked. A state may allow or disallow carrying a gun in public.

If such concerns, relative to carrying automatic firearms or other guns, bother you-- you probably need a constitutional amendment to change it. In fact, constitutional amendments may be required in many areas to bring the American democracy up to date and to clarify what the Founders meant by such freedoms as: free speech, freedom of the press, popular elections, freedom of religion, etc.

Since, "we the people" have been replaced by "the enlightened elites," are we ready to start to "provide for the general welfare" or shall we start a revolution for an enlightened democracy? If we do, it won't be nearly as tough as what the revolutionaries endured at Valley Forge.

Here are a few ideas we might want to consider in remodeling our much-respected Constitution, which has been an international gadfly for new governments. But gadflies don't live forever, and over time, they evolve.

Introduced here are a few of the ideas that have already made considerable progress through the states' legislatures. But there are of a few other ideas we might want to consider.

Following are possible considerations for a comprehensive amendment. These are in addition to the balanced budget proposals now circulating. There are some juicy discussions that should follow from these ideas.

Amendment to update the United States Constitution for the 21st Century:

1. The freedom of speech guarantee of the First Amendment is unlimited only as to expressing political ideas.

a. That freedom shall be limited relative to intelligent dialogue unimpaired by meaningless terms, including: vulgarities, improbable predictions, untruths, false news or false accounts of history, and hate directed at persons because of their religion, race, ethnicity, political leanings, sexual proclivities or identifications, or age.

b. Candidates for public office are held to these same standards. Violations of truthful speech or projected outcomes of a prediction will be ascertained by an impartial jury of non-aligned federal judges—and violators will sacrifice an adjudged number of votes in the election, or be found unworthy to serve.

c. If federal or state elections are proven to have been influenced by persons or groups, whether through social media or other means, not approved of by the candidates in writing, it will be considered to be espionage or treason and punished accordingly.

2. In order to make the concept of equality of opportunity a more possible and meaningful objective to promote the general welfare of the nation, and to increase the society's ability to advance maximally and to allow its citizens, and future citizens, to enjoy the possibility of achieving their greatest potential on their own efforts, these requirements are found to be necessary and required:

a. Income taxes be reduced to a maximum flat tax of 10%, except during a declared war.

b. All inheritance and wealth shall be taxed at 100% on the death of a citizen.

c. The spouse at the time of one's death is entitled to half of the community property without tax. The amount owned by the spouse or partner will be taxed at 100% at his or her death. Subsequent relationships, such as a marriage or partnership, will not be entitled to this 100% tax exemption.

3. Citizenship shall be earned. Children born of United States citizens shall be given a preferential advantage over children of non-citizens.

a. Children born in the United States of non-citizen parents shall not have automatic citizenship.

b. Well educated citizens being necessary to a modern democracy:

A written test in English will have an equal number of questions on: The Constitution, the history of the United States, the history of the world, logic and semantics, and environmental science.

4. The Second Amendment's right to bear arms as necessary for a well organized militia to repel foreign powers is hereby clarified.

a. The national military forces, the state national guards, and the state and local police are considered sufficient to repel an invading force.

b. Single shot rifles and pistols will be allowed for hunting.

c. Background checks shall be required of all gun buyers and owners.

d. No automatic or semi-automatic firearms may be possessed by any person living within the borders of the United States. Military and law enforcement personnel may be excepted.

5. A balanced budget and a 2% annual reduction in the national debt require that:

a. Taxes be adjusted annually to reflect the needs of the government.

6. In order to strengthen the separation of powers, these changes are made to the original Constitution:

a. Federal judiciary:

1) The reliance on common law to be replaced by the more common international law in which the wording of the law and its legislative intent are primary. In the West, this is referred to as Napoleonic law.

2) The selection of all federal judges, including Supreme Court Justices, would commence with nominations of an impartial, non-party affiliated, nomination committee of Federal and state supreme court judges. The list should include, as nearly as possible, a makeup reflective of the categories measured in the U.S. Census. The President will select his nominations from this list, with the suggestion that the ethnic and religious balances of the various Federal courts will reflect this balance.

b. Executive branch:

1) Elections will be entirely financed by federal government. No outside funding by individuals or groups will be allowed.

2) The Electoral College will be eliminated.

3) A majority of those casting votes will be required for the election of the president.

4) In the event that one party does not garner 50.01% of the votes for president, coalitions of parties can be formed to create that majority by transferring their votes to a selected candidate's party.

5) Data mining and other such methods of specialized communications to selected segments of the population will be prohibited.

6) Contributions of monetary value from individuals or special interest groups are prohibited.

7) The line item veto is possible for the President.

c. Legislative branch

1) Contributions of monetary value from individuals or special interest groups is prohibited.

2) All federal election expenses will be paid by the federal government. Media licenses may be contingent on the allowance of equal air time for all candidates.

3) A term limit of 12 years for any legislator is imposed.

d. Congressional districts will be determined by a non-partisan committee with the aid of digital analysis providing districts with no more than a 5% population differential, and with districts as nearly square as possible.

e. In order to keep citizens apprised of the actions of the government, every week a legislative and executive summary will be televised and individual emails will be forwarded to every voter with the pros and cons of each introduced law and the actual votes on each law recorded by the voter's representative and senator. The proposals and actions of the president will be similarly recorded. The summary will not exceed five pages but may include attachments.

EPILOGUE

CAN WE MAKE A DIFFERENCE-- LOTS OF NEGATIVES!

➤ It is getting easier and easier to snooker those who want to vote, and easier to discourage those from voting—those who would rather watch TV or play video games.

➤ We are seeing our people vote against their self-interests because they are victims of the old con artist trick of "bait and switch."

➤ It seems that most of us would rather have low taxes than happiness.

➤ Too many voters are relying on faith, and on opinions of friends and media people, than on verifiable facts.

➤ Our inability to see, or recognize, possible negatives in our human futures-- like forest fires, droughts, nuclear warfare, hurricanes and other fierce storms, terrorism that attacks our family, and other such likely occurrences. But we are quite aware that a happy afterlife awaits us.

We must—

➤ Think of the future because it will soon be NOW.

➤ Be willing to pay for what we want and what we have already overspent.

➤ Look beyond the obvious to the motivations of power, and to the basic assumptions of values, of those who would lead us.

THERE'S HOPE IF WE WILL SUPPORT AN OUTSTANDING PROGRAM OF EDUCATION

➤ There is good in the past and there is good in future, it depends on the issue.

➤ With an understanding of some basic physical science we may be able to understand the threats of climate change.

➤ With an understanding of some social sciences we may be able to see when politicians threaten our way of life.

➤ With an understanding of logic we may be able to see through the propaganda that so often confronts us.

➤ With a knowledge of history, we may be able to understand the positive and negative directions that social situations and politicians may influence us toward.